PRELATES AND PEOPLE

Ecclesiastical Social Thought in England

1783–1852

STUDIES IN SOCIAL HISTORY

PRELATES AND PEOPLE

Ecclesiastical Social Thought in England

1783–1852

by

R. A. Soloway

LONDON: Routledge & Kegan Paul
TORONTO: University of Toronto Press
1969

First published in 1969
by Routledge and Kegan Paul Ltd
and in Canada by
University of Toronto Press
Printed in Great Britain
by Cox and Wyman,
Fakenham, Norfolk
© R. A. Soloway, 1969

SBN 7100 6331 8
UTP SBN 8020 1610 3

For George L. Mosse

With gratitude and affection

Contents

Preface

I am deeply indebted to the staffs of numerous libraries and archives visited in both England and the United States. In particular I owe special thanks to the librarians and archivists at Lambeth Palace, the British Museum, the Bodleian Library and the National Register of Archives. In addition I am grateful for the assistance received in the Public and County Record Offices and the cathedral libraries and diocesan registries mentioned in the Bibliographical Note. Many other diocesan archivists and cathedral librarians carefully answered my written enquiries and were, as a result, most helpful. In this country the staffs of the Widener and Houghton Libraries at Harvard University and of the Newberry Library in Chicago were especially co-operative. I also wish to thank the Earl of Harrowby for his kindness while allowing me access to the Harrowby Manuscripts at Sandon Hall.

Professor Thomas Tentler of the University of Michigan patiently read and re-read most of the manuscript. His criticism was invaluable, and I believe he knows how grateful I am. Elizabeth Sumner was very helpful in preparing the final draft of the book, as was my wife, Maxine, whose interest in Church history, never very keen, has probably been destroyed forever. Professor Peter T. Marsh of Syracuse University in numerous discussions helped me to clarify many ideas, corrected many misconceptions, and taught me much about the nineteenth-century Church. If not enough, he is in no way responsible.

Several faculty research grants from the Horace H. Rackham Fund of the University of Michigan helped offset the expenses of research and manuscript preparation. I am most appreciative.

Richard A. Soloway

Chapel Hill, N.C.
August, 1968

Introduction

The reform of the Church of England in the first half of the nineteenth century was moulded considerably by the same pressures of industrialization, urbanization, and population growth that rapidly altered English society and its institutions as a whole. As one of those institutions, legally established, whose bishops sat in Parliament, and whose clergy were expected to support the State in their parochial ministrations, the Anglican Church and its episcopal leadership were particularly sensitive to the transformation of the country that took place from the later eighteenth to the middle of the nineteenth century. Already troubled by a spiritual revival that called attention to the secularity and neglect of their clergy, churchmen in the 1790's were staggered by the upheaval of European-wide revolution that seemed to threaten the very existence of Christian civilization. Even before recovering from that alarming experience, they were compelled to recognize very real institutional as well as clerical weaknesses in the Establishment. These weaknesses became increasingly obvious, and even dangerous, as decade after decade, English society rapidly expanded in ways that made the national Church often appear hopelessly archaic and irrelevant to the needs of an industrial, urban civilization.

This book examines the responses of the episcopal leadership of the Church in England and Wales to the transformation of the society to which they ministered. It considers primarily their social ideas and policies from the decade preceding the French Revolution to the middle of the nineteenth century; from that period when a few bishops began to worry about the effectiveness of their abuse-ridden Church to the time when the Establishment, ecclesiastically reformed and spiritually revitalized, looked forward to evangelizing the diverse multitudes who peopled the new age. By then the Church of England was more episcopal than at any time since the early eighteenth century. Convocation was

1

being revived after 135 years; bishops were resident administrators of their dioceses, overseeing an extensive network of social and religious projects; ecclesiastical discipline was more vigorously enforced, and in Parliament, the Church's interests were promoted regularly with skill and determination by prelates themselves.

Although much of the reform impetus within the Establishment was generated by the laity, especially in the earlier stages, men like William Wilberforce, Joshua Watson, Robert Peel, and Lord Liverpool were not simply riding roughshod over the objections of reactionary prelates.[1] On the contrary, episcopal consultation and co-operation in Church reform was increasingly the rule, not the exception. This does not mean that the bench was usually in the vanguard of reform; many of its members shuddered at the mention of the word. But in each episcopal generation there were important individual bishops who, though deeply conservative, were also realistic men who recognized that the Church was in a new age, faced with challenges demanding unprecedented adjustments on the part of its clergy. Recognition and accommodation to these realities were hardly uniform; but then few things were in the nineteenth-century Establishment. Parliamentary domination, the lack of a centralized ecclesiastical policy-making body, and the extraordinary independence of the Anglican clergy make it difficult, if not impossible, to discuss collective Church positions. Rarely was there a single Church position; there were usually party positions, or, more commonly, individual positions assumed by individual churchmen.

In such a particularized and fragmented ecclesiastical community the gradual reassertion of episcopal authority, especially with its close relationship to the government and Parliament, was particularly significant. It was very much in contrast to the eighteenth century when bishops intervened hardly at all in the administration of their dioceses and the lives of the parochial clergy. At that time, prelates' main functions were political, serving in the House of Lords, supporting the party or individuals to whom they were indebted for their episcopal thrones, and eager to please those in a position to translate them to an even more lucrative see. After that they were theologians, classical scholars, literary critics, and occasionally diocesan administrators as time, inclination, and transportation allowed.[2] Relations with their dioceses were usually formal: business was executed by archdeacons, secretaries,

---

[1] For the study of Church reform see, W. L. Mathieson, *English Church Reform 1815–1840* (1923); G. F. A. Best, *Temporal Pillars. Queen Anne's Bounty, the Ecclesiastical Commissioners, and the Church of England* (1964); Owen Chadwick, *The Victorian Church*, I (1966); Olive Brose, *Church and Parliament. The Reshaping of the Church of England 1828–1860* (1959).

[2] N. Sykes, *Church and State in England in the XVIIIth Century* (1934), Chaps. II, III.

and registrars. As Dr Best describes it, bishops' seals and signatures mattered much more than the bishops themselves, whose natural habitats were the West End and the universities. In their dioceses they were viewed as annual migrant visitors ordaining and confirming the years' accumulation of new clerics and new communicants.[1]

Diocesan affairs and ecclesiastical discipline sadly degenerated, reflecting and contributing to the disintegration of ecclesiastical and spiritual functions which scandalized Victorian and later critics of the eighteenth-century Church. In fact, by the 1780's, it was even beginning to trouble a few bishops alerted by the alarming growth of Methodism and the mounting criticisms of the Establishment. Ironically one of the first prelates to acknowledge the sad state of diocesan affairs, and urge the reassertion of inspiring episcopal leadership, was himself a veritable monument to clerical abuse. Nevertheless, in 1783, Richard Watson, the pluralistic (sixteen livings), nepotistic, non-resident Bishop of Llandaff (1782–1816) urged a fairer distribution of ecclesiastical revenue to improve parochial religion, and restore episcopal authority.[2] Sensitive to charges of opulence and diocesan neglect leveled at the bishops, Watson conceded the point by suggesting in a *Letter* to the Archbishop of Canterbury that a more equitable dispersal of Church resources would encourage episcopal residence and acquaintance with the clergy: 'by being better acquainted with their situations, prospects, tempers, and talents . . . (bishops) would be better able to co-operate with them, in the great work of amending the Morals of His Majesty's subjects, and of feeding the flock of Christ.'[3] Watson, appointed to one of the least affluent dioceses, understood the desire for translation that made bishops excessively dependent upon the laity, and placed the bench in a contemptible position. 'The laity, whilst they entertain such a suspicion concerning us, will accuse us of Avarice and Ambition, of making a gain of Godliness, of bartering the dignity of our Office for the chance of translation, in one word—Secularity. . . .'[4]

Watson was right, of course, but like most of his ecclesiastical contemporaries, he knew that Parliament governed the Church and had no intention of surrendering control. There was little sentiment, even on

---

[1] Best, *Temporal Pillars,* 359–60.

[2] Richard Watson (1737–1816), son of a Westmorland schoolmaster, Professor of Chemistry (1764) and Regius Professor of Divinity (1771) at Cambridge. An open supporter of the Whig cause, he owed his elevation to Llandaff to his former pupil Charles Manners, 4th Duke of Rutland, and to the Duke of Grafton, both of whom recommended him to Shelburne.

[3] R. Watson, *A Letter to His Grace the Archbishop of Canterbury* (1783), 20. In addition to a more equitable distribution of episcopal revenue, Watson urged the augmentation of poor livings from cathedral revenue.

[4] *Ibid.,* 11.

3

the bench, that it should. No bishop supported Watson's suggestions. Archbishop Cornwallis promptly died without replying; though there is no evidence that Watson's startling proposals contributed to his end. Only one of the twenty-four other prelates who were sent a copy of the *Letter* even bothered to acknowledge receiving it. Watson certainly was not surprised; knowing the dependence and timidity of his brethren he viewed his *Letter* as merely an opening wedge into a public discussion of the Church's problems. It would, as he predicted, take years of controversy before 'the utility of the changes was generally acknowledged.'[1] It took, in fact, more than fifty years before the newly-established Ecclesiastical Commissioners in 1836 partially equalized episcopal income, and, four years later, endorsed the redistribution of portions of cathedral revenue for use in overcrowded, urban districts.[2]

During those years, Parliament, without relinquishing control of the Establishment, increasingly shared it with an improving episcopate ready to assume a greater role in the administration and direction of the Church. Gradually, throughout the first half of the nineteenth century, the bishops loomed ever larger in the life of their dioceses, their ecclesiastical authority steadily strengthened by the passage of reform legislation designed to correct the worst clerical abuses, and extend the Church into the populous parts of the expanding nation. The bishops were not merely the passive agents of implementation of parliamentary Church reforms; they participated in the formulation of legislation and, when they disagreed with a particular measure, were often strong enough to stop it, or at least win a compromise. Moreover, as some of the bench began to understand that questions of Church effectiveness, and even survival, were closely linked to the economic and political forces at work in English society, they gradually took a wider view of their role in Parliament, and concerned themselves with social and political issues that seemed to bear directly upon the ability of the clergy to minister to the ever-expanding industrial society.

Only four of the bishops who guided the Church's progress in the

[1] R. Watson, *Anecdotes of the Life of Richard Watson, Bishop of Landaff, Written by Himself at Different Intervals, and Revised in 1814*, 2nd ed. (1818), I, 175.

[2] The Established Church Act of 1836 abolished livings held *in commendam* with sees, and established a scale of episcopal income ranging from £15,000 for Canterbury, £10,000 each for York and London, and so on down a scale to a minimum of £4,000 *per annum*. Although it was hardly a leveling of incomes, the richer sees were reduced somewhat to raise the poorer dioceses to an average of £4,000 to £5,000. The Dean and Chapter Bill of 1840 suppressed all non-resident prebends (about 360), sinecure rectories (68), and resident canonries above the number of four to each cathedral, with certain exceptions, and vested the money in the Ecclesiastical Commissioners. See Chadwick, *Victorian Church*, 136–7.

first half of the nineteenth century were born in that age. Most of their associates were born in the eighteenth century, before the French Revolution, and in most instances in the 1760's and 1770's. They were raised, educated and ordained in an eighteenth-century world, and began their ministry in a Church that had not yet adjusted to the past, when it began to suspect that it was not remotely in touch with the present. As eighteenth-century men, they brought to nineteenth-century problems ingrained rationalistic assumptions about human nature and social harmony. The Church they knew and loved reflected that harmony; it was rural, simple and pastoral, its patent charms captured in Southey's affectionate reminiscences. Its clergy formed an integral social and political alliance with the landed governing classes whose education, values and family connections they shared. No more than seventeen of the 104 bishops who led the Church between 1783 and 1852, when England was largely transformed from a rural to an urban country, ever held an urban living. Only two of them had any ministerial experience in a manufacturing or mining parish before their elevation to the bench.

This pattern of nominations remained, and, as the century wore on, the age of new appointments steadily increased so that the bench continued to be filled with prelates who had been born in the pre-revolutionary decades, and who had grown to maturity before the Napoleonic wars were finally over. Although two of Grey and Melbourne's fifteen nominees between 1830–41 were born in the first year of the new century, most of the remainder were born in the 1770's and 1780's. Had the Whigs come to power sooner, many of their episcopal appointments would have probably been elevated to the bench at a younger age. As it was, they averaged fifty-four years as compared to forty-six years for the twenty-three appointments made by the Tories, Liverpool, Canning, and Wellington, during the years 1812–30. The average age for all bishops installed between 1783–1852 was fifty. Victorian Prime Ministers in that period were especially partial to older candidates. With the exception of Samuel Wilberforce,[1] born in 1805 and raised to Oxford in 1845, Peel's bishops were closer to fifty-eight years old when nominated,

---

[1] Samuel Wilberforce (1805–73), son of the Evangelical reformer, William Wilberforce. Bishop of Oxford (1845) and Winchester (1869), he was a controversial and dynamic prelate who owed his initial appointment to royal favor, and to Peel's confidence that he could control the tumultuous situation created by the Tractarian controversy at Oxford. His antagonism of Palmerston and Disraeli (the latter modelled the worldly bishop in *Lothair* after Wilberforce) cost him further advancement until his close friend Gladstone, who would have raised him to Canterbury had he come to power six weeks earlier, moved him to Winchester. See A. Ashwell and R. G. Wilberforce, *The Life of Samuel Wilberforce*, 3 vols. (1880–2).

and were, therefore, like most of their predecessors, born before the French Revolution and raised in that tumultuous era. Despite the consternation caused by some of Lord John Russell's controversial episcopal selections between 1846–52, they were, if anything, the right age, all but one being born in the 1790's. For the first time, however, a majority of the episcopal appointments in the Victorian Church were men who were ordained after the revolutionary and Napoleonic wars.

Of the 104 bishops who occupied the twenty-six English and Welsh dioceses (increased to twenty-eight after 1836) between 1783 and 1852, twenty-five were already installed when Pitt assumed power in 1783. Four of these men were still alive after Waterloo; the last of them, James Cornwallis, Bishop of Lichfield–Coventry since 1781, died in 1824 at the age of eighty-two, a year after succeeding his brother to the family earldom. Although all of Peel's and Russell's appointments made in the 1840's lived well into the second half of the century, as did a few of Melbourne's and one of Liverpool's, most of the prelates who dominated the Church during the critical first half of the nineteenth century had already ended their careers by 1852, or shortly thereafter. The influence of those few who remained was fast eclipsed by a younger, more dynamic generation of churchmen, some of whom, like Samuel Wilberforce, already installed before mid-century, and others like Archibald Campbell Tait,[1] whose episcopal career was launched in 1856, dominated the Church in the mid-Victorian era.

This study concentrates on the four overlapping episcopal generations largely preceding that of Wilberforce and Tait; it examines the thought and policies of those prelates installed in the years before 1783, and from 1783–1812, 1812–30, and 1830–52.[2] For the most part they were men of the ruling classes; not only as a consequence of their being spiritual peers in the House of Lords, but often as a direct result

[1] Archibald Campbell Tait (1811–82), born in Edinburgh, raised as a Presbyterian. Succeeded Thomas Arnold as Headmaster of Rugby. Bishop of London (1856), Archbishop of Canterbury (1868). See R. Davidson and W. Benham, *Life of Archibald Campbell Tait*, 2 vols. (1891).

[2] Genealogical and career information has been compiled from such standard reference works as the *Dictionary of National Biography*, various editions of Burke's *Landed Gentry*, Burke's *Peerage*, and G. E. Cokayne, *The Complete Peerage*; also from Joseph Foster, ed., *Alumni Oxonienses* (1715–1886), J. A. Venn, ed., *Alumni Cantabrigienses*, Pts. I, II, J. LeNeve and T. D. Hardy, *Fasti ecclesiae anglicanae, or, a calendar of the principal ecclesiastical dignitaries in England and Wales* (1854), and Joseph Foster, ed., *Index Ecclesiasticus, or Alphabetical Lists of all Ecclesiastical Dignitaries in England and Wales since the Reformation* (1890). This *Index* is primarily a clergy list with a brief summary of careers for the period 1800–40. In addition, information has been utilized from published biographies when available, and cited accordingly.

of their temporal family connections and education. Although the social origins of four of the 104 members of the bench studied remain illusive, twenty-three of the other 100 were of noble families in which their father, brother or uncle bore a title at the time when their episcopal kin were elevated to a diocese. Four of this number were themselves sons of bishops, three of whom were closely related to peers. Still another prelate was connected to the peerage through his mother, while three more had the good fortune, or foresight, to marry bishops' daughters. Consequently, slightly more than one-quarter of the bishops between 1783–1852 were directly related to the peerage before their elevation, either through parental or marital associations. In addition, another prelate, Thomas Musgrave, later Archbishop of York (1848–60), married the daughter of a peer in 1839, two years after his appointment to Hereford.[1]

Although the extent of episcopal relationships with the landed gentry is much more difficult to determine accurately, it appears that the fathers of twenty-four of the 100 known bishops were of that class. At least three other prelates had mothers of the gentry, and ten were connected by marriage to recognized gentry families; as a result, thirty-seven members of the hierarchy were closely related to the non-noble, landed aristocracy. There is little question that the episcopate was heavily aristocratic: a compilation of male relations alone in the peerage and gentry indicates that forty-seven, or nearly half of the prelates whose genealogical origins are known, were of either class. When maternal and marital relationships are included, nearly two-thirds of the bishops fall into these elevated social categories. The preponderance of aristocratic alliances in the hierarchy is even more striking when the familial connections of the fifty-three bishops whose fathers were not of the aristocracy are examined more closely. The mothers of three of these men were the daughters of gentry landowners, ten more married into that class, and two into the peerage. Consequently, only thirty-eight of the 100 bishops already installed in 1783 or appointed over the next sixty-nine years lacked any direct familial relationship with the aristocracy, though it is likely that the four prelates whose genealogy is undetermined would probably fall into this category.[2]

---

[1] Thomas Musgrave (1788–1860), son of a wealthy Cambridge tailor and woollen draper, married a daughter of Lord Waterpark. Had a long career at Cambridge before his appointment to Hereford and later York (1848–60). Was a political Liberal, but a very conservative Evangelical churchman.

[2] For a comparative analysis of the French and English episcopate in the eighteenth century see Norman Ravitch, *Sword and Mitre. Government and Episcopate in France and England in the Age of Aristocracy* (The Hague, 1966). Ravitch carries his analysis of the English bench up to 1836, and

Nevertheless, the aristocratic nature of the Church's leadership in the eighteenth and nineteenth centuries is clear. Its development was a long-term reversal of sixteenth- and seventeenth-century trends. Aristocratic families apparently did not find the plundered Church after the Reformation a very enticing attraction for their younger sons. Professor Lawrence Stone has calculated that, of twenty-eight bishops in the 1630's, the fathers of nine were gentry, eight were clergymen, seven were merchants, one a yeoman, and three were artisans or below. It appears that the highest ranks of the clergy were generally regarded as inferior in status to the highest ranks of the legal profession, despite the presence of bishops in the House of Lords.[1] At the close of the reign of Charles II, only two prelates were sons of peers.[2] The rising importance of Parliament, the steady appreciation of episcopal landed income, the decline of anti-clericalism, and the general improvement of the clergyman's status in society, made the clerical profession, especially at the higher levels, increasingly attractive. Throughout the eighteenth century there was a steady rise in aristocratic representation in ecclesiastical positions in general, and on the episcopal bench in particular. As competition for these positions in the Church increased, familial connections were more important than ever. Of the twenty-six prelates already installed in 1783, eight were the sons or brothers of peers, and another was married to the daughter of a noble. Five additional bishops were sons of gentry parents, while three more had married into that class. This meant that half of the bench were sons of aristocratic families; when marital alliances are considered, more than two-thirds of the bishops were well-connected. At no time between 1783–1852 were less than half the episcopal nominees aristocratically allied by birth or marriage.

Eighteenth-century ecclesiastics were delighted by the trend, and nineteenth-century successors were worried that it might not continue. Though Archbishop Secker (1758–68) wished there were more opulent benefices to attract clergymen from the higher ranks of society,[3] his

---

[1] Lawrence Stone, 'Social Mobility in England 1500–1700', *Past and Present,* No. 33 (April 1966), 20.

[2] T. B. Macaulay, *History of England from the Accession of James II* (1849), I, 327. For an attempt to put Macaulay's analysis in perspective see C. H. Mayo, 'The Social Status of the Clergy in the Seventeenth and Eighteenth Centuries', *English Historical Review,* XXXVII (1922), 258–66.

[3] Sykes, *Church and State,* 226

---

though his general conclusions substantiate the aristocratic composition of the bench, they are based entirely upon male relationships and include a very large number of prelates whose genealogical connections are described as 'uncertain'.

colleague, Bishop Warburton of Gloucester (1760–79), thought it was no longer a problem. He rejoiced to see the sons of peers regularly entering the Church which 'has been of old the cradle and the throne of the younger nobility . . .' who left it after the spoliation of Henry VIII.[1] To those low-minded 'enthusiasts' who were unconvinced, and who suggested that the first leaders of Christ's Church were not especially hindered by a lack of social rank, Bishop Newton of Bristol (1761–82) conceded that there were probably some advantages in the Apostles being of a lesser station. Times had changed, however, and the benefits to be derived were, to eighteenth-century churchmen, no longer obvious. On the contrary, aristocratic clergymen 'may add strength and ornament to [the Church] . . . especially as long as we can boast of *some*, who are honourable in themselves as well as in their families; and whose personal merits and virtues, if they had not been nobly descended would have entitled them justly to the rank and pre-eminence that they enjoy.'[2]

The heavy laicization of the Established Church in the eighteenth century had brought the clergy ever closer to the dominant secular interests and values of the age. Not surprisingly, the hierarchy of the Church more closely resembled that of the State as Church and State, nearly split apart by the revolutions of the seventeenth century, were rejoined more tightly than ever under Parliament's domination. As clergy and laity adopted the same ideals and almost the same conduct, the spiritual and temporal estates became again what they had always been in medieval theory, twin dimensions of an indivisible unity.[3] Instead of feeling suffocated by the sweeping temporal embrace of establishment, Church leaders welcomed it as a blessing which permitted the laity and clergy to promote harmoniously common interests of material and spiritual benefit to all. Bishop Warburton's description of establishment as a mutual contract between the State and the majority Church based upon common interests and utility, made perfect sense to his and later generations.[4] Although there were rumblings of discontent in the closing years of the eighteenth century, disillusionment with the benefits of establishment was not really significant until the 1830's.

Church leadership by then was still heavily aristocratic; Liverpool

[1] William Warburton, *Letters From a Late Eminent Prelate to One of His Friends*, 2nd ed. (1809), 157.

[2] Sykes, *Church and State*, 186. See also N. Ravitch, 'The Social Origins of French and English Bishops in the Eighteenth Century', *Historical Journal*, No. 3, VIII (1965), 310–11.

[3] Best, *Temporal Pillars*, 70.

[4] W. Warburton, *The Alliance Between Church and State, or the Necessity and Equity of an Established Religion and a Test-Law Demonstrated* (1736).

even exceeded Pitt's strong preference for appointments from the better families of the realm. In this they reflected the wishes of the Crown even if they did not necessarily approve of royal intervention. Pitt, for example, was thwarted in his attempt to promote his old tutor, secretary, and ecclesiastical adviser, Bishop Pretyman of Lincoln, to Canterbury in 1804, when the king insisted on a man with better credentials for so lofty a position.[1] Though Pretyman, who had added the name of Tomline in 1803 to inherit the estates of an eccentric admirer, was of an old Suffolk family, George III refused to yield to Pitt's arguments and succeeded in elevating Charles Manners–Sutton, grandson of the Duke of Rutland, to the archiepiscopal throne.[2] George IV, who also occasionally demanded an appointment over the objections of his prime ministers, wrote to Manners–Sutton's successor, Bishop Howley of London,[3] shortly before his elevation to Canterbury in 1828, that it was 'very desirable' and good 'to connect the Bench, with the nobility of the Country; particularly when the heads of such noble families strongly support the Protestant Interests of the Country.'[4] The king in this instance was trying to strengthen the bench against the threat of Catholic emancipation, but his sentiments were certainly not contrary to prevailing notions of ecclesiastical patronage.

Liverpool, unlike Pitt, was much more concerned with the academic and theological credentials of candidates, as well as their political and

[1] George Pretyman-Tomline (1750–1827), son of Suffolk gentry, Bishop of Lincoln (1787) and Winchester (1820). Was also Pitt's biographer. A pluralist and a nepotist, he left over £200,000 (*Gentleman's Magazine* (Dec. 1827), 523).

[2] Pretyman to G. Rose, 13 Nov. 1804, *Pretyman Family Archives,* Ipswich and East Suffolk Record Office, T 108/45; also Pretyman to wife, 29 Dec.; 23 Jan. 1805; 5 March. When he learned that the Archbishop of York had fallen ill in January, 1805, Pretyman groaned at the thought of going to the north, but the old incumbent, Markham, survived another two years.

Charles Manners-Sutton (1755–1828), son of Lord George Manners-Sutton, Bishop of Norwich (1792) and Canterbury (1805). A reasonably active High Church prelate who managed to place seven of his relations in sixteen benefices.

[3] William Howley (1766–1848), son of a Hampshire vicar, Regius Professor of Divinity at Oxford (1809), Bishop of London (1813) and Archbishop of Canterbury (1828). He owed his appointment to Lord Abercorn, whose son he had tutored. A gentle, pious, and princely prelate, his very real generosity did not prevent him leaving a £120,000 estate. See S. L. Ollard and G. Crosse, eds, *A Dictionary of English Church History*, 2nd ed. (1919), 288–9.

[4] 23 Feb. 1827, *Royal Letters to Archbishop Howley*, Lambeth Palace Library, MS. 1754, f. 99.

familial qualities. Improvement, if not reform, was clearly on his mind as he labored to provide the Church with leaders who were both ecclesiastically and socially respectable in the broad spectrum of Anglican opinion. Given the diversity and partisanship of that opinion in the post-war world of the Established Church, it was no mean task. It seemed to some serious Church spokesmen that social criteria were perhaps more important than they should be in the age of Church improvement. Charles Lloyd, Regius Professor of Divinity and soon after Bishop of Oxford,[1] wrote in 1826 to Peel, his former pupil and now patron, that he could not accept Liverpool's belief that it was necessary to have men of family in the Church, especially when it led to the appointment to bishoprics of Lord George Murray and the Prime Minister's cousin, John Banks Jenkinson.[2] 'They have their advantages in a temporal point of view—but from their great professional ignorance these advantages are, in general, very largely counterbalanced.'[3] Lloyd, who did much to revive the study of theology for clerical candidates at Oxford, indicated how rapidly standards were changing when he cited professional competence as a desirable quality in a bishop.

The number of prelates related to the peerage fell rapidly after 1830. The peak had been reached during the preceding two decades when, between 1812 and 1830, Liverpool, Canning, and Wellington nominated seven of their twenty-three bishops from the peerage. Five of these were Liverpool's selections. In addition, five more prelates were related to gentry families, so that nearly two-thirds of the episcopal generation that came to power before the important election of 1830 were of the aristocracy. The general aristocratic nature of the bench did not change after 1830, but its social content was altered. Of the twenty-five bishops instituted between 1830–52, only two were of the peerage, and one of them, Edward Grey, Bishop of Hereford (1832–37), was the brother of the Prime Minister. It was an appointment Earl Grey had been reluctant to make. Not only did it leave him open to charges of nepotism, but he was continually plagued by his ineffectual brother for still

---

[1] Charles Lloyd (1784–1829), son of a Buckinghamshire schoolmaster, Regius Professor of Divinity (1822), Bishop of Oxford (1827). Deeply influenced Froude, Newman and Pusey, who attended his private lectures at Oxford.

[2] George Murray (1784–1860), son of Lord George Murray, Bishop of St David's (1801–3), and nephew of Duke of Atholl, to whom he owed his appointment to Sodor and Man (1814) and Rochester (1827). He was very High Church and sympathetic to the Oxford Movement.

John Banks Jenkinson (1781–1840), son of John Banks Jenkinson, brother of 1st Earl of Liverpool; Bishop of St David's (1825) and added Deanery of Durham in 1827.

[3] Lloyd to Peel, 15 May 1826, *Peel Ps.*, British Museum, Add. MS. 40342, ff. 348–9.

higher preferment.[1] Already suspicious that Edward leaned too closely towards the Evangelical party, the Prime Minister was further irritated when his brother regularly voted more like a Tory than a Whig in the House of Lords.[2] When, in 1836, Bishop Grey vainly solicited Melbourne for translation to the princely see of Durham —'a duty I owed to my family'—he wisely suspected that his brother would not be pleased, and received little support from that quarter.[3]

Melbourne, in fact, only made one appointment to the bench directly from the peerage, when, in 1840, he nominated Henry Pepys, brother of the first Earl of Cottenham, to Sodor and Man, and translated him to Worcester the following year.[4] His only other episcopal selection connected with the nobility was Charles Thomas Longley, the future Archbishop of York (1860–62) and Canterbury (1862–68), whose initial appointment to the newly-created diocese of Ripon in 1836 was promoted by his father-in-law, Sir Henry Parnell, first Baron Congleton.[5] The rapid decline of noble prelates was not entirely a Whig phenomenon; none of Peel's four nominees was of the peerage, nor, when the Whigs returned in 1846, were any of Lord John Russell's. If the number of episcopal appointments from the nobility fell sharply after 1830, new members of the bench continued to come from genteel families. Five of the thirteen recipients of Melbourne's patronage were the sons of gentry families, some very eminent, and a sixth was related by marriage. Half of Peel's choices were also of gentry parentage, and two of Russell's five nominees were related to old recognized landed families through mother or wife. Popular opinion, demanding a more serious and dedicated standard of clerical behavior, forced the government to be less obvious in succumbing to aristocratic favoritism. Moreover, in an era of reform, including ecclesiastical reform, it was increasingly important to appoint bishops who would support the government and offset the stubborn resistance to change still exemplified by several older Tory prelates. It is also possible that the sons of Whig peers were traditionally less attracted to a clerical career from the later eighteenth century onwards, as their opportunities for satisfactory preferment were limited by the Tory domination of ecclesiastical positions. Consequently, as Mel-

---

[1] Bishop Grey to Earl Grey, 9 Jan. 1833, and Earl Grey to Bishop Grey, 29 Aug., *Grey of Howick MS.*, The Prior's Kitchen, Durham Cathedral, Box 32/10a.

[2] Edw. Grey to Earl Grey, 28 Sept. 1826, *ibid.*

[3] Bishop Grey to Melbourne, 23 Feb. 1836, *ibid.*

[4] Henry Pepys (1783–1860), son of Wm. Weller Pepys, Bart. A Liberal prelate, resident, popular and conscientious.

[5] Charles Thomas Longley (1794–1868), son of a political writer and Rochester magistrate. Was Headmaster of Harrow (1829–36) before his elevation to Ripon. Was also Bishop of Durham (1856–60).

bourne discovered, it was not only difficult to find Whig clergymen of sufficient stature to be nominated to the bench, it was probably even more difficult to find them among the Whig peerage.

Of at least equal importance were the reforms within the Church that demanded an episcopate concerned with spiritual and ecclesiastical problems. The social and political perquisites of an episcopal career were still very attractive, but the opportunities for well-connected clerics to improve their lot steadily in the hierarchy were considerably reduced. The elimination of many cathedral dignitaries in 1840, following the partial equalization of episcopal revenue four years earlier, indicated that the Church was not only determined to use its financial resources more effectively, but, as Bishop Watson had urged fifty-three years before, to improve episcopal administration by discouraging the endless competition for translation to more lucrative sees. This competition had been especially advantageous to the politically compliant and the well-connected for over a century. Twelve of the twenty-six prelates on the bench in 1783 had been translated to their existing dioceses. From that year to the reforms of 1836 there were fifty-two additional translations with Pitt and Liverpool responsible for thirty-one of them. After 1836, however, episcopal mobility was strikingly reduced, and by 1852 only five translations, two of them archiepiscopal, had been permitted. Over the next twenty years, five additional moves took place.[1]

It is unlikely that the improving administration and discipline of ecclesiastical life left a large number of noble clergymen trapped in a family living far from an elevated *niche* in the hierarchy. Opportunities outside the Church for the privileged were greater than ever in the expansive society of the nineteenth century, and the sons of the nobility, if they chose to do anything, were taking advantage of them. Lord George Murray feared that it would only be a matter of time before there would be no more ecclesiastical dignitaries like him entering the Church. As a nephew of the Duke of Atholl and son of a bishop, Murray was particularly sensitive to Church reforms that might lead to a decline in clerical social standards. The episcopal reforms of 1836 and the cathedral reforms of 1840 indicated that the Church was abandoning all the social advantages won in the preceding century, and that it would 'drag on a mutilated and degraded existence. . . . It will soon sink into the state . . . where the clergy are but one degree removed from the labourer and the mechanic.'[2] A wiser generation had opposed this trend in the 1780's; Murray urged his to do the same.

[1] Thomas Lundeen, *The Bench of Bishops. A Study of the Secular Activities of the Bishops of the Church of England and of Ireland 1801–1871*, unpub. PhD. dissertation (University of Iowa, 1963), 138–9.

[2] G. Murray, *Charge . . . to the Clergy of His Diocese At the Triennial Visitation, Holden in July, MDCCCXL* (1840), 31.

13

Murray was only one of several prelates who feared that the harmonious ideal of a clerical hierarchy representing all classes, and paralleling the natural temporal hierarchy, was in danger. The comforting knowledge that 'the son of the highest peer, and the son of the humblest yeoman, along with every intermediate grade [are] engaged in the same course of pastoral duties, with equal earnestness and devotion' was threatened by the defection of those placed by providence at the top of the social pyramid.[1] Bishop Monk of Gloucester (1830–56),[2] when issuing this warning in 1835, recognized, as critics charged, that it might appear that 'the low-minded and worldly motive of pecuniary benefit' was a consideration of the well-born in entering the clerical profession. If anyone was guilty of such material weakness, however, it was not the individual interested in the Church, but his parents, who expected adequate recognition and advancement for their son.[3]

This concern about the social composition of the ecclesiastical hierarchy bothered Church leaders more and more in the 1830's and 1840's. Not only old Tory appointees like Murray and Monk fretted about leveling tendencies; young Liberals like Bishop Dension of Salisbury (1837–54) were uneasy as well.[4] Although he supported Church reform, Denison, like many moderate High churchmen, was never very happy about it. Stimulated by the Continental revolutions of 1848, Denison wondered if democratic notions were weakening the natural social hierarchy reflected in the Church. He devoted much of his visitation *Charge* of that year to warning of the dangers of drawing too heavily on the lower classes for clerical recruitment. It would in time severely curtail the influence and usefulness of the Establishment. France, where revolution had again erupted, suffered grievously from such a policy, he claimed; the excessive equalization of income in the French church had driven the better sort out, so that it is only among 'peasants and mechanics, in that part of the population entirely destitute of fortune, or even of the rudiments of education, that the Church is obliged to seek her ministers.' Denison explored the similar situation in Ireland and Scotland where, in contrast to the English clergy, they have 'none of the advantages of personal weight and consideration, of social and family

---

[1] James Monk, *A Charge Delivered to the Clergy of the Diocese of Gloucester, In August and September, MDCCCXXXV* (1835), 17.

[2] James Henry Monk (1784–1856), son of a military officer, Regius Professor of Greek at Oxford (1809–23), Bishop of Gloucester (1830). A very conservative High Churchman.

[3] J. Monk, *Charge* (1835), 18.

[4] Edward Denison (1801–54), son of a London merchant, later landowner and M.P. Though High Church and Oxford, was a Whig. A diligent, reforming bishop.

relations'.[1] The bishop realized that the changing composition of English society in his own lifetime made this a sensitive subject, and conceded that perhaps the national Church had of late drawn too few clergy from the middle and lower classes. Nevertheless he thought this an error on the side of caution, convinced that the clergy drawn from the higher orders at least had the interest of all levels of society at heart. If, however, the trend towards equalization within the Church continued, it would have a profound effect on the composition and character of the body of the clergy. For this reason Denison was opposed to further reforms that would have reorganized and expanded the number of dioceses to be financed out of still another redistribution of ecclesiastical revenue. As far as he was concerned, any further reduction of existing resources would make a clerical career even less appealing to men of good family, and in time this would be reflected to a disproportionate extent on the episcopal bench itself.

Denison, of lesser gentry parentage, was not in imminent danger of being swept away by a flood of low-born bishops. Nevertheless, there was an obvious increase after 1830 of prelates who lacked his or even higher genteel credentials. Fourteen of the twenty-four men elevated to the bench by Grey, Melbourne, Peel and Russell were of non-aristocratic families. At no time since the mid-eighteenth century had non-aristocratic appointments constituted more than 48 per cent of the new prelates. Yet 58 per cent of the episcopal generation elevated during the period 1830–52 could not claim a genteel pedigree. The sharp decrease in the number of bishops selected from the peerage was in part compensated by an increase in the number of appointments from the gentry, but even more so from the less-favored classes. This is what worried those churchmen already established in the ecclesiastical hierarchy. It is clear, however, that their new colleagues, if not always as well-born as they might like, were still at least well-connected.

Three of the non-aristocratic bishops had in fact married into the gentry and another into the peerage, so that in fact only ten of the twenty-four appointments after 1830 were completely unrelated to the aristocracy. When marital as well as parental relationships are evaluated, they reveal a slight upswing in the percentage of prelates born or married into the aristocracy. In 1783, 76 per cent of the bishops were so connected; between then and 1812, the percentage fell to approximately 62 per cent. Despite the increase in appointments from the peerage by Liverpool there was a decrease in those with gentry connections, so that the number of aristocratically-related prelates continued to fall, reaching slightly more than 56 per cent in 1830. The comparatively high incidence of non-aristocratic bishops appointed after 1830 who married

[1] E. Denison, *A Charge Delivered to the Clergy of the Diocese of Salisbury ... July and August, 1848* (1848), 23–25.

above their station actually reversed this trend, so that though the proportion of low-born prelates installed was probably greater than at any comparable period since the mid-eighteenth century, 58 per cent of them were still directly related by birth or marriage to aristocratic families.

Although a few of the fifty prelates between 1783–1850, lacking an aristocratic pedigree, were the sons of artisans, grocers, graziers, livery stable proprietors, and even a butler, most stood somewhat higher in the social scheme of things. Many bishops were in fact the offspring of bankers, merchants, attorneys, and, more often, military officers, government officials, and clergymen. In fact, thirty-two of the 100 bishops whose origins are known were sons of clergymen, and the mothers of an additional six were parsons' daughters. Consequently, approximately one-third of the prelates were at the top of what had become a hereditary profession. When maternal origins are included, the figure approaches two-fifths. As early as the 1630's, more than a quarter of the bishops were sons of parsons, and the figures for the later eighteenth century would suggest that the proportion remained fairly constant.[1] Of the bishops in power in 1783, one-quarter had clerical fathers. Information on the mothers of eighteenth-century bishops is too limited to be significant; although in all probability, if later trends are accurate for the earlier period, several additional prelates in 1783 had maternal grandfathers who were clergymen.

The hereditary characteristics of the bench were steadily extended in the next two episcopal generations: nearly a third of the bishops elevated between 1783–1812 had clerical fathers, and the proportions rose to over two-fifths between 1812–30. If maternal considerations are included, slightly more than half the prelates appointed in the latter period were carrying on their father's or maternal grandfathers' clerical profession. By the 1830's, however, as contemporary ecclesiastics noted, the Church was attracting a clergy of more diverse social composition, and this was in part reflected on the episcopal bench. In contrast to the previous episcopal generation, only one-fifth of the appointments made after 1830 consisted of sons of clergymen. The number of bishops whose mothers were clerical daughters does not appreciably alter this proportion. In all likelihood the Whig ministers who made most of the episcopal appointments after 1830 had nothing against clergymen's sons—only against Tory clergymen's sons. As the Anglican clergy was heavily Tory, politically and emotionally, the possibilities of finding suitable ecclesiastical appointments from that quarter were considerably reduced.

The Church hierarchy, closely related to the ruling classes by birth

[1] Stone, 'Social Mobility', *P. & P.*, 48.

and marriage, was further allied through education. Clergymen were not educated separately in seminaries; they received the same instruction as the laity. Although some of the bishops considered in the following chapters were in fact founders of formal clerical seminaries in their dioceses, none of them had been the recipients of a special education designed to prepare them for the Church.[1] More than half the bishops were educated in one of the seven foundation schools, usually Eton or Winchester, before moving on to Oxford or Cambridge.[2] All prelates attended one of the universities, and appointments to the bench usually reflected a long-standing custom of alternating the filling of vacancies between the two institutions. Melbourne broke the custom, nominating Cambridge men to nine of the thirteen sees he had to fill. Though he perhaps believed, as he claimed, that Cambridge produced ten able men to Oxford's five, his problem was more basic: it was difficult to find respectable churchmen from Oxford who were also reliable Whigs. Melbourne was determined to have co-operative bishops, but the search was often arduous and time-consuming, as revealed in his weary cry, 'Damn it, another bishop dead!' when he received news of still another vacancy.[3]

The improvement of university standards, and the revival of theological instruction in the first half of the nineteenth century, undoubtedly contributed to the improvement of clerical education and the quality of ministerial activity. In terms of advancement, however, the personal contacts made at school or university were probably still more important. Though scholarship, and occasionally even theology, were often routes to recognition and promotion, influential classmates or pupils were especially valuable ingredients for success in the Church, particularly when family connections were not all that they might be. The history of ecclesiastical patronage in the eighteenth and first half of the nineteenth century is more a history of whom one knew and whom one was related to, than it is a study of the rewards of merit and virtue. It is, in effect, a study of the same standards that prevailed in most English institutions.

As the quality of these standards improved in the nineteenth century, they reflected the changing expectations of a society in extraordinary transition. The law, Parliament, governmental agencies, local administration, were rationalized and reformed more in accordance with the utilitarian values and the economic and political realities of the age. The Established Church was inevitably affected. Its ecclesiastical leadership was still permeated with ambitious, place-seeking, mediocre party men who owed their advancement to family and friends. Many earnest

[1] In particular, Thomas Burgess, George Henry Law, and, more importantly, Samuel Wilberforce.
[2] Lundeen, *The Bench*, 43.
[3] Chadwick, *Victorian Church*, 122.

and dedicated clergymen whose very real merits were obscured by their distance from men of influence, or negated by their controversial opinions on troublesome issues, were undoubtedly neglected. What is surprising, however, is that the system produced as many capable and energetic prelates as it did to govern the national Church during its most trying period since the civil wars of the seventeenth century.

None of them were particularly original or daring men, though some of them were extremely intelligent and perceptive. They were, however, institutional beings, prelates of an ancient establishment. Conservative, sometimes utterly reactionary, innovation and reform were, for many of them, horrid concepts, and for others, at best, a necessity. Although, as a group, the episcopate was well educated, even learned, no single prelate of the age stands out as a great divine whose intellectual powers and example stimulated contemporaries. There was no Wesley, Newman, Pusey, Arnold, or Maurice among them to excite their times. Nevertheless these were the men who had to govern the Church when it was shaken and fragmented by Evangelical revivalism and High Church Tractarianism. More importantly, as this study emphasizes, they were also the men who had to guide, administer, and even reform the national Establishment in a period of unprecedented economic and social change that would have placed enormous demands on the most modern, perceptive, and innovative of social institutions. The Church of England was certainly none of these—something its leaders at first took pride in until they realized that their ideas and policies were perhaps the dangerous vanities of a bygone age.

I

<hr>

Social Speculation and
Revolutionary Upheaval

<hr>

1. THE NATURE OF SOCIETY

A decade or two before the outbreak of the French Revolution, English Church leaders were becoming increasingly uneasy about trends in social criticism. Too many contemporaries seemed interested in questions of social causation and inequality, as if existing rationalistic and theological explanations were unsatisfactory. Prying into established notions was disturbing to eighteenth-century bishops, but it was particularly worrying when the subject was the nature of society. Prelates were not very interested in wrestling with new social theories or critical analyses of inevitable, and natural, social problems. For most of them, the Bible and John Locke had explained the essentials; they saw no reason to enquire more deeply into the subject. As Professor Sykes has shown, the mitred guardians of the Establishment were primarily political functionaries whose interest in ecclesiastical matters was often ceremonious and superficial.

Episcopal interest in social questions was even more slender. Although many bishops certainly supported charitable and philanthropic projects, and annually delivered uninspiring sermons on behalf of the charity schools, few of them, until later in the century, could be considered in the forefront of social improvement. They were long accustomed to think of relevant problems in terms of papal threats, Nonconformity, deism, scepticism and religious enthusiasm. That the concerns of the Church might be re-examined in terms of the nature and problems of

19

society was a concept remote from most prelates' minds until the closing decades of the century. Then, prodded by Rousseau's ideas in particular, and the critical atmosphere of the times in general, a few Church leaders urged the imposition of restraints upon some of the far-fetched notions being propounded by restless social analysts.

It seemed that men were losing their perspective when they failed to see that periodic imbalances in society were inevitable, and that the exaggerated inequities that resulted for the less fortunate classes would in time be modified by a natural restoration of social balance. In the meantime, Christian charity and parochial relief would provide for those unable to stand the wait. Yet, despite such ancient truths, the explicitly antisocial criticisms of Rousseau, blaming individual misery and misfortune on the corrupting evils of propertied society itself, were, in varying forms, being preached by enthusiasts who refused to see that social causation was unscientific, unnatural, and unscriptural. To insist that the individual parts of society were a result of the whole was a violation of the most fundamental rational-empirical principles of modern science, as any Cartesian or Newtonian knew. To argue that social inequality was unnatural, the result of the wicked imposition of private property upon simple, unsuspecting men, was contrary to all that was known of human nature, the voluntaristic, contractual origins of society, and the progressive history of civilizations. Moreover, Rousseau's tardy warning to ignore the imposter who first arrogantly claimed, '*ceci est à moi*', and his lament that man was lost when he forgot that the fruits of the earth were for everyone, contradicted the Scriptural evidence of God's wrathful judgment when betrayed by this own creation—a judgment that in fact condemned man to labor inequitably for those fruits.[1]

Prelates thought they understood the reason for the assertions that the inequities of society were the results of social conditions and man-made distinctions: it was the result of the erosion of belief in a divinely-conceived hierarchical structure formulated in accordance with a predetermined plan. Eighteenth-century speculative thinkers, indefatigably seeking the rationally comprehensible natural laws governing man and society, neglected the truths of revelation and placed too much emphasis upon anthropocentric causation. The continual discovery of innumerable natural laws offering new insights into human behavior and the development of society made Scriptural explanations and justifications appear irrelevant and even ridiculous. Religion itself was often relegated to a derivative rather than a causal characteristic—more reflective of a society than formulative. Montesquieu, for example, included it along with climate, laws, governmental maxims, historical

[1] *Discours sur l'origine et les fondements de l'inégalité parmi les hommes,* in *Œuvres* (Paris, 1826), IV.

experience, customs and manners, as an intrinsic part of any social complex.[1]

In general, however, the diminution of divine causation and Scriptural explanation did not challenge concepts of the natural structure of society and the inevitability of inequality. Even deists or sceptics, while rejecting the supervision and intervention of an omnipresent God, did not deny the conservative assumption that existing societies were essentially derived from the nature of things. Utilitarian psychology and social contract theory both emphasized the importance of rational individual choice in the creation of the social community. English ecclesiastics, themselves very much products of their enlightened age, had little difficulty in accepting these general propositions and merging them into their broad concepts of natural religion. From their standpoint, rationally comprehended natural laws of social development did not conflict with the Scriptural explanation originating in the expulsion of fallen man from eternal paradise. Endowed with free will, and henceforth confronted with the problem of survival, man was plunged into a state of nature from which he had been developing ever since. When properly interpreted, the revealed laws governing that process did not really conflict with those that were natural and rationally discoverable. If anything, most English prelates believed, they were complementary. When, in the later years of the century, speculation started to expand in less comforting directions, and critics and reformers started overly emphasizing the causative factors of temporal conditions, propertied beneficiaries of those conditions thought it time to invoke less worldly explanations once more. Bishops, ostensibly the bridge between the spiritual and the temporal, were well suited for the task.

In 1769 Richard Watson, then Fellow of Trinity College, Cambridge, Professor of Chemistry, and later Bishop of Llandaff, felt it imperative to remind his contemporaries that the institutions of society were necessary as they existed. Contrary to recent suggestions, any defects in society were the result of individual failings, and those who agitated for social reforms were hopelessly ignorant of both revealed and natural law. Troubled particularly by domestic unrest over rising corn prices, Watson feared that critics were starting to draw some of their arguments from Rousseau's misguided writings. The implications of such an approach to natural phenomena far transcended periodic price fluctuations. Clergymen, the future prelate felt, should be especially sensitive to these developments as the parochial ministry had a primary role to play in the preservation of social harmony and continuity. 'Let us,' he urged, 'as ministers of the gospel of peace, co-operate in our proper stations with our superiors, in promoting harmony and good order in society, in preserving a due respect to the authority, and a proper confidence

[1] *L'Esprit des lois*, Bk. XIX, Chap. IV.

in the ability and integrity of those who are set over us.'[1] Watson, one of the most assertive clerical promoters of Old Whiggery, often did not practise what he preached. He vigorously opposed the American War and Lord North, and continually distrusted the ability and the integrity of the king as well as most of his ministers.[2] But his message, 'Christianity Consistent', was intended for transmission to the lower orders who were encouraged to show none of the ambition, contentiousness and neglect that he and many of his clerical brethren exhibited throughout their careers. In that sense, Watson was merely charting the course of social retrenchment followed by the Church during the tumultuous years of the French Revolution and in the early decades of the next century.

Society was, after all, as several bishops proclaimed, as much a divine creation as the Newtonian universe itself. To suggest that God created one but not the other was little better than atheism.[3] Deistic and materialistic descriptions of society developing independently of the creator were, according to Bishop Bagot of Bristol (1782–83), crude rejections of divine intelligence.[4] The refutation of such ideas was especially appropriate in a sermon in 1783 commemorating the death of the martyred Charles I. Free will, he preached, certainly allowed man to influence and participate in the development of his society, and in that sense it reflected the passions and prejudices of human nature. Nevertheless, society ultimately developed in accordance with a preconceived plan directly and continually involving the creator.[5] As in the universe itself, God demanded order and harmony in society; when men lost sight of that necessary truth, as some had of late, and many had in the preceding century, all ran the risk of being plunged into misery. Though he spoke to the highest peers of the realm, the Bishop of Bristol specifically urged the disgruntled poor to take note of his words.[6] As few among that lowly class spent much of their time perusing episcopal sermons delivered to the House of Lords, it was more likely they would receive the message from a less exalted clerical guide.

[1] R. Watson, *Christianity Consistent With Every Social Duty. A Sermon Preached at the University of Cambridge . . . March 9, 1769* (Cambridge, 1769), 15.

[2] See Watson's *The Principles of the Revolution Vindicated in A Sermon Preached . . . May 29, 1776* (Cambridge, 1776).

[3] Lewis Bagot, *A Sermon Preached Before the Lords Spiritual and Temporal . . . January 30, 1783, Being the Day Appointed to be Observed as the Day of the Martyrdom of King Charles I* (1783), 5–6.

[4] Lewis Bagot (1740–1802), son of Sir Walter Bagot, Bart., and brother of 1st Lord Bagot. Dean of Christ Church (1777), Bishop of Bristol (1782), Norwich (1783), St Asaph (1790).

[5] Bagot, *Sermon* (1783), 8.   [6] *Ibid.*, 13–14.

The moderate, aristocratic Bagot, charitable and industrious by the episcopal standards of the age, was repelled by the idea that society developed from a savage and disorderly state of nature and that all its advantages were 'the gradual work of mere human effort and ingenuity'. It troubled him that such naturalistic interpretations had permeated the Church itself when 'every power of the human mind, every affection of the human heart, is more than demonstration . . .' of the fallacy of those ideas. Furthermore, he was alarmed by the growing belief that society was essentially the work of fallible men; such a conclusion 'must either annihilate all social duties, both publick and private, or rest the obligation of them on false and insecure grounds.' Bagot was one of several prelates in the pre-revolutionary decade who wondered how far down the hierarchical social layers such naturalistic ideas had filtered. Was it just a matter of time before people on the lowest level would reject the evidence showing that God had placed man in society with all the 'various distributions of rank, wealth, power, and all the exterior circumstances of life'?[1]

Bagot's obscure successor at Bristol (1783–92), Christopher Wilson, basically agreed with but was not critical of the naturalistic premise that man formed society as a necessary means of self-preservation. 'Society is the natural object of his affections and attachments,' but man entered into it because the alternative state of nature was miserable and chaotic. Englishmen had caught a glimpse of that savage reality during the civil wars of the seventeenth century. Instead of denying the destructive nature of pre-social man, as did the more tender-minded Bagot, Wilson felt it should be frankly recognized so that men would be more willing to offer greater obedience to God and to authority.[2] Wilson, one of Pitt's first appointments to the bench, was typical in his easy reconciliation of rationally understood natural law with revelation. Few prelates of his generation found it a troublesome problem. Deists had, of course, failed to understand the continuing relationship between creative laws and the creator, and were blind to the obvious fact that natural religion and morality were in essence no different from the inspired precepts laid down in the Bible. Bishops Butler and Warburton had more than refuted claims to the contrary, and Archdeacon Paley resolved any lingering doubts.

This is what the energetic and influential future Bishop of St David's

[1] L. Bagot, *A Sermon Preached in the Cathedral Church of St Paul . . . June 5, 1788, Being the Time of the Yearly Meeting of the Children Educated in the Charity Schools . . .* (1788), 3–5.

[2] Christopher Wilson, *A Sermon Preached Before the Lords Spiritual and Temporal . . . January 31, 1785, Being the Day Appointed to be Observed as the Anniversary of the Martyrdom of King Charles I* (1785), 10–12.

(1803–24) and Salisbury (1824–37), Thomas Burgess,[1] meant in 1789 when he insisted that even if Scripture was ignored, 'the religion of Nature consists of certain notions of a superior being, collected from the works of creation. . . . [They] . . . are the unwritten will of God, and consist of certain universal and permanent principles conducive to the general good of society.'[2] A productive theologian and classical scholar before his elevation to the bench, Burgess, then chaplain to the powerful Barrington of Salisbury and (in 1791) Durham, explained that divine laws, as they regard society, 'originate from the two great principles of Self-Love, and Social Affection'. Common to all men, they embraced the natural laws of self-preservation and personal freedom. From the standpoint of these basic rights, Burgess agreed, all men are equal and independent, but when translated into social terms individual rights become modified by necessity.[3]

'Mutual protection and happiness are the ends of Society'; consequently, morality and good had to be judged in terms of those goals. Burgess added:

> Any moral good may be said to be intrinsically good, which conduces to those ends of Society. Whatever therefore contributes to the happiness of our fellow creatures, and to maintain the just rights of Society, is intrinsically good, because it promotes the peace and well-being of Society.[4]

The danger to society came when 'a pursuit . . . abstractedly and intrinsically understood . . .', and apparently not contrary to natural law, conflicted with the practical concerns of society. Burgess saw that danger emerging in his own time as social critics derived broad and disruptive conclusions from their analyses of individual natural rights, and accused society of violating those rights. Once speculative philosophy was permitted to intrude upon reality, the wildest conclusions were possible. He emphasized that 'the abstract and intrinsic nature of actions can form no rule for the general conduct of mankind. Such a rule would be susceptible of the worst perversions.'[5] Ultimately, social utility must be the final determinant, as individual utility was the initial motivation for the establishment of society. That which is in conformity with the fundamental purpose of society must also be in tune with natural law. As society had been a necessary and later development than the primitive

---

[1] Thomas Burgess (1756–1837), son of a Hampshire grocer, classical scholar, opponent of the slave trade, and close friend of Bishop Barrington, his patron. A serious, pious clergyman who revitalized the Church in the diocese of St David's. See John S. Harford, *The Life of Thomas Burgess, D.D.* (1840).

[2] T. Burgess, *Considerations on the Abolition of Slavery and the Slave Trade, Upon Grounds of Natural Religious and Political Duty* (Oxford, 1789), 39.

[3] *Ibid.*, 43–44.   [4] *Ibid.*, 27–28.   [5] *Ibid.*, 30.

state of natural individualism, it was erroneous and potentially harmful to abstract from the latter to condemn the former.

To some members of the Anglican hierarchy, such speculation was not only dangerous, it was also sheer nonsense. It was especially foolish when flowing from the pens and pulpits of Christian ministers. How could thinking and religious men believe their earliest ancestors once lived in a primitive and savage state of nature which they voluntarily abandoned to join together in society under acceptable political authority? George Horne, who briefly occupied the see of Norwich (1790–92) before his death, insisted that God had never created such people, left to themselves as savage beasts, uninstructed, eventually establishing a voluntary civil compact.[1] Dean of Canterbury for nearly a decade before his reluctant acceptance of the mitre, Horne was a sincerely devout High churchman who found natural law explanations of society thoroughly unconvincing.[2]

Horne could find no evidence that man ever lived in a state of equality and independence. From the time of his creation he was in a state of subordination, 'since from the beginning, some were born subject to others; and the power of the father, by whatever name it be called, must have been supreme at the first, when there was none superior to it. '[3] Scripture and rational understanding of familial dependency proved that the origins of society were patriarchal, and subordination was natural from the first presence of man on earth. Society and government developed from this basic familial-subordinate structure into warring tribes conquering and subordinating others. Over centuries, Horne concluded, these tribes combined to form states capable of controlling turmoil between the families and tribes within, and of protecting themselves from other states.[4] Scripture and history supported his account, he believed, and both were far more reliable than self-generating abstractions drawn from corrupt man's overweening pride in his reason.

Whatever modifications and qualifications Church spokesmen chose to place upon their varying interpretations of society, they all indicated

[1] G. Horne, 'A Discourse on the Origin of Civil Government', *The Scholar Armed Against the Errors of the Time; Or, A Collection of Tracts On the Principles and Evidences of Christianity, the Constitution of the Church, and the Authority of Civil Government*, 2nd ed. (1800), 271.

[2] George Horne (1730–92), son of a Kent clergyman, President of Magdalen College, Oxford, Vice-Chancellor of the University, Chaplain to George III. Owed his advancement to Lord North and the king.

[3] Horne, *Discourse*, 271.

[4] *Ibid.*, 272–6. Horne believed David Hume's 'false philosophy' had contributed much to this erroneous interpretation of social development. See *A Letter to Adam Smith, L.L.D. On the Life, Death, and Philosophy of His Friend David Hume, Esq.* (1799). First pub. 1777, and reprinted as late as 1836.

C

a genuine uneasiness about ideas of innovation and reform abroad in the land. The political and personal divisions, as well as the economic problems created by the American War, stirred up the feelings of clergy and laity alike. Catholic incursions, the explosiveness of the Gordon riots in 1781, Dissenter demands for admission to the universities, mounting criticisms of the Church by Methodists and enthusiastic Evangelicals, sent occasional tremors through the hierarchical pillars of the Establishment. Frequently, the prelates appeared more disturbed by a state of mind and a changing atmosphere than by specific events. Their often heavy and insensitive antennae seemed to sense a rumbling beneath the foundations of Church and State. It caused Bishop Prety-man of Lincoln to repeat on the eve of the French Revolution the many recent reminders that 'subordination of ranks, and the relation of magistrates and subjects, are indispensably necessary in that state of society for which our Creator has evidently intended the human species.'[1]

Like many of his brethren, Pretyman was prepared to invoke the deity on behalf of the *status quo*; he duly warned that whoever weakens and threatens the existing social and political structure 'by his words or by his actions, weakens the particular form which is duly established and justly administered in the community of which he is a member, sins against the ordinance of God.' And if, the new bishop portended, 'he should be the means of its entire destruction, he is guilty of the greatest crime which in his social capacity he can possibly commit.'[2] Six months later the Bastille fell.

2. THE FRENCH REVOLUTION

Over the next decade, Englishmen indulged in an orgy of self-evalua-tion, deprecation and condemnation, decrying every source of corrup-tion from adultery and duelling to an unsupervised reading of Erasmus Darwin's suggestive *Loves of the Plants*.[3] It was an era of moral self-flagellation in which people whipped themselves with dreary tracts on the evils of luxury, dissipation, religious indifference, and discontent, while intoning the stabilizing virtues of contentment, chastity, marriage,

---

[1] G. Pretyman, *A Sermon Preached Before the Lords Spiritual and Temporal . . . January 30, 1789, Being the Anniversary of King Charles's Martyrdom* (1789), 16.

[2] *Ibid.*

[3] The Revolution triggered a near-hysterical preoccupation with chastity in many quarters. Darwin was aware of this when he recommended that ladies be permitted to read his botanical studies only under the closest supervision. See his *A Plan for the Conduct of Female Education in Boarding Schools* (Dublin, 1798), 45–46; also *The Gentleman's Magazine*, LXV, Pt. II (Dec., 1795), 979.

home and the interdependent responsibilities of all members of society.[1] Once it became obvious that 'the French people, insensible of their own delirium [were] eager to spread the infection and to render all mankind as miserable as themselves', it was necessary to launch a national campaign of moral inoculation.[2] After all, Edmund Burke, the prophet vindicated, had recalled that France has always 'more or less' influenced English behavior, and ominously predicted, 'when your fountain is choked up and polluted, the stream will not run long, or not clear . . .'.[3] The sources of pollution were studied carefully in the waning years of the century, and all possible contamination isolated and exposed. Burke had provided some comfort by his assurances that the institutions of English society were not a site of infection. The pollutants were festering elsewhere, and were repeatedly traced to the corruption of social relationships brought on by the thoughtless behavior of the higher orders. Pious Evangelicals had of course been preaching against the dissolute behavior of the religiously indifferent rich for many years, but the Revolution provided them with a greatly enlarged congregation and chorus, many members of which hardly shared their spiritual enthusiasm or Low Church theology.

Warning cries of 'Reform or Ruin: Take Your Choice!' rang out from a wide variety of voices. The respected High Church barrister, John Bowdler, posed that alternative in 1797, and Englishmen considered it through eight successive editions. Like many others, Bowdler analysed the behavior of people in the middle and higher ranks, ranging from the lesser clergy, 'loose and neglectful in their duties', to the king himself, of whom he had no complaint. But below the monarch, among the nobility and gentry, 'do not Luxury, Corruption, Adultery, Gaming, Pride, Vanity, Idleness, Extravagance, and Dissipation, prevail too generally?'[4] Unfortunately things were not much better among the gentlemen of his profession any more than they were in medicine, commerce and trade. From such evidence, Bowdler wisely concluded that in the future all classes must 'BE GOOD!'[5] This was no different

[1] See R. A. Soloway, 'Reform or Ruin: English Moral Thought During the First French Republic', *The Review of Politics,* 25, no. 1 (Jan. 1963), 110–28.

[2] John Bowles, *The Real Grounds of the Present War With France* (1793), 5.

[3] Edmund Burke, *Reflections on the Revolution in France,* in *The Works of . . . Edmund Burke* (New York, 1813), III, 96.

[4] J. Bowdler, *Reform or Ruin: Take Your Choice! In Which the Conduct of the King, the Parliament, the Ministry, the Opposition, the Nobility and Gentry, the Bishops and Clergy, etc., etc., etc., is Considered and That Reform Pointed Out Which Alone Can Save the Country,* 2nd ed. (1797), 9–11.

[5] *Ibid.,* 26.

from what Frederick Howard, Fifth Earl of Carlisle, decided, nor the anonymous 'Belzebub', who chortled, 'I have always said that TOO MUCH LIBERTY AND LUXURY would make Britain my own.'[1]

Well above that satanic wisdom there was the exalted Burke's description of how 'the most licentious, prostitute, and abandoned . . . and at the same time the most coarse, rude, savage, and ferocious' manners and morals had destroyed the Old Régime.[2] This theme of moral and social corruption pervaded Burke's influential criticism as he reminded his contemporaries, 'all other people have laid the foundations of civil freedom in severer manners, and a system of masculine morality . . .'.[3] Even Richard Price, the Unitarian minister whose defense of the Revolution provoked Burke's *Reflections,* conceded that a remarkable 'accumulation of luxury, avarice, vice and venality' plagued both France and England;[4] he hoped that the French Revolution and its example would 'have ultimately in view a reformation of manners and virtuous practice'.[5]

Popular Evangelicals such as William Wilberforce and Hannah More joined with John Bowles and other High Churchmen not only to decry the uninspiring behavior of the upper classes, but to warn them of the deleterious effect it was having on their social inferiors.[6] How many 'amens' must have responded to Bowles's prayer, 'would to Heaven that the upper ranks could be prevailed upon to consider, before it be too late, how much the morals, and consequently the fate of their country depend upon them.'[7] While much of this criticism was inspired by religious revivalism, and fed upon a deep-rooted sense of personal sin, more of it was prompted by the awful crisis threatening the political and social structure of European society. The two motivating forces often became confused, but, more often than not, frightened critics of upper-class behavior were far less concerned with the salvation of souls

[1] F. Howard, *The Crisis: and Its Alternatives Offered to the Free Choice of Englishmen* (1798), 14. *Gentleman's Magazine,* LIX, Pt. I (June 1789), 508.

[2] E. Burke, *Four Letters Addressed to a Member of the Present Parliament on the Proposals for Peace With the Regicide Directory of France* (1796), in *Works,* IV, 368–9.

[3] Burke, *Reflections,* 54.

[4] R. Price, *A Discourse on the Love of Our Country, Delivered on November 4, 1789* (1789), 46–7.

[5] *Ibid.,* 15.

[6] W. Wilberforce, *A Practical View of the Prevailing Religious System of Professed Christians, in the Higher and Middle Classes in This Country, Contrasted with Real Christianity,* 6th ed. (1798). H. More, *Thoughts on the Importance of the Manners of the Great to General Society,* in *The Complete Works of Hannah More* (New York, 1857). I.

[7] J. Bowles, *A View of the Moral State of Society at the Close of the Eighteenth Century* (1804), vi.

than with the prevention of lower-class revolution. Believing as they did in a hierarchical society, it was logical and instinctive that they would concentrate upon the natural leadership of that society when it was in danger of neglecting or abusing its critical responsibilities.

Much to their discomfort, responsible and respectable critics found their fears justified when Jacobin sympathizers agreed that the higher orders had been far from exemplary in their treatment of the laboring poor. If the solutions of a Tom Paine, the American Joel Barlow, or a William Vaughan were hardly palatable to Wilberforce, Hannah More or John Bowles, they nevertheless jointly decried the want of under-standing and moral leadership by the propertied classes. Although republican agitators were basically concerned with political and social questions rather than those of moral behavior, Vaughan in his *Catechism of Man* (1794) defended the rights of the people on the grounds that the lower orders were more moral and better behaved than their betters. Why, he asked, should moral folk be ruled by those who are immoral, simply because of an accident of birth or good fortune?[1] There was no lack of evidence for such dangerous, leveling queries. The frightened propertied classes were filling books, newspapers, magazines, parliamentary debates, and the ears of innumerable congregations with more than enough examples of the rich's loose and thoughtless manner of living to keep a Jacobin well-armed.

All this contributed to an appalling sense of social disharmony and disintegration prodded by the stabbing fear of a revolutionary-minded laboring class no longer acquiescent in their natural state in the com-munity. Troubled clergymen had vaguely warned of such a possibility as they grew uneasy about the excessive secularization of explanations of individual and social behavior. When it was proposed by Rousseau and others that man was in fact a product of his own corrupt creation, society, rather than society being the result of individual corruption, the prospects for maintaining indefinitely the natural balance seemed to diminish. The French Revolution was startling testimony to what might be expected once the natural laws of social harmony were no longer respected.

Most members of the Church hierarchy responded slowly and cau-tiously to the Revolution until it took a more violent turn in 1792. They were certainly uneasy before then. Any sudden alteration of the *status quo* tended to cause a slight tremor in episcopal circles, and Burke's powerful analysis of events across the Channel did little to steady pre-latic nerves. Initially, however, since the Catholic Church appeared to bear the brunt of changes undertaken, Protestant bishops could readily

[1] W. Vaughan, *The Catechism of Man; Pointing Out From Sound Principles, and Acknowledged Facts, the Rights and Duties of Every Rational Being* (1794), ix-x.

29

find some soothing compensation. George Horne saw no reason at first to be alarmed. He was in fact amused by the impulsive prophecies thrown about during the opening months of the Revolution, and in a letter to George Berkeley, Vice-Dean of Canterbury, he lightly compared the warning of one Anglican parson that 'the devil is just broken loose' with Dr Price singing 'his *Nunc dimittis*, on the sight of paradise returning upon earth'.[1] Horne did not live long enough to witness the more somber evaluations which many of his episcopal associates made of such predictions.

Only one prelate, Watson, found anything good to say about the fall of the Bastille and French attempts to establish constitutional government. That Whig champion of English constitutionalism looked to Paris and saw the 'glorious prospect of the prevalence of general freedom and general happiness' in Europe. Civil and religious liberty were about to triumph, and despotic government would soon give way to 'lawful rule, and right supremacy'. Like many early sympathizers in England, Watson interpreted developments in France in the tradition of 1688, and concluded that princes would soon appreciate the importance of popular affection, liberty and loyalty.[2] During the following year, 1791, the bishop was less certain, but still hopeful that the main benefits of 'this wonderful Struggle' will be 'a Trial by Jury—an Habeas Corpus Act—and an incorrupt Administration of public Justice'. Perhaps influenced by Burke, whom he admired, and who shared his earlier views against the American War, a note of caution crept into his pronouncements. While continuing to rejoice in 'the Emancipation of the French Nation from the Tyranny of Royal Despotism', Watson was becoming uneasy about the French populace and 'popular and aristocratic Demagogues' whom he disliked more than monarchs. Possibly, he conceded, the French emancipation was more apparent than real.[3]

The disappointment Watson felt as the Revolution turned more violent contrasted with the feelings of horror and revulsion that swept the bench and the higher classes. Nevertheless, throughout the remainder of the decade he continued to believe that the bloodshed would run its course, and in time a better France and a better Europe would emerge. Although less positive than he had been during the American War, the bishop still felt it an error for England to fight against a revolutionary movement. Repeatedly he urged negotiations with the Directory which would secure France the fruits of its revolution and guarantee its bor-

[1] 15 Dec. 1789, *Berkeley Ps.*, British Museum, Add. MS. 39312, f. 108.
[2] R. Watson, *Considerations On the Expediency of Revising the Liturgy and Articles of the Church of England: In Which Notice is Taken of the Objections to That Measure, Urged in Two Late Pamphlets* (1790), 105–6.
[3] R. Watson, *A Charge Delivered to the Clergy of the Diocese of Landaff* (1791), 4.

ders. Burke's denunciations of a regicide peace were more reflective of ruling-class sentiments, but Watson suspected that the French would be better off temporarily under a democratic government than they had been under the Bourbons. In any event, the French should be permitted to work out their own destiny, and the bishop believed that in time they would revert to some modified monarchy.[1]

Internal unrest seemed much more dangerous to Watson than did the external military threat. An inhumane conflict was becoming transformed into a grandiose crusade that could drag on indefinitely while intensifying grave problems with the restive lower orders at home. The prelate frankly thought that the French government should be answerable for its sins to God and to its own people rather than to the English. Once the revolutionary government halted its offensive, there was no need to proceed against France any further.[2] Mutiny in the English fleet in 1797 and the imminence of rebellion in Ireland only strengthened Watson's conviction that the war had created a desperate situation internally. Consequently he advocated conceding to the victorious French all their conquests in order to end the war before 'adding a British republic to those of Italy and Germany'. That revolution, feared by so many of his colleagues who viewed France with unrelieved horror, now even panicked Watson. Peace alone would cause the 'fever of republicanism' to subside and give time to all established governments to remedy their defects.[3] What he despaired of most in the Revolution was its stultifying effect upon desperately needed reforms in England and elsewhere. Yet, 'it may be said to every man in England and Europe who attempts to reform abuses either in church or state—*desine, jam conclamatum est*'.[4]

The emergence of Napoleon and the spectre of invasion finally shattered Watson's hope that, if left alone, France would transform itself into a peaceful constitutional monarchy. Instead, tyranny triumphed once more. Watson no longer called for a generous peace, but for total mobilization. In one of his rare appearances in the House of Lords, the disappointed old prelate in 1804 recanted his Whig illusions about French republicanism. He would now 'rather live upon clap-bread and water, and be shod with the wooden clogs of Westmorland for the rest of my life, as a free subject of this limited monarchy, than be pampered with all the delicacies, cockered with all the luxuries of this luxurious town [London], as a slave of the French Republic.'[5]

To most ecclesiastics, it was incredible that any of their brethren might ever have felt otherwise. Samuel Horsley, the most powerful and articulate excoriator of French republicanism in particular, and change

[1] Watson, *Anecdotes*, II, 16–19. [2] *Ibid.*, 19.
[3] Watson to Duke of Grafton, 10 Oct. 1797, *Ibid.*, 46–47.
[4] *Anecdotes*, I, 222. [5] *Ibid.*, II, 191–2.

in general, was far more reflective of Church attitudes.[1] The parallels
that he drew were not with 1688 but with the terrible civil wars earlier
in the century that had torn English society apart. Horsley contended
that, during that dark period, contractual ideas of popular sovereignty
were introduced to inflame 'the phrensy of that fanatical banditti,
which took the life of the First Charles. In the madness and confusion,
which followed the shedding of that blood, our History holds forth an
edifying example of the effects . . . that are ever INTENDED, by the
dissemination of those infernal maxims, that Kings are the servants of
the people, punishable by their Masters. The same lesson is confirmed
by the horrible example, which the present hour exhibits, in the unparalleled misery of a neighbouring Nation. . . .' The execution of
Louis XVI, nine days before the annual January 30th sermon commemorating the death of the 'martyred' Charles, stirred the bishop to
heights of rhetoric from which he rarely descended during the long war
years that lay ahead. 'O my Country! Read the horror of thy own deed
in this recent heightened imitation! Lament and weep, that this black
French treason should have found its example, in the crime of thy unnatural sons!'[2]

In retrospect such savagery appeared inevitable to Horsley once the
French demolished their government, overthrew the altars, despoiled
and degraded the nobility, and forced the best citizens into exile. He
described the results:

> Her riches, sacred and profane, given up to the pillage of sacrilege and
> rapine! Atheists directing her Councils! Desperados conducting her
> Armies! Wars of unjust and chimerical ambition consuming her Youth!
> Her Granaries exhausted! Her fields uncultivated! Famine threatening
> her multitudes! Her streets swarming with Assassins, filled with violence,
> deluged with blood!

England had been fortunate in the quick restoration of Church and
Monarchy that followed 'our bloody deed', but it was impossible to
determine what would happen across the Channel now that 'Public
Justice [is] poisoned in its source . . .'.[3] The progress of the Revolution

---

[1] Samuel Horsley (1733–1806), son of a London clergyman, tutor to 4th Earl
of Aylesford and chaplain to Bishop Lowth of London both of whom were his
patrons. Bishop of St David's (1788), Rochester (1793) and St Asaph (1802).
An extravagant, pluralistic High Churchman, and competent scientist.
See Heneage Horsley Jebb, *A Great Bishop of One Hundred Years Ago:
Being a Sketch of the Life of Samuel Horsley, LL.D.* (1909).

[2] S. Horsley, *A Sermon Preached Before the Lords Spiritual and Temporal . . . January 30, 1793, Being the Anniversary of the Martyrdom of
King Charles the First. With an Appendix Concerning the Political Principles
of Calvin* (1793), 22–23.

[3] *Ibid.*, 23–24.

was an unrelieved catastrophe for Horsley; there could be no compromise, no reconciliation. Certain that the Christian world was engaged in a fateful struggle, the bishop felt England was the last outpost to resist. He demanded in 1798 that the clergy be mobilized into an armed militia for the final defense. Other prelates, equally alarmed by the naval mutiny, the resistance in Ireland, and predictions of imminent insurrection at home, nevertheless had reservations about the propriety and military value of clerical warriors. At a special meeting at Lambeth Palace, old Archbishop Markham of York urged the bishops to 'check the arming influenza of their inferior brethren', and most agreed.[1] Horsley, however, continued to insist he was ready 'to level the musket, and to trail the pike', if necessary, and, after his translation in 1802 to the more exposed diocese of St Asaph, he helped to organize the local militia, and encouraged it to exercise and drill on the palace lawn.[2]

As Watson had feared, the struggle against the French had become transformed into a holy war for the preservation of Christian society. While he repeatedly appealed for peace, Horsley insisted there could never be any reconciliation with bloody regicides at war with mankind. During the debates in 1801 preceding the Peace of Amiens signed the following year, Horsley opposed the government, though not 'insensible to the miseries of war . . .', and well aware of his clerical obligation 'to stop the effusion of human blood'.[3] Not even Bishop Porteus's measured warning that after nine years of war, and now two years of famine, the distress of the lower orders was so severe that a respite was absolutely necessary, was sufficient justification.[4] Horsley knew that in so cataclysmic a struggle, peace could not last until one party was ultimately defeated. A temporary withdrawal would only benefit the forces of darkness, for internal vigilance and repression would be relaxed and the Jacobin levelers would quickly revive.[5] But Horsley's opposition was founded upon even more forbidding assumptions. By the dawn of the new century he, like several of his clerical associates and many laymen, was utterly convinced of the existence of a grand international conspiracy directed against Christian civilization and unfolding in accordance with apocalyptical and millenarian prophecies. Given this belief, the establishment of peace would have little effect upon the elaborate machinations inexorably undermining the foundations of Christian society.

[1] Jebb, *Great Bishop*, 117–19.   [2] *Ibid.*, 172–3.
[3] Cobbett's *Parliamentary History* (1801), XXXVI, 179–81.
[4] *Ibid.*, 183.   [5] *Ibid.*, 182, 191.

3. CONSPIRACY AND MILLENNIUM

E. P. Thompson, in his illuminating and provocative study of the English working class, has described the appearance of millenarian prophecy and activity among the lower classes in the 1790's and the opening years of the nineteenth century. In accordance with his general thesis about the revolutionary nature of working-class thought and action in this period, the author associates millenarianism with the frustrations of a deeper democratic revolutionary impulse diverted and projected into prophetic fantasies.[1] Millenarian illusions, however, were more widespread than Thompson has suggested. They were prevalent among the higher orders as well, where they often became confused with revelations about age-old super-secret societies dedicated to the destruction of monarchy and religion. In the early months of the Revolution, the fashionable and learned, if somewhat erratic, Mrs Piozzi, earlier Mrs Hester Thrale, the wife of the wealthy brewery owner, wondered if the end of the world was approaching. The King's insanity, the death of Emperor Joseph II, 'the French struggling to obtain that Liberty they will not know how to use; the Rage for emancipating Negro Slaves, the Number of Jews lately baptized into Protestant Churches . . .', and many other signs pointed in that cosmic direction. According to her system of historical dating, the approaching year 1800 would leave only two centuries more before a third division of two thousand years would be completed; two thousand from the creation to the deluge; two thousand to the coming of Christ; and another two thousand more 'from his crucifixion to his second appearance in Glory, preceded by a flaming world'.[2] Mrs Piozzi believed in 1790 that her great-great-grandchildren would probably see 'the closing scene'. Four years later, events had caused her to revise her timetable and to conclude, 'so I shall live to see the great Prophecy completed, and our Saviour's *second* coming will then be most surely at hand.'[3]

She saw great significance in exaggerated reports of Jewish conversion, which she interpreted as a prelude to Christ's return. Others, like James Bicheno, a later fervent proponent of Malthusian prophecy as well, emphasized the destruction of papal power in France, and by citing numerous biblical prophecies and mystical numbers, interpreted it as the prelude to the kingdom of Christ being established on earth.[4] Al-

---

[1] Edward P. Thompson, *The Making of the English Working Class* (1965), 116–19.

[2] K. C. Balderston, ed., *Thraliana–The Diary of Mrs Hester Lynch Thrale (Later Mrs Piozzi) 1776–1809*, 2nd ed. (Oxford, 1951), II, 744.

[3] *Ibid.*, 869.

[4] J. Bicheno, *The Signs of the Times: Or, the Overthrow of the Papal Tyranny in France* (1793).

though the Privy Council in 1795 was sufficiently alarmed to lock up in an asylum the retired naval captain Richard Brothers when his interpretations of the Book of Revelation prophesied the end of monarchy and the triumph of the honest poor, Parliament was willing to listen to those of an obscure clergyman, Elhanan Winchester, who assured the legislators that the millennium was upon them. After passing through the three great periods of 'woe'—Mahomet's reign, the triumph of the Turks, and now the French Revolution—mankind was fast approaching the restoration of the Savior's universal rule. 'Then we who are alive and remain, shall be caught up with them in the clouds, to meet the Lord in the air! And so shall we ever be with the Lord.'[1] Whether or not many M.P.s shared Winchester's conviction of an ultimate elevation, some of them were unsure enough to listen to two of these prophetic sermons in a three-week period in 1793.

The variety and extent of such prophetic speculation was in part stimulated by the spiritual excitation of religious revivalism preceding the Revolution. Startling events in France added new dimensions to spiritual enthusiasm that often fed upon portentous signs and a quickened sense of imminence. But many people ostensibly uninfluenced and even hostile to the spiritual awakening could not escape a gnawing sense of confrontation that increasingly clashed with their ingrained confidence in rational explanation. Both attitudes were prevalent in episcopal circles, the latter much more than the former.

Bishop Porteus, more sympathetic to the Evangelical revival than most of the bench, believed, like many of his contemporaries, that the French Revolution could best be explained as a result of the immorality and irreligion that had corrupted French society and dissolved natural hierarchical bonds.[2] Consequently he welcomed and endorsed the innumerable appeals for moral rejuvenation and exemplary behavior on the part of the higher orders in England before the French example made an irreversible impression upon the inferior classes. Tom Paine, and leveling Jacobins like him, were already at work with their deplorable 'democratical' tools etching into the simple minds of the poor the exaggerated lessons of French fanaticism. Alarmed though he was, Porteus

---

[1] Elhanan Winchester, *The Three Woe Trumpets of which the First and Second are Already Past and the Third is Now Begun under which The Seven Vials of the Wrath of God are to be Poured Out Upon the World. Two Discourses Delivered in Parliament February 8 and 24, 1793* (1800), 69–70.

[2] Beilby Porteus (1731–1808), son of a Virginia landowner who emigrated to York in 1720, Royal Chaplain (1769), Bishop of Chester (1776), of London (1787). Was anti-Calvinist, though pro-Evangelical. A decided opponent of the slave trade, early patron of the Church Missionary Society and Bible Society, he was a pluralistic but energetic, improving prelate by the standards of the day.

shied away from the growing assumption that the crisis was in fact part of a greater scheme of things beyond human control. That mankind was plunged into a period of severe testing, there was no denying; whether it was, as some saw, the fulfilment of biblical prophecy leading to the millennium or the day of judgment, he did not pretend to know. All Porteus would say in 1794 was that mankind was caught up in 'awful and portentous times' that required the most serious attention to obligation and responsibility.[1]

The rest of the bench were at first equally cautious. Most of them thought of themselves as rational, suspicious of enthusiasm, and advocates of a moderate natural theology conformable to a balanced mind that found it difficult to give credence to agitated prophets ranting about the apocalypse or the second coming. Conspiracy, however, was more logical—the product of perverted free will contaminated by the defects of the human mind violating the rational laws of nature. Consequently, if the leaders of the Church were initially unable to swallow prophetic, millenarian explanations of the disintegration of European society, many of them readily accepted proof of a fantastic human plot designed to achieve that ominous end.

When, in 1797, the *émigré* Jesuit, the Abbé Augustin Barruel, revealed that the French Revolution was the culmination of efforts by a grand international conspiracy led by the Freemasons, Encyclopedists, and the mysterious Bavarian *Illuminati*, his propositions found ready acceptance on the episcopal bench. In his four-volume *Mémoire pour servir à l'histoire du Jacobinisme*, Barruel traced the conspiracy from the medieval Order of Templars to the Enlightenment, where it fell under the control not only of the Freemasons but of their atheistic, literary, and political allies, Voltaire, Turgot, Condorcet, Diderot, d'Holbach, and d'Alembert. From 1776 onwards, Condorcet, in alliance with the Abbé Sieyes, had constructed the Jacobin revolutionary organization that finally launched the Revolution.[2] Barruel had been influenced in his Masonic illusions by the conspiratorial notions of the Scottish mathematician, John Robison, whom he met in London. The latter's *Proofs of a Conspiracy against all the Religions and Governments of Europe, carried on in the secret meetings of Freemasons, Illuminati and Reading Societies* appeared the year after Barruel's *Mémoire* and gave them added authority.[3] If English clergymen were naturally cautious of the claims of

[1] B. Porteus, *A Charge Delivered to the Clergy of the Diocese of London* . . . (1794), 28–30.

[2] A. Barruel, *Mémoire pour servir à l'histoire du Jacobinisme* (1797–98). See also Norman Cohn, *Warrant For Genocide—The Myth of the Jewish World-Conspiracy and the Protocols of the Elders of Zion* (1967), 25–27.

[3] J. Robison, *Proofs of a Conspiracy against all the Religions and Governments of Europe, carried on in the secret meetings of Freemasons, Illuminati*

a French Jesuit, their substantiation by a safe, respectable, Scottish scientist went far to dispel serious doubt.

Shortly after Barruel's *exposé* appeared and before Robison published his *Proofs*, Lord Liverpool suggested that Bishop Watson, who had recently given Paine a sound drubbing in print, would be the proper person to clothe the arguments of the Abbé in 'a Protestant dress' to give them wider circulation and effect.[1] He picked the wrong man. As a devoted Lockeian rationalist and a confirmed Whig Protestant, Watson found it difficult to reconcile his ideas and feelings about the Revolution with those of an *émigré* Jesuit who represented much that was wrong with France and the Catholic Church before the Revolution. Moreover, Watson welcomed the civil constitution of the clergy and the redistribution of Church property.[2] He himself had been advocating similar reforms for the Established Church for more than a decade.[3] In addition he long thought it possible to interpret the assault on the Gallican Church not as dangerous precedent, but as a step in the direction of international religious toleration and co-operation long resisted by the Papal powers.[4] While he was not prepared simply to reject Barruel's explanation, Watson could not give 'full credit to what had been asserted, the existence of a conspiracy among the philosophers of France and the *illuminés* of Germany to pull down altars and thrones'. The bishop saw that the 'progress of literature and the cultivation of science had, in every country, roused into activity the human intellect, and spurred it to shake off the shackles of superstition and the chains of arbitrary power', but he did not think that this added up to an organized conspiracy. Though in England 'some precipitate and self-sufficient spirits would outrage common sense, and, in over-stepping the bounds of sober investigation, would cease to distinguish the Christian religion from its corruptions, and equitable government from continental despotism', he doubted Barruel's explanation would help restore perspective.[5]

Several of Watson's episcopal brethren had no such reservations. George Pretyman of Lincoln informed his clergy in 1800 that the Abbé Barruel and Professor Robison had conclusively proven the existence

---

[1] Sir John Dalrymple to Watson, 25 April 1797, *Anecdotes*, II, 37–38. See Watson's *An Apology for the Bible in A Series of Letters Addressed to Thomas Paine* (1796).

[2] Watson, *Charge* (1791), 6–7.

[3] See Watson's *Letter to the Archbishop* (1783) and *A Charge Delivered to the Clergy of the Archdeaconry of Ely . . . June 12, 1788* (Cambridge, 1788).

[4] Watson, *Considerations*, 107–10.   [5] Watson, *Anecdotes,* II, 38–39.

---

and Reading Societies (Edinburgh and London, 1797). *Proofs* went through five editions in two years.

of 'a regularly digested plan for the extirpation of all belief in Christianity'. It was part of a 'formidable conspiracy' launched several years earlier, and the prelate thought it important that he validate the evidence in order 'to guard against the effect of contradictory assertions, industriously spread, and often hastily adopted without examination'.[1] Pretyman had himself hastily seized upon Barruel when the *Mémoire* appeared three years earlier and had perverted the Abbé's arguments into a condemnation of the Catholic Church. The conspiracy, like the Revolution, was a divine instrument designed to destroy the power of the Roman religion, and end 'the cruelty, the tyranny, and the impiety of the Church of Rome'.[2] Although previously silent on the spate of prophecies circulating for several years, Bishop Pretyman now recalled that many of them could be interpreted to show that the destruction of the Roman Church would precede the triumph of the true faith. Various analyses of the Book of Revelation indicated that the end of the eighteenth century would be a period of great calamity, but, the bishop reflected, it might also lead to a great era of spiritual improvement. Over the next few years Pretyman satisfied himself that millenarian prophecies, in spite of their often obscure form, could clearly be seen unravelling. In such times as these, he preached to his clergy, we must especially examine them 'as they furnish the only satisfactory explanation of these recent and marvellous occurrences, which tend to stagger the belief of philosophizing Christians, and fill the less learned . . . with apprehension and alarm'.[3]

The notion of a grand conspiracy seemed to release Church leaders from the restraints of reason and moderation as they fumbled for explanations of the Revolution. Conspiracy, of course, provided essentially simple and comprehensible answers to conservative and frightened minds. Many prelates had suspected that some great, nefarious scheme was afoot, and Barruel and Robison not only confirmed their suspicions but made them respectable. Moreover, the approaching end of a century was itself an apocalyptic stimulant that took on added significance in such times. The cautious Porteus, who, in 1794, had hesitated to take a position on the possibility of hidden causes, claimed in 1798 that his private fears had now been verified by Barruel's and Robison's revelations. He confessed that he did not realize how deep the foundations of irreligion had been laid and how widely the principles had been spread, but now we see it 'secretly and silently undermining . . . the great bul-

---

[1] Pretyman, *A Charge Delivered to the Clergy of the Diocese of Lincoln . . . June and July, 1800* (1800), 8–10.

[2] Pretyman, *A Sermon Preached . . . Before His Majesty, and Both Houses of Parliament . . . December 19th, 1797, Being the Day Appointed For a General Thanksgiving* (1798), 10–12.

[3] Pretyman, *Charge* (1800), 11–12.

warks of morality and religion. . . .'.[1] France had disintegrated, but thank God, 'our good sense and judgment influenced by the Holy Spirit and the purity of our faith', had thwarted the conspiracy.[2] The struggle nevertheless continued, and though Porteus was not certain if there were *Illuminati* about, he knew there were societies in England with similar aims, and working amongst the lower classes. The miners of Cornwall and the colliers of Newcastle were selling their Bibles to purchase Tom Paine's *Age of Reason*; it was clear that the systematic distribution of such atrocious literature could not be the work of a few unconnected individuals, but required a united organization of considerable size.[3]

Like many of his contemporaries, Porteus had also come to believe that the international conspiracy was a necessary agency of the deity who was actually directing the 'confusion and disorder in the world . . . to those important purposes designated in the prophecies of holy writ (more particularly in those relating to the rise, progress, and establishment of the power of Antichrist) . . .'.[4] Predictions of the Antichrist rising from the chaos of revolution were plentiful in the 1790's, and the emergence of the apparently invincible Napoleon certainly strengthened the argument. In 1796, Samuel Horsley recognized that 'we are fallen upon times which [are] perhaps [more dangerous] than any which the Christian Church hath seen, since its first struggles with the powers of darkness in the first centuries'.[5] An upheaval of such unprecedented proportions indicated that something of enormous significance was to happen. 'The signs of the times are such as may create an apprehension that the hour of trial is not far distant.'[6] The opening of the new century four years later was carefully watched for further signs, and Horsley

[1] Porteus, *A Charge Delivered to the Clergy of the Diocese of London in the Years 1798 and 1799* (1799), 8–9. Porteus, alarmed by the events of 1797, had delayed his triennial visitation so as not to have to summon the clergy from their posts, where they were needed to combat conspiracy and prepare for the French invasion.

[2] *Ibid.*, 11.

[3] *Ibid.*, 13.

[4] *Ibid.*, 42–43. Porteus added this section in a note; it was not included in the text of the *Charge* when delivered. He was still uncomfortable about millenarian prophecies, but thought the matter too pressing to avoid discussing it. He particularly recommended that the clergy read Henry Kett, *History, the Interpreter of Prophecy: Or, A View of Scriptural Prophecies and Their Accomplishment in the Past and Present Occurrences of the World*, 3 vols. (Oxford, 1799). This work reached a fifth edition in 1805.

[5] Horsley, *The Charge . . . Delivered At His Primary Visitation in . . . 1796* (1796), 33.

[6] *Ibid.*, 52.

saw them as a prelude to the millennium. It was clear that the world was faced with its greatest crisis 'since the moment of our Lord's departure from the earth'.[1] The French Encyclopedists, Condorcet, the Bavarian *Illuminati*, and especially Voltaire, 'the crafty villain', had done the work of Antichrist before he came. The way had been paved; Horsley saw rising 'out of the raging sea of Anarchy and Irreligion . . . the dreadful Apocalpytic Beast . . . in its ancient form . . .'.[2]

The purpose of the French Revolution was now clear to the bishop; it was the vehicle for the appearance of Antichrist. God, he recalled in 1805, employs natural causes and events for His ends, but it must not be forgotten that He also wills those ends. The case for Antichrist is clear; it is foretold he will rise and will fall before the second advent. Not having heard yet of Austerlitz, Horsley thought that Trafalgar was the turning-point.[3] It was not, and shortly before his death in 1806, the old bishop wrote resignedly to his half-brother in India that Napoleon would remain master of Europe—at least of the southern part—and would 'settle a considerable body of Jews in Palestine, which will open the door to him for his conquest of the East, as far as the Euphrates. He will then set himself up for the Messiah, and a furious persecution will take place in which his friends in Palestine will at first be his principal instruments, but will at last turn their weapons towards his destruction.'[4] Whether this would be followed by the wholesale conversion of the Jews prophesied as a prelude to the second coming is not made clear in the bishop's letter.[5] Four days later he was dead.

Horsley's strange predictions were not simply the paranoic ramblings of a frightened old man, though there were certainly indications of this in the later years of his life. The French Revolution was a shock from

[1] Horsley, *The Charge . . . Delivered At His Second General Visitation in . . . 1800* (1800), 3.

[2] *Ibid.*, 7–11. Horsley not only praised Barruel and Robison, but Bishop Pretyman for defending them in his *Charge* of the same year.

[3] Horsley, *The Watchers and the Holy Ones. A Sermon Preached . . . December 5, 1805, Being the Day of Public Thanksgiving For the Victory Obtained by Admiral Lord Viscount Nelson Over the Combined Fleets of France and Spain Off Cape Trafalgar* (1806). In case there were any doubts, Horsley emphasized that the defeat of 'the vile Corsican' was God's doing, not ours, and was in accordance with some grand divine plan soon to be revealed.

[4] 30 Sept. 1806, Jebb, *Great Bishop*, 224–5.

[5] Horsley's speculation about Napoleon's association with the Jews was perhaps prompted by the Emperor's summoning an assembly of French Jews to Paris in 1806 to confirm their loyalty and recruit their assistance in controlling money-lenders. This 'Great Sanhedrin' as the meeting was called, after the supreme Jewish court of antiquity, convinced many persons that Napoleon was indeed the Antichrist appearing as the Messiah to the Jews. See Cohn, *Warrant for Genocide*, 29 ff.

which he never recovered. He raged incessantly against it, and against any attempt to establish peace with any of the régimes that came to power after 1793. But the conspiratorial and millenarian atmosphere of the age was widespread in ecclesiastical circles as well as among younger clergymen whose episcopal careers had not yet begun. Chief among them was the ultra-High Church pluralist Vicar of St Mary-le-Bow, William Van Mildert, who later, as Regius Professor of Divinity and successively Bishop of Llandaff (1819–26) and Durham (1826–36), stood as firmly as any churchman against the nineteenth century.[1] Baptized by Horsley in 1765, Van Mildert greatly admired and shared many of the strong opinions of that powerful prelate. During the year of the former's death, 1806, Van Mildert published the Boyle Lectures he had been delivering at St Mary-le-Bow since 1802, in which he was thoroughly convinced by Barruel's and Robison's revelations.[2] Within the context of apocalyptical prophecy, they made a great deal of sense. 'According to some interpreters of eminence . . .', the prediction of the 'rise, growth and downfall of the Papal and Mahometan powers . . .' had been fulfilled.[3] These were necessary steps to the arrival of the millennium, but others were still to come. The death and resurrection of the Two Witnesses, and the conversion and restoration of the Jews, still lay in the future, although it was likely that these events would soon synchronize. But the reign of the Antichrist was not yet over, though Van Mildert believed the day would not be very distant. The decay of the Papal See and the Ottoman Empire was rapid, but it was not clear whether the coming of the Two Witnesses to restore truth would be in the Protestant Church in the west, or in the remnant of the Greek Church in the east.[4] Van Mildert, who throughout his career steadfastly opposed any further extension of religious toleration to Dissenters, feared that their corrosive influence would interfere with the Witnesses appearing as Protestants. Socinians and Quakers were especially dangerous and were probably in

[1] William Van Mildert (1765–1836), grandson of a Dutch merchant and son of a Surrey distiller; pluralistic and non-resident, he was actually fined £110 in 1800 in one of the earliest instances of more stringent residency requirements being enforced. Was a favorite of Liverpool, who elevated him to Llandaff and gave him the deanery of St Paul's on condition that he resided half the year in London. During the tense coronation of George IV in 1820 Van Mildert was so frightened that the Queen would cause a riot at St Paul's that Liverpool told him to stay at Llandaff until it was over. He did. (See *Liverpool Ps.*, British Museum, Add. MS. 38288, ff. 154, 170).

[2] W. Van Mildert, *An Historical View of the Rise and Progress of Infidelity, With a Refutation Of Its Principles, and Reasonings: In A Series of Sermons Preached For the Lecture Founded by the Hon. Mr Boyle, in the Parish Church of St Mary-le-Bow, From the Year 1802 to 1805* (1806), I, 382–3, 401–2.

[3] *Ibid.*, 442.   [4] *Ibid.*, 452–3.

D

league with the conspirators whom Barruel and Robison described. The Socinians were welcomed by the atheistical philosophers and their leader, Frederick II of Prussia, because their rational perversions helped destroy Scripture; while the Quakers, with their '*fanatical* pretensions to *Inspiration*', maligned the Sacraments and the Christian priesthood.[1]

Turning to the Jews, Van Mildert concluded that their survival, in spite of endless persecution, was in accordance with God's plan, and, though they had yet to convert, there was no longer any doubt that sooner or later they would do so. All of these signs pointed to the millennium. Whether it would be preceded by the actual resurrection and triumph of the saints raised from the dead, or the renovation of the Church to flourish one thousand years after the conversion of the Jews, was not clear. What was certain, however, was that the true Church would have to face trials and tribulations similar to those recently undergone. After a thousand years the devil would make one final and fierce assault, and would then fail forever.[2] As the dating was confused, Van Mildert did not know how far along the prophetic road to the advent man had stumbled. He did know, however, that 'the nearer the awful day of the Lord approaches . . . more madly does the world rage against its Creator and Redeemer, the more desperately does it rush on its own ruin, and scoff at the Divine judgments with increased audacity and contempt'. The world was certainly raging, rushing, and scoffing. Quoting St Peter (iii. 3), 'there shall come, in the last days, Scoffers, walking after their own lusts . . .', Van Mildert saw the fulfilment of still another prediction of 'the approaching close of the Christian dispensation upon earth'.[3]

As in the case of the Jewish people who grew worse as the fateful day approached, the pattern was repeated in recent times. It could be traced from the confused deism of Lord Herbert of Cherbury to the infidels of the eighteenth century, until it was finally transformed into a great international anti-Christian conspiracy under the auspices of Freemasons, the *Illuminati*, Frederick the Great, and Voltaire. In England, Tom Paine and William Godwin were in many clerical minds the principal agents of the conspiracy.[4] Bishop Horsley for a time feared that their dangerous ideas were being introduced into the Sunday schools, which were fast becoming nurseries of revolution. Van Mildert lamented that the Channel had not been wide enough, nor was the horrid example of France sufficient to protect the English from a 'generation of vipers' who conspired with their atheistical cohorts on the Continent to create nothing short of a 'universal Apostacy', and to deprive 'the Redeemer of *all* the Souls for whom his precious blood was shed'.[5]

[1] *Ibid.*, 409–11.　　　[2] *Ibid.*, 455–9.　　　[3] *Ibid.*, 394–5.
[4] *Ibid.*, 406–7.　　　　[5] *Ibid.*, 397.

This was strange talk for rational men well acquainted with the laws of nature and human behavior. Before the Revolution, they had kept reason and revelation well in balance, and if there was too great a conflict, they had tended to reconcile it in favor of the former. But the scope of the upheavals in the last decade of the century was too great to be coped with in a completely rational way, and gradually the defensive barriers of reason began to crumble before incredible events. Confused, and at times terrified, many people crowded into the inner sanctuary of suspicion, conspiracy and fantasy, where garbled history and illuminated revelation retrospectively merged into frantic explanation. The voice of rational religion and natural theology was strangely quiet. It was as if it had had its hearing, but now seemed hopelessly inadequate for the frenzied needs of enlightened churchmen who were no longer confident that they understood the natural laws of human nature and social cohesion.

One new member of the bench recoiled at this trend, and sought to restore some rational balance and perspective to the Church's analysis of recent events. John Randolph, elevated to Oxford in 1799, privately confessed his deep concern about the conspiratorial-millenarian exaggerations that were thrown about.[1] He for one could not take Barruel and Robison seriously, and could not understand how so many of his fellow bishops could.[2] He told his clergy in 1802 that though there might be some indications of conspiracy and prophetical happenings, the evidence was slight and unconvincing.[3] The explanation of the recent momentous events could best be explained by a knowledge of human nature and history rather than by an enthusiastic reading of apocryphal texts or dubious accounts of grand international machinations. As a former Professor of Moral Philosophy and Regius Professor of Greek and then Divinity, Randolph thought he had thoroughly studied the cause of the Revolution—'the Will of Man!' That gift, when unguided by reason, 'its natural superior', was influenced by the passions, and led man to a dangerous course of innovation and change.[4] The collective 'general Will', which is ever necessary to moderate the errors and

[1] John Randolph (1749–1813). Son of a President of Corpus Christi College, he had an academic career as Professor of Poetry, Greek, Moral Philosophy and Regius Professor of Divinity before his elevation to the bench.

[2] Randolph to Rev. T. Lombard, 20 Nov. 1800, Bodleian Library, MS. Top. Oxon., d. 355, f. 22.

[3] J. Randolph, *A Charge Delivered to the Clergy of the Diocese of Oxford . . . in June, MDCCCII* (Oxford, 1802), 5. Randolph was much more disturbed by Methodist 'schismatics' than he was about Antichrist.

[4] Randolph, *A Sermon Preached Before the Lords Spiritual and Temporal . . . March 12, 1800, Being the Day Appointed For A General Fast* (Oxford, 1800), 7.

extravagances of individual wills, is not always able to prevail and the wildness in unreasoning man can then collectively as well as individually burst forth. If often leads to chimerical illusions and innovations tending towards the creation of ideal societies beyond the ability and the needs of mankind.[1] This was nothing new in human history. Englishmen had tried it in the seventeenth century, and now France is 'in pursuit of this phantom which continually flies before [it]'.[2] That was no excuse, however, for rational contemporaries to fly off on the wings of their own fantasies.

Randolph did not mean to suggest that the hand of God was not in evidence. On the contrary, he was certain providence was punishing man as it always did when he exceeded the bounds of free will rationally exercised in accordance with the teachings of Scripture.[3] In permitting the growth of deism and Socianism, man had neglected religious truth and had relied entirely on reason.[4] He had again entered on the course of innovation, forgetting that it is God who 'steers the ship into port . . .'. It was especially alarming this time because in contrast to the seventeenth-century civil wars, there was an abandonment of religion. Instead of delusionary sects emerging we have 'a torrent of infidelity . . . and the abandonment of all restraint'.[5] The bishop acknowledged that divine retribution was also behind the crop failure of 1800, but as he was even uncomfortable with this direct supernatural explanation, he quickly cautioned that God's actions are really too difficult to grasp, and dropped the subject.[6] Unlike many of his fellow churchmen, Randolph refused to be carried away by the hysteria of the times. As great as the danger was, it did not come from newly discovered conspiracies of *illuminati* or the appearance of Antichrist. It came from long-recognized sources: from religious enthusiasts, Roman Catholics, Socinians, and agitated men following their passions rather than their reason.

Randolph's was the voice of the eighteenth-century churchman who saw the crisis of the day in terms of human nature drifting away from the comprehensible verities of moderating rational religion. As he moved up the ladder of preferment to Bangor (1807–9) and finally London (1809–13)[7]—the calm, strong-willed Tory prelate continued to maintain that the tumult of the era was man's making, whether it be in France or England. The former had succumbed to enthusiasm and a perverted (i.e. unreasonable) sense of free will. But there was no real evidence of universal corruption. England had so far avoided destruction in spite

---

[1] *Ibid.*, 9–11.   [2] *Ibid.*, 13–15.   [3] *Ibid.*, 3.
[4] *Ibid.*, 5.   [5] *Ibid.*, 15–16.   [6] *Ibid.*, 20–21.
[7] In 1800 Randolph was also offered the Primacy of Ireland by Pitt, but refused 'to get embroiled' in that 'fearful country'. The very idea, he told a friend, terrified his wife. Randolph to T. Lombard, 1 Feb. 1800, Bod. Lib., MS. Top. Oxon., d. 355, ff. 1–2.

of the rantings of home-grown enthusiasts and dangerous visionaries proclaiming the possibility of an equalitarian society. Although some of Randolph's contemporaries, like Bishop Huntingford of Gloucester (1802–15), remained convinced that the Revolution was a manifestation of an awful conspiracy of infidels 'against all European governments, against all European religion, and more especially against Christian religion', they began to realize that England was likely to survive the holocaust.[1] In 1814, with the coming of peace, Huntingford still cited Barruel and Robison as evidence of this plot that led us 'to a dark abyss of unparalleled foulness . . . which, as it indicates the most hideous distortion of reason, and exposes the blackest dye of viciousness in heart, so it is novel in the history of all that was ever suggested to any aggregate body of human beings, by the world, the flesh, or the devil'.[2] But like Randolph's successor at London, William Howley, who also long nurtured the illusion of conspiracy, Huntingford knew that England had stepped back from the fateful abyss.[3]

4. REVOLUTION AND CLERICAL REFORM

The critical factor in the salvation of the country during the long years of revolution and war was, in the minds of contemporaries, the acquiescence of the lower orders in the natural state of English society. Although the lurid temptations placed before them by Tom Paine and his equalitarian minions had enticed some of the laboring sort away, most of their class had rejected the grand conspiracy. Church spokesmen who had joined with lay moralists to urge the higher classes to an appreciation of their moral and social responsibilities were delighted that their efforts had been rewarded. It even appeared that many of the wealthy were attending church with greater regularity than at any time in recent memory.[4] Within clerical circles, however, another explanation for the preservation of social stability rapidly gained credence. This was the belief that the revolutionary flood had been stanched at the Channel

[1] George Isaac Huntingford (1748–1832), son of a Hampshire clergyman, became Warden of Winchester school, where he had Henry Addington as a pupil. Addington, later Viscount Sidmouth, was his patron and saw him elevated to see of Gloucester and, in 1815, Hereford.

[2] G. I. Huntingford, 'Discourse On Thursday, July 7, 1814, Being the Day Appointed For General Thanksgiving to Almighty God On the Restoration of Peace', in Henry Huntingford, ed., *The Posthumous Works of . . . G. I. Huntingford, D.D.* (1832), 439.

[3] W. Howley, *A Charge Delivered to the Clergy of the Diocese of London . . . in the Year 1814* (1814), 12.

[4] This was noted as early as 1798 in *The Annual Register*, 229. In describing the 'avenues to the churches filled with carriages', the writer wryly noted that 'this novel appearance prompted the simple country people to inquire what was happening'.

45

because of the heroic efforts of the parochial clergy. At the urging of their bishops, they had, by their zealous ministrations, erected insurmountable barriers to atheistic disaffection. When it was all over, and the French were at last safely defeated, the indolent Bishop of Ely (1812–36), Bowyer Edward Sparke,[1] roused himself sufficiently in 1817 to congratulate the Anglican clergy for exerting themselves 'most strenuously and successfully in stemming the torrent of sedition and disloyalty' that had earlier threatened to inundate the country.[2] He only hoped that the new generation of ministers would be as successful in coping with the post-war unrest that was again troubling English society.

Since the opening years of the new century, prelates had similarly been congratulating themselves and their clergy for surviving. Porteus knew that the continuation of the Establishment was dependent upon the perpetuation of the existing social institutions of the realm, and, in 1803, claimed that both had persisted during the previous terrible decade because of the stabilizing endeavors of the Establishment ministry.[3] To prelates raised on the Warburtonian idea of the utilitarian function of an Established Church as a political and social agency of the state, it appeared that the Anglican clergy had justified their privileges. One of Porteus's successors at Chester (1800–9), Henry William Majendie,[4] asserted that the passage of legislation in 1803–4 to reduce clerical non-residence, cut down pluralism, and assist impoverished curates who were not paid enough by absentee incumbents, was above all an expression of appreciation from a legislature grateful for the important benefits 'derived from the unremitted exertions of the Clergy, during the last ten years especially'.[5] The measures were in fact the result of mount-

---

[1] Bowyer Edward Sparke (1759–1836), son of a Middlesex squire, owed his preferment to the Duke of Rutland, whose tutor he had been. An apparently insatiable nepotist and pluralist, even for those times, Sparke, his son and son-in-law enjoyed more than £30,000 a year in Church endowments between them.

[2] B. E. Sparke, *A Charge Delivered to the Clergy of Ely . . . in the Year MDCCCXVII* (1817), 8.

[3] B. Porteus, *A Charge Delivered to the Clergy of London in the Year 1803* (1804), 18.

[4] Henry William Majendie (1754–1830), grandson of a Huguenot *émigré*, and son of an Anglican clergyman who was a Canon of Windsor and tutor to the Prince of Wales and Duke of York. Majendie followed in his father's footsteps as a canon and as preceptor to Prince William, later William IV. Owed his elevation to Chester and, in 1809, to Bangor, to the royal family.

[5] H. W. Majendie, *A Charge Delivered to the Clergy of the Diocese of Chester . . . In the Months of July and August, 1804* (1804), 20–21. The legislation in question was 43 Geo. III, c. 84, and 44 Geo. III, c. 2. See Best, *Temporal Pillars*, 222.

ing criticism both within and without the Church directed against some of the more outrageous abuses of the Anglican ministry—abuses that threatened to render the Establishment ineffective at the parochial level at a time when revolutionary, Jacobinical ideas were being preached and distributed in every locale in the country. The introduction of these initial, inadequate reforms, at a time when the idea of reform was anathema to the governing classes, indicates how disturbing clerical abuses had become. Nevertheless, Majendie was sure that gratitude, not criticism or dissatisfaction, prompted Parliament into 'unequivocally and judiciously acknowledging its obligations to the Church . . .'.[1] The bishops were less magnanimous; they defeated the first of several attempts to compel non-resident clergy to pay curates an adequate wage.

Without actually denying the momentous task of pacification and acquiescence undertaken by the clergy in the revolutionary years, few of Majendie's episcopal brethren shared his illusions of parliamentary appreciation and generosity. On the contrary, the Revolution had sharply intensified what the religious revival had already outlined—the Established Church was so weighed down with internal physical and spiritual abuses that it might soon prove completely inadequate for its special secular role as a stabilizing agency of the State and its religious role as a guide to eternal salvation. Although the former responsibility was exaggerated in the atmosphere of crisis, the latter took on renewed meaning, not only because of the religious revival, but because the connection between spiritual relevancy and social and political influence could no longer be ignored. To an Established Church that owed its privileged position primarily to political utility rather than popular affection, this was an increasingly worrisome development that was to trouble Church leaders throughout the first half of the nineteenth century.

Plagued by non-residency, pluralism, secularity and indifference, the Church suddenly seemed in the 1790's a weak barrier to revolution, and many of its leaders knew it. Bishop Watson had been repeating his suggestions for ecclesiastical reform since 1783. With the exception of an occasional anonymous rebuttal from a contented parson, Watson's ideas were launched into a void of clerical indifference. The closest thing to an episcopal response to his proposals for redistributing ecclesiastical revenue came obliquely from Samuel Horsley in 1786, when he concluded that the great inequality that admittedly exists in the Anglican Church, 'this evil in the domestic life of the minister of the Gospel, I will venture to predict, no schemes of human policy ever will remove'. Inequities were inevitable, Horsley explained, and they 'arise from the nature of our Calling; in part from the corrupt manners of a world at enmity with God; but primarily, from the mysterious councils of Providence; which, till the whole world shall be reduced to the obedience of

[1] Majendie, *Charge* (1804), 16.

the Gospel, admit not that the ministry should be a situation of ease and enjoyment'.[1] With thousands of curates eking out a bare subsistence serving several parishes for pluralistic non-residents, many of whom were themselves holding additional cures to obtain an adequate income, and with episcopal incomes ranging from less than £500 to over £20,000, it was clear that uniform Scriptural obedience was a long way off.[2] No one knew this better than Watson, who saw that his *Letter to the Archbishop* was only the beginning of a long and often bitter public discussion of the Church's problems.[3] Solutions, he believed, were at least a generation or two away.

The bishop was right; but the upheaval created by the French Revolution quickened the pace, as it placed the question of clerical responsibility and effectiveness in a very different and critical perspective. The occasional prelatical voice calling for an improvement in clerical standards, residency, and parochial diligence, usually to thwart Methodist itinerants canting about 'the new birth', was soon joined by an episcopal chorus reasoning, urging, pleading and even threatening the clergy to prove their utility to the State and God by making their parishes secure. Watson, himself the embodiment of clerical abuse, warned in his 1791 *Charge* that unless those friendly to the Church were prepared to initiate some reform it might soon be undertaken by 'ruder hands'.[4] He praised the example of the National Assembly redistributing church revenue to provide more equitably for all the clergy. Without advocating equality of income, Watson did believe that much could still be done within the Establishment to improve inadequate incomes and eliminate the most serious abuses—pluralism and non-residence. These were disgraceful scandals that undermined parochial religion and caused the clergy to be held in contempt by a growing number of 'the rude and undisciplined part of mankind'.[5] Unlike their betters, the multitudes did not understand that woefully inadequate incomes in thousands of livings necessitated pluralism and non-residency. Though the possessor at that time of four rectories and an archdeaconry, which, along with his diocese, he rarely visited,[6] the prelate spoke longingly of some future time, though

[1] S. Horsley, *A Sermon Preached At the Anniversary Meeting of the Sons of the Clergy . . . May 18, 1786* (1786), 18–20.

[2] See Best, *Temporal Pillars*, 196 ff., 545.   [3] *Anecdotes*, I, 175.

[4] *Charge* (1791), 5.   [5] *Ibid.*, 6. See also Watson's *Considerations* (1790).

[6] Watson continued to acquire livings and to manage his estates throughout his career, blaming his pluralism and non-residency on Pitt's refusal to translate him to a more lucrative see. As he explained in 1797, 'it is not my fault that some of the best years of my life have been thus employed; had I met with the encouragement of my profession, which would have enabled me to make a moderate provision for eight children, I never should have commenced an agriculturist . . .'. *Anecdotes*, II, 118.

he might not live to see it, when such evils would be eliminated.[1] Watson had felt the previous year that the time to start was propitious, and reminded those who might stubbornly resist 'that more constitutions, civil and ecclesiastical, have been overturned, by what is called firmness in their rulers, than by well-timed condescensions to popular requisitions'.[2]

Such thoughts were on Bishop Porteus's mind when in his primary *Charge* to the clergy of London in 1790 he warned about taking 'public esteem' and the support of the legislature for granted. They were based upon the clergy's ability to promote 'most effectually the peace, the morals, the good order, the welfare, and the happiness of the community'.[3] Unlike Watson, he found nothing admirable in the actions of the National Assembly; instead, he saw an example of what happens when an established clergy loses the confidence and justification for its privileged position. If it should happen, he ominously predicted, we will be open to all our adversaries, 'and our properties and revenues will be swept away, like those of our brethren, in a neighbouring kingdom, whose despoliation . . . has been no less owing to their non-residence, their secularity, their dissipation, their loss of public esteem, than ever to the subversion of their civil government'.[4] Watson viewed the National Assembly's actions as redistribution and equalization; Porteus and most of the bench saw them as despoliation, even if they were not too chagrined about it at the time. But, like Watson, Porteus was aware that pluralism, non-residency and the poverty of the lesser clergy were serious threats to the favored position enjoyed by the Anglican ministry. Unlike him, however, he was not yet prepared to go any further than personal exhortation.

That was more than enough for some of his frightened colleagues who wanted nothing whatsoever to do with reform of any kind. Porteus's non-resident successor at Chester, William Cleaver, cautioned that tampering with existing institutions was a very dangerous business. 'Considering the uncertainty of events, which no human wisdom can secure, the certain detriment, to which all attempts to change subject the general happiness, and the quality of moral, as well as natural evil, which is inseparable from them . . .' it is much better to be satisfied with 'present advantages . . .'.[5] He was not so satisfied himself as to reject

[1] *Charge* (1791), 7.

[2] *Considerations*, 90.

[3] B. Porteus, *A Charge Delivered to the Clergy of the Diocese of London . . . in the Year MDCCXC* (1790), 25.

[4] *Ibid.*

[5] W. Cleaver, *A Sermon Preached Before the Lords Spiritual and Temporal . . . January 31, 1791. Being the Anniversary of King Charles's Martyrdom* (Oxford, 1791), 12.

translations to Bangor (1800) and finally St Asaph (1806) while continuing to reside at Brasenose College, where he was Master.[1] All the while he continued to maintain the fear that of all reforms, that of the Church was most dangerous because it was the principal support of the monarchy and the constitution. When the Gallican Church was altered, it paved the way to disaster.[2]

The inclination of the hierarchy was clearly for retrenchment, but the weaknesses of the Church were too apparent to permit an easy withdrawal from reality. The old Bishop of Hereford, John Butler, in 1792 described that reality in rare quantitative terms. Shortly after his translation from the see of Oxford to Hereford in 1788, Butler sent out visitation queries and compared the results with the diocesan survey last made in 1747. The decline in church attendance was so distressing that he was unwilling to divulge the figures. They were by no means very high in 1747, and given the increase in population since that time the results were even more alarming. Butler predicted that if the trend continued for another forty years the results for the Church would be deplorable.[3] As explanation he gave the usual eighteenth-century criticism of excessive luxury and materialism encouraged by the prosperity of the age, and also suggested that since the energies of so many clergymen were devoted to replying to attacks on the faith, they had neglected their parochial functions.[4] That battle had been won, he concluded, and it was now necessary for the clergy to return to their parishes and preach 'animating Evangelical Truths' to their fast-disappearing flocks. 'The present state is Disgraceful and DANGEROUS'; a revival was long overdue.[5]

Butler was no religious enthusiast. A moderate Broad churchman and former Whig pamphleteer who, like Watson, owed his elevation to Oxford in 1777 to his political services, he converted to Toryism after 1783, and gained translation to Hereford. He would have been content to live out the remainder of his long life in the tranquillity of his new diocese, but the upheaval of the 1790's made such complacency too difficult. Similar evidence to that of Butler's was being gathered in other dioceses, sometimes by the bishop and occasionally by interested clergy. In 1800 there appeared a particularly disturbing report based upon statistics gathered in seventy-nine of the more than twelve hundred

---

[1] Cleaver (1742–1815), son of a Bucks. schoolmaster, and brother of Ewesby Cleaver (1746–1819), Archbishop of Dublin, owed his advancement to his former pupil at Cambridge, the Marquis of Buckingham.

[2] Cleaver, *Sermon* (1791), 14.

[3] John Butler, *Charge to the Clergy of His Diocese . . . In the Year 1792* (Hereford, 1792), 5–7.

[4] *Ibid.*, 7, 11.

[5] *Ibid.*, 13–14.

parishes in the largest diocese of the realm, Lincoln.[1] The survey, conducted by several reform-minded Evangelical clergymen in Lincolnshire, and published with the approval of Bishop Pretyman, revealed that out of an approximate population of fifteen thousand people, less than five thousand had anything to do with the Church, and of these only eighteen hundred could be considered communicants. Since the communicants were drawn from the adult population of the parishes, which was estimated at approximately eleven thousand, less than one-sixth of persons above the age of fourteen could be classified as devoted participants in the life of the national Church. The compilers of the report concluded that not only had family religion largely disintegrated, but it was difficult to get parents to send their children to Sunday schools when they were established in a parish. Furthermore, sick persons rarely called for clerical comfort any longer, at least 'scarcely ever before the last extremity'.[2]

Any number of reasons were given for this lamentable situation. 'Profane, obscene and seditious writings' undoubtedly encouraged disaffection from the Church, and they especially flourished in an atmosphere of Sunday drinking, grazing of cattle, raucous wakes, feasts, dancing, cock-fights, and races. Churchwardens were slack in their responsibilities and magistrates failed to enforce legislation against vice. Although Dissenters were hardly a problem with their eight small meeting-houses, the Methodists were more disturbing with some thirty-eight assorted places of worship. Admittedly, some Methodists also attended Anglican services, but a second group did not, and even attended chapel during the time Church services were being performed. A third group followed 'and encouraged a wandering tribe of fanatical teachers . . . from the lowest and most illiterate classes of society'. These were often 'raving enthusiasts' who were 'deluding the minds of the ignorant multitude'.[3] The latter group was described as wild and dangerous, openly assaulting the Church and all authority. Their subversive purpose was obvious in such dreadful times, and it was urgent that the legislature act quickly before 'all useful connection between the Clergy and their parishioners' was destroyed.[4] Once that happened, and

---

[1] *Report From the Clergy Of A District In the Diocese of Lincoln Convened For the Purpose of Considering the State of Religion In the Several Parishes In the Said District, As Well As the Best Mode of Promoting the Belief and Practice of It; And of Guarding, As Much As Possible, Against the Dangers Arising to the Church and Government of this Kingdom, From the Alarming Increase of Profaneness and Irreligion On the One Hand, and From the False Doctrines and Evil Designs of Fanatic and Seditious Teachers On the Other* (1800).

[2] *Ibid.*, 6–7.   [3] *Ibid.*, 7–9, 20–21.

[4] *Ibid.*, 16.

the statistics indicated it might not be far off, not only the Church, but the State itself would be in peril.

Having run through the gambit of excuses, the writers of the *Report*, like more and more of their contemporaries, also recognized that much of the problem could be traced to the failures of the Anglican ministry itself. Though the clergy had become more 'zealous and industrious' as a result of recent attacks on Christianity, their efforts fell far short of the needs. Recognizing the sensitivity of the issue, the authors qualified their charge by explaining they were making a general observation rather than reporting on specific enquiries into clerical behavior. They agreed that many of their brethren's failures were exaggerated by enthusiasts 'who pretend to a more than common zeal and concern for religion', but who injured their cause by misconstruing and aggravating 'perfectly innocent . . . little faults incident to the infirmity of human nature in all orders and conditions of men . . .'.[1] Those 'innocent little faults', readily catalogued in nearly every study of the Georgian Church, had by the end of the eighteenth century largely sapped the spiritual energies of the Establishment, and made its teachings irrelevant to millions of laymen unable to distinguish between religion and those who preached it. The secularity, neglect and indifference of the latter had done much to diminish a vital interest in the former. This did not mean, as many Anglicans claimed, that great numbers of people were abandoning the national Church for Dissent. The *Report* of the Lincolnshire clergy certainly did not indicate this, nor did most statistical returns in the early years of the new century. In spite of the rapid growth of Methodism, far more Englishmen, especially among the classes who dropped away from the Anglican communion or never entered it at all, remained outside any organized religion—a fact borne out by the great religious census taken a half-century later.[2]

It is significant that remedies suggested in the Lincoln *Report* stressed above all the revival of parochial religion dependent upon a conscientious resident clergy determined to eliminate religious indifference. Though the clerical authors talked vaguely about legislative restrictions on itinerant enthusiasts, they emphasized the restoration of Church and family religion guided by devoted clergy who provided adequate services and were themselves perfect Christian examples, avoiding levity, unbecoming dress and common discourse. Only by the re-establishment of responsible clerical influence at the parochial level was it possible once more to impart not only the lessons of Scripture, but those of 'industry and subordination'.[3] That, after all, was what an Established Church was for.

Even without the benefit of statistical revelation and the cautious prodding of the moderately Evangelical clergy who examined the state

[1] *Ibid.*, 13–14.   [2] See Conclusion.   [3] *Report*, 18–22.

of parochial religion in Lincolnshire, it was becoming apparent to Church leaders that something had to be done about clerical abuses that threatened to leave multitudes of poor, restless Englishmen to the pestiferous enticements of rootless, leveling religious and secular enthusiasts. Samuel Horsley, who had found little to criticize in the Church ten years earlier, before his elevation to the bench, was by 1796 castigating the parochial clergy for being negligent, pluralistic and non-resident to the extent of threatening the Established Church 'with the greatest danger'.[1] Considering that the times were more perilous than at any period since the first three centuries of Christianity, it is not surprising that Horsley had become much more sensitive to weaknesses in the main line of defense.[2] Whatever support the Church received from the great majority of Englishmen was primarily 'for its good services in civil life'. It was utility, not religious conviction, that assured their friendship, but 'they will be our friends no longer, than while we act it well. They consider the emoluments and privileges of the order, as a pay that we receive from the public, for the performance of the part assigned us.' Horsley solemnly warned that if that performance was neglected it would only be a matter of time before the Church would find its property confiscated, and its privileges abolished.[3]

It was no longer possible to avoid the criticism being heaped upon the clergy by friend and foe alike. Although Horsley preferred to believe it was more a question of form than substance, nevertheless even the appearance of indolence and greed was sufficient to scandalize the Church and 'give a handle to our enemies, and perhaps may provoke God to employ the fire of persecution, to purge away the dross'.[4] It is time, he said, that we, like the Apostles, must follow 'the policy of the serpent united with the harmlessness of the dove'.[5] Like many of the bench, he appreciated the aristocratic Bishop Courtenay's conclusion that it did not matter whether the 'supineness and secularity' of the clergy were a reality that threatened disaster; the fact that it was believed was sufficiently alarming.[6] Whatever the condition of clerical spiritual life, it was more important that all ministers be at their post, if only for political reasons. People in such tumultuous times, Courtenay said, are overly sensitive to sinecures and unfulfilled duties, and they are 'apt to be attended with much murmur and discontent. . . . Thus . . . from

---

[1] Horsley, *Charge* (1796), 31.   [2] *Ibid.*, 1, 52.   [3] *Ibid.*, 25–26.
[4] *Ibid.*, 27.   [5] *Ibid.*, 1.
[6] Henry Reginald Courtenay, *A Charge Delivered to the Clergy of the Diocese of Bristol* (1796), 5. Courtenay (1741–1803), son of H. R. Courtenay, M.P. and grandson of 1st Earl Bathurst. Held considerable cathedral preferment, elevated to Bristol in 1794 and Exeter in 1797. Married a daughter of Earl of Effingham, and in 1835 one of his sons became the 11th Earl of Devon.

political motives alone, in regard to our own interest, and with a view to satisfying the public mind, we are called upon to shew ourselves properly in those respective stations in which we are placed.'[1] As a non-resident, pluralistic prelate, Courtenay, like Horsley and most other bishops, understood the various requirements of economy, educational leisure, and social intercourse that dictated non-residency and pluralism; yet the younger clergy at least had less excuse than their elders, and it might be expected that they would be more diligent in their attendance to duty.[2] Horsley vaguely threatened to do something about it, and Courtenay contented himself with the hope that only those clergy for whom it was absolutely necessary would absent themselves from their parishes. Few bishops were yet inclined, or in a position, to go any further.

[1] *Ibid.*, 7
[2] *Ibid.*, 8; also Horsley, *Charge* (1796), 28–29.

II

<hr />

Inequity and Poverty, 1783–1815

<hr />

1. LOWER-CLASS DISAFFECTION

The revival of parochial religion and the re-establishment of moral stewardship on the part of the upper classes were the principal alternatives to revolution proposed by Church and lay leaders during the French Revolution. Many of them had been severely shaken by the prospect of a great anti-Christian conspiracy that threatened to unleash the explosive passions of the disaffected poor against their betters. In that context, the misery of the lower classes as described by Tom Paine, and contrasted with the resources of the country being 'lavished upon kings, upon courts, upon hirelings, imposters and prostitutes . . .',[1] took on ominous meaning. In spite of the obvious importance of moral exhortation, it seemed clear to many people that it would take more than pious homilies to refute the Jacobinical charges being leveled against the ruling classes. The philanthropic physician, John Coakley Lettsom, was only one of the innumerable humanitarians of the day who warned the rich that unless they 'hear the cries of the poor, the time will come when they must hear the loud voice of want and misery'.[2] If the poor were being enticed into massive disaffection from the values and natural laws of English society, it was in part a result of their resistance having been weakened by prolonged physical deprivation. When Lettsom described the 'evil . . . accumulating' that threatened to

<hr />

[1] T. Paine, *Rights of Man*, in Philip S. Foner, ed., *The Complete Writings of Thomas Paine* (New York, 1945), I, 405.

[2] Thomas J. Pettigrew, *Memoirs of the Life and Writings of the Late John Coakley Lettsom, M.D., LL.D.* (1817), II, 45.

'burst through the mound of oppression', he was talking about poverty and recent important analyses of its extent and effects in English society.

The important, pioneering studies of Frederick Morton Eden and Patrick Colquhoun describing the condition of the laboring classes were the most important systematic articulations of a growing interest and concern about the relationship of economic and social conditions to lower-class behavior.[1] The tradition of eighteenth-century environmentalism pointed in this direction, but the French Revolution gave such investigations increased importance. For Lettsom, John Howard, Jonas Hanway and many other enlightened humanitarians, the relationship between severe material deprivation and the brutalization of the poor was long established. Evangelicals, prepared to crusade on behalf of unfortunate Negro slaves, were gradually persuaded to consider more than the moral and spiritual welfare of the suffering poor at home. In 1796, Wilberforce, who had established the Proclamation Society in 1787 to prevent the further corruption of lower-class morals by immoral and blasphemous publications, led Evangelicals into the Society for Bettering the Condition of the Poor.[2] The Yorkshire reformer had not abandoned his mission to purify the morals of his age; six years later he launched the Society for the Suppression of Vice.[3] But he realized that such problems could not be completely separated from social and economic conditions, and willingly joined in the philanthropic efforts of Sir Thomas Bernard to improve the physical welfare of the laboring classes.

Similar voluntary efforts mushroomed over the next two decades as propertied Englishmen, motivated by Evangelicalism, traditional Christian virtues, humanitarianism and a keen sense of survival, combined to assuage the fluctuating sufferings of the poor. For the national government and the local magistrates, the extension of outdoor relief and continual increases in the burdened Poor Law rates seemed the most propitious course to follow. Where such measures were unable to check the spread of infectious leveling doctrines, and discontent manifested itself in dangerous ways, civil authorities, often encouraged by moraliz-

[1] Sir F. M. Eden, *The State of the Poor; or An History of the Labouring Classes in England, from the Conquest to the Present Period*, 3 vols. (1797); P. Colquhoun, *A Treatise on the Police of the Metropolis* (1796); *The State of Indigence and the Situation of the Casual Poor in the Metropolis Explained* (1799); *A Treatise on Indigence Exhibiting a General View of the National Resources for Productive Labour* (1806).

[2] R. I. and S. Wilberforce, *The Life of William Wilberforce* (1838), I, 130–34. See also *Reports of the Society for Bettering the Condition and Increasing the Comforts of the Poor*, 5 vols. (1798–1808).

[3] Wilberforce, *Life*, 130; also F. K. Brown, *Fathers of the Victorians. The Age of Wilberforce* (Cambridge, 1961), 428–36.

ing vigilants, were prepared to enforce repressive legislation passed in the closing years of the century. These diverse approaches converged on one common assumption—whatever the failings of the upper classes, moral or humanitarian, the critical question of social stability and order ultimately had to be answered in terms of the attitudes and condition of the laboring poor. The salvation of society depended upon the practical as well as the moral enticements presented by the guardians of the Constitution as an alternative to the bloody, unnatural allurements of democratic fanaticism.

The Established Church as one of the most solid, unyielding pillars of society was quickly drawn into the swirl of fear, recrimination and the hurried search for stability. Criticized implicitly by the energy and enthusiasm of the Methodist and Evangelical awakening, and explicitly by newly-inspired Dissenters and old political opponents, it was now violently assaulted by revolutionary zealots who, delighted by the destruction of the State Church in France, warmly recommended the example to England. Prelates were especially disturbed by scathing attacks on their princely lives and their indifference to the sufferings of the poor and their own lesser clergy. It was certainly irritating to bear the occasional barbs and even blatant condemnations of a Charles James Fox or a Lord Abingdon in the relative privacy of the Houses of Parliament. But it was downright frightening to know that Paine's description of religion as a trade, extracting money 'even from the pockets of the poor, instead of contributing to their relief', was being read and repeated by laboring folk throughout the country.[1]

Fox, angered by episcopal opposition to Catholic relief, could thoroughly annoy the hierarchy by reminding them that religion had existed for centuries without secular assistance, and the Anglican alliance with the State was in no way founded 'on the purity of their Christian doctrines, but merely on promises of mutual support'. His contrasting of earlier divines appealing to Scripture with modern bishops appealing to secular authority as 'contemptible and shameful' was not likely to result in an invitation to one of Archbishop Moore's Sunday concerts at Lambeth Palace. But abuse was to be expected if prelates chose to participate in the political arena. Acceptance of it became more difficult, however, when Fox suggested in the early days of the Revolution that the recent treatment of the Church in France ought perhaps to have some influence on the English bench.[2] Then the conditioned episcopal response, 'The Church is in danger!', had a slightly more sincere, even hysterical ring to it. It soon rose to a crescendo, loudly intoning against the republican claim that the national churches were the

[1] T. Paine, *Letter to Camille Jordan* (1797) in *The Theological Works of Thomas Paine* (Boston, 1859), 204.

[2] *Parl. Hist.*, XXVIII (1790), 397-9.

common property of all the people. Paine's Quaker origins merged with his democratic ideals as he described the role of organized churches and their holdings:

> They are national goods, and cannot be given exclusively to any one profession, because the right does not exist of giving to any one that which appertains to all. It would be consistent with right that the churches be sold, and the money arising therefrom be invested as a fund for the education of children of poor parents of every profession, and, if more than sufficient for this purpose, that the surplus be appropriated to the support of the aged poor. After this, every profession can erect its own place of worship, if it choose—support its own priests, if it choose to have any....[1]

The leaders of the Established Church, for decades to come, labored desperately and determinedly to purge such noxious poison before it contaminated the great laboring masses, and eroded the other necessary foundations of English civilization.

In formulating their defense, Church spokesmen did not stress the comparative merits of their religion. They were less concerned about convincing the lower classes of the spiritual beauties of the Anglican faith than they were in reconciling them to the necessary realities of natural social inequality. The generalized principles of natural religion had so deeply permeated the hierarchy of the Establishment that even the most pious prelates, Beilby Porteus, Thomas Burgess or Lewis Bagot, did not dwell upon any particular spiritual comforts for the poor unique to the Church over which they presided. All of them worried about the growth of Dissent and Methodism; they understood the appeal of revivalistic preaching; yet they offered no real, inspiring alternative.

When in 1793 Porteus charged the clergy of his London diocese to realize that 'there never was . . . in the history of this island, a single period in which the personal residence and personal exertions of the parochial clergy, were ever more wanted, or more anxiously looked up to, and expected and *demanded* by the general voice of the whole nation, than at this moment', he was only in part speaking of spiritual exertions.[2] The 'general voice' could more accurately have been described as belonging to the propertied classes, and they demanded that the poor be reassured that the inequities of rank, wealth and power were indeed part of a grand design to maximize human happiness. Failing that, they should at least be made to understand that socially disruptive behavior would not only bring down upon them immediate earthly retribution, but a far greater eternal punishment as well. Since the parochial clergy

[1] Paine, *Letter*, 207–8.
[2] B. Porteus, *Works*, R. Hodgson, ed. (1811), VI, 322.

were a principal means of propagandizing as well as controlling the lower orders, it was, as Porteus and many other prelates pointed out, incumbent upon them to respond vigorously to the threat of Jacobin equalitarianism.

No rational person could deny that God had created his entire universe on a hierarchical scale ranging from plants and animals to man himself. Each species and sub-species was particularly adapted to specifically assigned functions. At every stage or level, explained Bishop James Yorke of St David's (1774-79), 'some are of a superior species, and more distinguished texture; whilst others are formed of coarser and more ordinary materials'.[1] Yorke was clearly woven of finer stuff; the youngest son of Lord Chancellor Hardwicke, he proceeded to the See of Ely (1781-1808) and the Deanery of Lincoln after his six-year tour as the non-resident Bishop of St David's, immediately followed by a brief pause at Gloucester. Such a variety of occupations, conditions, and pursuits was, according to the persuasive Bishop Horsley, 'no less essential to the public weal, than the diversity of members in the natural body, and the different functions of its various parts are essential to the health and vigor of the individual'. This applied to mobile prelates as it did to all men, but, as he cautioned during the discussions on inequality preceding the Revolution, this did not mean that the differences in 'the elegance and lustre of their exterior form . . .' excluded a relative happiness and contentment for all classes. On the contrary, Horsley insisted that 'the quality of real happiness, within the reach of the individual, will be found, upon a fair and just comparison, in all the ranks of life the same'.[2]

Events in France and unrest at home indicated that a great many people were unconvinced. As some bishops had feared, the transfer of equalitarian ideas from the state of nature to society had occurred, and a deluded generation, convinced that society was responsible for their misfortunes, had suddenly run amok and threatened to carry the rest of the civilized Christian world with them. But before that had happened, several prelates, while accepting the divine and natural inevitability of wealth and poverty, conceded that the distinction between them had perhaps become too sharp to be reconciled to the impartial dictates of the creator. It is true, Yorke granted, that reason and revelation confirm that man was created for universal happiness; although the same evidence clearly proves equality was not a consideration. Nevertheless, though man had been deprived of his sublime condition, 'it is improbable that the bulk of mankind should be predestined to incessant toil and want; or to groan under oppressive infirmities and grief: whilst the more

[1] J. Yorke, *A Sermon Preached In the Cathedral Church of Lincoln On Opening the New County-Infirmary* (Lincoln, 1777), 5.
[2] Horsley, *Sermon* (1786), 5-6.

favoured few, indifferent to their sufferings, should riot in ease and abundance'.[1]

Such a notion was revolting to the bishop's harmonious concept of the creator as rational and benevolent—'the father of mercies, and God of all consolation'. Inequality then was ordained, but the excesses of inequality which admittedly exist are the consequence of human perverseness, and corrupt the 'moderate and beautiful' inequities originally designed by the deity. Nothing could be done about it, of course; the poor must be content to suffer the additional evils perpetrated by their betters. At the same time, they should not blame their maker for the misery in which they so frequently found themselves. It was never His intention that any of His species should bear so disproportionate an amount of suffering.[2] Yorke went as far as any prelate in conceding the responsibility of society for many individual afflictions endured by the laboring poor. He did so, however, not out of personal compassion, but in defense of the involvement of the creator whose presence deists and sceptics denied. He was merely reacting to the common enlightenment charge that a rational, merciful and creative being could not participate in the perpetuation of so much cruelty and unhappiness, but had, in fact, withdrawn, if ever involved, from overseeing the human condition. On the other hand, Yorke could not abide Calvinist enthusiasts explaining everything by trumpeting the wrathful vengeance of Jehovah against His fallen progeny.

While many episcopal contemporaries certainly shared Yorke's rational compromise, none of them, especially after the fall of the Bastille, was prepared to discuss openly the question of social causation. They would go no further than to join in the campaign to bring the upper classes to their moral senses. The laboring classes were aroused and already suspicious that their misfortunes were made and could be unmade on earth rather than in heaven. If anything the emphasis was upon proving that society was not only divine, but completely antithetical to individual rights of equality. Such rights, Bishop Cleaver of Chester maintained, 'can only be supposed in a state of unassociated existence'. Man had abandoned that state to achieve 'the greatest degree of personal security, and enjoyment, which is consistent with the greatest good obtainable for the whole of Society'. This greater individual and collective good 'cannot be supposed to exist without the relation, each to the other, of inferior, or superior'.[3] In 1791, Cleaver wondered whether the French were losing sight of reality. By 1793 there was no doubt. The French had clearly gone mad. Horrified and enraged by the execution of Louis XVI, Bishop Horsley launched his thirteen-year holy war against the Revolution which ranged from anger and fear to hysteria, paranoia,

[1] Yorke, *Sermon* (1777), 6–7. [2] *Ibid.*, 7.
[3] Cleaver, *Sermon* (1791), 11–12.

and, near the end of his life, expectations of the millennium. As far as he was concerned, the endless discussions about the origins of government, authority, society and natural rights had finally created the widespread insecurity needed for the triumph of conspiracy and insurrection. Where Horne had merely found such speculation unsettling and foolish in its neglect of Scriptural explanation, Horsley found it heathen, futile and utterly destructive.[1] Man always lived in society, and under government, he fumed; to attempt to place him in a state of independent nature previous to a contractual arrangement with authority was pure fiction. To deduce societies and governments from a non-existent state of nature was 'an absurd and unphilosophical creation of something out of nothing'. Even worse, there was implicit in such deductions the right of any generation to repudiate the compact, and, if it deems it beneficial, to revert to an independent state of nature.[2] The present generation of savage Frenchmen was a perfect example.

As man was always intended to live in a state of civil society deriving authority from the divine will, the principle of subjection to authority was never a voluntary compact, but 'a conscientious submission to the will of God'.[3] Horsley made it clear he was not reviving discredited divine right arguments of the previous century,[4] nor was he endorsing any particular form of government or society—only those already in existence. Irrespective of form and substance, these were 'the work of human policy, under the control of God's overruling Providence', and each individual was religiously bound to submit.[5] Change, the bishop insisted, must never come from individual action; it must, as Burke had shown, come from within society itself through orderly and gradual means. Horsley complained that in recent years men had forgotten their worldly state was a divine condition, and as a result had concocted dangerous schemes for the alteration of civil society if 'the People' were dissatisfied. These concoctions, he angrily concluded, 'we abominate and reject, as wicked and illegitimate'.[6]

Horsley's influential words were certainly heard and endorsed by guardians of the Establishment who nevertheless were reluctant to repudiate Lockeian contractual notions about the origin of society and government. Without necessarily rejecting deeply ingrained assumptions of utilitarian motivation as the explanation for natural man's transition into civil society, all agreed that subordination and inequality were necessary corollaries of that conclusion. A future prelate, Huntingford, had learned his lessons well when he warned that order and harmony were no less essential to society than to God's universe as a whole;

---

[1] Horsley, *Sermon* (1793), 1–2.   [2] *Ibid.*, 4–5.   [3] *Ibid.*, 6–7.
[4] Horsley was reacting to criticisms of a High Church revival of divine-right preaching by some frightened clergy in the 1790's.
[5] Horsley, *Sermon* (1793), 8–10.   [6] *Ibid.*, 19.

61

consequently, it was inevitable that there would be 'high and low, rich and poor in the same society . . . as that there should be young and old . . .'. All rational men could see that 'our wisdom and duty is to acquiesce in the general law of distinct ranks in which man is formed to experience the greatest degree of happiness'.[1] In addition to being irrational, it was also futile and dangerous to anticipate any decline in social distinctions as society advanced; on the contrary, distinctions naturally increased in direct proportion to the growth of population.[2]

Reason might by itself persuade a man that no individual could have any claim on providence to place him in a more exalted position than others, but, as the old Whig Bishop of Peterborough (1769–94), John Hinchliffe, argued shortly before his death, reason coupled to experience and faith proved 'the interests of Civil Society, even the very existence of it requires, that there should be . . . subordination of rank and authority . . .'[3]. The Gospels alone confirmed these truths, which are, Bishop Pretyman asserted:

> in direct opposition to the system of modern innovators . . .
> God himself makes one man to differ from another; that the distinctions of high and low, rich and poor, are the appointments of Divine Providence, and are made the sources of various duties, the bonds of mutual affection.[4]

Not only would society disintegrate without the blessings of inequality, but Christianity would be unable to exist. It is, Pretyman believed, fundamentally a religion of inequality dependent upon the exercise of 'compassion, gratitude, and humility . . .'. These virtues could not be exercised unless 'there is a diversity of ranks; and a contentious and turbulent spirit can never be reconciled with the Gospel graces of gentleness, forbearance and contentment'.[5]

The militant Horsley suggested that the responsible classes of English society had been too indiscriminate in their exercise of these and other graces. As far as he, the Bishop of St David's, was concerned, brotherly love could no longer be radiated to all men, but only to reliable brethren

[1] G. I. Huntingford, *Discourses On Different Subjects* (1795–97), I, 298–9.

[2] Huntingford, *A Discourse Preached Before the Corps of Hampshire Fawley Volunteers . . . March 19, 1797* (1797), 12.

[3] John Hinchliffe, *Sermons . . .* (1796), 145. Hinchliffe (1731–94), son of a Westminster livery stable operator, had an academic career at Westminster School, where he was briefly Master, and at Cambridge, where he was Master of Trinity. He owed his advancement to the Duke of Grafton. A strong liberal who supported Catholic emancipation, he was given the deanery of Durham in 1788 in order to remove him from Trinity.

[4] G. Pretyman, *A Charge Delivered to the Clergy of Lincoln . . . In May and June 1794* (1794), 21.

[5] *Ibid.*

who would not abuse it. To those who turned to the gospels of equality and revolution, we must 'abjure all brotherhood. . . . They have no claim upon our brotherly affection. . . . Miserable men! They are the gall of bitterness and in the bonds of iniquity.'[1] It was not Christian love and charity such wretches deserved, but the Treasonable Practices Bill and the other repressive measures of which Horsley was the principal episcopal advocate.[2] He was fed up and frightened by all the talk of the 'rights of the people', whether by Whigs or Jacobins, and frankly 'did not know what the mass of the people in any country had to do with the laws but to obey them . . .'.[3] When challenged by Lord Lauderdale, Horsley repeated, but clarified, his angry outburst. The rules of conduct were clearly laid down in statutes and customs, 'an equal rule to all, liable to no sudden change or perversion—to no partial application from the passion or the humour of the moment . . .'. The disgruntled people in society may petition, but nothing more. His statement would stand:

> I will maintain it under the axe of the guillotine, if, through any insufficiency of the measures which may now be taken, the time should ever come when the prelates and nobles of this land must stoop their necks to that engine of democratic tyranny.[4]

Since a desire for martyrdom was not among the more prominent qualities possessed by eighteenth-century prelates, the impulsive Horsley was not overwhelmed with episcopal promises to join him at the scaffold. Not that many of his colleagues were less alarmed by the continued success of the French armies, and the vigorous activities of home-grown Jacobins spreading their incredible nonsense about the 'rights of man'. They were thoroughly frightened by real and imagined republican conspiracies, and as a body deplored the distribution of the *Age of Reason* and the *Rights of Man* among 'the mechanic, the manufacturer, the farmer, the servant, the labourer'.[5] Repression, therefore, was undoubtedly necessary as a temporary expedient until the clergy and the ruling laity were able to assure themselves that the laboring poor were still in possession of their senses. Ultimately, however, churchmen knew that security was dependent upon the lower orders rationally and religiously understanding the reasons for the existing composition of society. Along with that understanding would come the confidence that temporary and periodic distress would continue to be ameliorated by the charitable obligations borne by the upper classes. If this was no longer acceptable to men deluded by the unnatural nonsense taught by

[1] Horsley, *Sermon* (1793), 24–25. [2] *Parl. Hist.*, XXXII (1795), 269.
[3] *Ibid.*, 257–8. [4] *Ibid.*, 267–8.
[5] Porteus, *Charge* (1794), 23. Porteus described Paine's writings as '*irreligion made easy*' to the great bulk of mankind and rendered intelligible to every capacity'.

disaffected, fanatical visionaries, it did not mean that the nature of things had changed; only man's fallible perception had been distorted. Until it was clarified, churchmen feared society would be likely to remain in a state of turmoil.

2. POVERTY RE-EXAMINED

Several Church leaders in the pre-Revolutionary years wondered if the apparent confusion about the natural structure of society was not related to growing misunderstandings about the relationship between wealth and poverty. They pondered the problem while justifying inequality; a few saw that the dissatisfaction with traditional explanations was perhaps related to an increased questioning of established methods of poor relief in the 1770's and 1780's. Englishmen had become more conscious of the steady rise in the poor rate since the accession of George III. As the heaviest of the local rates, it had by the end of the American War risen to approximately two million pounds *per annum*; while the enforcement of the workhouse provisions introduced in 1722 had, with other stringent measures designed to reduce the number of paupers, been increasingly ignored by the administrative justices.[1] Poor Law bills of 1776 and 1782 incorporated this more humane and flexible trend in the distribution of relief funds.[2]

The liberalization of relief, and the rising costs of maintaining the poor on the rates, were not only disturbing the ratepayers upon whom the levy fell, but also early proponents of *laissez-faire* economics concerned about the artificial subsidization of unproductive laborers. In addition, concern was developing over the puzzling question of population growth and decline; David Hume in 1752 and, more directly, Robert Wallace in 1761 had raised the spectre of overpopulation which Malthus was to articulate with such striking impact nearly a half-century later.[3] But the growing interest in poverty and its relief was also stimulated by enlightened humanitarian thought which was increasingly translated into philanthropic efforts to ameliorate the wretched conditions brought to light by individual reformers. Little encouragement

---

[1] *Parliamentary Papers* (1817), Report from the Select Committee on the Poor Laws, VI, 155–7.

[2] S. and B. Webb, *English Local Government From the Revolution to the Municipal Corporations Act: English Poor Law History* (1927–9), VIII, 422.

[3] Hume, 'Of the Populousness of Ancient Nations', in *Essays Moral, Political and Literary*, Pt. II, No. 11; Wallace, *Various Prospects of Mankind, Nature and Providence* (1761), and his *A Dissertation on the Numbers of Mankind in Ancient and Modern Times ... With an Appendix Containing Additional Observations and Some Remarks on Mr Hume's Political Discourse, Of the Populousness of Ancient Nations* (Edinburgh, 1753).

was found in Joseph Townsend's important analysis, published in 1786, of poverty and its alleviation. Not only did he conclude that the misery of the laboring poor was inevitable and necessary; he felt that efforts to alter their condition would prove futile. In all likelihood sufficient relief would have a negative effect of diminishing the motivation needed by indigent laborers to pursue their harsh, rudimentary and ignoble tasks.[1]

Although the expansion of Poor Law relief and the rapid development of lay philanthropy had largely stolen the charitable thunder from the Church, many clergymen, through tradition and inclination, as well as through parochial influence and administrative responsibilities, were intimately involved in the whole problem of providing for the poor. As the tempo of discussion and criticism picked up in the 1780's, so did the interest of several ornaments of the hierarchy. Without showing much originality, they nevertheless began devoting a greater portion of their thinking to the troublesome question of the nature of poverty and the role of society in its amelioration. Almost invariably, however, it was considered in terms of the broader and more worrying problem of the natural relationship between classes. Taking their cue from stimulating Evangelicals, and even more reluctantly from enthusiastic Methodists, prelates began punctuating their social pronouncements with the cautious reminder that irrespective of class or function we are all God's children. Such commonplace homilies were clearly a far cry from George Whitefield's shocking revelation to the indignant Duchess of Buckingham that she had 'a heart as sinful as the common wretches that crawl on the earth',[2] but they did indicate an awareness of a need to reiterate that there was an inevitable spiritual equality, whatever necessary temporal inequities were experienced. Even the promise of an ethereal leveling had to be made with the greatest caution, however; for, as Bishop Hinchliffe recognized, so fundamental a Christian principle was not easily admitted by the rich or the poor. The former opposed it from vanity, and the latter from envy and discontent.[3]

The bishops were not very comfortable with it either, however, and they were really much more anxious about convincing the poor, and perhaps themselves, of the inevitability of poverty than they were in echoing enthusiastic nostrums about the equalitarian nature of human corruption. Hinchliffe conceded that 'while some men are possessed of an abundance far greater than what either the comforts or conveniences

[1] Joseph Townsend, *A Dissertation on the Poor Laws by a Well-Wisher to Mankind* (1786); also his *Observations on Various Plans Offered to the Public, for the Relief of the Poor* (1788).

[2] J. W. Bready, *England Before and After Wesley. The Evangelical Revival and Social Reform* (1938), 211–12.

[3] J. Hinchliffe, *A Sermon Preached . . . June 1, 1786, Being the Time of the Yearly Meeting of the Children Educated in the Charity-Schools . . .* (1786), 2.

of life require, there are multitudes, who, with all their care and industry, find it difficult to procure the necessary support of a miserable subsistence'.[1] Such was human nature, for as men and their dispositions and ambitions vary, so will their situations in life.[2] Hinchliffe's disposition and ambition, with the Dukes of Devonshire and Grafton assisting, had carried him from his father's Westminster livery stable to the Mastership of Trinity College, Cambridge, the See of Peterborough, and to the Deanery of Durham as well. Consequently, churchmen well understood that while it was no difficult task convincing the rich 'of the necessity or utility' of inequality, the poor were rather less enchanted by the logical arguments of their betters.[3] Poverty, Hinchliffe agreed, was undoubtedly an inevitable manifestation of natural law, existing in all ages. But in each age there were comprehensible and immediate reasons for the form it took which could be isolated and explained, even if little could be done to correct the condition. In his own time, poverty was largely the result of the inability of the economy to absorb 'the numbers of the poor [who] are daily increasing, while fewer means present themselves . . . for the gain of an honest subsistence'.[4]

Other Church spokesmen were openly suspicious of such rationalistic explanations, and saw implicit in them the arguments of social causation, no matter how explicit Hinchliffe and others were in reaffirming that whatever the immediate cause of distress, it was always ultimately linked to divine necessity. The pious George Horne preferred a less-qualified explanation:

> God could have ordained that all should have been rich. But he has not so ordained. Poverty, with every other evil, came in, upon man's transgression.

Class and function were necessary results of original sin. Labor, the function of most men, was an unfortunate but inevitable manifestation of their corruption, as was the lower class it created. 'If none were poor, none would labour, and if some did not labour, none could eat. . .' It was as simple as that—'as the case has stood since the fall'. One of the most devout of contemporary High Churchmen, Dean Horne was not only disturbed by naturalistic arguments about the nature of poverty, but he was also troubled by the growing assertions that the Poor Law and indiscriminate charity were only perpetuating poverty. Perpetuating poverty! But of course every true Christian knew that it was perpetual—'the poor shall never cease out of the land'. What, he asked, was love and charity, if not the Christian's acceptance of that reality?[5]

[1] *Ibid.*   [2] *Ibid.*, 5–6.   [3] *Ibid.*, 6.   [4] *Ibid.*, 12–13.
[5] G. Horne, *Charity Recommended On Its True Motive, A Sermon Preached . . . Before the Governors of the Benevolent Institution for the Delivery of Poor Married Women at Their Own Habitations . . . March 30, 1788* (1788), 10.

It appeared to some that so fundamental an explanation of poverty smacked too much of an Old Testament wrathful determinism inimical to the progressive improvement of the human condition. A few years before the French Revolution caused him to doubt the possibility of such advancement, Samuel Horsley rejected the idea of passive resignation and periodic amelioration. Poverty was unquestionably a necessary result of human sin, but it was nevertheless a real evil that men must seek to eliminate as much as possible. While it was true that the Gospel taught that 'the poor shall never cease out of the land', it did not mean that God had determined a fortune or lack of it for each class.[1] If He had, He would have in effect sanctioned a state of 'epicurean indolence', in which 'Industry, of all qualities of the individual the most beneficial to the community, would lose the incitement of its Golden dreams; and Sloth, of all the vices of the individual the most pernicious to the community . . .' would rule unrestrained.

Few bishops knew better than the pluralistic, high-living Horsley how much the fortunes of man were always in a state of flux, 'governed by an intricate combination of causes, of which no sagacity of human forecast may predict or avert the event'.[2] His prophetic ability was no more reliable in matters of personal fortune than it was on the outcome of the French Revolution. He lived lavishly, his coach regularly drawn by four horses, and he died heavily in debt. Perhaps if he had received Durham as he requested, instead of the less lucrative Rochester, his heirs would not have had to sell the clothes in which he died in order to reduce some of his remaining debts.[3] But the way Horsley lived, and the amounts of charity he distributed, especially to the poorer clergy, suggest it would not have made much difference. There was, then, a personal note in Horsley's description of poverty as a relative rather than an absolute evil, resulting from complex and often indeterminate causes:

> The individual's means of subsistence will not always correspond with other circumstances . . . they will sometimes fall greatly short of what belongs to the particular sphere, which upon the whole he is best qualified to fill with advantage to the community. . . . *This* is the evil to which the name POVERTY properly belongs. . . .[4]

He reasoned that the employment of subsistence standards to measure poverty failed to differentiate between the various levels and expectations of social classes, so that poverty could be seen to exist in all ranks of life.

[1] Horsley, *Sermon* (1786), 7.   [2] *Ibid.*, 8.
[3] Horsley to Pitt, 28 May 1791, *Chatham Ps.*, Public Record Office, 30/8/146. Joseph Farington, *The Farington Diary*, James Greig, ed. (1922–28), VIII, 96.
[4] Horsley, *Sermon* (1786), 8.

He is truly poor, whose means of subsistence are insufficient for his proper place in Society, as determined by the general complication of his circumstances; by his birth, his education, his bodily strengths, and his mental endowment.

Social analysts, by dividing society into simplistic categories of rich and poor, concentrated upon the basic provisions of food, lodgings and clothing without understanding that there were varying expectations and needs which also constituted subsistence at every level. Laborers, Horsley elucidated, needed 'mattock and spade', merchants needed capital, and the professions education. The lack of this 'previous competency' was surely also poverty, as the individual's industry would be insufficient without it. But instead of considering such poverty an evil, the bishop surmised that the 'instability of the individual's prosperity . . . is essential to the general good'.[1]

Since the possibility of lapsing into poverty was a calamity threatening all ranks, it kept society from fossilizing into rigid classes and subclasses based on permanent fortunes. On the contrary, the threat of impoverishment not only encouraged industrious activity on the part of individuals in all ranks of life, but actually went a long way towards promoting class harmony. Poverty then, according to Horsley's empirical analysis, is merely the 'expedient that the merciful Providence of God guards civil life against the ruin which would otherwise result from the unlimited progress of its own refinements'.[2] Faced with the danger of losing their relative subsistence, all men are continually trying to improve their condition. As a student of science and an editor of the great Newton's works,[3] Horsley realized that the social benefits he derived from his analysis of human nature would be no more obvious to the laboring poor than would be the principles of the Newtonian universe. They were none the less true 'as the common good demands, and the constitution of the world accordingly admits'. Consequently, as some of his brethren argued from Scripture, and 'as it is most truly said, . . . the evil of Poverty is a public good. . .'. But, the bishop cautioned, only when it is precisely defined: 'The danger of Poverty, threatening the individual, is the good: Poverty in *act* . . . is to the community, as well as to the sufferer an evil.'[4]

Horsley's interesting attempt to introduce an individually oriented, social-utilitarian perspective into the mounting number of clerical sermons and tracts on the subject of poverty was certainly unique in episcopal circles. Without bowing to the arguments of social causation, he reaffirmed the safer and more widely-held belief that poverty was essentially an individual condition to be corrected by individual effort. At the

[1] *Ibid.*, 9–10.   [2] *Ibid.*, 10–11.
[3] *Isaaci Newtoni Opera Quae Exstant Omnia*, 5 vols. (1779–85).
[4] *Sermon* (1786), 12.

same time he agreed that it was perhaps a more complex problem than previously understood, and by describing poverty as a necessary affliction relative to all classes, he hoped to subvert the case presented by equalitarian critics who concentrated upon the isolated misery of the laboring classes. Instead of being deprived of their rightful place in society the laboring classes were in fact governed by the same natural laws of human motivation activating people at all levels. Relative to their station, the laborers stood to gain as much as their betters who worked to avoid the evil of actual poverty. Original sin, after all, had touched all of mankind, and the deprivation and necessity resulting from that fateful transgression always had, and always would, affect all men equally. That some were apparently more equal than others was the result of individual choice, and it applied whether one was a humble day laborer or a peer of the realm. Within their respective stations, each possessed the individual capacity, understanding and motivation to affect their material welfare as they affected their spiritual welfare.[1] God, by the necessity of labor, the teachings of Scripture, and the gift of free will, had provided the stimuli and the means for both.

This kind of relativistic sophistry encouraged numerous prelates to discourse time and time again upon the many advantages the poor enjoyed as compared to the rich. Uncomplicated, unexposed to the material and fleshly inducements of a luxurious age, and unburdened with political and social responsibilities, the lower orders were able to keep earlier hours, enjoy the delights of the open air, and with 'cheerful spirits and active limbs', live a comparatively healthy life.[2] Richard Watson was another episcopal witness to the restless, dissatisfied, overindulgent, unhappy, unhealthy existence endured by the wealthy; he could not but be impressed by the contrasting of such suffering with the natural, simple, healthy lives led by the poor.[3] Whatever their position all men must, as Hinchliffe preached, 'run with patience the race that is before them'. Unfortunately, as he and his brethren knew, 'the poor and afflicted' were easily beset with 'the sin of distrust', and often attributed an illusory happiness to their betters. It was irrational and unfair of the inferior orders; all that was required of them was patience, contentment and resignation. But the rich had to be actively engaged in attempting to close 'the breach of distinction, to comfort the afflicted, to instruct the ignorant . . . to deal . . . superfluities to the wretched; and thereby convince them, that the ways of Providence are just'.[4] Even

---

[1] S. Horsley, *The Charge to the Clergy of His Diocese, Delivered . . . in the Year 1790* (Gloucester, 1791), 11–13.

[2] Yorke, *Sermon* (1777), 11.

[3] R. Watson, *A Sermon Preached Before the Stewards of the Westminster Dispensary At Their Anniversary Meeting . . . April, 1785* (1793), 8–9.

[4] Hinchliffe, *Sermon* (1786), 9–11.

before the outbreak of the Revolution, Church leaders were worried that the task was becoming more difficult.

Nevertheless, no matter how great the dissatisfaction of the lower orders, the realities of revelation as manifested in the operation of immutable natural laws divided mankind into rich and poor, and that was that. This did not mean, as some of the more enlightened bishops qualified, that assignments were determined on an individual basis. Only the general condition was established. As Watson insisted, each individual was free to determine where he would reside on the hierarchical scale, for 'the end aimed at, by the men of every profession and every trade, is to advance themselves from a state of poverty to a state of riches, or from the possession of a smaller portion of wealth to that of a larger'.[1] But men, being afflicted by vice and folly, often failed in their quest, and lapsed into that state all sought to avoid.

Few bishops in the later eighteenth century analysed the problem of poverty in such individualistic utilitarian terms. Watson's conclusion that poverty was essentially an individual failing within a natural, generalized condition, and that any person through 'honesty, diligence, and frugality', could rise out of it, was more representative of the thinking expressed by the next generation.[2] Most Church spokesmen still thought of poverty and the poor as an integral and necessary state explained and justified by Scripture and reason. They did not try to isolate the individual pauper from that state. While accepting many of the eighteenth-century utilitarian principles of human nature, and agreeing with Watson that all men were in part motivated by material, acquisitive drives, they were still too closely bound to traditional Christian concepts of inevitability to analyse poverty as an individual rather than a generalized condition.

All assumed as a matter of course that property was an integral part of the natural condition of things, just as they did the Lockeian concept that all men possessed it in their labor. But few of his episcopal contemporaries echoed Watson's conclusion that whether or not a person chose to add to this natural possession was entirely dependent upon the extent of his individual corruption. Nevertheless, it was clear that 'all the pursuits of mankind, whether they be laudable or disreputable, have a natural tendency to introduce a disparity of property; to establish the great distinction of the human species into Rich and Poor'. This could be agreed upon without specifically analysing the personal nature of the poor, and it was further proof that the equalization of property as a solution to poverty was unnatural and irreligious. It rejected the property value of individual labor, which was as diverse as the persons who owned it, and conflicted with the 'natural appointment of God himself—*The rich and the poor meet together, the Lord is the maker of them all . . .*'.[3]

[1] Watson, *Sermon* (1785), 3.   [2] *Ibid.*, 5.   [3] *Ibid.*, 3.

Equalitarian solutions also ignored the realities of subsistence labor which would exist even if the rich were to lose their superfluities; 'for if all men were upon a level, he who is now doomed to labour must labour still . . .' to procure the necessities of life. If anything, the superfluities of the wealthy helped the poor by providing them employment and the opportunity to rise above mere subsistence.[1] The mistake of the poor, as Watson conceived it, was in taking their poverty personally. In providing private property as an incentive to personal improvement, God had not singled out any individual for wealth or poverty. Impartial, He judges His children on their prescribed responses to the respective trials and responsibilities which they face in their relative stations.

Watson's comparatively lengthy discussion of the nature of poverty was uncommon in episcopal circles. The Church leaders of his generation simply took it for granted, and in contrast to those of the next generation were yet unmoved by the realities of industrialism, population growth and a keener sense of rapid social change. Moderately troubled by new ideas of social causation, and annoyed at the rising costs of poor relief, some questions and objections were raised without really giving much serious thought to answers. In spite of his confidence in the opportunity for individual self-improvement, even Watson never suggested that such improvement would in any way alter the nature of society and existing social relationships. Like all of his brethren, he believed the poor could be persuaded not to blame their betters for their lowly condition. They should instead thank God for having provided His unfaithful children with an opportunity for repentance irrespective of their temporary earthly status. Watson suggested they might in fact also blame themselves for their misfortune. The vast disparity of wealth, position and influence in society was, he knew, irrelevant to the issue.

The turmoil generated by the French Revolution indicated otherwise. Watson's earlier preachments on poverty were reprinted in 1793 under the title *The Wisdom and Goodness of God in Having Made Both Rich and Poor*. The Bishop of Llandaff's comforting words were added to those uttered by such eminent divines as William Paley and Samuel Parr, as they increased their efforts to convince themselves, if not the poor, of the necessity and advantages of poverty.[2] All the dubious contrivances about relative responsibilities and temptations were dispensed with increasing frequency, with Archdeacon Paley adding boredom to the mounting list of afflictions patiently borne by the unhappy rich.[3]

[1] *Ibid.*, 6–7.

[2] W. Paley, 'Reasons for Contentment Addressed to the Labouring Part of the British Public', *Works* (Philadelphia, 1836); S. Parr, 'On the Beneficial Effects of Labour', *Works*, J. Johnstone, ed. (1828), V.

[3] Paley, *ibid.*, 496–500; Parr, *ibid.*, 252–3.

If, however, the poor chose to ignore these obvious truths, there were others more to the point. In 1793, the moderate, learned Dean and future Bishop of Rochester (1802–8), Thomas Dampier, after describing the comparative enjoyments of the poor, bluntly warned them that in a confrontation with the rich they could only lose and compound their misery.[1] The affluent possessed the necessary reserves to see them through tumultuous times, but the poor man, if deluded by equalitarian panaceas, must 'bear the utmost fierceness of the Storm which tears up the foundations of Society, and be a trembling witness of the Ruin of that System which was used to give him Security in his Property, his Liberty, and his Life'. Cruel and harsh though it was, if the lower orders were so mad as to disrupt the established order of things, they would suffer grievously, and find themselves cut off from that benevolence which they counted on in hard times. More succinctly, 'the Happiness and Virtue of a poor Man consists in studying to be quiet and to mind his own Business...'.[2]

As the disgruntled poor were unlikely to receive these lessons from cathedral pulpits, elevated churchmen more often than not were merely reassuring each other and their wealthy, privileged congregations. Far more laborers learned of their good fortune and responsibilities from the vast libraries of cheap, moralistic literature published and distributed throughout the revolutionary years to counteract the pernicious influence of Paine's writings. Hannah More, the most famous and successful of the moralizers, was initially encouraged in her *Cheap Repository Tracts* by Bishop Porteus, Bishop Barrington, and Archbishop Moore.[3] Barrington's chaplain, the future Bishop Burgess, not only welcomed

[1] T. Dampier, *A Sermon Preached In the Cathedral Church of Durham... On the Opening of the Public Infirmary Of That City* (Durham, 1793), 6–7.

Dampier (1748–1812), son of a lower master of Eton, tutor to the Earl of Guildford, and later Master of Sherburn Hospital, was translated to Ely in 1808. An undistinguished prelate, he was an eminent bibliophile whose great library sold for nearly £10,000.

[2] *Ibid.*, 10–11.

[3] Shute Barrington (1734–1826), son of 1st Viscount Barrington, was chaplain to both George II and III, and never held a parish living; his entire career was built on cathedral appointments. Elevated to Llandaff by the king in 1769, and, despite Shelburne's protests, to Salisbury in 1782. Moved to Durham in 1791. A generous, even pious prelate, sympathetic to Evangelicalism, he perhaps owed his religiosity to having been one of the few men of his age to have survived a lithotomy.

John Moore (1730–1805), son of a Gloucester grazier, tutored the sons of the Duke of Marlborough, a favorite of George III. Elevated to Bangor in 1775, and, after Bishops Lowth and Hurd declined it, to the See of Canterbury in 1783. An amiable, nepotistic pluralist, he left an estate of over a million pounds.

Mrs More's pious tales, but contributed some of his own to the 'annals of good conduct'. In contrast to Mrs More and the popular Sarah Trimmer, Burgess sought to publish 'true stories' of lower-class virtue.[1]

All such efforts were designed to support Mrs More's goal of saving 'the profligate multitude that want to be drawn off from that pernicious [Paineite] trash, the corruption of which is incalculable'.[2] Well aware of the growing literacy of the poor as Sunday schools were extended throughout the land, their supporters were especially sensitive to the charges made by opponents of lower-class education that there was no guarantee that the poor would confine their reading to safe literature. Burgess, an eminent classicist, had personally written simplified spelling books for the schools to assure that the poor were properly indoctrinated as early as possible.[3] But it was necessary during the 1790's to provide them with even more wholesome material than that being offered by Jacobin fanatics. Horace Walpole might have playfully chided Hannah More for her cruelty in 'making the poor spend so much time in reading books, and depriving them of their pleasure on Sundays',[4] but he certainly understood her plea, 'From liberty, equality, and the rights of man, good Lord deliver us!'[5]

In their pious defense of the *status quo*, Will Chip, or Jack, the village blacksmith, two of Mrs More's rustic saints, readily agreed with episcopal assurances that society was a necessary integral blending of unequal functions and duties.[6] For these solid, fictitious lads there would have been no difficulty in rightly responding to the all too real lordly Bishop Murray's rhetoric: 'If all mankind were masters, how would they exist without attending to the cultivation of the earth, which has been cursed upon our account?' Yet if all 'were reduced to the common drudgery of life, from whence would come employment, protection, encouragement and reward?'[7] Wise and virtuous Jack wished that the higher orders would always set the proper example for the likes of him,[8] but understood the bishop was absolutely right in saying that in spite of occasional failings, 'the children of men must all be dependent upon

[1] T. Burgess, *Moral Annals of the Poor, and Middle Ranks of Society, in Various Situations, of Good and Bad Conduct* (Durham, 1795).

[2] W. Roberts, ed. *Memoirs of the Life and Correspondence of Hannah More* (1834), II, 429.

[3] Harford, *Life*, 104.   [4] Roberts, *Hannah More*, 435.   [5] *Ibid.*, 357.

[6] H. More, 'Village Politics', *The Complete Works* (New York, 1857), I.

[7] G. Murray, *A Sermon Preached on the 16th of December, 1792, at a County Church in the County of Kent* (Maidstone, 1792), 5.

Murray (1761–1803), son of 3rd Duke of Atholl and father of Bishop Murray (1784–1860). Though elevated to St David's in 1801, spent most of his career working on the telegraph (a species of semaphore), and in 1796 was appointed Director of the Telegraph at the Admiralty.

[8] More, *Works*, 61.

F   73

each other'. Though the poor 'are ever in the world; they are necessary to the rich, and are upon the whole equally happy; the rich are as necessary to the poor, and have many sources of uneasiness unknown to those below them'.[1]

A principal cause of that uneasiness for the revolutionary generation and those to follow was the unpredictable behavior of their laboring inferiors. It was perfectly obvious to every right-thinking Englishman like Bishop Pretyman that 'private property is essential to the very existence of civil society'. Whatever the wild interpretations about the community of goods extracted from ill-perceived notions of primitive Christianity, 'it is not to be believed that the Gospel . . . would destroy, in any respect, or weaken, a principle which is the foundation of every social comfort . . .'.[2] Many wrong-thinking people were clearly unconvinced. If, as feared, equalitarian ideas had darkly stained the coarse fabric of lower-class life, it was also recognized that the severity of want was a major inducement to disaffection. The more analytical enquiries into the condition of the poor, and the means of ameliorating their distress, indicated that it would take more than pious tracts and confident expositions on the nature of hierarchical society to keep the lower orders acquiescent and complaisant.

3. POOR RELIEF RECONSIDERED

To conservative, traditionally-minded Churchmen, the best way to cope with a problem was the old way. As applied to poverty, this meant charity and the Poor Law. Critics, however, were becoming less enamoured with these solutions, fearful that relief had become indiscriminate, exorbitant and perhaps self-perpetuating. Yet both were too deeply imbedded in the ancient structure of the Church and the State to be easily removed by the doubts of a Joseph Townsend and his followers. Furthermore, after insisting that poverty was a necessary characteristic of society sanctioned by Scripture and natural law, it would seem that one could not logically deny the Christian obligations which were required by the same laws. Still, several prelates in the 1780's were troubled by denials of that type. In 1788, Bishop Bagot allowed that the Poor Law was sometimes abused and perhaps encouraged indolence and other vices; but this was a failure of administration rather than principle. The State had wisely provided, 'a fixed and permanent maintenance for the poor and helpless'; if there appeared to be more people on the rates and the costs were rising, it indicated not corruption and decay, but a natural result of increased wealth, prosperity, extended commerce,

[1] Murray, *Sermon* (1792), 5.

[2] G. Pretyman, *Elements of Christian Theology Containing Proofs of the Authenticity and Inspiration of the Holy Scriptures* . . . (1799), II, 560.

improved husbandry and an increasing population. Instead of complaining, Bagot believed men should be cheered by such developments and willingly pay whatever was legally necessary, and more, as needed.[1]

Charges that relief was not only self-perpetuating, but an interference with the natural operation of economic laws, were countered by Bishop Horsley with a warning that the divine origin of inequality also entailed a divine responsibility for the relief of the poor. The rich could not have it both ways. Although it is not clear whether Horsley had read Townsend's critique of the Poor Law, his response in the same year it appeared (1786) was nevertheless to the point:

> It may seem a presumptuous deviation from the Creator's plan, that any should become suitors to the public charity, for a better subsistence than their own labour might procure. Poverty it may seem, can be nothing more than an imaginary evil; of which the modest will never complain, which the intelligent never will commiserate, and the politic never will relieve. . . .

Not only was this attitude contrary to reason, sound policy, and benevolent feelings of philanthropy, it violated the precepts of the Gospel. Moreover it 'can never be more indecent, or less worthy of regard, than when it us used by those, who profess to be strangers and pilgrims upon the earth, and have a balm for all the evils of the present world in the certainty of their prospects in a better country'.[2]

Eighteenth-century bishops, in contrast to their more spiritually earnest successors, did not usually emphasize to the poor assurances of a divine compensation for their inordinate earthly sufferings. Horsley, for one, did not like people justifying the abrogation of their charitable responsibilities on such shabby grounds. Furthermore, it had the ring of enthusiasm and spiritual equalitarianism which few prelates found very pleasing. Heavily encrusted with the precepts of natural theology, they tended to discuss religious truths as exemplified in virtuous daily living rather than in terms of ultimate spiritual rewards. Largely unaffected by religious revivalism and the nascent principles of political economy, Horsley's episcopal generation still viewed poverty as an individual misfortune perhaps, but a social necessity which did not necessarily suggest some distressing personal fault on the part of the poor. Whatever their spiritual and administrative defects, they were still committed to an older Christian idea that did not consider poverty a terrible sin, and the poor especially sinful. Utilitarianism and sin-centered revivalism was moving in that direction, but with the possible exception of Richard Watson, bishops were not particularly harsh on the poor. They were, instead, removed from them.

[1] L. Bagot, *A Sermon Preached . . . June 5, 1788, Being the Time of the Yearly Meeting of the Children Educated in the Charity Schools* . . . (1788), 6–7.
[2] Horsley, *Sermon* (1786), 6–7.

Nevertheless, as providence has 'so wonderfully . . . interwoven the public and the private good . . . the public is . . . interested in the relief of real Poverty . . . for Providence hath so ordained, that so long as the individual languishes in Poverty, the public must want the services of an useful member'.[1] Horsley emphasized those services had to be provided within a constricted sphere; for the poor, as a result of early-formed habits, and the more important 'natural bent of genius', cannot readily move from one rank to another and still be useful members of society. As a mechanic would be useless if elevated to the pulpit, the bar or senate, the statesman or scholar would be a poor tradesman, and the courtier a failure at the plough.

> Thus every man's ability of finding a subsistence for himself, and of being serviceable to the public, is limited by his habits and his genius to a certain sphere; which may not improperly be called *the Sphere of his Political Activity*. Poverty, obstructing the political activity in its proper sphere, arrests and mortifies the powers of the citizen, rendering him not more miserable in himself than useless to the community; which, for its own sake, must free the captive from the chain which binds him, in order to regain his services.

Consequently, in addition to the Christian responsibility to aid the poor, there was also a practical utilitarian reason which would benefit society as a whole. Even if an individual as a result of accident, disease, age—'the extinction of the natural powers of the animal'—could not be useful any more, he was still entitled to relief. Any other policy would contradict 'the very first principles, or rather the first idea of all civil association; which is that of a union of the powers of the Many, to supply the wants and help the infirmities of the solitary animal'. Implicit, then, in the origin of society was a fundamental obligation to assist effectively all those 'on whom the mischief falls'.[2] As long as poverty was a providential result of the social condition, the poor were not to be despised or neglected.

Admittedly, there was some danger that too great a reliance upon the rates would diminish the fear of poverty, and the corresponding advantages such fear provided by stimulating men to industry. It was commonly accepted that legal relief was never intended to 'change the dread of want in the lowest orders of the people, into an expectation of a competency . . .'. Otherwise, statute law would be in conflict with the natural inclination of men to avoid the unpleasant state of poverty, and to seek to improve themselves. Rather than relying too much upon the Poor Law, it was important to encourage its supplementation from private charity—'a duty which all individuals owe to the public . . .'.[3]

They also owed it to God of course, but it is significant that obligations derived from the Gospels were rarely mentioned by the bishop.

[1] *Ibid.*, 11.   [2] *Ibid.*, 12–13.   [3] *Ibid.*, 14.

Private beneficence was praised primarily because it was 'the most natural and the best method of relief', closely conforming to the utilitarian motivations and responsibilities of civil society. Since poverty 'is to the community, as well as to the sufferer, an evil; and since, in the formal nature of the thing, it is an evil from which the individual cannot be extricated by any efforts of his own; Policy, no less than humanity, enjoins that the community relieve him', collectively and individually.[1] In any event, Horsley concluded, the occasional relief of some, and the perpetual relief of others, was a small price to pay for the blessings of a well-balanced, harmonious society.

During the terrible years of the French Revolution, Horsley relentlessly encouraged and supported the persecution of those among the lower orders who preferred Paine's analysis of society to his own. But to others who agreed with him, and kept quiet, he was very generous indeed. The most outspoken prelate of his age, Horsley's influence and ideas were virtually unchallenged by his contemporaries on the bench. Coleridge was to praise him as the only clergyman of that generation who represented what the 'clerisy' should be. A powerful divine who promoted learning and culture, he was the only prelate comparable to those of the seventeenth century—'the one red leaf, the last of its clan . . .'.[2] Although some of his less militant brethren questioned his increasingly irrational refusals ever to contemplate peace with France again, they accepted his rational explanations about inequality and poverty, and could see no reason for changing the tried and true methods for coping with those inevitable problems. A few bishops, such as Barrington, Porteus, and later, Burgess, placed slightly more emphasis upon the sinful origins of human want, and the Gospel-inspired obligations for relief, but even their mildly Evangelical modifications did not diverge in substance from the natural-law, utilitarian interpretations made by Horsley.

Only Bishop Watson openly differed; in contrast to Horsley, the Whig prelate's conviction that poverty was a personal failing made him reluctant to concede the social value of relief. On the one hand it minimized the responsibility of lazy, imprudent men for their condition; on the other it suggested that relief was a natural right. Troubled by a de-emphasis of individual responsibility implicit in Rousseau's arguments, and opposed to the modification of relief requirements, Watson, in 1785, tried to shake the pre-Malthusian optimism of people who believed that God had provided the means to support the entire human race. He did not deny it, nor did he challenge the necessity of the Poor Law. But such support was only feasible if all men continually endeavored to fulfil their responsibility to improve themselves. Man had entered into society not

[1] *Ibid.*, 13.
[2] S. T. Coleridge, *Essays on His Own Times, Forming A Second Series of the Friend*, his daughter, ed. (1850), I, xxv.

only to protect his property, but also to enlarge it if possible. The individual would thereby benefit himself and his family as well as the rest of society, without detracting from the progress of others.

> God . . . never meant that the idle should live upon the labour of the industrious, or that the flagitious should eat the bread of the righteous: He hath therefore permitted a state of property to be everywhere introduced; that the industrious might enjoy the rewards of their diligence; and that those who would not work, might feel the punishment of their laziness.[1]

Eight years later, in 1793, Watson, in an appendix to his earlier comments, claimed that England was very generous—perhaps too generous—to its poor. Although initially he had cautiously approved of the Revolution in France, he had long since repented of his short-sightedness and could not understand why the English poor would be attracted to pernicious Jacobin doctrines.[2] Already, 'the provision for the poor in this kingdom is so liberal, as, in the opinion of some, to discourage industry'. What else was to be done for them?[3]

Watson, a wealthy, improving Westmorland landowner, calculated that the total rental of lands in England and Wales did not 'amount to more than eighteen millions a year; and the poor rates amount to two millions. The poor then, at present, possess a ninth part of the landed rental of the country; and, reckoning ten pounds for the annual maintenance of each pauper, it may be inferred, that those who are maintained by the community do not constitute a fortieth part of the people'. In fact, the bishop concluded from this statistical legerdemain, 'an equal division of land would be to the poor a great misfortune; they would possess far less than by the laws of the land they are at present entitled to'. When the amounts contributed and subscribed by private benefactors were included, the poor were so obviously at an advantage under the existing system of inequality that proposals to share the land in common 'cannot but excite one's astonishment, that so foolish a system should ever have been so much as mentioned by any man of common sense'.[4]

Equally upsetting to Watson and other critics of the rising cost of relief during the war was the persistent demand by republican enthusiasts such as Paine and William Godwin that the poor were entitled to assistance as a right. Both insisted that the right to subsistence extracted from the property their labor created was due to all men whether employed or not.[5] In 1796, prompted by the reappearance of Watson's sermon describing the divine

[1] Watson, *Sermon* (1785), 2. [2] Watson, *Charge* (1791), 4.
[3] Watson, *Sermon* (1793), 24. [4] *Ibid.*
[5] Paine, *Rights of Man*, Pt. II, Chap. 5; Godwin, *An Enquiry Concerning Political Justice and Its Influence on General Virtue and Happiness*, 2 vols. (1793), Bks. II, VIII.

wisdom in creating rich and poor, Paine denied that the distinction was in any way natural or divine. Poverty was entirely the creation of civilization; it derived from the accumulation of private property, and was dependent upon the participation of all men in society. Property-owners therefore had a clear obligation to all members of society who made their wealth possible by participating in the social contract, but they had in addition a special responsibility to the laborers at whose expense unequal wealth was accumulated.[1]

Bishop Horsley, who loathed Paine and shuddered at the mention of his name, nevertheless shared shared similar ideas on the responsibilities of the propertied classes towards the poor. Although they formed very different conclusions about the nature of government derived from social compact, they did react similarly to the growing interpretation of poor relief as merely the right to work rather than the right to receive minimum support whenever necessary. Paine's Quaker humanitarianism and Horsley's Tory, natural-law, Christian paternalism led them to the belief that poor relief was implicit in the nature and purpose of civil society. The old bishop would have been horrified to contemplate so wicked an intelectual alliance.

Elsewhere, however, clerical attitudes were becoming less tolerant of the poor. When established in 1797, the Evangelical Society for Bettering the Condition of the Poor made it clear, that it had no intention of distributing relief merely because of need.[2] The Reverend John Venn, organizing a branch at Clapham two years later, explained:

> Before any relief is granted, information should be particularly sought concerning the moral character of the applicant, particularly if he is accustomed to attend public worship; whether he sends his children to school, and trains them in the habit of industry.

If an applicant lacked the necessary moral and utilitarian qualities he was to be denied assistance. Indiscriminate relief interfered with individual moral and physical improvement; 'the very character of a man who subsists on charity is changed. He has lost his boldness, his fortitude, his openness, his manliness, and is become mean, abject, pusillanimous and often deceitful.'[3]

Evangelicals held no monopoly on that analysis. Though obsessed with the reformation and salvation of the sinful soul, and prone to view outward misery as a sign of inner corruption, they also reflected the heightened feelings of dislike and distrust of the lower orders increasingly evident during the frantic closing years of the eighteenth century.

[1] Paine, *Agrarian Justice, Opposed to Agrarian Law, and to Agrarian Monopoly* (1797).

[2] See *First Report*, T. Bernard, ed.

[3] M. Hennell, *John Venn and the Clapham Sect* (1958), 144–5.

There was a pervasive feeling that everything had gone wrong; previous policies were inadequate, even dangerous. High churchmen, terrified by the Revolution—'this awful crisis of our fate'—and suspicious of Evangelical and enlightened philanthropic approaches to the lower classes, joined the growing numbers who pointed an accusing finger at the extension of relief. The ultra-High Churchman, Jonathan Boucher, angrily denounced it as 'mercy without justice . . .'.[1] He deplored the fashion of philanthropy and the charitable efforts of 'religious enthusiasts'. Their intention was 'spurious and false, whilst it shews itself only being indulgent to folly, and tolerant and forgiving chiefly towards vice'. He was not alone in his conviction that the poor had been made restless and dangerous by extravagant promises of perpetual relief.

> The injury done to pure morals, legal justice, genuine loyalty, and true religion, by that ape of *mercy*, modern philanthropy; which under the pretence of befriending the whole human race, disturbs the peace and destroys the happiness of all its own nearest and dearest connections.[2]

The message was getting through. When, in the more trying months of the war, the London magistrate, Patrick Colquhoun, set up soup kitchens in the Metropolis, he defensively assured critics that his measures were carefully designed to discourage sloth and indigence, and preserve the traditional social and economic balance of the country. In practice, it meant just enough nourishment to keep the poor from starving.[3] The balance was preserved.

Bishop Burgess was one of the few prelates who wondered at what cost to Christian principle. In 1802, clearly troubled by the attacks and qualifications on charity during the previous decade, Burgess urged his fellow man 'not to be too scrupulous about the objects of his benevolence. Charity shrinks from the cold scrutiny of minute enquiry. God, we know loveth a cheerful giver.' Preaching on the eve of his elevation to the See of St David's, Burgess noted that cheerful givers were yielding to suspicious benefactors angry at their impoverished beneficiaries, and fearful that perhaps their efforts were only encouraging unrest and perpetuating individual indolence. What mattered, Burgess replied, was not that many undeserving people received charity, but that one person in genuine need was helped. God was the best judge of the sincerity and motivation of both receiver and giver; it was presumptuous of man to take that complex evaluation upon himself.[4]

These quaint sentiments, rare enough in the previous half-century,

[1] J. Boucher, *A Sermon Preached at the Assizes Held at Guildford, July 30, 1798* (1798), 21-22.

[2] *Ibid.*, 8-10. [3] Pettigrew, *Lettsom*, 357.

[4] T. Burgess, *Charity, The Bond of Peace and of All Virtues. A Sermon Preached . . . September 2, 1802* (Durham, 1803), 8.

virtually disappeared from episcopal thought in the next several decades. They were replaced by the more scientific analyses of political economists trying to cope realistically with vexatious problems of rising rates, overpopulation and rapid economic and social dislocation. Since 1795, when the Berkshire justices for the Speenhamland hundred decided, in the interests of social order and humanity, to supplement the inadequate wages of impoverished agricultural laborers, the cost of relief had risen rapidly as the system, endorsed by Parliament, quickly spread through other counties. By 1801, as Arthur Young revealed, a typical Suffolk laborer was receiving an average wage of nine shillings per week, supplemented by six shillings from the rates in order to obtain the barest essentials for his maintenance.[1] What had been initiated as a temporary expedient soon became a permanent adjunct to the Poor Law, discouraging migration to less destitute areas, and driving the rates higher every year. In 1803 the cost of relief had reached £4,267,965, more than twice the cost ten years earlier. Before the war ended the figure soared to over seven million pounds.[2] But most Englishmen, no matter how disgruntled by the excessive costs, would have had to agree with George Canning's conclusion that the rapid expansion and flexibility of relief measures had prevented serious rioting and even revolution in many agricultural districts.[3]

Although the post-war bench was filled with prelates who increasingly opposed the expansive additions to the Poor Law, and in time the Poor Law itself, only Richard Watson spoke out against it during the war. Not that he was any less alarmed at the prospect of the poor rebelling; in fact he repeatedly urged Pitt to terminate the external conflict before internal conditions became so desperate as to reach an 'irresistible height'. The mutiny in the fleet and the Irish rebellion in 1797 portended the worst disaster, and he pleaded with the Prime Minister to recall the troops from the Continent, level a tax on all wealth in the country, and employ a mercenary army to defend it. If a sufficient tax were exacted, the national debts could be paid off, oppressive levies eliminated, and the economy rejuvenated. Moreover, as a result of so great a national sacrifice to fill the coffers of the land, 'the corrupting influence of the poor would be diminished—the poor rates would be reduced . . . and the French would be so astounded by our magnanimity that they would accede to peace'. All Europe, the bishop promised, would see the folly of fighting so 'high spirited a people'.[4]

---

[1] J. Steven Watson, *The Reign of George III 1760–1815* (Oxford, 1960), 528.
[2] *Parl. Ps.* (1817), VI, 155–7.   [3] Watson, *George III*, 529.
[4] Watson to Pitt, 15 Feb. 1797, *Chatham Ps.*, P.R.O. 30/8/187. Also Watson to Duke of Grafton, 10 Oct., in *Anecdotes*, II, 46–47, and Watson's *Address to the People of Great Britain* (1798), 2.

Pitt made no such inflated claims for the income tax enacted the following year, but Watson was confident that the government was on the right track. He was soon disappointed when the new revenue, instead of ending the war and assuaging discontent, was quickly swallowed up in new campaigns. Not only were the lower orders still a threat, but the cost of maintaining more and more of them continued to rise. In 1796 he had complained to the Prime Minister of the disproportionate burden falling on parishes unfortunate enough to have surplus laborers. Ever ready with a scheme, the bishop proposed that the government take the average of the rates in every parish for the preceding seven years and freeze them at that figure. If the Poor Law was then rigorously enforced and paupers set to work 'either in an house of correction or in a school of industry . . .', an end would be put to the idleness and profligacy which the current looseness permitted. During years of prosperity and plenty, the fixed rates would accumulate and a surplus would be made available for periods of distress, or even employed to pay off the national debt. If at any time the surplus was insufficient to meet the needs of the deserving poor, a national grant should provide the difference. Watson believed that the poor were the responsibility 'of the public at large', not just the local landowners.[1] Certain as he was that the 'present state of our poor is a disgrace to our polity', he tried once more in 1800 to arouse Pitt's interest. As the national census was to be taken for the first time the following year, the bishop recommended a shilling be collected from each person counted. Estimating the population at approximately ten million, he calculated raising £500,000 to apply to the construction of workhouses, almshouses, and a reduction of the rates.[2]

Pitt remained unimpressed by Watson's repeated attempts to shift the burden of poor relief to the nation as a whole. The prelate's episcopal colleagues were even less enthusiastic, and were perfectly content to avoid tampering with established institutions no matter how great their abuses. During the debate in 1800 over measures to be taken to aid the needy during the severe grain shortage of that year, Archbishop Moore, supported by Barrington of Durham, believed that the legislature should do nothing whatsoever. The wealthy, nepotistic archbishop, himself of humble origin, lamented 'the inconveniences and distress which the lower orders of society must unavoidably suffer'; nevertheless he felt the safest and most prudent course to follow would be for the upper classes to set some meaningful example for their destitute inferiors. Specifically, he urged their lordships to sign an agreement 'to diminish' the use of flour in their family meals, and discontinue all pastry.[3] Barring-

[1] Watson to Pitt, Feb. 1796, *Anecdotes*, II, 32–33.
[2] Watson to Pitt, 30 Nov. 1800, *Chatham Ps.*, P.R.O. 30/8/187.
[3] *Parl. Hist.*, XXXIV (1800), 1496–7.

ton agreed such a sacrifice could not but impress the poor who 'naturally looked up to the example of the higher', and in his enthusiasm suggested that 'the retrenchment' be extended to include other luxuries as well.[1]

By the opening of the new century, Church leaders wanted to hear nothing of innovation. They had held their breath during the terrible preceding years, and increasingly held their tongues as well. The speculation about the nature of society, inequality and poverty, before the fall of the Bastille, and in the years immediately after, tapered off. As far as most prelates were concerned there had already been too much speculation on such subjects, and the tragic results were only too apparent. Though staggered by the French Revolution, they had little understanding or interest in the dynamic forces of political, economic and social change altering the society to which they ministered. These forces were not a meaningful influence on their formative and pastoral years as they were to be on those of their successors after Waterloo. Consequently, most bishops of the revolutionary era examined them defensively, superficially, yet with a certainty that they were essentially irrelevant to the nature of things. The new forces and the speculation about them meant change and innovation—a disruption of God's harmonious, natural universe. Though many of the next generation of churchmen who came to power near or after the end of the war also tried to reject the changes occurring in their lifetimes, it was much more difficult by then to ignore them or pretend they were irrelevant to the Church and society.

In the early years of the new century, however, even Bishop Watson, one of the most interesting and active thinkers on the bench, if one of the least active diocesans, ceased his theorizing upon questions of social organization and the poor. He contented himself with repeating his conclusions of three or four decades earlier, certain that poverty not only made people happier, but more virtuous.[2] Even the Luddite disturbances in 1811–12 failed to prod the old bishops into renewing their pleas, explanations and warnings to the lower classes. The breaking of competitive machinery was an economic grievance not beyond the understanding of an eighteenth-century clerical squirearchy, who did not now equate it to equalitarian insurrection as they did the political and social demands of lower-class agitation in the 1790's.

England had survived the revolutionary plague. To deeply conservative, traditional minds, that in itself, even without Burke's assurances, was sufficient proof of the rightness of the existing social and political institutions of the realm. In the end, even the savage French had to

[1] *Ibid.*, 1501.

[2] R. Watson, *A Charge Delivered to the Clergy of the Diocese of Landaff, in June 1809*, in *Miscellaneous Tracts On Religious, Political, and Agricultural Subjects* (1815), I, 205–6.

return to a system of authority, hierarchy and inequality as the only guarantee of order and stability. The interdependency of class and the relativity of responsibility in the natural, well-ordered society had been severely tested, theoretically and practically, and had not been found wanting. It was clear, as the greedy, pluralistic, nepotistic, endlessly place-seeking, aristocratic Bishop of Bristol, George Pelham, confidently exclaimed in 1806:

> The happy people of this kingdom enjoy the best security: where the interests of individuals are so connected, that material changes must affect the whole community: where the elevated situations, which wealth or power give, must be supported by the industry and labour of the indigent: and where they, on the other hand, receive protection and comfort from those, whose station they do materially uphold.[1]

Though he lived another twenty-one years, moving to Exeter (1807) and finally Lincoln (1820), Pelham hardly noticed the changes in society affecting 'the happy people' and the relationship of the Established Church to them. He had little in common with the more diligent, serious young clergymen already starting to fill the vacant places on the bench in the post-war years—clergymen for whom the problems of poverty, population and social discontent were very serious issues requiring considerable thought and analysis. Not only because they affected the general happiness and welfare of society, but because they specifically related to the spiritual revival and utility of the national Church. But where the earlier generation of Church leaders had discussed the questions within the context of Rousseau's criticism and Lockeian concepts of natural-law, the new generation was to discuss them in terms of political economy.

[1] G. Pelham, *A Sermon Preached Before the Lords Spiritual and Temporal . . . February 26, 1806, Being the Day Appointed For a General Fast* (1806), 8–9.
Pelham (1766–1827), son of 1st Earl of Chichester and cousin of Duke of Newcastle, was also close friend of the Prince Regent whose gala parties he attended at the Brighton Pavilion. Continually badgered Prime Ministers for more preferment to help improve 'poor Mrs Pelham's health' which was apparently rejuvenated by periodic transfusions of ecclesiastical advancement. See Pelham to Liverpool, 9 and 10 May 1825, *Liverpool Ps.* B.M. Add. MS. 38300, ff. 60–65. After still another request for Durham, Liverpool, in a letter of 13 March 1826, Add. MS. 38301, f. 116, sharply told Pelham there would be no more preferment. The bishop died the following year.

III

❖❖❖❖❖❖❖❖❖❖❖❖❖❖❖❖❖❖❖❖❖❖❖❖❖❖❖❖❖❖❖❖❖

Poverty and
Political Economy

❖❖❖❖❖❖❖❖❖❖❖❖❖❖❖❖❖❖❖❖❖❖❖❖❖❖❖❖❖❖❖❖❖

1. WATERLOO TO PETERLOO

In many ways the coming of peace in 1815 was more troublesome to the Church than the war. Reform was in the air; it was only a matter of time before the instability of conditions and the burdens of the long conflict would no longer satisfy as excuses for avoiding change. In 1792, William Windham had asked, 'Who would repair their house in a hurricane?'[1] and the obvious answer to that rhetorical query had for nearly twenty-five years justified clerical and lay reluctance to tamper seriously with existing institutions and policies. The Church, faced with the task of keeping the lower orders content, had made some hesitant moves towards improving clerical residence, and, prompted by the Nonconformist challenge of Lancastrian schools, had since 1811 turned its attention to educating the children of the laboring poor. By the end of the war dedicated High Church laymen in conjunction with the archbishop and other prominent clerics had already made the government aware of the necessity of extending the resources of the Establishment into crowded areas lacking provisions for worship in the national faith.

The repeated disturbances and eruptions of violence that followed in the troubled years immediately after Waterloo gave such measures a new urgency. The condition of the laboring poor, and the reasons for it again seemed an especially pertinent issue when it was feared that the lower orders might once more be on the brink of revolt. As disturbances

[1] Watson, *George III*, 302.

85

spread from agricultural to manufacturing areas, the Church seemed more incapable than ever of coping with the enlarged, active laboring classes who were clearly less and less responsive to the traditional exhortations and pious homilies of their clerical guardians. Not even the elevated leaders of the Anglican Establishment were able to ignore any longer the tenuous relationship the Church had in many areas with large segments of the working population. There had already been warnings of this in the later years of the preceding century when a few ecclesiastics had cautioned their clergy about lower-class disaffection. George Horne, in 1786, complained that parsons were too far above their poor parishioners and were turning them away.[1] The disturbing *Report* of the Lincolnshire clergy in 1800 only confirmed what several troubled churchmen had already concluded—the lower orders were seeking spiritual alternatives in the camp of Dissent, or forgetting their spiritual needs entirely.

The problem took on more meaningful perspective as statistical evidence of the extent of demographic growth and movement began to pile up in census returns, diocesan questionnaires, and in numerous publications devoted to the question of population. When compared with the information being gathered on Church extension during the previous century, demographic acceleration sharply contrasted with the depressing stagnation that had set in since the time of Queen Anne. It was already clear that Methodism and revived Nonconformity were perfectly willing to take full advantage of the situation. Moreover, ecclesiastics could hardly be insensitive to the heightened criticism of their enemies, who not only berated the Church for its spiritual apathy and material greed, but, in accordance with the changing values of the age, deplored it as useless to the mass of the populace. This charge particularly rankled with clergymen who took a confident pride in the belief that it was mainly through their placating efforts that the lower orders had remained loyal during the long years of revolutionary temptation.

Yet after Waterloo the laboring poor again appeared to have learned nothing from the experience of the preceding twenty-five years. Unlike the Luddite disturbances earlier in the decade, which hardly caused a stir among the easily panicked hierarchy, post-war conflicts seemed much more dangerous. Not only were potential revolutionaries driven by comprehensible economic grievances, such as rising prices, wage reductions and unemployment, but they were again tempted by political and social reforms. These ranged from the extension of the franchise and redistribution of parliamentary seats, urged by the revived Hampden Clubs, to the redistribution of property demanded by the wild followers

[1] Horne, *The Duty of Contending for the Faith. A Sermon Preached . . . July 1, 1786* (Oxford, 1786), 20.

of the land reformer, Thomas Spence. The provocative oratory of Henry Hunt at huge open meetings such as that held on Spa Fields in 1816—but one of many preludes to the fateful meeting on St Peter's Field, Manchester, three years later—and the cutting pen of William Cobbett, combined to stir up terrible memories of the 1790's. Reports pouring into the Home Office seemed to confirm the worst fears. When a window in the Regent's coach was pierced by a stone or bullet at the opening of the 1817 session of Parliament, who could not recall a similar attack on George III in 1795?

Certainly not Archbishop Manners–Sutton, nor the new, frightened Bishop of London, William Howley. Nor would they soon forget the eccentric, democratic Lord Cochrane breaking up their attempts in 1816 to revive the Association for the Relief of the Manufacturing and Labouring Poor. When originally established during the distress of 1812 there had been no difficulty. But four years later the prelates were unable to join with several dukes, Wilberforce, and the Chancellor of the Exchequer, Vansittart, in a public subscription meeting, without being howled down.[1] It seemed that such traditional, benevolent solutions were no longer satisfactory. What would be acceptable was distressingly apparent.

As in the 1790's, the bench readily supported the repressive legislation enacted in 1817 that put an end to mass meetings, the Hampden Clubs, and caused Cobbett to flee to America, as they did the extension of this legislation into the Six Acts quickly passed after Peterloo two years later. Although some prelates realized the difficulties were in part caused by post-war readjustments in the economy, they feared there were more perverse motives at work. Ignorant and deluded people, they knew, usually blame their rulers for their problems, and this in itself was not unexpected. But attacks on the Church and its clergy, especially bishops and clerical magistrates, indicated that the agitation was part of a wider plan of revolution. Even a cursory retrospective glance at France reminded Bishop Sparke that 'the transition from infidelity to disloyalty is but too easy; they who do not fear God will not long honour the King'.[2]

As the similarities between the dangers of the 1790's and those of the present day were obvious, Sparke exhorted his clergy to exert themselves once more to preserve the Constitution as they had done in that earlier decade.[3] Sparke knew how to go about it. One way was to place one's children and relatives in lucrative preferments. He did so to the extent of provoking a scurrilous pun explaining how to traverse the Cambridge fens at night by following the illumination provided by the 'little Sparkes'

[1] Elie Halévy, *The Liberal Awakening 1815–1830*, E. I. Watkin, trans. (1961), 12–13.

[2] Sparke, *Charge* (1817), 6–8.   [3] *Ibid.*, 9.

planted in all the good livings. Another was to encourage and praise those clerical magistrates, such as the Reverend Henry B. Dudley, who urged the Home Office to call out the troops against disgruntled laborers in the Isle of Ely. Dudley did so after rejecting an attempt by other magistrates to negotiate a wage increase of two shillings a day, and pressure the local farmers to pay the full wages of workers being subsidized by the rates.[1] The Regius Professor of Greek at Cambridge, and future Bishop of Gloucester (1830–56), James Henry Monk, was greatly relieved when the Ely rioters were finally in jail. Understanding priorities, he feared that their schemes, if they had 'no worse effects, would certainly have interfered with our College Examinations, which are now in progress'.[2]

The fact that clerical magistrates were often antagonistic to the poor laborers was exploited by critics of the Establishment who readily described un-Christian and uncharitable parsons harassing the unfortunate of their parishes. At Peterloo, two of the frightened magistrates who summoned the troops were Anglican clergymen, and one of them read the Riot Act.[3] The laboring classes were slow to forget, and the clerical magistrate long remained an anti-Establishment symbol of a materialistic upper-class Church wedded to propertied interests, and indifferent to the spiritual and physical welfare of the poor. The new Bishop of London, Howley, was sensitive to these charges when in 1816 he was reluctant to have anything to do with repressive measures against the troublesome laborers. But he finally conceded after the riots of that unsettled year that he could see no reduction of 'that enormous mass of evil . . . without the decided interposition of the Legislature'.[4]

Others, less troubled by the role of the clergy in promoting and enforcing repressive legislation, wondered what else could be done if the poor refused to accept humbly and peacefully divine visitations. Henry Phillpotts, later Bishop of Exeter (1831–69), then the magistrate-vicar of St Margaret's, Durham, insisted that

> they [the poor] must not deem it a hardship, if the peculiar circumstances of the times require of them to submit for awhile to a homelier, and, it may be in some instances, a scantier fare, than in more prosperous seasons

[1] R. F. Wearmouth, *Methodism and the Working Class Movements of England 1800–1850* (1947), 22.

[2] Monk to Samuel Butler, 30 May 1816, *Butler Ps.*, British Museum, Add. MS. 34584, f. 166.

[3] Mathieson, *Church Reform*, 27. Although the Church was increasingly uneasy about the secular and anti-working-class implications of clerical magistrates, in 1832 there were still 1,354, one-fifth of the total number of magistrates, who were performing this dual function.

[4] Howley to Charles Bowdler, 16 Sept. 1816, *Howley's Letter Book*, Lambeth Palace, uncatalogued MS. 75.

they have been enabled to enjoy. Least of all may they join in that foolish and wicked cry, which has already been heard in some parts of our island, as if all the distresses we are compelled to bear may be attributed to our rulers: as if reform in the government will bring with it the remedy for every evil.[1]

Burke had prophesied and a generation had found out where illusory ideas of reform could lead. Then, as now, the lessons taught by the learned author of the *Reflections on the Revolution in France* were pertinent. It was sheer folly for men to blame natural distress on the failure of statesmen, but if they do, Phillpotts quoted, 'Let government protect and encourage industry, secure property, repress violence, and discountenance fraud, it is all that they have to do; the rest is in the hand of their master and ours'.[2]

As far as Phillpotts was concerned, there was nothing more to be said. That the poor were less than convinced was clear from the outbreak of strikes, riots and mass meetings in the manufacturing districts of Lancashire and Yorkshire in 1818–19. Try as they might to convince the workers they must resign themselves to temporary providential visitations, the clergy were unable to dissuade many of them from the belief that low wages, unemployment, and the combined power of magistrate-supported manufacturers had at least as much to do with their misfortunes. The explosion on St Peter's Field, Manchester, on 16 August 1819, followed by bitter recriminations and the panicky passage of the repressive Six Acts in November and December, seemed a logical if unfortunate result of post-war discontent. Old Bishop Pretyman–Tomline, who had welcomed his pupil, Pitt's, stern measures against the threat of revolution in the 1790's, was still around to welcome those instituted by Liverpool's government two decades later. Decisive action was necessary in both eras, and the Lincoln prelate assured the Prime Minister that 'all well-disposed' persons would support any measures

[1] H. Phillpotts, *Two Sermons . . . On Occasion of the Late Harvest, and of the Attack on the Prince Regent, When Passing From the Parliament House, 28th January 1817* (Durham, 1817), 16.

Phillpotts (1778–1869), son of Herefordshire gentry who had fallen on hard times, married a niece of Lord Eldon. Extremely politically active Tory clergyman and strong anti-Catholic controversialist until persuaded by Wellington to support emancipation. Appointed to Exeter in 1830, but Whigs delayed his installation until he surrendered the rich living of Stanhope, Durham. A bellicose ultra-High Church prelate, Phillpotts spent nearly £30,000 on some fifty lawsuits during his career. Sympathetic to the Oxford Movement, and an early supporter of Miss Sellon's sisterhood at Devonport, he was the principal episcopal defender of the pre-reform Establishment. Ceased to participate in public or diocesan affairs in 1862. See G. C. B. Davies, *Henry Phillpotts, Bishop of Exeter* (1954).

[2] *Ibid.*, 17.

he believed necessary to check 'the revolutionary proceedings in the North'.[1]

As long as the government was in a repressive mood, it seemed to the new Bishop of Llandaff (1819–26) and Dean of St Paul's, William Van Mildert, that the legislature should also be encouraged to add another Bill against blasphemous libel. Van Mildert, who had been Regius Professor of Divinity at Oxford, was the deeply conservative voice of respectable High Church orthodoxy. His more moderate successor as Regius Professor and later Bishop of Oxford (1827–29), Charles Lloyd, said rightly of Van Mildert that his knowledge of the exact doctrines of the Church of England was so great that orthodoxy oozed out of his pores, and he would talk of it in his dreams.[2] No wonder he was so upset by the vituperative assaults on the Establishment preceding Peterloo, and intensifying after it. The literary swipes of a Byron or a Shelley and the utilitarian condemnations of Bentham's anonymous *Church of England Catechism Examined* (1817) were tame when compared with the bitter charges William Hone, Richard Carlile and other extremists were leveling against the higher orders.

The deistic Carlile, who not only published new editions of Thomas Paine and his American disciple, Elihu Palmer, but selected works of Voltaire and Diderot as well, was already being persecuted for blasphemy both by the government and Wilberforce's Society for the Suppression of Vice. Bishop Van Mildert applauded the action, but insisted that even stronger laws were needed. Blasphemy and irreligion had permeated the lower orders, where 'learning and argument are no longer antidotes . . .'.[3] Feelings against the Church were running so high after Peterloo that the new prelate was sure the *Age of Reason* and other wicked works had turned the lower orders deaf to the teachings of their spiritual counsellors. Consequently, suppression of all such literature and declamations dangerous to the national faith was as necessary as the other contemplated forms of restrictive legislation.

The bench of course sided with the government and its interpretation of the events at Manchester. No bishop then in power expressed any sympathy for the people who were killed or injured, nor did any of them suggest that the authorities might have acted presumptuously, if not irresponsibly. Only one episcopal voice, and that belonging to Edward Stanley, a Whig prelate of Melbourne's era, disputed the official version.[4] Stanley's modest eyewitness account of Peterloo, which he priv-

---

[1] Pretyman to Liverpool, 29 Oct. 1819, *Liverpool Ps.*, British Museum, Add. MS. 38280, f. 261.

[2] F. W. Cornish, *A History of the English Church in the Nineteenth Century* (1910), I, 72.

[3] Hansard's *Parliamentary Debates*, XLI (1819), 987–8.

[4] Edward Stanley (1779–1849), son of Sir J. T. Stanley, Bart., and brother

ately jotted down for friends two months after the event, and his testimony at a trial three years later, gave considerable credence to the charge that local magistrates, some of them clerical, had launched a grave and unprovoked assault on a peaceful assembly. Vicar of his family's living of Alderley, Cheshire, for many years before his elevation to Norwich (1837–49), Stanley was visiting in Manchester in a house next to St Peter's Field on the day of the assembly. He saw no symptoms of riot or disturbance before the meeting, and described the people as 'sullenly peaceful'. No weapons, stones, or clubs were anywhere in evidence, and he only heard angry statements after the attack by the local militia.[1] Without denying that Henry Hunt, who was scheduled to address the crowd, and Richard Carlile, were dangerous men, the future bishop consistently maintained that he saw no necessity for the cavalry to attack what was an orderly meeting of well-dressed men, women and children.[2]

Henry Phillpotts no more believed Stanley in 1819 than he did years later when both were on the bench, and his ultra-High Church views and policies repeatedly clashed with the Broad Church tolerant liberalism of his episcopal brother. Nevertheless, in the aftermath of Peterloo, Phillpotts saw the need to mollify some of the anger which he feared would erupt into widespread rioting. It was this, rather than any sense of guilt or compassion, that led him to urge restraint on all sides. Public meetings and declarations condemning the government and the Prince Regent for congratulating the magistrates at Manchester were prejudicing normal legal procedures. Ever the frustrated barrister, Phillpotts, who had contemplated studying law before taking orders, pleaded that the courts be allowed to determine the existence of a revolutionary plot, and the culpability of magistrates trying to carry out their obligations in so confused and dangerous a place as Manchester. If the magistrates' reports to the government upon which the Regent premised his congratulations were incorrect, an enquiry would soon reveal the truth. In the

[1] E. Stanley, *Narrative of the Proceedings At St. Peter's Field Manchester, August 16, 1819* (Westminster, 1819), British Museum Add. MS. 30142, ff. 78–83.

[2] F. A. Burton, ed., *Three Accounts of Peterloo by Eyewitnesses Bishop Stanley, Lord Hylton, John Benjamin Smith, With Bishop Stanley's Evidence At the Trial* (Manchester, 1921), 35.

of 1st Baron Stanley. A Broad Churchman and the most liberal prelate on the bench, Stanley was a diligent, reforming bishop who revitalized the See of Norwich. A close friend of Thomas Arnold, Lord Shaftesbury, and father of Dean Stanley, the bishop was an energetic supporter of education, museums, temperance societies, mechanics, institutes, missionary societies and interdenominational co-operation. See A. P. Stanley, ed., *Memoirs of Edward and Catherine Stanley*, 2nd ed. (1880).

meantime, things were chaotic enough without violating the right of trial by jury, and mobs, 'in maintaining the Bill of Rights, violate Magna Charta'.[1]

Phillpotts, who had no qualms about the suspension of *habeas corpus* in 1817, and who spent much of his stormy career bullying, prosecuting, or arbitrarily condemning his less compliant clergy, was rarely so solicitous of the rights of his fellow man. But then he was certain that an enquiry or trial would certainly prove the magistrates were conscientiously acting to thwart an insurrection. The Assizes at Lancaster had already come to that conclusion, and Phillpotts was disturbed that responsible people could conclude otherwise.[2] As he wrote privately to a friend after the appearance of his public plea for objective restraint,

> the feelings of Englishmen must have undergone a strange Revolution if they could have remained insensible to the merits of those real patriots who in spite of personal danger, and multiplied annoyances of every kind, have contributed so largely to save us from the horrors of revolution in its worst form.[3]

In such a charged atmosphere, it is not surprising that many anxious clergy took an active interest in the various theories and explanations of lower-class conditions and behavior which multiplied after the war. They were especially interested in the writings of their more learned clerical brethren who saw that any understanding of the laboring poor required a thorough comprehension of the nature and causes of poverty. Within the context of the times this also meant an understanding of Malthus and the new laws of political economy which were being revealed in more detail with each passing year, and gradually becoming part of the clerical frame of reference.

There is no evidence that Malthus's *Essay on Population*, published first in 1798 and seriously revised in 1802, was read by any member of the bench elevated before the end of the war. Yet within a few years many of the Church leaders who were to guide the Establishment through the critical years of reform were considering the relationship of the Church to the lower orders not only in Malthusian terms, but within the general context of political economy. Unlike most of their episcopal elders, they had even read the earlier works of Robert Wallace, Adam Smith and Joseph Townsend. Furthermore, they were familiar with, and quoted from, the important evidence presented by Frederic Morton Eden and Patrick Colquhoun. If they missed the first edition of Malthus's

---

[1] H. Phillpotts, *A Letter to the Freeholders of the County of Durham. On the Proceedings of the County Meetings, Holden on Thursday 21st October Instant and Particularly on the Speech of John George Lambton, Esq. M.P.* (Durham, 1819), 26.

[2] *Ibid.*, 27.

[3] 6 Dec. 1819, *Phillpotts Ps.*, Exeter Cathedral Library, ED 11/72.

Essay, they certainly read one of the later editions, and in time supplemented it with at least a second-hand knowledge of the works of Jeremy Bentham, David Ricardo, J. R. MacCulloch, James Mill, and many of their disciples.

2. CHRISTIANITY, MALTHUS AND POLITICAL ECONOMY

Political economy was a supplementary revelation for some clergy and a repugnant perversion of traditional Christian values for others. Whatever their reaction, the post-war generation of Church spokesmen were deeply affected by the changing emphasis of social and political analysis. As the problem of poverty and the proliferation of the poor was a major concern of advocates of political economy, as it was to the Church, interested clergy were quickly drawn into the swirling controversies that developed after Waterloo. Reconciling the new dogma to the teachings of the Gospels was a difficult and often explosive task; several of the most influential clergy nevertheless spent a fruitless half-century attempting it. Although they often approached the question from very different vantage-points, their conclusions, often complementary, pointed to a striking departure from the Church's traditional teachings about the nature of poverty, and the responsibilities of believing Christians towards its amelioration.

As early as 1807, Bishop Watson had been asked by a Bath clergyman to take up his persuasive pen once more on behalf of the faith.[1] This time it was to refute the pernicious assertions of Parson Malthus, as in the past it had broken the anti-Christian assaults of Edward Gibbon and Tom Paine.[2] The clergyman described Malthus's *Essay on Population* as an insidious attack upon the Gospels designed to bring benevolence into contempt, and encourage magistrates to oppress the poor if they dared to have large families. It was a monstrous rejection of Christ's teachings to infer that the poor had no right to live unless they could obtain subsistence entirely by their own labour. Since Malthus was an Anglican minister rejecting the principles of Christian charity, Watson's correspondent believed that the Church, not 'politicians', should repudiate the false teaching of one of its own errant brethren. Yet no spokesman for the national faith had spoken out against the *Essay,* and the angry cleric wondered why not.[3]

---

[1] Watson, *Anecdotes,* II, 324.

[2] See Watson, *Two Apologies, One For Christianity, in a Series of Letters Addressed to Edward Gibbon, Esq. The Other for the Bible, in Answer to Thomas Paine* ... (1820). By the time of Watson's death in 1816 the *Letters ... to Gibbon,* first pub. in 1776, had passed through eight editions, and those to Paine, first pub. in 1796, through eleven editions.

[3] *Anecdotes,* II, 324–7.

93

He received little satisfaction or enlightenment from the old Bishop of Llandaff. In fact Watson confessed that after an initial glance he had not bothered to read the book. As he explained:

> perceiving that the author was endeavouring to shew the utility of bringing down the population of the earth to the level of the subsistence requisite for the support of man (a proposition wanting no proof, since where there is not food man must die), I thought his time and talents would have been better employed in the investigation of the means of increasing the subsistence to the level of the population.

The bishop had missed the point. In contrast to his protesting correspondent, he faulted Malthus's reason rather than his faith. From the latter standpoint, however, Watson felt justified 'in thus neglecting to peruse a book thwarting the strongest propensity of human nature, and contradicting the most express command of God, Increase and multiply!' What troubled him far more was that the fundamental premise was empirically without foundation, for rational scientific enquiry clearly indicated that man had hardly begun to draw upon the earth's potential to sustain life. Consequently he was 'persuaded that the earth had not in the course of six thousand years . . . ever been replenished with anything like one half the number of inhabitants it would sustain'.[1]

Watson was an old man content with improving his estates in Westmorland. He had fought his battles in a different age, and against different enemies—scepticism, deism, and finally leveling Jacobinism. Aware though he was that the times were changing rapidly, and certain that the Church would eventually have to change with them, he preferred to leave the inevitable problems of that change to a new generation of prelates. Malthusian arguments spoke to the future, not to the past; they spoke to nineteenth-century bishops, not to those of the eighteenth, secure in their elevated station, presiding over an unchallenged State institution whose property and privileges were guaranteed by law, rather than by popular spiritual appeal. That the Church was becoming less and less relevant to large numbers of people who found it not only spiritually vacuous, but inimical to their social and economic condition, was a possibility the retrenched Establishment only haltingly considered. The idea that Tom Paine's rancorous appeal, and the Methodist revival, spoke to the same point—the Anglican Church was separated from and even viewed as hostile by large numbers of the lower orders—was something Watson's brethren were unwilling to consider. They hoped that once the long war was over everything would be the same as before.

A younger generation of clergy, many of them ordained during the revolutionary years, were less sanguine about that possibility. Theirs was an age of rapid transition, and whether they liked it or not, they recog-

[1] *Ibid.*, 328–9.

nized it, and thought increasingly in terms of adjustment and accommodation. If Malthus was correct, things would become even more difficult in the years ahead. It was this realization that led the future Evangelical Bishop of Chester (1828–48) and Archbishop of Canterbury (1848–62), John Bird Sumner, to attempt a reconciliation of Malthusian principles with the 'wisdom and goodness of the Deity'.[1] During the closing years of the Napoleonic wars, while still an assistant master at Eton and Vicar of Mapledurham, Oxfordshire, he labored over a two-volume *Treatise On The Records Of The Creation* which, when it appeared in 1816, proved to the satisfaction of many clergymen and laymen alike that the lessons of the *Essay on Population* were not incompatible with those of Scripture.[2] Malthus had derived his information from Adam Smith, David Hume, Wallace, Townsend and Richard Price; Sumner felt a few loftier sources could only help the argument. Their addition allowed him to endorse the validity of Malthus's conclusions without accepting his pessimism.

Sumner conceded Malthus's point that the population indeed expanded geometrically while the means of subsistence had only increased arithmetically. But he also believed that 'it is impossible to suppose, that the ratio of increase among men, and its consequences, were not present to the contemplation of the Creator'. Since the multiplication of all species followed a divine design, the fecundity of every living creature, animal or human, was regulated. For example, Sumner cited short-lived creatures such as rabbits, insects, and codfish which gave birth to many, if not thousands of offspring. In contrast, the long-lived eagle laid a single egg, an elephant bore a single calf, and a whale no more than two cubs. 'It would be contrary to all just analogy to believe that brute animals received an attention denied to the human race. . . .'[3] The careful balance maintained between the sexes was further evidence of divine forethought. Quoting from Alexander von Humboldt's *Political Essay on the Kingdom of New Spain* (1811), Sumner noted the number of male births exceeded those of females in Europe and South America because the hazardous employment faced by men, including going to war and sea, required a counterbalance, 'a foresight which can only be attributed to the original mandate of Providence'.[4]

---

[1] J. B. Sumner (1780–1862), son of a Warwickshire vicar, brother of C. R. Sumner, Bishop of Winchester, and cousin of Samuel Wilberforce. A gentle, moderate, pious and hard-working prelate, Sumner was a strong supporter of Church reform.

[2] J. B. Sumner, *A Treatise On the Records of The Creation, And On the Moral Attributes of the Creator; With Particular Reference to the Jewish History, and to the Consistency of the Principle of Population With the Wisdom and Goodness of the Deity,* 2 vols. (1816).

[3] *Ibid.,* II, 133.   [4] *Ibid.*

Malthus was also right in contending that in every inhabited country there would always be as many people as could be supported at all, and always more than could be supported well, but, Sumner added, the author of the *Essay* misinterpreted his own brilliant findings.[1] Overly pessimistic, he exaggerated the need for vice and misery, for 'positive checks', while overlooking the grand and benevolent plan of the creator. Consequently, Malthus assumed that if the population of a country proceeded unchecked, even for a short period, it would so far surpass the power of the land to produce sufficient subsistence, that only the death of a part of the population would allow others to survive.[2] Fortunately, Sumner argued, things do not proceed that way. The deity is ultimately in favor of progress and civilization; both would suffer grievously without the urge and need to procreate.

> Every exertion to which civilization can be traced proceeds, directly or indirectly, from its effects; either from the actual desire of having a family, or the pressing obligation of providing for one, or from the necessity of rivalling the efforts produced by the operation of these motives in others.[3]

As for all other species, God provided 'an instinctive principle in our nature' suitable to His plans for us. The creator desired that

> the human race should be uniformly brought into a state in which they are forced to exert and improve their powers: the lowest rank, to obtain support; the one next in order, to escape from the difficulties immediately beneath it; and all the classes upward, either to keep their level, while they are pressed on each side by rival industry, or to raise themselves above the standard of their birth by useful exertions of their activity, or by successful cultivation of their natural powers.[4]

The procreative instinct was not to be deplored or feared; on the contrary it is a necessary motive force for social development as well as individual improvement. Private property, so essential to a stable progressive society, came into being as a result of population demands upon common property. Sumner described common property as a luxury of abundance; while the value of property 'originates with its scarcity'. A state of abundance is always ultimately self-defeating and temporary since the population will continue to expand indiscriminately so long as there are sufficient resources to provide for it. Once the population becomes too great for the existing means of support, labor is required to supplement it; 'as soon as it demands labor, it becomes valuable'.[5] Steeped in Locke and Adam Smith, Sumner, like most of his contemporaries, believed that the value of property was initially determined by a quantity of human labor 'resulting from the necessities imposed upon

[1] *Ibid.*, 108.   [2] *Ibid.*, 165.   [3] *Ibid.*, 133.
[4] *Ibid.*, 132.   [5] *Ibid.*, 108–9.

man by the constitution of things'.[1] Overpopulation in effect provided the spur to human industry which created private property and, in time, civilization.

Although population pressure was necessary and beneficial, there was no denying the 'inheritance of want, and pain, and misery that accompanied it'.[2] Sumner's Evangelicalism easily merged with his political economy to emphasize the sinful and fallen nature of man. Human corruption, after all, created want in the first place. Men seemed to have forgotten that earth was never meant to be a utopia; it is a place of testing and trial; a temporary passage to an ultimate disposition of each individual case. Persons who suffer during periods of overpopulation could at least be comforted by the knowledge that their maker had considered their 'general welfare' by 'the establishment of universal industry, and . . . the quick and wide diffusion of the beneficial results of that industry . . .'.[3]

Sumner's Evangelical persuasion was basically Arminian in its emphasis upon free will. Predestinarian Calvinism had little influence upon his religious or his utilitarian economic views. Individual choice remained the principal source of improvement in the temporal as well as in the spiritual world. As a result, he believed a balanced ratio between population and subsistence might eventually be established when all men realized that the abolition of paradise entailed an individual obligation to labor as well as to satisfy the original command to 'Increase and Multiply'.[4] Unfortunately too many Englishmen had ignored their responsibility while obeying the command, and had lapsed into a state of dependent indolence. Adam Smith had sketched out the course of recovery when he showed that an intelligent division of human labor would make it possible to multiply two or three hundred fold the productive powers of man.[5] The *Wealth of Nations* was an important corrective to the *Essay on Population* for it showed how a rapid multiplication of the species could in fact be channelled into more effective labor and provide the necessary production to support an enlarged populace. Sumner saw the appearance of such important ideas as further indication that God had not forgotten. The natural laws of population which originally provided men with the industrial initiative necessary for the creation of civilization were also capable of directing them to 'universal welfare' through 'universal labor'.[6]

If the first positive result of overpopulation was the emergence of private property, the second, which inevitably followed, was the development of social class. Leveling, revolutionary fanatics were completely mistaken when they asserted the division of ranks was *imposed* upon mankind. Not only did rank emerge naturally from the necessary

[1] *Ibid.*, 113–14. [2] *Ibid.*, 136. [3] *Ibid.*, 139. [4] *Ibid.*, 141–2.
[5] *Wealth of Nations*, Bk I, Chaps. I, II. [6] *Treatise*, II, 147–9.

appearance of private property reflecting the realities of individual industry and fortune, but the social inequality that resulted provided the stability and order for human progress. Turning to David Hume's *Essays,* John Millar's *Origin of the Distinction of Ranks* and Montesquieu's *Spirit of the Laws* for evidence, Sumner explained how, as a result of hard work, good health, a productive family and greater ability, some men were more successful than others in accumulating property. The less industrious or the less fortunate members of society gradually became laborers dependent upon the surplus created by their more successful neighbors. Neither in ancient nor in modern times has human regulation been able to stop this 'silent operation of nature overpowering the feeble bulwarks . . .' of man-made restraints.[1]

This had been the fatal flaw in the arguments of Rousseau and William Godwin. Sumner felt that Malthus, in the first edition of the *Essay,* was absolutely right in his refutation of the latter along with all the deluded equalitarians and distracted optimists who nearly destroyed European civilization. The 'Records of Creation', as well as history, made it clear that if land was divided equally at any stage among fifty families, in less than a century it would be held by twenty in very unequal shares upon whom everyone else would be dependent for support.[2] Malthus, Sumner mistakenly thought, had been too depressed by the prospect of a suffocating crush of unrestrained population, to recognize that the real danger of people like Godwin was their utopian misinterpretation of natural law which encouraged people to seek solutions in impossible panaceas. Human improvement and expanding population were perfectly compatible so long as they were rightly understood. Population growth not only encouraged internal industry, but contributed to communication and interchange around the world.[3] Migration spread the fruits of human advancement, industry, arts and culture, to the rest of mankind, and Smith had described the advantages of colonization to an advanced civilization as well as to a backward colony. Ultimately, Sumner was certain, population expansion would be regulated by an 'elastic adaptation to the various circumstances . . .', in accordance with the divine plan.[4]

More specifically, Sumner cited Smith's calculation showing that the population of North America doubled every twenty-five years in comparison with the five hundred years it took for the same rate of growth to occur in Europe. Although, in his opinion, Smith had underestimated the rate of growth during the eighteenth century, he did not feel it altered the argument whether the difference was ten- or twenty-fold. Malthus had reinforced the evidence of natural demographic adjustment by showing that in New Jersey the proportion of births to deaths from 1736 to 1743

[1] *Ibid.,* 121, 127. [2] *Ibid.,* 122. [3] *Ibid.,* 149.
[4] *Ibid.,* 161, 164; *Wealth of Nations,* Bk IV, Chap. VII.

was 300 to 100; while in France and England it was no higher than 120 to 100. These figures seemed to confirm the sagacity of divine intention and the natural laws of population which 'do not require that the population should be reduced, by depriving of existence those who have been once brought into the world: but . . . provides by a natural check, that the existing number shall never exceed the actual demand of the country itself for labourers'.[1]

In spite of his unconcealed admiration for Malthus, Sumner shared the concern expressed by many critics and opponents of the *Essay* who were repelled by the approval of such 'positive checks' as famine, war, epidemic and vice as natural means of population control. Concentrating on the second and later editions of the work, in which Malthus sharply modified his position and stressed the importance of 'preventive checks', such as moral restraint, Sumner emphasized his fellow parson's moderating qualities.[2] He nevertheless still hoped that the author of the *Essay* might further 'correct or qualify those expressions . . . [that] have created a wrong impression in the minds of many readers'. Sumner could see no place for divine forethought in Malthus's severe conclusion that man was deterministically bound to a disastrous course of mass starvation. God would want no part of it. Moreover, he still felt the *Essay* underestimated the effectiveness of preventive checks in avoiding the frightful consequences predicted:

> If prudential restraint, i.e. the *preventive check*, is disregarded, who can doubt that famine, war, or epidemics will arise? just as bankruptcy will come upon a man who takes no care of his fortune; or disease will follow the neglect of prudential rules for the management of the constitution. But it is *not necessary* that the prudential check should be violated; neither, therefore, is it *necessary* that famine and pestilence should carry off a redundant population.

On the contrary, dangerous overpopulation would in fact be contained 'by the simple effect of that division of property, which obliges every man, before he brings a family into the world, to see the means of providing for it within his reach . . .'.[3]

Confident as he was in the reasonableness and the utilitarian motivation of his fellow man, Sumner was sure that enlightened self-restraint, prudently exercised, would come into play at the right juncture and would provide a sufficient check to dangerous overpopulation. Specifically, marriages would voluntarily be delayed, because, as Malthus himself explained, 'the only plain and intelligible measure with regard to marriage is the having a fair prospect of being able to maintain a family'.

[1] *Ibid.*, 165.
[2] T. R. Malthus, *An Essay On the Principle of Population* . . . 2nd ed. (1803), see Preface.
[3] *Treatise*, II, 166.

Sumner calculated that would be when a healthy man has the power 'of earning such wages, as at the average price of corn, will maintain the average number (4) of living children to a marriage'. Furthermore, once he decides to marry, a man must ceaselessly labor to enjoy any comforts; 'thus labour has a perpetual stimulus and a daily reward. Without labour, nature gives nothing anywhere.'[1]

Malthus, as his defender pointed out, had come to a similar conclusion in later editions of the *Essay*, and in other writings in which he leaned heavily upon the importance of the preventive check of marital restraint. Sumner particularly referred to the *Observations* in which Malthus warned of the importance of reasoned restraint to prevent the sexual instinct, a natural and necessary provision of the creator, from becoming 'a moral poison'.[2] The later archbishop of the Victorian Church was still too much the eighteenth-century naturalistic utilitarian to deny that sexual relations were not only immediately satisfying, but often highly laudable: not in crowded England, however, where reason had to exercise 'her peculiar province, in keeping the right balance . . .'.[3] As he explained:

> If the inclinations were indulged with as little restraint and consideration in old countries, as in the empty wastes of America, some melancholy corrective, as famine, pestilence, or the sword, must soon ensue, and bring things to a level. But man, being moderated by reason, as well as impelled by passion, has the means within his power of keeping clear of any such desperate condition. Where a space appears, in which the principle of population may act unlimitedly, the natural desire is also the law of reason. But under the different appearance which most European countries present, rational prudence interferes as a check to the natural desire, and by setting before every individual his own best interests, actually, though perhaps unconsciously, determines the rate in which population shall proceed.

Population control was above all simply a question of enlightened self-interest. Sumner avoided discussing positive checks. There was no need of violence and cruelty, 'nothing contrary to the nature of man as a reasonable and accountable being'.[4]

Sumner's treatise made a striking impression on his post-war episcopal generation. Many of the prelates who came to power before 1830 were familiar with the general principles of political economy, but drew their demographic conclusions from the census, diocesan returns, and from

[1] *Ibid.*, 169.

[2] *Ibid.*, 90; Malthus, *Observations on the Effects of the Corn Laws, and of A Rise or Fall in the Price of Corn on the Agricultural and General Wealth of the Country* (1814).

[3] *Ibid.*

[4] *Ibid.*, 166–7.

the Reverend Richard Yates's important studies of the impact of population growth upon Church facilities.[1] There is little evidence, however, that any more than a few of them studied Malthus directly. There is considerably more evidence that, after 1816, Church leaders learned their Malthus from Sumner, for it was the *Records of Creation* rather than *An Essay on Population* which they often cited in discussions about the relationship of the Church to overpopulation and poverty.

One of Melbourne's first appointments to the bench, William Otter, a classmate, traveling companion and life-long friend of Malthus, recalled how little appeal the comfortless prognosis of the *Essay* had to Churchmen until Bishop Sumner revealed 'a bright side to this law of nature'.[2] Otter, who became Bishop of Chichester in 1836, understood that Malthus's ideas contradicted optimistic traditional beliefs in the economic and spiritual advantages of population growth, but felt his old friend had been unfairly maligned. After Malthus's death in 1834, he tried to place the *Essay* in perspective, when he pointed out the difficult times in which it was written. In the midst of war, economic unrest, and the constant danger of insurrection and revolution, it was not surprising that Malthus had perhaps been misled into undue pessimism. Sumner had saved the day, and rescued a brilliant work from undeserved obloquy; 'they who have read the . . . *Records of Creation* will remember how ingeniously and beautifully he has shown that, in the hands of a gracious Providence, this principle [population pressure] is made subservient to the most beneficial and improving ends; being the great moving cause which, by the necessities it creates, and the fears and hopes it suggests, excites the best energies of mankind into action, overcomes their natural indolence, and gives spirit and perseverance to their most valuable labours.'[3] Otter believed Sumner's arguments had been so compelling as to cause Malthus in the subsequent (1817) edition of the *Essay* to modify, correct and even omit several expressions.[4]

[1] R. Yates, *The Church in Danger: A Statement of the Cause, and of the Probable Means of Averting That Danger, Attempted in a Letter to Lord Liverpool* (1815); *The Basis of National Welfare; Considered in Reference Chiefly to the Property of Britain, and Safety of the Church of England in a Second Letter to Lord Liverpool* (1817). See Best, *Temporal Pillars*, 147–51.

[2] W. Otter, 'Memoir of Robert Malthus', in T. R. Malthus, *Principles of Political Economy Considered With a View to Their Practical Application*, 2nd ed. (1836), xlvii.

Otter (1768–1840), son of a Nottinghamshire vicar, private tutor to Lord Ongley, met Malthus at Jesus College, Cambridge. One of his daughters married a son of Malthus. A pluralist, he vacated all preferment to become first Principal of King's College, London, in 1830. Otter was a moderate Whig and a conscientious bishop.

[3] *Ibid.*   [4] *Ibid.*, liii.

The Provost of Oriel College, Oxford, and later Bishop of Llandaff (1828–49), Edward Copleston, was also an admirer of Malthus's writings, but recognized that they often seemed to contradict all known evidence of God's great benevolence.[1] Like Otter, he praised Sumner for having first seen the possibility of reconciling the laws of population with the divine commands of the creator who had formulated them. Three years after the *Records of Creation* appeared, the influential Copleston described the author to Sir Robert Peel as 'not only an advocate, but an able and ingenious expositor of the whole system—one who has beautifully developed the high moral and religious blessings which in the eyes of many candid persons . . . hang over [Malthus's] . . . discovery'.[2]

Although Copleston, because of an early interest in the new ideas of political economy, was one of the few important Church spokesmen of his generation who clearly read Malthus as well as Sumner, he did not notice that the former had also raised the question of overpopulation and divine forethought. In the last two sections of the first edition of the *Essay* the author discussed the problem of good and evil, and insisted, 'we should reason from nature up to nature's God and not presume to reason from God to nature'. An examination of nature reveals that 'the world and this life [is] the mighty process of God, not for the trial, but for the creation and formation of mind, a process necessary to awaken inert, chaotic matter into spirit, to sublimate the dust of the earth into soul, to elicit an ethereal spark from the clod of clay . . .'.[3] Whatever trials and vicissitudes—'the roughness and inequalities of life'—men experience, these are necessary results of divine stimuli to activate the improvement of body and mind. Without such prods, 'the mass of mankind . . . would be sunk to the level of brutes, from a deficiency of excitements . . .'. Quoting Locke's utilitarian explanations about pleasure-pain motivation, Malthus described the role of evil and suffering as 'necessary to create exertion, and exertion seems evidently necessary to create mind'.[4]

---

[1] Edward Copleston (1776–1849), son of a Devonshire rector, a liberal Tory who built his career at Oxford. Close friend of Lord Grenville, whom he supported for Chancellor in 1809, and of Lord Dudley. As a bishop he supported Church reform, and conscientiously tried to revive the Establishment in Wales.

[2] Copleston, *A Second Letter to the Right Honourable Robert Peel . . . On the Causes of the Increase of Pauperism and On the Poor Laws* (Oxford, 1819), 23.

[3] Malthus, *Essay* (1798) Chap. XVIII. Malthus was probably influenced by Dean Tucker's earlier study of *Theology*. See James Bonar, *Malthus and His Work* (1885), 34–35.

[4] *Essay* (1798), Chap. XVIII.

When applied to demography, God required the exercise of labor to procure food while allowing population to increase more rapidly than agricultural production. Although Malthus recognized this resulted in 'much partial evil', an understanding of the creator's purpose proved 'a great overbalance of good' would result. As Sumner was to contend nearly twenty years later, the constancy of nature indicated the stimulus of overpopulation had always been necessary, and always would be; 'had population and food increased in the same ratio, it is probable that man might never have emerged from the savage state'. Malthus then, like Sumner, was confident, in spite of his gloomy calculations, that 'the principle, according to which population increases, prevents the vices of mankind, or the accidents of nature, the partial evils arising from general laws, from obstructing the high purpose of creation'.[1]

The brief explanation of the divine origins and reason for overpopulation contained in the first edition of the *Essay* was omitted in later editions. Malthus planned to develop this theme later in a separate essay, but never got around to it. Sumner, in contrast, built his entire argument upon it without ever recognizing that Malthus had also concluded, 'evil exists in the world not to create despair but activity'. He nowhere acknowledged he was amplifying the controversial parson's premise that the laws of population were necessary to stimulate the development of man's physical and intellectual resources. Repelled by Malthus's passive acceptance of vice and misery as 'positive checks' to dangerous overpopulation, Sumner, like most of his contemporaries, failed to note the stated probability, 'that moral evil is absolutely necessary to the production of moral excellence'.[2]

An early work on Malthus has suggested that since the premises in the *Records of Creation* were largely developed from later editions of Malthus's *Essay*, perhaps Sumner never read the first edition.[3] Far more people, it is true, read the greatly modified second edition (1803) and those that followed, than the more pessimistic and alarming initial publication of 1798. Yet Sumner seemed well aware of the propositions in the first edition, and certainly realized the nature of the changes and modifications Malthus made in later editions. Like Otter, he was always puzzled about the persistence of anti-Malthusian sentiment, despite the more humane alterations that were added. Otter certainly read the first edition of his close friend's work, yet he also never suggested the *Essay* had considered the laws of population in a religious context. It was the Reverend Thomas Robert Malthus who first wrote:

The partial pain, therefore, that is inflicted by the Supreme creator, while he is forming numberless beings to a capacity of the highest enjoyments, is but as the dust of the balance in comparison of the happiness that is communicated, and we have every reason to think that there is no more evil in

[1] *Ibid.* [2] *Ibid.*, Chap. XIX. [3] Bonar, *Malthus*, 38.

103

POVERTY AND POLITICAL ECONOMY

the world than what is absolutely necessary as one of the ingredients in the mighty process.[1]

But it was the Reverend John Bird Sumner who made it acceptable to a generation of churchmen absorbing and trying to reconcile the truths of political economy with their reviving concepts of a Christian society.

Not only did Sumner bring the natural laws of population into line with the divine command and the human instinct to multiply, but he also satisfied the long-held secular belief that an expansive economy and a powerful state required an enlarged population. For more than a century and a half, mercantilists, physiocrats, followers of Adam Smith, and even contemporary political economists viewed population growth as a healthy sign. James Mill, Nassau Senior and James MacCulloch were not alarmed by Malthus's predictions. They were more confident of the possibilities of economic and technological expansion to cope with an enlarged populace than they were with Malthus's more humanistic claim that the question of the production of wealth should be secondary to the practical realities of overpopulation.

Few Churchmen doubted that God would provide for His creation; and their confidence complemented that of the wealthy laity, optimistic, after the war, about the great age of economic progress in which they lived. Even before the start of the long hostilities, the well-known agriculturalist Arthur Young was no more successful than the unknown Parson Malthus in convincing people of the dangers of overpopulation.[2] Bishop Watson spoke for most of the clergy and the great majority of Christian laymen when he shrugged off their conclusions with the assured conviction that the earth had hardly begun to be cultivated.

In 1796, two years before Malthus's *Essay* appeared, the much younger Edward Copleston won a prize at Oxford for a physiocratic-styled essay, *On Agriculture*, in which he labored to the same conclusion instinctively reached by Watson. In striking contrast to the pessimistic ideas Malthus was formulating in spirited debates with his father over William Godwin's utopian prognosis for society,[3] Copleston promised

the vast increase of population, which is the constant result of plenty, adds vigour to the state, and is the foundation of all its comparative importance. Nor is this to be dreaded by any country as a dangerous acquisition; as amassing a burden, which it must either hereafter discharge, or itself become a prey to intestine tumult. The earth is a never-failing

[1] *Essay* (1798), Chap. XIX.
[2] A. Young, *Proposals to the Legislature for Numbering the People, Containing Some Observations on the Population of Great Britain, and a Sketch of the Advantages That Would Probably Accrue From An Exact Knowledge of Its Present State* (1771).
[3] See Preface to 1st ed. of Malthus's *Essay*.

resource for the exertions of labour; and as superior skill and industry are employed, its produce will be proportionally advanced.[1]

Later, after reading Malthus and the other political economists of the day, Copleston concluded that the analysis of population growth in later editions of the *Essay* was quite sound, but the conclusions were less reliable. There was never any doubt in his mind about the ability of mankind to produce enough to sustain itself.

Temporary setbacks would of course occur, but confident clerics knew they would usually be the result of maldistribution or poor economic policies. In the aggregate, however, there would be accumulative progress. Meanwhile, if the lower orders would learn the value of the preventive checks described by the Reverends Malthus and Sumner, the way to wider prosperity and greater happiness would be considerably eased. Above all, Otter explained, the laboring classes had to understand the Malthusian truth that 'no efforts of the Poor or of the Rich can possibly place the Labouring Classes of Society in such a state, as to enable them to marry generally at the same age in a fully peopled country, as they may do with perfect safety in a new one'. Otter, in quoting his famous classmate, explained that imprudent marriages were 'inevitably followed by a train of wretchedness and want'.[2] Not only was it imprudent and unreasonable to indulge the passions to the extent of creating misery, it was also sinful. Otter and Copleston spoke for a great many Englishmen when they endorsed Sumner's practical suggestion to discourage the poor from marrying before the age of twenty-five.[3] Seizing upon the recent developments in lower-class education as a wonderful opportunity for the clergy to inculcate the virtues of enlightened self-interest, Church leaders urged children be taught early 'that prudential check upon marriage which, whether deliberately imposed, or adopted only through habit and custom, is absolutely essential to the well-being of society'.[4]

Within this Sumnerian context, Malthusian pronouncements on the law of population were much less offensive to religious sensibilities, and, perhaps more importantly, to the feelings of progressive material optimism increasingly evident in the post-war decade. Furthermore,

[1] E. Copleston, 'On Agriculture', in *The Oxford English Prize Essays* (Oxford, 1830), II, 7.

[2] W. Otter, *A Sermon Upon the Influence of the Clergy in Improving the Condition of the Poor . . . Preached at Ludlow, the 26th of May, 1818 . . . To Which is Added an Appendix Containing the Plan of a Provident Society for a Country Village* (Shrewsbury, 1818), 36–37.

[3] *Ibid.*, Sumner, *Treatise*, II, 313–17. See also the views of Samuel Whitbread and Joseph Austin in *Reports of the Society for Bettering the Condition of the Poor*, III.

[4] Copleston, *Second Letter*, 102–3.

proponents of Sumner's compromise welcomed the enlightened possibilities of doing something about the costly perpetuation of poverty. If they did not share Malthus's unhappy vision of an overpopulated future, they certainly welcomed his sharp attack on the Poor Law and the corruption of poor relief.[1] Annoyed at soaring relief costs, and suspicious of the negative effects of indiscriminate charity, many people hoped the basic lessons of political economy would explain to the poor the reasons for their misery, and guide them out of it. Clerical supporters of this position knew that there were larger reasons as well for the perpetuation of poverty, but did not necessarily find them incompatible with temporal scientific explanations. Both aimed at the same goal—the contentment of the restless poor.

The real danger then, as some of the post-war spokesmen of the Establishment saw it, was not from starving multitudes ravaging an agriculturally exhausted land, but from irreligious hordes wallowing in self-perpetuating poverty, ignorant of the reasons for it, and threatening the security of both Church and State. From the standpoint of ecclesiastics, the critical problem was not physical subsistence or even the frustration of the virtuous, natural sexual instinct; it was the nourishment of spiritual resignation and the repression of all dangerous passions. Consequently, the bishops did not simply recoil in fear and bewilderment as they became cognizant of the extent of demographic change in their dioceses. Surprisingly few of them really complained about the *fact* of population growth and mobility. What was worrying was the often painful realization that the facilities and even the values of the Church were woefully inadequate to cope with the accumulating masses of laboring humanity congregating beyond the hearing and control of the national ministry.

Although Church leaders in the post-war years continued to support legislation and the old clerical-gentry alliance to keep the lower orders content in their station, it was becoming obvious to the more perceptive among them that not only did labor mobility make it difficult to maintain the old forms of co-operation, but the laboring poor were themselves a different problem. There were more of them than ever before, they were often literate and they were accumulating in urban areas where the gentry and clergy would have little direct influence on their behavior. As a result, the poor were more susceptible to alternative ideas, which they were increasingly able to read themselves, and seemed willing to act upon in ways likely to alter drastically a society already in a state of exceptional transition.

[1] Malthus, *Essay* (1798), Chap. V. Malthus discussed the Poor Law in more detail in later editions.

3. INEQUALITY EXPLAINED

In spite of the enduring hostility and scepticism of several of the more traditional Tory pillars of the Establishment, many of the new generation of clergy, destined for places in the hierarchical firmament of the reformed Church, believed with Sumner that there was no essential conflict between the new laws of political economy and the inspired regulations of revelation. Inequality and poverty were no less necessary conditions, but they could now be understood more thoroughly and their worst features eventually moderated. Christian charity and benevolence towards the poor were not repudiated; they were only more carefully regulated to encourage the even greater divine gift of individual free will. Once the poor understood how to exercise that gift properly, it would perhaps even be possible for their Christian brethren to love them once more.

In the meantime, the poor were feared, pitied and sometimes held in contempt, while their pastoral shepherds undertook the exasperating, often frustrating task of guiding them to the shrine of contentment where the divine and natural laws determining their condition would be clearly revealed. Sumner's study of the 'Records of Creation' was not only an attempt to certify Malthus's Christian credentials, but an effort to re-think the question of poverty within the context of new ideas in a new age. The continued threat by the lower orders to society, even after Waterloo, made it patently clear to clergy and laity alike how necessary it was.

Unwilling to concede that there was anything fundamentally wrong with the structure of civil society, Sumner and his supporters claimed that the real source of disturbance could be traced to individual misunderstandings about natural causation. The disgruntled and disaffected poor simply did not understand why things were the way they were. Although personally of a strong Evangelical persuasion, Sumner was concerned that the excesses of enthusiastic preaching were contributing to the poor's social confusion. In 1815, the year before the *Records of Creation* appeared, its author warned his more Calvinistic brethren to preach less of the sinfulness of man to the lower orders, even if it was attractive and filled the church. Obviously they were not offended, since 'the lower classes, unless they are truly religious, usually *are* gross sinners, and therefore, are neither surprised nor shocked at being supposed so themselves . . .'. More dangerous, however, especially during times of great unrest, was that the poor

feel a sort of pleasure which need not be encouraged, when they hear their superiors brought down to the same level: and . . . it seems to furnish them with a sort of excuse for their sins, to find that they are so universal, and so much to be expected of human nature.[1]

Sumner also felt there was some question about the validity of so sinful a description of man, made in God's image, and likely still to possess many of the positive characteristics of the divine love that entered into his creation. To preach the contrary was 'to court . . . dangerous applause'.[2]

Considering the state of lower-class religion, it was hardly spiritual enthusiasm that drove the laboring poor to smash machines, riot and strike throughout the second decade of the nineteenth century. Never again did Sumner even intimate that it was. The explanation he gave the following year, which many of his clerical counterparts were to repeat over the next three decades, was that the poor were lamentably ignorant of the natural causes of their misery. Until they understood them, and made necessary adjustments, their state could not effectively be improved. As the only rational species, a 'creature of education and discipline . . .', man alone was capable of conscious self-improvement.[3] The 'Records of Creation' proved that God had created all living things with precise useful limitations regulating 'the extent of their capacity by an impassible decree'.[4] Human limitations were the most flexible, and Sumner insisted there was a divine obligation on all persons, irrespective of their station, to take advantage of their preferential nature. God had empowered and charged man, unlike other animals, 'to become the artificer of his own rank in the scale of beings . . .'.[5] This applied to the poor as well as the rich, but it was not a call to social and economic leveling; it was a call to personal betterment within the necessary order of things.

Central to Sumner's explanation of poverty was the distinction he and many others made between poverty as a natural class distinction and as an economic condition. The two had become confused in the minds of rich and poor alike in recent years; consequently they failed to understand that poverty was an inevitable condition determined by God and confirmed by natural law. Indigence, however, was an economic condition which if properly understood could be corrected without violating the natural hierarchical order of things. As he carefully explained,

these conditions, it must be ever remembered, are essentially distinct and separate. Poverty is often both honourable and comfortable; but indigence can only be pitiable, and is usually contemptible. Poverty is not only

[1] J. B. Sumner, *Apostolic Preaching Considered in An Examination of St Paul's Epistles* (1815), 115.
[2] *Ibid.*, 119–20.   [3] Sumner, *Treatise*, II, 22–24.
[4] *Ibid.*, 16–17.   [5] *Ibid.*, 21.

the natural lot of many, in a well-constituted society, but is necessary, that a society may be well constituted. Indigence, on the contrary, is seldom the natural lot of any, but is commonly the state into which intemperance and want of prudent foresight push poverty: the punishment which the moral government of God inflicts in this world upon thoughtlessness and guilty extravagance.[1]

The problem for the poor then, as Sumner analyzed it, was not one of escaping poverty, but of avoiding a dependent state of indigence which made the natural state of poverty unbearable to those who were in it, and distressing to those who had to observe and support it. So long as some of the poor abused their rational gifts and natural instincts by marrying too soon and producing more children than they could possibly support, indigence, as Malthus explained, would plague all levels of English society.

Reckless and improvident during prosperous times, the laboring classes quickly became destitute and dependent at the slightest fluctuation in their fortunes. Their thoughtless breeding not only cut the margin of flexibility which their human qualities allowed them, but it created a labor surplus that diluted the available wages naturally allotted to their support. More and more of them, Sumner and his contemporaries complained, threw themselves upon the local rates, which only served to subsidize and perpetuate irrational folly. But this was essentially the result of fallacious thinking; misery was not an inevitable consequence of poverty; nor, as some charged, was it a natural result of economic expansion. 'It is very soothing to our indolence and self-satisfaction, to charge upon the constitution of the world, that is, upon the ordinances of the Deity, the various evils of poverty and ignorance which confront us on every side. . . .'[2] But it was wrong, Sumner insisted, as it was wrong to contend 'that the condition of the majority of the community must always be deteriorated, as the community itself advanced in opulence'.[3] Like many of his clerical generation, he was hopeful that the newly-conceived systems of lower-class education would be 'nurseries of prudence and restraint' which the children of the poor would learn along with their ABC's.

Sumner did not see in this, however, any danger to the natural state of inequality, necessary for the progress of the human community. Conscious of the equalitarian delusions generated by the French Revolution, and often cited by enemies of lower-class education, Sumner emphasized that the new proposals could in no way interfere with the original constitution of human nature from which 'inequality uniformly finds its way, in spite of every obstacle. The stream, which is constantly setting against the barriers raised to oppose it, has a source so deep

[1] *Ibid.*, 92.   [2] *Ibid.*, 290.
[3] *Ibid.*, 308.

109

and permanent, that it has always, at no distant period, either found a channel, or forced one.'[1]

Sumner's examination of the development of society revealed men accumulating the surplus of their labor, while others were 'eager to exchange their labour for a portion of that superfluity'. From this nascent inequality, the arts of civilization developed, and a certain portion of society, exempted from labor, applied itself to literature, philosophy, the arts—the cultivation of genius. Consequently, there exists in every society a chain of innumerable links formed from the 'colossal fortunes of the highest rank, to the large and increasing class who are obliged to give their daily labour for their daily subsistence'. It is, Sumner believed, the natural 'union of all the various classes' comprising civilization that gives the community its 'strength and opulence'.[2] Even such critics of inequality as Rousseau and the Abbé Raynal, who questioned rank and condition, thereby poisoning the minds of so many people, could not deny that 'wherever equality is found to exist . . . mankind are in the lowest and most savage state'. Carelessness and indolence constituted the freedom applauded by equalitarian enthusiasts, and Sumner described it as an emphasis upon nothing but the perfection of an existence incompatible with man's progressive, rational faculties. 'It can never be allowed that the perfection of existence is compatible with insensibility to improvement, or of happiness, with ignorance of rational enjoyment.'[3]

The author of the *Records of Creation* could find no evidence in Scripture or in history to support the horrid notion that 'the evils of society . . . owe their birth to civilization . . .'. On the contrary, they 'spring up in spite of it; and are to be referred to the nature of man, not to the constitution of society. The same course of argument might reject agriculture, because weeds thrive quickest in the richest soil.'[4] Rousseau's charge that the first expropriation and acceptance of property was the start of human misery, as if crime, war and murder were unknown to the savage, was completely without foundation. In reality, not until 'the first blow had been given to the system of equality by recognizing that division of property which secures to every man the fruit of his own labour', did he begin to progress.[5]

The people who populated Sumner's community were formed not in heaven but in the market-place of eighteenth-century speculative thought where various explanations of human nature were regularly hawked. He settled on the common utilitarian interpretation of man as an acquisitive creature constantly questing after personal gratification—'the chief excitement of civilized life'.[6] The savage, however, only feeling motivations of rudimentary necessity, is limited to the uninspiring condition

[1] *Ibid.*, 128–9. [2] *Ibid.* [3] *Ibid.*, 30–31.
[4] *Ibid.*, 32. [5] *Ibid.*, 42–43. [6] *Ibid.*

of unprogressive equality. Like any respectable Enlightenment social theorist, Sumner drew comparisons with primitive peoples, but without ennobling or romanticizing their condition. Describing the Indians of North and South America as crude, degraded, struggling for subsistence 'at the utmost verge of the habitable globe . . .', he could not conceive how reasonable people could contemplate emulating their values. Paralyzed by equality of rank and condition, the wretched savages would always wander indolently close to famine, in 'careless ignorance and indifference to all improvement'.[1]

Contrasted to these pitiable creatures was civilized, utilitarian man, driven by enlightened, competitive self-interest, stimulated by experience and reason, his natural desire for personal acquisitions propelling his entire society forward. Sumner admitted that on the surface it was perhaps un-Christian for individuals to neglect the general good, and struggle merely for self-advancement at the expense of fellow Christians.

> But the other side of the picture shows individual advantage terminating in public benefits, and the desire of aggrandizement which is stimulated by ambition or domestic partialities, contributing towards the welfare of the community at large.

No matter what their situation in life, Sumner believed that all individuals have 'both opportunity and inclination for vice . . .', and he could not accept the sentimentalized notion that somehow the vices of savages were less obnoxious than those of civilized people. 'Ferocity, intemperance, and revenge, if . . . not worse, certainly are not better than avarice, rapacity, or luxury'. Furthermore, 'the savage vices have no compensation of delicate taste, refined manners, improved understanding, or exalted virtues'. As far as he could determine,

> a contest for riches or power does not more disturb the harmony of life, than the disputed possession of a palm-tree or a cabin: but the latter produces no other fruit than private rancour or revengeful malice: the former enriches the state by the addition of two active and useful citizens.[2]

While this type of utilitarian casuistry was not likely to make much of an impression upon impoverished, competing laborers trying to survive the unemployment and rising prices of the post-war years, it was a telling blow to the lingering argument of eighteenth-century equalitarian naturalism. Antipathetic not only to a hierarchial social structure, but to a rapidly changing industrial economy as well, the folly of equality was too obvious for rational men to deny. Of more importance, however, Sumner's defense of utilitarian economic motivation was widely accepted by the clergy during the next few decades, and closely allied the Church to the policies and justifications of political economy. It meant that clergymen who, in the previous century, closely reflected and promoted

[1] *Ibid.*, 37–38. [2] *Ibid.*, 32–33.

the values and interests of the landed gentry were, as the economic and social winds began to shift, prepared to be blown along in new directions. It was not that the Anglican ministry abandoned its long alliance with the squirearchy; instead it extended it where necessary to include the new moneyed interests profiting from the industrial expansion of the age.

Many die-hard Tory parsons refused to make that accommodation and were thankful they ministered to congregations uncorrupted by the incursion of mining and factory populations. But others very much in the mainstream of secular life and thought were not unimpressed by the new economic realities and the exciting ideas they generated. Clerical acceptance and defense of political economy was welcome to the propertied interests who found the criticisms of government restriction, the defense of natural wages, and assaults on the excessive cost of poor relief most congenial. That it was less welcome to the accumulating masses of laboring poor in the manufacturing and mining areas of the realm, or to the surplus laborers in the distressed agricultural districts of the south, only dawned very slowly upon the ecclesiastical economists formulating the Church's position in the industrial age.

If, in the meantime, the archaic Christian virtues of charity and compassion were aroused in the minds of the more traditional clergy, and if, as Sumner admitted, all might at first be appalled by the vast wealth of a few and the great poverty of the many, even when linked by gradations, it had to be seen in terms of a broader ulterior destination; otherwise it would make no sense.[1] The Christian justification for inequality ultimately derived from the human condition being a state of probation, rather than perfection. Were it otherwise, Sumner explained, we might dwell upon Platonic concepts of 'ideal excellence . . .'. Unfortunately, such exalted notions were incompatible with the state of mankind. Virtue, after all, was not an ideal, but 'an active and energetic habit, arising from the various relations of human life, and exercised in the practice of real duties . . .'. Virtuous behavior was itself a natural result of inequality, to follow Sumner's reasoning, for 'as you increase the number and variety of those relations, you enlarge its sphere of action, and in proportion as you bring down the conditions of mankind towards an uniform level, you lower the standard and reduce the degree of moral excellence'. God, then, favored and encouraged inequality because it greatly increased the opportunities for His fallen children to exercise a wider variety of virtues under varying conditions. Knowing all too well the weaknesses and strengths of His creation, and desiring the merits of individual improvement, the deity in His infinite wisdom provided 'the nursery most suited to their formation, and the theater most fitted for their exercise'. In them, equality played no part; even if it would perhaps

[1] *Ibid.*, 85.

diminish many crimes, it would still 'affect only a small part of the moral guilt of mankind', while eliminating the countless occasions inequality provided for the uplifting expression of free will.[1]

Raising that hoary hierarchical nostrum once more, Sumner, as if it were a new bride, dressed it in something old and something new. Eighteenth-century homilies from the gospel of natural religion were spiced with the teachings of the new book of political economy. At the same time, the Evangelical defender of the newly-merged faith also reverted to an earlier state of Protestant fundamentalism. In contrast to his predecessors in the previous century, the future prelate placed much more emphasis upon the sinfulness of man, the transitory nature of his earthly vicissitudes, and the omnipresent reality of a stern, omniscient divine judge. Eighteenth-century churchmen had not rejected this Scriptural asseveration so important to Arminian revivalists, but, imbued with the sensible principles of natural religion and morality, they tended to ignore it. Their conclusions about the individual in an unequal society were derived more often from Locke than from Jehovah. The contamination and endless suffering of the entire species as a result of an individual's failing, while undoubtedly true, was nevertheless repugnant to enlightened individualism and irrelevant to the rational comprehension of the principles of natural religion.

The generation of Church spokesmen appearing in the second and third decades of the new century had also been raised on the works of Butler, Warburton and Archdeacon Paley, but their rationalistic theology was considerably altered not only by Evangelical enthusiasm, but by a reviving sense of ecclesiastical purpose and spiritual confidence. It affected prominent clergymen of every party within the Church. Evangelicals such as Sumner, his younger brother Charles, and Henry Ryder, as well as High Churchmen like John Kaye, Christopher Bethell, Charles James Blomfield, Phillpotts and Copleston, were enthusiastic at the prospect of the Establishment once more becoming a vital spiritual institution. They and many of their brethren over the next half-century saw the Church not only reformed and newly aware of its history and purpose, but determined to guide millions of the neglected, sinful, laboring poor through the treacherous interlude of mortality. However, instead of moderating the harsh social and economic conclusions of natural law, buttressed by the imposing logic of political economy, the revived Church all too often complemented them, and provided their advocates with the added blessing of revelation as well as reason.

They sought to teach the lower classes that life was a continual conflict of pleasure and pain in an imperfect state of transition. Man was especially fortunate, Sumner said, in that the 'elastic adaptation of the mind to its permanent situation . . . equalizes the apparent inequalities

[1] *Ibid.*, 76–78.

of fortune; and blunts the edge of imagined hardships . . .'. The loss of this perspective agitated the poor, and led the rich to pursue apparently beneficent policies which were not really suitable. 'Those who commiserate the condition of the industrious poor, are for the most part persons, who, born in a different sphere, and accustomed to a different manner of living, have learnt to consider the superfluities of their station no less important to human nature generally, than use has rendered them to their own enjoyment.' Excessive generosity, while personally rewarding, was in fact retrogressive when it prompted the wealthy to act on unscientific assumptions about the poor without understanding their habits, their values, their relative concepts of pleasure and pain. As Bishop Horsley had explained to his generation, the poor had very different expectations and disappointments than their betters, and Sumner repeated this to his. But where the late prelate had nevertheless emphasized the Christian social responsibility of broad charitable relief, his successor wanted it sharply curtailed. After all, since the chimney-sweep can be happy in situations 'disgusting to men of taste and refinement', there is no reason and much danger in interfering with so natural an arrangement.

> Habit, which reconciled the soldier to his tent and the sailor to his deck, reconciles the peasant to his cabin. The want of those superfluities which are supplied by affluence, is as little distressing to the poor, as the mere possession of them can be satisfactory to the rich; and a probable assurance that the necessaries of life will not be wanting, is the only thing which can be justly considered an indispensable condition of comfortable existence.[1]

In economic terms this meant an absolute minimum subsistence which would in no way confuse basic utilitarian motivation and values.

Social critics such as Godwin and Paine were as wrong as well-meaning philanthropists in their distorted descriptions of the poor as worn, exhausted, frustrated wretches, bearing the misery of perpetual labor until their bodies and minds were stultified, or they were driven to revolt. Godwin's sarcastic and melancholy conclusion that such men were at least 'happier than a stone', had little relevance to reality, and again exemplified the inability of the higher ranks to appreciate the desires of the poor.[2] Sumner and the social analysts of the Establishment knew better. They knew the poor were actually relatively happier than the rich, and got 'more actual enjoyment from the satisfaction of [their] . . . hunger by the most frugal fare, with an appetite sharpened by air and labour, than those receive whose table is regularly spread with sumptuous variety'.[3]

[1] *Ibid.,* 267–9.   [2] *Ibid.,* 270–1. Godwin, *Enquiry,* 3rd ed. (1797), I, 445.
[3] *Treatise,* II, 274.

Reverting to what had been an occasional argument for contentment in the 1780's and 1790's, Sumner and his contemporaries in the post-war years discussed it at length. In addition to the usual sophistries about the comparative advantages of poverty and the gentle pleasures of the pastoral poor, it was necessary to pay some attention to the blessings enjoyed by the accumulating factory workers in the expanding manufacturing towns. The young Vicar of Mapledurham had in fact read inconclusive reports condemning conditions in the factories as 'oppressive to . . . bodily strength and faculties', but as far as he could tell the workers were not demonstrably affected. True, Sumner observed this from his rural college living, or the playing fields of Eton, but he was certain it was valid; 'not only from what we know of human strength, and its gradual adaptation to the burden imposed upon it, but from what we see of the recreations of the poor, which are, in favourable seasons and climates, invariably athletic and active'.[1]

The future bishop of the most industrialized diocese in the country had not yet been disabused by experience and the later reports of the great enquiry commissions investigating the working and living conditions of the laboring classes. Consequently, he confidently cited cases of workers in foundries, forges, mines, and factories, as well as some who labored in poor climates in the open air; they were all healthy, long-lived, and reared large families of thriving children. Too many of them as a matter of fact. All this was possible because nature had provided for the needs of the laboring classes by endowing them with the capability of adjusting to their necessary environments.[2] To suggest otherwise was to deny the great foresight of the creator. Those who allowed their credulity or compassion to run away with them should therefore remember that if the ship-bay's hammock, the peasant's hut, and the mechanic's truckle-bed may appear unhealthy and loathsome to them, they are, to their occupants, 'the best furnished apartment and the softest down'.[3]

Sumner's lengthy analysis, if not completely accepted by many clergymen unreconciled to the new political economy, was nevertheless reflective of the atmosphere of self-delusion permeating the Church in the years after Waterloo. Long terrified by the threat of revolution from a rapidly enlarging laboring population, the awakening Church found itself alarmingly out of touch with it. Not only had the Establishment lost much of its effective contact in traditional agricultural areas as a result of indifference, non-residence and spiritual apathy, but it was clearly without the means and often the will to establish any viable relationship with the great numbers of poor workers increasingly inhabiting the neglected manufacturing and mining towns. Escape into a logical fantasy, built upon necessary assumptions translated into natural law,

[1] *Ibid.*, 280.　　　　[2] *Ibid.*, 284–6.　　　　[3] *Ibid.*, 276.

was a common reaction of conservative churchmen confronted with staggering problems they feared to contemplate.

Yet the days were numbered in which spokesmen for the national Church could seriously comfort themselves, if not the laboring poor, with assurances that the lower orders were actually healthier and happier than the rich. To say it was to will it perhaps, but not even fanatical sacerdotalist papists attributed that power to their priests. It is difficult to know who the future Whig Bishop of Chichester (1831–6) and Durham (1836–56), Edward Maltby, was trying to convince when, as a result of the death in childbirth of Princess Charlotte in 1817, he believed the poor would henceforth be willing 'to acquiesce with more cheerfulness in their own situation, and to repine less at the distinctions and advantages of their superiors, when they see it so plainly declared, that even the highest classes are subject to the afflictions of death'.[1] Since not even the most servile worshipper of rank suggested that immortality was a perquisite of superior station, Maltby, like so many of his contemporaries, was seizing upon any opportunity to reaffirm an almost desperate belief in the relativity and universality of happiness and suffering.

For several years he had been defending the necessary subdivisions of society, 'which make up the general mass of convenience, knowledge and happiness . . .'. As all social advantages are reciprocal, it is perfectly reasonable 'that the poor should toil with their hands in order to supply the natural or artificial wants of the wealthy . . .', while the rich distribute and employ 'their substance and the cultivation of their intellectual powers, for the protection and support of the lower orders'.[2] God would judge the performance of each class according to their relative obligations.

Maltby, the pluralistic magistrate-vicar of parishes in Huntingdonshire and Lincolnshire, was at the same time well aware of the unemployment and rising costs that made it difficult if not impossible for the laboring poor to fulfil their toilsome responsibilities. He wrote to Lord Hardwicke in 1815 that he had never seen things so bad, and urged the

---

[1] E. Maltby, *A Sermon Preached . . . November the Nineteenth, Being the Day Appointed For the Funeral Of Her Late Royal Highness the Princess Charlotte Augusta, Consort of His Serene Highness the Prince Leopold of Saxe Coburg* (1817), 18–19.

Maltby (1770–1859) son of a Norwich Presbyterian weaver, pupil of Samuel Parr, chaplain to Bishop Pretyman-Tomline, who was married to a cousin of Maltby. A competent Greek scholar and a moderate Whig, he was Earl Grey's first episcopal appointment. Although he had tutored Pusey in 1817, he was a vigorous anti-Tractarian. Resigned in 1856; died three years later, leaving his large library to Durham University.

[2] E. Maltby, *A Sermon Preached Before the University of Cambridge June 29, 1806* (Cambridge, 1806), 8–9.

legislature to come to the aid of the desperate agricultural workers before it was too late.[1] Regaining his perspective soon after, Maltby, who long remained an enemy of government interference in the economy, suggested that perhaps people were taking 'an hasty and superficial view of things . . .'. Sobered by the death of the young princess, he decried the envy the poor conceive 'against the fancied happiness of others. Peasant! dost thou murmur at thy humble lot?' That was the least of the laborer's sins. He also agitated, rioted and, according to numerous spies and the Home Office, plotted a great revolution: all this in spite of the fact that he had a good, healthy wife who prepared 'a frugal, but sufficient meal' at the close of the day, and lovely, sturdy children who shared this good fortune and well-being.

> Each day's rising sun sees thee go forth to the labour, that nerves thy limbs with strength, and stamps thy brow with independence; and still, on thy return, art thou greeted with smiles by thy spouse, and with endearments by thy children![2]

The non-resident Maltby, often occupied with his duties as chaplain to his cousin's husband, Bishop Pretyman-Tomline, and as a prebendary of Lincoln, could not conceive how the poor could be disquieted, discontented and embittered when their satisfactions were denied even to the greatest family of the realm. He admonished them, 'learn thou to check thy murmurings, which are as unreasonable as they are ungrateful . . .'.[3] Yet Maltby did not have to peruse the local Bills of Mortality to learn that the death of poor mothers and their children in childbirth was not unheard of even in picturesque, idyllic cottages filled with rustic love. If clerical visitation of such cottages was a later characteristic of the revived Church, many parsons still knew that between rhetoric and reality a wide gap certainly existed.

The preaching of pious rationales could not alter the worrying truths of extensive indigence, lower-class unrest, and increasing relief costs. It was frankly puzzling; Maltby's friend, the Malthusian William Otter, could not understand how a country of such affluence and power, possessed of abundant capital, industry and skill could be so 'overwhelmed with a pressure of Indigence which threatens to sap the foundation of its Prosperity . . .'. Shame and disgrace, so long attached to parochial dependence, seemed to be disappearing in the midst of prosperity. Young and healthy people, 'as well as the aged and infirm, crowd with willing steps, to the Parish Pay Table, and even the Parish Workhouse'.[4] Though Otter tried to explain it away in Malthusian terms of

---

[1] Maltby to Hardwicke, 13 Jan. 1815, *Hardwicke Ps.*, British Museum, Add. MS. 35700, f. 297–8; also 4 Feb., f. 312–13.

[2] Maltby, *Sermon* (1817), 19–20.   [3] *Ibid.*, 21.

[4] Otter, *Sermon* (1818), 4–5.

population surplus, errant Poor Laws and the discouragement of individual initiative, he remained troubled that something still undefined was wrong when he compared the great misery of the laboring poor with the wealth of the country as a whole.

4. ECONOMIC CAUSATION

Sumner, Maltby, Otter and other clerical economists in the Malthusian camp all accepted the inevitability of poverty, but believed that any particular instance of excessive suffering within that general condition was the result of the individual sufferer's ignorance and imprudence. In their eagerness to defend the natural and revealed laws of social inequality they utterly rejected Rousseau's panacea of social causation with its violent overtones of revolutionary equalitarianism. However, at least one influential churchman, Edward Copleston, who shared their predilection for political economy and its coalescence with Scripture, was uncertain whether their enthusiasm for inevitability and individual causation did not obscure as much as it illuminated.

Earlier in his career, when still a Fellow of Oriel and Poetry Professor, Copleston would have agreed with them entirely. In 1805, for example, he bluntly reminded misguided proponents of equality, 'the poor shall never cease out of the land'—a Gospel truth verified by reason and experience.[1] At the same time, however, in contrast to many of his more conservative and frightened brethren he welcomed the diversity and extent of social analysis evident in recent years. 'The result of these enquiries has been to shew the folly of attempting to prevent in the first instance, by any peculiar conformation of civil society, the unequal distribution of worldly goods among men.' Property had nothing to do with the causes of inequality and poverty in the world, and, if anything, actually minimized the effects of the latter.

> The riches of a few are the spontaneous growth of a well-compacted system, in which the efforts of many are combined, and rendered infinitely more productive to each individual, than the same efforts would be, if single and unassisted. For if you were to remove the class of rich . . . you would not by so doing, better the condition of others: you would only add to the numbers of the poor, and increase their poverty.

Copleston was confident that scientific investigations had in the end confirmed the teachings of Scripture, and both agreed 'that want and distress are inseparable from human society—that we must, be our national prosperity what it may, we must either suffer it or see it'. Try as we may to mitigate the inevitable, pain, want and misery 'are neces-

[1] E. Copleston, *A Sermon Preached for the Devon and Exeter Hospital . . . August 11, 1805* (1805), 3.

sary to the condition of man in this life, and must by an immutable law of nature be endured more or less, in all states of society'.[1]

After the war, however, Copleston, who had continued to study political economy, began to appreciate that there was a closer connection between poverty and social and economic policies than he had once believed. Like many of his contemporaries, he was puzzled by the growth of poverty in the midst of economic expansion. If anything the poor should have benefited from increased productivity. Certainly much of it was their own fault, but by 1819 Copleston wondered if individual causation had not been overly exaggerated, and whether economic conditions beyond the control of the poor really determined the extent of poverty. After a close reading of the economic literature of the day, particularly the recent writings of David Ricardo, Copleston decided that the laboring poor, especially those in agriculture, were caught in a period of rising prices in which their wages, naturally, lagged far behind.

The poor were really victims of economic conditions beyond their control, and Copleston questioned the widespread assertion that 'our labourers have lost the spirit of independence, and prefer the certain pittance of parish allowance to the earnings of laborious industry'. He believed it time 'to recollect how ill-requited that industry has been, even when most willing and most productive . . .'. No matter how diligent and frugal he was during times of plenty, the laborer 'was still unable to do more than to provide a bare subsistence . . .' which did not permit him to save. At the first 'unfavourable season' he was plunged into 'a situation of absolute penury and dependence'. Necessity, not desire, drove them in increasing numbers to the parochial magistrates for relief, 'and when they had tasted of its eleemosynary succour, scanty as it was, and ought to be, and most sparingly administered, still the difference was not so great between wages and alms—between their present lot and their former condition—as to make them look back with regret upon that condition, or to strive eagerly for its recovery'.[2]

In writing of this in 1819 to Peel, his former pupil at Christ Church, Copleston made it clear that he did not think the depreciation of wages relative to prices could be legislatively remedied. Long an advocate of *laissez-faire* economy, and recently impressed by Ricardo's analyses, Copleston recognized that the availability of surplus labor would naturally induce employers to keep wages as low as possible. 'The age is too enlightened to think that a regulation of wages by law can give effectual relief; that Government can create food, or a demand for labour . . .'. Nevertheless, the government not only could, but should remove 'many obstacles to that principle of self-correction which the analogy of nature

[1] *Ibid.*, 5–7.
[2] Copleston, *Second Letter*, 82–83.

119

teaches us is the universal law to her constitution'.[1] The principle obstacle Copleston wished to start with was the instability of currency lacking a fixed value in gold or silver, and compounded by the continued suspension of specie payment undertaken during the war. Ricardo, and other spokesmen for the manufacturing middle class, continually urged a policy of fiscal retrenchment which would halt the rapid depreciation of the bank-note, and contain the inflationary evils in the economy.[2] The government, faced with a severe debt since abolition of the income tax in 1816, repayment of earlier loans, a heavy drain on specie to the Continent, and a bad harvest in 1816–17, preferred to delay a return to specie payment.

In spite of governmental hopes to the contrary, a committee of enquiry appointed in 1818 under Peel's chairmanship was convinced by the advocates of hard currency. Legislation, passed the following year, established the necessary controls and timetable for the Bank of England to return to specie payments.[3] Peel's old tutor was not uninfluential in persuading him to end 'the pernicious effects of a variable standard of value', and he invited Copleston to join him in a discussion of the matter with William Huskisson and the London banker, Alexander Baring.[4] Copleston emphasized the impact of a depreciated currency upon the poor, and argued that as the government should not interfere with the natural law of wages, it should also avoid any '*artificial*, any *superfluous*, any *arbitrary* and *coercive*' measures contributing to the depreciation of the value of wages.[5] The use of non-convertible bank-notes in place of specie resulted in bullion leaving the country at an unfavorable rate, and the government then had to buy it back with paper notes worth more than the gold. Bank paper and coinage were not in fact equal, and so long as people acted as if they were, the currency in circulation would decrease in value.[6]

[1] Copleston, *A Letter to the Right Hon. Robert Peel, M.P. For the University of Oxford, On the Pernicious Effects of a Variable Standard of Value, Especially As It Regards the Condition of the Lower Orders and the Poor Laws* (Oxford, 1819), 37.
The title page proclaimed 'Laissez nous faire!'
[2] David Ricardo, *Proposals For An Economical and Secure Currency, With Observations on the Profits of the Bank of England* (1816).
[3] 59 Geo. III, cap. 49. Halévy, *Liberal Awakening*, 50–53.
[4] W. J. Copleston, *Memoir of Edward Copleston, D.D. . . . With Selections From His Diary and Correspondence* (1851), 86. Archbishop Whately said Copleston's currency and free trade proposals antagonized Tory landowners and delayed his elevation to the bench. See R. Whately, ed., *Remains of the Late Edward Copleston . . . With an Introduction Containing Some Reminiscences of His Life* (1854), 28. Actually Copleston's early conversion to Catholic relief was probably more important in causing the delay.
[5] Copleston, *Letter*, 38.   [6] *Ibid.*, 50–54.

Like Ricardo and others, Copleston recognized the commercial advantages of flexible and mobile currency, and agreed that any return to specie must be gradual, so as not to disrupt the economy.[1] A sudden reversion to 'natural money' would only compound the misery of the laboring class, since the circulation of money would be curtailed, and production cut back. Moreover, as Ricardo had explained, the poorest land which requires the most labor to cultivate is always the first to be left fallow when demand falls, thereby increasing the number of laborers without employment.[2] The long war had compounded the problem by creating artificial demands and artificial measures.[3]

Rising prices were necessary to encourage production, but Copleston, in spite of Ricardo's logical explanation, wondered if wages had to lag so far behind. With the currency depreciating, the situation forbode disaster. The rich not only grew more prosperous from rising prices and low wages, but were in a much better position to ride out fluctuations in the economy. They could if they wished hold back selling their goods or crops until the prices rose even higher. Laborers, however, had no insulation and were continually forced to sell their labor in order to buy the immediate necessities of life. Clearly they could not withhold their labor, nor could they wait out price fluctuations. A stable currency would at least provide a foundation for recovery, otherwise, Copleston maintained, the lower classes would sink deeper into hopeless despair. There was no escaping the fact that the poor 'must buy, and they must sell, and that immediately [since] the parties with whom they deal are intent upon gain'. Gradually, the laboring classes adjust to their 'harder condition of life; to inferior food, lodging and clothing', and unless a sudden demand for labor comes to their aid, this gradual decay of standards continues until their 'condition is permanently and irrecoverably degraded'.[4]

To those of his troubled colleagues who could not understand the existence of such great poverty in so prosperous a nation, Copleston assured them it was not a unique occurrence. He had traced similar situations back to Elizabethan times when wage-earners were incapable of paying the rising price of provisions. The establishment of the Poor Law was the direct result, though it had been 'sometimes absurdly attributed to the suppression of the monasteries'. As in their own day, the instability of currency had created 'a violent disturbance of the established economic relations . . . and the lower classes being the last to obtain redress, sunk into that state of abject dependence, from which they

---

[1] *Second Letter*, 2.

[2] *Ibid.*, 6–8. Ricardo, *On the Principles of Political Economy and Taxation* (1817), esp. Chaps. II, V.

[3] *Second Letter*, 13.

[4] Copleston, *Letter*, 29–31.

slowly emerged through the natural corrective of a diminished population aided by the general improvement of the next century, and the greater steadiness of our currency; but into which they are now again plunged by the operation of a similar cause'.[1] If the upward cycle could be started again by stabilizing the currency, increasing the value of money, and enhancing the purchasing power of wages, the entire country would benefit. Naturally employers would eventually reduce wages when they realized the improvement, but Copleston felt that until that time the laborer would gain as the employer had profited when the value of money was depressed.[2] It was hardly a permanent solution, but then there was no solution to poverty. The workers' improvement would be temporary until their wages were once more diminished to the point of subsistence. Only a continual labor shortage would obviate that recurring condition, but Malthus and Sumner had shown why there was little prospect of that happening.

But the inevitability of poverty was not the question troubling clerical economists. What really bothered Copleston and his ecclesiastical generation as they rose to power, was the obvious widening of the gap between rich and poor, and a gnawing fear that the moderating gradations of wealth necessary in a harmonious society were fast disappearing. Sumner had been quite explicit in his contention that a natural economy, though necessarily unequal, should not concentrate great wealth in comparatively few hands. The most favored state was always the one in which there was a reasonable proportion of 'opulence, competency and poverty'.[3] This meant a gradual distribution of wealth from the highest to the lowest ranks; Sumner warned, 'the civilization is always least advanced, where any of the intermediate steps are wanting'.[4]

On the eve of great progress and prosperity following a long war for the preservation of Christian civilization, was it possible that it would all be subverted by some gross imbalance in the natural quest for self-enhancement? The possibility troubled several Church leaders over the next several decades, and prompted Copleston in 1819 to caution Peel that the situation was already severe. Employers were accumulating 'vast wealth' from the sweat of their deprived workers, and their material success stimulated others to embark upon a similar course. Life in England was beginning 'to wear a new embroidery, woven by the humble toil of beings who are left to grovel on the earth, and to perish obscurely when their work is done, destined never to enter upon the fruits of their own labour'.[5]

Pain and privation were undoubtedly necessary if the poor were to have an opportunity to exercise the divine virtues of patience, resignation and contentment, as well as to demonstrate their confidence in an

[1] *Ibid.*, 32–33. [2] *Second Letter*, 35–36. [3] Sumner, *Treatise*, II, 323.
[4] *Ibid.*, 74. [5] Copleston, *Second Letter*, 47–48.

ultimate reward. At the same time the misery of others was expected to stimulate among the upper class 'acts of love and charity which are perhaps the most efficacious towards fitting us for the enjoyments of a higher state of being'.[1] Yet there was mounting evidence that the poor had been recently provided with more than enough chances to fulfil their obligations, without succeeding to stimulate the hearts of employers who paid wretched wages in the knowledge that the poor laborer could survive with the aid of a supplementary parish dole. True, the Gospel taught that the poor would always be among us; but Copleston, Sumner, Otter and several others wondered if there need be so many of them.

Paupers were perhaps an inevitable result of the class interests and conflicts implicit in a Ricardian analysis of wages and rents, but Copleston was not happy with the idea, or the reality. The latter suddenly induced him near the end of his *Second Letter to Peel* to urge employers arbitrarily to raise the wages of their workers. Unnatural though it was, he suggested losses in profits might be compensated by leaving the least fertile lands uncultivated. Even if still lower profits were forthcoming, Copleston felt in the long run that the natural laws of economy would create a beneficial balance. Surplus laborers would leave the land and enter some new occupation, 'but the labour that is *retained* ought surely to be paid adequately . . . and not be driven to solicit extraneous and indirect assistance'. What Copleston wanted was nature expedited by landowners paying laborers a greater wage, 'which by the slow operation of the principles of human society must one day or other take place'. Was it too much, he wondered, to expect from 'the more enlightened class' a firmness of character and 'more personal sacrifice' than might be expected from the ignorant lower orders? By helping nature along, the harmful interference of authority could be avoided; the raising of wages 'does no more than quicken the march of justice, and smooth the way for her passage'.[2] Otherwise, the alternative would be to allow a further institutionalizing of poverty, and the denial of the benefits of a well-balanced natural, unfettered economy to the greatest number of people.

Subsistence wages were not truly natural wages, because they were in fact inadequate and required subsidization. Property-owners should see that the larger rates they paid and complained about could be more effectively and humanely applied to wage increases. At the same time it would go a long way to promote greater harmony between the classes. As a Tory clergyman still attached to a pastoral social system heavily

[1] E. Copleston, *An Enquiry Into the Doctrines of Necessity and Predestination In Four Discourses Preached Before the University of Oxford* (1821), 60–61. Also Sumner, *Treatise*, II, 323–4.
[2] Copleston, *Second Letter*, 107–9.

encrusted with at least the ideal of gentry paternalism, Copleston emotionally rejected the Ricardian conclusion that the landed interests of the country were naturally antipathetical to those of the middle and laboring classes.[1] In accepting many of Ricardo's iron laws of political economy, he at the same time appealed to farmers and the landed gentry to melt down their harshness by reducing profits and coalescing their natural interests with those of the masses of laboring poor. Not only should the landed classes be prepared to increase wages, but Copleston proposed they eventually repudiate the protective corn laws recently enacted on their behalf.[2]

Although he was an advocate of an economic system oriented towards middle-class moneyed interests, Copleston was not interested in promoting the welfare of manufacturers, merchants and bankers. Like many of his colleagues, he found their demands and desires were exaggerated and harmful to the agricultural society which he much preferred and had long defended.[3] Furthermore, the welfare of factory workers was not relevant to his position. In contrast to agricultural laborers they were much more mobile, and in a position to sell their labor wherever it would bring the best price. But the agricultural laborers, constituting the greatest number of Englishmen, lacked such opportunity and flexibility, and were plunging deeper and deeper into a quicksand of immobilizing indigence. Without repudiating the utilitarian laws of competitive self-interest, the clerical economist surmised that they had been distorted to place the blame for poverty entirely upon the poor. Many people were undoubtedly guilty of wilful pauperism, but all too often 'no account is taken of those who are able and willing to work, but have no employment'.[4] Opportunity and a realistic subsistence wage free from parochial subsidization and based upon sound currency were the most important means of restoring the social economy to natural harmony, where 'all the several interests will speedily settle of their own accord into the right places'.[5]

If not a passionate or compassionate defender of the poor, Copleston, in contrast to many of his clerical brethren, at least acknowledged that there were very real social and economic reasons for their condition beyond any individual guilt they might have to bear. In their enthusiasm to refute the dangerous assertions attributing poverty to the man-made evils of a hierarchical society, parsons and prelates had, if anything, exaggerated utilitarian individualism, and sanctified it with religious

---

[1] Ricardo, *Principles*, 391.   [2] Copleston, *Second Letter*, 9.

[3] Copleston, in his prize-winning essay 'On Agriculture', described it as 'the primary and most powerful agent in civilizing mankind, so likewise will it be found the best and surest support of national power, wealth and happiness', 4–6.

[4] Copleston, *Second Letter*, 53–54.   [5] *Ibid.*, 109.

justifications of free will. Copleston did not disagree, but was wary when he found employed laborers were little better off than unemployed laborers. Moreover the natural principle of subsistence wages was self-defeating if it was determined to be at such a low level that the poor were continually at the mercy of economic and demographic fluctuations.

Yet he knew Ricardo was right, and in spite of his appeals Copleston believed that wages would in all likelihood be kept at a deplorably low level; not, as Malthus proposed, to discourage population growth, but, as Ricardo explained, to maximize profits. He accepted Sumner's analysis of the former, and along with Ricardo, James Mill, and Bentham, was confident there was still much land to be cultivated, new technology to be employed, and free trade to be encouraged to expand greatly the international distribution of food. Periodic overpopulation would be controlled by the moral education of the poor rather than by their compounded misery. Until that time, however, all Copleston could recommend aside from stabilizing the currency was that employers voluntarily restrain their natural self-interest, and pay their laborers more. No Anglican Church leader was yet prepared to go much beyond Copleston's wishful suggestion.

IV

❖❖❖❖❖❖❖❖❖❖❖❖❖❖❖❖❖❖❖❖❖❖❖❖❖❖❖❖❖

The Poor Law Attacked

❖❖❖❖❖❖❖❖❖❖❖❖❖❖❖❖❖❖❖❖❖❖❖❖❖❖❖❖❖

1. POOR RELIEF RECONSIDERED

General discussions about the nature and causes of poverty after the war invariably turned to the role of the Poor Law. Although complaints had multiplied earlier as relief rates increased steadily after the adoption of wage supplements in 1795, the age of the Poor Law, and the fear of tampering with established institutions during the French Revolution, precluded any sustained attack upon it for the duration. After the war, however, opponents, armed with new weapons hot from the forges of political economy, launched their assault. Their ranks were swelled by ratepayers who had little knowledge of Malthusian arguments against the self-perpetuating characteristics of institutional relief, but who recoiled at the enormous expenditure of £5,072,028 in 1815. This was nearly three times the amount distributed at the start of war. The economic dislocation after Waterloo forced relief costs up to £6,910,925 in 1817, and a high of £7,870,809 the following year.[1] Few propertied Englishmen would deny that the poor had become a very heavy burden indeed.

All Christian societies were of course expected to carry that burden one way or another, but clergy and laity alike increasingly questioned whether the unique English system of institutionalized relief was in fact the best way to fulfil their obligations. The extrapolations of Malthus or Ricardo indicated that it was not. Unless serious reforms were undertaken it was feared the country would eventually be inundated with starving paupers, or the natural laws of a utilitarian economy would be

[1] *Parl. Ps.* (1817), VI, 155–7; Halévy, *Liberal Awakening*, 40.

126

so flagrantly violated as to impede social progress. Significantly, Joseph Townsend's plan, first published in 1786, was reprinted in 1817.[1] Among its more attractive features was one reducing the relief rates annually to one-tenth of the existing amount over a ten-year period. Another of Townsend's suggestions, that of a compulsory subscription to a common fund proportionally withheld from wages, aroused considerable interest, but would have been a risky proposal in the midst of so much worker discontent. John Curwen, in print and in Parliament, urged a parochial assessment levied on every species of wealth in order to distribute the burden of relief more equitably.[2]

Compalints and advice poured in from every direction: from radical utilitarians, undogmatic, conservative landowners, from clergymen, agrarian socialists and, of course, from William Cobbett. The Parliamentary Committees, established in 1816 to examine the problem, were confronted with mountains of unsolicited evidence to assist the attempt to work out a compromise to cut the cost of relief without infuriating the desperate poor. In 1817, under the chairmanship of Sturges Bourne, the Commons Committee criticized the excessive growth of outdoor relief in preceding years, recommended reducing the discretionary powers of local magistrates to grant special assistance, and urged a reorganization of the vestries to give rate-paying landlords great control over the administration and distribution of relief funds.[3] Parliament, in endorsing the Report through legislation enacted in 1818–19, also made the requirements for individual assistance more stringent by insisting that able-bodied paupers must prove they were unemployed for reasons beyond their control.[4] This was the first important step away from the more humane interpretation placed on the Poor Law during the previous century.

The bishops of the Church were silent. Many lesser clergy expressed their opinion, usually in support of tighter restrictions, but no prelate spoke. Most of them, as rate-paying landed proprietors and allies of the government, were probably content, along with the gentry, to welcome the more stringent measures without further antagonizing critics who delighted in pointing to the hard-heartedness of an Established Church impervious to the sufferings of the unfortunate populace. Genuinely compassionate, charitable bishops, such as old Barrington at Durham,

[1] Townsend, *A Dissertation on the Poor Laws* . . . (1817). Sumner reviewed it favorably in *The British Review*, X, no. XX (1817).

[2] J. Curwen, *Sketch of a Plan . . . for Bettering the Condition of the Labouring Classes of the Community, and for Equalizing and Redressing the Amount of the Present Parochial Assessment* (1817). See also his speech in the Commons, *Hansard*, XXXIV (1816), 871 ff.

[3] *Report From the Select Committee on the Poor Laws; With the Minutes of Evidence Taken Before the Committee* (1817).

[4] 58 Geo. III, c. 69; 59 Geo. III, c. 12 and c. 50.

Burgess at St David's, and the first avowed Evangelical on the bench, Henry Ryder, listened in silence as the hierarchy and the clergy were lacerated by accusations of selfish materialism and the abandonment of their impoverished charges.[1]

Lesser dignitaries came to the defense, and attempted to justify support of a tougher Poor Law by proving that social legislation was all too often in conflict with Scripture. Charles Goddard, Archdeacon of Lincoln, explained the problem in 1817:

> Religion supposes that all according to their stations and in some way or other (the poor especially), should 'work that they may eat': in other words, it receives into its code, industry on the part of Christians, as also the proper concomitant virtues of temperance and frugality, as express duties; and if, of late years, and in contradiction to their original intention, and in fact to their earlier operation, the Laws of this Country have not concurred with this, the religious view of the subject, [they] have presented to the poor, facilities for eating without work. . . .[2]

Others, a minority, believed this was cutting the line of Christian charity very thin indeed, and deplored the influence of Malthusian political economy on established ideas of assistance. But the debate was carried on beneath the lofty heights of episcopal hierarchy.

Several clergymen who would ascend those favored heights during the next two decades were less reticent than their predecessors. John Bird Sumner, who had gone to such lengths to square Malthus with Scripture and natural law, was still troubled about the implications of the *Essay on Population* for poor relief. Acknowledging that the Poor Law had encouraged too many recipients of assistance to have children, Sumner also knew how important parochial relief was when a man was completely destitute, or a family abandoned. Moreover, in spite of the obvious evils of wage supplementation undertaken in the 1790's, he realized that the rates provided a livable income for many hard-working laborers whose pay was simply inadequate.[3] Instead of criticizing the wage policies of employers, as Edward Copleston did, Sumner was satisfied that a satisfactory wage balance was achieved by use of the rates. They subsidized not only low wages, but cheap goods as well; 'the injury does not fall upon the contributor to the rates, as is commonly

---

[1] Henry Ryder (1777–1835), son of 1st Baron Harrowby and brother of the 1st Earl, was a pious, energetic parish priest. Dean of Wells (1812), Bishop of Gloucester (1815), Lichfield-Coventry (1824). His appointment was carried by his brother over strong opposition against the bishop's Evangelical views. Though a pluralist, Ryder was a vigorous preaching and reforming prelate.

[2] C. Goddard, *District Committees and National Schools. Two Sermons Preached in . . . 1817* (Windsor, 1818), 23.

[3] Sumner, *Treatise*, II, 88, 290.

supposed, who, if he did not pay these, would pay much more in the enhanced price of every article from the augmented wages of labour'.[1] While such reasoning undoubtedly delighted landlords and farmers who relied upon the rates to maintain their ill-paid laborers at a subsistence level, their enthusiasm was hardly shared by many others who protested at the enormous increase in the levy immediately after the war.

For Sumner the troublesome problem of the current Poor Law was not really economic; it was moral. He was not concerned that the laborers were inadequately paid; that all balanced out in low prices. But he was disturbed by claims that the rates discouraged prudence, responsibility and gratitude.[2] Even more distressing, the poor increasingly expected to be relieved as a right derived from noxious principles of revolutionary equalitarianism and social causation. Much of the harshness of political economy grafted to clerical social thought in the first half of the nineteenth century was motivated by a determination, sometimes conscious, often unconscious, to destroy the lingering infection of *The Rights of Man*. Though apparently dormant for long periods of time, it would, like 'low fever', periodically erupt and spread rapidly through laboring-class districts.

To suggest that because a man's condition is determined by society he has the *right* to expect its assistance and protection when he cannot or will not work was to deny the human need for 'an urgent stimulus to manual exertion . . . [and] a strong and sensible incitement to the exertion of the mind', if there was to be progress. The nature of man being what it is, Sumner did not find it surprising that stimulation was often a crude and materialistic 'love of gain'. Pitiful as it may seem, experience proved 'the gratification of vanity or appetite' was necessary; 'the vast and complicated machine of human society . . . was originally actuated, and is kept in continual activity, by each individual's desires of bettering his own condition'.[3] Sumner, an Evangelical, in contrast to many followers of that stricter persuasion, was not distressed by the accumulation of luxury. It was a natural result of the acquisitive stimuli that drove competitive men to a natural means of pleasurable gratification.

Adam Smith had conclusively shown that man would labor in society only if individual satisfaction was adequate. But the Scottish economist had recognized, and Sumner agreed, that there is not a manufacture, even after the exclusion of all luxury, that does not require processes very 'inconsistent with the most desirable state of human existence'.

Consequently people labor on the roads and canals, go down into mines, cultivate the soil, not for its own sake—such labor is not

<hr/>

[1] *Ibid.*, 300. [2] *Ibid.*, 301. [3] *Ibid.*, 56–57.

pleasurable—but for more important personal gratifications that they seek and need. This did not mean, however, that most people must constantly suffer in a perpetual state of deprivation in order to be properly stimulated to labor. The learned Smith had also determined that 'servants, labourers and workmen of different kinds, make up the far greater part of every political society. . . . No society can surely be flourishing and happy, of which the far greater part of the members are poor and miserable.'[1] At the same time, Sumner added, no society could be flourishing and happy in which the natural acquisitive motivation of a large number of the populace was eroding. Institutionalized relief was a principal cause. Established initially out of necessity and Christian compassion, it had, after some three hundred years, been corrupted by the poor into a right rather than a privilege to be permitted with caution and restraint. And more important, it was no longer received with a deep sense of gratitude, obligation and acquiescent humility.

Clerical complaints about the ingratitude of the laboring poor became commonplace in the post-war years. Considering the huge outlay in private and public assistance, it was baffling to many parsons, confident of their charitable righteousness, why the poor were so dissatisfied and belligerent. How could the laboring multitudes, as one of them put it, turn on people who have such 'a charitable and benevolent heart'? The puzzled cleric, the Reverend T. T. Walmsley, High Church Secretary to the National Society for Educating the Children of the Poor, was not wrong in his assurances that no other civilized country 'can exhibit such a variety of systems for every species of misery . . .'. It was as if there was 'a general concurrence, of every individual who has ability to do so, to divide amongst themselves the sum of human misery . . .'.[2] Yet everywhere there were riots, machine-burnings, and alarming reports of insurrectionary activity.

In the aftermath of Peterloo, Thomas Whitaker, pluralist Vicar of Whalley and Blackburn, was astounded 'that our persons and houses were threatened, and that property, the only source of bounty, was not regarded as the fruitful, yet appropriated source of munificence, but as an object of plunder and pillage'.[3] That the 'working commonalty' should follow 'the lying and impudent vagabonds' who bring nothing but words to them, instead of their natural protectors, indicated to what extent right and wrong had become inverted in the minds of the poor. They demanded as a right what was willingly given them from charity.

[1] *Ibid.*, 71; Smith, *Wealth of Nations*, Bk. I, Chap. VIII.

[2] T. T. Walmsley, *A Sermon Preached in the Parish Church of All Hallows, Lombard Street . . . December 21, 1817, For the Benefit of the City of London National Schools* (1817), 5.

[3] T. D. Whitaker, *A Sermon Preached . . . In Aid of A Subscription For the Relief of the Poor in the Town of Blackburn* (Blackburn, 1820), 15.

In so doing, the preacher lamented, they cut themselves off from the benevolence of their betters, and it was necessary to repress rigorously their dangerous demands. Whitaker was not unaware of the sufferings of the poor, and spoke of the 'hunger, thirst, nakedness, the shivering nights', they endured 'under a thin and time-worn covering of rags'.[1] Unlike many of his brethren, he did not hesitate to condemn the cutting of workers' wages by rapacious businessmen 'who had just emerged from their own rank', and he specifically warned factory-owners, 'woe unto him that buildeth his house by iniquity, and his chambers by wrong; that useth his neighbour's service without wages and giveth him not for his hire'. The parson even suggested that the 'opulent and honourable persons' comprising the highest ranks seek measures 'to compel those who are growing wealthy by wrong, no longer to defraud the hireling of his wages'.[2]

Whitaker, in contrast to many of his colleagues, was not critical of poor relief, and believed it should be cautiously resumed and even extended to those who were 'politically tainted'. There was no reason why innocent children and wives should suffer, but all assistance ought to be accompanied by the reminder that in spite of real or imaginary hardships, the 'short pressures of this life' are but a prelude to eternal happiness.[3] Gradually, he hoped, the poor would again realize the only real claim they had upon the property of their betters was derived from an individual Christian desire to aid the unfortunate. Only meekness and humble gratitude on the part of the needy stimulated that desire; the riotous proclamation of wilful demands deadened it.

> While you demand . . . we refuse; when you begin to supplicate, from that moment, we bestow. While you continued to lift the sword to our throats, so long we repel your threatenings with disdain—but condescend to supplicate, and you receive. We crush the stubborn; we spare the vanquished. This is as it should be.[4]

This was not the voice of a political economist. Whitaker disliked middle-class manufacturers and their natural laws of rapacity and social irresponsibility. He saw the country on the brink of class warfare because mutual responsibilities had been permitted to decay. Typically, he longed for the preservation of a paternalistic squirearchy functioning through clerical agents, and prayed the riots of 1819 were but 'the single burst of a volcano'.[5] The laboring poor, having realized their precipitous folly, would, he hoped, allow everything to be as before.

Many of his clerical brethren had abandoned such illusions. They had finally realized that social problems were not simply questions of lower-class quiescence. A penetrating analysis of the new laws of economy

[1] *Ibid.*, 19. [2] *Ibid.*, 17. [3] *Ibid.*, 24.
[4] *Ibid.*, 15. [5] *Ibid.*, 22.

showed that the rich as well as the poor were victims of unnatural social and economic relationships permitted to develop unchecked. Central to the problem was the Poor Law, which had, William Otter insisted, 'shed too often a malignant influence upon all who are connected with it . . .'. It introduced 'suspicion, churlishness, hardness of heart, on the part of those who give; discontent, clamour, falsehood, ingratitude, and, sometimes, unfounded indignation, on the part of those who receive'.[1] As the pluralist rector of two Shropshire parishes, Otter was aware of the need for assistance in that county, but it was clear to him the expansion of parochial relief only aggravated the difficulties.[2] He had studied the Report of the Select Committee on the Poor Law in 1817 and agreed with the conclusion that difficulties arose through population growth, poor harvests and price fluctuations. Nevertheless, in spite of periodic rises and slumps, 'the main evil is progressive'.[3]

Townsend realized it as early as 1786; Malthus explained it, and, in the second edition of *An Essay on Population* (1803), offered a more practicable solution than his predecessor. So long as the poor were relieved without increasing production, they would continue to suffer, and eventually all society would be similarly depressed. Considering the enormous increase of relief costs during the preceding two decades, it was clear to Otter in 1818 that his old friend had been more than vindicated in his description of English poor relief as 'puerile and ineffectual'. Malthus had warned that

> the price of labour, when left to find its natural level, is a most important political barometer, expressing the relation between the supply of provisions and the demand for them; between the quantity to be consumed and the number of consumers; and taken on the average, independently of accidental circumstances, it further expresses clearly the wants of the society respecting population; that is, whatever may be the number of children to a marriage necessary to maintain exactly the present population, the price of labour will be just sufficient to support this number, or be above it, or below it, according to the state of the real funds for the maintenance of labour, whether stationary, progressive, or retrograde.[4]

The innovation of wage supplements had made a shambles of the natural level, and excessive liberality and humanity had undermined the effectiveness of the old Poor Law entirely. Otter, like Malthus, urged a hard line be taken in the future; he advocated a clause be inserted in the revised measure denying relief to any legitimate or illegitimate

---

[1] Otter, *Sermon* (1818), 6.

[2] Not to be outdone by his father, who had been a triple pluralist, Otter added another vicarage to his livings in 1825.

[3] Otter, *Sermon* (1818), 4–5.

[4] Malthus, *Essay* (1803), Bk. III, Chap. V.

children born one and two years respectively after the new law was enacted. Furthermore, it was the responsibility of the clergy to explain the possible consequences of imprudent marriages to the laboring ranks.[1]

Malthus's description of the Poor Law perpetuating poverty by encouraging overpopulation, and sapping the 'spirit of independence' among the poor seemed perfectly obvious to many of his contemporaries, even if they did not necessarily share his long-range conclusions. If the Malthusian analysis of lower-class psychology was correct, simply raising wages, as some suggested, would not only be fruitless, but self-defeating. So long as parochial relief existed as an alternative, the laboring classes would not think of their future, and would continue to expend all their income on subsistence and drink. Even more distressing, they would find little reason to repress their reproductive instincts. Not understanding the real causes of their misfortune, the poor were discouraged from saving during prosperous times, confident that the rates would sustain them when confronted with hardship once more.

> A man who might not be deterred from going to the alehouse from the consideration that on his death or sickness he should leave his wife and family upon the parish, might yet hesitate in thus dissipating his earnings, if he were assured that in either of these cases his family must starve, or be left to the support of casual bounty.

In the years after the war Malthus converted many of his clerical brethren to his conclusion 'that if the poor-laws had never existed . . . though there might have been a few more instances of very severe distress, the aggregate mass of happiness among the common people would have been much greater . . .'.[2]

In 1816, Sumner was not convinced of this conclusion, but his experiences of the next few years brought him around. Where in the *Records of Creation* he accepted the development of institutionalized relief as necessary and often beneficial, he became more severe in later articles submitted to the *Edinburgh Review*, the *British Review*, and the 1824 edition of the *Encyclopaedia Britannica*.[3] Submitting a solicited article in 1822 on the Poor Law to Macvey Napier, an editor of the *Edinburgh Review*, Sumner interjected, 'you will perceive that I am a decided enemy of the system; and in fact I become more so every day, from what I see of its effects.'[4] Like most clerical Malthusians of his day, the future archbishop was disappointed that the legislation of 1818–19 did not

---

[1] Otter, *Sermon* (1818), 10.

[2] *Essay* (1803), Bk. III, Chap. VI.

[3] 15 Jan. 1822, *Napier Ps.*, British Museum, Add. MS. 34613, f. 12; also *British Review*, X, no. XX (1817), 333–50.

[4] 25 April 1822, *Napier Ps.*, Add. MS. 34613, f. 53.

effectively correct the problem. But being cautious, he was sensitive enough to know that it was an explosive issue, and would 'require a large degree of political courage' to make any practical alterations.[1]

That courage, as far as Otter and Edward Maltby were concerned, had been found wanting. Consequently it was likely that 'the present generation of paupers will be succeeded by another still more destitute, and more reckless of their posterity', while the rates grow more intolerable.[2] Actually the rates decreased after 1819, falling to a low level of £5,736,900 in 1824.[3] Improved economic conditions had as much to do with the decline as did the legislation based on Bourne's Report, but as far as Maltby could see the cost was still too great, because the principle was as fallacious as ever. The injunction, 'that if any would not work, neither should he eat . . .' (Thessalonians iii. 10–13), was no less valid than before prosperity returned, and it applied to the invariable laws of political economy as it did to the revealed laws of Scripture. The moderation of distress only exacerbated the issue, since the continuance of relief was an unnecessary violation of 'the generous and charitable spirit enjoined by Christianity . . .'. The 'lazy and designing', Maltby warned in 1822, are more content than ever to exploit 'that bounty, which was intended for the benefit of the industrious and the comfort of the afflicted'.[4] He was vague as to how one should determine these classifications, but like many of his generation he spoke in generalities of how charity had always been corrupted by the greedy and the indolent, but never to so great an extent. Even St Paul had excoriated those who abused so 'beautiful and useful a system', proclaiming 'that they, who would not contribute their share of industry to the community, should not receive any advantage from the bounty of the public'.[5] Maltby was pleased that the apostles were on his side.

The future occupant of the diminished, but still very lucrative See of Durham, conceded that though the Poor Law was originally established in the Christian spirit, it had become 'an excuse for the idle; or . . . a resource to busybodies; or . . . an encouragement to the discontented'. Maltby was but one of many people who believed that the disturbances of the preceding decade had been largely fomented by lazy troublemakers who, instead of engaging in daily labor, had, as a result of being subsidized by the rates, been able to wander about doing mischief. Individual

---

[1] *Ibid.* Although Sumner was paid £30 for the article it apparently was never published (*ibid.*, f. 146).

[2] W. Otter, *Reasons for Continuing the Education of the Poor at the Present Crisis: A Sermon Preached . . . 16th of March, 1820* (Shrewsbury, 1820), 12.

[3] Halévy, *Liberal Awakening*, 43.

[4] E. Maltby, 'Sermon V (1822)', in *Sermons* (1819–22), II, 70.

[5] *Ibid.*, 75–76.

unemployment was no excuse; it was time the laboring classes understood that

> wherever the labour of an whole family can procure a sufficient sustenance, though it be scanty, yet there is no moral, no religious, and . . . no legal claim upon the bounty of the public.

Maltby, from his acquaintance with the great Whig families of the realm, knew that every rank and station was 'exposed to some diminution of their former comforts', so why should the poor be any exception? By applying for relief unnecessarily and refusing to exert 'their utmost pains to procure a maintenance, they only increased the amount of general difficulty'. His experience as a Huntingdonshire magistrate convinced the vicar of the rapid disappearance of 'a becoming pride in a poor man not to be indebted to the public bounty for that which his own honest and unremitting labour could procure . . .'. Alas, too many had lost that ancient virtue, and took advantage of 'a fund, of which not one mite should be ever paid without urgent and visible necessity'.[1] Again, Maltby was ambiguous and imprecise about requirements, but the tone of his argument, like that of many others, was hostile and severe. The poor were fast becoming an enemy, indifferent to their own fate as well as that of others; inimical to their own prosperity and to that of society as a whole.

2. THE POOR LAW DEFENDED

Some influential clergymen were disturbed by this antagonism, and by the overly speculative and exaggerated tendency simply to blame the Poor Law. Edward Copleston certainly shared many of the reservations expressed by critics of relief, but felt that those who deplored the Poor Law as a major source of poverty were confusing symptoms with causes. The Poor Law did not cause poverty, but was a result of it. During particular periods of economic distress, practical and temporary means of relief have always been dispensed by societies, he explained.[2] A careful review of the history of the Poor Law from the sixteenth century to the present day showed 'one thing is certain; that this increase of poverty cannot be attributed, as has been the common theme of modern times, to the Poor Laws themselves. They grew out of the state of things. . . .' In each age the reason for their need was different; Copleston believed that in his own time the reason could be traced to the instability and depreciation of currency.[3]

He calculated that, in spite of the vexatious rise in the annual

[1] *Ibid.*, 83–84.
[2] Copleston, *Second Letter*, 40.
[3] *Ibid.*, 46–47.

expenditure for relief, in proportion to the increased size of the population, *per capita* assistance had in fact decreased. Considering the recent postwar fluctuations in the economy, the disruptive experience of nearly twenty-five years of war, as well as the inadequacy of depreciated wages in a time of rising prices, Copleston found something optimistic in the decline in 'the ratio of pauperism . . .'. To bemoan and decry the loss of 'the spirit of industry and self-support' among the laboring poor was to ignore very real evidence that they were more energetic. 'There is', he was sure, 'a *moral elasticity* in the character of this people, which though borne down by the accumulated pressure of many difficulties, is yet unbroken and unimpaired.' Copleston predicted a rebound from poverty once the economy was stabilized in accordance with right principles. In the meantime, 'the spirit of independent industry' vital to the poor permitted a safer dispensation of relief because of the reluctance to resort to it. While many of his contemporaries looked at aggregate costs, trembled at laborer unrest, and lamented the end of lower-class virtue, Copleston maintained that the decrease in real wages since the war had far exceeded the costs of relief.

> When this vortex had by degrees absorbed all the aged, the helpless, and the infirm, it was stern necessity alone, and not lazy indifference or choice, which compelled at last the hardy labourer himself to assert a privilege, which nature has conferred only upon orphan childhood, decrepitude and disease.[1]

The English laborer was not exactly inundated with such clerical testimonies of confidence in the early nineteenth century. Feared, even hated, he was continually berated for his individual corruption and the wretched conditions he created. But Copleston, without denying the sacred and necessary obligation of the poor to remain patient and contented in their state, and without for a moment admitting that relief was anything other than a privilege, conceded that the lower orders were often victims of economic conditions beyond their control. It would be a mistake then to alter the Poor Laws very much when they were at the same time necessary and utilized by proportionally fewer people. Furthermore, he opposed the imposition of a fixed ceiling on the rates, since the needs of enlarged future generations would probably be quite different;[2] it is necessary that 'we . . . be careful how we make provisions to bind posterity, founded upon the limited experience or the peculiar circumstances of our own times'.[3]

Copleston feared many well-meaning people were being frightened into an inflexible position against Poor Law relief and its recipients because of the erroneous conclusions of Parson Malthus. He nevertheless praised him for citing misinterpretations of the purpose of the laws

[1] *Ibid.*, 89–90.   [2] *Ibid.*, 91.   [3] *Ibid.*, 82.

which had erroneously confused morality and benevolence with practical legislation.

> It is the high distinction of the *Essay on Population* to have demonstrated . . . that all endeavours to embody benevolence into law, and thus impiously as it were, to effect by human laws what the Author of the system of nature has not effected by his laws must be abortive—that this ignorant struggle against evil really enlarges instead of contracting the kingdom of that evil—that it not only must fail, but that it involves great mischief both during the attempt and in its consequences.

Whatever modifications Malthus made in later editions to adjust his conclusions more closely 'to the goodness of God, and the duty of benevolence in man', many of his initial criticisms about the corruption of poor relief remained sound.[1] But the author of the *Essay* was wrong in his basic contention that the Poor Law encouraged excess population by holding out a promise of food and employment. Copleston deplored the arguments of those extreme Malthusians like James Bicheno, who condemned aid to the pauper because it purportedly allowed the 'gratification of his natural wants without any exertion on his part'.[2] These ideas fed the erroneous conclusion that paupers were as well off as independent laborers and did not hesitate to plunge into a poverty-perpetuating marriage. Yet from the earliest days, Copleston countered, 'the dreadful severity of laws against mendicity, and the precarious support of the poor from alms in their own residence, cannot have held out any encouragement to thoughtless and improvident matrimony'.[3]

The Poor Laws as conceived were certainly no inducement. Fear, pride, or religious virtue all serve to keep the poor off the rolls until they are truly desperate, and neither the language nor the effect of the Laws justified the contention that they encouraged overpopulation and perpetual impoverishment.[4] Copleston noted that Malthus had modified his earlier charge, and, in an appendix to the 1806 edition of the *Essay*, said he would 'not presume to say positively they tend to encourage population'. More recently, in the *Additions* of 1817, he acknowledged several other causes as well, though he still urged the gradual abolition of institutionalized relief.[5] At the other extreme, however, there were people like Thomas P. Courtenay, who denied any relationship between the Poor Laws, population growth and poverty. Copleston felt they were

---

[1] *Ibid.*, 22–23.

[2] *Ibid.*, 26–27; James Bicheno, *An Inquiry Into the Nature of Benevolence, Chiefly With a View to Elucidate the Principles of the Poor Laws, and to Show Their Immoral Tendency* (1817).

[3] *Ibid.*, 46.   [4] *Ibid.*, 28.

[5] *Ibid.*, 30–31; Malthus, *Additions to the Fourth and Former Editions of An Essay on the Principle of Population* (1817).

also guilty of facile exaggeration.[1] Malthus's evidence, and that drawn from Sir Frederick Morton Eden's *State of the Poor*, did indeed reveal an important connection. It showed that though the principle of the Poor Laws was sound, their ill-conceived extension and flaccid administration had corrupted their original purpose.

When he turned to the subject of administration, Copleston sounded more like a critical nineteenth-century clerical economist; he particularly deplored the late eighteenth-century trend towards humanity and flexibility in the Poor Laws. Gilbert's ill-conceived Acts of 1782 and 1796 not only improved conditions in the workhouses, but gave legal sanction to the practice of occasional relief so as not to disrupt families. Samuel Whitbread's abortive attempt in 1796 to establish a minimum wage for agricultural laborers and Pitt's 'incredible' plan the following year to pay a premium to large families—'to make the parish allowance in such cases a *right* and an honour'—were further indications of the economic *naïveté* of the preceding generation. The adoption of wage supplements based on the average price of grain was the unfortunate outgrowth of such fallacious thinking.[2] All this took place on the very eve of Malthus's epic publication, that 'blazing beacon . . . the rock upon which all former projects, and all legislative measures split . . . one that lies in the mid-channel of our navigation, and yet had been only occasionally perceived, by hasty and transient glimpses of men who never dreamt of the importance of what they saw'.[3]

Having seen the danger of confusing voluntary benevolence with legal relief, Malthus, Copleston believed, in spite of some initial miscalculations, had warned of the harm it would inevitably cause. Confident though he was that the poor were essentially victims of social and economic conditions, and would not, from some inner character fault, flock to the relief tables without genuine need, Copleston had no intention of making things very pleasant for them when they reached that desperate stage. Though the Poor Laws were basically sound in principle, they were unsound in practice because the degree between mere subsistence and actual comfort had been blurred. No one could deny that if relief was so inadequate as to lead 'to the extinction of life, it is horrible—if to the bare preservation of it, it is a limitation which ought to operate at *all times*'.[4] That is all the law should do—'preserve life'. To do more, 'it has been demonstrably shewn would multiply misery and distress, and in the end defeat itself'.[5] Copleston agreed with political

[1] T. P. Courtenay, *Copy of a Letter to the Right Hon. William Sturges Bourne, Chairman of the Select Committee of the House of Commons Appointed for the Consideration of the Poor Laws* (1817). Courtenay, a member of the Committee, disagreed with Bourne's Malthusian views of the Poor Law. See also Copleston, *Second Letter*, 31.

[2] *Ibid.*, 78–79.   [3] *Ibid.*, 80.   [4] *Ibid.*, 92.   [5] *Ibid.*, 28–29.

economists who accepted fluctuations in the amount of relief distributed so long as it did not approach a competitive level with the wages paid independent laborers. When in doubt it was always best for magistrates to err on 'the lower side', the side of inadequacy, as the errors end with themselves, 'whereas those on the side of indulgence have a tendency to increase in a geometric ratio'. If the indigent were treated too rigorously it was always possible to increase the dole; 'the error of indulgence tends to disturb and alter the standard itself by which it is measured, and thus to blind the judgment of mankind against all future correction'. Once this was understood, Copleston held out the prospect 'that it may be possible to provide by law for *preserving* life, without encouraging *propagation* of it'.[1]

This 'cheering inference', as the minister described it, should certainly have pleased Malthusians, if not the ignorant poor, for it necessitated an end to outdoor relief, and the supplementation of inadequate wages from the rates. The Berkshire magistrates had exceeded their power in 1795, and others had fallen into the same error over the years, encouraged by irresponsible legislation.[2] It was intolerable and unscientific to permit sometimes a single justice to distribute arbitrarily other people's money. Not only should a minimum of two magistrates be required, but like the overseers they should have 'the stoutest, not the kindest hearts', particularly in times of severe distress.[3] Wages and alms needed to be sharply separated, and the latter 'so controlled, and scantily paid' as to force laborers to seek any other conceivable means of support. 'If adequately paid, and indulgently treated, it must have a strong tendency to perpetuate or even to propagate itself.'[4] Since Copleston, in contrast to many people who shared his views, did not believe the poor would willingly avoid employment if it was available, the problem was to keep them from being corrupted while awaiting a favorable upturn in the economy. By corruption he meant the debasement of their natural and moral sense of individual self-interest to a point where it was irredeemable.

To keep that utilitarian quality alive, for the sake of the poor as well as for society as a whole, Copleston recommended stimulating it by the revival and extension of the parochial workhouse. When initially established under George I, the workhouse system had indeed led to a lowering of the rates, but over the years 'their notorious failures, as places of productive labour', and their general neglect, allowed the costs to rise once more.[5] The physical growth of the population was undoubtedly a factor, but the clergyman also attributed it to the decline in the fear and terror the workhouses had once struck in the mind of the lower orders. When they lost the ability to frighten, they lost their efficiency.

[1] *Ibid.*, 28–30.   [2] *Ibid.*, 34–35.   [3] *Ibid.*, 94–95.
[4] *Ibid.*, 97–98.   [5] *Ibid.*, 81.

Gilbert's foolish Act of 1782, and the general trend towards humanizing relief, further undermined the utility of the workhouses. By calling for their remodeling, and establishing guardians of the poor, the whole concept of relief came to be 'conceived in the false spirit of humanity . . .'. Once the comfort of the poor became a consideration, the institutionalization of outdoor relief and wage supplements logically followed. These measures, Copleston complained, 'spread the infection of pauperism through the body of the people—legislating still upon the false assumption of a *right* to support, and upon the mistaken basis of active benevolence'. Was it not time to return to the original spirit of the Poor Law, he asked? The workhouses operated in that spirit were still a good idea if not planned for 'the *comfort and domestic situation and happiness* of . . . poor persons'. They would, when conceived within the framework of our understanding of human nature, deter 'lazy applicants for parochial relief, by the conditions they hold out of confinement, labour, and personal control . . .'.[1]

In 1819, when trying to convince Peel of the folly of seriously overhauling the Poor Laws, Copleston argued that it was more prudent and feasible to strengthen the viable features of existing legislation rather than try to legislate for unforeseen future fluctuations in the economy. As the workhouses were a long-standing and logical part of the Poor Laws, they could, under the supervision of strict overseers, become the prudential alternative to what was fast becoming a legalized charity. He complained to his old pupil about the 'querulous sensibility, fostered by somber descriptions, in verse and prose, of Workhouses and Village Poor, which tends only to breed discontent, and to propagate the most erroneous notions of the duty of Government, and the defects of civil institutions'. In making relief an emotional issue, 'seditious demagogues' stirred up 'weakened intellects of persons unaccustomed to deep reflection, not with a view to awaken active benevolence, but to make them repine at the evils incident to social life'.[2] Years later, when Bishop of Llandaff, Copleston was to sit in silence while his colleague and friend, Henry Phillpotts of Exeter, mounted attack after attack on the workhouse system established in 1834. Not even Charles Dickens's 'sober descriptions' aroused him to defend the scheme he had long favored. He had learned too much in the intervening years.

But in 1819 Copleston felt the workhouse was an important lever with which to pry law and charity apart, and break up their unnatural union. Of course, no amount of relief would eliminate poverty, but anything that encouraged cautious discrimination would at the same time be less likely to discourage industry, frugality, and domestic responsibility on the part of the lower classes.[3] So long as laborers were invited to

[1] *Ibid.,* 75–78.   [2] *Ibid.,* 25–26.
[3] Whately, *Remains of . . . Copleston*, 223.

neglect these virtues they would; so long as employers were permitted to use the rates to avoid paying a living wage, they also would. As a Ricardian economist, Copleston knew 'that a rise in wages is a diminution not of rent, but of profits', and if employers did not understand the laws that determined it, they certainly understood the effect.[1] He also knew that appeals for a voluntary increase in wages would fall on ears tuned to the natural calls of acquisitive self-interest. But if laborers could no longer be paid from the rates, these same natural laws would assure the payment by employers of at least a subsistence wage. For redundant laborers it would temporarily mean the workhouse, and the continued stimulation of their utilitarian senses. When things got better they would fly to seek employment.

A residual advantage of confining the poor would be the encouragement it gave to labor mobility. Laborers, rather than separate from their families, would prefer to move elsewhere in search of employment, and Copleston believed that the free circulation of surplus labor was essential to a sound economy. Consequently he joined with those political economists who opposed attempts to enforce strict parochial residence as a requirement for relief. Since the unimpeded circulation of labor benefited the economy as a whole, there was no reason, he argued, why the risks could not be shared by a wider segment of the community. In areas attracting surplus labor, and where there was an excessive relief burden because of an increased number of factory workers, Copleston proposed that the counties as well as the local parishes might bear part of the load. After all, the manufacturing areas grew wealthy at a rate far exceeding occasional losses, yet when unemployment occurred factory workers were relieved from rates paid by non-manufacturing landlords. Considering the 'occasional case' where a major factory failed, and an excessive burden was thereby placed on the local parish, Copleston suggested that 'some provision . . . seems in reason and equity to be called for, in order to protect landed property from the consequences of failure in commercial speculation'.[2] He suggested loans to manufacturing workers temporarily unemployed, as well as to those who agreed to move elsewhere in search of work.[3] Perhaps, he posited, commercial interests should contribute to the county rates so as to minimize the burden borne by parochial landed contributors.[4]

Living in a glasshouse, Copleston, like many Anglican churchmen, was cautious when throwing stones about. Critics of the Establishment were already complaining about the selfish materialism of the Church, and urged that a larger portion of the tithes and other clerical revenue be allocated for poor relief. Anglican parsons of means bristled at the erroneous assertion that the poor had been robbed of their right to such

[1] Copleston, *Letter*, 36–37.   [2] Copleston, *Second Letter*, 92–93.
[3] *Ibid.*, 100.   [4] *Ibid.*, 93, 101–2.

assistance when the monasteries were dissolved in the sixteenth century, and the resources of the Church expropriated by the laity. Copleston, describing monastic alms as 'an ostentatious, wasteful, lazy, bounty', insisted that the poor never had any right to them whatsoever. Moreover, most relief before the Reformation had come from the parochial clergy, not the monks. This did not mean, however, that the poor ever had any legal right to non-monastic clerical assistance either. A proportional allotment of the tithe to that purpose was formerly a matter of ecclesiastical custom and regulation, but was never sanctioned by law.[1] If the care of the poor became a legislative concern after the Reformation, Copleston emphasized that it was never intended to diminish the necessary charitable responsibilities of clergy and laity alike. It would have been an unforgivable violation 'of those social affections and sympathies, which the God of nature has implanted in us . . .', and which make us aware of our mutual dependence on each other.[2] Long suspicious of the ineffectiveness of individual giving, however, Copleston endorsed the growing number of voluntary subscription societies as the most prudent compromise between indiscriminate charity and institutionalized relief.

Years later, in his *Letters . . . to Peel*, Copleston feared the balance had been tipped away from voluntary assistance and complained,

> we have an imperfect sense of moral obligation, and a low degree of benevolence. . . . Man would be virtuous, be humane, be charitable by *proxy*. . . . To throw off the care of want, and disease, and misery upon the magistrate, is to convert humanity into police, and religion into a statute book.

To make the receipt of charity a right and benevolence compulsory 'is a contradiction in terms . . . and if we attempt to transplant it from our own bosoms to the laws, it withers and dies . . .'.[3] Again, the source of the error could be traced to the eighteenth century, where successive generations failed to heed the sensible advice of wise Bishop Warburton and illuminate their 'romantic' ideas of the state by 'the light of revealed religion'.[4] The result, Copleston complained, was the unnatural intrusion of civil society into the most basic and sacred relationships between Christian men.

To restore the balance it was not necessary to eliminate the Poor Law, but merely to emphasize its least attractive features. Once compassion and humanity were removed from relief legislation, they would be returned to their rightful place in the benevolent hearts and minds of

[1] *Ibid.*, 41. Copleston drew heavily upon evidence in Eden's *State of the Poor.*

[2] Copleston, *Sermon* (1805), 12–13; also 'Sermon on Christian Liberality', in *Remains*, 223.

[3] Copleston, *Second Letter*, 18–19.

[4] *Ibid.*, 21; Warburton, *Alliance Between Church and State*, Bk. I, Chap. III.

Christian stewards. In many ways Copleston reflected an ambiguity felt by other clerical economists. On the one hand, as a Christian minister he sympathized with the laboring poor, felt they were unjustly maligned, and feared for their welfare if their principal source of aid, the Poor Law, was eliminated. But, on the other hand, as a student of political economy he knew the deleterious effects of guaranteed relief on human nature. In the end, in spite of his defense of the poor and his recognition of economic causation, Copleston came to conclusions similar to those advocated by people who ignored external causes, and who decried the personal vices of indigent wretches perpetuating the poverty in which they consciously wallowed.

There was certainly no guidance from the bench; not until Copleston's generation began assuming positions of ecclesiastical prominence in the next decade did bishops start speaking out on the relationship of the Church to poor relief. The only other member of that generation to enter the debate in the post-war years was Copleston's friend, Henry Phillpotts, later Bishop of Exeter. Like Copleston and many other contemporaries, he deplored the confusion of humanity and sympathy with legalized relief. But as a strict Durham magistrate, he felt little kindness or confidence in the 'dangerous rabble' who had constantly to be restrained by a strict enforcement of all laws. In an open *Letter to Sturges Bourne* during the discussion of the Poor Law revision in 1819, Phillpotts boldly proclaimed:

> Upon the whole, unfashionable as the doctrine may be, I am not ashamed to avow my conviction, that infinitely greater mischief continues to arise to the community at large, and especially to the poor themselves, from the humanity, than from the hard-heartedness of those with whom they have to do.[1]

Although he welcomed the mounting sentiment for a harsh administration of the Poor Law, he agreed with Copleston that it would be unwise to alter it very much. But unlike his friend, Phillpotts did not argue in terms of utility. He was no political economist; he profoundly disliked their ideas. Nor did he protest from any sense of Christian charity or compassion—Phillpotts rarely felt compassion for anyone—but out of a fear of the changing social and economic structure of the country which he believed political economy encouraged, and which he found utterly repugnant throughout his long life. As one of the fiercest, unregenerate Eldonite old Tory churchmen of the nineteenth century, Phillpotts, who married a favorite niece of the reactionary Lord Chancellor, never ceased his lamentations about the sorry course of labor

[1] H. Phillpotts, *A Letter to the Right Honourable William Sturges Bourne, M.P., on a Bill Introduced by Him Into Parliament, ' To Amend the Laws Respecting the Settlement of the Poor'* (Durham, 1819), 24.

migration, urbanization and industrialization. Consequently when Bourne proposed to allow paupers to establish parochial residence for purposes of relief after only three to five years in a location, Phillpotts bore down on what was to him a dangerous encouragement to labor circulation. Instead he demanded a rigorous enforcement of the existing statute requiring a person be relieved only in his natal parish. If people were allowed to establish new residences, society would remain in a constant state of flux. There would be an even greater emigration of agricultural laborers to the towns, 'a mischief of which it is hard to say, whether it be more formidable to the morals and happiness of the people, or to the peace and security of the State'. Well aware of census returns, the Durham cleric was troubled by the contrast between urban and rural population expansion; 'already it is not an uncommon thing for rural laborers to live in the adjacent towns; and never can this take place without injury to those characteristic excellences which were wont to distinguish the English peasant'.[1]

A revised Poor Law, he warned, would accelerate the trend, and the towns would welcome the influx. Phillpotts calculated that the farmer, deeply concerned with the parish, was also concerned with each pauper and the cost of relieving him. But the citizen was not similarly involved, as the cost of each new burden was spread over so many citizens, he was not aware of it, and was less determined to curtail unnecessary relief. Country people, after all, were very cautious about increasing rates, and were reluctant to build cottages for the poor in their parishes. City employers, however, welcomed inexpensive surplus labor, while speculators derived great profits from the rental of tenements. The result, of course, was the rapid weakening of the traditional and necessary bonds of English society.

> The lower orders of our countrymen will be forced to herd together in towns still more completely than at present, out of the reach of that kindly intercourse with their superiors, which ought to elevate and improve the characters of both parties. What little yet remains of the connexion of the country gentlemen with a respectful and attached peasantry will be sacrificed to a low and sordid calculation of the profit to be derived from a transfer of the burthen of their relief; it will be succeeded by a selfish and retired luxury on one side, and the turbulence and lawless violence of lazaroni on the other.[2]

Phillpotts found it incredible that the government would encourage such developments by permitting the poor to qualify for assistance elsewhere than their home parishes. Social connections were disrupted and individual independence discouraged. Furthermore he could see nothing inhumane about driving paupers back to their birthplace after they had lived elsewhere for years. Sentimental descriptions of old and friendless

[1] *Ibid.*, 20. [2] *Ibid.*, 21–22.

people being sent to workhouses in a parish they hardly knew, and under the direction of a cruel overseer who resented their return, did not move the future bishop. Actually, he countered, most overseers had long violated the law and sent relief to other parishes to prevent a pauper from returning home. That was an abuse which, like so many abuses, originated in thoughtless compassion. Country parishes thereby rid themselves of many poor residents, 'and thus largely contributed to people the suburbs of all our principal towns with a squalid, half-fed, unemployed, and profligate rabble'.[1]

Society and the poor would benefit by a return to a strict workhouse system, as Copleston proposed, provided it was not weakened by tender sensibilities which prevented people from being separated from their families and friends. Sympathy, Phillpotts believed, would be misplaced in such cases, as it would be if the complaints of soldiers whose subsistence depended upon a willingness to be separated from their families and die in remote garrisons were taken seriously. Why, he asked, should the poor be any exception?[2]

His fear and antipathy towards the towns led to Phillpotts closing his mind to recurrent suggestions that urban areas should be taxed as part of a wider system of county relief. Though he was aware that much of the pressure for revising the Poor Law resulted from manufacturing towns not providing for paupers, but sending them back to their old parishes when aged or infirm, Phillpotts still did not feel that the towns should be responsible. In reality, he argued, the towns, as a whole, did not benefit from the labor of the poor; only a few individuals profited, and they were not assessed on the basis of their profits in any event. Also, he doubted if the towns really gained very much from increased property values, greater trade and expanded consumption. Since the workers were only paid subsistence wages, they purchased few consumer goods and did not encourage increased production.[3]

These conclusions were derived more from Phillpotts's contempt of urban growth than from a serious analysis of town economics. If the towns became an important source of poor relief, he feared they would draw even more agricultural laborers into a new and fragmented society beyond the control of the landed gentry. Difficulties would only be compounded, he continued with some perception, because most of the wealthy factory-owners and tradesmen lived in different parishes away from the poor where the levies on their landed property were relatively light. If the rates were extended to the towns, was it not likely they would fall heaviest on the poorest parishes where the inhabitants were least able to afford them? Was it not also likely that it would create even greater tensions in those smouldering districts? Curwen's plan to tax all forms of wealth, rather than just landed property, 'might be fair, if it were

[1] *Ibid.*, 23. [2] *Ibid.*, 24–25. [3] *Ibid.*, 15–17.

practicable', he told Bourne, 'but . . . there are such great difficulties in the way of any such tax, so many sound reasons of policy against it, that no prudent legislature would venture on the experiment'.[1] As for Copleston's recommendation to Peel that a county-wide rate be collected to assist the urban poor, Phillpotts dismissed it with the flimsy warning it would only encourage excessive expenditure by local officials and make things even worse.[2]

Grumble though he did about a manufacturing system that allowed a few men to get rich on the labor of thousands of poor factory workers without having any responsibility to provide for them when they became old or unemployed, the conservative parson refused to permit industrialists the same obligations as the squirearchy; that would have given them a permanence and respectability he preferred not to contemplate. He frankly wished that agricultural laborers would stay on the farms, and hoped that those who had already left for the towns would, even in quest of relief, return. While reluctantly conceding that urban growth was perhaps unavoidable in the progress of human affairs, he did not have to like it, and hoped it could be delayed as long as possible.

The expanding towns not only disrupted ancient social relationships, they also threatened the Church with a social structure that allowed 'the most numerous and the most ignorant part of the people' to be removed from the reach of religious instruction and communication with their spiritual guides.[3] That those guides might have to follow after and provide critical directions to the laboring masses accumulating rapidly in urban areas, was a concept of pastoral duty which Phillpotts and many of his brethren were slow to adopt. The Anglican Church, as they conceived of it and loved it, was never meant for that new world. Phillpotts believed much of the recent criticism of the Establishment came from the towns, and was encouraged by sentimental and clever overseers who permitted the poor to congregate in manufacturing areas. A return to stringent residence requirements, he hoped, would slow down and even possibly reverse the social tendencies of recent years. A revision of the ancient Poor Law in any other direction was but another fateful step along the treacherous path towards the unknown. Phillpotts strongly opposed taking it while a Durham clergyman in 1819. He bitterly and tirelessly resisted when, as the Bishop of Exeter a decade and a half later, he was asked to consider it again.

There was more in the limited revisions of 1818–19 to please Phillpotts than there was to satisfy the more aggressive critics of the Poor Law. Without really altering the structure of relief, requirements were made more severe, and more extensive controls placed on distribution. Malthusians, such as William Otter, were disappointed, but knew the House of Commons with its present composition could not pass a

[1] *Ibid.*, 15–16.   [2] *Ibid.*, 19–20.   [3] *Ibid.*, 26.

measure at that time capable of reconciling all opinions. This being the case, there was nothing more to be done than to try to educate the poor to Burke's formula of 'Patience, Labour, Frugality, and Religion'. Malthus had himself come to accept that the only real remedy for poverty lay in 'the prudence and foresight of the labouring classes'. Only then, Otter predicted, would the poor stop their 'canting lamentation' about their condition, and an end be made to the threat that 'the present generation of paupers will be succeeded by another still more destitute, and more reckless of their posterity'.[1]

Not only was it necessary to educate the lower orders to the truths of economic redemption that would come from the virtues of thrift and family planning, but they had to be provided with an opportunity for exercising them. Malthus, Samuel Whitbread, Patrick Colquhoun and Sir Thomas Bernard had all seen the value of savings banks and associations for the poor, and clerical economists also shared their vision. Sumner was an early supporter, but realized that great commercial establishments could not be bothered with small accounts and that the proliferating county banks were unreliable. Local benefactors were urged to establish savings banks for the poor, and guarantee them through investing boards of trustees. Sumner calculated that if the poor were guaranteed a 5 per cent return on their money, they would welcome the opportunity. This would in time relieve the rates from all burdens except those created by orphans, the abandoned, and the genuinely destitute.[2]

Copleston also thought savings banks were a fine idea, but cautioned against supporting mutual-aid societies as well among the poor, since it was unnatural to expect a poor man to save for another. Savings banks were more in tune with human nature, and the individual motivation of enlightened self-interest. If the poor man could be taught to see that simple truth, the possibilities of improvement were striking. 'The more unrestrained power of withdrawing his deposit invests him with the character of a proprietor, and tends to nurture all those qualities which naturally spring from the possession of property—prudence, frugality, self-respect, dread of mendicity and dependence'.[3] Clerical, utilitarian hearts beat faster at the exciting prospects concocted. Working couples would delay marrying while conscientiously building up their individual savings accounts, and would then be in the position of collectively warding off impoverishment and providing for their children in much greater security.[4] George Davys, the young Victoria's tutor, who was eventually rewarded with the See of Peterborough (1839–64), treated the subject on a different level in one of his many pious tales for

---

[1] Otter, *Sermon* (1820), 11–12.   [2] Sumner, *Treatise*, II, 304–7.
[3] Copleston, *Second Letter*, 104–5.
[4] Otter, *Sermon* (1818), 36–37; Sumner, *Treatise*, 317.

the poor.[1] Prosperous 'Will Wise' explained to his old friend, the perpetually indigent 'Ralph Ragged', how, after abandoning the pub seven years before, he saved four shillings a week until he accumulated nearly ninety pounds. In time he met, courted (for several years), and eventually married good 'Mary Manage', a woman of similar prudence who, over the years, saved an additional sixty pounds. The Wise family lived happily ever after in simple security.[2] It was clearly a marriage made in a Malthusian heaven.

Even Edward Maltby, who in sermon after sermon described the poor as susceptible to 'idleness and dishonesty' as if they were generic characteristics, saw a ray of hope in both savings banks and mutual-benefit societies. He envisaged the day when 'healthy and robust men' would no longer 'upon the first appearance of distress . . . fling aside the rugged and manly independence of their forefathers, and without a scruple and without a blush, throw themselves upon the bounty of the parish'.[3] Clergymen were increasingly urged to extend the scope of their social instruction to the poor. It was no longer enough simply to preach the passive virtues of patience and contentment to the lower orders; the ministry was also to become an agency for economic activism as they educated their less fortunate parishioners in the truths of enlightened economic self-interest. Preaching in support of the Buckden Amiable Society in 1819, Maltby cautioned the poor man to 'take care that no one receives injury through his idleness, his intemperate pleasures, or his dishonesty'. All classes must be just, he concluded, and the poor were unjust when improvident. Unless they took advantage of the economic opportunities provided them the entire community suffers.[4] Otter, who early established a savings and sickness institution in one of his parishes, poured forth Scriptural injunctions to alert the laborers to their newfound advantages. Exhorting from Proverbs to 'drink the waters of our own cistern, and of the rivers that run out of the midst of our own well' he interpreted it to mean 'we are to depend upon our own exertions and resources and not upon the labours of other men'. Furthermore, if the pauper would but study the example of Christ, and the teachings of St

---

[1] George Davys (1780–1864), a simple, undistinguished clergyman, safe enough to have tutored the young Victoria for fifteen years. Was rewarded with various preferments, including the deanery of Chester (1831) and, though a Tory, with the See of Peterborough. Melbourne was not happy. He was a likeable prelate who steadily promoted his relatives to cathedral stalls and voted against the Whigs. See Chadwick, *Victorian Church*, 159–61.

[2] G. Davys, *The Savings Bank, A Dialogue Between Ralph Ragged and Will Wise* (n.d.).

[3] Maltby, 'Sermon X' (1819), in *Sermons*, I, 186–7.

[4] *Ibid.*, 179–81.

Paul, 'it is scarcely credible that [he] would willingly forfeit his character and his hope as a Christian, and barter the conscious worth of honest, independent Industry, for the sense of a degrading dependence upon Parish Relief'.[1]

Since industry was not always sufficiently rewarded to protect a large family against the 'miseries of want', frugality was just as important. Otter was unable to come up with any precise quotations exhorting the poor to save for a rainy day, but was confident such prudence was 'implied' in all Scriptural references to work. Unfortunately there was no positive equivalent to St Paul's dictum, 'that if any man would not work, neither should he eat!' The closest lesson Otter could find, and even he admitted he was stretching things somewhat, was the exhortation to Timothy, 'If any provide not for his own, and especially those of his own house, he hath denied the faith, and is worse than an infidel'.[2] To interpret that as an endorsement of savings banks and mutual-benefit associations required remarkable confidence in the compatibility of the Gospels and treatises on political economy. Otter had that confidence, as did many of his brethren who were within a few years of reaching the influential summit of ecclesiastical leadership.

3. CRITICISM AND INNOVATION

As the disturbances and fears of revolution prompted by economic dislocation receded before the prosperity of the 1820's, Church leaders were less inclined to contribute to the general discussion of poverty and poor relief. For one thing the issue seemed less pressing than in the confused and troubled years after Waterloo, and it took a great deal of stimulation to arouse Anglican ministers to take a position on social issues. Furthermore, theorizing about social problems took second place to the practical extension of Church and educational facilities which, if unable to alter the economic condition of the lower orders, could at least explain the necessary reasons for it, and provide that spiritual comfort which guaranteed contentment. Even the short-lived economic crisis of 1825, which led to the collapse of several banks and a severe recession in the cotton industry, failed to revive the frantic atmosphere of 1816 or 1819. The economic impact tended to be regional, and the strikes, riots and machine-breaking in Lancashire and elsewhere by unemployed weavers lacked the political overtones of earlier unrest. In general, the causes were recognized to be economic rather than ideological, and the widespread use of charity to meet temporary needs met with little criticism even from those who a few years before

---

[1] Otter, *Sermon* (1818), 20–22.
[2] *Ibid.*, 26–27.

149

warned that it would produce 'nothing but a beggarly and miserable population'.[1]

Charles James Blomfield, Bishop of Chester since 1824, shared those sentiments, but agreed in 1826 to be chairman of a committee to administer relief to the distressed weavers in his diocese and at Spitalfields.[2] The King donated £1,000, and another £3,750 was raised at a charity ball at Covent Garden. Drawing upon these and other contributions, Blomfield and his committee opened relief offices in February and distributed the funds to thousands of impoverished weavers. He was appalled by the suffering of the Spitalfields silk-weavers displaced by mechanization and the abolition of protective duties and, in spite of strong *laissez-faire* beliefs, vainly urged Peel at the Home Office to seek artificial support from the legislature.[3] Blomfield soon recovered from his brief lapse into sentimental expediency, and two years later, as the new Bishop of London (1828–56), he repudiated the whole idea of charitable collections for temporary relief. His experience with the weavers and the poor in general convinced him the money was wasted and little permanent good accomplished. Rather than continue to launch annual appeals to raise funds to assist the London poor through the winter, Blomfield convinced Peel that the money could be utilized more effectively if applied to the construction of new churches in populous areas.[4] The bishop, who was himself a generous and beneficent clergyman, was of course not opposed to charity as such. What troubled him was the regularity of assistance and expectation. When individually or thoughtlessly distributed, charity was self-perpetuating. As the leading clerical

---

[1] W. V. Vernon, *A Sermon Preached at the Musical Meeting For the Benefit of the Derbyshire General Infirmary . . . October VIII, MDCCCXXII* (York, 1822), 9, 13. Vernon, a York prebendary, was the son of Archbishop Vernon-Harcourt.

[2] C. J. Blomfield (1786–1857), son of a Bury St Edmunds schoolmaster, a prize-winning classicist at Cambridge, where he was so tense and studious that he developed digestive problems. Owed his early preferment to Lord Bristol, a family friend, was non-resident, and tutored noblemen's children. Met Lord Spencer this way, who also supported his ambitions, and added to his pluralistic holdings. Nevertheless was an active parochial clergyman, Archdeacon of Colchester (1822), Bishop of Chester (1824) and London (1828). Blomfield, though never very popular, was the most powerful bishop of his day. A leader of Church reform and a strong figure in Parliament, his influence was considerable. Resigned in 1856 and died soon after. See A. Blomfield, ed., *A Memoir of Charles James Blomfield . . .* 2 vols. (1863). For his role in Parliament see Brose, *Church and Parliament*.

[3] P.R.O., H.O. 43/36.

[4] *Ibid.*, 44/18. In a letter of 23 Dec. 1828, Peel informed the Lord Mayor of London that the annual appeal for winter relief funds would cease, as would the traditional royal letter launching the campaign. *Ibid.*, 115/1.

architect of Church reform and extension, Blomfield was certain that donations funneled into schools and churches would have a lasting effect upon the amelioration of the poverty of the next generation, if not the present one.

The Bishop of London's cautious sniping at the ineffectiveness of perpetual relief was reflective of a gradual reassertion of clerical criticism in the closing years of the decade. It was in part prompted by the growing competition for funds to finance the accelerating extension of the reinvigorated Church. The generosity of the rich was not without its limitations, and ecclesiastical leaders feared that continued appeals and enlargement of charitable relief could only be at the expense of new churches and schools. Blomfield's predecessor, the new archbishop, William Howley, had warned his clergy for years not to put too much pressure on public charity, for 'by attempting too much we may lose all'.[1] Like most of the bench he presided over, the archbishop believed that the expansion of Church institutions to cope with the enlarged population should receive top priority. But Blomfield was fast becoming the real power in the Establishment, and he, like many of his episcopal generation, had been well educated in the utilitarian criticism of poverty. As they moved into positions of influence, the lines of argument in terms of political economy had already been established. To give them even more meaning, several bishops were able to hold out the added inducement of a vigorous and reviving national Church prepared to educate the poor to prudence and self-reliance once they were weaned from their dependence upon the soured milk of indiscriminate charity and perpetual relief.

Many clergymen resisted the shift in the Church's attitude towards poverty. The old Rector of Bishop Wearmouth, Robert Gray, on the eve of his elevation to the See of Bristol in 1827, was especially disturbed by the reviving attacks on poor relief. A former Bampton lecturer (1796) and a conscientious parochial minister for twenty-two years, Gray had little understanding or sympathy for new-fangled notions of poverty and poor relief. As far as he was concerned, the care of the poor was and always had been a parochial problem that should be faced at the local level by utilizing whatever expedient measures helped the unfortunate. He had opposed the more stringent Poor Law proposals of 1818–19, and disliked the continuing pressure for an extension of the workhouse system. Essentially an eighteenth-century Tory parson deeply suspicious of centralization, Gray warned that the workhouses were a step towards oppression. Poor relief was a Christian and an individual act best administered in the houses of those who needed it. If, as some of his younger colleagues complained, the poor would not save for periods of distress, it had always been so. Nevertheless the

[1] Howley, *Letter Book*, Lamb. Pal., 31.

obligation to assist them was religious and enduring. Moreover it should never be forgotten that relief was 'most gratefully received' within the parish where 'the connexions of life are least broken and dissevered'.[1]

Poor old Gray, elevated to the bench at the late age of sixty-five, reluctant to leave his quiet parish, was thrust into an era of breaking connections. He was to die seven years later, in 1834, with his palace burned to the ground by Reform Bill rioters, the Irish Church 'looted', a savage, centralizing Poor Law enacted, and cries of disestablishment in his ears. They were hard times for eighteenth-century Tory bishops and Gray's last days would have been more comfortable had he bowed out a bit earlier. Yet some of his generation, such as Howley, four years younger, and George Henry Law, a year older, had already been on the bench for several years, and were to live on well into the 1840's. They were, however, more flexible, and if they could not really believe many of the ideas of their younger brethren, they at least recognized the importance of their arguments, and, when possible, compromised. Their criticism of poor relief or the Poor Law was not a result of some newly conceived appreciation of the truths of political economy; it was instead inspired by a gnawing fear of the disintegration of the most traditional and essential social relationships.

Bishop Law first confronted the problem when translated from Chester to the agricultural diocese of Bath and Wells in 1824.[2] In 1828, after having visited nearly every parish in his diocese, Law sadly concluded that the Poor Laws 'have torn asunder the sacred ties of social and domestic life'. He was dismayed that the dependence of agricultural laborers upon the parish rates had literally become a way of life in many parts of the south and south-west. Parents were simply unable to support themselves from the wages of their own labor, and had come to accept the inevitability of their children being similarly assisted. 'The children, on their part, supported by eleemosynary contributions, lose the benefit of that paternal superintendance, of that maternal love, which no other substitute can ever adequately supply.'[3] He had never seen anything like it in Carlisle, where his father had been bishop, nor had such a blight

[1] R. Gray, *A Sermon Preached at Bishopwearmouth, On Sunday 11 March 1827, On Occasion of the Resignation of the Rectory of That Parish* (Sunderland, 1827), 10–11.

[2] G. H. Law (1761–1845), son of Bishop Edmund Law of Carlisle (1769–87) and brother of Lord Chief Justice Ellenborough. An active, pious clergyman, Law was nevertheless extremely cool to the Church reforms of the period.

[3] G. H. Law, *The Spiritual Duties of a Christian Minister. A Charge Delivered to the Clergy of the Diocese of Bath and Wells . . . in July, 1828* (Wells, 1828), 25–26.

infected his huge diocese of Chester. Yet it was now clear to the worried prelate that any institution, no matter how long established, that corrupted the most natural familial relationships must be seriously defective.

Law worried about the harm done to the family; other clergy feared for the necessary relationships between superior and inferior classes. Samuel Butler (1774–1839), Headmaster of Shrewsbury School, Archdeacon of Derby, and later Bishop of Lichfield (1836–9), unmoved by the misery of the laboring poor, complained that institutionalized relief minimized the effective control that benefactors had over recipients of charity. The dispensation of aid was an important means of maintaining 'kindly feelings' between classes, as well as an essential control by which the higher orders expressed approval or disapproval of the individual behavior of the poor. 'But when the principal stream of charity runs in wider channels, and is swallowed up in great and distant societies . . . the feelings of real charity are liable to be absorbed in the vortex of speculative, and sometimes abortive benevolence.' Butler, a Whig, like many Tory-clerical defenders of rural parochial society, distrusted the proliferation and expansion of voluntary charitable societies, almost as much as he did the extended costs and structure of the Poor Law. Both tended towards the same end: the destruction of the 'moral effect' of charity, beneficial to giver and receiver, and the 'social effect', necessary to the preservation of a hierarchical society. Charity, as always, must begin at home, he maintained, and excessive 'sentimentality' was as damaging to that fundamental principle as was the legalistic institutionalizing of assistance.[1]

Butler could hardly be accused of being excessively sentimental about the poor: he tried to think about them as little as possible, since he found the subject unpleasant. John Bird Sumner, however, thought about them a great deal, and as he did, grew less confident that their wretchedness could really be alleviated by the implementation of the laws of political economy any more than by the futile, self-perpetuating Poor Laws. In 1820 he was still hopeful that the clergy could prepare the children of the lower classes for the sufferings that lay ahead during their state of trial, while at the same time inculcate the utilitarian principles of prudence, restraint, thrift and foresight.[2] Six years later in a study of the *Evidence of Christianity*, Summer considerably tempered his optimism and reflected that perhaps all the clergy could really do for the poor was 'soften the roughest, and sweeten the bitterest, and exalt the humblest of human labours . . .'. In contrast to the *Records of Creation*,

[1] S. Butler, *A Charge Delivered to the Clergy of the Archdeaconry of Derby . . . June 18 and 19, 1829* (1829), 10–11.

[2] J. B. Sumner, *The Encouragements of the Christian Minister. A Sermon Preached . . . August 22, 1820* (1820), 6–7.

published ten years earlier, the *Evidence of Christianity* was much more restrained about the possibilities of improving the condition of the bulk of the population, and much more spiritual in emphasis. Life for most people would remain 'inevitably poor and laborious', perpetuated from generation to generation. Only the gentle beauties of faith could provide relief and dignify 'the lowest stations and the meanest pursuits'.[1] There was no corresponding comfort to be found now in the poor's comprehension of the natural laws of economic self-interest.

After succeeding Blomfield to the See of Chester in 1828, and surveying the huge manufacturing diocese, Sumner's growing pessimism was, if anything, reinforced. During his primary visitation in 1829 he offered the disheartening prognosis:

> Circumstances are at work in every part of this country, not more affecting its manufacturing than its agricultural population, which leave little to expect for a large proportion of its inhabitants except hardships and difficulties. . . .[2]

The new bishop no longer spoke of an 'effectual remedy', as he had in younger days. There were only opportunities for ministers to 'affect the heart of a poor man' by the principles and faith of the Gospels and prevent him from eternalizing his inevitable earthly suffering by the commission of sin. This did not mean reconciling him to the principles of Malthus and Ricardo, but 'to hardships and privations, as the intended trial of his faith, the lot of many of God's most approved servants'.[3] Although Sumner was particularly dismayed by the rioting and machine-breaking by unemployed hand-loom weavers in several of the manufacturing towns of his diocese, his gloomy fatalism preceded his elevation to the bench, and, if anything, deepened over the next decade. In spite of tireless efforts to cope with the rapid increase of population and the social effects of industrialization, the prelate was repeatedly plagued by an overwhelming sense of futility that did not begin to wane for many years.

Other members of the bench, certain that the revived Church had a more vigorous role to play, felt that wise policies, encouraged by an active national clergy, could certainly improve the state of things. The outbreak of disturbances in agricultural districts in 1830 quickly revived the whole issue of poor relief. As laborers, under the leadership of 'Captain Ludd's' imaginary successor, 'Captain Swing', smashed threshing machines, burned mills and terrorized the countryside in

[1] J. B. Sumner, *The Evidence of Christianity, Derived From Its Nature and Reception*, 2nd ed. (1826), 404–6. This work went through seven editions in Sumner's lifetime.

[2] J. B. Sumner, *A Charge Delivered to the Clergy of the Diocese of Chester . . . in August and September, MDCCCXXIX* (1829), 26–27.

[3] *Ibid.*, 19–20.

sixteen southern and eastern counties, the revolution across the Channel took on ominous proportions. With the Continent in flames once more, and the French monarch in exile, anxious Englishmen readily imagined what inspired their laborers to threaten farmers, clergymen, and the overseers of the Poor Law. The disturbances were in fact comparatively mild, but they certainly stirred up the most alarming memories. When coupled to the great agitation following the failure of the Reform Bill the next year, and its passage the year after, it is not surprising that propertied people whose lives had largely been spent in an atmosphere of war, revolution and social instability were haunted by all sorts of woeful precedents. Clergy and laity alike knew that something had to be done about the poor. The question could be avoided no longer.

Bishop Law, usually a mild and compliant Tory prelate, lashed out at Wellington's late government, in which his brother, Lord Ellenborough, had been a member, for neglecting the agricultural laborers in spite of many warnings he and others had given. Perhaps also distressed by Whig victories in the election of 1830, he claimed that rioting, agitation, ferment and terror could have been avoided by the defeated government, 'by enquiry, by timely concession, and a due regard to the real sufferings of the poor'.[1] Earlier in the year he had described the abysmal life led by the laboring classes in his diocese, where men were yoked together like oxen to haul coal. Grateful though he was that they bore such degradation with Christian patience, Law doubted they would do so indefinitely.[2] He repeatedly presented petitions to Parliament, 'the father of the poor', cataloguing the misery its suffering children endured with 'heroic fortitude', but could not get the government to act.[3]

The poor, as was inevitable, had finally acted instead. Law was reluctant to grant concessions while being threatened by rioting laborers, but he hoped their real needs were now apparent, and that remedial measures would be forthcoming as soon as possible.[4] It seemed to the old bishop that the causes of misery could be isolated and at least partially corrected. Overpopulation, a decline in agricultural exports, enclosures, and the consolidation of small farms had combined to drive thousands of people to relief tables.[5] Even where employment was available, the laborer was so inadequately paid that it was expected he would need supplementary assistance. But it was not the poor who were at fault; they had not corrupted the ancient Poor Law. Law charged the upper

[1] G. H. Law, *Remarks On the Present Distresses of the Poor* (Wells, 1830), 24.

[2] *Hansard*, XXII (1830), 1003–4.

[3] *Ibid.*, XXIII (1830), 1121–2; also Law's *A Pastoral Letter On the Present Aspect of the Times, Addressed to the Clergy, the Gentry, and Inhabitants of the Diocese of Bath and Wells* (Wells, 1831), 11.

[4] Law, *Remarks*, 25.   [5] *Ibid.*, 8–9.

classes with destroying the feelings of mutual interdependency by forgetting 'the poor man is as necessary, and as important to the rich man, as the rich man can be to the poor. The land is of no use to one, without the cultivation of the other'.[1]

Society, Law reminded the rich, is a coherent whole involving a diversity of ranks and stations, with relative duties and rights. Protection and employment were a specific responsibility of the higher orders as manual labor was the assigned function of the lower. Any disruption of that careful balance threatened the peace and stability of society. Although the scales had been tipped against the poor in recent years, it was the result of fluctuating variables that could be minimized by the efforts of the rich. But, in fact, the upper classes had abrogated their responsibilities and deprived the laboring poor of employment and a fair wage. Bishop Law knew little political economy. Ricardo and all the theories about natural wages were irrelevant to him. He was concerned with divine stewardship, not with scientific calculations of profit and loss.

> We are called upon therefore, by every principle of humanity and justice, to reverse, in this respect, the present order of things: to pay the labourer that which he fairly earns, and to pay it to him as his right, and as his due. Thus shall we secure the willing and effectual services of the labouring classes of the community, and remove from their minds, every ground of discontent and murmuring.[2]

So long as the poor were denied their rights, derived as they were from the natural structure of society, there would be disharmony and turbulence. Law was disturbed that many people viewed employment and a sufficient wage as a privilege derived from natural competition. This contradicted all revealed and rational evidence that proved that the lower classes were expected to perform manual labor. Not to provide them an opportunity to do so, and reward them sufficiently, was unnatural and un-Christian.

Law predicted, 'when ... the laborer is adequately paid; then and not till then, the source of our present evils will be eradicated, and the face of content will, again, illumine the cottage ... '.[3] The alternative was demonstrated by the violence of 1830. If Great Britain was to retain power and influence; if she wished to avert the horrors of disaffection, and turbulence, she must procure sufficient employment, and pay, for an increased and increasing population. By granting them they would be received by the lower classes as a great boon. 'It is therefore the part of wisdom ... not [to] wait till it be demanded as a right. ...'[4]

When Edward Copleston, who had been elevated to the See of Llandaff the previous year (1829), pleaded for higher wages ten years earlier during the disturbances of 1819 it had been a sudden expediency,

---

[1] *Ibid.*, 11.   [2] *Ibid.*   [3] *Ibid.*, 19.   [4] *Ibid.*, 12.

almost an afterthought, and contrary to his belief in Ricardian economics. The venerable Bishop of Bath and Wells had no such limitation upon him. Still very much a product of the eighteenth century, he argued in terms of natural harmony and rational coherence complementing the revealed laws of Scripture. Utilitarian ideas of individual self-interest were only viewed as socially integral, not personally and materially exclusive. Man, for Law, was always a social rather than an economic being, and any consideration of his welfare had to be seen in those terms. Equitable wages were, for him, the most direct way of restoring social harmony. But he also recommended providing the poor with a small piece of land as a means of reviving their sense of independence and responsibility as well as helping them through periodic hard times.[1] If the amount of land was kept small, in proportion to the size of the laborer's family, it would help inculcate the values and virtues of the propertied classes without really interfering with the necessary gradations and functions of the various orders.

The redeeming value of a little plot of land was often on the mind of social theorists and reformers in the early nineteenth century. Arthur Young in 1800 urged that every laborer who was the father of three or more children be given half an acre for planting potatoes, and enough grass to feed two cows.[2] Agricultural allotments and agrarian communities, ranging from the utopian schemes of a Charles Fourier to the elaborate constructs of Villeneuve-Bargemont based upon experiments in the Netherlands, were much in evidence in England and on the Continent.[3] Even Archbishop Manners–Sutton in 1817 briefly flirted with Robert Owen's plan to put the poor into 'Villages of Co-operation', where, after an initial capital grant from taxes, they would pay their own way while becoming useful, industrious, self-disciplined and temperate.[4]

Copleston in 1819 was strongly opposed to the various agricultural allotment plans being circulated; if the poor were provided with land even at minimal rental, it would become 'a sort of outdoor workhouse', and would not have the necessary effect upon teaching them to save. Since it was likely that the allotted land would only be cultivated in seasons of distress, there would be 'a positive deduction from the national wealth at all other times'. Of equal concern, however, was the

[1] *Hansard*, XXII (1830), 1003–4; also *Remarks*, 13–17.

[2] A. Young, *The Question of Scarcity Plainly Stated and Remedies Considered. With Observations on Permanent Measures to Keep Wheat at a More Regular Price* (1800).

[3] Jean Paul Alban de Villeneuve-Bargemont, *Économie Politique Chrétienne, ou Recherche sur la Nature et les Causes du Paupérisme, en France et en Europe, et sur les Moyens de le Soulager et de le Prévenir* (Brussels, 1837), 595 ff.

[4] Thompson, *English Working Class*, 782.

likelihood that agricultural allotments would seemingly recognize and sanction a class of poor as permanent, and 'possessed of positive rights and interests in their corporate capacity—an error which naturally arises out of the certainty that there will always be poor in the land'. The teachings of the Gospel were never meant to be interpreted as justifications for interfering with the natural regulation of the economy. The poor, after all, usually compromise nothing more than 'the aggregate of individuals, who from time to time may have lost their station as competent members of society'.

> They have no *political* relation whatever—they are essentially dependent upon the *charity* of others—and they should not be taught to expect any legal rights or exclusive advantage arising out of that situation. By the nature of things theirs is a lower condition than any employment however menial—and it is an inversion of the order of things to make it the title to privileges of any kind.[1]

Bishop Law strongly disagreed with such arguments both from experience and outlook. Class relationships for him were still governed by rural Christian concepts of paternalistic responsibility, *noblesse oblige* and reciprocal gratitude, rather than by iron laws of competitive self-interest and *laissez-faire* theories which abrogated the natural role of the various ranks in society. The new ideas of political economy were 'alarming symptoms of the present day', in which 'we cannot but observe and lament, that the strong tie which had for ages bound together the Clergyman, and his Parishioners, the Landlord and his Tenants, by a sense of benefits mutually conferred and received, appears now to be inauspiciously weakened, if not entirely rent and torn asunder'.[2] For nearly thirty years he had tried to preserve that tie, and had rented small pieces of land to the laboring poor. It provided them with resources corresponding to the size of their families, kept them busy and out of the pubs, and encouraged a profitable utilization of leisure time.[3] Having extended the practice to his new diocese he claimed to have rented to over two hundred tenants at Wells, not one of whom had been in trouble with the law, and only two of whom, both aged, received any parochial assistance. Law not only believed the legislature should adopt the plan, but urged the clergy to attach the poor more closely to the Church by providing them with small parcels of land. Anticipating a battle over tithes, the persistent prelate even recommended they be commuted to land for the poor.[4]

[1] Copleston, *Second Letter*, 99–100.
[2] G. H. Law, *A Charge Delivered to the Clergy of the Diocese of Bath and Wells . . . May and June 1831* (Wells, 1831), 19.
[3] Law, *Remarks*, 13–17; *Hansard*, X (1832), 128.
[4] G. H. Law, *Reflections Upon Tithes, With a Plan For a General Commutation of the Same*, 2nd ed. (Wells, 1832), 23–24.

Basically, however, old Law spoke for those who feared and lamented the disintegration of pre-industrial England. His allotment plan was partially designed to keep the surplus poor from migrating to the great towns. He joined with Henry Phillpotts and others in deploring the multitudes of agricultural laborers who were daily flocking to the manufacturing and mining districts, carrying away in their pitiful little sacks, not only their meager belongings, but a way of life in which the landed rich at least found much comfort. Hopefully, the bishop believed that if wages could be raised, and 'if by the blessing of God, each poor man be enabled to occupy his rood of land, a larger population may be provided with the means of sustenance, and England may again be blessed with a people, virtuous, contented and happy'.[1] Population growth was something to be welcomed, not feared. If some of his younger brethren cared to quote Malthus's *Essay on Population*, Law was prepared to rebut them with older and more reliable quotations from William Paley's *Moral Philosophy*. Though it certainly dated him, the Bishop still found more comfort and truth in Paley's lesson that 'the object, at which every statesman should aim, as the greatest benefit to his country, is not the diminution, but the increase of population . . .'.[2] It was not, however, eighteenth-century moral philosophy, but nineteenth-century political economy that triumphed in the composition of the Poor Law Enquiry Commission of 1832, and in the severe Poor Law Amendment Act of 1834.

[1] Law, *Charge* (1831), 18.
[2] W. Paley, *The Principles of Moral and Political Philosophy* (1786), Bk. VI, Chap. XI; Law, *Remarks*, 7–8.

V

The Poor Law Reformed

1. THE POOR LAW AMENDMENT ACT: 1832–34

Angered and frightened by the disturbances of the preceding two years, critics of the Poor Law in 1832 ascribed the demoralization of the laboring classes to the diverse and lax methods of implementing the requirements for relief. Despite the expenditure of more than seven million pounds, one-fifth of the nation's budget, little progress was evident, and the poor seemed as dangerous as ever. The cost of assistance had declined from the record eight million pounds disbursed in 1818, but it was gradually rising once more; this in spite of the puzzling fact that the price of bread had diminished by one-third over the previous decade. As contemporaries believed that there was a direct relationship between the price of bread and the cost of subsistence, suspicions and antagonisms about the administration and effectiveness of poor relief were greater than ever.

The rates were administered individually in the thousands of different parishes in the country, and reached recipients in numerous ways. Some magistrates employed the Speenhamland system; some required paupers to work on the roads; others utilized a labor rate system whereby rate-payers, on the basis of their real rental or property, hired a number of paupers, and still other parishes simply paid employers to hire the poor at fixed rates. Workhouses, where they existed, were populated by indigents, orphans and the able-bodied. This haphazard intermixing of the private natural economy with public works was particularly grating to the efficient, administrative sensibilities of Benthamite reformers. But even less doctrinaire critics agreed that there was something wrong with a system so inordinately expensive and usually administered by farmers and publicans who readily used the Poor Law to their own advantage. Although the Select Vestry Act of 1819 permitted greater administrative authority to those who paid the highest rates, only one-fifth of the parishes had adopted it, and the less wealthy parishioners continued to dominate the distribution of relief. Overriding all of the costs and complaints about administrative diversity was the obvious fact that the Poor Law, no matter how enforced, had again failed to do what it was above all expected to do—keep the laboring poor content in hard times.

The composition of the Poor Law Enquiry Commission, dominated as it was by such ardent political economists as the Malthusian, Sturges Bourne, and the Benthamite disciples, Nassau Senior and Edwin Chadwick, precluded much attention being paid to the homely suggestions of a Bishop Gray or the agricultural proposals of a Bishop Law. Significantly, the clerical appointments to the Commission, the chairman, Bishop Blomfield, and Bishop Sumner, were, with Nassau Senior, already convinced that the Poor Law should be abolished.[1] In testimony before the Emigration Committee in 1827, Blomfield had expressed his growing disillusionment with existing relief measures, and felt that a dramatic new approach should be taken.[2] Gradually, however, he, along with Sumner and the rest of the Commissioners, accepted Chadwick's practical argument that it was not possible at that time to abolish the Poor Law. Both prelates were persuaded to define the problem in Benthamite administrative terms, rather than as one of Malthusian economics. Chadwick's detailed investigation of Berkshire convinced the Commission that the Poor Law did not automatically increase surplus population, but instead decreased productivity by encouraging subsidized pauper labor to compete with independent workers.[3] Like Bentham and Mill, Chadwick accepted the premise that expanded productivity would readily accommodate a growing population.

By redefining the Poor Law as an administrative problem, rather than as a demographic or moral problem, the Commissioners concluded that if paupers could be forced to enter the free labor market or not interfere with it, there would not only be a drop in the rates, but an increase in productivity. In practice this meant making relief as unattractive as possible on the Benthamite 'less eligibility' principle that the

---

[1] See Sumner's article on the Poor Law in the 1824 ed. of the *Encyclopedia Britannica*; N. Senior, *Three Lectures on the Rate of Wages, Delivered Before the University of Oxford in Easter Term, 1830* (1831), v; also Senior's *A Letter to Lord Howick, On a Legal Provision for the Irish Poor; Commutation of Tithes, and a Provision for the Irish Roman Catholic Clergy* (1831). Senior called for an end to all relief for the able-bodied poor.

[2] Samuel Finer, *The Life and Times of Sir Edwin Chadwick* (1952), 44.

[3] *Ibid.*, 44–48.

pleasure-pain alternative would soon cause the poor to avoid the less attractive experience of rigorous workhouses, and take whatever steps were necessary to find gainful employment. Once paupers were off relief, employers would be able to employ in capital expansion the funds they previously paid in rates, which would in turn encourage greater production and wider prosperity.[1]

The Commission was prodded in this direction by the new Archbishop of Dublin, Richard Whately (1831–63).[2] As Senior's former tutor and later successor as Professor of Political Economy at Oxford (1829–31), Whately shared his belief in MacCulloch's theory of a fixed wages fund. Artificial subsidies could not alter the basic economic fact that there was only so much money available for wages, proportionate to the number of laborers, and it was ridiculous and futile to believe that wages could be arbitrarily raised so long as the number of laborers and the available wage fund remained unchanged.[3] Wages were derived from profits, Ricardo had shown, so until increased production created more employment and profits, nothing would really alleviate existing conditions. Whately agreed that the existing Poor Law seriously interfered with that increase by subsidizing unproductive labor, and withdrawing needed productive capital from the general economy. He was confident that if *laissez-faire* principles were applied, agricultural production would outstrip the geometric increase in population which was worrying his Malthusian contemporaries.[4]

Consequently Whately urged Senior and Chadwick to do everything possible in the rewriting of the Poor Law to discourage the indigent from seeking relief, and to minimize the costs of maintaining them at the expense of others. The archbishop suggested, among other things, that all paupers be tattooed on the foot or some other place so that if they were caught begging or seeking more relief, they could be punished as chronic burdens to society. Ever conscious of minimizing the costs of assistance, the thrifty prelate also added:

> Pray suggest, in your report on paupers, that any female receiving relief should have her hair cut off; it may seem trifling, but *hae nugae*, etc. . . . A

---

[1] *Ibid.*, 72–74.

[2] Richard Whately (1787–1863), son of a Hertfordshire clergyman, Fellow of Oriel College, where he was close friends with Keble and Newman. A strong Liberal, opposed to religious disabilities, he eventually broke with his old friends. Though a vigorous defender of education in Ireland, he was much too tolerant of Catholic sensibilities to be a very popular Protestant bishop. See E. J. Whately, *Life and Correspondence of Richard Whately*, 2 vols. (1866).

[3] Senior, *Three Lectures*, Lect. I.

[4] R. Whately, *Introductory Lectures on Political Economy*, 2 parts (Dublin, 1831–2).

good head of hair will fetch from 5s. to 10s., which would be perhaps a fortnight's maintenance. . . . Indirectly, the number who would exert themselves to save their hair is beyond belief. One of our maids is ill of a fever, and we have almost been driven to force to make her part with her hair, though her life is in danger. I am certain she would have cheerfully worked and fared hard for any length of time to save it.[1]

If the poor were to have their quaint little vanities, there was no reason not to turn them to advantage. One could waste no opportunity to promote the inculcation of virtuous habits and motives in such strange creatures. Whately took considerable pride in his refusal to give any alms to beggars on the streets. When distributing charity in his parish and at Oxford, he had never hesitated to have applicants searched, and made them turn their pockets inside out. Furthermore, as an active member of a Society for the Suppression of Mendicity, Whately had steadfastly denied help to any person who was unwashed or unshaven. No washing of the feet for that clergyman—'Breakfast or beard!' was his motto, and if some obstinate lout chose the latter it was clear that he was a professional beggar, or had something to hide.[2] That he might, like the poor servant girl terrified at the loss of her hair, have some pride, some crude dignity, was simply not conceivable. It was enough to make a utilitarian bishop wonder about the odd and perverted sense of pleasure-pain priorities preferred by the lower orders.

Whately, like so many of his clerical contemporaries, thought of himself as a charitable Christian, and proved it over the years by contributing to many relief societies in England and Ireland. During the terrible famine of 1846–9 he personally gave away nearly £8,000 while bitterly resisting the introduction of outdoor relief as likely to perpetuate the misery, and blaming the disaster on the extension since 1838 of the Poor Law into Ireland.[3] While distributing large sums from his private fortune, he grumbled, 'the idlers are eating up the country', and wrote to Senior in 1849 that the only cause he knew of 'why the country should be worse off now than it was ten years ago' was the corrupting influence of the Poor Law.[4] If the government had not intervened (though it did so only after millions were starving) the archbishop was certain that the famine would have quickly ended once the poor came to see that their only relief lay in hard work and greater production.

This was the same advice he had given to his former pupil nearly twenty years earlier. Unless production was increased, it was not possible to improve the condition of the poor except at the expense of the rest of the community. 'You are trying to lengthen the blanket by cutting off a strip at one end and sewing it on at the other.' In those clear instances when it was necessary to distribute food, it should be 'bestowed

[1] Whately to Senior, 2 July 1832, in Whately, *Life*, I, 163.
[2] *Ibid.*, 149–50.   [3] *Ibid.*, 117–18.   [4] *Ibid.*, 152.

as a *reward*, not on those in want merely, but on those of *extraordinary* sobriety, industry, and general good conduct'. But, he added, it was preferable to give, or sell cheap, coals, clothing or other articles instead of food, because they were not 'subtracted from the total stock', but were produced as a result of the demand. 'As for food, I like particularly to have all the bones and scraps that would otherwise be wasted, collected for soup; *that* does increase the quantity of food.'[1]

The archbishop's specific culinary advice was soon to grace the menus of workhouses throughout the land, while his general analysis found a friendly reception from the principal architects of reform on the Commission of Enquiry. Though less harsh in their criticism of the individual poor, both episcopal representatives shared Whately's deep conviction that the Poor Law, as constituted, was clearly corrupting the laboring classes. Blomfield and Sumner were also both beneficent prelates who, during their long careers, donated much of their income and time to charitable causes. But like so many nineteenth-century clergymen, their motivation for giving seemed to have more to do with a sense of utilitarian function and obligation than it did with a feeling of Christian compassion. It was often a form of role obligation essentially split off from any genuine emotional involvement with the suffering poor. Their innumerable charitable activities steadily reinforced the clergy's conviction that the Anglican Establishment was again vigorously fulfilling its traditional function as guardian and protector of the poor and ameliorator of social antagonisms. Charity, at the same time, defended them from the perhaps unconscious feeling that in spite of all the schools they financed, all the churches they built, and all the beneficent societies they patronized, they did not truly love millions of God's unfortunate children. Though the clergy often sympathized, they rarely empathized. More often, they distrusted the poor, feared them, and in some instances clearly loathed them. Since the lower orders could not be loved as they were, it was necessary they be changed. It was necessary to strip them, scrub them clean, and reclothe them in the reassuring and recognizable garments of middle-class virtue. That the cleansing process would be difficult and often painful there was no doubt; but then the dirt of poverty was ground in deeply. The harsh abrasive of unsentimental political economy would certainly scour it out, and in time it might be possible for God's ministers truly to welcome the poor as brethren once more.

The bishops on the Commission of Enquiry shared the belief of the other members that there must be no turning back along any course that suggested still more relief. This was made clear in 1833, when Blomfield opposed Bishop Law's plans for providing the poor with small plots of land, and another measure requiring landowners to hire unemployed laborers in times of severe distress. Although the principle

[1] *Ibid.*, 76–77.

of relief through employment appealed to him, he argued that the proposal was unfair to proprietors, and but another step in the fruitless direction of institutionalized assistance. Nothing would be done to discourage imprudent marriages, nothing to discriminate between the conscientious and the negligent laborer; it would in fact only aggravate the disease without alleviating the symptoms. The existing Poor Law already curtailed the free circulation of labor, Blomfield explained, and to encourage this still further by guaranteeing employment would be self-defeating.[1] Bishop Law could reply that the reality of conditions demanded the employment of the laborers in preference to direct relief, but his brother of London insisted that the need or the demand for relief was not sufficient justification when the cumulative effects would further corrupt the laborer's character, comfort and happiness.[2]

Blomfield, like many clerics, was also aware that any new burdens on the rates might be at the expense of clerical tithes, already under severe attack by landowners. Only after a compromise amendment protecting tithes was passed did he reluctantly consent to the temporary hiring of the unemployed.[3] He trusted that the report being prepared by Chadwick and Senior would, if approved, soon put an end to such futile recourses to outdoor aid. Certainly that was a principal aim of the document when it was issued in February, 1834.[4] Various types of outdoor relief which had accumulated over the years were to be abandoned, and, in the spirit of the original Elizabethan statute, able-bodied paupers would henceforth earn their relief primarily in workhouses. Predicated on Chadwick's interpretation of Benthamite utilitarian psychology, workhouse life and labor obviously would be less desirable than that enjoyed by the poorest laborer who remained off the rates. Settlement laws were to be simplified and made more stringent in an attempt to encourage surplus laborers to migrate to areas, mainly in the manufacturing north, where they might find employment. In an attempt to control the very real problem of widespread illegitimacy among the poor, the legislature, after some heated debate, agreed to the Commissioners' Malthusian solution of placing the full burden of support upon the mother. The new bastardy clauses deliberately abandoned the traditional search for the father of an illegitimate child, and insisted that the mother could obtain relief for herself and her child only by entering a workhouse.

Equally striking in its departure from tradition was the Benthamite administrative structure developed by Chadwick to provide uniformity and ensure the vigorous enforcement of the new law. The establishment of three national commissioners, and the reorganization of the country

---

[1] *Hansard*, XVIII (1833), 671–3.   [2] *Ibid.*, 678.   [3] *Ibid.*, XIX, 467.

[4] Report From His Majesty's Commissioners For Inquiring Into the Administration and Practical Operation of the Poor Laws, *Parl. Ps.* (1834), XXVII.

into new administrative units (Unions) under the direction of elected guardians, was viewed as a necessary if disturbing attempt to undermine the idiosyncratic administration of poor relief by local authorities. Whatever fears of centralization and the diminution of local control were felt by the propertied classes, they feared the growing burden of poor relief even more. Consequently, the opposition never mustered more than fifty votes, and the new Act, in spite of its revolutionary implications, passed through Parliament by August, less than four months after its introduction.

2. EPISCOPAL DOUBTS AND DEFENSES

Church support of the Poor Law Amendment Act was a most sensitive issue. It was the first major piece of social legislation that clearly bore the imprint of the Establishment both in formulation and defense. To a reinvigorated Church exhausting enormous energy and vast funds in an effort to win the laboring populace over, the role of the episcopate in overhauling the principal means of poor assistance had profound implications for the Establishment's relations with the lower classes. The presence of two bishops, one of them chairman, on the Commission of Enquiry was supposedly a guarantee that the interests of the poor would be humanely represented. Instead, as usual, their spiritual guardians clearly sided with the propertied classes, and presented the Church's many enemies with another sensational example of its hostility towards the laboring masses. It was no surprise to the working classes, long since convinced that the Anglican clergy were at best indifferent to their welfare. It was also no surprise to Bishop Blomfield, who had to defend the measure in the House of Lords. He was well aware that the poor saw the new Act as a blow directed against their welfare.[1] He had been reluctant to serve on the Commission when it was established, knowing full well the severe obloquy that both he and his Church would suffer. As the bishop expected, contempt and vituperation were quickly forthcoming, and even he had to admit that on the surface at least the new Poor Law did not 'bare a kindly feeling towards the poor . . .'. He trusted that in time, however, the harshness employed would be justified.[2]

Many of his brethren were not as confident. Church revenues were being sharply criticized and investigated; Dissenters and radicals were calling and petitioning for the disestablishment of a Church no longer representative of the beliefs of a large proportion, perhaps a majority, of the nation. Under such conditions nervous churchmen were unenthusiastic at the prospect of denying relief to the poor and further alienating large numbers of them. Beneficed clergymen were particularly sensitive

[1] *Hansard*, XXV (1834), 914.   [2] *Ibid.*, 1079–80.

to ever more persistent claims that the poor had a right to a large portion of the Church's revenues, and if the wealth of the Establishment was rightfully distributed, the paupers of the realm would be properly relieved. Furthermore, tenants and landowners were certainly not unsympathetic to the added proposition that the commutation or the abolition of tithes would make the burden of the rates bearable while at the same time permitting greater investment and increased production.

The Irish were already in rebellion against the tithe, and it was clear to less inflexible prelates that unless a compromise was worked out at home, English proprietors would prevail upon the reformed legislature to solve the problem arbitrarily. But none of the bishops was ready to concede to the demands of the poor and their defenders that the lower orders were being deprived of ecclesiastical relief as the result of clerical misuse of charitable endowments. Trollope's wardens there might be in the Church, but the hierarchy knew that they were few and far between, and probably as innocent and guileless as the timorous Septimus Harding. Unfortunately too many people were coming to believe that the grasping Archdeacon Grantlys were more typical in their abuse of the endowed patrimony of their less fortunate parishioners. Long before the first of the Barsetshire revelations appeared in 1855, Blomfield, who was to be satirized in it, along with Henry Phillpotts and Samuel Wilberforce, as one of Theophilus Grantly's disagreeable sons, was troubled by the growing distrust of the Church's management of charitable trusts.[1]

In 1823, the year before his elevation to the bench, Blomfield responded to Henry Brougham's investigations into the question, and warned the radical reformer that the diversion or reduction of Church revenue would actually do great injury to the lower orders; 'the difference will soon be felt and deplored, not only by every charitable institution, but by the poor of almost every parish throughout the kingdom'.[2] He was sure that any objective analysis of charitable contributions would prove that the clergy, rich and poor, gave far more to the needy than did the laity. Pointing to a recent £1,300 endowment made by the princely

[1] Anthony Trollope, *The Warden*, Chap. VIII. See T. B. Lundeen, 'Trollope and the Mid-Victorian Episcopate', *Historical Magazine of the Protestant Episcopal Church*, XXX (1961).

[2] C. J. Blomfield, *Remonstrance Addressed to Henry Brougham, Esq. by one of the 'Working Clergy'* (1823), 26. Blomfield's reference to the 'working clergy' was a sarcastic rebuke to Brougham and others who so distinguished the lesser clergy from the dignitaries of the Church. Blomfield was particularly disturbed by Brougham's criticisms of the abuse of charitable endowments contained in Brougham's *Reports From the Select Committee on the Education of the Lower Orders in the Metropolis* (1816–18), and which led to the appointment of Commissioners to examine educational charities.

Bishop of Durham to a clergy-orphans' school, Blomfield compared it to the £10 and £20 contributions made by several of the nobility. These proportions, he felt, would probably prevail for most charitable ventures, ranging from education to the distribution of food and clothing.[1]

The care of indigent clerical orphans, whose fathers were probably the victims of the atrocious maldistribution of Church revenue in the first place, was not likely to pacify William Cobbett and others who increasingly charged that the Poor Law only existed because the Church abandoned its legal obligations towards the poor after the monasteries were suppressed in the sixteenth century.[2] Copleston had responded briefly to the charge in his *Letters . . . to Peel* in 1819, decrying monastic relief as more harmful than helpful in its perpetuation of indigency. Moreover, it had been completely inadequate, and in 1531 even Charles V had to establish poor laws in the Netherlands in spite of an abundance of monastic institutions.[3] Later, however, members of the episcopate, sensitive to growing disapprobation about their material wealth, were reluctant to defend Church endowments too vociferously. They had become more conscious of public opinion during the 1820's, and their own improving standards made them somewhat embarrassed by the often exaggerated riches attributed to them. The reports of the Ecclesiastical Revenues Commission established in 1832, while showing the lamentable extent of the maldistribution of Church revenue, also substantiated episcopal claims that in general critics had inflated and imagined figures.

In the meantime the bishops welcomed the trenchant rebuttals of lesser dignitaries like the Bishop of London's Chaplain, William Hale Hale, who repudiated any legal claims that the poor might make upon tithes. With Blomfield's approval, Hale, who was also a canon of St Paul's, insisted that there had never been a legal division of Church revenue or property to provide specifically for the lower orders. The monasteries, perhaps, had received endowments prescribing specific provisions and amounts for the poor, but, Hale maintained, the beneficed clergy never had such restrictions upon them.[4] With obvious High Church irony, the chaplain concluded that whatever legal rights the poor had were dissolved along with the monasteries; 'if the poor have been at all defrauded, the guilt lies not at the door of churchmen, but at

---

[1] Blomfield, *Remonstrance*, 27.

[2] W. Cobbett, *A History of the Protestant 'Reformation' in England and Ireland Showing How That Event Has Impoverished and Degraded the Main Body of the People in Those Countries* (1824), Chaps. V, VI, XVI.

[3] Copleston, *Second Letter*, 41, 46.

[4] W. H. Hale, *An Essay On the Supposed Existence of A Quadripartite and Tripartite Division of Tithes in England For Maintaining the Clergy, the Poor, and the Fabric of the Church*, 2 parts (1832–3), 28–29.

that of the laity, whose families have been enriched by the plunder or purchase of Church lands'.[1]

Few Anglican clergymen would have disagreed 'that the poor always have had a claim upon [them] . . . for assistance under poverty and distress, but . . . the measure of their charity has never been regulated in England, by reference to any principles of the statute or canon law'.[2] Charitable endowments, they understood, were usually left to the discretion of the Church, and in no way impinged upon clerical property. In general that discretion had been wisely exercised to the satisfaction of most churchmen, and until recent years at least there had been no complaints from the poor. That was as it should be, for Hale was certain that an examination of canon or common law before and after the Reformation showed that the poor 'had no other claims, but that which the poor ever will have upon the property of the rich, whether ecclesiastics or laymen, the claim of Christian charity'.[3] That was why, even before the dissolution of the monasteries, 'the legislature had always accounted it the duty of the people at large, and not of the Clergy only, to maintain the poor'.[4] Hale buttressed his case with evidence showing that as early as 1349 there were laws requiring local communities to support the poor by permitting begging—something Henry VIII also authorized in 1530.[5]

Copleston, and his episcopal colleagues, could only applaud such clear and perceptive reasoning. But the Bishop of Llandaff was concerned that it might appear as if the Church were trying to minimize its relationship with the poor. While many clergy were certainly not averse to that prospect, Copleston and other Church leaders saw the dangers and heard the criticisms of those who harped upon the unrepresentative nature of the national Establishment. He assured them that if the poor had no legal claims upon the property of the Church, they were nevertheless major beneficiaries of it.

> A moment's reflection is sufficient to convince us, that it is the rich and not the poor, who would reap the fruit of . . . a spoliation. The property of the Church is emphatically the inheritance of the poor. It is given, that the Gospel may be freely preached *to them*. It is their portion in the land in which they live; their bread of life springs from it; and whoever alienates, or lessens this portion, does, in some degree, take from the common stock destined to their comfort and instruction.

The suggestion that the poor might draw upon their inheritance early to provide for less ethereal nourishment was not warmly received by their episcopal benefactor. He reminded the proponents of such short-sighted material solutions that 'the costly ointment poured on the Saviour's feet, might, it is true, have been sold for much and given to the poor. But

---

[1] *Ibid.*, 31.   [2] *Ibid.*, 6.   [3] *Ibid.*, 11.   [4] *Ibid.*, 33.
[5] *Ibid.*, 35–36, 38–39.

the sentiment met with no encouragement from our Divine Master; nor is it recommended by the character of him by whose lips it was uttered'.[1]

If the bishops agreed that an enforced distribution of clerical revenues and endowments to the poor was illegal and unsound, they were less united in their feelings about the disposition of wealth in general. Some deeply distrusted the economical efficiency of the revised Poor Law, and feared for traditional personal class relationships weakened by the decline of local charity. Bishop Law repeatedly questioned whether want and suffering could really be ameliorated in a society regulated 'by some fixed rule of distribution, by stern unbending laws'. He doubted that peace and order could long be maintained under such a system, and insisted that charity was a necessary mollifying agency within the structure of rigid social laws. Charity, he was certain, was most effective when applied 'to those we know first . . .'.[2]

Charity as a form of social control was too deeply ingrained in the structure of paternalistic parochial relief to be easily discarded in favor of less personal, distant arrangements. The gentle, paternal Bishop Law worried not only about the social implications of centralized workhouse relief, but the effect on the poor as suffering Christians. For others, such as the Archdeacon of Derby, Samuel Butler, soon to be elevated to the See of Lichfield, the latter consideration was of minor importance. He had long insisted that the clergy would be wise to approve relief not just on the basis of poverty, but on 'the moral conduct of the claimants' as well. To sober, honest and industrious paupers who attended church and sent their children to Sunday school, he usually gave four or five shillings. Remaining funds were distributed among the less deserving. He was pleased to recall in 1834 that in the preceding year he had given but one shilling each to twelve applicants from the hamlet of Middleton, because they were persons who were never seen at church. Obviously such magnanimity troubled him somewhat, for he followed the dole up with a personal investigation and triumphantly discovered that several of the recipients were in fact not 'in a miserable state of destitution', but were quite comfortable[3]—probably a result of their wandering from parish to parish begging a shilling here and a shilling there from indiscriminate parsons.

Actually Butler, like many stricter ministers, preferred to distribute food and clothing rather than money; especially if it was possible to get

[1] E. Copleston, *A Charge Delivered to the Clergy of the Diocese of Llandaff in September, MDCCCXXXIII* (1833), 13–15.

[2] G. H. Law, *A Sermon Preached On Sunday, July 12, 1835 . . . in Aid of the Royal Dispensary for Diseases of the Ear, and the Deaf and Dumb, Dean Street, Soho Square* (1835), 6, 10–11.

[3] Butler to W. Bateman, 12 Jan. 1834, *Butler Ps.*, Add. MS. 34589, f. 4–5.

the indigent to pay some nominal sum. He was sure 'the poor like it better than a mere dole—the latter destroys their independence, the other mode sustains it. It gives that sort of mutual co-operation between rich and poor which tends to promote kind feelings on both sides'.[1] While Butler and clergymen like him were probably not favorites of the twelve paupers from Middleton and millions like them, whatever influence they had over them was threatened by the new Poor Law Amendment Bill. Not only did the revised Act remove the poor from the direct and personal supervision of their local superiors, but it cut them off from their local clerical guardians. 'Nothing ought to be admitted which tends to separate the interests of the poor from the superintendence of their ministers.' Butler was perceptive enough to realize that the poor would probably rejoice in that separation at first, 'but the day will assuredly come when they will sorely lament the loss of their best and kindest, and often their only, protector'.[2]

This was all that really worried the Archbishop of Canterbury, William Howley, and once assured that workhouses would be provided with Anglican chaplains he was content to leave the defense of the Church in the hands of Bishop Blomfield.[3] The latter, even more than Samuel Butler, knew how antagonistic the new legislation was to the poor. But he agreed with Bishop Maltby that so long as the poor man 'throws the burthen of his support upon the hard-earned means of his industrious neighbour', he would remain corrupt and beyond the reach of the ministry. Maltby told his clergy they must understand that while coping with the expected anger of the poor, 'Divine Providence when it laid man under the original curse of earning his bread by the sweat of his brow, mercifully sweetened the morsel by annexing to the exercise of industry the pride of independence, and the comfort of rest, which is rendered so grateful by exertion'.[4] The workhouses would guarantee the return of that exertion, and derivative moral and material advantages would soon follow.

Blomfield explained during the early debates over the new Act that the Poor Law Commission's aim was to return the laboring class as far as possible to the independent condition they enjoyed about a half-century before.[5] In spite of the great changes of the new age, the bishop conceived

[1] *Ibid.*

[2] S. Butler, *A Charge Delivered to the Clergy of the Archdeaconry of Derby . . . June 26 and 27, 1834* (1834), 4.

[3] *Hansard*, XXV (1834); see debates in July on the Poor Law Amendment Bill, when the question of workhouse chaplains was raised several times, 455, 474–5.

[4] E. Maltby, *A Charge Delivered to the Clergy of the Archdeaconry of Chichester . . . in September, 1834* (1834), 23–24.

[5] *Hansard*, XXIV (1834), 1073.

of improvement as a return to the virtues and values of a less confused and corrupted era where the poor were not only industrious and independent, but attached to an Established Church relevant to their condition in life. The first step in that direction was an end to outdoor relief. The poor must be returned to their natal parishes and forced into the union workhouses. It was 'one of the greatest boons which could be conferred on the labouring classes', who, in spite of their initial bitterness, would develop prudence, foresight and an independence which eschewed relief as disgraceful.[1] Ultimately, however, the real hope lay with the younger generation. Blomfield strongly argued for separating children from their parents, and educating them beyond their disruptive influence. Evidence showed that such children were always the best servants.[2] Chadwick and Senior agreed and endorsed the general idea of separating the aged and children in different workhouses. However, in practice, mixed workhouses remained, although the guardians did not hesitate to segregate parents from their children.[3]

The only open episcopal conflict during the debates on the new law came over the question of the bastardy clauses.[4] Bishop Phillpotts, who deplored the whole prospect of political economists interfering with established parochial society, seized particularly upon the Malthusian idea of requiring the mothers of illegitimate children to bear alone the responsibility for the care of their offspring. While it was true that the Commissioners had compiled considerable evidence documenting the sorry state of lower-class morals, Phillpotts questioned the assumption that female promiscuity was so much at fault. Illegitimate children were, after all, still the result of a union which, if not conceived in heaven, was nevertheless conceived in nature. Both parties were thus responsible. The Bishop of Exeter had no sympathy for expedient explanations about the practical problems of locating fathers, and protecting innocent men from false accusations. Human law, he countered, no matter how difficult to enforce, must reflect divine law, and this meant in questions of bastardy, mutual accountability.[5] Drawing as he often did upon his earlier legal studies to support his theology, Phillpotts quoted Blackstone on English law and Erskine on Scottish law to prove the legality of his point.[6]

Welcoming another opportunity to club the loathsome Whig government, and throw a few sharp jabs at the compromising and influential Bishop of London, Phillpotts queried the logic and Christian spirit behind a proposal to send a wretched mother to a workhouse to support

---

[1] *Ibid.*, XXV, 581, 583–4.   [2] *Ibid.*, 1059–60.

[3] J. L. and Barbara Hammond, *The Age of the Chartists* (Hamden, Conn., 1962), 71; Finer, *Chadwick*, 85–86.

[4] U. R. Q. Henriques, 'Bastardy and the New Poor Law', *Past and Present*, No. 37 (July, 1967), 103–29.

[5] *Hansard*, XXV (1834), 586–92.   [6] *Ibid.*, 1066.

her child, and thereby ruin any future prospects for either of them. Would a poor-house make her any more chaste? Would a scheme of such gross injustice, which deprived a helpless woman of all support until she was driven to a workhouse, really conform to the needs of the poor and the teachings of Christ? Was it natural that women who were not designed to assume such burdens be forced into so unnatural a condition? Did the spiritual and temporal peers of the realm really believe that God sanctioned a man setting aside a woman he has humbled, and approved of legislation which in effect justified and encouraged the abandonment of children?[1] On the contrary, such thinking would lead to 'other horrid evils' far worse than the immorality in question—'all for the sake of frightening women into chastity'.[2]

These were telling blows, and Bishop Blomfield knew it. After his defense of the bastardy clauses in the House of Lords, he had his speeches corrected and published in order to explain to angry critics of the Church the logic which permitted him and several of his episcopal colleagues to endorse what seemed to be a patently inhumane and un-Christian measure; one 'which seems to wear on the surface something of unkindness towards the most interesting portion of the community'.[3] This cautious understatement was followed by assurances that the improved morality and happiness of the laboring poor would justify the policies. Stung particularly by Phillpotts's barbs about violating divine responsibilities, the London diocesan refused to concede that the bastardy clauses were un-Christian. As he could find no express law on the subject in Scripture, he believed it was right to enact laws most consistent with God's desire to check immorality.[4]

When, as the evidence collected by the Commission showed, the overwhelming number of lower-class women marrying were already pregnant, drastic measures to improve the morality of such people were in order. Blomfield did not see this being achieved if the holy state of matrimony was debased by forced marriages. Worthy sentiment though it was, human law could not always be based on divine law; human nature and the human passions made it impossible. Some comfort was at least found in the knowledge that a mother by nature must always suffer more than the father of her child. In that sense, the bishop reflected, the bastardy clauses were merely an extension of natural law. Blomfield also questioned his brother of Exeter's interpretation of statute law. Bastardy laws had always been directed against the woman, and he claimed that existing laws could be traced back to the time of James I. Fathers were required to do no more than pay something for the support of the child, but, Blomfield insisted, this was to assist the parish rather than the mother. The new clauses were not then a break from the general

[1] *Ibid.,* 610–12. [2] *Ibid.,* 1067–72.
[3] *Ibid.,* 4. [4] *Ibid.,* 612.

tradition of bastardy laws, and at the same time they promised to put an end to unjust accusations of paternity.[1]

In a very real sense, the bastardy clauses were a direct result of a growing obsession about domestic morality, as a fundamental pillar of social stability, which had been intensifying since the French Revolution. The fear of social disintegration and an awareness of continual rapid change had encouraged a reaffirmation of those virtues and institutions —the home, the family, and unsullied chastity—which seemed so essential to the traditional maintenance of the well-ordered society. The awareness that such values were not exalted among the laboring classes was increasingly disturbing to their betters, who had already enshrined them before the young Victoria came to the throne. During the disturbances of the immediate post-war years, episcopal complaints about lower-class immorality were not very common. The severe scrutinizing of manners and moral behavior was not yet a characteristic of the Anglican hierarchy, in spite of Evangelical prodding. Providing the laboring folk kept quiet, and did not disturb the tranquillity of the *status quo*, most prelates were content to mouth traditional eighteenth-century platitudes about rational, moderate, virtuous living. With the exception of a Porteus, a Burgess, or a Barrington, few bishops really put their hearts into it, and only occasionally their heads.

The tone of episcopal exhortation changed rapidly in the 1820's and 1830's as a new generation of earnest, spiritually active prelates assumed command of the Establishment. Whether in the preachments of Evangelicals like Ryder or the Sumner brothers, or High Churchmen like Blomfield or Bethell, more austere qualities of the religious revival were increasingly evident. Blomfield, for example, was as strong a Sabbatarian and as dour a moralist as most Evangelicals. His support and defense of the bastardy clauses was only one facet of his continuing campaign to pass legislation correcting the wanton and dissolute behavior of the lower orders. In many ways he was William Wilberforce's successor. When in 1830 he joined with Bishop Law to urge tighter licensing laws for pubs, Blomfield went a step further and proscribed not only beer, but skittles as well.[2] He protested that he was not trying to restrict the few amusements of the laboring poor, as the Press, several magistrates (who were probably pub-owners), and some clergy complained; rather he simply wanted the workers to indulge in games of 'a much more manly character' and to stop dissipating their energies and meager resources.[3]

It became apparent from the depressing evidence of lower-class immorality gathered by the Poor Law Enquiry Commissioners that some of the 'manly games' engaged in were not quite what the good bishop had in mind. His championing of the severe bastardy clauses was promp-

[1] *Ibid.*, 597–9.   [2] *Hansard*, VI (1831), 214.   [3] *Ibid.*, 750.

ted as much by the shock to his moral sensibilities as it was by his confidence in Malthusian logic. The lines of Victorian rectitude were converging rapidly when Blomfield focused on the woman, and insisted that under no condition must she be rewarded for her folly, and thereby encouraged to repeat it. She was to receive neither material nor spiritual comfort. The most influential prelate of his age, Blomfield endorsed the practice, and supported those of his clergy who refused to 'church' women after the birth of illegitimate children.[1] There would be no blessings; there would be no easy forgiveness. They would go to the workhouse with their infants, fully aware that the Church and God would not condone and consequently encourage such behavior.

To those sentimentalists who found such an attitude very hard indeed, the bishop could point to the alarming testimony revealed by the Commission. He could also invite them to examine the learned and influential study of the Scottish clergyman, Thomas Chalmers, on the *Christian and Civic Economy of Large Towns*. From it they would learn how the complete removal of parish aid to unwed mothers laid 'an instantaneous check upon the profligate habits of the people . . .'. Chalmers's study also proved that illegitimate children were actually better cared for than those on the rates, when they remained under the 'guilty affection' of their mothers, who managed to raise them as best they could.[2] The bishop and the other Poor Law Commissioners had no intention of recommending that such 'guilty affection', in spite of its obvious advantages for the child, be permitted to mothers and their children outside of the workhouse. Why should they, when the poor themselves refused assistance to unwed mothers? The friendly and benefit societies gave no relief to such people, nor would they help men who asked support for a child born out of wedlock. Female friendly societies, Blomfield argued, actually expelled any unmarried member who became pregnant.[3] The poor already recognized what their superiors were slow to learn: the number of bastards relieved would rapidly decline as funds were cut off. Triumphant in such logic, the bishop concluded that if the poor solved the problem that way, the rest of the nation should not hesitate to follow their wise example. Probably the poor would have preferred that the clergy learn other lessons from their plight, but a selective understanding of the behavior of the lower orders was easier to reconcile to the preconceptions motivating their spiritual guardians.

Blomfield carried the day; the bastardy clauses passed the Lords by 93 votes to 82. If the temporal peers were convinced, their spiritual

---

[1] C. J. Blomfield, Letter Copy Book 358, f. 25, *Fulham Ps.,* Lambeth Palace Library.

[2] T. Chalmers, *The Christian and Civic Economy of Large Towns*, 2 vols. (Glasgow, 1821–23), II, 240; *Hansard*, XXV (1834), 10, 1086–7.

[3] *Hansard*, XXV, 12–13.

counterparts were at least cautious. Only the Prime Minister's brother, Edward Grey, the innocuous Bishop of Hereford, voted with the Bishop of London. Nine other prelates sided with Phillpotts against the clauses.[1] The aristocratic Tory Bishops, Murray of Rochester and Bagot of Oxford (1829–45), were typical in their reluctance to endorse any measure that threatened to break up families, though they believed that something had to be done to restore 'the prosperity, the independence, and the respectability of the English poor!'[2] In addition they understood Phillpotts's anxiety about the consolidation of parishes into unions with its threat to local influence. The Exeter prelate, more distressed than ever by the growth of the towns, added the old warning that the children of the agricultural poor would be sent to urban workhouses and encouraged to emigrate to the manufacturing towns, where their morals were bound to suffer.[3] Though several of his episcopal colleagues certainly shared his concerns, Phillpotts was the only bishop to sign parliamentary protests against the new law, particularly those sections pertaining to bastardy and administrative reorganization.[4] In so doing, he launched a long career as the most relentless and vigorous opponent of the Poor Law Amendment Act in the House of Lords.

3. RESISTANCE AND RECONSIDERATION

From the time of its inception the new legislation was under continual assault. The Tory press hammered away at the abuses of centralization and the evils of the workhouses. In the House of Commons John Walter, the editor of *The Times* and Thomas Wakeley, editor of *The Lancet*, joined with the factory reformer, John Fielden, to denounce the cruel and oppressive measure. The addition of Benjamin Disraeli and other sentimental Tories to their ranks in 1837 strengthened the cause. In the House of Lords, Bishop Phillpotts, unsupported by any of his epis-

[1] *Ibid.*, 1096–1102.

[2] *Ibid.*, 1061. Also Richard Bagot, *A Charge Addressed to the Clergy . . . August, 1834* (Oxford, 1834), 12–13.

Bagot (1782–1854), son of 1st Baron Bagot and nephew of Bishop Lewis Bagot. A kind, timorous man, he was at first sympathetic to the Oxford Movement until pressures on him forced him to clamp down after the publication of Tract 90. Ill and on the edge of a nervous breakdown, he was translated to Bath and Wells in 1845. Incapacitated soon after, his diocese was administered by the Bishop of Gloucester and Bristol. He never completely recovered.

[3] *Hansard*, XXV (1834), 1099. Approximately ten thousand people were encouraged to migrate to the manufacturing towns before the depression of 1838 curtailed the efforts of migration agents working with Poor Law officials in agricultural districts. See Finer, *Chadwick*, 124.

[4] *Hansard*, XXV (1834), 1102.

copal colleagues, presented one petition after another describing countless abuses of the new system, and calling for amendments or repeal. He
pleaded with the peers to again become the protectors of the poor, prevent families from being destroyed by arbitrary rules, and reverse the
frightening treatment of poverty as if it was a crime.[1]

A series of three good harvests after 1834 accompanied by small
wage increases eased the way for the implementation of the new Poor
Law in the south. Although the cessation of outdoor relief was bitterly
resented, there was little direct resistance. In spite of Chadwick's desire
to take advantage of the prosperous times to implement the legislation
as rapidly as possible in the northern manufacturing areas, where resistance was greatest, the Commissioners moved more cautiously there.[2]
Nevertheless, by 1838 only 1,000 parishes remained outside of the new
unions, most of them in the north, where the use of the Poor Law had
largely been restricted to hand-loom weavers during periods of temporary
unemployment.[3] Town workers had not become permanent recipients
of outdoor relief like so many laborers in the south, and attempts to
introduce the new stringent legislation as if their situation were the same
led to open resistance by workers and magistrates. The depression which
became severe in 1838 only served to inflame further the explosive resistance to the attempts of the Commissioners to override local relief
measures and employ their new system. Riots, threats to Assistant Commissioners and refusals even by elected guardians to implement the
orders of the Poor Law Commissioners nullified their futile efforts.
Stirred up by vigorous arguments of the Anglican parson, George
Stringer Bull, the renegade Methodist, J. R. Stephens, Richard Oastler
and John Fielden, protests poured in against the attempts to curtail
outdoor relief. Some 250,000 persons in 1838 alone signed petitions. This
resistance received a decided boost from the elections following the
death of William IV in 1837. The Whigs lost a great many county seats
to the Tories on the Poor Law issue.

Bishop Phillpotts had warned of serious trouble as petitions from the
north began arriving. He pointed out that the Poor Law had always
been primarily an agricultural measure which, if properly administered,
was perfectly sound.[4] But as factory workers were often unemployed
only for short periods of time, every effort should be made to keep
them out of the workhouses, and keep their families together until
employment was again available. As far as the Bishop of Exeter was
concerned, the workhouses were prisons designed to punish the innocent
incapable of finding employment as well as those unwilling to seek it.

[1] *Ibid.*, XXXVII (1837), 835–9; XXXVIII, 1146.
[2] Hammond, *Age of the Chartists*, 61–63; Finer, *Chadwick*, 120.
[3] *Ibid.*, 147.
[4] *Hansard*, XXXVII (1837), 835–7.

He could not understand how a Christian legislature could allow the new law to continue unamended.[1] In one speech after another Phillpotts described the horrors of the workhouses where parents were wrenched from each other and their children, and where the diet was scandalously insufficient. In 1838 he presented a petition from the guardians of the Dudley union complaining that the Commissioners would not allow them to increase the meager food ration to the inmates. The bishop asked how paupers, many of them temporarily unemployed from the forges, were to keep their strength on a miserly ration of bread, cheese and one and a half pints of gruel a day. A physician he employed to study the diet reported that it was indeed inadequate and unhealthy, as the guardians had warned.[2] Addressing himself to the evidence, Lord Melbourne reminded the peers that medical men were not always the best judges of such questions, 'for this was a dietary for persons in health, and medical men were more conversant with that for persons who were sick . . .'.[3]

That was the kind of irrefutable logic that appealed to the likes of the Earl of Radnor, who applauded the Prime Minister, and described all of the complaints as groundless. Furious, but with icy contempt, the bishop asked:

> Were they to be told by the noble Earl, who was revelling in wealth, well employed, . . . who enjoyed great riches . . . and who was possessed of one of those noble fortunes which had descended from one of the ancient aristocracy of England—were they to be told by such a man, forsooth, that this was a groundless complaint? Were they to be told, that labouring men, who were accustomed to earn their bread by the sweat of their brow . . . working and toiling . . . before heat issuing from iron furnaces, a task which none of their Lordships, not even the strongest of them, would be able to endure for a single hour, ought only to have such a sustenance given to them as would neither support them when in health, nor preserve their health until the season of employment returned, and that to complain that no better sustenance was afforded to them was a groundless complaint?[4]

The Earl's short, weak reply was not likely to satisfy the aroused prelate; but then nothing less than repeal would have at that point. When in 1839 the Poor Law Commissioners were required to seek renewal of their authority, Phillpotts, rising to the scent of still another legal battle, filed a suit in the Court of Queen's Bench challenging their power. The bishop knew it was hopeless, and soon withdrew the charges; but he had made his point.[5] Rioting in Birmingham and disturbances in other manufacturing towns only confirmed his dire warnings about the de-

[1] *Ibid.*, 841–3. [2] *Ibid.*, XLI (1838), 741–5. [3] *Ibid.*, 746.
[4] *Ibid.*, 756–8.
[5] *Ibid.*, XLIX (1839), 741–4.

178

structive nature of the new Poor Law. On numerous occasions he had described in the Lords the 'filthy and freezing conditions' in various workhouses, decried the destruction of the familial relationship among the poor, and compared their treatment with that of the Negro slaves. He showed how illegitimacy had not been curbed by the savage bastardy clauses, how baptisms had declined, vaguely inferred that infanticide had increased, and wondered about the mysterious deaths of idiot paupers in the workhouse at Crediton.[1]

Yet Phillpotts had little love or sympathy for the poor. He had been a harsh magistrate when a clergyman at Durham. During the cholera epidemic of 1831–2, despite appeals that he at least make an occasional appearance in Exeter, the bishop who had shortly before been elevated to the See, refused to enter the city.[2] As soon as the disease was detected in his diocese in the summer of 1832, he left for his villa in Teignmouth, confident in the knowledge that he could discharge his duties as well in one part of the diocese as another.[3] Although the canons of the cathedral were perhaps less able to use that excuse, they nevertheless followed the example of their new diocesan and quickly absented themselves from the area. Some 345 people died of the cholera in Exeter that summer. Phillpotts did not return until late October, when the disease had passed.[4] It was an inauspicious start for the already unpopular bishop whose absence, along with most of the cathedral clergy, was in sharp contrast to the work carried on by Evangelicals and pious Nonconformists, as well as his own son, newly ordained and recently arrived in his Cornish parish.[5] Thomas Latimer, the radical editor of the *Western Times* in Exeter and life-long opponent of Phillpotts, never hesitated to remind his readers that their diocesan had run away.[6] If Christian compassion meant a possibility of contamination, the bishop preferred to exercise other virtues. Excoriate the workhouses as he did year after year, Phillpotts managed to avoid ever visiting one. He admitted privately and weakly in 1844 that all his evidence was received second-hand, because he feared that in the light of his declared hostility it would appear that he

[1] *Ibid.*, LXIII (1838), 986–7; LX (1841), 978–93; LXXIII (1844), 107–30.

[2] Davies, *Henry Phillpotts*, 142–3.

[3] Phillpotts to Rev. T. Baker, 29 July 1832, *Phillpotts Ps.*, Ex. Cath., ED 11/3.

[4] Davies, *Henry Phillpotts*, 145.

[5] *Ibid.*, 143. Phillpotts knew how unpopular his appointment was in Exeter, where it was commonly believed that he had dropped his strident opposition to Catholic emancipation in return for episcopal preferment. See Phillpotts to R. Barnes, ? Nov. 1830, *Phillpotts Ps.,* Ex. Cath. ED 11/4, and 5 Nov. 1830, *Phillpotts Letters*, Devon County Record Office, P.R. 17/20, No. 9.

[6] Richard S. Lambert, *The Cobbett of the West. A Study of Thomas Latimer and the Struggle Between Pulpit and Press at Exeter* (1939), 55.

was spying if he ever entered a workhouse.[1] It was ironical that the principal defender of the rights of the poor was a bishop who, whenever possible, sought to avoid any contact with them.

In contrast to the arguments of his close friend, Copleston, and others, Phillpotts insisted that the poor had a *right* to subsistence which had been violated in 1834 when it was arbitrarily converted to a *privilege*. That right was implicit in the Scriptural injunction to be fruitful and multiply, and reaffirmed in the Elizabethan Poor Law, 'the Magna Carta of the poor'.[2] The new Poor Law, that 'great production of Malthusian philosophy . . .', sought to deny both divine and statutory law. Phillpotts conceded that Parson Malthus had been a kind, sincere, even benevolent man who corrected his initial opposition to subsistence for unproductive paupers. But his successors ignored his moderation in later editions of the *Essay on Population* and other writings, with tragic results.[3] What it really added up to, and what lay behind the tireless assaults launched by the bishop, was the fear that the Malthusians and their allies had, in undermining the parochial structure of society, seriously weakened the Church as well as the State. Originally he believed it was a Whig conspiracy, and had hoped for a return to Tory government and Tory values. By 1844 he had seen his hopes fulfilled for the preceding three years, and was angry and frustrated that it had made little difference. Peel was not Lord Eldon; it was no wonder Phillpotts was so upset. The bishop had warned the clergy and laity alike in 1837 that locking the poor in workhouses would exclude them from the parochial religious life of the community and threaten their necessary and integral relationship with the higher classes. Rejecting the defenses raised by such diverse spokesmen as Melbourne, Brougham and Wellington, he complained that the rich and poor were no longer to meet together in the House of the Lord or anywhere else, and all the advantages of mutual association were being lost.[4] Not even Negroes in the West Indies were excluded from the parish church.[5] The proprietary pew system was scandalous enough in its separation of classes before God, and in its preventing the poor from kneeling and praying at the side of the rich; but the Poor Law went a step further and excluded the poor from the parish church entirely.[6] Providing workhouse chaplains was no alternative. Not only were there not enough of them, but, he complained to a clergyman, the poor were still being deprived of 'their best friend, the Minister of their parish'. The whole system was an 'abomination'. The rich suffered as much as the poor because the wretched were removed from their view and beyond their reach—'a most iniquitous interference with the merciful

[1] Phillpotts to T. Baker, 19 Aug. 1844, *Phillpotts Ps.*, Ex. Cath., ED 11/3.
[2] *Hansard*, LXXVI (1844), 1816.   [3] *Ibid.*, 1818–20.
[4] *Ibid.*, XXXVII (1837), 845–6.   [5] *Ibid.*, LXIII (1838), 986–7.
[6] *Ibid.*, XXXVIII (1837), 1840–1.

design of that author of all good, who for the good of all, ordained that the rich and the poor meet together'. Even more distressing, the rich preferred it that way: another clear sign of the deplorable characteristics of the new age.

> How can these things be without grievous desertion of the plainest duties of the rich? Alas! Alas! I tremble for England—It is possessed by the work of Daemons. . . .[1]

During the previous year, 1843, Phillpotts had created a considerable stir by urging his clergy to revive the offertory in their services as a means of raising alms to assist the poor and protect them from the Poor Law. By so doing 'the *parochial* connexion of our people' would be preserved, as well as 'the precious sympathies of neighbourhood, which it is the undeniable tendency of this Law . . . to destroy'. In accordance with the Rubric the plate would be passed after the sermon, and the clergyman and the churchwardens would then determine how the collection would be used.[2] Low Church clergy and laity deplored the revival of such a Popish measure, and their suspicions of their prelate's High Church sympathies for the Puseyites were further aggravated. But the idea was also opposed by ratepayers, who were regularly taxed for the maintenance of the poor, and who were certain that they were already sufficiently sympathetic.

Bishop Phillpotts received no support from the rest of the bench during his years of opposition to the Poor Law. While most of his colleagues had real reservations about its implementation, they were reluctant to oppose the government and to encourage the mounting agitation against the new measure. On the contrary, they continually reprimanded clergymen for supporting petitions against the Poor Law, and warned of the great evil that could result from ministers stirring up opposition to the law of the land.[3] Phillpotts had been accused of this by Lord Melbourne and others, but many Tory parsons sympathized with the Exeter prelate in his condemnations.[4] The Reverend Edward Duncombe, for example, was not alone in his angry charge that the new Poor Law was an expediency devised for the protection of property while abandoning responsibility for the maintenance and protection of the poor. It was, as he described it, 'a *Union* against the working classes—*a union* to say "go find work, for if you remain on our estates we shall no longer let you

[1] Phillpotts to T. Baker, 19 Aug. 1844, Ex Cath. ED 11/3.
[2] H. Phillpotts, *A Letter to the Clergy of the Diocese of Exeter On the Use of the Offertory, Especially With Reference to the Missionary Exertions of the Church, and to the State of Spiritual Destitution in the Manufacturing Districts of England* (1843), 14.
[3] See for example the complaints of Bishops Stanley and Grey in *Hansard*, XXXVIII (1837), 1914–15.
[4] *Ibid.*, 1146.

have cottages, but you must go to the workhouse . . .".[1] It was a conspiracy to drive people off the land to the industrial towns, and he was appalled that the Bishops of London and Chester had so little respect for 'the existing rights of the poor', and acted from expediency rather than justice. Expediency, he reminded them, could be a two-edged sword.[2] Duncombe could not understand why landlords were not required to provide small plots for the poor to cultivate as a spur to industry and frugality and a genuine protection against periods of distress. Like Bishop Law, he believed it would benefit industrial workers as well as agricultural laborers.

To those who feared for the rights of the landlords, the parson reminded them that the government purchased land for railroads and canals to benefit the rich, so why not land to aid the poor? Let the poor work to supplement their miserable wages; do not imprison them in workhouses:

> Give the people a little diversity of work and some expanse of mind beyond the mill, the factory and its webs—to lead them to study nature itself, instead of driving them to revel in the sophistry and philosophy of ill-directed reason. The real policy for the security and prosperity of all property, is to identify the agricultural and commercial interests. . . . Give them something to go back upon when work is scarce and slack. . . .[3]

This fear of social disintegration and class alienation underlay much of the anti-Poor Law agitation. It drove the Edward Duncombes, the George Stringer Bulls, the Walter F. Hooks, and many other clergymen to find some way to restore meaningful relationships between all classes. Although their efforts were a long way from W. G. Ward's Tractarian ideal of a primitive Church undominated by rank or station and devoted to the laboring poor, the various ideas all reflected the realization that the Church had in fact largely abandoned its role as protector of the poor.[4] The Poor Law reforms were the most glaring manifestation of it, and were simply too much for many members of a revived and active clergy to accept.

Bishop Otter was the only prelate openly to suggest that clerical opposition was exaggerated; in 1838 he defended the clergy from government charges that they were working against the new Poor Law. If anything,

---

[1] E. Duncombe, *The Present Crisis: Church Reform* (1835), 53–54. Duncombe, Rector of Newton-Kyme, Yorkshire, was, unlike Phillpotts, both an Evangelical and in favor of Church reform. Yet he warmly praised that pillar of the unreformed High Church for his vigorous resistance to the new Poor Law.

[2] *Ibid.*, 57.　　　　　　　　　　[3] *Ibid.*, 52.

[4] W. G. Ward, *The Ideal of a Christian Church Considered In Comparison With Existing Practice* (1844).

Otter replied, it was surprising how few had taken any position at all, but had simply accepted and supported the measure. His recent visitation of the diocese of Chichester convinced him that the clergy were generally favorable and, if not, had at least refrained from any interference.[1] As Otter's agricultural diocese had been organized into unions quickly with his full support and with minimal resistance during the prosperous years after 1834, he was predisposed from his experience to believe that the new scheme was working well. But he was also persuaded by his deep commitment to the teachings of his close friend, Malthus, and was extremely irritated by the abuse heaped upon the author of the *Essay on Population* following the passage of the Poor Law Amendment Act. Archbishop Whately in 1835 had urged Nassau Senior to write a short account of Malthus's views to be used against his enemies, and even more against his professed friends, 'who have made him a tool for noxious purposes'.[2] Otter undertook the task in a *Memoir* attached to an edition of *Principles of Political Economy* published in 1836, two years after Malthus's death.

The bishop agreed with critics that Malthus's ideas were of major importance in the creation of the new Poor Law. But the old law had become corrupted by the failure to understand the natural laws of population. In spite of the warnings raised in the *Essay* nearly forty years earlier, 'the evil it contemplated had lately risen to so great a height as to threaten the most serious mischief to society, and to call for the strongest measures . . .'. Had it not been for Malthus the situation would have been much more serious, and the solution even more obscure and difficult—'if any way could have been found at all, short of a convulsion of society'.[3] Otter knew that the revised Poor Law was 'a great experiment . . . upon the result of which, the due and harmonious adjustment of the relations between the rich and the poor will hereafter mainly depend'. But as the measure was founded on the basis of Malthus's work, he was confident that they would stand together. Instead of creating greater class conflict, the Malthusian principles in action would moderate existing tensions and wind tightly the loosening bonds of society. The new laws would not just benefit the wealthy by diminishing their burdens and assigning the 'parochial odium to others, but . . . the poor themselves will derive and eventually be conscious of, in the elevation of their minds, the bettering of their condition, the improvement of their morals and habits, and especially the softening of that harsh temper and disposition towards the other classes of society, at present one of the worst features of the times . . .'.[4]

Few of Otter's episcopal colleagues were so certain. Even Blomfield's enthusiasm for the law he helped to draft soon waned. Faced with bitter

---

[1] *Hansard*, XLI (1838), 1064–5.   [2] Whately, *Life*, I, 301.
[3] Otter, *Memoir*, xlvii.   [4] *Ibid.*, xix–xx.

opposition from within the Church against the various measures of Church reform he sought to implement, and aware of the serious resistance to the Poor Law, the pragmatic prelate decided to concentrate his efforts where they would be most beneficial. Blomfield never once defended the new Poor Law after it was passed in 1834; not even when provoked by the antagonistic Phillpotts. By 1842 he was again endorsing the distribution of charity to distressed unemployed workers, recalling his efforts in the 1820's on behalf of the unfortunate weavers in Spitalfields and Bethnal Green. Praising the 'quiet resignation of those sufferers' and forgetting his earlier opposition to such measures, the bishop supported an appeal for contributions, hopeful that the workers would recognize that those above them were not insensible to their sufferings.[1]

Blomfield understood by the 1840's that the new Poor Law could not really be employed as its drafters had envisaged. Firm resistance, intensified by severe depression and the rise of Chartism, not only made the government reluctant to press on with the inflammatory measure, but made cautious clergyman shy away from so dangerous an innovation. Moreover, local magistrates in the northern unions steadfastly refused to co-operate with the Poor Law Commissioners, In 1839, despite hopes that outdoor relief would be greatly reduced, four-fifths of the relief given was still in the form of outdoor assistance, and the number of paupers being relieved in that manner actually increased from 1,000,000 in 1839 to 1,200,000 in 1842. The following year the Commissioners bowed to reality and sanctioned a wider use of outdoor labor in the depressed north.[2] At that time in some towns such as Sheffield as much as one-tenth of the population was on relief, and there existed neither the facilities nor the inclination to drive them to workhouses.[3] Proponents of the new law could take some comfort in the fact that the overall rates were driven down from £6,750,590 in the early 1830's to £4,886,702 in 1844.[4] But this was largely a result of stricter enforcement in the agricultural districts of the south. In the manufacturing north, the new Poor Law remained a dead letter. Even Bishop Phillpotts felt partially vindicated when in 1844 the hated bastardy clauses were revoked.

The other Church representative on the Poor Law Enquiry Commission, Bishop Sumner, had also come to realize the danger and futility of pushing ahead in the face of such vigorous opposition and severe economic dislocation. As the conscientious diocesan of a great manufacturing diocese, he was well aware of the effects of the depression and the angry resistance and hostility felt in the industrial towns. But Sumner had grown increasingly pessimistic about relieving poverty before the Poor Law confrontations began, and it is difficult to know

[1] *Hansard*, LXIII (1842), 777. [2] Hammond, *Age of the Chartists*, 65.
[3] Finer, *Chadwick*, 181. [4] *Ibid.*, 93–94.

why he accepted a place on the Commission. His earlier enthusiastic confidence in the truths of Malthusian economics had gradually given way before his stronger Evangelical feelings of despair and resignation; his experience at Chester only fortified that attitude. Significantly, neither during the months of heated discussion preceding passage of the Poor Law Amendment Bill which he helped draw up, nor in the years after, did Sumner defend his position.

While Blomfield weighed the practical implications of the new measure and concluded it could not be implemented for economic and political reasons, his Evangelical colleague at Chester pondered whether in fact the real difficulty was in its being contradictory to divine wishes. More often he returned to the fundamentalist conclusion that since life is a great testing-ground, poverty could not be alleviated to the extent that the reformers had suggested. During the harsh depression year of 1839, Sumner thought the workers were perhaps exaggerating their misery by looking to the present world alone.[1] By implication he also inferred that elaborately-conceived schemes to end their poverty were suffering from the same faulty perception. Dwelling more and more on this theme, the bishop recalled that poverty was the result of sin, as was the necessity to labor, and wondered if the attempt to eliminate one would not also undermine the other. There was, he felt, a real danger that a great alleviation of poverty would only encourage the greater evil of idleness, something which God never sanctioned. The widespread sinful scenes on workless Sundays only illustrated 'how little the nature of man is fitted for a state in which there should be no poverty, no want, no need of labour . . .'. Certain as he was that 'nine-tenths' of the misery in the world was the result of sin, the bishop felt that perhaps the emphasis of recent years had been ill-conceived, and tended to forget the Gospel reality that 'the poor ye have always with you . . .'.[2] There had been, he believed, too much emphasis upon the elimination of poverty, and not enough upon simply making it more bearable.

In practice it meant that Sumner, like Blomfield, turned again to the role of private charity. He concluded that the stress on the Poor Law had greatly weakened confidence in the efficacy of individual giving as harmful to industry and injurious to the moral character of the poor. Agreeing that the Poor Law had been 'a vicious system, which was alike calculated to injure the character of the labourer and of the employer . . .', the prelate insisted that it did not mean that intelligent, judicious, private benevolence was harmful. If anything, it was needed more than ever 'because it will be long before the body of labourers can recover from the

---

[1] J. B. Sumner, 'David's Purpose' (1839), in *Christian Charity, Its Obligations and Objects, With Reference to the Present State of Society, In A Series of Sermons* (1841), 174.

[2] 'The Gospel, A Blessing', *Ibid.*, 131–3.

effects of a system which had continued for forty years in operation, and of which they had not been the authors but the victims'. Bishop Sumner did not advocate a return to the unrevised Poor Law. At the same time, however, he did not endorse the new measures he had lent his name to a decade before. Instead he was content to agree again that public charity was open to many objections, and should only be employed to remedy 'greater evils', but private charity, 'essential to the nature and condition of mankind', was the approach he personally preferred.[1]

Sumner recognized that there were places 'where the evil is become so deeply seated as to defy the efforts of ordinary benevolence, and require public aid and legislative authority'. Nevertheless he hoped that whatever measures Parliament felt compelled to take would 'originate in private observation and interposition. Individual attention leads the way to general conviction, and public measures follow.'[2] What particularly irritated the bishop and several of his usually compliant brethren by the 1840's was that the breakdown of individual attention had greatly contributed to the severity of the situation. He began, for the first time in his long career, to criticize the wealthy for allowing poverty to become so extensive. Sumner was hardly a visionary, and had no illusions 'that the land can be cleared of misery and want. No exertions of benevolence can counteract the effects of sin. . . .' Still there was no question in his mind that 'the condition of a large portion of our community would have been different from what we actually find it, if there had not been wanting on the part of the higher classes that attention to the lower, which both humanity and Christianity require . . .'. He was especially censorious of those 'who employ the labour, and so promote the increase of the working classes'; he wished that they had 'paid due regard to the welfare of those whom they caused to congregate'.[3]

Several of Bishop Sumner's ecclesiastical colleagues were pressing the wealthy to accept more of the responsibility for the spiritual problems, which their acquisitive enterprises created for the Establishment. The latter was unable to provide enough churches and schools for the laboring population. At the same time Bishop Sumner was also urging the wealthy to take a greater role in relieving physical misery. The class bitterness stirred up by Chartism and socialism was alarming. It was not enough simply to abandon implementation of the new Poor Law; it was necessary to re-establish a sense of mutual obligation and responsibility between the rich and the poor. Sumner was hardly alone in his conclusion that the indifference of wealthy employers was of primary importance in creating so much tension. Would the inflammatory new measures have had to be introduced at all if the rich had been willing to double the amount of charity they distributed? Sumner thought not, and calculated that their standard of living would not have changed

[1] *Ibid.*, vi–viii.   [2] *Ibid.*, xiii.   [3] *Ibid.*, x.

appreciably, especially if the charity came from capital rather than 'from luxuries and superfluities'—if it had come 'from that which is annually employed in adding to accumulated opulence: in adding field to field, and business to business, and factory to factory, and hoard to hoard'.

> Indeed, if one fourth part of that capital which has been used of late years for the purpose of extending commercial and manufacturing concerns, had been devoted to purposes more conducive to the glory of God and the real welfare of the community, the reward would have been immediate and the other three-fourths producing, at this moment, a far more valuable return.[1]

The bishop believed that it was possible to determine how much charity was necessary to ameliorate the condition of the poor without requiring any change in the 'general habits' of the rich. Of a total national income of £474,129,688, £12,000,000 was already being spent on the poor: £5,000,000 from the rates, and an equal amount from private donations. An additional £1,000,000 each came from religious societies and parochial charities. Sumner proposed that if an additional expenditure of £500 per thousand people was privately donated, all the real needs of the poor would be satisfied. This sum would in effect double the amount of private benevolence, and while not necessarily reducing the poor rates, it would at least prevent them from rising.[2] Of most importance, however, the extension of private giving would go a long way to heal the breach between rich and poor, and do much to restore shattered class harmony.

Sumner had not completely lost his earlier faith in the natural laws of political economy; only in their application outside of a traditional Christian, charitable framework. He still opposed the artificial raising or subsidizing of wages as interfering with the natural machinery of the community.[3] But he realized that in prosperous countries the 'close and violent contrasts' of wealth and poverty created 'a very anomalous appearance'. This was inevitable, however, and complain as one might, 'money is accumulated in large masses: population verges hard upon the means of subsistence; or, in other words, the demand for employment is greater than the demand for labour'. Legislation could neither produce nor correct the situation, but 'like every other providential arrangement, the evils which belong to it have a corresponding remedy'. In that case it was the acknowledgment that 'we are every one members one of another' (Rom. xii. 5), and if one class of society suffers, all others

---

[1] *Ibid.*, xvi.

[2] *Ibid.*, xiii–xvi. Sumner derived his statistics from James MacQueen, *General Statistics of the British Empire* (1836).

[3] Sumner, *Christian Charity*, 25.

'suffer with it' (1 Cor. xii. 26).[1] Rational political economists had for-gotten these truths, and others too, when they contemplated not only the relief of poverty but its eventual elimination. They had allowed their reason to carry them beyond revelation which truly explained the cause and necessity for labor and poverty. In their enthusiasm they had neg-lected the traditional and proven ways of dealing with the inevitable result of human sin: ways which placed individual responsibilities upon the rich as they placed individual obligations upon the poor.

What it meant to Sumner in practice was an increased concern with the alleviation of particular incidents of severe distress, rather than any hope for the sustained reduction of inevitable poverty. Perhaps through some personal spiritual failing he had lost sight of that divine reality in 1834. The agitation and disturbances of the next few years, as well as the continued extraordinary growth of workers in his huge diocese, not only reminded him but frightened him. It drove him and many others into issuing a revived call for individual Christian charity, and to re-buke not only the corrupt and factious poor, but their thoughtless betters as well. When nineteenth-century bishops started to criticize the rich, things were indeed serious.

The criticisms were often the result of frustrations felt by clergymen overwhelmed by the magnitude of their ministerial tasks in the towns. The revised Poor Law had not helped the problem, but only exacer-bated class tensions and made the Church even more contemptible than before in the eyes of the working classes. By 1841 the guardians were in rebellion, demanding local discretionary powers.[2] In those agricultural areas where workhouses had been established, alarming reports of con-ditions continued to be heard. In spite of Chadwick's dream, it was some-times impossible to make conditions in the workhouses less appealing than outside, and when diligent attendants tried to conform to the Ben-thamite 'less-eligibility' standard, the results were often gruesome. Bishop Phillpotts alone was the most eminent clerical critic of these conditions, but a hostile press and numerous petitions validated his lurid tales. When the Andover workhouse scandal broke in 1845, and it was revealed that inmates were so starved as to fight over the putrid gristle and marrow of the animal bones they were crushing, it should not have been a surprise. The enquiry that followed confirmed the worst suspicions of the critics, and the replacement of the inept Commis-sioners by a new Poor Law Board in 1847 was the final blow.[3] Within five years local guardians were expressly confirmed in their practice of providing the poor with outdoor relief at their discretion.

Churchmen were further disappointed when the Poor Law did not

[1] J. B. Sumner, *A Charge Addressed to the Clergy of the Diocese of Chester
... May and June, MDCCCXLIV* (1844), 22.
[2] Finer, *Chadwick*, 195–6.   [3] Hammond, *Age of the Chartists*, 69–70.

even become an effective means for providing paupers with a basic Christtian education. Chaplains appointed by the guardians were often unsatisfactory and difficult to obtain because of low salaries and the unattractive congregations. Though Bishop Blomfield continually urged guardians to raise chaplains' salaries and provide decent places for worship, he had no means of compelling them to comply.[1] Nonconformist ratepayers and guardians were not overly eager to fulfil the prelate's requests, but there is little indication that their Anglican counterparts were any more compliant.

A few Church leaders whose episcopal careers came later, such as the future Bishop of St Asaph (1846–70), Thomas Vowler Short, and Sumner's successor at Chester (1848–65), John Graham (1794–1865), sought to defend the amended Poor Laws. The latter in 1841, when he was still Master of Christ's College, Cambridge, and Chaplain to Prince Albert, praised 'the wholesome strictness of the revised law', and although it had caused much excitement, he approved very strongly. 'As a friend to the poor', he sincerely believed that if they would but give it time, the law would be of great benefit in 'bringing them back to habits of industry and frugality and temperance; by rekindling in their breasts a spirit of honest independence'.[2] But many clergymen and some bishops were wondering if either the poor or the Church could afford such friends much longer. One of them, Edward Stanley of Norwich, who had earlier approved of the amended Poor Law, by 1846 was endorsing a Christian version of Robert Owen's village communities, proposed five years earlier by J. M. Morgan. Like Archbishop Manners-Sutton thirty years before, Stanley hoped that communal villages of three or four hundred families would prove to be the answer. Half the common agricultural production would be applied towards paying off the initial loan

[1] Letter Copy Book 382, *Fulham Ps*, ff. 289–90.

[2] J. Graham, *A Sermon Preached . . . March 16, 1841, Being the Day On Which the Foundation Stone Was Laid of the Cambridge Victoria Benefit Societies Asylum* (Cambridge, 1841), 6–7. Graham, a strong supporter of the Friendly Benefit Societies, believed they could help workers during periods of unemployment without destroying their independence as the old Poor Law did (p. 11). See also, T. V. Short, *Parochialia: Consisting of Papers Printed For the Use of the Parish of St George's Bloomsbury, During the Years 1834–1841* (1842), 18–19. Published when Short was elevated to the bench in 1841, these tracts emphasized the importance of saving associations, benefit societies and education as means of freeing the laboring classes from their eleemosynary dependence on society.

Short (1790–1872), son of a Cornish clergyman, was a Liberal moderate High Churchman who owed his early advancement to Brougham. Appointed to Sodor and Man in 1841, he was translated by Russell to St Asaph in 1846. Was a serious, hard-working bishop who spent half his income on improving the see before resigning in 1870.

until the land and houses became the property of the laborers. Each village would, of course, include a church and houses for the clergy. The initial capital of £45,000 was to be provided by a new Church of England Self Supporting Village Society. The liberal, Broad Church Stanley joined with the High Church, Young England idealist, Lord John Manners, in supporting the utopian scheme. However, since the community would need 183 years of stable prices to pay off the investment, the workers would be unable to acquire the property before the year 2030. It was hardly an immediate solution to a pressing problem. Furthermore, Owen's authentic disciples were shocked by the wasteful proposal to spend £4,500 of the capital upon a church and parsonage.[1]

Considering recent episcopal denunciations of Owenite socialism as atheistic and leveling, Stanley's endorsement of Morgan's plan was a bold move. But then the Bishop of Norwich was a singularly independent person who recognized that relationships with the laboring poor had become so strained that all avenues of reconciliation ought at least to be explored. Most prelates understood this by the 1840's, even if many of them could not overcome their instinctive dislike of innovation and ecclesiastical flexibility. Yet it was difficult to disagree with the perceptive and very capable Edward Denison when, in 1845, he frankly concluded that poverty, and the Church's attitude towards it, seriously threatened the revival and survival of the Establishment as a national institution. Elevated to the See of Salisbury in 1837 at the age of thirty-six, Denison was a diligent, reforming bishop who spent long hours visiting the poor, even during the cholera epidemics. During his seventeen years at Salisbury he preached regularly on Sundays when in the cathedral town, and donated more than £17,000 to charity, saving nothing from his episcopal income. Even the critical Samuel Wilberforce modestly conceded that Denison was one of the few prelates of the age as capable as he.[2]

Reviewing the efforts of the Church to regain the confidence of the laboring classes in recent years, Denison questioned whether the Establishment had been as realistic and as independent as it should have been; whether it really understood the complexity of the problem. 'It is plain and easy to lay down in the abstract the duties of the parish priest ministering to a population, on a large part of which poverty presses, as it now does on our own, while the wealth of the more opulent class is collected into fewer hands, and is in them increased.' It was simple to ask clergymen to preach contentment to the poor and promise them a better life in heaven, while telling the rich of their stewardship, and of their blessed task to help the deserving poor. But he knew how difficult

[1] Chadwick, *Victorian Church*, 348.

[2] Wilberforce to W. E. Gladstone, 26 Dec. 1851, *Wilberforce Ps.*, Bodleian Library Dep. D. 204, ff. 281–6.

it was for serious ministers to do it 'with faithfulness and tenderness, with boldness and discretion'.[1] It was in effect difficult to translate social and economic realities into spiritual justifications, no matter how disagreeable those realities might be.

Denison articulated what many perceptive churchmen knew: in spite of a determined effort by the ministry, preaching to the poor was as difficult as ever because the Church had become completely identified with the interests of the rich and the legislation of the propertied classes. The Poor Law was a perfect example—a product of secular, material thought rather than of Christian spiritual feeling and obligation. Though by ordination and law the clergy were responsible for the harmonizing of parochial poor relief, 'the current of modern legislation has in a great degree run counter to this intention of the Church, and has interrupted the connexion between the parish priest and the most destitute members of his flock'.[2] Law and Phillpotts had warned of this a decade earlier, before Denison was even on the bench. Now the young prelate openly opposed clergymen participating in the administration of the Poor Law, as reform-minded clergy had earlier pushed for an end to clerical magistrates. The nature of the law, he said, 'does not bear with it the gracefulness of charity, or have the character of almsgiving of Christian men'.[3] The workhouses were the most distressing manifestation of what the bishop clearly felt was un-Christian legislation. Not only was it reprehensible to force the virtuous poor into indiscriminate contact with the 'idle, and careless, and profligate, who will be habitually inmates of these houses', but they would have a frightful effect upon children whether they be illegitimate or not.[4] Again, he was sorry that the Church had become associated with such wretched places and identified accordingly in the minds of the suffering poor.

Denison was defining in social terms what the Tractarians were arguing in theological and historical terms; the Church had allowed itself to become an instrument of the State and secular interests which had resulted in a steady erosion of its Christian independence. As the Tractarians deplored the reality of the Church controlled by a legislature comprised in part of Nonconformists and Catholics, and whose sacred doctrines were ultimately subject to the interpretation of a lay committee, so Bishop Denison deplored the necessary association of the Church with the doubtful policies of the ruling orders that only intensified class antagonisms. Personal charity and an ameliorative relationship between pauper and priest were fundamental qualities of a true Christian society. But the cold impersonality of class relationships had, he feared, in his own lifetime split the Church off from great multitudes

[1] E. Denison, *A Charge Delivered to the Clergy of the Diocese of Salisbury . . . in April and May, 1845* (1845), 43–44.

[2] *Ibid.*, 44.   [3] *Ibid.*, 45.   [4] *Ibid.*, 48–49.

of children who had lost their way. On the basis of Christian necessity, both for the good of the poor as well as the Church, there is, he insisted with careful restraint, 'a most cogent reason for the exercise of some further discretion on granting outdoor relief'.[1]

That discretion was soon forthcoming; by mid-century Denison and others like him who were trying to reinvigorate the Establishment and make it a national spiritual institution once more, were relieved that the contentious, inflexible Poor Law had been sufficiently modified so as to stand in the way no longer. But perhaps the damage had already been done. Denison partially realized himself that the association of the Church with the Poor Law Amendment Act was more a symptom of the Establishment's weakness and dilemma than it was a cause. The clergy had never been enthusiastic about the new measure; yet they were too closely associated with and reflective of the interests of the wealthy propertied classes to overcome their own coolness towards a severe act which could only infuriate the laboring classes, and weaken the Church's great efforts to attract the poor to the hundreds of schools and churches still being erected in all parts of the country. To an earnest ministry dedicated to the critical task of social reconciliation as well as the salvation of souls, it was an unhappy situation.

[1] *Ibid.*, 49.

VI

Church and Social Legislation

1. EARLY FACTORY CONDITIONS

The Church's awareness of the social and religious implications of economic change tended to be governed by the difficulty it encountered in reaching the laboring populace. As more dedicated clergymen with each passing decade saw their educational efforts continually frustrated by the necessitous demands for child labor, and their revivalistic exertions ignored or spurned by countless multitudes who found the national faith irrelevant or inimical to their needs, they were forced to re-evaluate not only the teachings and structure of the Establishment, but its applicability to social and economic realities. This meant that churchmen had to think about those realities, and in time concede a direct relationship between social conditions and individual and collective human behavior. They were, like most interested Englishmen, assisted by the remarkable expansion of parliamentary enquiry that introduced legislators and the public at large to the way millions of their working countrymen of both sexes and all ages lived, labored and died.

Awareness was one thing; improvement another. Clergymen born and raised in the atmosphere of the Georgian Church did not think of the Establishment as an instrument of social action, capable of affecting social conditions. Such conditions were, after all, natural manifestations of a hierarchical society, and it was certainly likely that tampering with them would actually do more harm than good. The French Revolution sufficed to quiet those who might have thought otherwise. Yet, in 1806, the Bishop of Exeter, John Fisher (1748–1825), questioned whether

193

Christianity had not become too aloof from social realities, allowing the world to become 'a *spiritual* and moral WILDERNESS . . .'.[1] Fisher, who built his career tutoring such notables as Queen Victoria's father and Princess Charlotte, was nevertheless aware that the Church was not sufficiently 'condescending to men of low estate . . .', and was much too ineffective among the lower orders. He suspected that this resulted, in part, from a setting aside of the social principles of Christianity for individual selfish satisfactions. Struck by the 'blighted corruption' into which the children of the London poor were born and raised, the bishop recalled that 'Christianity is a social principle of action, and will not permit us, for a moment, to rest in a selfish acquiescence in our own personal progress and sustainment . . .'.[2] Like many Church leaders of the next decade, Fisher first became aware of social conditions through the education of the poor. As Vice-President of the newly established British and Foreign Bible Society (1804), and a strong supporter of Sunday schools, he was distressed to learn of the extent to which poverty, especially in the towns, interfered with meaningful clerical ministrations.

Such episcopal solicitude, however, was comparatively rare that early in the century, and ideas of Christian social action were alien to the whole tenor of Establishment thought. Fisher himself spoke only in the vaguest of generalities. Moreover, in 1802, the year before his elevation to the bench, he showed no interest in the elder Sir Robert Peel's Health and Morals of Apprentices Act, containing protective regulations for parish apprentices sent to cotton and woollen factories. Only one prelate, Henry Majendie of Chester, even mentioned the measure. Since many of the factories in question were in his diocese, Majendie urged that his clergy 'especially shew themselves forward to co-operate with the Civil Magistrate in correcting such irregularities, as are known to be injurious to the principles and health of multitudes of children of both sexes engaged in large manufactures'. The remainder of the bench did not oppose the Act with its provision for religious instruction on Sunday. There was no episcopal dissent from Majendie's conclusion that the new legislation was 'excellent, benevolent and judicious'.[3] Still, the bench believed that economic and social legislation was beyond their prescribed area of political activity and saw no reason to enter the debate.

Information on working-class conditions was slow to make any

[1] J. Fisher, *A Sermon Preached . . . June 5, 1806, Being the Time of the Yearly Meeting of the Children Educated in the Charity Schools . . .* (1806), 2.

[2] J. Fisher, *A Charge Delivered to the Clergy of the Diocese of Exeter . . . 1804 and 1805* (1805), 23–24.

[3] Majendie, *Charge* (1804), 19–20.

impression on the bench, in spite of Eden's and Colquhoun's independent studies that revealed the extent of misery endured by the laboring poor. Few bishops had any experience with the realities of poverty and deleterious labor. One of the few who did, Bishop Porteus, as early as 1786 recognized that factory life in his diocese of Chester was perhaps having a harmful effect on workers. Though an energetic supporter of Sunday schools and an ardent Sabbatarian by the standards of the day, Porteus was troubled enough to ask his clergy to leave plenty of time on Sunday for the poor to enjoy some rest and relaxation. 'This relaxation is necessary for *all*, but *especially* for those who are confined at work in trades or manufactures during the whole week; and still more, where they are employed in a constant course of labour (different sets succeeding each other) *day and night*, which I am told is the case in some of the cotton manufactures.' He was moved to discuss the matter after having studied a report of the physicians of Manchester on a deadly fever that ravaged the town of Radcliffe two years before. As contributing causes to the epidemic, which had been especially hard on children, the doctors had pointed to oppressive hours, confined space and limited relaxation. Now that the reasons were clearly understood, Porteus closed the subject, certain that 'there can be no doubt, but that the proprietors of the cotton mills, and other factories, where children are accustomed to work, will, on every principle of charity, compassion, and sound policy, conceive themselves bound to observe most punctually and religiously those excellent regulations'.[1]

The natural and scientific justifications allowing factory-owners to ignore such recommendations were not yet spelled out, though the letters were being arranged by the grammarians of political economy. If Porteus was disappointed with the response to the physicians' report, he never mentioned it. His attention turned towards the slave trade and, during the French Revolution, towards the inculcation of social reliability rather than social improvement. Even if working and living conditions were as deplorable as some studies indicated, nothing much could be done while Christian civilization tottered on the brink of revolutionary anarchy. The times called for a reaffirmation of established social principles, policies and institutions, not innovation. Although episcopal arguments to the contrary were lacking, except in matters regarding the overseas slave trade, there were clergymen, considerably lower in the hierarchy, whose hearts felt 'no small anxiety' at the condition of the poor. William Jones, Vicar of Broxbourne, Hertfordshire, for example, saw the poor 'crowded together in dark courts and narrow alleys, in cellars, or in garrets; where damp, stagnated air, and accumulated filthiness, injure their health, and facilitate the progress of

[1] B. Porteus, *A Letter to the Clergy of the Diocese of Chester Concerning Sunday Schools*, 2nd ed. (1786), 21–22.

contagious diseases'. From the church registers of births and deaths, he also noted how epidemics 'which might almost be called by the frightful name of plague . . . rapidly cleared off a great number of poor people', such as Hoddesdon experienced in 1803. Noting in his diary that mainly the poor were afflicted, Jones 'verily believed the disorder . . . has been generated from *poverty* and *filth*. The poor, notwithstanding the assistance of parishes, and the charity of benevolent individuals, were so reduced by the severe pressure of the times, that they had not anything like strength remaining, which might resist, or throw off, distemper in any form.'[1]

As awareness of such conditions reached those more favorably placed in the Church, reactions varied. The Evangelical Dean of Wells, Henry Ryder, soon to be Bishop of Gloucester, ran soup kitchens for the poor and personally distributed food and clothing on a regular basis in his two Leicestershire parishes as well as in the parishes of the deanery.[2] William Howley, Regius Professor of Divinity at Oxford, two years before his move to London in 1813, confessed to Lord Aberdeen that there was no rational way to cope with widespread misery; 'it is neither in our power nor is it our duty to attend solely in these cases to dry reason. Affliction is to the mind, as pain is to the body: Insensibility is an unnatural state: But reason and duty suggest the propriety of submitting to bodily mental anguish and bodily torture with manly composure and pious resignation'. The suffering poor, like all people, had to understand that this life is but a prelude to an eternity.[3]

The distributors of charity and the preachers of resignation did not deny the unhappy conditions in which the poor labored and lived. They assuaged and explained them in traditional ways. When, after the wars, the movement for factory legislation was resumed and the elder Peel, with Robert Owen's assistance, sought to extend the protective measures he had encouraged earlier, a new generation of Church leaders was starting to make itself heard. Conscious of the rapid expansion of the laboring population and the existing inadequacies of Church facilities, they slowly began to understand that their schools and new places of worship had to be seen and planned in the context of social and economic conditions they hardly comprehended. Like it or not, if the revived Establishment was to capture future generations of laboring children for the national faith, its guardians had to take a more active interest in the lives led by those children and their parents.

Yet Church leaders knew very little about the conditions that were to

[1] W. Jones, *The Diary of the Rev. William Jones, 1771–1821*, O. F. Christie, ed. (1929), 138–9.

[2] Ryder to Dudley Ryder, 15 April 1812, *Harrowby MS.*, V, ff. 105–6, Sandon Hall, Staffordshire.

[3] 4 Nov. 1811, *Aberdeen Ps.* British Museum, Add. MS. 43195, ff. 5–7.

frustrate their revivalist efforts and make the Church appear meaning-less to multitudes of workers who viewed it as a hostile creature of the wealthy classes. This can be seen in John Bird Sumner's hesitant apprai-sal of working-class conditions in 1816. God, according to that clergy-man, had not only fashioned the laboring man's constitution to adjust to the harsh, manual conditions of his trial, but had also provided him relative satisfactions conformable to lower-class standards. This was true for factory workers as well as other laborers, and Sumner could not believe that the former were more unhappy than the generality of their class, except perhaps in those factories where there was limited space, only tolerable air to breathe, monotonous repetition of function, and dis-solute, gregarious surroundings. The possibility that this description might be the rule rather than the exception did not occur to Sumner, who consequently believed that factory laborers were either quite healthy, or, if not, only suffered when employers were a little thoughtless. In par-ticular, Sumner recommended the example of Owen's model factory at Lanark, and urged the reforming industrialist to publish a detailed ac-count of it to serve as a model for other factory-owners.[1] Although Owen complied, he understood long before Sumner how little influence it had on men of his class.

While undoubtedly there were abuses in the factories, Sumner was sure the charges were exaggerated, though he did not visit a factory until a decade later, when Bishop of Chester. He could not accept the lament-able descriptions of child labor presented by early advocates of factory legislation. Troubled by the contradictory medical reports gathered by people on both sides of the question, Sumner, like most contemporaries, chose those that were accommodating to his preconceptions. Citing from Dr Jarrold's *Dissertations on Man*, Sumner argued that children in cotton factories were as healthy as those living in any great town. It was true that the pallor of their skin and their clothes covered with cotton make them look 'forlorn', but there was no evidence that they were unhealthy. If it was true for children, it applied with equal force to adults. Instead of complaining about the mechanization of industry which brought people together into factories, Sumner welcomed it as a means of relieving overcrowding in homes where domestic industry had flourished.[2]

Factories, as far as Sumner was concerned, were no more guilty of dulling the mind than they were of wrecking the body. Adam Smith had raised the possibility that mechanization and the routine division of labor might stultify the mental faculties, but Sumner could see no evi-dence of it. Factory work might not be intellectually stimulating, but the

[1] J. B. Sumner, *Treatise*, II, 280–3. Sumner learned of Owen's work from the Society For Bettering the Conditions of the Poor, *Reports*, VIII.
[2] *Ibid.*, 282.

clergyman found it difficult to cite many vocations, among either the illiterate or educated classes, which contributed to the improvement of the mind. A true enrichment of the intellect required both leisure and commitment, for which few occupations provided. Sumner belonged to one that did, and, like generations of his clerical brethren before him, found it difficult to understand the effects of one that did not. This was not to minimize the limited possibilities for improvement that did exist for town workers: 'in point of fact, the manufacturer derives a superiority over the peasant, from his constant intercourse with society, and the collision of various minds to which he has been accustomed from his youth. And as for the mechanic, whose labour does not confine him to a single spot, whose work demands the frequent resources of his ingenuity, and who is constantly interested in the pursuit of some new employment or operation, none of the evils of manufactures must be considered as applying to him.'[1]

As an early clerical convert to Malthusian economics, Sumner was suspicious of intensifying arguments for legislative interference into factory conditions. While he admittedly had little first-hand experience with industrial expansion, and in the *Records of Creation* primarily discussed agricultural laborers, he did believe that the principle of free labor in an unrestricted market was necessary for an improving economy. From a Malthusian standpoint, free labor would encourage worker migration from overpopulated areas, and promote a more productive redistribution of the labor force. What this would mean for his Church, thoroughly unprepared for the great swelling of urban manufacturing centers, did not yet occur to this future bishop of areas such as Liverpool and Manchester. There is no indication of his response to the elder Peel's argument that the principle of free labor, while sound, could not be applied to little children who were in no position to know their own minds. It is, however, unlikely that he was one of the thousands of signatories to petitions in 1818–19 calling for legislation restricting the overworking of children before the age of sixteen.

Many clergymen, along with doctors, shopkeepers, manufacturers, artisans, and workers, did sign such pleas which were presented to the House of Lords by the one episcopal advocate of legislation, George Henry Law.[2] An influential Tory prelate, then Bishop of Chester, Law threw his weight behind Lords Liverpool, Holland and Kenyon as they fought off the free labor resistance of the aristocratic spokesman for political economy, the Earl of Lauderdale. Bishop Law joined the battle in 1817, when, on a visit to Stockport, he was shocked at the conditions under which children labored in the mills.[3] Energetic and paternalistic,

[1] *Ibid.*, 283.   [2] *Hansard*, XXXIX (1819), 340.
[3] R. B. Walker, 'Religious Changes in Cheshire, 1750–1850'. *The Journal of Ecclesiastical History*, XVII, No. 1 (1966), 91.

Law had the uncommon episcopal habit of actually visiting many of the parishes in his diocese. He soon discovered that the example of Stockport was not unique. He urged the appointment of a committee of enquiry and brought in long petitions from Lancashire, Cheshire and Lanarkshire. Lauderdale suggested that the petitioners were either bribed, unreliable, or were northern agitators stirring up workers in Manchester and elsewhere. Law countered with still more petitions, including some from parents of factory children and others from children above the age of sixteen who also begged protection.[1] Moreover, the bishop, having personally confirmed many of their complaints through extensive visits to factories throughout his huge diocese, was in no mood to have *his* word questioned by doubting opponents.[2]

Lauderdale managed temporarily to block the passage of Peel's measure, which had been largely drafted by Owen. Striking out with dire warnings about interfering with property and trade, he then calmed troubled consciences with medically confirmed evidence that children were actually healthier as a result of their labor in the factories. Law, along with Liverpool and other allies, contradicted these claims with medical testimony, substantiated by the parents of children in the factories, who, as Law said, certainly knew the state of their offspring's health. Furthermore, Law claimed, it was misleading to interject free trade arguments since the children in question were hardly free agents. No one could believe that children would work fourteen or sixteen hours a day if they had any choice.[3] Only a paternalistic Parliament could protect the poor worker, and it was indisputably clear from his diocese alone that the legislature must act.

When it did so in 1819, instead of all the textile factories, as Owen, Peel and Bishop Law wanted, only the cotton mills were affected.[4] Children under sixteen were to be protected, and could not work more than twelve hours a day, while all those under nine were completely excluded from the mills. It mattered little, however, since Owen's important proposal to appoint salaried factory inspectors, which had been in Peel's Bill since it was first proposed in 1815, was finally dropped. It meant that inspection remained in the hands of local magistrates and clergymen, and there was no indication that they would be any more diligent than they had been in the past. This did not greatly trouble the bishop, who was hopeful that the evil, now pointed out, would be voluntarily corrected. Having carefully exonerated the factory-owners from wilful inhumanity and misrepresentation during the debates, Law felt that they, too, would see the dangers of excessive child labor.[5] As their workers exhibited patience and resignation, so they might exercise

[1] *Hansard*, XXXIX (1819), 347–8.   [2] *Ibid.*, 655.
[3] *Ibid.*, XXXVIII (1818), 793–4.   [4] 59 Geo III, c. 66.
[5] *Hansard*, XXXVIII (1818), 793.

kindness and charity in this 'vast theater of action [life], presenting scenes of misery—and virtue'.[1]

True to the purple, Bishop Law was a cautious and deeply conservative churchman, willing to forgo the centralizing innovation of a factory inspectorate. From the clergy in his own diocese he received considerable information and support and was confident that they would continue to oversee conditions and correct abuses in their parishes. No other bishop joined in the inspectorate debate, their sermons and charges not even alluding to the question. For, in spite of the fact that powerful Church leaders were now more conscious than ever of the need to extend the ministry into crowded manufacturing towns by establishing schools and constructing new and enlarged places of worship, this did not imply to them any Church responsibility for the physical well-being of those laboring masses they were attempting to reach. The fears and tensions of the post-war years, together with the tragedy at Manchester in 1819, undoubtedly made the hierarchy even more reluctant to trifle with social and economic matters already brought to the boiling-point by fanatical enthusiasts and other enemies of an orderly society. But it is even more likely that the guardians of the Establishment still understood their functions and those of the Church in precise categories which kept political and economic questions separate from spiritual considertions. They did not yet see that, in an age of great transformation, their additional function of social preservation and class reconciliation precluded their keeping categories and functions so neatly compartmentalized. Spiritual enhancement in the towns could no longer be separated from physical improvement. Like it or not, churchmen would have to be concerned with the dirty, diseased, foul-smelling bodies of the working poor if they were to reach beneath the grime to cleanse their corrupt and sinful souls. Law and his colleagues on the bench scarcely contemplated that disagreeable prospect in 1819. Law never once suggested in two years of debate that the physical condition of the poor was relevant to the spiritual ministrations of the Church. Before his long career was over, Law knew that it was; meanwhile, a new generation of clergy had emerged, more sensitive to and interested in the connection between social conditions and spiritual effectiveness.

2. MINES AND FACTORIES, 1832–50

By the end of the next decade, several prelates were less reticent about committing themselves to questions of social legislation. Disturbances in

[1] G. H. Law, *The Necessity and Advantages of an Habitual Intercourse With the Deity. A Sermon Preached . . . October 31, 1819* (Chester, 1819), 8–10, and *A Sermon Preached . . . June 13, 1813, Being the Time of the Yearly Meeting of the Children Educated In the Charity Schools* (1813), 2.

the agricultural counties and agitation in manufacturing districts confirmed the growing impression that the Church's efforts to promote spiritual and social contentment were being hamstrung by economic and social conditions beyond its control. Although Church leaders were little prepared to do much about it, some of them were prodded into openly supporting renewed efforts to obtain meaningful restrictions on child labor and improvements in working conditions. While Bishop Law was promoting land allotments for distressed agricultural laborers in 1830-1, a few of his colleagues, including both archbishops, welcomed the enquiries of the Select Committee of 1832 and those of the Factory Commission the following year, which led to the Act of 1833.[1] Under its provisions children under thirteen were limited to a nine-hour day or a forty-eight-hour week, except in silk mills, where ten hours' work was permitted. Furthermore, no child under nine was to work in any mill except a silk mill, and no one under eighteen could work at night. Children between the ages of thirteen and eighteen could not be worked for more than twelve hours a day or sixty-nine hours a week. Especially meaningful to the Church was the provision requiring that children under thirteen have two hours' schooling each day. The establishment of travelling inspectors, absent in earlier legislation, gave the new measure some teeth.

Archbishop Howley, when Bishop of London during the debates of the post-war years, had never even acknowledged the existence of a factory in the country. He was willing to learn, however, and in 1832 not only presented petitions in favor of regulatory legislation, but deplored the system of 'cruelty and oppression' that kept children in factories for thirteen to sixteen hours a day. It was a disgrace to a Christian and civilized nation to allow such exploitation to continue 'merely for putting money in the pockets of the master manufacturers'.[2] The timorous, often inarticulate Howley was speaking with what, for him, was uncommon bluntness. His old Tory archdeacon, Joseph Pott, had been less gentle with manufacturers, whom he described as 'the worst of . . . seducers . . . , rootless, scribbling, mercenary men, whose discontents are the growth of uncontrolled desires, of envious and ambitious thoughts; who live by fraudulent dissimulations and dishonourable calumnies; who care not whom [they] strip, the nobler sort of their good name, the poor man of his hope . . . '.[3]

While invective would not alter the reality of an industrial world Pott and many other eighteenth-century clergy abhorred and feared, Bishop

[1] 3 and 4 Wm. IV, c. 103.

[2] *Hansard*, X (1832), 985-6.

[3] J. H. Pott, *The Scandals of Impiety and Unbelief, And the Pleas Made For Them by Their Abettors, Considered In A Charge Delivered to the Clergy of the Archdeaconry of London . . . May 4, 1820* (1820), 23.

Ryder hoped that legislation and good intentions perhaps could. Factories, Ryder thought, need not be so destructive of workers, as he recalled 'the ever memorable instance of the Scottish manufactory [Owen's] in the valley of Dale—where, in twelve years, out of three thousand children successively employed, only twelve died, and not one was brought before a magistrate for any serious offense'. That record, Ryder believed, 'should satisfy us that such a consummation is not a mere dream of benevolent enthusiasm'. There were other similar instances of enlightened manufacturers—concerned with the welfare of their workers, yet able to profit. Nevertheless, the bishop realized that legislation was necessary to destroy the 'virtual tyranny, which has been exercised by some of the higher over the lower classes of the mercantile community, and . . . to enable the poor man to make the best—at least his own—use of his little weekly earnings, and to profit by his children's earliest *safe* and *suitable* exertions, without ruining their constitutions by premature and excessive toil in an unwholesome atmosphere'. Ryder, of course, wished that 'moral superintendence' and the daily inculcation of religious knowledge could be attached to these temporal improvements and welcomed the minimal educational provisions that were included.[1]

Given the more obvious truths of political economy, many churchmen were strong advocates of *laissez-faire* policies, and doubted the wisdom of legislative interference. Blomfield, who was to take a very active role in the promotion of social legislation in the 1840's, was clearly unenthusiastic about it in 1830. Though he agreed to participate as a member of a 'Manufacturers Relief Committee' to assist the unemployed workers in industrial districts, he had little faith in such unnatural measures.[2] He steered clear of the debates over legislation in 1832–3, but his views were soon made known in the discussions of the Poor Law revisions his Commission proposed. In 1831 Edward Stanley had exemplified caution by warning against being panicked into regulatory measures because of riots and disturbances in manufacturing and agricultural areas. Economic fluctuations, mechanization, and temporary unemployment were, like all occasional abuses, an unfortunate but necessary aspect of progressive change. It had been the case in the development of printing, the introduction of the plow, harrow, watermill, and, since 1815, power looms and other machines.[3] Stanley was certain that the poor would be much worse off without these developments.

---

[1] H. Ryder, *A Charge Addressed to the Clergy of the Diocese of Lichfield and Coventry . . . August, 1832* (1832), 25–26.

[2] Blomfield to Lord Francis Leveson Gower, 13 June 1830, *Peel Ps.*, Add. MS. 40338, f. 190.

[3] E. Stanley, 'A Country Rector's Address to His Parishioners . . . With Reference to the Disturbed State of the Times (1831)'. in *Addresses and Charges* (1851), 4–8.

Richard Arkwright, he recalled, was assailed when the spinning jenny deprived the poor of employment, but in less than twenty-five years a half million people were employed in cotton manufacturing, 'all getting plenty of money, and rearing families in comfort . . .'. Consequently, he was reluctant to see any interference from the legislature or from individuals which would disrupt the functioning of a free competitive society. Any action that caused a rise in cost of consumer goods—a breaking of machines, or a combining for higher wages—actually injured the lower classes. The reduction of working hours or the raising of wages cut into profits; and, in a competitive society where all things are reduced to a 'just scale', an easy acceptance of this is not possible beyond a point. The competitive system kept prices within a natural range, but if workmen asked for 'unreasonable wages', resisted machinery, or demanded that other restrictions be imposed, the whole public suffered from higher prices. As the poor were the greater part of the public, Stanley concluded that they would suffer the most.[1]

Later, after leaving his family living in Cheshire in 1837 for the See of Norwich, Stanley, like many prelates of his generation, became more flexible in his attitude towards social and economic problems. In 1831, however, still certain that the laws of *laissez-faire* political economy were applicable, his argument avoided specific reference to the child-labor problem, and was largely supportive of those opposed to regulation. Yet, upon his elevation to the bench, he became one of the strongest episcopal advocates of liberal, national education; he quickly learned, as more and more of his contemporaries recognized, that so long as the children of the poor were confined to factories for most of their waking hours, or forced to enter them at an early age, the Church's hold on them would be brief and superficial. Times were changing, however, and by the 1830's it was becoming clear to Church leaders that they could no more remain unconcerned about the physical conditions of the populace than they could about the physical condition of the Church itself. The well-being of the one seemed, more than ever, dependent upon the improvement of the other. The Whig victory and mood of reform in 1830 delighted and encouraged Stanley's predecessor at Norwich, Bathurst, who hoped that, at last, 'some regulations [will] meliorate the condition of the labouring poor, who . . . have been sadly ground down'.[2]

In spite of the legislation of 1833 (which did not go into effect until 1836), relief was slow in coming. The Poor Law Amendment Act of 1834 suggests that the enthusiasm of old Bathurst was perhaps ill-founded. But within the Church as in the country as a whole, the atmosphere was changing—accelerated, perhaps, by the disaster of the new

[1] *Ibid.*, 11–12.

[2] Bathurst to daughter, 24 Jan. 1831, in *Memoirs and Correspondence of Dr Henry Bathurst . . .*, Mrs Thistlethwayte, ed. (1853), 373–4.

Poor Law—and when the next wave of factory legislation broke, a few more ecclesiastics were ready to help guide it into constructive channels. Undoubtedly, Chartist and socialist agitation, and the realization that both movements were hostile not only to established society in general, but also to the Established Church in particular, motivated these ecclesiastics to see a necessity for some meaningful concessions. At the same time, however, a decade of parliamentary reports and debates documenting the incredible conditions in the laboring world often shocked the sensibilities even of Anglican clergymen who themselves began to hear a slightly hollow ring in the mechanically repeated and often empty homilies, on the inevitability and necessity of suffering.

It would be an exaggeration to describe ecclesiastical involvement as a sudden outpouring of a compassionately aroused social conscience. That conscience was stirred up very slowly, and in general conformed to that of the government's. The bishops who endorsed the mining, factory and sanitation legislation of the 1830's and 1840's, for example, were more often followers than leaders, supporters than formulators, in these efforts. That, after all, had long been the position of the hierarchy, and, whatever religious and administrative conflicts it had had with the government, their interests were still too closely allied to permit the introduction of significant social alternatives. Like the government and the legislature, they recognized that some social conditions were too deplorable and dangerous to be allowed to continue unalleviated, since the working classes and many of their allies from the higher ranks were no longer willing to endure them peacefully. Such conditions interfered with the security of the State and the effectiveness of its spiritual arm. None the less, only a small minority of the bench ever felt moved to enter the debates, and with the exception of the Corn Law discussions, their attendance and voting remained minimal.

Revelations contained in the Commission's report on child and female labor in the mines issued in 1842 opened up a decade of social legislation by immediately rallying support for the quick passage of regulatory laws to keep women, and boys under ten, above ground.[1] Bishop Stanley, who had been cool to restrictive factory legislation a decade earlier, now presented several petitions against the employment of women and children in the mines, and decried their wretched, bestial working conditions. Like many of his contemporaries, he was particularly shocked by the gross immorality and sensuality that flourished underground in the presence of impressionable children.[2] Stanley, who thought that ten-year-old boys were too young to enter the pits, urged, in vain, a minimum age of thirteen.[3]

The Bishop of London, Blomfield, who had suffered much abuse because of his close association with the hated Poor Law Amendment

[1] 5 and 6 Vict., c. 99.   [2] *Hansard*, LXIII (1842), 196.   [3] *Ibid.*, LXIV, 1166.

Act of 1834, had generally remained silent on social questions throughout the remainder of the decade. But his energetic work in Church extension and reform had increasingly brought him into contact with the economic and social realities of working-class life, and any illusions he might have had earlier about the folly of legislative interference were dispelled. His *laissez-faire* days were over when in 1842 he insisted that the legislature was not only able, but was obligated, to step in and remedy the great evils existing not only in the collieries then under investigation, but in manufacturing towns as well. He no longer had patience with the claims of a mine-owning Lord Londonderry, or an Earl Fitzwilliam, that children in the factories and the collieries were as healthy as those in agricultural districts. When the latter peer called for still another enquiry into working conditions of children, Blomfield curtly replied that no more reports were needed to show the evils of a system 'which was eating into the very vitals of the country'. All statistical evidence showed a higher mortality rate in the factories and the mines, and it was clear that whatever misfortunes agricultural laborers suffered, they were 'fearfully aggravated among the manufacturing population'. With or without more study, the bishop frankly doubted that the Lords could really form a very accurate estimation of the condition of those classes from whom they were so far removed.[1]

Changing attitudes were clearly evident in the greater interest churchmen showed in the abortive Factory Act of 1843, especially in its provisions for the education of factory children under Establishment control. While lowering the age-limit of employment from nine to eight, the measure also cut the number of hours of work from eight to six and a half in textile factories, thus acknowledging the necessity for providing more time in school and reaffirming the special educational privileges of the national faith. Church leaders were naturally disappointed when Nonconformists angrily protested, petitioned against, and finally forced the withdrawal of a measure that would enhance the influence of the Church. During the following year, when it passed without the educational clauses, the bench, to quiet Dissenter fears, remained silent, even though many of its members undoubtedly welcomed the twelve-hour day for all women and the reduction of hours for children between the ages of eight and thirteen. The bishops now felt that they were clearly on the side of the angels, in contrast to hardened Nonconformists whose stubborn resistance alone prevented the bestowal of even greater benefits on factory children.

During the debate over the critical Ten Hours Act of 1847, the episcopate was prepared to take a more active role than ever before. Newer prelates like Charles Longley, John Lonsdale, James Prince Lee and Samuel Wilberforce joined with Blomfield and Connop Thirlwall to

[1] *Ibid.*, LXIII, 199.

place the Church squarely behind the important measure. Blomfield had spent too many years compromising with reality to tolerate the abstract philosophical objections of orthodox political economists whose ideas he now felt had little application to the practical problems of the working classes. Reason and charity required the bending of rigid philosophies to alleviate unacceptable misery. He no longer believed that government which governed least, governed best: rather, government that governed paternally, governed best, and it must interfere to prevent excessive injury to so many of the population unable to protect themselves. Blomfield knew, as opponents claimed, that if women and children were limited to a ten-hour day, it would, in effect, mean the same for all adults; but the physical and spiritual salvation of the young was too important to balk at what was, in any event, a just result. For too long had children been considered factory instruments for making money, and if their 'natural guardians' (parents) would not stop it, the legislature had to. Hope lay with the future generation, and, unless it was given time for moral and physical improvement, the troubles of recent years would be frequently repeated.[1]

Blomfield fluctuated between angry rebuttal and cautious conciliation. To those who doubted the severity of factory conditions he replied that the mills were prisons holding the helpless workers to a ceaseless process of manufacturing that injures their health and brings on early death. Statistics, not sentiment, showed that factory workers had twice as high a death-rate as other urban employees. The bishop knew, of course, that the mill-owners really had the best interests of their workers at heart, and he certainly shared their opposition to legislative interference. Unless it was undertaken, however, there would be an even more rapid physical deterioration and moral degradation of a large portion of the most helpless classes. Opponents had used the same arguments against the twelve-hour limitation and other improving measures, complaining that output would be curtailed, yet mechanization had and would continue to compensate for the difference. Underlying Blomfield's argument was always the question of Church extension. What most troubled him was that working-class children had insufficient time to attend the National Society schools. He therefore concluded that even the proposed ten-hour day was grossly inadequate to educate factory children religiously and to guarantee the security of the nation.[2]

Although Blomfield's open adherence to the short-time cause was late in coming, the Church in general had been cool to a measure that all too often seemed embroiled in dangerous agitation. In 1833, the principal clerical promoter of the measure, George Stringer Bull, 'the Ten Hours parson' of Bierley, said that only two of seventy Manchester clergymen

[1] *Ibid.*, XCII (1847), 925–6.   [2] *Ibid.*, 927–30.

of all denominations supported him.[1] Among the early supporters, however, was the reticent Archbishop of York, Vernon-Harcourt. Although he never spoke on that or any other question of social legislation, the archbishop gave Bull twenty pounds in 1833 to assist the Ten Hours movement.[2] Gradually churchmen began to associate themselves with the short-time advocates, especially when it became clear that many respectable and responsible persons, both Tory and Whig, found merit in the cause. Charles Longley, the first bishop of the newly established diocese of Ripon, recalled years later, when Archbishop of Canterbury (1862–8), how he had given his support to the Ten Hours Bill shortly after his elevation, and how delighted he had been when the measure was finally passed.[3]

Longley, like several other prelates, was influenced by the workers' own determination, as well as by the Chartist threat. Where Blomfield had argued in terms of paternalistic responsibility, some of his brethren concluded that it was no longer a question of treating the laboring poor as if they were helpless children. On the contrary, in recent years they had shown themselves capable of both formulating and agitating to satisfy their own desires. Connop Thirlwall, Bishop of St David's (1840–75), understood this by insisting in 1847 that the principal reason for passing the Ten Hours Bill was that the workers had considered all the consequences and still wanted it. Consequently, it was an issue of common sense, not political economy. The workers had heard all the dire prophecies of economic disaster, unemployment and reduced wages, but were still determined to obtain short time. To them it was not a restraint of freedom, but an attempt to restrain the abuse of freedom by employers and their 'pernicious system of coercion'.[4]

Thirlwall found support from the new Bishop of Oxford, Wilberforce, who shared his view that the workers indeed knew their own minds better than their employers, and were perfectly right in their demands. Wilberforce, who was one of the first leaders of the Church to recognize that the workers had class aims and minds of their own which were perfectly comprehensible within the context of their experience, saw the Ten Hours Bill as a manifestation of these facts. He vigorously supported the measure, ridiculing the disasters portended by opponents. He thought it unfounded nonsense to claim, as many political economists did, that profits were made in the last one or two hours of the day, and that the workers themselves were generally in favor of retaining the longer day. Such arguments had been bandied about since the question was first raised by the elder Peel in 1815 and had been maturing ever since under

[1] Hammond, *Age of the Chartists*, 288.

[2] J. C. Gill, *The Ten Hours Parson: Christian Social Action In the Eighteen-Thirties* (1959), 113.

[3] *Ibid.*, 189.   [4] *Hansard*, XCII (1847), 944–5.

the guidance of the greatest of human passions—the love of gain. In fact, however, the principle of interference had proved to be beneficial, and the creation of wealth at the physical and moral expense of people was certainly unlawful. Employers who were content to cite the individualistic laws of political economy instead of the Gospels could have solved the problem if they had acted individually in their workers' best interest; since they ignored their needs, however, the legislature was forced to respond. The alternative, as Wilberforce described it, was combination and violence, which would endanger not only manufacturers, but the country as a whole.[1]

Three years later, in 1850, Wilberforce, along with Lonsdale, opposed a compromise measure designed to end the abuse of shift work which raised the working day to ten and a half hours, although reducing it to seven and a half hours on Saturdays. Their ally, Lord Ashley, agreed to the proposal because it established a normal work day and a Saturday half-holiday, but Wilberforce argued that any alteration of the Ten Hours Act without worker approval was a breach of contract.[2] Although the bishop was not clear about how worker opinion might be solicited, he knew that, unless consulted, the operatives would lose whatever recent confidence they had acquired in the House of Lords as a fair and impartial seat of justice. Lonsdale backed Wilberforce and questioned the wisdom of allowing a few unscrupulous manufacturers, who resorted to a shift system to keep their factories open fifteen hours a day, to set aside all the proven advantages of the ten-hour day. Like his brother of Oxford, Lonsdale thought it very dangerous to interfere with so great a boon to the workers.[3] Only two prelates supported the successful compromise measure: Maltby of Durham, and Prince Lee of Manchester. The latter's brief tenure in that new see had convinced him that many mill-owners were absolutely ruthless and, given the opportunity, would exploit their workers, especially children. However, by establishing opening hours from 6 or 7 a.m. with equivalent evening closing hours, allowing an hour and a half for meals, many abuses might be prevented by having all workers arrive and leave at the same time. He was certain that the operatives would accept an increase of two hours' work, during

[1] *Ibid.*, 941–3. [2] *Ibid.*, CXII (1850), 1366–7.

[3] *Ibid.*, 1358–60. John Lonsdale (1788–1867), son of a clergyman, educated Eton, Cambridge, studied law at Lincoln's Inn, but took orders. Held numerous livings, was Chaplain to Archbishop Manners-Sutton, and owed his career to episcopal patrons. Was Principal of King's College, London, in 1839, a position he refused when the college was first founded. Elevated to Lichfield in 1843 on Howley and Blomfield's recommendation. A serious, non-controversial diocesan who markedly improved the see, supported Lichfield Theological College and F. D. Maurice when he was removed from King's.

the week, compensated by quitting two hours earlier on Saturday.[1] It would not only prevent the rotation of children on shifts which started as early as 5 a.m. and ended at 8 p.m., but would also provide all workers with more leisure time and a less rigorous pace of labor.

3. HEALTH, HOUSING AND CORN

By the middle of the century the episcopate could no longer be described as indifferent or hostile to the physical needs of the working classes. As late as 1830, thirteen bishops had voted, less from conviction, more from party obligation, with the government against a proposal of the Duke of Richmond to establish a Select Committee to enquire into the condition of the working classes.[2] Such a vote was not repeated. Two years later the Church neither opposed Michael Sadler and his successor, Lord Ashley, in their promotion of investigations into working-class conditions, nor resisted any of the enquiries that followed over the next two decades. Voting with the majority, the attitude of the bench reflected changes in attitude among the ruling class. Relatively few Church leaders were prepared to enter debates and take a leading role in the area of labor legislation; those few, however, indicated an appreciable change in clerical attitudes and concepts of the clergy's role in the new age. Several of these prelates were newer appointments, more conscious of economic and social realities; older bishops, like Blomfield, Law and Charles Richard Sumner, however, were certainly as influential, if not more so, than their newer brethren. Some, like Longley, Lonsdale, Prince Lee Lee, Stanley and Thomas Musgrave, were Whig favorites, but Wilberforce, Bethell and Blomfield were Tory standard-bearers, the latter two appointed before the triumph of the Whigs in 1830. Their party allegiance within the Establishment ranged from Evangelical to High Church. They all agreed, however, that the clergy's social responsibility to the working classes could no longer be limited to charity and Scriptural explanations of the divine wisdom of social acquiescence.

Charles Richard Sumner, among the earliest of prelates to recognize that winning the lower orders would require more than schools and additional churches, tried to explain to the clergy of his new diocese of

---

[1] *Ibid.*, 1365-6. James Prince Lee (1804-69), son of the Secretary and Librarian of the Royal Society, educated at St Paul's and Cambridge. Was a master at Rugby under Arnold; Headmaster of King Edward School, Birmingham (1838) where he taught three later bishops, Benson, Lightfoot and Westcott. After several persons rejected the appointment to the new See of Manchester, Prince Lee, after disproving scurrilous charges that he was a drunkard, accepted it in 1848. Though somewhat despotic and overly pedagogical, he was an admirable diocesan organizer and administrator.

[2] *Ibid.*, XXIII (1830), 438-40, 476.

Winchester in 1829 that they had to expand their parochial interests to be effective among the poor. The bishop saw that overpopulation and economic change were creating intolerable living conditions for laborers crowded into inadequate cottages and tenements. The problem, he noted, was compounded by the unwillingness of landlords to maintain such places adequately and become liable for higher rates. A devoted advocate of statistical enquiry, Sumner had already begun analyzing his new diocese. In one parish he described 210 persons crowded into twenty-nine dilapidated cottages, providing aggregate space of 347 by 282 feet. This indicated an average space of twelve feet by ten into which eight to ten people, occasionally of different families, were crowded. Several people were forced to sleep in the same bed, and in many cases children had to sleep under the bed of their parents.[1] Sumner believed that such conditions could not be ignored, not only for humane reasons, but because they interfered with the effective ministrations of the clergy. Although he knew that it would be extremely difficult to improve the situation, he thought an evident desire to do so was important, hoping that appropriate corrective measures would, in time, follow.

Sumner's tepid and cautious reference to the connection between social conditions and clerical effectiveness was not likely to produce a Church crusade against the physical degradation endured by millions of laborers and their families. It is difficult to find other contemporary episcopal references to the question, while Sumner's brief discussion of the problem was largely an isolated aside to the clergy of that generation. Yet, twenty-five years later episcopal pronouncements were filled with statements on working-class conditions and the importance of clerical assistance in their improvement. In 1854 Sumner spoke to his clergy again, but now emphasized that it was their duty to be engaged directly in the '*total*' improvement of the working population. The minister must convince the poor man that he is not alone, 'that there is a Christian neighbour who cares for him and yearns to raise him in the scale of beings . . . [and] humanize the grossness of his nature . . .'. The old prelate was not speaking of mere spiritual enhancement. He did not think it was possible any longer to preach to the poor in a context of social statics; the clergy should not be exclusively concerned, as they had been for generations, with making the poor satisfied with their place in society. The Church, he believed, as never before, must enter the field of adult education—support institutes, reading-rooms, libraries, lectures, local displays of nature and art—and be primarily concerned about sanitation, the improvement of living and working conditions, as well as the further reduction of working hours. It was time for the national Church to see that the laboring population had places of recreation, the

[1] C. R. Sumner, *A Charge Delivered to the Clergy of the Diocese of Winchester In September and August, 1829* . . . (1829), 48–49.

opportunity to commune with nature or plant a garden. The growth of 'rural parties' or days in the country provided a wonderful opportunity for the ministry to seek further to raise the quality of working-class life.[1]

Sumner, like many of his colleagues, was distressed by the quantified details of working-class alienation from the Church revealed in Horace Mann's recent report on the 1851 religious census. Instead of comforting the bishops with evidence of how far the Church had come in the past half-century, it showed them how far it still had to go. Several of the newer prelates in the previous decade thought the Church was already well on the way into a new era of understanding and co-operation with the lower orders. Wilberforce in 1848 encouraged the clergy to become social reformers, to fight prostitution, oppose blood sports, support prison reform, endorse sanitary health measures, improve and humanize the Poor Law, and, in general, endorse any proposal that would increase the comfort and well-being of the laboring population.[2] As Thomas Musgrave, the Evangelical Archbishop of York (1847–60) surmised, improving their miserable living conditions will make the poor more receptive to us.[3] Their physical deprivation largely resulted from atrocious housing and sanitation, which not only demoralized the laboring classes but numbed them to their ministers' spiritual message.

When still Bishop of Hereford in 1845, Musgrave had warned his clergy that it was no longer possible to restrict their efforts to the spiritual welfare of their laboring parishioners. If the Church was to succeed as a national institution, it must promote the temporal as well as the religious good of the poor. 'It is idle to expect that persons depressed by severe poverty and wretchedness will always be so well conducted, or so accessible to the pastor's warnings and advice, as those who are in easier and more comfortable circumstances.' Dioceses and parishes varied in their social composition, but the enhanced responsibility of the clergy remained the same. Concentrating on his own agricultural diocese, Musgrave explained:

> Without entering on the question whether the manufacturing and mining, or the purely agricultural labourers are in the better condition, our lot is cast almost exclusively among the latter, with the exception of a very few parishes. And we cannot shut our eyes to the fact that their social state admits of amendment. Their dwellings are often dark and confined, sordid and cheerless, with little or no space for profitable employment on

[1] C. R. Sumner, *The Home Work of the Parochial Ministry. A Charge Delivered . . . In October, 1854* (1854), 32–33.

[2] S. Wilberforce, *A Charge Delivered to the Clergy of the Diocese of Oxford . . . 1848* (1848), 13–14.

[3] T. Musgrave, *A Charge Delivered to the Clergy of the Diocese of York, June and July, 1853* (1853), 12–13.

their own account, or for recreation. The natural tendency of this privation is to degrade and demoralize the character of the inmates.

Consequently the clergy must be concerned with better housing and living conditions. Ideally, as Law had preached more than two decades earlier, each cottage should have some land to cultivate by spade husbandry. Musgrave appealed to the ministers to use their influence on local landowners, for it 'would elevate the honest and industrious poor in the social scale, and at the same time contribute to the security and happiness of all'.[1]

Certainly the most influential episcopal spokesman for clerical involvement in social issues was Bishop Blomfield. His support of factory legislation derived from an expanded awareness of general working-class conditions. A strong supporter of Edwin Chadwick, and the prelate most responsible for the amended Poor Law, he was privy to the deplorable conditions reported by the Poor Law Commissioners. Appointed as a result of their Report in 1838, a Select Committee on the Health of the Towns reported in 1840. Its shocking revelations of the deplorable housing conditions, filth and disease in which the laboring poor lived was strengthened by Lord Normanby's personal visit to Bethnal Green—an experience which made him a lifelong advocate of sanitation reform.[2] The Whig Home Secretary was but one among many who were exposed for the first time to the unbelievable conditions in the towns. Simultaneously the new Tory government both slowed the passage of legislation, bowing in 1841 to landlord pressure, and strengthened its case by establishing in 1843 a Commission on the Health of the Towns. Its decision was strongly influenced by the appearance the previous year of Chadwick's startling *Report on the Sanitary Conditions of the Labouring Population*. In 1839, at Chadwick's request, Blomfield had called for an enquiry into the health and sanitation of the working classes, and Lord John Russell had ordered the Poor Law Commissioners to proceed.[3] The resulting *Report* appeared under Chadwick's name when the cautious Commissioners refused their sanction because of the criticisms made of the London Water Commissioners and the hopeless Commissioner of Sewers.[4]

Chadwick's evidence exposed the incredible state of both sewerage and the disposal of filth and waste from domestic and factory sites. In the new manufacturing towns more than one in every two children died before the age of five. Local administration was desperately inadequate, and too often patently corrupt, to cope with the enormous problem. Chadwick's Benthamite remedy proposed a centralized admini-

---

[1] T. Musgrave, *A Charge Delivered to the Clergy of the Diocese of Hereford, June, 1845* (1845), 21–22.

[2] Finer, *Chadwick*, 161.   [3] *Ibid.*, 162–3.   [4] *Ibid.*, 211–12.

stration which would utilize engineering and medical experts to solve sanitation problems and to regulate the further extension of towns. The Royal Commission on the Health of the Towns not only accepted Chadwick's evidence and conclusions, but had him write most of their initial reports on conditions in some fifty towns.[1] Appearing in 1844–5 and causing a further sensation, these reports prompted the establishment of the Health of Towns Associations, the Association for Promoting Cleanliness Among the Poor, and the Society for the Improvement of the Conditions of the Labouring Classes. The first of these organizations, avowedly propagandist in favor of Chadwick's proposed legislation, included some of his old enemies such as Lord Ashley and Charles Dickens. The latter two organizations were concerned with establishing bath- and wash-houses for the poor and to construct model sanitary housing at a nominal return of 4 per cent. Chadwick opposed the housing plan as too benevolent and destructive to a free market, differing on on this point with his closest political ally, Bishop Blomfield.[2]

For support, however, Chadwick knew that he could count on Blomfield as well as J. B. Sumner and Stanley. Although the fall of Peel's government in 1846 weakened Blomfield's political influence, both the other prelates had the ear of Lord John Russell, who, for example, raised Sumner to Canterbury in 1848. In addition to supporting legislative action, they also encouraged the more traditional voluntary forms of improvement. Disturbed by the Poor Law Commissioners' report of 1838, and increasingly aware of conditions in London, Blomfield in 1839 had tried to launch a private subscription drive in London to provide sanitary facilities for the poor. He quickly discovered, however, that the improvement of slum conditions was a very different problem from that of raising money for schools and churches. Though funds were contributed, Blomfield soon despaired to learn that propertyowners opposed improving their buildings, even at other people's expense; the money collected had to be returned.[3] Two years later, when Bills to control building and sanitation were pending, the bishop welcomed the government's interference, but was disappointed when Peel's new administration took a more cautious tack to avoid antagonizing aroused landlords. Nevertheless, Blomfield continued his private efforts, attempting to focus voluntary energies on the Society for the Improvement of the Conditions of the Labouring Classes. He was reluctant to promote measures deflecting support from what he thought was the most necessary improvement—better and cleaner living conditions.[4] When, in 1848, Lord Ashley suggested the establishment of another infirmary in a working-class district, Blomfield doubted that the poor would consider it a great boon. In the first place, he wrote, hospitals

[1] *Ibid.*, 232.   [2] *Ibid.*, 237–9.   [3] *Hansard*, LVI (1841), 536.
[4] 18 Oct. 1849, Letter Copy Book 382, *Fulham Ps.* f. 399.

and infirmaries already in poor areas lack funds; to establish another would only cut the resources available and cause others to collapse. Also, he was certain that the poor would much prefer a clean, comfortable, habitable dwelling *now* to the promise of medical facilities *if* they need them some day. The more involved in such questions the prelate became, the more he was persuaded 'that the best mode of carrying out one great object which we have in view, will be to appropriate our funds to the providing of decent and comfortable habitations for the poor'. He still hoped that landlords provided with a model example would see the great advantages of improvement. He believed Ashley was on the right track in promoting model housing, and felt that such ventures 'will be the most appropriate, and most truly beneficial kind of memorial, as far as the physical and social status of the labouring classes can be assisted by our efforts'.[1]

Equally important to Blomfield was the promotion of personal cleanliness among the poor. Chadwick's reports had shown what dirty creatures the laboring classes were, explaining this distressing fact in terms of an absence of the most minimal fresh-water provisions. In 1845, the Commission's second report on the health of the towns commented: 'It is only when the infant enters upon breathing existence, and when the man has ceased to breathe—at the moment of birth and at the hour of death—that he is really well washed.'[2] In 1842, Liverpool and Leeds established wash-houses and baths at a maximum cost of twopence, and in 1846 similar scattered efforts in various towns were combined into the Association for Promoting Cleanliness Among the Poor. Episcopal support was readily forthcoming. Blomfield, who was influenced by the innovation in Liverpool, saw it as a new area of benevolent involvement, but cautioned that, while the bath- and wash-house would not supersede the obligations of providing food and clothing to the destitute, 'it will render the poor man's dwelling more comfortable, cleanly, and healthy; it will improve his domestic condition and personal habits, and it will spare him expense: and in all these ways it will dispose and enable him to extricate himself from the depths of poverty'.[3]

Both in public and in private Blomfield joined the fight to get the laboring poor cleaned up and revive those 'appetencies for nobler objects which counteracted the baser attributes of our nature'. As a strong backer in 1846 of the Bath and Wash Houses Act which permitted boroughs to establish them from the rates, the bishop argued that cleanliness raised the poor man from extreme destitution and helped relieve 'the urgent pressure of misery . . .'. Moreover, and perhaps of

[1] Blomfield to Ashley, 29 April 1848, *ibid.*, 397, ff. 93–96.
[2] Hammond, *Age of the Chartists*, 101–2.
[3] 24 March 1846, Letter Copy Book 377, ff. 377–8, *Fulham Ps.*

most importance, it made him more accessible to moral teaching. Ever more conscious of the difficulties that the Church was encountering in populous working-class districts, Blomfield questioned how much of a spiritual impression the ministry could make on the laboring man without some improvement in his desperate physical condition. The expansion of the cities was steadily compounding the problem as the poor were being forced out of areas to make room for new streets. Invariably they were pushed into already overcrowded slums which were filthy and disease-ridden. Blomfield did not know if anything could be done to prevent the dispossession of people that improvement entailed, but he shuddered at the frightful toll it took in morals and mortality. Knowing that families of five and six children lived in one small room, it was not surprising to Blomfield that death-rates were rising, and diseases were more prevalent in the towns. Wash-houses, he believed, would be a very great relief to such people.[1]

Blomfield, like several of his more socially active brethren, had long since learned how difficult it was to appeal to material vested interests in moral and spiritual terms. They had learned that the gospel of enlightened self-interest, once believed easily reconciled to reason and revelation, was, in fact, subject to a variety of interpretations not always in the best interest of religious improvement. The earlier wish of sanitation-minded prelates, that bathing and washing facilities be voluntarily constructed throughout the country, was not fulfilled, and Blomfield turned to the legislature as the only hope. As in Liverpool, the baths would not be free; there would be a charge of twopence to discourage idle use and to prevent competition with private bath-houses.[2] Also there was no danger of social leveling when, as in Westminster, the baths could be divided by class—one shilling for the middle classes, and threepence for mechanics. Middle-class water was constantly replenished and fed through a filter bed to lower-class baths.[3] Furthermore, it was obvious that people of taste and discretion would not willingly bathe with their inferiors for the sake of saving a few pence. Even at the low cost of working-class baths, Blomfield calculated a return of 7 to 10 per cent on the investment, thus requiring no maintenance from the poor rates. Whatever the financial result, however, it was secondary to 'the beneficial effects of bathing and washing on the poor [which] were most striking to all those who came into contact with them'.[4]

Bath-houses were but one stage in the greater battle for sanitation, and during the long and bitter struggle over the Public Health Act of 1848 Blomfield and Sumner repeatedly endorsed Chadwick's efforts to

[1] *Hansard*, LXXXVII (1846), 104–6.
[2] *Ibid.*, 107–8. Also 1 July 1846, Letter Copy Book 395, f. 184, *Fulham Ps.*
[3] Hammond, *Age of the Chartists,* 101–2.
[4] *Hansard*, LXXXVII (1846), 107.

create effective centralized machinery in the face of bitter local opposition. Cries of centralization and oppressive interference made little impression upon them as they urged the establishment of boards of health throughout the country. Blomfield sought to strengthen the Act when it came up from the Commons by inserting an amendment requiring the establishment of a board in a locale whenever (1) the mortality of children under five exceeded 38 per cent of the total deaths, and (2) where epidemics were responsible for 20 per cent of the deaths. As the measure was being hammered through in the midst of a severe cholera epidemic, the latter clause was particularly pertinent. Although another of Chadwick's allies, Lord Morpeth, revised and simplified Blomfield's amendment in the Commons by replacing it with an overall seven-year average death-rate of 23 per cent (which was 2 per cent above the average), the central Board of Health was somewhat strengthened in its struggle to get municipalities to establish boards.[1] The Act remained weak, however, gutted by factionalism and compromise. London successfully resisted the control of the general Board of Health as the local vestries fought bitterly to retain authority. In 1854, when the controversial five-man Board of Health was allowed to run out its six-year tenure, Blomfield and Sumner vainly fought to retain it, continuing their defense of the controversial Chadwick to the end.[2]

Although the center of Blomfield's own diocese, London, remained a cesspool, much progress had been made. By 1854, of the 284 places which established boards of health, 170 of them were elected. Of these, 157 were towns, in most of which at least one-tenth of the ratepayers, in accordance with the Public Health Act, had initiated their establishment.[3] Conflicts remained after 1854, and the sanitary improvements of the towns proceeded more slowly and cautiously. By then, however, it was reasonably clear where the Church stood on such matters. Blomfield and Sumner had closely allied the Establishment to the cause of improving the living conditions of the laboring classes, a position it would continue to take in the second half of the century. Several prelates, such as Stanley, Lee, Longley, Lonsdale and C. R. Sumner, were particularly active at the local level, while most others were content to let Blomfield carry the fight not only in his own huge diocese, but nationally as well. For some older Tory bishops like Phillpotts or Monk, it was about time that the towns were made to pay for the enormous misery and evils their greedy, materialistic proprietors created by luring the laboring poor away from their healthful, secure lives in stable, agricultural parishes. A few unregenerate *laissez-faire* Whigs like Maltby were suspicious of the whole trend to try and legislate away social misery. But most bishops, confronted with the practical problems of ministering to industrialized areas in their dioceses, had concluded in

[1] Finer, *Chadwick*, 325.   [2] *Ibid.*, 426, 468.   [3] *Ibid.*, 436–7.

the course of the 1840's, if not before, that it was no longer possible to separate the revival and extension of the Church from its disruptive social and economic environment.

The change that had taken place can be seen in the reaction to the return of cholera in 1847. When it had last struck, in 1832, more than eighteen thousand people died. Church leaders simply accepted it as a divine visitation and, if they did not flee before the disease, they remained remarkably silent in the face of it. By the next decade, however, many churchmen had experienced and were educated in the realities of lower-class sanitation and, although ignorant of how the cholera was transmitted, recognized some connection between filth and disease. Chadwick, whose influence on Blomfield and J. B. Sumner was considerable, refused to listen to suggestions that the disease was carried by water, but insisted that it was airborne, rising from filth and permeating the atmosphere in crowded, unsanitary districts.[1] Whatever the physical cause, the importance of the spiritual implications was unquestionably in episcopal minds. The cholera, coupled with the potato failure in Ireland and poor harvests in parts of England, clearly portended a period of divine retribution. The outbreak of revolution on the Continent in 1848 indicated a Godly wrath transcending national boundaries.

While the clergy were naturally expected to render spiritual aid by enabling parishioners to understand and accept the inevitability of these periodic visitations, Blomfield believed that much more could be done. During the cholera epidemic which opened the previous decade, the Bishop of London had resigned himself to the situation and, like most clergymen, was satisfied with Archbishop Howley's proclamation of a day of fasting and humiliation. In 1847, however, Blomfield told his clergy that since the disease hit the poor the hardest, because of 'a want of cleanliness, and, in an inferior degree, intemperance, and an insufficiency of wholesome food', there was something they could do. The bishop urged the ministers to establish local committees in slum areas to improve sanitation and provide sufficient nourishment for the needy. He was confident that the clergy, better than anyone, knew and understood the real condition of the poor, 'and of the nature and extent of that evil, which is sometimes, no doubt, the result of their own ignorance or carelessness, but much more frequently, at least in the metropolis and other great towns, of deficiencies which they have no means of supplying, and of obstacles to cleanliness, which it is the duty of other persons to remove'.[2]

Blomfield knew that it was no longer possible to explain away social misery with simple-minded appeals to individualism and descriptions of

[1] *Ibid.*, 335.

[2] C. J. Blomfield, *A Pastoral Letter to the Clergy of the Diocese of London* (1847), 5–8.

P
217

divine opportunities for self-improvement. The intemperance and misery of the poor, which the rich saw as a consequence of some individual failing, are the results, not the causes, of poverty. Unless they are relieved, 'it will be an empty mockery to tell those who are borne down and crushed by its weight, that they would be less miserable, if they were less filthy'. What else could they be, he angrily queried, when forced to live packed together in 'miserable tenements or apartments . . . at rents, the excessive amount of which cripples their means of comfort and cleanliness'. He subsequently deplored 'the inadequate supply of water; the want of all provisions for ventilation; the absence of all convenience for personal ablution, and household washing—these, and the disgraceful state of the sewerage in the most crowded parts of the metropolis, are causes, which engender, or aggravate disease, and hurry great numbers of our fellow-creatures and neighbours to an untimely grave'.[1]

The incredible revelations of working-class conditions in recent years now precluded any ready acceptance of them. Blomfield insisted that not only must the rich provide a decent life for those who provide the labor from which the wealthy alone benefit, but the nation as a whole had to realize and accept the truth—the poor were victims of a society which herded them into the most loathsome conditions, and then disavowed responsibility for the lamentable results. Contrary to popular belief, the poor are not naturally filthy and inclined towards self-destruction. If appliances within their means were provided, they would take full advantage of opportunities to alter their lives. Blomfield believed that the clergy had a major responsibility in seeing that such opportunities were forthcoming. After all, he suggested, if tens of thousands of fellow Christians live, at this very moment, 'in the very neighbourhood of our most sumptuous palaces and halls, in the extreme depths of physical, social, and moral degradation, and exposed to the most imminent danger of perishing by disease, *that* is not entirely, often not at all, their own fault; but the fault of those, whose duty it is, not only to teach them the benefits of cleanliness and decency, but to do something towards furnishing them with the means of being cleanly and decent, which under their actual circumstances is nothing less than an impossibility'.[2]

In spite of Blomfield's attempts to rally his clergy, he, like Chadwick, was frustrated by local resistance and bitter conflicts between local officials and the new Board of Health. Before the epidemic finally abated in the fall of 1849, fourteen thousand people died in London alone.[3] This time, however, the Church took an active role in relief, and many of the clergy in newly established churches and districts in slum areas worked diligently to help their frightened and susceptible parishioners. A new generation of devoted, earnest ministers, willing to accept

[1] *Ibid.*, 9–10.   [2] *Ibid.*, 8–9.   [3] Finer, *Chadwick*, 346–7.

the unattractive pulpits in desperately overcrowded parishes, were already hard at work when Blomfield spoke to them of the changed responsibilities of the Church in an urban world. Unless those responsibilities were vigorously assumed, spiritual efforts would be in vain. Archbishop Sumner, the old Malthusian and early critic of governmental interference, was converted when he realized that church extension and education were making little meaningful headway in the pestilential districts of the metropolis and in the towns of his former industrial diocese. In supporting Shaftesbury's efforts in 1852 to get the legislature to take a stronger position in cleaning up the slums, Sumner said that, frankly, he could no longer see any other alternative.[1] Even the episcopal architect of the Church's expansion and reform, Blomfield, who had placed such hope in the physical presence of churches and schools, sadly confessed in 1851 that every year confirmed his belief that new churches and schools in the towns would do little good unless the physical condition of the laboring classes could be relieved from the lowest depths of degradation which blocked out the light and comfort of the Gospel.[2]

This growing awareness and involvement in the physical problems of the lower orders was closely connected with the resurgence of the Church as a *national* institution and the conscious efforts of many of its clergy to make it relevant and receptive to all classes. The Oxford movement and the bitter controversies surrounding the Hampden, and later the Gorham, appointments had underlined the dependency of the Church upon Parliament, while the spread of Chartism and the preachments of socialism painfully revealed its restricted dependency on the propertied classes. Both this lack of independence from secular authority and a sense of alienation from perhaps a majority of Englishmen were increasingly troublesome and vexatious to serious churchmen dedicated to a revitalization of the national faith. For example, Bishops Wilberforce and Thirlwall were led during the heated debates over the repeal of the Corn Laws in 1846 to decry various attempts to persuade or threaten the bench to vote one way or the other. Wilberforce, while supporting his patron, Peel, nevertheless insisted that the Church could no longer sit as the representative of one class. It was dangerous and destructive of the Constitution.[3] He shared Thirlwall's conviction that all class positions must be set aside, since the Establishment's concern lay with the general welfare of the mass of the community. As Thirlwall interpreted it, it was a question 'of life or death to the people of this country'. If the Church rejected their hopes, it would tell the great mass of the populace that there was no immediate prospect for their improvement.[4]

Like Wilberforce, Thirlwall was angered by those landlords who pressured clergy and bishops to work against repeal when, in fact, the

[1] *Hansard*, CXX (1852), 1299–1300.   [2] *Ibid.*, CXVIII (1851), 1844.
[3] *Ibid.*, LXXXVII (1846), 320–1.   [4] *Ibid.*, 310.

clergy as a body had taken no position on it, while the bishops were guided by their own personal convictions.[1] Thirlwall and the other prelates were well aware of the argument that a reduction of grain prices would also reduce clerical tithes, which were commuted on a seven-year average of the price of corn; but, Thirlwall insisted, they must be ready to face this sacrifice for the greater good of the masses. Although Wilberforce supported repeal, he was also irritated by inducements of anti-Corn Law proponents who calculated that the bishops, with their fixed incomes, would benefit from lower prices.[2] All such arguments missed the essential point: the patient and long-suffering poor of the nation were counting on them to make a decisive move to alleviate their long trials. Consequently, he pleaded with his brethren and with the peers at large not to think in narrow class terms for the benefit of the few, but of the greater good of all. 'Your power is indeed great: but there are some things which it cannot effect: it cannot stand . . . against the rising tide of a great nation's convictions.'[3] More restrained than his loquacious brother of Oxford, Thirlwall had few illusions that repeal would solve the severe problems of the age; at least it offered some hope of improving to a small degree the comfort and happiness of the laboring classes, however, while collectively it would be substantial. Any improvement in the condition of the working classes had to be supported, he felt, and this hope dare not be rejected. It had become a national issue, not a class issue, and advocates of repeal hoped that the leaders of the Church would side with the nation.[4]

Wilberforce and many of his colleagues believed that the Anti-Corn Law League was indeed representative of popular opinion. The clergy most in contact with the populace realized it, and while many joined in supporting repeal, others were unwilling to sign petitions to preserve the restrictive measures. The clergy, Wilberforce claimed, knew that the end of protection would mean a reduction of their already meager incomes, but the justice of the measure prepared them to accept the results. The ministers of the poor, knowing as well as anyone that things could not go on as they were, would welcome an end to the want and misery they saw all about them.[5]

Other Tory prelates, like Phillpotts, Monk, Bethell, Murray, Gilbert, Bagot, and Short, disagreed and voted against repeal. They were joined by Edward Copleston, who had gradually abandoned his faith in political economy, and by Charles Richard Sumner, who, as in 1832, split with his brother on this explosive issue. Those most closely identified with the older Tory landed interests and values, Phillpotts, Monk, Murray and Bethell, went further and signed a protest against the Bill when it was passed on 25 June 1846. Sixteen prelates voted with the

[1] *Ibid.*, 303–8.　　[2] *Ibid.*, 320–1.　　[3] *Ibid.*, 335–6.
[4] *Ibid.*, 312.　　[5] *Ibid.*, 326–30.

majority on the critical Second Reading, unpersuaded by Phillpotts's vigorous defense of protection. The crusty Bishop of Exeter viewed repeal as another nail in the coffin of squirearchical, Tory England, hammered in by urban manufacturers, confused farmers, and political economists in order to avoid paying higher wages. What the poor really needed was not cheap bread, but a fair remuneration for their labor. How could a reduction of tariffs raise wages, the bishop asked; by bringing English laborers into competition with the serfs in Poland? On the contrary, wages would probably be further reduced. Repeal of the Corn Laws was a dangerous measure, raising false hopes and leading to even greater disappointment and frustration.[1]

Phillpotts also did not view with the same equanimity as some of his brethren the prospect of a reduction of clerical income. As a bitter opponent of many of the financial reforms in the Church and the redistribution of revenue imposed in the preceding decade, he felt that the proposed Bill would further alter the state of clerical temporalities. If these were diminished in any way, both rich and poor would undoubtedly suffer. Phillpotts insisted that his brethren were wrong to discuss the measure in terms of class interest. The land-owning protectionists, he explained, were not against repeal because of class interests, but because of their higher desire to preserve religion and morality by keeping the Church strong. As a result, the prelate pleaded, it was in the bishops' interest to oppose the Bill and preserve the troubled Constitution.[2] Strong Tory though he was, even Wilberforce, who admired the Bishop of Exeter, found it difficult to swallow Phillpotts's specious analysis, and in effect told him so. The selfless vote, as far as he was concerned, was the vote for repeal. That was what would benefit the greatest number of people.[3] The Church would be strengthened when the clergy thought not of itself or one class, but of the nation.

On the question of the Corn Laws the political economists were right, Wilberforce continued, and so long as the protection of agriculture was 'an unnatural state of things', the protectionist landowners could not be considered friends of the laborers. God provided all the protection that was necessary for agriculture through the soil, the sun and the dew, and the fruits of His assistance should be available to all at the cheapest prices. Wilberforce was convinced that only through free competition would farming techniques and agricultural production keep up with the expansion of the manufacturing population, whatever might be felt about the advantages or disadvantages of an industrial economy.[4] Wilberforce had much sympathy for an idyllic, older, less-complicated, rural England, and understood the repugnancy of smoke-filled, crowded, pestilential and dangerous manufacturing towns to the sentimental pre-

[1] *Ibid.*, 316–18.   [2] *Ibid.*, 314–16.   [3] *Ibid.*, 320.
[4] *Ibid.*, 322–4, 331–3.

221

servers of a more innocent era. It was a time for realism and action, however, explained Wilberforce privately, 'we cannot maintain our manufacturing population without free trade. Whether it is a blessing to have a manufacturing population is another matter. . . .'[1]

Most of Wilberforce's episcopal brethren thought it was no blessing. Like the intelligent, reform-minded Edward Denison of Salisbury (1837–54), many of them went through considerable soul-searching and practical calculation before they could bring themselves to vote on the measure.[2] Not since the Reform Bill of 1832 had nearly the entire bench been so involved in a non-ecclesiastical piece of legislation. But, like that earlier Bill, the repeal of the Corn Laws seemed to affect the whole structure of the Constitution and raised a critical question for the Church. Deeply involved in trying to extend its influence over uncounted millions of workers beyond its reach, the revived, energetic Establishment found itself confronted with a measure that placed it squarely in the spotlight. Repeal was a vital issue to the laboring classes, as it was to protectionist landowners who bitterly resisted it and ripped the Tory Party apart when they eventually lost. If the bishops had supported the landed interests, or simply kept out of the issue, they would have acted true to form. Not only were they swayed, however, by the great divisions within the propertied ranks themselves, but they were also faced with the question of supporting the administration of one of their best friends and closest allies. It was, of course, easier for Whig prelates, who voted as a bloc for repeal. Joining them, however, were eight Tories, including Archbishop Howley, Bishop Blomfield, Sumner and Kaye. While all were certainly desirous of supporting Peel, of even greater importance by 1846 was their conviction that young Wilberforce, who was their spokesman during the debates, was essentially right in his contention that it was in the best interests of the Church, spiritually and institutionally, to promote a measure which, like many other measures in that reforming decade, would associate it once more with the interests of a majority of Englishmen.

4. DANGEROUS ALTERNATIVES: CHARTISM AND SOCIALISM

Nothing prodded episcopal interest in social legislation more than the alternatives proposed by the working classes themselves. Several bishops throughout the 1830's were troubled by the growth of combinations and the prospect of the lower orders being swayed by dangerous political and social ideas that portended serious conflicts with their betters. When, at the end of the decade, Chartists and Owenite socialists, stimu-

[1] Wilberforce to C. Anderson, 4 March 1846, *Wilberforce Ps.*, Dep. C. 191, II.
[2] *Hansard*, LXXXVII (1846), 447–9.

lated by economic depression and bitter resistance to the new Poor Law, began demanding political reforms and attacking private property, latent fears of a great class confrontation were quickly revived. Church leaders were especially sensitive, since many Chartist and socialist spokesmen were particularly blunt in their condemnation of the Establishment as a selfish, material, plundering, un-Christian institution uninterested in the welfare of the poor. Corrupt, hypocritical, the Church only pretended to minister to the needs of all people, when in fact it was the despotic agent of the oppressive ruling classes.[1] Chartists were not content with verbally assaulting the clergy; they often invaded their churches, disrupting the services and frightening parson and parishioner alike. Frequently the intruders asked the minister to preach from texts describing the worth of labor, the need for just reward, and the sins of wealth. Unfamiliar with sermonizing upon such Scriptural sources, the preacher would often condemn the troublemakers from the pulpit, or sternly preach on more familiar subjects: passive obedience, the folly of worldly interests, or any other theme guaranteed to infuriate the Chartists and drive them from the church.[2] Few ever returned. Some sought to establish their own churches embodying simple Gospel truths they thought were long since forgotten by the Anglican Church, and most of the Dissenting denominations as well.

Bishops were especially contemptible in their dual capacity as princes of the Church and tyrannical peers of the realm. The redistribution of excessive episcopal wealth by the recently formed Ecclesiastical Commission made little impression upon hostile workers who believed the bishops were merely juggling their ill-gotten gain, not renouncing it. The bishops of 'the Pious Pickpocket', as one Chartist paper labeled the Church, were grossly overpaid when their labor was compared with that of the average working man.[3] In November 1841 Bishop Stanley had to be guided through a Chartist crowd assembled with a musical band to disrupt his sermon in Norwich Cathedral.[4] Not surprisingly, Chartist journals sided with Dissenters and other critics of the Establishment in calling for a complete separation of Church and State. Though they did not incorporate the demand as one of their proposals for political reform contained in the great petition, Chartist spokesmen kept up a steady barrage against the national Church, calling for the abolition of tithes and rates, the institution of voluntary support for bishops and clergymen, and their election by congregations. It was patently clear to the bench what lay in store for them if working-class notions of parliamentary reform were ever adopted. Furthermore, despite the massive expenditure

[1] H. U. Faulkener, *Chartism and the Churches. A Study in Democracy* (New York, 1916), 28–29.

[2] *Ibid.*, 35–37.   [3] *Ibid.*, 32–33.

[4] *Ibid.*, 39.

of time and money by the Church for the education of the lower classes, the ungrateful Chartists also demanded a national system of non-sectarian, popular education.[1] Years of accumulated working-class resentment of the national Church, only occasionally acknowledged by some of the more realistic pessimists in the Establishment, burst upon the Establishment at a time when it was straining to appeal once more to the inferior sort. Its apparent failure was trumpeted by a movement openly hostile to it, yet able to gain more than a million signatures on behalf of a radical reform petition. No wonder bishops were alarmed and despondent.

To compound their despair, several prelates confused socialist efforts to establish Robert Owen's 'New Moral World' with the goals of Chartist agitators. Many participants in Owen's abortive Grand National Union, including Bronterre O'Brien and William Lovett, had turned to Chartism. In general, however, they did not share Owen's grand schemes for social transformation. Owen himself thought the political emphasis of Chartism a mistake, and vigorously promoted his socialist alternatives. Although both movements were particularly contemptuous of the Church and favored disestablishment, the socialists were in general stridently anti-religious, and had little use for any denomination. Owen's unbelief was as shocking as his condemnation of private property, and, given the fundamental conviction of the age that the preservation of the latter was dependent upon the destruction of the former, it is perfectly understandable. Chartism, as even a bishop occasionally recognized, was at least in the tradition of political reform agitation that had appeared after Waterloo and again after 1826. That it was drawing more and more upon the laboring classes was certainly disquieting, but then economic discontent was becoming more pronounced at that level than ever before. Owenite socialism, however, hand abandoned its earlier utopian emphasis upon voluntary agricultural and industrial co-operatives that could even attract the support of the conservative old Archbishop Manners-Sutton. In its place it had substituted a fundamental social transformation unwilling to compromise with natural political and economic realities. Although Owen himself, anti-democratic and hardly a revolutionary, counted on argument and example rather than barricades and guillotines to establish the 'New Moral World', many frightened Church leaders saw all the agitators together in one great kettle, boiling up a most fateful storm.

Henry Phillpotts looked into the bubbling cauldron, held his breath until the hissing steam of the Chartist threat was released, and then screamed for the damnable Whigs to cover the pot. Furious that Melbourne in 1839 had presented Owen to the Queen, whose father, the Duke of Kent, had once patronized the reformer, the Bishop of Exeter,

[1] *Ibid.*, 33–35.

accused the government of encouraging the spreading agitation.[1] He had long suspected the Whigs of plotting the most nefarious schemes against the Establishment, and some time earlier in the decade had scribbled on a scrap of paper:

gRey
mElbourne
dVrham
hOlland
aLthorpe
rUssell
sTanley
rIchmond
gOderich
. . . . . .[2]

If the sum of the ministry at that time did not add up to 'Revolution', Phillpotts feared it was just a matter of time before it would. By 1840 with a slight alteration of position it was possible to complete the loathsome word by the addition of the Home Secretary, Normanby.

With his typical lack of charitable restraint, Phillpotts repeatedly lacerated Normanby, virtually accusing him of collusion with the enemies of society, because the government refused to return to the Six Acts of 1819 and rigorously enforce the laws against sedition and blasphemy. Finally, after months of harassment, Normanby bluntly informed the warring prelate that he detested and held him in the utmost contempt. Phillpotts, the model of injured innocence, retreated assuring Normanby and the House of Lords that he felt no such vindictiveness.[3] Apparently he did so only towards Whigs, socialists, Chartists, Evangelicals and anyone else who disagreed with him. It was most apparent when the crusty prelate was frightened, and in 1840 he was certainly that. Early in the year he had presented a petition from Birmingham, signed by four thousand people, describing the alarming spread of Owen's 'wicked influence'. Unable to accept the government's claims that the socialists had done nothing illegal, he was certain that any society dedicated to the French international aim of altering the laws and religion of peaceful lands must be culpable of something. As far as Phillpotts was concerned, all the worker agitation of the day was a result of seditious missionary activity in the French tradition, and Owen's publication, *New Moral*

---

[1] H. Phillpotts, *Socialism. Second Speech of the Bishop of Exeter in the House of Lords, February 4, 1840, On Moving An Address to Her Majesty; With the Queen's Gracious Answer* (1840), 3, 12. Also *Hansard*, LI (1840), 530–1.

[2] *Phillpotts Ps*. ED, 11/72 (2), Ex. Cath.

[3] *Hansard*, LV (1840), 1224–36.

World, was another treasonable call for the destruction of society. Not only did it decry property, religion and the family, but it revived noxious eighteenth-century claims that man was not responsible for his condition. With the sacred ties of Christian civilization once again threatened by deluded men proposing to improve their condition by radically altering their society, the government chose not to prosecute. It was criminal.[1]

Armed with a steady flow of petitions and clergymen's reports on the progress of the conspiracy, Phillpotts added to his arsenal 'blasphemous' excerpts from socialist speeches and writings. In addition, he was prepared to cite innumerable crimes committed in the factory towns by socialists *and* Chartists. These ranged from domestic brutality to incest and even infanticide; all apparently justified by socialist denunciations of a corrupting environment. Other mad revolutionaries openly proclaimed that the monarchy and the Church were *passé.* It was no wonder when the *New Moral World* called upon the lower orders 'to place us in an entirely new situation, such as . . . was never contemplated before. Under that system there was to be no private property—no marriages—no religion'. He disagreed with those who argued that Chartism was something separate from socialism; perhaps it was less openly blasphemous, but workers throughout the industrial north were nevertheless exposed to the grotesque teachings of both groups.[2] Like all of his colleagues, Phillpotts was sorely aware that it was in exactly these manufacturing areas where the Church was least effective, and he grew frenzied at the thought.

As if their teachings were not sufficiently repugnant, socialists, with the support of men of 'means and education', were building lecture halls, buying property and, as in the case of Coventry and Lincoln, even being allowed to preach their 'foul doctrines' in the guildhalls.[3] As Phillpotts had feared when opposing the Municipal Corporation Bill five years earlier, the towns were apparently coming under the control of irresponsible municipal officials who lacked a deep attachment to English traditions. To Phillpotts this meant Radicals and Nonconformists. The government refused to panic; Melbourne and Normanby insisted that as foolish and disgusting as many socialist arguments were, Owen and his followers had done nothing illegal. Since the rejection of the Chartist petition the previous year, 1839, the government was content to allow Owen his proselytizing, confident that the 'New Moral World' was not imminent, despite the dire threats and warnings regularly leveled by the Bishop of Exeter. If the government was certain, many peers were not. Phillpotts successfully carried a motion calling

[1] *Ibid.,* LI, 237–8, 510–31.
[2] Phillpotts, *Socialism* (1840), 4, 8, 11–12.
[3] *Ibid.,* 11–12.

for an address to the Queen urging the establishment of an enquiry into the entire problem.[1] Not surprisingly, he was warmly endorsed by his episcopal colleagues, who were genuinely alarmed by the prelate's revelations.

Blomfield, whose relations with his brother of Exeter were barely cordial by 1840, nevertheless supported his demand for prosecution. Some years before, Blomfield confessed, he had urged the Home Office to take action against the socialists, but it had declined to do so. Unimpeded, they had since acquired money and property as well as a large following among those classes ruled by appetite and passion and held in check only by 'all the motives and restraints of religion . . . '.[2] It was necessary to rally the upper classes against the threat through an open policy of exposure and prosecution. At the same time there was reason to hope that 'the lower classes of the community . . . were not yet so fallen into the delusions which had been spread for them as to be insensible to the great weight and influence of the united opinion of all the learned, and wise, and pious in the land'.[3] Copleston was slightly more cautious and saw some merit in Melbourne and Brougham's contention that persecution would only give a wider exposure to Owen's absurd doctrines. Nevertheless he felt that if argument and reason proved insufficient in combating the menace, strict prosecution for sedition and blasphemy was clearly necessary.[4]

It is difficult to tell who frightened poor Archbishop Howley more, Phillpotts or the socialists. Already upset by the worker disturbances of the preceding year, the Bishop of Exeter's speech on February 4th greatly alarmed the mild archbishop. Only a few years before, Owen's speculations were nearly isolated and of little consequence; suddenly, they had spread like a 'pestilence over the country', and threatened to overthrow religion itself. It was incredible that ideas of common property, the abolition of marriage, necessity in place of duty was tolerated by people from the higher classes. His brethren were absolutely right. Exposure and prosecution were the only ways to deal with so diabolical an evil:

> Vice is a monster of such hideous mien,
> That to be hated needs but to be seen.[5]

There was no disguising the fact that all of the bishops who spoke on the question were prompted in part at least by their distrust and dislike of the Whig government. Archbishop Whately in Ireland bluntly charged that High Church Tory prejudices prompted the debate. He had little sympathy, he wrote Nassau Senior, for the members of that 'party

[1] *Hansard*, LI (1840), 1176–7, 1191.
[2] *Ibid.*, 537–9.   [3] *Ibid.*, 1214–17.
[4] *Ibid.*, 1207.   [5] *Ibid.*, 1203–7.

who are incessantly railing at all those who wish to make the labouring classes rational, and to found religion on conviction, instead of faith (i.e. on itself)—a party supported and patronized by prelates, who then wonder to find the people, whom they have left defenceless, overpowered by their assailants'. Whately had nothing but contempt for those who thought that repression and prosecution were the answer, as if one could 'exercise parental guardianship over these helpless innocents by silencing with secular coercion those who are misleading them'. Chartism and socialism, he contended, were the direct results of the refusal of the Church to permit the practical, rational education of the lower classes. Comprehending the principles of political economy, the poor would not only understand their relative position in society, but would accept their religion from a rational basis of conviction rather than from a system of 'vague imposition'. Whately was not really worried about socialism; he always believed that a much greater danger came from blind High Churchmen like Phillpotts who opposed the truths of political economy and the creation of an inter-denominational system of public education, even in Ireland. He found it difficult from his vantage-point in Catholic Dublin to understand how his fellow Protestant bishops could condemn the socialists for their criticisms of Christians, when they 'revile in gross terms seven millions of their fellow [Christian] subjects . . .'. If, he asked, 'the Socialists are to be prohibited from disgusting and irritating the mind of a fellow subject who is, as they maintain, erroneous in his belief, has he a right to disgust and irritate his Roman Catholic fellow subjects for being in his judgment erroneous in theirs?'[1]

Whately was raising an extraneous issue for most of his brethren, Whig and Tory alike. The rise of Chartism and socialism was a clear warning not about the evils of religious intolerance, but of the dangers of class alienation and class conflict. It was true that Phillpotts, Blomfield, Copleston and Howley were frightened and fed up with the Whig government, pushing the Church into further reforms, establishing educational inspectors, drawing episcopal candidates from the ranks of the Broad Church clergy, and refusing to provide them with the means of coping with the working poor in their own way—building still more churches in the populous districts. It was not surprising to them therefore that the entire country was in danger from policies calculated to weaken the national Church. Without agreeing with these causes, many liberal prelates certainly felt the danger of the effects. Longley joined with Bishop Otter of Chichester, shortly before the latter's death in 1840, in deploring 'that moral disorder which prevails through a large portion of our social system, and is pregnant with so much alarm . . .'. They meant that separation, 'by a broad and dark line, of those who labour with their hands from their employers, producing selfishness on

[1] Whately, *Life*, I, 451.

one side, sullenness and discontent on the other . . .'.[1] It was difficult to disagree with Otter's warning that if it went on much longer the conflict between the middle and lower classes, already 'an evil of great magnitude, already deeply rooted in our system', would seriously wound the Church, 'and finally subvert the whole fabric of society'. Only the clergy could restore class harmony. But it was no longer sufficient merely to teach the poor their responsibilities. It was absolutely necessary that the middle classes recognize that their interest and participation in the restoration were critical to its success.[2]

At the same time some Church leaders refused to make any such concessions to the claims of socialists and Chartists and feared the rich would be panicked into leveling concessions. Class interests and differences 'this alloy of imperfection' were entirely natural, irrespective of form, so that benefits far exceeded disadvantages. Prince Albert's Chaplain, John Graham, in 1841, thus defended the 'splendid mansions, magnificent equipages, and costly furniture' of the rich as vital to the poor. The trappings of wealth provided employment and wages, 'just as the life-blood, in the human frame, circulates from the heart through the extremities of the body back to the fountain from which it came'.[3] Graham, then Master of Christ College, Cambridge, and a strong Whig *laissez-faire* utilitarian, raised many of the old arguments about the necessity of inequality not only as a result of human sin, but as the essential spur to human progress. Unwinding the virtues of property, 'the mainspring of social improvement, the foundation both of domestic comfort and national wealth . . .', the future Bishop of Chester ticked off the well-worn mutual benefits and services binding 'the several ranks of society together by the tie of common utility . . .'. Delivering the expected response to his own litany, Graham intoned the relativity of class happiness as he descanted upon the heart-filling example of the prudent, temperate, kind worker devoted to his station and his God-fearing family. Nearly a half-century of profound economic and social change was swept away by the mellifluous winds of Graham's sentimental certainty; there stood revealed the worker, returning home, 'his children looking out to hail with their little voices his return; his industrious helpmate ready to receive him with the house in order, the table spread, and her own face lighted up with cheerful contentment and honest pride'.[4] The possibility that they might be all returning home from the factory together, or that their domestic bliss could be interrupted by the children going off to their work-shifts in no way intruded

[1] C. T. Longley, *A Sermon Preached . . . May 11, 1840* (1840), 17–20. Also W. Otter, 'Letter to the Rural Deans, 1840', in *Pastoral Addresses* (1841), 73–74.

[2] Otter, *ibid.*, 75–77.

[3] Graham, *Sermon* (1841), 2–3.   [4] *Ibid.*, 8–10.

upon this saccharine antidote to worker disaffection. As far as Graham
and like-minded churchmen were concerned, the entire problem was the
result of 'evil-disposed persons' trying to possess the minds of the working classes with a notion that there is an unfair degree of hardship
attending their condition.[1]

Without denying this likelihood, even the very conservative John
Kaye now appreciated the inadequacy of such an explanation and defense. However much the prelates of his generation had buttressed themselves against change by repeating the old, naturalistic arguments about
inequality and social inevitability, neither Kaye nor most of his contemporaries felt as comfortable reverting to them any longer. Only
Bishop Maltby with his unwavering belief in Paley and political economy continued to sound as he did three decades earlier, occasionally
joined by a newcomer like Graham. But when Kaye, who had managed
to seal himself off from the industrial realities of the country for many
years, warned that we are on 'the eve of a great conflict . . .' which does
not involve the simple question of reforming this or that civil or ecclesiastical policy, it was clear that most Church leaders, consciously or not,
realized that the old eighteenth-century natural law explanations and
utilitarian justifications would no longer suffice. The largest class in
society no longer listened.

Consequently the question posed by Kaye in 1840 was 'whether the
whole frame of society is to be changed, and a new system introduced,
founded on different views of the best mode of prompting the general
happiness, and designed to effect an entire revolution in the relations in
which men have hitherto stood, both to each other, and to the community'. The Chartist and socialist agitation was horrifying, but symptomatic of 'a ferment in the public mind, threatening danger to all existing
institutions . . .'. Even the Church, long attacked on doctrinal grounds,
was under assault 'because it is an institution, closely connected with the
other institutions of the land . . .'.[2] Alarmed further by the strikes and
riots that followed the rejection of the second and even larger Chartist
petition in May, 1842, Kaye was particularly depressed by the class
bitterness and hatred which had resulted in the necessary elements of
society 'arrayed in more determined hostility against each other . . .'.[3]
There was no doubt that God desired mutual co-operation as essential
to individual and collective prosperity, yet men of different stations
raged against each other in blind fury. Kaye, appealing for Christian

[1] *Ibid.,* 1–2.

[2] J. Kaye, *A Charge Delivered to the Clergy of the Diocese of Lincoln . . .
in MDCCCXL* (1840), 5–6.

[3] J. Kaye, *Two Sermons: One Preached . . . October 12, 1842 . . . the Other
. . . October 13, 1842, At the Annual Meeting of the Governors of the Notting-
ham Infirmary* (1842), 17–18.

unity as the one common ground upon which all classes could meet in a spirit of mutual assistance and co-operation, recognized that a lack of Christian charity had so permeated English society as to preclude a meaningful dialogue between rich and poor.[1] He was frankly puzzled as to how individual misery and ignorance could have become translated by Chartists and socialists into a collectivized threat to the necessary gradations of society.

Times had clearly changed. The apparent determination of millions of workers to reject the wisdom of their betters and provide their own solutions to those problems most real to them could not be ignored. Bishops like Kaye felt that something was clearly wrong with English society if it drove the most populous class into the arms of Chartists and socialists. It was slowly dawning upon churchmen that their priorities and those of the laboring populace were dangerously dissimilar. Perhaps economic and social conditions, as well as political impotence, were really primary concerns to the working classes, and were sufficiently important to interfere with their hearing the even more important truths communicated by the national Church. If so, then principles of clerical social action had to be expanded in such a way as to convince the lower orders that at least some of their priorities, and those of their parson and bishop, were not necessarily incompatible. On the eve of the great social reforms of the 1840's some Church leaders already understood this. The seemingly sudden appearance of Chartism and atheistic socialism certainly opened the minds of several others, so that episcopal support of improving social legislation was commonplace by mid-century. It was, however, conceived as a policy of preservation rather than change. The alleviation of social misery was a way of making the working classes more amenable to the divine ordinance that man is born to labor inequitably. As J. B. Sumner cautioned, 'when we can take winter out of the year, and make all a perpetual spring, we may take labour out of the world, and place man once more in Paradise'.[2] In case overzealous reformers had any doubts, Paradise was not about to be regained.

[1] *Ibid.,* 8–9.
[2] J. B. Sumner, *Christian Charity, Its Obligations and Objects, With Reference to the Present State of Society, In A Series of Sermons* (1841), 101.

VII

<><><><><><><><><><><><><><><><><><><>

Church and Social Conflict

<><><><><><><><><><><><><><><><><><><>

1. LOWER-CLASS ALIENATION

Throughout the first half of the nineteenth century churchmen were increasingly burdened with an ominous feeling of social disintegration. They had first sensed it during the French Revolution, when it was feared that class antagonisms, exacerbated by republican visionaries, threatened to obliterate the natural social relationships governing all levels of society. Relieved that their heroic ministrations had apparently stemmed the tide of lower-class disaffection, clergymen were nevertheless aware that class relationships had undergone a severe strain. Their confidence in the stability of a stratified, but harmonious social order had been seriously shaken. That confidence was never to be regained; it was a permanent casualty of the economic and social revolution, already underway before the French Revolution, and in the long run far more disruptive. Try as they might in the years after Waterloo to maintain and extend the social harmony that they believed had been on the edge of collapse in the 1790's, clerical leaders found their task complicated by a mutual dislike and distrust between rich and poor unlike anything they had known in pre-revolutionary days. To an improving Church already proud of its conciliatory and useful political and social role during the years of revolutionary bitterness and war, it was evident that the great gaps that had appeared in the structure of society were still in need of repair.

Bishop Ryder, upon his translation to Lichfield in 1824, spoke of the clergyman's role as 'the cementer of social union, the organ of kindly communication between the rich and the poor of the land. He is at once the object of respect and the friend to each'.[1] These were comforting words predicated upon eighteenth-century social ideals. But nineteenth-century ministers were finding that the harder they endeavoured to apply their adhesive talents to all classes in society, the greater the antagonisms seemed to become. Although their task was facilitated by the rapid extension of Church facilities and schools, each passing year revealed that the gaps between rich and poor were growing wider, and the prospects for a harmonious reconciliation dimmer. Furthermore, as the laboring population increased rapidly, its hostility towards those spiritual guardians seeking to reconcile it to whatever direction the governing classes steered society, seemed to become more bitter. As an agency of the State, and as social and political allies of the propertied orders, the Establishment's position was always compromised and was at best tenuous when it purported to represent the interests of all classes. Time and time again, as the Poor Law reform clearly indicated, the Church was committed to policies antipathetic to the interests of the very class it was most desperately trying to reintegrate into the pattern of social harmony. The laboring poor understood this long before it permeated clerical minds bemused by idyllic eighteenth-century notions of a naturally blended social hierarchy in which any excessive gradations were smoothed out by the gentle explanations and assistance of the local parson.

The Revolution had made some churchmen conscious of the many poor people completely separated from the national Establishment, and they knew that the Anglican clergy had lost much of its persuasive hold on the lower orders. The unique *Report* of the Lincolnshire clergy in 1800 substantiated sporadic charges that the laboring classes, even in stable agricultural districts, were often entirely beyond the preaching of their parish priests. Most churchmen readily blamed it on schismatic Methodists and other wandering enthusiasts who invaded stable parishes, but it was becoming increasingly difficult to ignore the deleterious effects of non-residence, pluralism, and a scandalous spiritual dullness among the clergy. Even before the fear of revolution exaggerated the problem an occasional bishop struck out at such abuses. Lewis Bagot, translated from Bristol to Norwich in 1783, delivered the sharpest rebuke to clergymen heard before the reform agitation of the next century. Troubled by the decline of religious values and the diminishing influence of the Church, Bagot indicted the clergy for failing to perform their duties zealously and preach the Gospel. While it was undoubtedly true that the censure of the clergy was sometimes unfair, it was no longer possible to deny that it also was often justified. 'We must rigidly censure and correct ourselves . . .' after recognizing that we have been neither diligent

[1] H. Ryder, *A Charge to the Clergy of the Diocese of Lichfield and Coventry, at the Primary Visitation* (Stafford, 1824), 13.

nor zealous in the performance of parochial duties. A candid examination would reveal that the clergy, though not guilty of gross immorality, were culpable of carelessness, indifference, and neglect of their solemn obligations. Bagot concluded that at best the ministry performed 'the stated and occasional duty', but recoiled at that description: 'the stated and occasional duty! Good God! is this their care, their anxious concern for the souls of those, of whom they are to give account to their Redeemer?'[1]

This was strong, almost enthusiastic language for a prelate, and was certainly a rarity in the long-neglected diocese of Norwich, not to mention the Church at large. Bagot threatened a number of reforms to consolidate parishes, reduce pluralism, non-residence, and generally improve clerical standards. Ever conscious of tradition and proprietary rights, however, he indicated that he had no intention of interfering with present arrangements, only those in the future.[2] These were the pious, but ineffective hopes of a worried diocesan conscious of decay in his church. Bagot focused his criticism upon the parochial clergy, and, in contrast to Bishop Watson, never suggested any failing at higher levels in the Establishment. At the same time he understood what some of his episcopal generation and most of the next were to learn: if the Church was to survive as a meaningful national institution, relevant to all classes, it had to meet revolutionary challenges, whether religious, political, or economic, by a revival of parochial life.

The success of the Sunday school movement and the introduction of the National Schools even before the revolutionary wars were over indicated that the message was getting through. The passage of legislation to improve residency and assist stipendiary curates, inadequate though it was, also pointed to an expanded awareness of parochial deficiencies. That multitudes already separated from the Church would have some place to worship once returned to the fold was seemingly assured by the decision in 1818 to extend the physical Church into populous areas where large numbers of laboring Englishmen were effectively excluded by the severe lack of facilities. All of this suggested that having held the line against revolution, the Church, supported by the government, was prepared to correct a few glaring deficiencies and reassert its traditional role as the great spiritual and social mediator of a hierarchical society.

To several Church leaders the problem was simply one of restoring the eighteenth-century ideal of a rational, harmonious social balance. The Establishment was to guarantee that all of the component parts were carefully integrated into the societal whole in accordance with proven

---

[1] L. Bagot, *A Charge Delivered to the Clergy At the Primary Visitation* (Norwich, 1784), 8–12.

[2] *Ibid.*, 17–18.

natural laws. As the extra-cautious and deeply conservative Bishop Howley continued to believe, all individuals were an integral link in the great social chain, 'which never is broken without disturbance and injury to those which immediately adjoin it'. During the long years of revolutionary conspiracy and war the Church had labored to keep the links connected, and even started to reforge those weakened by abuse and neglect. Unwilling to accept the mounting evidence that the old links of social cohesion could not readily be welded with the new metals being wrought by rapid economic and social change, Howley was not alone in his simplistic, naturalistic defense of the eternal balance still raised in 1826:

> Society is in fact a piece of machinery, disposed with consummate art and contrivance, of which the several parts are so skilfully interwoven, with such due proportion and reference to one another, as to provide compensation for the defects and imperfections of all, and minister to their preservation and safety. How beautiful the arrangement by which the calm prudence of age and the ardent activity of youth, the powerful engines of man and the amiable qualities of the softer sex, are wrought into one harmonious system, in which the rich and the poor, the mean and the mighty, the wisdom that plans and the labour that executes, have each their separate place, their several interests, and yet are so closely connected, that no member can suffer without some injury to others![1]

It was not the move from Fulham to Lambeth Palace two years later that provided Howley with a broader perspective that shattered his confidence. It was rather the accumulation of evidence revealing the magnitude of the Church's problems with the laboring classes that caused him reluctantly to concede that the balancing qualities of the Establishment had become so distorted as to allow the social machinery at times to gyrate wildly, and perhaps even fly apart. More slowly and less fully than some of his younger brethren, the archbishop was coming to recognize that the problem of reintegrating the working multitudes into the national Church was more complex than merely providing them with new churches in which to harangue them with old lessons about patience and contentment. If Howley could understand that, then there were few of his colleagues on the bench who could not.

The workers also understood it and acted upon it by their indifference or hostility to a Church so closely allied to the propertied classes. As the poor became further and further alienated in the nineteenth century, they found little comfort in the preaching of clergymen who tried on the one hand to exhort them to be acquiescent in the righteousness of their exploitation, and, on the other, supported severe measures against them

---

[1] W. Howley, *A Sermon Preached At the Fifty-Second Anniversary of the Royal Humane Society . . . 9th April, 1826* (1826), 8–9.

when they could no longer bear their misery with patience and contentment. Worker discontent and disaffection were naturally frightening to their betters, but to some Church leaders they were also disillusioning and puzzling. It caused some of the more perceptive of them not only to berate the poor, but to wonder about the effectiveness of their efforts in assuring the continuance of class harmony. Pitt's old tutor and ecclesiastical adviser, George Pretyman-Tomline, considered himself one of the architects of lower-class contentment during the long wars. When they were over he wondered what had gone wrong, recalling how essential the 'well-ordered poor' were to the success of the war effort, and to 'our comfort, safety and prosperity, private and public—the very basis of a prosperous society'. It had seemed to him that the poor had understood it as well as the rich! Yet the lower orders were becoming indifferent to society, and even to their own fate. The bishop was alarmed by what he considered to be a dangerous post-war trend, and hoped that the new educational schemes would soon correct it.[1]

Correction, as some of the younger clergy understood, meant reconciling the working classes not to the old, but to a new society containing large congregations of laboring poor. As William Otter and others pointed out, urbanization had created new and peculiar problems for the Church as multitudes of people were being pressed closely together in daily life and labor where they were becoming aware of their collective strength. In the aftermath of Peterloo, Otter reminded his congregation of Paley's warning about the dangers of confederations and combinations of men sharing sectarian or other interests. Not only was the warning ignored, but the laboring poor were congregating in towns, 'where they form . . . an isolated class, without that due admixture of ranks, and orders, which in all other cases tends, by the infusion of benevolence, respect and intelligence, to temper and soften the whole mass'. Their relationship with their masters was taking on a new and disturbing character for they saw them only for business, and rarely derived any of the moral and social virtues that traditionally resulted from a close proximity of the inferior with his betters. Otter perceptively noted that 'the capitalists who have made their fortunes, generally retire to more peaceful and pleasing spots for the enjoyment of them', leaving behind the clergy to inculcate alone the desirable qualities which usually come from a steady acquaintance with persons of 'superior education'. It was not surprising, therefore, that the Dissenters were more successful in the manufacturing towns, because the upper classes were not available for guidance and consultation.[2] He, of course, forgot that many of

[1] Unpublished sermon on Heb. x. 24, n.d., *Pretyman Family Archives*, T. 108/24.

[2] Otter, *Sermon* (1820), 31–32.

the urban industrialists and bankers were themselves Dissenters and financed the efforts of their ministers in the populous areas.

Otter was less concerned about religious distortions than he was about social distortions. He feared that the isolated poor soon became angry and envious, convinced that 'wealth and happiness are inseparably united . . .'. They lacked a natural perspective and thus failed to see that happiness and unhappiness were scattered 'with an even hand by Providence over the different ranks of life'. Consequently only the pleasures of the upper classes are apparent to the poor instead of their benevolent virtues. When discontent arises there is 'no superior mind, no revered person—*pietate gravis et meritis*—to soothe their murmurs and to direct their thoughts'.[1] This was perfectly evident in Manchester and Leeds, where the laboring classes, crowded together, were effectively split off from superior guidance, and in times of distress acted accordingly. This is what troubled Henry Phillpotts and other opponents of the Poor Law revisions in 1818–19, who feared that they would encourage more rural emigration and a further breakdown of the traditional landed society.

Spiritual dangers also lurked in social changes. John Kaye, the new Bishop of Bristol (1820–7), was fearful in 1821 that the altering social patterns would accelerate the spread of infidelity through the lower classes where it had once only been present among the upper orders.[2] Hostility to the Church was rapidly spreading; 'men in the obscurest walks of life have caught the contagion, and have learned to think and to speak of the Gospel as a mere imposture, as a scheme devised by crafty men for the purpose of holding their fellow-creatures in a state of subjection'. So heinous an idea was not socially dangerous when believed by the wealthy infidel, for he was at the same time concerned with the preservation of his position. He understood that even if he rejected Christianity, it still has 'the powerful tendency . . . to render men peaceable and contented with their condition'. Since men of the lower ranks lack such a concern, 'and rather than desire permanence in society they see change as synonymous to advantage', it was always to the advantage of the rich to give at least the appearance of being religious.[3] Yet, at a

---

[1] *Ibid.*, 32.

[2] John Kaye (1783–1853), son of a Hammersmith linen-draper, was a brilliant student at Cambridge, where he was tutor of 2nd Marquess of Bute. Master of Christ Church (1814), Regius Professor of Divinity (1816), he revived patristic studies. Elevated to Bristol in 1820, was translated to Lincoln in 1827. An able, deeply conservative High Church prelate, Kaye was an energetic improver of his diocese, and an influential member of the bench.

[3] J. Kaye, *A Charge Delivered . . . At His Primary Visitation in August, 1821* (Bristol, 1821), 6–7.

time when the upper classes were in fact more supportive of religion than at any time in the preceding century, their example was being lost on their inferiors as they came less and less into contact.

Religious arguments by Church leaders on this problem were uncommon. The fear of social change and class disintegration predominated, even in Kaye's worried analysis of what was wrong with the poor. The minister in that context was not envisioned as the guardian of the faith, but as 'the connecting link between the different ranks and degrees of society, the corner-stone of our political and social fabric'. By education the Anglican parson was at a level with the great, yet by duty and charity he conceived of no person beneath him. Such was the inviting picture of the clerical social ameliorator drawn by John Bird Sumner in 1820. Having the perspective of all classes, the minister was the critical ingredient in the maintenance of peaceful class relationships in an age of rapid change. This was especially true in the larger towns. To those who were critical of supporting the expansion of the Establishment in populous areas, Sumner asked:

> Take away the Minister of the Gospel, and who will remain to stand between the employer and his labourer, between the magistrate and the offender? Who will be the almoner of the rich man's bounty? Who will direct the poor man's industry into the most useful channels?[1]

The alarm generated by the agitation and disturbances of the post-war years gradually diminished during the more stable decade of the 1820's. Society seemed less likely to be torn apart by class conflicts when the ruling classes were willing to moderate many of the harsh legal penalties directed against the poor, and after 1824 even permit them to combine to improve their condition. Charity was readily available during difficult periods, and the Poor Law continued to provide varieties of relief. Church leaders pushed ahead with schools and church extension, hopeful that before another crisis struck a new generation of workers would be prepared to face it with Christian conviction and fortitude. Bishop Howley's plaintive description of the well-balanced, harmonious society perhaps even seemed a possibility.

Yet some churchmen realized that the temporary decline of worker agitation in no way halted the inexorable process of economic and social change that was relentlessly altering the country. Philip Shuttleworth (1782–1842), friend of Lord Holland and tutor to his children, sounded a warning note in 1825. That ardent Whig, who was to become the short-lived Bishop of Chichester in 1840, agreed that it was very nice to comfort oneself with pastoral pictures of the poor laboring man earning his bread by the sweat of his brow, yet humbly and religiously doing his duty cheerfully, regularly, and piously—comforting yes, but no longer

[1] Sumner, *Sermon* (1820), 16–17.

accurate. It was, he claimed, an exaggerated sketch of the past which if not extinct was at least becoming comparatively rare. The close contacts of population, the pace of 'business activity' and the refinements of wealth and luxury had done much to eliminate it. In their wake these developments tended to leave intensified social differences, so that the line separating the lower from the superior classes had become more sharply defined. There had been no halt in the continued exclusion of the working classes from the luxuries, the arts, the pleasures of life. Shuttleworth described them 'in the laborious and often unhealthy and degrading preparation of which they are the necessary instruments, without reaping the civilizing effects resulting from their enjoyment'.[1] The gap was particularly wide in the great manufacturing towns where the workers were almost completely cut off from any meaningful contact with those who benefited from their labor. Increasingly envious and dissatisfied, the workers were a threat to themselves and the rest of society. But having recognized the problem, he predicted that 'the debasing profligacy of a thronged population' was unlikely to diminish. Shuttleworth believed that all that could be done was to educate the workers in the solid religious justifications for the apparent inequities under which they suffered.[2]

Although Shuttleworth's solution was less than inspired, his analysis was significant. Not only did he warn of the growing alienation of the working classes, but he recognized that it was in large measure a result of economic and social developments that were perhaps to the poor's disadvantage and drove them further apart from the rest of the society. Moreover, he did not try to moderate the situation with silly prattle about how happy the laboring poor really were when they evaluated their blessings. Another Whig prelate, Edward Maltby, as late as 1831, might still drone on with comparisons of the healthy poor and the haggard rich; how much stronger their children were as a result of their robust outdoor upbringing and early labor; and how the rich, tempted by their fortunes, missed the advantages of a simple, industrious and useful life.[3] But the clerical power of self-delusion had been greatly reduced by the evidence of the post-war years, and such confident pronouncements were few and far between. More common was Bishop Law's almost apologetic plea to his clergy to face up to the 'temporal concernments of the poor'. The widespread disturbances in 1830–1 revived the issue, and Law was joined by several new prelates who recognized that although

[1] P. N. Shuttleworth, *A Sermon Preached . . . the 5th of July, 1825, at the Fourteenth Annual Meeting of the Hampshire Society for the Education of the Infant Poor on the Plan of the Rev. Dr Bell in the Principles of the Established Church* (Winchester, 1825), 14–16.

[2] *Ibid.*, 18.

[3] E. Maltby, *Sermons Preached In the Chapel of Lincoln's Inn* (1831), 295–7.

poverty was an eternal condition, it was seriously affecting the stability of society and could not be ignored any longer. In agricultural districts it was clear, as others had warned earlier, 'that the strong tie which had for ages bound together the Clergyman and his Parishioners, the Landlord and his Tenants, by a sense of benefits mutually conferred and received, appears now to be inauspiciously weakened, if not entirely rent and torn asunder'.[1]

If the problem was serious in agricultural districts, it was far worse in the towns. Blomfield in 1832 interpreted the loss of upper-class authority in the urban areas as a result of the disintegration of the ancient alliance between gentry and clergy. During questioning by the Common's Committee on Sabbath Day Observance, the London prelate was asked whether it would not do much good if the higher classes 'concurred with the clergy and with the magistrates in acting by admonition and not by legal means?' Blomfield had no doubt of it, except in the towns. 'I do not think the higher classes have their legitimate influence there, as they have, or may have, in the country, where, if they could go hand in hand with the clergy, I have no doubt it would be so.'[2] As the old forms of influence had broken down in the cities, the bishop believed that the legislature should intervene with the passage and enforcement of strict Sabbatarian laws as one means of controlling the urban poor. William Wilberforce and other founders of Evangelical societies for the rejuvenation of morals had been advocating such a measure for years, and welcomed the support of the influential High Church prelate whose enthusiasm for Sabbath legislation exceeded that of any of his episcopal colleagues. Most in fact were quite wary of so provocative an approach to the reinstitution of controls on the lower orders. Broad Churchman though he was, Samuel Butler was representative in his belief that there were already sufficient laws regulating Sunday behavior. It was only a question of enforcement. But even there he was cautious as he warned that Sunday should not be made a hateful day for the laboring poor. Zealous legislators did not seem to appreciate the wide differences that existed between a metropolitan and a country population, and all too often expected them to act the same on their one day of rest. It was ridiculous not to expect that

> they who have been confined in the close and heated air of manufactories and shops, in narrow streets, and crowded and ill-ventilated apartments, for six days continually, naturally wish to breathe a freer and a purer air, and to enjoy a refreshing relaxation on the seventh. To debar them from their usual and only gratification, that actual rest from their labours . . . would be as oppressive as it fortunately is impossible.[3]

[1] G. H. Law, *A Charge Delivered to the Clergy of the Diocese of Bath and Wells . . . in May and June, 1831* (Wells, 1831), 18–19.
[2] *Parl. Ps.* (1831–2), VII, 502.   [3] Butler, *Charge* (1834), 6–8.

It was true, of course, Butler admitted, that refreshing relaxation was all too often found in gin-shops, drunkenness and licentiousness, but if existing laws were enforced it could be stopped. If the law tried to do more it would just be broken and held in contempt. Furthermore, it would make religion even more distasteful to workers who would find a day of gloom and austerity rather than a merciful rest to the body and cheerfulness to the soul.[1] As far as Butler was concerned, Sabbath laws were another enthusiastic Evangelical scheme destined to drive the laboring classes even further from the Church. His continued opposition brought him much criticism, but he steadfastly insisted that the voluntary principle was preferable to penal exactments in religion as well as in life in general.[2] That was about as much support as the laboring poor ever got from Butler.

It was, however, a difficult dilemma for the directors of the national Church. Their ranks were certainly improving as perceptive, serious, and hard-working clergymen were filling the vacancies on the bench as well as at lower levels. As a result, it was becoming more obvious to the hierarchy that the alienation of the working classes was not just an occasional explosion of discontent, linked to one or two particular policies of the ruling order, but was an enduring aspect of the changing times. Church leaders might repeat descriptions of the responsibilities of the clergy to provide the connecting link between rich and poor, and the 'friendly feeling' between all classes, but, as Thomas Vowler Short complained in 1835, 'the complicated state of society and property . . .' was making it very difficult 'to know how to arbitrate between conflicting claims'. It seemed to him that 'the working part of the community' were not unfair in asking 'what right the governing part of our predecessors had to mortgage the labour of the present generation?'[3]

Older spokesmen could still agree with the Bishop of Durham's usual reply about the 'reciprocal obligations' of a hierarchical and mutually interdependent society from which there results 'the union and happiness of the whole', but it was apparent to more and more of his brethren that the parts as constituted did not necessarily add up that way.[4] Alarmed by worker hostility, they could only murmur 'amen' to Bishop Otter's prayer for the improvement, 'and especially the softening of that harsh temper and disposition towards the other classes of society, at present one of the worst features of the times . . .'.[5] How could they

[1] *Ibid.*, 9.

[2] 7 June 1837, *Butler Ps.*, B.M., Add MS. 34594, f. 129.

[3] Short, *Parochialia*, 27; also *National Education, and the Means of Improving It* (1835), 5.

[4] E. Maltby, *A Sermon Preached . . . June VI, MDCCCXXXIX At the Yearly Meeting of the Children of the Charity Schools* (1839), 2.

[5] Otter, *Memoir*, xx.

have responded otherwise when basic to their entire concept of society was the assumption that 'the safety and comfort of the whole depend upon the security and connexion of the several parts; as the strength of a chain fails, if a single link be snapped asunder'?[1] Metaphorically and realistically the links seemed weaker than at any time since the French Revolution. Short and others knew it, and hoped that the inculcation of religious principles would convince the laboring man that the chain must be kept intact and the social compact observed, even to his own hindrance.[2]

2. THE REFORM BILL

While the Church labored to secure the loyalties of the inferior multitudes it suddenly found its efforts at stabilization and retrenchment undermined by its supposed allies in Parliament. Not only was the religious monopoly of the Establishment threatened by the repeal of the Test and Corporation Acts in 1828, but of far more consequence most of the restrictions on Catholics were removed the following year. Although Pitt had been able to obtain the support of only two prelates (Watson and Shipley) when he attempted to abolish restrictions on Dissenters,[3] by Wellington's time the bench believed that the Establishment was secure and the restrictive laws of little value. Furthermore, their improved religious sensibilities made them feel that the sacrament was debased when employed as a test for secular office. Consequently, several bishops, including such cautious prelates as Howley and Van Mildert, spoke for the passage. Catholic emancipation was far more traumatic for the Church, however, and only loyalty to the government and fear of the veracity of Wellington's prediction of revolution in Ireland sufficed to split the episcopal ranks on the issue. Even at that only eight prelates, five of them elevated since the last vote in 1824, supported emancipation, while sixteen others continued to oppose it.[4]

It appeared to many churchmen that the trusted Tories had, with brutal haste, betrayed the Establishment and the Constitution, and had left both exposed to the destructive machinations of a non-Protestant Parliament. If such Church stalwarts as Wellington and Peel were willing to support a measure that was so clearly dangerous to the Establishment, episcopal spines shivered at the thought of what the Whigs would do to society as a whole once they gained power. When they did so in 1830 the Anglican hierarchy, still reeling from the blow they suffered the

[1] Maltby, *Sermon* (1839), 2; also *Sermons* (1831), 271–3.

[2] Short, *National Education*, 6.

[3] *Moore Ps.,* Lambeth Palace Library, SR 166; also Watson, *Anecdotes,* I, 261–2.

[4] *Hansard*, XXI (1829), 694–5.

preceding year, alarmed by the outbreak of revolution again on the Continent, and nervous about pillaging and rioting in several agricultural counties, now had to contemplate that great leveling assault on the social and political foundations of the Constitution, the Reform Bill. To a Church so intimately attached to the existing structure of things, basic political reform appeared another stage in the unravelling of the threads of social stability which had been carefully and patiently drawn together largely as a result of clerical efforts during the preceding tumultuous decades.

Though ill in June, 1831, Bishop Van Mildert was eager to visit the clergy of his diocese and bolster them for the unknown dangers that lay ahead. In a mood reminiscent of the revolutionary years, he warned, 'we all ought to prepare ourselves for such a state of things as none of us yet have lived to witness. I pray God they may prove less disastrous than at present we are warranted in expecting.' The enemies of the Church had only grown bolder and stronger since concessions were made to them in 1828–9 and were now seeking to strengthen the House of Commons at the expense of the king and the House of Lords, knowing full well how firmly the aristocracy supported the Establishment.[1] In spite of appeals and warnings from friends and enemies alike that the failure of the Reform Bill would endanger the entire bench, Van Mildert remained adamant. No further concessions should be made to the innovators, and the Church must hold firm against the threats of Earl Grey, Lord Durham, or Henry Brougham and refuse to compromise. A month before the bishops joined in defeating the measure in October, 1831, Van Mildert made it clear that he had not yielded: 'if Lord B[rougham] expects me to come forth with a plan of Church Reform he will be grievously disappointed and still more so if he supposes that my vote for the Parliamentary Reform Bill can be purchased by fears and menaces of the impending fate of the Church'. There was no convincing the old prelate 'that the Church will be more safe or last one year longer by supporting that measure which can answer no purpose but to whet the appetites of the radicals and atheists and to give them an increase in power which no Government . . . would long be able to resist. . . .'[2]

Reform was in the air, and Van Mildert knew that once it triumphed in the political realm it would surely invade the Church. Moreover the changing, critical utilitarian standards of the day were being directed more often against the real and imagined abuses of the Establishment.

[1] Cornelius Ives, ed., *Sermons On Several Occasions, and Charges of William Van Mildert . . . to Which Is Prefixed A Memoir of the Author* (Oxford, 1838), pp. 119–21.

[2] Van Mildert to Archdeacon Thorpe, 10 Sept. 1831, in Edward Hughes, 'The Bishops and Reform, 1831–1833: Some Fresh Correspondence', *English Historical Review*, LVI (1941), 467.

Non-residency and pluralism continued to be decried at the same time as they were steadily being reduced, but now the issues were more ominous. Growing attacks upon tithes and the amount and distribution of Church revenue posed the critical question of property rights and the spectre of spoliation. Bishop Gray of Bristol raised the point directly during the early stages of debate in the spring of 1831. Not only was the Reform Bill a perilous constitutional innovation, but it was also a dangerous infringement of the rights of property. Once Parliament sanctioned one kind of spoliation by eliminating the franchise in some areas, even decayed boroughs, there was no telling what species of property would be safe. He worried for the stability of society if Parliament could deprive people of any kind of property without consent.[1] Gray, like most of his colleagues, was especially sensitive to such an issue with all sorts of charges and reform proposals flying about the spires of the Church. Church leaders knew that much of the criticism directed against the Establishment came from the towns where the Anglican ministry was largely uninfluential, and unpopular. These were exactly the areas that would be enfranchised by the Reform Bill, and their representatives might well be hostile Dissenters and even Papists.

Although twenty-one bishops voted against the measure when it was defeated by forty votes in October, many of them realized that some degree of reform was inevitable and perhaps even desirable. They believed, however, that the government's Bill went too far in extending the urban franchise at the expense of ancient privileges. The bench was not clear as to what would constitute a safe adjustment but hoped that something better could be worked out in committee. Some of its members felt that the reformers were being driven too far by agitated public opinion whipped up by a hostile press—'a new engine of frightful power', as Bishop Copleston described it. That prelate, elevated to Llandaff two years before, knew that some sort of reform measure would be passed in 1831 and hoped the Church party 'will be moderate but firm . . . not sticking for everything that can be called a right, if the public opinion or feeling, or even prejudice, is universal against it'.[2] Copleston, who had been an early advocate of educational reform at Oxford, was thoroughly familiar with the obstructionist, conservative tendencies of the Anglican clergy.[3] Consequently he warned that though concession to unenlightened opinions might seem undesirable, it 'is not cowardly, and it certainly is prudent'. Yet he shared the fear of many of his brethren 'that the advocates for parliamentary reform will do too much at once' and turn all power in the state over to the House of

[1] *Hansard*, III (1831), 1333–4.

[2] Copleston to W. Copleston, 26 Jan. 1831, in *Memoir*, 139.

[3] See E. Copleston, ed., *Letters of the Earl of Dudley to the Bishop of Llandaff* (1840), 5.

Commons. 'The only thing that has kept us from pure democracy has been the influence of the crown and the nobility, or great proprietors in the representative body.' True, the bishops were particularly fearful for the Church, but Copleston warned those who saw the danger of democracy and disliked the Establishment that they would only be temporarily pacifying the republicans if they sacrificed the interests of the Church. Their time for leveling would soon come. He hoped Lord Grey and Brougham understood and would defend the constitution.[1]

Copleston's old friend and new colleague on the bench, Henry Phillpotts, doubted that the Whigs were much interested in such a defense. Furious that the new ministers had delayed his consecration to Exeter until he surrendered his rich *commendam* living of Stanhope, Durham, Phillpotts described them as 'slaves of the newspapers'. Their plans for reform 'have all the air of coarsest flattery of the lowest and most ignorant of the revolutionary talkers of the day'.[2] When the government introduced its proposal in March 1831 with its extensive disenfranchisement of the smaller boroughs and enhancement of town and county representation, Phillpotts assured his secretary that 'the Revolutionary Bill' would be thrown out and the irresponsible ministers would dissolve Parliament 'at whatever hazard to the peace'. Confident though he was that they were 'universally despised for their blundering imbecility' he knew there was really 'no security against their prowess for mischief'. He had repeatedly argued in private that the concept of 'a safe reform' was contradictory, and that abuses could be individually corrected without throwing the country into the hands of democratic fanatics.[3]

Although the Bill passed its Second Reading in the Commons on March 23rd by a single vote, the government was defeated in committee the following month and, as Phillpotts feared, the country was faced with a new election. Clearly it was a 'visitation', and the bishop prayed that God would extend His Grace to help England endure its hour of trial. After warning his secretary, Ralph Barnes, to keep his name out of it, Phillpotts endorsed and financed the printing of cheap tracts to 'offset the effects of the Jacobin press'. He wanted the tracts distributed to the Devon and Cornwall county electors in an all-out effort to defeat Whig candidates in the diocese. In the meantime he continued to heap venom upon the reformers; though in a rare moment of self-control he would not trust himself to give his opinion of the loathsome Brougham.[4] Like most of the bench, Phillpotts was particularly disturbed by disenfranchisement. In spite of his hatred of the towns he recognized that enfranchisement, if carefully done, was a logical result of social change.

[1] Copleston, *Memoir*, 139–40.
[2] Phillpotts to R. Barnes, Dec. 1830, *Phillpotts Letters*, D.C.R.O., P.R. 17/20, No. 28.
[3] *Ibid.*, 24 March 1831, No. 84.   [4] *Ibid.*, n.d. April, No. 100.

But one could not take place at the expense of the other without removing the foundation of the constitution and assuring the collapse of the superstructure. Simply put, his logic, which he described as 'not only defensible, but reasonably impregnable', led to the conclusion that you could no more constitutionally disenfranchise an M.P. than you could a peer. Phillpotts meant a spiritual as well as temporal peer, and the preservation of the former was, in his mind, dependent upon the security of the latter. As a result he prayed God would somehow make 'this great and appalling crisis' a source for the furtherance of His truth.[1]

In spite of such prayers and propagandist tracts, the reformers won an even larger majority in the General Election and brought forward a second Bill in June. By then it was clear that the bishops were at odds with that popular opinion they so deplored, but few of them yet realized how strong it actually was. Phillpotts had some sense of its intensity and was reluctant to come to Exeter once his sentiments on reform were known. Already distrusted for his High Church views by many of the Evangelical clergy and parishioners in his diocese, and suspected of owing his appointment to Exeter to his reversing his position as a bitter opponent of Catholic emancipation, Phillpotts's opposition to the Reform Bill made him even less popular.[2] Throughout the spring of 1831 he offered one excuse after another for not coming to Exeter. For some unexplained reason, his physicians were reluctant to permit him to visit the cathedral city of his diocese. They did not, however, prevent him from travelling to Durham where he had a stall, or to Cornwall by boat, carefully bypassing Exeter. When the excuses wore thin and criticism mounted, Phillpotts added still another:

> I hear that the people of Exeter, or somewhere or other, are displeased at my not having gone thither. I really cannot submit to be the slave of their opinions. I wish to do my duty, and they who think I wish to neglect it, must enjoy their own notions on the subject.[3]

Self-righteous independence aside, Phillpotts was simply frightened that he would be hooted or assaulted in some other way. When in the middle of May he finally conceded that a visit might be politic he made it very brief, stayed much longer in Cornwall, and then went directly by sea to London.

[1] *Ibid.*, 2 May, No. 101.
[2] Phillpotts strongly denied that he had been promised promotion by Wellington for changing his position on Catholic emancipation. He told his secretary that he had made no step to get the bishopric, and wished some way could be found to make this clear to 'cool and moderate men'. 5 Nov. 1830, *Phillpotts Letters*, No. 9.
[3] *Ibid.*, 7 May, 1831, No. 103.

Although Phillpotts and most of his colleagues did not enter the debates, long before the Reform Bill ever reached the House of Lords the spiritual peers were depicted as unalterably opposed to the progressive desires of the populace. This is what the sensible Bishop of London, Blomfield, had tried to avoid when, after the introduction of the first Bill in March, he wrote to his close friend Bishop Monk that 'it has been thought prudent to abstain from all episcopal conference on the Reform Bill till we see whether the measure will come before us. If it should, much, I think, will depend upon its shape, and upon the weight of majority which sends it to us. . . .' Personally, however, he viewed the proposed measure in the same light as Monk—'Caput inter nubila condit'. There was nothing to do but wait and 'trust in Providence'.[1] When the new Parliament, more radical than its predecessor, convened, Blomfield saw the handwriting on the wall and was convinced that it was far more dangerous for the House of Lords, and particularly the bishops, to obstruct passage than it was for them to let it through. Like several of his fellow prelates, Blomfield hoped that the Bill would be modified in committee to make it possible for more bishops than the old, liberal Bathurst and the new Whig appointment, Maltby, to support the government.[2] The former was delighted that reform was imminent, and warned his alarmist colleagues on the bench that if the Church was in fact in danger, as they claimed, the threat 'arises not so much from a restless spirit of *innovation* in some, as from an *obstinate adherence* to *antiquated abuses* in others, who, unobservant of the change in public opinions, are regardless of the consequences which must result from this change'.[3]

There is no question that the Church leadership seriously misjudged the sentiment of the nation both in stubbornly opposing all reform, or, as the more realistic among them hoped, in holding out for concessions. Archbishop Howley spoke for the latter sentiment when, during the pre-divisional debate on 7 October, he conceded that some reform was needed to correct obvious abuses, and had hoped that a cautious, unified proposal might have been worked out co-operatively by both parties.

[1] Blomfield, *Memoir*, I, 163–4.　　[2] *Ibid.*, 165.

[3] Henry Bathurst, *Memoirs of the Late Dr Henry Bathurst, Lord Bishop of Norwich* (1837), II, 123–4.

Bathurst (1744–1837), son of a Tory squire and nephew of Lord Bathurst, he was a kind, lax, nepotistic eighteenth-century Latitudinarian. Elevated to Norwich through his uncle's influence in 1806, he was correctly warned that his support of Catholic emancipation and his general liberalism would prevent his being translated. Lived the life of a Whig squire, playing whist and hunting until the age of eighty. Was offered Archbishopric of Dublin by Earl Grey in 1831, but as he was then eighty-seven tried vainly to have it offered to his son. Though the most liberal prelate on the bench, he was also perhaps the worst diocesan administrator, and the neglect of his see was shocking to improving ecclesiastical sensibilities.

But the government had refused to modify its 'extensive experiment', and this left responsible churchmen no alternative but to vote in the negative. Whatever the result, he was prepared to face it. If, as some predicted, violence would follow, he would at least be consoled in his few remaining years (he lived until 1848) that he acted on the sincere belief that the Reform Bill endangered the constitution.[1] Phillpotts predicted that the Lords would destroy 'this detestable Bill' by forty votes, although he expressed in private a willingness to approve a modified version.[2] His prediction was nearly accurate as he, along with twenty of his episcopal brethren, joined with twenty other peers to defeat the measure. It was an aristocratic Tory triumph: of the twenty-one prelates opposed five were of the peerage, one a baron, and seven others were gentry.

The triumph was short-lived. Bishops were hooted and burnt in effigy; Blomfield and Ryder were warned not to preach in London and Lichfield; the archbishop was mobbed in Canterbury, and old Gray of Bristol saw his palace burned by an angry mob. Anti-clerical feeling reached even greater heights than in the years immediately after Waterloo, and the growing demands for serious Church reform and disestablishment were suddenly more pressing than ever. Some clergymen like Walter F. Hook, laboring to bring the Anglican faith to the urban populace, bemoaned the loss of 'a magnificent opportunity of attaching the people to the Church'. By failing to champion the Reform Bill the Church confirmed the conviction too commonly held 'by the vulgar mind' that the leaders of the Establishment were 'opponents rather than champions of the great Christian principles of liberty and justice'.[3]

In the aftermath of the defeat the harried episcopate reacted in one of two ways; some became even more entrenched in their opposition, while others acknowledged that they had grossly misread the sentiments of the populace, and would, out of conviction or expediency, change their position the next time around. Infuriated by government charges of episcopal collusion, and appalled by anti-clerical demonstrations throughout the country, Phillpotts, a few days after the vote, vented his spleen on the accursed Whigs, as he spoke for the forces of continued resistance. Ignoring Gray and Blomfield's futile attempts to restore order, the Bishop of Exeter recalled the Prime Minister's earlier warning to the bench to 'put their house in order' or face grave dangers, and charged the government with fulfilling that prophecy by inciting the nation against the episcopate. Confiscation and popular violence had been suggested, and now encouraged. Having remained silent during the long months of debate before the vote, Phillpotts could stand it no

[1] *Hansard*, VIII (1831), 302–4.
[2] Phillpotts to Barnes, 7 Oct. 1831, *Phillpotts Letters*, No. 149.
[3] W. R. W. Stephens, *Life and Letters of W. F. Hook* (1878), I, 149.

longer and launched his long and heated career in the House of Lords by antagonizing the usually moderate Gray into charging him with 'a foul and calumnious aspersion . . .'.[1] The Earl was just the first of a long line of distinguished Whigs who would be thus goaded by the infuriating prelate. As Greville once said of Phillpotts, he 'would have made a great Bishop in the days of Bonner and Gardiner, or he would have been a Becket, or, still better, a Pope either of the palmy days of Papal Power or during the important period of reaction which succeeded the Reformation. He seems cast in the role of a Sixtus.'[2]

Sixtus in the steam age was perhaps anachronistic, but the bellicose Phillpotts roared on, leading the fight against reform. More convinced than ever that the Reform Bill was tantamount to revolution, he bitterly assailed Blomfield in particular, and those of his colleagues in general, who turned round while 'truth and reason will stand still'.[3] He compared his own time with the initial stages of the French Revolution up until June 1792, when the king fled. Then, as now, everything was done under the guise of constitutional reform. Overcoming angry protests and interruptions from the floor, he predicted that if the delicate constitutional balance was tipped in the direction of more democracy, monarchy and aristocracy would be overwhelmed as it had been in that earlier epoch. Moreover such reform would provide a precedent for giving the Irish Catholics control of their government, and with reform of the Irish Church clearly in the offing the preservation and protection of the Anglican community in Ireland could not be ignored. Consequently, in opposing the Reform Bill bishops were fulfilling their sacred and constitutional responsibilities as guardians of the Establishment.[4]

What horrified the twelve bishops who again voted against reform, as well as some of the eleven who supported it, was the tremulous conviction that this was just the beginning. As George Monk described it, the Bill was the first of a series of changes that would certainly alter the Constitution. He was not opposed to correcting electoral abuses, nor to the enfranchisement of towns, but the Bill 'raised the spectre of perpetual change'. In spite of widespread agitation, Monk knew that the country was opposed to the measure and was merely being bullied by the rabble and radical republicans who joined with Catholics and Dissenters against the Church.[5] Public opinion was a difficult concept for eighteenth-century clerical minds to grasp, and when it appeared to disagree with policies of Burkeian retrenchment, bishops like Lord George Murray of Rochester described it as 'popular clamour' or 'mob clamour', and, as such opinion was fickle, it was folly to succumb to it.

[1] *Hansard*, VIII (1831), 473–7.

[2] C. C. F. Greville, *The Greville Memoirs*, L. Strachey and R. Fulford, eds. (1938), IV, 84.

[3] *Hansard*, XII (1832), 274.   [4] *Ibid.*, 279–86.   [5] *Ibid.*, 405–6, 409.

That aristocratic prelate was certain that the 'tide of rational opinion' had turned the 'tide of popular clamour' and it was now possible to reject precipitate action. No man had a greater respect for the people than he, 'so long as they maintained their respective and private stations . . .'. These, however, did not include matters connected with legislation, and he for one would never disgrace nearly five hundred years of his ancestors by voting for any measure that threatened to confuse the natural hierarchy.[1]

That hierarchy, however, was already more confused than ever by social and economic forces severely straining the bonds of tradition that the Church sought to keep closely wound around the existing structure of society. Although he agreed with Murray, and wished with all his heart that what he said was so, the deeply conservative Van Mildert knew that public opinion favored reform and that it was inevitable. He lamented the restlessness and innovation of the age, and deplored the widespread desire to destroy the old and set subject over ruler. These were signs not of progress as many claimed, but of decline. Times had changed; the spread of learning had altered a sound society. Political reform would only accelerate that alteration. Atheism, infidelity and the eventual annihilation of all ancient institutions would inevitably follow.[2] After his first vote against reform, Van Mildert suffered much abuse from the local Whig gentry and magistrates, and even feared for his personal safety.[3] He was resigned to the belief that it would be much worse the second time, but was determined to persevere.

Expediency, not perseverance, seemed a much more realistic course of action for nearly half of Van Mildert's episcopal brethren. The reality of a Whig government and the shock of explosive reform sentiment had sunk in. Although Archbishop Howley continued to oppose the Bill, Vernon-Harcourt of York, who had absented himself from the vote the previous year, not only endorsed reform in 1832, but claimed that he would have done so in 1831 had his episcopal duties permitted him to attend. The archbishop, who in reality had been reluctant to vote against the government or his associates, now rationalized that all that was involved was a reform of the House of Commons, and so long as that body approved, Lords could have no objection.[4] Moreover Harcourt privately

[1] *Ibid.*, 401–3.　　　　　　[2] *Ibid.*, 48–50.
[3] Van Mildert to Thorpe, 2 Nov. 1831, in Hughes, *E.H.R.*, 468.
[4] *Hansard*, XII (1832), 1043–5.

Harcourt (1757–1847), son of 1st Baron Vernon, was a simple, benevolent man, who was elevated to Carlisle in 1791 and to York in 1807. He was a generous, humane bishop who regularly spent more than his total income on diocesan improvements. In 1831 he inherited the Harcourt estates through his wife, and in 1838, at the death of 3rd Earl Harcourt, he added the name, but declined the title.

informed Lord Grey that in spite of the hostility of some of his colleagues (particularly Phillpotts), he would give the same support to the Whigs as he had given to other governments.[1] When Grey resigned in 1834 Harcourt wrote of his 'sincere regret' and thanked him for his protection of the Church.[2]

Not many of the archbishop's associates on the bench were as yet so reconciled, but, as in 1832, several of them had come to realize that a prudent acquiescence to reform was a necessary corollary of the age. In opposing the first Reform Bill, Bishop Kaye believed that his decision was the lesser of two evils.[3] For the same reason he supported it the following year. Like Copleston and others who thought it 'madness to resist' again, Kaye made his peace with reality. Copleston was speaking for most prelates when he confessed that he 'was in error as to the degree and the extensive prevalence of public opinion on this subject, not understanding, as I now do, what a strong hold the question has acquired in the minds of the middle classes, and of those just above them'. Still, he could not overcome his recollections of the French Revolution, and hoped that in order to avoid republicanism the franchise could continue to be based upon a variety of qualifications.[4] Copleston claimed that he and many of his fellow prelates had opposed the first Bill in order to gain time for further consideration and concession.[5] There was no longer any time.

Blomfield had felt this to be the case even before the first vote, and when he was unable to persuade Howley, or even his close friend, Monk, he deliberately absented himself from voting on the pretense of his father's death, which had occurred shortly before.[6] When accused of inconsistency and perhaps trimming his sails to the prevailing winds (as Phillpotts suggested), Blomfield countered that it was well known he had favored approval, but could not bring himself to vote against those with whom he always agreed. But the time for neutrality was over; the experiment had to be undertaken, and though the result would be unknown, it was the wisest policy to seek to control it. He knew that many feared an attack upon ecclesiastical property would follow, but he believed that reform might actually diminish agitation 'against our

---

[1] 7 Jan. 1833, *Grey MS*. Also Maltby to Gray, 14 March 1832.

[2] 11 July 1834, *ibid*. Grey replied and assured the archbishop that he was always anxious to support the Church, and there was no danger so long as it could 'be brought to adopt reasonable and timely Reforms', 12 July.

[3] *Hansard*, XII (1832), 244–6.

[4] Copleston to Lord Goderich, 27 Nov. 1831, *Memoir*, 148.

[5] *Hansard*, XII (1832), 287–8.

[6] Blomfield, *Memoir*, I, 167–8.

venerable institutions'.[1] The alternative he had repeatedly posed to Monk as he attempted in vain to gain that bishop's vote:

> I am so convinced that a great political convulsion will follow upon the rejection of a new Bill without a second reading; and, on the other hand, that if the second reading be carried by a new batch of peers, it will be all over with the House of Lords and the Church. . . .

The hostility towards the bench was so intense that Blomfield did not think it feasible that the bishops simply stay away and take no part in the debates or the decision. Instead he wished that they not only participate, but that most of them 'may be induced to vote for the second reading, reserving to themselves the liberty of supporting any amendments in Committee'.[2]

Prodded by the warning that it was up to the bishops whether or not new peers would be created to pass the Reform Bill, Blomfield worked vigorously behind the scenes to round up episcopal support.[3] The Whigs knew that he was the key, and that his support was critical. The influence of the more inflexible prelates like Van Mildert had been considerably diminished as a result of the explosion that followed the triumph of their policies. Now it was up to the leader of the more realistic, conciliatory bishops, Blomfield. Greville in his diary quoted Lord Holland as saying after one of the debates in February 1832, 'the Bishop's the man; and in the evening at Lord Grey's I found they were all full of the Bishop'.[4] By then Blomfield had already secured ten votes and was vainly working on that of the archbishop.[5] Among those whom he had won over was the frightened Bishop Law, who immediately after the vote in 1831 had taken a house in Torquay for six months to flee from the populace at Wells and wait out the expected insurrection.[6] In addition John Bird Sumner, who blamed 'the odious Bill' for everything, including his brother Charles's severe illness, was persuaded to reverse his position, and in so doing voted against his recovered, but unyielding brother.[7] Phillpotts condemned them all, and tenacious as ever joined

[1] *Hansard*, XII (1832), 268–71.

[2] 24 Nov. 1831, Blomfield, *Memoir*, I, 171.   [3] *Ibid.*, 171–2.

[4] Greville, *Memoirs*, II, 275.   [5] Blomfield, *Memoir*, I, 172.

[6] H. Beeke to Phillpotts, 20 Nov. 1831, *Phillpotts Ps.*, Ex. Cath., ED/11/7.

[7] Sumner to Mrs C. R. Sumner, 16 Nov. 1831, in G.H. Sumner, *Life of Charles Richard Sumner, Bishop of Winchester* (1876), 202.

C. R. Sumner (1790–1874), younger brother of J. B. Sumner, and like him, a moderate Evangelical. Owed his advancement to Lord Conyngham, whose son he tutored, and to George IV, whom he met through Conyngham's sister, one of the king's mistresses. Though Sumner was still only a curate, the king offered him a stall at Windsor. Liverpool refused. The king bestowed other cathedral preferment and royal sinecures on him, made him his chaplain, and in 1826 Liverpool consented to raise him to Llandaff and also

with seventy-two peers in signing Wellington's protest after the battle was lost. His effigy was burnt in Durham (where he still held a stall), his name was greeted with hearty groans, and in general he continued to suffer abuse longer than any of his fellow prelates.[1] Of course he also encouraged it more than they did, but it is difficult not to share Greville's grudging admiration of that stern Tory bishop tottering, as Phillpotts liked to believe, on the brink of martyrdom. 'It would be an injury to compare this man with Laud', Greville wrote, 'he more resembles Gardiner; had he lived in those days he would have been just such another, boiling with ambition, an ardent temperament, and great talents. He has a desperate and dreadful countenance, and looks like the man he is.'[2]

Unfortunately for Phillpotts and his followers, dreadful countenances and violent rages were less potent weapons in defense of the Church and society than were conciliation and compromise. The Tory hierarchy had been severely shaken during the previous three years. The implications of Catholic emancipation stood out more starkly than ever in the light of great political reforms instituted by men determined, so it seemed, to overhaul every institution in the country. That the Church would be next there was no doubt. Its finances were already under investigation, and Blomfield and others had started preparing for that inevitability before the Reform Bill was passed.[3] The sensible proposals of an Edward Burton or Peel's brother-in-law, Lord Henley, were being circulated along with the extravagant, comprehensive concept of the Church detailed by Thomas Arnold.[4] At Oxford a small group of men, distressed

[1] Davies, *Henry Phillpotts*, 138–9. Phillpotts signed more protests against Bills passed in the Lords than any bishop in the nineteenth century, and, with two exceptions, more than any temporal lord. He signed on sixteen occasions. See James E. Thorold Rogers, ed., *A Complete Collection of the Protests of the Lords*, 3 vols. (Oxford, 1875); also Lundeen, *The Bench*, 101.

[2] Greville, *Memoirs*, II, 287.

[3] An Ecclesiastical Revenues Commission was established in 1832. See Report of the Commissioners of Enquiry into the Ecclesiastical Revenues of England and Wales, *Parl. Ps.* (1835), XXII. Also Best, *Temporal Pillars*, Chaps. VI–VII.

[4] Burton, *Thoughts Upon the Demand for Church Reform* (Oxford, 1831); also *Sequel to Remarks Upon Church Reform . . .* (1832); Henley, *Plan of Church Reform* (1832); Arnold, *Principles of Church Reform* (1833). See Best, *Temporal Pillars,* Chap. VI, for an excellent discussion of these and other Church reform proposals.

gave him the deanery of St Paul's. Translated to Winchester in 1827, at age of thirty-seven. His support of Catholic emancipation in 1829 cost him the king's favor. Sumner, his early career notwithstanding, turned out to be a serious, conscientious prelate, one of the important diocesan reformers of the age. Suffered a stroke and resigned in 1869.

by the trend in reform and determined to resist further Erastian encroachments on the Church, were preparing to launch a series of 'Tracts for the Times' that would chart the course to institutional as well as spiritual revitalization and independence. These were ostensibly friends of the Church. Its enemies were even more vigorous, to the extent of convincing Dissenter leaders in 1834 that the time for disestablishment was ripe. Their petitions insisting that the Anglican Church no longer had the right to claim that it was a national church, favored by the majority of Englishmen, was a final blow to that harried institution convinced it was being assaulted by unstoppable forces of innovation.

But measures were already being discussed to force the Church to adjust to social and political realities it instinctively preferred to ignore. The great era of Church reform was about to begin with the establishment in 1835 of the Ecclesiastical Commissions.[1] The trauma of the Reform Bill had in a sense eased the way within the Church itself by shocking many of its leaders into an awareness of how much society had changed, and how little the Establishment had adjusted to new realities. Whether they approved of Church reform was, after 1832, less relevant than their recognition that it was expedient in an age of altering standards and values. To the surprise of some prelates, the Church was not disestablished, and in fact survived the most dire predictions of some of its gloomy spokesmen. Yet it ministered to a society that appeared no more cohesive than before. The extension of the franchise did not mean the end of aristocracy and the establishment of republican government as some hysterical opponents had predicted. If anything the industrial, urban middle classes seemed perfectly content to support the hierarchical structure of English society now that they had achieved their representational goals. Furthermore the newly enfranchised towns welcomed the efforts of the reforming Church to bring religious morality and social contentment to those troublesome multitudes who found little to admire in the great Reform Bill, and were more antagonistic than ever to their immediate social superiors. Much to their despair, the older Tory prelates on the bench who reluctantly endured the realities of reform, as well as the newer Whig appointments committed to that course, also had to acknowledge that social cohesion seemed further away than ever. The years surrounding and following the passage of the Reform Bill were filled with conflict and bitter divisions in the country. The angry resistance to the new Poor Law was one indication. The startling emergence of Chartism and Owenite socialism was another. Reform tensions within the Establishment itself threatened to plunge the Church into a debilitating factionalism not seen since the early years of the eighteenth century. Fears of chaos and social disintegration, that

[1] *Ibid.,* Chap. VII.

legacy of the French Revolution never very far beneath the surface of nineteenth-century clerical thought, quickly revived.

3. CLASS WARFARE: CHARTISTS AND SOCIALISTS

Charles Thomas Longley, who, through the efforts of his father-in-law, the Whig financier and pamphleteer, Sir Henry Parnell, was the first appointee to the new industrial See of Ripon in 1836, soon recognized that he governed a diocese in the midst of a hostile world of disinterested and antagonistic sinners. For the former Headmaster of Harrow (1829–36) the extent of lower-class alienation was a shock. Though dedicated and hard-working, Longley, by 1840, felt overwhelmed; like many of his associates he feared the dissolution of 'the fabric of civil society . . .' that threatened to 'carry us backwards in the course of civilization, to the confines of the savage life'. That fear was not prompted so much by the social and economic conditions endured by the working classes as it was by the failure of the Church to reach the lower orders and teach them the reasons for their state in life as well as the rewards that would ultimately follow their patience, prudence, and moderation. Longley knew that living and working conditions could not be divorced from clerical concerns, but the natural course of improvement would likely be too slow to prevent the disruption of society unless the Church was able to provide meaningful remedies. When he described 'that most appalling condition in which . . . such vast masses of our working population [are] . . . placed . . .', he did not mean slums, mines and factories; he meant their distance from an Anglican minister. It left them open to seditious ideas so long as there was a 'want of a sufficient antidote to the infection'.[1]

Four years more of Chartist disturbances, worker agitation and riots, all in an exaggerated atmosphere of atheistic socialism, convinced Longley and others that the disease continued unabated and the nation stumbled towards 'a great national calamity'. God's wrath was being invoked for permitting 'dense crowds of immortal beings' to grow up unaware that they even possessed a soul to be saved and a mind to be purged of anti-Christian and anti-social ideas. With Jeremiah-like solemnity, he described recent disturbances in 1844 in Ripon and elsewhere as a final divine warning that 'our social well-being' is indeed in danger. The 'din of civil commotion has been heard among us—the tide of distant insurrection, gradually rolling onwards, soon crossed our own borders, penetrated into the heart of our diocese, and threatened for a while to involve everything in the vortex of a popular despotism'. Still, Longley preferred to believe that worker disturbances were not prompted by 'the urgency of temporal want', a conclusion concurred in by many

[1] Longley, *Sermon* (1840), 17–19.

harried manufacturers and colliery-owners. He was a bishop after their own hearts when he explained that it was far more serious, because 'the principles of discontent and insubordination' were deeply rooted in 'hearts undisciplined by religious restraints', and this situation was likely to become a permanent rather than a periodic condition in the body politic.[1]

Cataclysmic signs and ominous prophecy had largely receded from episcopal thought in the decades after Waterloo. The shock, pessimism, and periodic hysteria that contributed to the portentous interpretations of the revolutionary era gave way to a general confidence and optimism by the 1820's. Buoyed up by the economic expansion and the general prosperity of that period, English society appeared to be entering an era of indefinite material progress. The Establishment, strengthened by parliamentary and voluntary grants for church extension, welcomed the opportunity to bless the great material advancements of the new century with divine approval. Though worried and divided over Catholic emancipation in 1829, few prelates saw in it the hand of the divine. If the disturbances abroad and at home in 1830–2, accompanied by cholera, were briefly interpreted by some as a clear manifestation of God's displeasure, that disquieting conclusion tended to moderate with the epidemic.[2] Facing unparalleled pressures to reform in the 1830's, the bishops readily attributed the Church's difficulties to everything from the Reformation to the Reform Bill and on everyone from Wesley to Newman. Few, however, thought to attribute them too directly to God. Unquestionably it was a time of testing, but it lacked the atmosphere of imminent confrontation endured by the previous generation of Church leaders.

The seemingly sudden explosion of radical lower-class organization and agitation that accompanied the depression of the late 1830's and the following decade changed this as it made even the most complacent prelates aware of how little impact the revived Church had actually made on the laboring multitude. English society seemed more fragmented than ever; the cement of clerical guidance had been spread too thin and not far enough down the social pyramid. The broad foundation was crumbling, and the entire structure appeared to slip towards the

---

[1] C. T. Longley, *A Charge Addressed to the Clergy of the Diocese of Ripon . . . in September, 1844* (1844), 7–9.

[2] Howley prodded Earl Grey for over a year to urge the king to sanction 'some public expression of religious humiliation and penitence, and of trust in the mercies of God for deliverance . . .' from the cholera. Grey was less confident of divine support and frankly thought people would scoff. Nevertheless, he finally agreed. Howley to Grey, 21 Dec. 1830, 19 Nov. 1831; Grey to Howley, 21 Nov. 1831, *Grey MS*. Also Howley to Bishop Burgess, 4 Nov. 1831, *MS. Eng. Letters*. C. 136, f. 56, Bodleian Library.

edge of disintegration. This feeling punctuated old Archbishop Howley's vague, apocalyptical warning to Bishop Kaye in 1840 of an approaching conflict 'between the principles of evil and good. . . . The prevalence of the former would convulse the civilized world.' Howley, though constitutionally hostile to change, had been pressurized and persuaded to support Church reform, but his second thoughts haunted him. Without much conviction he professed to feel that 'moral and physical power' still lay with 'the better side', but predicted that a grave struggle would ensue before the issue was resolved.[1]

The frightened archbishop's clergy were treated to the same gloomy prognosis when, in his visitation *Charge*, he dredged up once more the memory of the French Revolution, 'which, like a dormant volcano, bursting forth on a sudden, spread terror and desolation over Europe'. Since that time 'the antagonist powers of good and of evil have been in constant activity, and the period seems to be approaching which will decide the issue of the conflict.' Howley had been a young clergyman of twenty-five when he first 'beheld with dismay and astonishment, infidelity avowing its principles and mustering its hosts for the battle against all that was reverenced as sacred by the Christian World, in the hope of subverting the throne and the altars by force of arms. At that moment when opposition seemed to be hopeless, the powers which it brought into the field were dispersed and confounded by the hand of an overruling Providence.' God, he believed, had found His people wanting and had visited them with revolution and war, finally rescuing them from tyranny and anarchy. Now, seventy-six years old, Howley saw the great conspiracies of the previous century revived once more. The forces of evil, long preparing 'in darkness and secrecy', were again coming into the open with their 'hostile designs against our Established Church'. Above all, he was alarmed at their influence over the vast working populace who still lay beyond the reach of the ministry. Chartists and socialists, the new agents of evil, were leading them into a coalition with the traditional enemies: unbelievers, Dissenters, schismatics, and lately, 'professors of liberal sentiments'.[2]

Longley, who was not even born when the French Revolution broke out, and not yet ordained when the long wars finally ended, nevertheless recalled how a great nation could be destroyed by turning from God. The seeds of infidelity and atheism, planted in earlier generations, are still capable of blossoming, he warned, and though we may indeed be favored by Providence, there were grave signs reminding us that such preference must be deserved. The condition of the great mass of the

[1] 27 July 1840, *Kaye Deposit*, B/5, 10, f. 18, Lincolnshire Archives Office.

[2] W. Howley, *A Charge Delivered At His Ordinary Visitation in September 1840* (1840), 14–17.

lower classes in this 'present complicated state of society' was a clear warning that until they are in the Church the foundations of society will be insecure.[1] But Longley, unlike Howley, was a believer in the laws of political economy, as interpreted by Sumner, a comfort denied to the unhappy archbishop. Frightened though he was by the overwhelming population in his industrial diocese, Longley at least understood the social and economic reasons for it, and never faulted what was unquestionably part of a larger divine plan of natural law. The poverty, the misery, the loathsome working and living conditions in the manufacturing towns of his diocese were less relevant to worker discontent, than was the workers' ignorance of the natural laws that governed all classes of society. Until the clergy could successfully impart those laws, the lower orders would not be responsive to the soothing balms of the Church. This was the task he repeatedly set for his ministers in the 1840's, hopeful that they could accomplish it in time.

The alternative to this, or some less modern solution, was as one prelate after the other posited, social chaos. They felt that they were in a desperate race against the forces of anti-civilization and class warfare. They evoked the imagery of a savage, unrestrained sea of humanity boiling up and finally spilling over the weakened breakers of social order. As in all things, Bishop Phillpotts was more extreme and more dramatic than his colleagues. The lessons of political economy seemed beside the point when he graphically described a nation of 'irreligious savages' grown up all around them; 'men without hope and without God in the world'. The future looked grim:

> there is laid up a store of woes for England, the elements of a wider and more irreparable devastation, than any which the history of man has ever yet recorded. Every year aggravates the danger. Every alternation of commercial prosperity and depression brings to the reflecting mind fresh assurances of the approaching convulsion.

The unreconstructed Tory bishop had never been reconciled to a commercial and industrial England, and he probably felt a perverse satisfaction in seeing his repeated warnings about the disintegrating and alienating effects of political economy apparently coming true. To those who had long delighted in the material prosperity of the realm, and confidently predicted that the natural laws of economy would eventually assure the greatest happiness for the greatest number, he contemptuously added:

> the very glut and surfeit of national wealth in which we are now revelling —the unparalleled activity of our manufacturers—the growing demand for labor in all the branches of industry and every field of speculation—

[1] C. T. Longley, *A Sermon Preached . . . June II, MDCCCXLII, At the Yearly Meeting of the Children of the Charity Schools . . .* (1842), 6–7, 10.

while they do indeed, protract the day, are only accumulating materials for a more deadly explosion.

The belief that the volatile charge could be diffused by education, or by still greater prosperity, Phillpotts thought illusory; only religion could prevent a revolutionary conflagration. 'If it be not supplied—if the purifying spirit of the Gospel be not breathed upon the corrupt and fermenting mass—a contest will and must come—God only knows how soon—a contest of classes.'[1]

Phillpotts, like Howley and many other members of the bench, had grown from young manhood to nearly middle age during the revolutionary and Napoleonic years. Few were able to suppress a shudder at the prospect of reliving those years again under even more terrifying circumstances. Yet it seemed to many of them that similar dangers to religion and to society were again present, and the possibility of internal collapse greater than ever. The propertied classes may now as then win many a bloody victory, Phillpotts warned, but until the vast population of the country is spiritually cared for, the source of evil remains. So long as it does, the war will be renewed again and again, and 'the ultimate issue cannot be doubtful—the overthrow of this empire of Mammon by its own serfs'.[2] Phillpotts was the spokesman for a past suffused in the stabilizing qualities of a rural paternalism overseen by the comforting interest of squire and parson. Powerfully, emotionally, but nevertheless irrelevantly, for a half-century he decried the economic and social changes that destroyed his ideal and created an urban working class seemingly on the verge of plunging the country into brutal class warfare. Whether or not prelates shared Phillpotts's unfaltering attachment to a rustic, uncomplicated, preindustrial England, they certainly felt, as Blomfield warned Peel, in 1843, that the workers were dangerously alienated from their superiors. 'Two things', he concluded, 'are necessary, in order to replace the social system in a healthy state: a more direct and friendly intercourse between the different classes of society, and the general inculcation of Christian principles.'[3]

Chartism and socialism, Blomfield claimed, were logical, if deluded, attempts by those persons 'kept so far asunder by the difference of their worldly conditions' to find satisfactory alternatives.[4] Wilberforce and Connop Thirlwall perhaps understood this better than any of their episcopal contemporaries. Thirlwall, unlike Wilberforce, welcomed the

[1] H. Phillpotts, *A Charge Delivered to the Clergy of the Diocese of Exeter . . . in 1845* (1845), 50–51.

[2] *Ibid.*, 51.

[3] *Peel Ps.*, British Museum, Add. MS. 40537, ff. 178–9. Blomfield was soliciting Peel's endorsement of a new Association for Promoting the Relief of Destitution in the Metropolis.

[4] *Ibid.*

technological and industrial advancements of the age while recognizing the grievous social disruption they caused.[1] He believed, however, that the Church and the legislature understood that it was no longer possible to remain indifferent to the condition of the working classes, or merely offer good wishes for individual improvements. Together, he predicted in 1849, it was possible for the secular and spiritual forces of the country to solve 'the great problem of our day: to unite liberty with order, stability with progress: that stability without which there can be no happiness, with that progress without which there can be no peace'.[2]

Wilberforce was less optimistic than Thirlwall, and far more critical of an industrial society that 'tends to make us a luxurious, a selfish, and so a low-minded people', and created such bitter class divisions. He was appalled at the sacrifice of 'those bands of children . . . in the vast idol temples of our manufacturing greatness . . .',[3] and by the rich man treating his workers as 'occasional instruments for getting certain necessary operations done, or [as] troublesome competitors for charity, disturbing his cherished ease'.[4] Though describing himself as a 'liberal Tory', Wilberforce dissociated himself from 'modern liberalism . . . the Devil's creed: a heartless steam-engine, un-Christian, low . . . utilitarian creed which would put down all that is really great and high and noble: all old remembrances and customs: merely to let up what is low and multiply such miserable comforts as going very fast through the air on a railroad—and for this purpose it would overturn the Church; that is Christianity; and worship the very devil if his horns were gold and his tail was a steam-engine'. His was an age that saw the 'breaking down the character of the old English country gentleman . . . one of the finest characters in the world'. As a local, religious, kindly man, the squire kept society together, and did 'more good than all the vile bushels of *useful knowledge* which have turned the heads of all the half-learned

[1] C. Thirlwall (1797–1875), son of a London clergyman, brilliant student at Cambridge, studied law at Lincoln's Inn, called to the Bar in 1825. Abandoned law and entered the clergy in 1828 as more convenient to his literary ambitions. Lost his tutorship at Cambridge in 1834 for supporting degrees for Dissenters. Already known in liberal circles, he was given a living by Brougham in 1834 and elevated to the See of St David's in 1840 after Melbourne carefully read his translation of Schleiermacher's *Essay On St Luke*, and was satisfied by his moderate Broad Church views. Thirlwall also translated *Niebuhr's History of Rome*, and wrote an eight-volume *History of Greece* (1835–47). Quickly learned Welsh and devoted himself to the revival of the Church in his diocese. Resigned in 1874. See C. Thirlwall, Jr., *Connop Thirlwall, Historian and Theologian* (1936).

[2] C. Thirlwall, *The Advantages of Literary and Scientific Institutions for All Classes. A Lecture Delivered . . . December 11th, 1849* (1850), 36–37.

[3] S. Wilberforce, *A Charge Delivered . . . In June, 1841* (1841), 30–31.

[4] *Ibid.*, 15. Also *A Charge Delivered . . . November, 1844* (1844), 11–12.

traders in the universe'.[1] Rural poverty and the cruel exploitation of marginal agricultural laborers had little place in the 'Young England' Wilberforce hated to lose, though even a casual reading of the Poor Law Commissioners *Reports* would have revealed that 'Christian steward-ship' was perhaps less fashionable in agricultural areas than Wilberforce imagined. 'Benumbing selfishness' was not an urban monopoly.

Wilberforce's attention, however, was drawn to the manufacturing towns where the fierce heat from the flame of material acquisitiveness was 'melting away' class bonds. There the rich worshipped property and neglected responsibility; consequently, like all mighty nations before, England had become 'the prey of the untrained, violent needy'. The unequal distribution of property is nowhere tempered by 'a common bond of unity'. These were symptoms of 'a highly unnatural, and in many respects, diseased state of society; and the craving for their redress is not in itself evil. It becomes evil only when it seeks the mock-ing, selfish world as its redressor; instead of seeking, as it ought to, the power of Christ's Church.'[2] This, Wilberforce explained, is what Chartism and socialism were all about. What was to be expected, he asked, when to the worker's pleas we respond with the 'somewhat unpalatable truths of political economy . . . the iron sinews of a pro-claimed necessity, which must always sound as a taunt in the sufferer's ear'. Was this the way to restore 'the old bonds of mutual affection and respect—of natural care on the one side, and generous trust upon the other . . .'? Clearly it was not, and frustrated, angry workers sought new bonds. The disintegration of a society comprehensible to the poor carried over to religion as well. The workers find still more sects and divisions; consequently they seek in their common interests, 'and the jugglery of sensual promises, a cement strong enough to hold together their pretended social system'.[3]

With considerable perception Wilberforce defended the logic of the working classes' desire to combine in movements that appeared relevant to their needs. In Chartism, and even in socialism, they mistakenly sought a security, once present in the family and the Church, in a society of mutually interdependent relationships. Their quest should be en-couraged, but diverted towards the Church once more where social integration and security could be provided by the revived clergy. By what other means, he asked, was it possible to show the rich 'the fearful danger of wealth, and [the poor] . . . the dignity and blessedness of Christian poverty'.[4] Certainly not by Whigs—those 'shabby, word-

---

[1] Wilberforce to C. Anderson, 21 Aug. 1837, *Wilberforce Ps.*, Dep. C. 191, I.

[2] S. Wilberforce, *A Charge Delivered . . . In September and October 1840*, 2nd ed. (1840), 33–35.

[3] *Ibid.*   [4] *Ibid.*, 36.

eating, pocket-picking . . . sacreligious villains as ever poisoned fresh air"[1]—presenting 'our virgin Queen' to Robert Owen 'in his character of great natural philanthropist'. By so dignifying that 'chief apostle [of] . . . a debasing sensual atheism', the government only encouraged the propagation of socialist doctrines at a time when large segments of society were particularly vulnerable. The Chartists were certainly 'unhappy men', Wilberforce sympathized, but the socialists were 'the outward exhibition of the deep moral disease . . . the infidelity of the age'.[2]

His antipathy for liberalism notwithstanding, Wilberforce, in his less vituperative moments, suggested that Chartism and socialism were not only manifestations of economic change and a misguided policy of political economy, they could also be traced to the failure of preceding generations of churchmen to come to grips with reality. As a result, many of the problems of his day were the 'outgrown sins of the coldness of heart of the preceding century'. Chartism and socialism were two of those sins—'the headstrong violence of men entrusted for the first time with some measure of political power, and who whilst groaning under the sufferings which are more or less necessarily connected with the unequal distribution of wealth, have been taught to believe it possible by merely earthly machinery to redress this manifold evil'. What were these working-class eruptions but 'the outgrown religious dissent of the preceding generation? What are they, but the moral history of those who have run through all sects, until, in the vexation of their weary spirits, they believe that all religion is sectarian; and who, therefore, having given up with Christianity the first principles which hold together family and social life, are now groping blindly after an impossible unity amidst the pollutions of a low and selfish sensuality?' Comparing the social unrest of his age with the spiritual unrest of the preceding age, Wilberforce continued, 'what then, again, is this, but the fruit of that practical unbelief, which did, in the last generation, drive whole masses of our countrymen to seek amongst dissenters from our national communion, that reality and earnestness of personal piety, of which, alas, so little trace was visible in the Church? . . . How again the sins of that age are become the scourges of this.'[3]

Wilberforce was in effect arguing that Chartism and socialism were essentially secularized forms of Methodist dissent. The modern laboring poor, like their eighteenth-century predecessors, found little comfort in the national Church, and had broken away. Their defection was much more serious, however, for it not only threatened the unity of the faith, but the very survival of the Church and all other social institutions. It

[1] Wilberforce to Anderson, 13 April 1837, *Wilberforce Ps.*, Dep. C. 191, I.

[2] S. Wilberforce, *A Letter to the Right Hon. Henry, Lord Brougham, On the Government Plan of Education*, 3rd ed. (1840), 37–39.

[3] Wilberforce, *Charge* (1842), 29–31.

was a mistake to vent fury upon the unfortunate, deluded poor who flocked to the banners of the new secular forms of dissent. Like the Methodists of an earlier age, they were, in the final analysis, the fault of the Church, and its failure to provide for their spiritual security irrespective of the economic and political policies that complicated its sacred task. Wilberforce was certainly more insightful than most mid-Victorian prelates, even if his solutions were rarely more inventive than those of his contemporaries. By the 1840's, however, Church leadership in general realized how poorly adapted the Establishment was to the social and spiritual needs of a severely class-ridden society. The political leveling of Chartism, and the social and economic leveling of socialism, only underlined the inadequacies of clerical attempts at social reconciliation. This realization not only permitted greater flexibility in diocesan policies, but to a considerable extent explains why the emergence of Christian socialism, after the collapse of Chartism in 1848, met with so little opposition from the bench.

If bishops raised little opposition to Christian socialism they also showed little interest in the movement. The participation of Frederick Dension Maurice, a moderate High Churchman, and Professor of History and Theology at King's College, London, at first probably went a long way towards calming episcopal fears. Obscure, often mystical, Maurice nevertheless was concerned with a problem troubling the most influential churchmen in the country—effectively communicating with the alienated working poor. Few bishops by mid-century were prepared to reject openly any scheme that might entice the lower classes to listen to the preachments of an Anglican minister—even if that minister was the Hampshire vicar and novelist, Charles Kingsley. In spite of occasional exaggeration, Kingsley's reassertion of the early Christian principles of communal brotherhood did not directly question the even more sacred right to private property.[1] Though perhaps too sympathetic to the aspirations of the Chartists for most prelatical sensibilities, Kingsley's sermons emphasizing Scriptural responsibilities and restraints on the rich were not usually provocative enough to encourage a bishop to take a position that seemed contrary to the interests of the poor. Whether or not Church leaders read the more extreme articles of the former Owenite socialist, John Malcom Ludlow, in the *Christian Socialist* (and there is little evidence they did), it was difficult to disclaim the general Christian socialist plea for the Church to leave its sanctuary and go into the world. Bishops of all persuasions were now urging their clergy to involve themselves in every act of common life, though they rarely encouraged, as Ludlow and Maurice did, the reorganization of society.

[1] Torben Christensen, *Origin and History of Christian Socialism 1848–54* (Copenhagen, 1962), 24.

When reorganization took the form of associations or co-operative societies, some prelates like J. B. Sumner or his successor at Chester, John Graham, might worry about their impact on an individualistic, *laissez-faire* economy. But they were conflicted when confronted with the ideal of trying to end the antagonism between capitalist and worker by showing the worker the direct benefits of capital when responsibly employed. Prelates had toyed with co-operative ideas since the early years of the century, and as recently as 1844 had shown no opposition to the successful Rochdale Co-operative and the movement that followed its establishment. Bishop Stanley openly supported it in 1846 and welcomed the Owenite inspiration behind co-operative ventures. Wilberforce and the Catholic Dr Wiseman both purchased suits from the tailor's co-operative established by Christian socialists in London in 1850, though it has been suggested that they were for their footmen rather than for themselves.[1]

The only prelate to question openly the growth of Christian socialism was John Kaye. During twenty years on the bench he had seen a new world born and wondered in 1849 where it would all end. Chartism and socialism were manifestations of that new world, and had little to do with the Christian society he knew. Yet their followers were now seeking to associate Christ with 'schemes for the reconstruction of the fabric of society to the community of goods which subsisted for a short time among the first converts at Jerusalem'. To such people rank and property aroused feelings of envy and cupidity which they falsely believed would be eliminated by communism. Kaye argued that such a concept inverted the order of things; the community of goods in Jerusalem was not the cause, but the result of the extinction of these evil feelings within the converts. The community of goods in Jerusalem was voluntary and its continuance implied a total change in human nature. Obviously no such overwhelming change occurred, for the community did not long continue, nor was it ever to succeed in other churches where it was tried. Invariably voluntary communism degenerated into a compulsory, tyrannical system. It was inevitable, for all such schemes which assume the perfectibility of man and accordingly seek the reconstruction of society are in conflict with all we have learned from Scripture and experience.[2]

If men were to derive all sorts of chimerical concoctions for social improvement from Scripture it would be at the expense of a sound reading of the Gospels. After all, Kaye recalled, the Apostles did not seek to alter social structure or meddle with social distinctions. On the contrary,

[1] Chadwick, *Victorian Church*, 355.

[2] J. Kaye, *A Charge Delivered . . . in 1849*, in *Nine Charges Delivered to the Clergy of the Diocese of Lincoln, With Some Other Works* (1854), 354–6.

they spread the word among all classes so that necessary reforms would come naturally and voluntarily so as to benefit all men. In more recent times the triumph of such an approach could be seen in the successful abolition of slavery without violent social disruption.

> Without interfering with the relation between the master and slave, it gave to both correct views of that relation; of the spirit in which the one ought to require, the other to render, obedience: it taught the master to aim at winning the affections instead of working upon the fears of the slave; and thus, having first corrected the abuses of the system, it succeeded at last in abolishing the system itself.[1]

Unconsciously perhaps, Bishop Kaye cited an example often used by the enemies of the factory system in equating the misery of the workers with that of the Negro slaves. The lesson to be learned nevertheless remained the same.

While other prelates undoubtedly shared Kaye's reservations about Christian socialism they kept quiet about them. Ten years earlier there would have been an episcopal chorus of agreement, but by mid-century the leaders of the Church were so conscious of the hostility of the working classes and their very real difficulties in reaching them, they were reluctant to repudiate too quickly an opportunity to show the workers that there were paths of Christian improvement and co-operation open to them. Blomfield, for example, was well aware of 'agents of socialism and infidelity' constantly spewing their poison in the poorer parts of his diocese. Clergymen were alarmed by the size of socialist crowds, especially on Sunday mornings; Blomfield repeatedly urged the establishment of evening institutes as educational counter-measures.[2] He was, however, more cautious about Christian socialism, and would neither support nor condemn the movement. If workers were going to listen to socialist proponents it was better that the lessons came from Scripture than from Owen. When in 1851 Kingsley suggested in a sermon that the Gospel preached liberty, equality and fraternity, episcopal toleration was severely tested. Caught up in his own enthusiasm of the moment, the preacher condemned all systems of society favoring the accumulation of capital in a few hands, and urged the disenfranchized poor not to judge the Church by its clergy. He implied that the clergy supported a system in conflict with the biblical promise that the poor are free, made equal by baptism, and guaranteed by a communion proclaiming their brotherhood as an absolute and eternal right.[3]

In the uproar that followed, Blomfield inhibited Kingsley from further preaching in the diocese, but quickly withdrew the inhibition when the minister was able to show the old bishop from the text of the sermon that

[1] *Ibid.*, 356–8.
[2] 9 Sept. 1851, Letter Copy Book 385, ff. 373–5., *Fulham Ps.*
[3] Chadwick, *Victorian Church*, 358–9.

when he spoke of freedom, he meant the freedom to do right, not to act as one liked. The equality of which he spoke was not an encouragement to license, but to develop as far as possible unequal talents.[1] Although he remained suspicious, Blomfield recognized that in many ways the Christian socialists were able to generate a religious enthusiasm among the working classes and open a spiritual dialogue that would perhaps otherwise never take place. Consequently he refused to condemn the movement even after most of the respectable Tory journals like the *Quarterly Review* had accused the Christian socialists of teaching everything from the destruction of capital to the communal sharing of wives.[2] Blomfield insisted that more time was needed before a final judgment could be made.[3] He never made one. When in 1853 he presented the successful motion that cost Maurice his theology professorship, it was based upon Maurice's rejection of hell and the doctrine of eternal punishment. It is difficult to determine how much of a role his involvement in Christian socialism entered into the decision.

The days of Christian socialism as an organized movement were in fact already numbered. Ludlow had resigned in 1851, opposed to the rapid expansion of co-operatives, and aware that many churchmen, including Maurice, were not really interested in the establishment of a socialist society. Thomas Hughes, for example, never felt comfortable about the associations, and believed that Christian socialists could be more effective as individuals. The economic collapse of several co-operatives and the gradual return of prosperity only exacerbated the internal differences. The future lay in education, not co-operatives; it was to the Working Men's College that Maurice turned after his dismissal from King's College. In 1855 he formally acknowledged that Christian socialism, as an organized movement, was finished.[4] Its socialist origins were romantic and utopian from the start, steeped in nostalgic notions of a simpler, more primitive pre-industrial Christian society. Its relationship to the more dynamic concepts of socialist change emerging in the 1840's was at best superficial. Christian socialists did not really want to upset the social and economic structure of their country; they wanted to make it conform more closely to their romanticized notions of Christian community. That Establishment bishops were willing to tolerate Christian socialism perhaps indicates, as clearly as anything could, how harmless the movement really was.

[1] Blomfield to Kingsley, 27 June 1851, Letter Copy Book 385, f. 242, and 3 July, f. 249., *Fulham ps.* Chadwick *Victorian Church*, 359, 362.

[2] *Quarterly Review*, LXXXIX (1851), 491, 522–4. Also Chadwick, *Victorian Church*, 362.

[3] Blomfield to Rev. W. Blunt, 30 Jan. 1852, Letter Copy Book 398, f. 160, *Fulham Ps.*

[4] Christensen, *Christian Socialism*, 351–66.

Christian socialism had emerged from the general realization within the revived Church that it was unable to ameliorate class conflicts in an industrial age so long as it was associated with and only able to preach to one part of the nation and not the other. The situation for many churchmen was not only politically and socially dangerous, but spiritually intolerable. The Church was separated from its sacred purpose of ministering to the needs of all people, but especially to those whom the Gospel singled out as most in need—the suffering poor. Their redemption then was not only a question of practical necessity, as had been emphasized since the French Revolution, but an act of deep religious conviction as well. Whether it added up to anything more meaningful for the laboring populace is questionable when one of the most perceptive, innovative churchmen of the age could envision nothing more rewarding than the restoration of feelings of 'mercy and charity' among the rich, and 'patience and cheerful industry amongst the poor . . .'.[1]

4. RICH AND POOR IN CHURCH

As the Church became more conscious of its inability to communicate its social and religious message to the huge laboring multitudes, some of its leaders began to understand that all the efforts made to reach the lower orders were being compromised by the reality that the Establishment was still socially too exclusive. In spite of its claim to be a national institution charged with a legal and divine responsibility to preach the truth to all men irrespective of their station in life, the Church was captured by deeply ingrained upper-class propensities that seriously interfered with its credibility among the poor. They also interfered with the Establishment's vital utilitarian role as the moderator of social antagonisms. If, however, churchmen were unable even to integrate the laboring poor into the class-ridden, proprietary churches of their parishes, their prospects for integrating them into society as a whole were not very bright. Increasingly, troubled clergy worried about the absence of the lower classes from church, were becoming sensitive to the contradictions of preaching the equality of all men before the Lord to congregations which were manifestly unequal in the House of God. No sane parson would deny the necessity and natural inevitability of economic, political and social inequality. But many of them, inspired by Evangelical revivalism or a deep sense of the renewed purpose of a truly catholic national Church, wondered if the inequities of the temporal world were congenial or even relevant to the spiritual world.

In practice the question was closely related to the vexatious problem of appropriated sittings. The rental of pews was not only a necessary

[1] Wilberforce, *Charge* (1844), 20.

source of clerical revenue, but it had become intricately enmeshed in questions of proprietary right and social status so that by the nineteenth century appropriated sittings far outnumbered available free spaces, and in a great many churches completely eliminated them. Free sittings, where available, were usually far in the back, in galleries, or along the sides of the nave where all too often the poor were effectively cut off from the sight and much of the sound of the service. The churches in effect merely extended the proprietary and social hierarchical realities of life. The congregations might well have comprised all God's children, but in the Anglican churches, as well as in many Dissenting chapels, it was clear that the deity had His favorites.

When in the early nineteenth century the realities of population growth and mobility began to dawn upon concerned churchmen they understood that the impact upon the Church was in that area where it was least competent to cope—the providing of facilities for the laboring poor. Proprietary chapels and endowed churches benefited those who could afford to rent seats in them. This effectively excluded the poor, a result which caused few pew-holders much anguish. But by then large numbers of workers could not have cared less. They had found refuge in a Methodism not yet respectable and thus exclusive, or, as was more probable, simply drifted away from any form of religious worship.

After the war, when Church leaders set about trying to bring them back, they interpreted the problem largely in terms of providing physical rather than spiritual space. The Church Building Act of 1818 and the voluntary Church Building Society both emphasized the construction of churches in which the seats would at least be half free. In addition the bishops, with some hesitation, began to encourage pew-holders to leave their seats open, and urged the clergy to keep proprietary restrictions to a minimum. Evangelicals had already raised the question in the later years of the preceding century. Charles Simeon was but one of many clergymen of that persuasion to decry pews locked by people who 'would neither come to church themselves, nor suffer others; and multitudes from time to time were forced to go out of church for want of necessary accommodation'.[1] They were increasingly joined by active High Churchmen who retaliated by denouncing Evangelical proprietary chapels, but who also understood the extent of exclusionary practices throughout the Establishment as a whole. It was, after all, the very High Churchman Charles Daubeny who had established the first free chapel in Bath in 1798 to combat Methodist defections, and his example was certainly in evidence over the next two decades. If it was rarely feasible to duplicate Daubeny's generous efforts, it was

[1] W. Carus, ed., *Memoirs of the Life of the Reverend Charles Simeon* (1847), 39, 54.

possible to gather support for the construction of new galleries, and the rearrangement of benches in old churches, as well as provide free sittings in the new edifices constructed.

Caution, however, was drilled into the mind of every parson fearful of angering the wealthier members of his congregation. Bishop Howley set the tone in 1818 when, after complaining about the restrictive evils of proprietary pews, he warned the more enthusiastic of his clergy:

> yet ought we to labour with all Christian meekness, and toleration of human infirmity, to ameliorate feelings, and eradicate notions, which operate in direct opposition to the dictates of Christian charity: and if at first our exhortations are fruitless, to wait for more favourable opportunities of renewing our suit.[1]

Many Anglican parsons from conviction or financial necessity were willing to wait a long time for their chance, as evidenced by the complaints against proprietary sittings throughout the next three decades. More serious clergymen and more vocal critics found closed pews in conflict with their improved concepts of Christian community.

The extra cautious Church Building Commissioners were not very likely to lead an aggressive assault upon such traditional practices in spite of their recognition of the need for more open sittings. Bishop Ryder in 1821 had to resist firmly an attempt by the Commissioners to levy a small charge on the sittings designated for the poor in a new church in his diocese. The prelate explained that the 'great poverty of the Inhabitants and the extreme and long continued prevalence of Dissent . . .' made such a proposal inexpedient.[2] Ryder clearly recognized that the poor were not attending the church, and that it was highly unlikely that they would pay for the privilege of doing something they preferred not to do when it cost them nothing.

Yet wealthy Anglicans seeking the moral rejuvenation of a lower class denuded of feelings of independence and 'manly responsibility' believed that a minimal pew rental would help in the re-establishment of such basic virtues. The inculcation of the proprietary instinct was a favorite objective of nineteenth-century Englishmen who could find little reason why all people should not be modelled after them. Samuel Butler, who had become thoroughly fed up with the refusal of the poor to learn what was in their own best interests, by 1838 doubted the value of free seats. Discussing the enlargement of a church in his diocese which contained only a dozen free sittings out of a total of four hundred, Bishop Butler agreed that perhaps a few more places for the poor might be added, but he preferred that most of the new arrangements be rented out at a low

---

[1] W. Howley, *A Charge Delivered to the Clergy of the Diocese of London . . . in July and August, 1818*, 2nd ed. (1818), 20–21.

[2] Ryder to Ch. Blg. Comm., 15 Sept. 1821, *Minute Book*, V, H.M.C.B.N.C.

rate. 'Experience has taught me', he confided, 'that the poor will come much more thankfully to church when they have a seat which they can *bona fide* call their own, than when they are accommodated with entirely free ones.'[1]

Butler had not believed this to be the case before he was elevated to the bench. On several occasions in previous years he complained of the lack of free sittings for the poor, and did not blame them for staying away or turning to Dissent when the national Church failed to provide for their needs.[2] Always suspicious of the excessive faith placed in the construction of new churches, Butler in 1835 pointed out that there were countless old churches lacking free facilities for the poor which were completely ignored. For far less money than it cost to build new edifices, many of the older churches could construct free galleries and seats to care for the lower classes. Still smarting over the attacks by Dissenters and Radicals on the Establishment during the preceding year, Butler conceded that the poor had indeed been excluded from the Church as a result of proprietary pews and excessive population growth. It was not surprising that they were turning to Dissent.[3]

Among the prelates who were willing to attack the sensitive problem openly, Butler's earlier views were certainly more typical than his later arguments. Ill and dying in 1838, he had abandoned any real hope of winning the lower orders over to the Church. He had never really cared for the idea very much in the first place, and as he diligently excluded as many children of the poor as possible from Shrewsbury School when Headmaster, he was not much disturbed if the Establishment remained primarily the Church of the propertied classes. During his short three-year tenure on the bench he consistently resisted innovative attempts by his clergy to attract the lower orders, arguing that if the laboring classes wanted to come to church they would be welcomed. If not, it merely showed how tenuous their concern was for their own and their children's welfare. The Church could get along perfectly well without such people. To an Establishment seeking to re-establish its national credentials, and defending its privileged endowments, Butler's indifference was no longer acceptable. As an Established Church, its clergy were responsible, as Bishop Kaye said, for bringing the Gospel to 'the very door of the humblest cottager'. The great advantage of a State Church was its guarantee of regular parochial ministers rather than periodic itinerant preachers, and the assurance that even poor congregations, unable to

---

[1] 12 Nov. 1838, *Butler Ps., Add. MS. 34592, f. 153.

[2] S. Butler, *A Charge Delivered to the Clergy of the Archdeaconry of Derby . . . June 22 and 23, 1825* (1826), 12. Also *A Sermon Preached . . . August 24, 1830* (1830), 10.

[3] S. Butler, *A Charge Delivered to the Clergy of the Archdeaconry of Derby . . . June 25 and 26, 1835* (1835), 10–15.

endow a parson voluntarily would be provided with spiritual guidance.[1] Even Kaye knew that in practice the fulfilment of the ideal was less than perfect, but the principle was nevertheless valid. In time it would be justified once more.

By 1836, Parliamentary grants and voluntary contributions had provided for over 600,000 new sittings of which 400,000 were free and open.[2] Most of these were in newer populous areas and did not encroach upon the existing proprietary preserves of the better sort. Nevertheless it was discouraging to active proponents of extension to see so many of the open pews unoccupied week after week. Some of the more perceptive of them began to realize that the rebuilding of integrated congregations was not simply a problem of providing more seats and galleries for the laboring classes. The Bishop of Chester, J. B. Sumner, in 1838 noted the demoralizing effects of poverty on church attendance, and wondered if it was not unrealistic to expect the depressed poor to mingle readily with their betters even once a week.

> Those who are in this state are naturally reluctant to mingle themselves with the richer: they are unwilling to exhibit poverty and rags in contrast with wealth or splendour. The very act of attending the house of God requires in them something of an effort; and they are moreover continually and importunately tempted to withdraw themselves. . . .

Not only were the lower classes put off by the psychology of their poverty, but, Sabbatarian arguments notwithstanding, many of them were required to spend their Sundays 'in pursuit of gain'. As an alternative, Sumner suggested the use of school-rooms or lecture-halls as places of worship for the laboring people so they would not be ashamed to attend services. Expedient measures of that type had been employed earlier in the diocese and had led to the establishment of many workers' churches in Lancashire.[3] In effect, what the bishop was suggesting was the abandonment of social mixing in many of the churches. Economic and social realities were apparently too strong to permit even spiritual integration any longer.

From the standpoint of many members of the wealthier classes this was a perfectly sound compromise. Every prelate was bothered by the complaints of rich pew-holders protesting the construction of galleries and free sittings that encouraged the lower orders to come to services.

[1] J. Kaye, *A Sermon Preached . . . August 29th 1834* (1834), 16.

[2] *The First and Second Reports From His Majesty's Commissioners Appointed to Consider the State of the Established Church With Reference to Ecclesiastical Duties and Revenues* (1836), 62–63. Also in *Parl. Ps.* (1835), XXII, and (1836), XXXVI.

[3] J. B. Sumner, *A Charge Delivered to the Clergy of the Diocese of Chester . . . in 1838* (1838), 62–63. Sumner took several of his ideas from Henry Wilberforce's *The Parochial System. An Appeal to English Churchmen* (1838).

Blomfield in his testimony before the Committee on the Observance of the Sabbath in 1832 explained that it was the object of the Church Building Commissioners to intermingle as much as possible the seats of the rich and the poor so as to afford the latter nearly the same facilities for hearing which the former enjoyed. But he confessed that they had been repeatedly thwarted in their efforts, 'on account of the objections which were made by the richer classes to too great an intermixture of the poor among them, objections which it was absolutely necessary to attend to because the whole income of the Minister depends on the pew rents accruing exclusively from the richer classes'.[1]

For those Church leaders seriously committed to the fulfilment of national religious responsibilities, the close connection between property and endowment was a serious dilemma. Not only did it impede a rational reorganization of parochial administration, interfere with ecclesiastical discipline, and leave earnest clergymen confused by their knowledge of spiritual righteousness and the realities of expediency, but it increasingly exacerbated class tensions. Critics of the Establishment never tired of pointing to the exclusiveness of the Anglican communion, and they were increasingly joined by a worker press that often revealed the depths of contempt in which the laboring classes held the clergy of the national Church.

Blomfield was not alone in his efforts to minimize these antagonisms. Repeatedly he had to prevent wealthier members of congregations and their ministers from reducing the number of free sittings and relegating the poor to aisles and the back of galleries, if not driving them completely from the Church. To one of many clerical requests for permission to appropriate some free seats for wealthier parishioners, the bishop sharply replied that not only was it un-Christian to displace the poor from their accustomed place, but it was likely that they would quit the Church altogether.[2] With cries of disestablishment still ringing in his ears in 1835, Blomfield seriously doubted whether the Establishment could survive too many more defections from the populous and impressionable lower orders. Ten years later, and more conscious of class tensions than ever, the Bishop of London was still fighting the same battle. Much more aware now of the psychological implications of unequal services, and segregated and inferior sittings, Blomfield continually urged his clergy to minimize the differences of social and economic inequality at least in church. He personally scrutinized the plans of new and rebuilt churches to see that there was an adequate proportion of free seats conveniently located. In addition he did not hesitate to insist on the lowering of pew rents to bring seats into the

[1] Blomfield, *Memoir*, 325.

[2] Blomfield to Rev. J. Hutchinson, 7 and 12 Dec. 1835, Letter Copy Book 344, ff. 334, 354, *Fulham Ps.*

range of 'little tradesmen' and other people of lesser income.[1] When necessary he was perfectly prepared personally to endow free seats when he did not feel there were sufficient numbers of them, and the minister was reluctant to accept a lesser income.[2]

As the most powerful prelate on the bench, the Bishop of London saw his efforts as designed to ameliorate bitter class divisions and antagonisms within the Establishment, and restore to it its historic role as the harmonizer of all classes. It was to apply not only to the living, but to the dead as well. Blomfield insisted that his clergy make no distinction between rich and poor even during funeral services. All too often such services for wealthier members of the congregation were held in the church while the dead of the poor had to take their final leave from the churchyard. It was, as the bishop wrote, 'an invidious and improper distinction',[3] but one not untypical of the oppressive class mentality of the Anglican ministry.

What in the early years of Church reform had been an embarrassment was by the 1840's a compelling and critical issue. Older prelates such as Blomfield and Phillpotts, and the leaders of the new generation such as Samuel Wilberforce, were no longer content with the gentle prodding and patience advocated by the careful Howley years before, and long practised by their brethren. With the country tottering on the brink of imagined class warfare, conservative minds became radical. High Churchmen especially led the attack. Alarmed by the inability of the Establishment to cope with the multitudinous laboring masses, and frustrated by Erastian limitations upon its policies, they saw in the failures of the Church the failures of society to appreciate its integrating powers. If it was not manifested within the churches themselves, it was no wonder that society as a whole was riven by class hatred.

Phillpotts, long aroused by the evils of the Poor Law, and convinced that the Church had largely abandoned the lower orders to Whig hyenas and socialist revolutionaries, added his authoritarian voice to the discussion of Church responsibility. As an ultra-High Churchman and the principal episcopal defender of the Tractarians, the Bishop of Exeter was more explicit about the secular corruptions undermining the purity of the Church. Closed pews and the relegation of the laboring classes to undesirable parts of the Church were typical of the social and political disharmony that plagued his terrible age. It was incongruous to make 'the very worship of God an occasion of injustice to man—of usurpation of the rights of the poor'. By permitting wealth to determine the relative station of men worshipping God was an interference with a process of divine evaluation. Only in church did 'the rich and the poor

[1] Letter Copy Book 378, f. 7, *ibid.*
[2] Letter Copy Book 377, f. 63, *ibid.*
[3] 14 May 1845, Letter Copy Book 376, ff. 270–1, *ibid.*

meet together; not equal, indeed, in God's sight, but distinguished by qualities, which will make many who think themselves to be the first to be the last, and the last first'.[1]

Although it was true that many free sittings had been added to new and old churches during the past two decades, Phillpotts knew that the best seats were still sold or rented, and the poor thrust into remote galleries. The rights of the poor had been usurped; they were 'ROBBED of their rightful inheritance . . .'. Equally distressing was the increased use of pew rents instead of church rates for the maintenance of the churches. Bowing to the pressures of the enemies of the Church, maintenance had 'been shifted from property and fastened upon poverty. The poor have been taxed in the provision made by God and many for their souls, in order that the rich may . . . evade a payment, too light for the most sordid among them to feel as any real burthen'. It was not surprising, he told the people of Plymouth, that the only church built in their city with adequate free sittings received from local contributions less than one thousand of the six thousand pounds of construction costs; nor was it surprising that the poor felt unwanted in the Church.[2]

What was the alternative? The castigating prelate was vague, for after decrying the renting of pews, he stopped short of demanding that the practice should be abolished. In the end he merely endorsed the already existing practice of contributions for the erection of more free seats in better sections of the churches, and hoped that the contributions would equal the illegal rentals being charged.[3] As was so often the case, a bishop could point directly to an abuse which he rightly believed to be harmful to the Church. All too often he would then exaggerate its causative effects, rather than recognize that it was symptomatic of a wider problem. But even within his limited frame of reference, he was unable to take the next step, and recommend a meaningful way to rectify the evil. It was a cruel dilemma for conservative men distressed by practices and policies they believed fundamentally harmful to their Church and society, but still so integrally a part of the ruling circles of that society that the prospect of assertive reform was even more alarming to them. It was as perplexing to an old prelate such as Phillpotts as it was to a new, young episcopal dynamo like Wilberforce.

The former, unable to accept the failures of the Church of his youth, contented himself with railing at governments (Whig, of course) and a laity whose material and proprietary interests corrupted the pure faith

[1] H. Phillpotts, *A Charge Delivered to the Clergy of the Diocese of Exeter . . . in 1842* (1842), 88.

[2] H. Phillpotts, *The Widow's Mite. A Sermon Preached . . . 1844 in Obedience to the Queen's Letter, In Behalf of the National Society. To Which is Prefixed, A Pastoral Letter to the Inhabitants of Plymouth* (1844), 4, 6–7.

[3] *Ibid.*, 8.

and its dissemination. Wilberforce in contrast never knew the Church as Phillpotts, Blomfield or Howley knew it. Born in the nineteenth century, raised in an environment of Evangelical criticism, he was one of the leaders of a new clergy ready to criticize the Church as well as the State, and willing to recognize that many of the failings of the Establishment were largely a result of spiritual apathy and stunted values among many previous generations of its ministers. This did not mean that the State was blameless. On the contrary its dominance over the Church was a principal factor in the emergence of so restricted a spiritual sphere of influence. But for Wilberforce's generation of churchmen, moving into positions of episcopal leadership in the second half of the century, even that dominance was increasingly viewed as much a symptom of the failure of the earlier Church as it was a cause. They would, throughout the remainder of the century, struggle to restore some balance which was as spiritually and socially satisfying as it was politically practicable.

They would to a considerable degree be guided by the disturbing evidence compiled in the census of 1851, which, among other things, documented what had been recognized by some Church leaders and many Church critics—the national Church was not a spiritual commons where the rich and poor met in social harmony, and where the bonds of social hierarchy were strengthened as the result of a mutual recognition of duty and responsibility. It had been hoped that the Anglican clergy, themselves representative of all ranks, 'binding together in the equality of the common priesthood the sons of the highest noble and of the meanest peasant', would have provided a model for Christian society.[1] They had not done so; irrespective of their origins, the Anglican clergy in general ministered primarily to the middle and upper classes. Encouraged by the religiosity of enlarged congregations, ministers tended to overlook how few of them contained many members of the most populous class in the country. A year before his elevation to Oxford, Wilberforce told the clergy of his archdeaconry:

> We look, it may be, every Sunday, at our well-filled churches, and we forget, for the moment, in the presence of those we see, the multitude we see not; the mass behind; whom misery, as well as sin, whom want of room, want of clothes, indolence, neglect, or utter wretchedness, are shutting out from our fellowship, and severing from civilization and religion. Yet there they surely are. In all our great towns thin walls separate luxury from starvation. The two classes live in absolute ignorance of each other: there are no points of contact between them; the two streams nowhere intermingle: selfish respectability degrades one set; whilst misery and recklessness, which soon turn into vice and wickedness, weigh down the other.[2]

[1] Wilberforce, *Charge* (1840), 36.
[2] Wilberforce, *Charge* (1844), 15–16.

What especially distressed Wilberforce was the realization that in spite of all the great reform efforts of the nineteenth-century Church, the Establishment still reflected the disharmony of society as a whole. It was exclusive, upper class, and, in spite of his High Church propensities, too clerical. More concerned with education and respectability than with spiritual worth and earnestness, it had excluded many capable people from its ministry, and drove pious laymen into Dissent. As a result, it was difficult to claim any longer that the Anglican Communion represented a national faith.[1] It was not 'the equal home of the richest and the poorest . . .'. The poor, and even many humble people above them, had been driven away; it breaks 'our people into separate and unsympathizing classes, and thus sows amongst us broadcast the deadly seeds of intestine discord. The unity of the Church's worship, in which the rich and poor might mix together freely, would be a blessed safeguard from this danger.'[2]

But Wilberforce knew, as did his contemporaries, that the question of mixing was as sensitive as any of the problems of social reconciliation. Consequently he was cautious to temper his often imprudent remarks by explaining that he did not necessarily advocate the physical mixing of classes in church, but rather a reduction of excessive numbers of appropriated pews which deprived the poor of good seats, and their spiritual rights. Proprietary pews were, after all, 'suitable to our national character, they tend to foster habits of family religion, and, by preventing the inconvenient confusion of different classes, they may, whilst they protect his rights, be even more welcome to the feelings of the poor man than of the rich'.[3] It is doubtful that Wilberforce was really satisfied with his own arguments, for he returned time and time again to the question of equal sittings throughout the 1840's, and repeatedly moderated his enthusiastic pleas for common worship, an end to illegal pew-holdings, and the equality of all before God. In 1843 he assured protesting critics and over-zealous churchwardens that he did not mean to advocate open pews, and agreed that rank and station were transient and external realities that in no way interfered with the divine truths of spiritual equality. To try to impose this equality upon congregations, 'to insist on intermixing all . . . is to aim at an artificial equality which we do not feel, and which would not be maintained, by its most strenuous advocates in dress or manners'. To attempt to implement it in church would be 'to bring affectation into the house and worship of the Lord'. It might also have brought in more of the poor, but Wilberforce knew that it would be at the expense of the rich, who insisted that even in church any visions of equality be restricted to God. As he gently put it, equality would be harmful to family devotion, and create uneasiness

[1] *Ibid.,* 29–30.   [2] Wilberforce, *Charge* (1842), 19.
[3] *Ibid.,* 15.

among the rich and the poor. It would, he vaguely suggested, inflict a more serious wound than many suspect.[1]

During the revived Chartist disturbances of 1848 and under the impact of a fear of revolution spreading from the Continent, Wilberforce, now as Bishop of Oxford, again hammered on his theme of the importance of integrating the poor equally into the Church, and permitting them to worship in common with their betters. He could not help but believe that restricted pews still drove the poor from the Church, and as their religious feelings declined so did their acceptance of the comparative hardships of their lot. If only the 'highest and lowest of the parish gather all together as equals in the sight of God . . .' would internal peace be preserved. He described with eloquence and feeling the misery endured by the laboring classes, and was genuinely saddened that they could find so little alleviation from it in the comforts of common worship with people of all classes. Yet again recognizing that perhaps he had gone too far, Wilberforce quickly retreated from the implications of his emotions and explained to both the clergy and the churchwardens of his diocese that he did not mean to violate 'the orderly distinctions of men of various ranks and manners' by indiscriminate seating. The equality of which he spoke was only spiritual. All he meant was that the poor be allowed to use empty pews, and be provided sittings out of the dark corners of the church.[2]

Wilberforce spent a great deal of time talking himself in and out of positions before thinking through the implications of what he was saying. Emotional, loquacious, often propelled by instinct rather than calculation, the Bishop of Oxford was nevertheless not untypical in the ambivalence he felt about Church policies. It was perfectly evident to him as it was to others that the Church had been unable to promote class cohesiveness in spite of its massive efforts to restore the lower orders to the Establishment. The economic and social changes of the preceding half-century had occurred at a rate too great for the Church to cope with. Moreover the newer generation of bishops was perfectly willing to admit that the eighteenth-century Church had been particularly guilty of neglecting its flocks, and had allowed the multitudes to grow up beyond the reach of the ministry. All of the efforts of the nineteenth-century clergy had resulted in restoring the firm attachments of the propertied classes to the Church, but had made little impact upon the most populous part of the nation. The question of appropriated sittings was symptomatic of the general malaise. Great efforts had been made since 1818 to correct the deficiency of free places for the poor. Yet only about one-third of the seats provided by the Church Building Act were

[1] S. Wilberforce, *A Charge Delivered . . . November, 1843* (1843), 6–7.

[2] S. Wilberforce, *Address to the Churchwardens of the Diocese . . . September and October, 1848* (1848), 7–9. Also *Charge* (1848), 56–57, 60.

free, although the proportion was higher in the populous towns. By the middle of the century only four million of the approximately nine and half million sittings available in Establishment churches were clearly unappropriated.[1] A great many of these remained empty week after week, year after year.

Church leaders were becoming aware of this even before the religious census of 1851 confirmed it. Whether they blamed the Reformation, the government, industrialization and urbanization, or their apathetic predecessors in the eighteenth century, the Church was no longer the cement of society. Romantic and nostalgic reminiscences about an uncorrupted pastoral and harmonious past, while soothing, were no longer very significant. Nevertheless, throughout the first half of the century, one clergyman after another sought to solve the Church's inadequacies by a resurrection of idyllic social relationships, and a parochial structure which had in fact never existed. Social harmony rather than spiritual satisfaction had too long been the principal task of the Established Church in regards to the laboring classes. It had blinded the clergy to the possibility that eighteenth-century society appeared to be so much more balanced and restrained than their own because it was economically and socially much less in flux, rather than because of the harmonious social truths blended together by the Church.

[1] *Census of Great Britain, 1851. Religious Worship In England and Wales, Abridged From the Official Report Made by Horace Mann, Esq., to George Graham, Esq., Register General* (1854), viii, 106.

VIII

❖◇❖◇❖◇❖◇❖◇❖◇❖◇❖◇❖◇❖◇❖◇❖◇❖◇❖◇❖◇❖◇❖

People, Towns and Churches

❖◇❖◇❖◇❖◇❖◇❖◇❖◇❖◇❖◇❖◇❖◇❖◇❖◇❖◇❖◇❖◇❖

1. POPULATION GROWTH

Ecclesiastical ideas about society in general and the poor in particular were continually pressed into new directions by the massive weight of a mobile and enormously enlarged population during the first half of the nineteenth century. Relentlessly, decade after decade, the number of people increased at a rate never less than 13 per cent, and as high as 18 per cent. As a result, the population in England and Wales more than doubled, expanding from 8,892,536 in 1801 to 17,927,609 in 1851.[1] Because this ever-enlarging populace was concentrated in new and even older towns where the Church was physically and psychologically at its weakest, the staggering difficulties of ministering to it were intensified. Most clergymen held living in rural or semi-rural agricultural parishes, and counted upon the support of local gentry. Considering that of 10,693 livings surveyed in 1821 at least five thousand were in the hands of lay proprietors, most of them landowners, the clerical-gentry alliance was based, not only on mutual social and religious interest, but on economic necessity as well.[2] The Anglican parson, like his episcopal superior, was an integral part of the traditionally landed social and political establishment that governed the country throughout the eighteenth and much of the nineteenth century. By both affinity and necessity, he readily cooperated with those who shared his education, attitudes, and politics and whose patronage he needed.

Towns held few attractions for such a clergy. While an Evangelical

[1] *The Census of Great Britain in 1851* (1854), 90.
[2] Best, *Temporal Pillars*, 47.

minority, eager to obtain any living, might endure the discomforts of a poorly endowed, overpopulated urban parish, most Anglican parsons lacked a sense of missionary zeal and preferred the leisurely pace, status, and social cohesion of a rural cure. The clerical ideal of a well-paid, simple, pastoral living could hardly be fulfilled in the unhealthy slums and dingy housing estates of enlarged manufacturing and mining towns plagued by disease, Dissenters, and a variety of itinerant enthusiasts. Nothing was constant in an urban, manufacturing parish; and, until spiritual revitalization or economic interest became sufficient inducements, clergymen were reluctant to enter that crowded, polluted atmosphere. Only the lucrativeness of the London living of St Botolph's, Bishopsgate, persuaded Blomfield in 1820 to abandon his hopes of a rural or academic appointment providing 'a comfortable income, and the literary leisure which is a principal object to me'.[1] In fact, he received the offer, on Bishop Howley's recommendation, only after another clergyman, upon discovering that the parsonage was bothered by rats 'which being in the bones from the neighbouring churchyard . . . occasion an offensive smell . . .', refused it.[2]

With the urban population increasing at a rate nearly twice that of the rest of the country, eighteenth-century pastoral attitudes and ideals were rapidly bruised by the persistent blows of nineteenth-century economic and demographic reality. London's population alone expanded from 958,863 to 2,362,236, nearly one and a half times, during the first half of the century. Estimates of manufacturing and mining town population in the same period show an increase of nearly two and a quarter times; and, by the middle of the century, approximately half the population, 8,410,000, lived in urban areas.[3] A large proportion of these people were immigrants. In 1851, of 3,336,000 people over the age of twenty living in London and the next largest sixty-one cities in England and Wales, only 1,337,000 had been born there. London, Leeds, Norwich and Sheffield had the highest proportion of native-born residents, none, however, exceeding 50 per cent. In some towns, such as Manchester (Salford) and Bradford, three-quarters of the population were immigrants; while nearly one-seventh of Liverpool's population had come from Ireland.[4]

This meant that the Church had to cope not only with a rapidly expanding population in areas where it suffered from a serious shortage of churches and clergy, but also with an unparalleled mobility among its

[1] Blomfield, *Memoir*, I, 17.

[2] Howley to Liverpool, 13 April 1820, *Liverpool Ps.,* Add. MS. 38284, f. 133.

[3] *Census*, 1851, 15.

[4] J. H. Clapham, *An Economic History of Modern Britain. The Early Railway Age 1820–1850* (Cambridge, 1939), 536–7. Also, Hammond, *Age of the Chartists*, 23.

existing parochial congregations. Vast numbers of people were emigrating from small, rural parishes where the local clergyman, if resident, was not only important to the administration and cohesiveness of society, but, like the parish church, was a visible symbol of the national Establishment. Although this may have been a questionable advantage, given the character of many eighteenth-century clergymen, it certainly appeared so when compared to the complete absence of any visible minister or church spire in inflated urban parishes. Even where urban clergy were resident and zealous, they could not begin to follow the expanding parochial boundaries which weaved through the crowded and pestiferous alleys proliferating as fast as the laboring multitudes who populated them. It is not surprising that so few of the rural immigrants ever resumed any contact with the parish church. Their earlier association, if not already broken before emigrating, did not usually inspire them into overcoming the great organizational and clerical deficiencies that rendered the urban Church largely invisible and meaningless.

The Church in the early nineteenth century had barely begun to adjust to the changes of the eighteenth century. During the fifty years preceding the census of 1801, the population of Great Britain had steadily increased from perhaps 7,250,000 to 10,578,000. During the following thirty years, the population growth in England and Wales alone exceeded five million, the rate of increase reaching as high as 18 per cent in the second decade.[1] Yet the physical and institutional structure of the Establishment remained essentially unchanged. The number of parishes, hardly altered in the preceding century, mostly remained inviolate throughout much of the first half of the new century. Incumbents and patrons of town parishes were deeply committed to the defense of their proprietary rights, bitterly resenting and resisting attempts to subdivide their grossly enlarged cures with an entailed loss of parochial fees. Critics might complain of such selfish materialism on the part of clerical shepherds while so many of the flock blindly wandered perilously close to eternal destruction, but the clergy of the Establishment were too integral a part of English propertied society not to worship at more than one altar.

Established in the sixteenth century, the number and composition of episcopal dioceses had also fossilized. In spite of the huge influx of people into northern manufacturing and mining districts, the province of York until the 1830's still encompassed only 2,000 of the nearly 12,000 parishes, and but six of the twenty-six sees. This static character of the eighteenth-century Establishment was especially evident in its failure to make even a minimal effort to provide adequate facilities for worship in enlarged areas. An Act passed amidst the High Church enthusiasm of Queen Anne's reign provided for the erection of fifty new churches in

[1] *Census*, 1851, 88–89.

London.[1] Tithe-payers and existing patrons, fearful of greater burdens and a decline in the value of their holdings, combined with Whig distrust of sacerdotal claims and popular apathy to frustrate the anticipated expansion. Ten of the proposed edifices were constructed in the course of the century, making London the center of what little extension there was.[2] Only one church each was built in Bristol, Birmingham and Macclesfield to contain the enlarged trading, mining and manufacturing population appearing in those towns in the later years of the century.[3] Manchester-Salford erected two churches in the years preceding the French Revolution to provide services for the nearly 95,000 people who flocked to those once-sleepy towns. Drawing upon all its resources in the area, the Establishment could provide no more than eleven thousand places should the working populace care to attend an inadequate once-weekly service.[4]

Church lethargy contrasted sharply with the expansionist efforts of many Dissenter congregations. Although the parish of Sheffield increased from 14,105 people in 1736 to 45,758 in 1801, the Establishment erected only one church (in 1788) and, as it was subscribed, the poor were effectively excluded. Dissenters, during the same period, constructed five additional chapels for a total of eight—five more buildings than the Anglicans possessed. In general, the chapels were considerably smaller than Establishment churches, but not until 1821, when Sheffield's population reached 65,000, did the Church erect another structure.[5] Of the fifty-nine new places of worship constructed in Manchester-Salford between 1741 and 1830, forty-one belonged to independent denominations, and largely preceded the Church's building program launched in 1818.[6] Although the Dissenters estimated in 1811 that they comprised no more than two million of the population, an official enquiry into parishes of over one thousand inhabitants revealed that the number of Nonconformist chapels exceeded Anglican churches, 3,438 to 2,533.[7] Particularly striking was that while the Establishment figures had altered little throughout the preceding century the Dissenters, since 1740, when they possessed 533 chapels, had provided more than 2,900 additional places of worship.[8] Although most of these were proprietary chapels

---

[1] 9 Anne, c. 22.

[2] Elie Halévy, *England in 1815*, E. I. Watkin and D. A. Barker, trans., 2nd ed. (1949), 399.

[3] L. E. Elliott-Binns, *The Early Evangelicals. A Religious and Social Study* (1953), 172.

[4] Wilberforce, *Life*, II, 163.

[5] E. R. Wickham, *Church and People in an Industrial City* (1957), 47–48.

[6] H. W. C. Davis, *The Age of Grey and Peel* (Oxford, 1929), 151.

[7] Halévy, *England in 1815*, 428.

[8] J. W. Bready, *England Before and After Wesley* (1938), 292.

with established fees and therefore not particularly designed to attract the masses of urban laborers moving into the towns, they do reveal in comparison the virtually somnolent state of Church expansion before the end of the Napoleonic wars. Until then, the awakening had been slow; now, however, as many Church leaders were still trying to wipe away the cobwebs, volumes of private and official statistics ominously revealed a society in great flux.

The growth of statistical enquiry in the early years of the nineteenth century had a striking effect upon the Church. Already in the throes of self-criticism, prodded by the Evangelical Revival and intensified by the fearful outbreak of international revolution, the Establishment became increasingly conscious of its privileged role in English society. Private studies and visitation returns had in recent years suggested that the Church was losing ground. The establishment of the decennial census in 1801 provided statistical data which, when compared with diocesan and parochial figures, supported the worst fears of reform-minded clergymen: there existed a large gap between population and church facilities.

Episcopal interest in the question had been decidedly limited until the implications of census figures compiled in the early nineteenth century began to be interpreted in ecclesiastical terms. Bishop Porteus, the only prelate of his generation indicating an interest in demographic questions, seemed to appreciate their possible relevance to his diocese. He not only read population literature, but also circulated it among his friends and acquaintances.[1] Upon elevation to the See of Chester in 1777, he was well aware of its population growth and understood how the establishment of factories encouraged it. The only task he saw for the Church, however, lay in combatting the moral and religious laxity that accompanied the expanding wealth and luxury of the age.[2] Although calculating in 1781 that the diocese had increased by more than 250,000 people since 1717, Porteus did not indicate that any particular problems followed from that development. In some parts of the see, the extent of growth ranged from four- to six-fold or more, while Liverpool's population alone had risen from 5,000 to 35,000 since the opening of the century. Parts of Manchester formerly comprised of a few hundred people now contained over 11,000, while two of the archdeaconries in the diocese had increased by 95,000 during a half-century.[3] These figures, when compared with others contrasting the number of Catholics in the diocese in 1767 (67,916) and

[1] Porteus to 1st Earl Liverpool, 28 May 1781, *Liverpool Ps.*, Add. MS. 38216, f. 172.
[2] B. Porteus, *A Letter to the Inhabitants of Manchester, Macclesfield, and the Adjacent Parts, on Occasion of the Late Earthquake in Those Places* (Chester, 1777), 22.
[3] *Parl. Hist.*, XXI (1781), 1376–9.

1780 (69,376) clearly indicated a proportional decrease of papists—a point Porteus made in 1781 during the agitation and riots accompanying proposals for Catholic relief.[1]

The bishop made no allusion to the virtual absence of church extension or parochial reorganization during the century to adjust to the demographic realities he described. Relieved that the papists had not expanded in his diocese, Porteus drew no further significance from his statistics. Not until eight years later, after his translation to London, did he suggest that extensive urban parishes created special problems for the clergy. Porteus told the clergy then that it was his experience that the most devoted ministerial exertions might be insufficient and ineffectual 'unless the laws, and the magistrates will, in certain cases, come in to our aid, especially in large and populous towns'. Aid, according to the bishop, did not mean new parishes, churches and clergy, but rather an enforcement of anti-vice legislation to control the temptation and corruption so apparent in urban locales.[2]

Although an occasional prelate saw some need for institutional reform or reorganization to improve clerical effectiveness, it was far more common for diocesans to appeal for better residency and a more diligent performance of parochial functions. The Methodist challenge and Evangelical criticism was seen as a much greater problem than worker mobility and the growth of towns. Since the religious revival was concerned with individual behavior and salvation, it challenged the energy and zeal of the Establishment's ministers, rather than its physical and organizational structure. Consequently, because of both the terms of the challenge and the existence of little pre-revolutionary sentiment favoring an institutional resurgence which smacked of High Church sacerdotalism, the episcopal defenders did not respond to the challenge by proposing a resurgence of the institutional Church. Reflecting the views of their society, the leaders of the Establishment proposed instead that what the growing multitudes of the towns needed was more preaching and exhortation to recognize their sinfulness and redeem their souls through a patient resignation to the *status quo*. Ideally, should this prove inadequate, the law stood behind the clergy and was prepared to deal quickly and harshly with the unregenerate. Such was the goal pursued by Evangelicals like Wilberforce who oriented their efforts to obtain more rigorous legislation for the punishment of immoral and blasphemous behavior. Porteus, Barrington, and a few other prelates welcomed the move. The intense excitement of the Revolution streng-

[1] B. Porteus, *A Letter to the Clergy of the Diocese of Chester Containing Precautions Respecting the Roman Catholics, 1781* (1782), 4.

[2] B. Porteus, *A Letter to the Clergy of the Diocese of London*, 2nd ed. (1789), 15–16. Porteus was a strong supporter of Wilberforce's Proclamation Society.

thened their hand as the towns suddenly assumed an exaggerated importance. Those warrens of laboring humanity were no longer just objectionable vice-pots brewing the usual ingredients of human sin; they were also filled with active and potential revolutionaries, reading Tom Paine and conspiring to drown the constitution in their odious mixture. As pressure was applied to the clergy to reach such people before it was too late, the magnitude of the problem began to sink in. A few prelates realized, however, that advocating more preaching to the poor was one thing; getting them within earshot of a clergyman was quite another.

After nearly a decade of urging his clergy to minister to the urban poor as never before, William Cleaver, Porteus's successor at Chester (1787–1800), recognized that the expanding Lancashire and Midland towns of his diocese were virtually unaffected. Though a non-resident residing at Brasenose College, where he was Master, Cleaver paid enough attention to his diocese to understand that in addition to the population continuing to expand rapidly, existing places of worship were hopelessly inadequate for 'an increasing and unequal population'. Not only did such a situation cause an exclusion of many workers from the Church during perilous times of wild temptation, but it also explained, to the bishop's satisfaction at least, why the lower orders were defecting to Dissenter chapels. For the first time, the implications were recognized and spelled out by a member of the bench as Cleaver warned:

> If we suppose the population of this Diocese, and probably of some others, to exceed the means of accommodation in public worship upon the Establishment nearly by one half, and that excess still to receive a constant and rapid augmentation, it is evident, that the Establishment must by a continued decrease in the proportion, at no very distant period, lose its due weight and influence in the political constitution of these kingdoms.[1]

Distrustful of Evangelicals and other enthusiasts, the bishop insisted that doctrinal matters were not involved in the diminution of Anglican influence. The problem was primarily physical, and was fast approaching a magnitude requiring the attention of the legislature.

2. LACK OF CHURCHES

Three years before, in 1796, George Isaac Huntingford, Warden of Winchester and future Bishop of Gloucester (1802–15) and Hereford (1815–32), had 'with the utmost deference and submission' cautiously hoped that the legislature would recognize the growing difficulties in

---

[1] W. Cleaver, *Charge Delivered to the Clergy of His Diocese* (Oxford, 1799), 12–13.

populous areas. He praised the efforts of the High Church Archdeacon of Sarum, Charles Daubeny, who was currently building at Bath the first free church in England, and suggested that the government might encourage such subscription efforts throughout the country.[1] Neither Huntingford's hesitant proposal nor Cleaver's direct warning made any impression on a government deeply involved in financing and fighting an exhausting war, or upon most Church leaders ignorant or indifferent to conditions in such alien places as manufacturing and mining towns. Few were prepared to go further than Shute Barrington when in 1797 he gently asked 'the opulent proprietors of estates and mines' in the diocese of Durham to think about providing churches and schools for the increased but 'very useful part of our labouring poor' in the mining areas.[2] They ignored him, and he dropped the subject.

In the opening decade of the new century, however, others picked it up. Slowly, hesitatingly, a few members of the bench seemed to grasp the meaning of some of the statistics compiled in the first census of 1801. Complaints from more serious clergymen, like those who compiled the Lincoln *Report* of 1800, also started to make an impression. Of equal importance was the personal awareness among several prelates of conditions in London. It is not surprising that the metropolis was the focal point of episcopal discussions of population growth, as it was the one city in which most bishops spent considerable time. The Bishop of Chester would rarely if ever visit Liverpool or Manchester, while the Archbishop of York spent little time in Leeds, Sheffield, or Hull. Yet both were often in London and Westminster. As a result the non-resident Bishop of Llandaff, Richard Watson, who knew little of conditions in his own diocese, complained of the serious lack of churches and free sittings in London. In a letter to Wilberforce in 1800 Watson proposed the building of several large churches without appropriated seats and open to all classes. They should be simple structures staffed by diligent clergymen who provide two services every Sunday and teach the catechism during Lent. The Bishop, feeling that the churches should be built from public funds, suggested that Wilberforce raise the question with Pitt. Twenty churches, he estimated, could be built for £100,000; if a charity box was placed at each door, it would be filled by the many country families periodically coming to London and wanting to distinguish themselves from the lower classes by voluntary donations.[3]

---

[1] G. I. Huntingford, *A Sermon Preached . . . June 2, 1796, Being the Time of the Yearly Meeting of the Children Educated in the Charity Schools . . .* (1796), 23–24.

[2] S. Barrington, *A Charge Delivered to the Clergy of the Diocese of Durham . . . MDCCXCVII* (1797), 23–24.

[3] Watson, *Anecdotes*, II, 111–13.

When no action followed, Watson publicly made the same proposals three years later. It is perhaps ironic that one of the earliest proponents of church extension was the most prominent and belligerent 'Old Whig' on the bench. Watson, however, was growing alarmed at conditions in London and elsewhere, where the concentration of the lower orders in large numbers was a clear danger to the State. By 1804, having seen the results of the census, he warned that churches are 'not sufficiently numerous in large Towns, or in this Metropolis. Near a million of Inhabitants are here congregated, on an Area of a few square Miles: and additional Churches are certainly wanted for this immense Population.' Watson was confident that the legislature would soon take the matter into serious consideration and provide simple and capacious buildings open to 'the Common People, as well as their Superiors'.[1] In addition, he believed that the government should provide attractive salaries for the clergy in order to engage men of first-rate preaching ability.

Watson received little support from the Bishop of London. While recognizing deficiencies in the Metropolis, and complaining that the lower orders were either excluded from attending church or driven to independent chapels, Bishop Porteus went no further than tepidly conceding that Parliament would eventually have to consider the matter.[2] The aging prelate retained the illusion that voluntary societies, cheap moralistic literature, and exemplary behavior by the upper classes would continue to assure the poor's attachment to the Establishment until some vague future time when clerical abuses and the want of churches would be alleviated. Other prelates, however, especially High Churchmen concerned about the institutional structure of the Establishment, were more alarmed by the new statistical compilations indicating that such an attachment was increasingly difficult to maintain. John Fisher of Exeter, soon to be translated to Salisbury, was jolted by 'the magnitude of the evil'. In six of the Metropolis's western parishes, containing a population of 204,000, there were only 24,310 places in church. As a great many of these sittings were proprietary holdings, the lower orders were effectively excluded. In some of the parishes, such as the prostitute-ridden area around St Giles, there were two thousand places for over 23,000 people; while the largest parish considered, Marylebone, had 7,050 seats for a population of over 64,000. If such discrepancies extended to all of London, Fisher complained, 'the evil would appear to prevail in a still more alarming degree'. It was indeed 'a melancholy spectacle . . . which calls for immediate attention, if we have any regard to the divine protection, or to the permanence of that holy religion which is our only

[1] R. Watson, *A Sermon Preached Before the Society For the Suppression of Vice . . . May, 1804* (1804), 6–7.

[2] *Hansard*, IV (1805), 453–4.

safeguard and consolation in the accumulating perils and struggles through which we are destined to pass'.[1]

Fisher's plea for legislative support was echoed repeatedly as more and more churchmen became aware of the extent of the population and the limitations of Church facilities. High Churchmen were especially active in demanding that the State fulfil its obligations to the Established Church by providing the means for bringing the growing multitudes into the fold. Their position was considerably strengthened by the support of Archbishop Manners-Sutton and the translation of John Randolph to London after Porteus's death in 1809. The archbishop finally acknowledged the problem by admitting that the population, particularly in some large towns, far exceeded the machinery by which the Establishment's beneficial effects could be communicated.[2] Randolph, in contrast to Porteus, was an aggressive High Church prelate who openly held his predecessor's moderate Evangelical sympathies in contempt. During his primary visitation in 1810 he asserted that 'the want of Churches, or of sufficient accommodation in them in proportion to the inhabitants . . .' was in large measure the result of substituting proprietary chapels for adequate church facilities. It was clear that he felt the Evangelicals, with Porteus's acquiescence, had been especially guilty of this, as well as of a variety of other things. Although recognizing that the pressures of the times had perhaps impeded the passage of legislation needed to erect new churches in populous areas, he was confident that it was merely a matter of time before matters would be rectified. Meanwhile, he suggested, wealthier parishes could build churches like those in Hackney and Marylebone to accommodate the growing population, for it is 'undeniable that the call upon us is pressing, as Christians, to make provision that the means of public worship be adequate to the growing commerce of the country'.[3]

Evangelicals, furious that most of the *Charge* was directed against them and their emphasis upon simple, spiritual preaching, delighted in pointing to the locked pews and luxurious decoration in the churches at Hackney and Marylebone, the former a center of High Church activity, and contrasted them with the simplicity and accessibility of free churches at Bath and chapels in St Giles and Plymouth Dock. As one anonymous 'Episcopalian' sarcastically concluded, 'but after all, it will probably be found that the best way to prevent tabernacles and meeting houses from springing up on every side, will be to provide the new Churches and

[1] J. Fisher, *A Sermon Preached Before the Lords Spiritual and Temporal . . . February 25, 1807, Being the Day Appointed For a General Fast* (1807), 10–11, 16–19.

[2] *Hansard*, XIV (1809), 857.

[3] J. Randolph, *A Charge Delivered to the Clergy of the Diocese of London . . . MDCCCX* (Oxford, 1810), 25–27.

Chapels with that very sort of preachers which it seems to have been the principal object of this Charge to disparage'.[1] Actually, the preceding year, 1809, marked the first of eleven £100,000 annual grants by the government to Queen Anne's Bounty to augment poor livings and encourage residence. Priority was to go to livings in the more populous areas, and on a scale proportionate to the size of the population served by the minister.[2] The pious Prime Minister, Spencer Perceval, also supported the necessity for more churches in expanded areas, and in 1811 worked out a plan to erect them in industrial towns.[3] The financial difficulties associated with prosecuting the war delayed its presentation to Parliament, while Perceval's assassination the following year left its implementation to his successor, Lord Liverpool.

As in the case of education, High Churchmen seized the initiative, recognizing that the National Society's efforts to inculcate the poor with Church principles would be largely negated if places of worship were not provided. In 1814, John Bowdler, Joshua Watson, and James Alan Park, later a Justice of the Common Pleas, rallied other leaders of the High Church party, including Archdeacons Daubeny and George Owen Cambridge, to support their appeal to the new Bishop of London, William Howley, jointly to press the government into action. To the cautious but sympathetic new prelate, they pointed out that 'not a *tenth* part of the Church of England population in the west and east parts of the metropolis, and in populous parts of the county of Middlesex, can be accommodated in our churches and chapels'. While their travels throughout the nation reassured them that the majority of the people were still attached to the Established Church, 'one great cause of the apparent defection from the Church, and of the increase of sectaries, and Methodism, is the want of places of worship'. Overjoyed by the end of the war, they urged, 'let us show our thanks by immediately dedicating to God's honour a number of free churches and chapels, sufficient to supply the wants of all God's faithful worshippers in the Established Church of England'.[4]

Although premature, their joy was revived by the second defeat of Napoleon at Waterloo the following year, whereupon Bowdler drew up, and 120 prominent laymen signed, a petition to Liverpool which expressed 'extreme alarm at the danger to which the constitution of the

[1] *A Letter Respectfully Addressed to the Lord Bishop of London After A Perusal of the Charge Delivered At His Lordship's Primary Visitation in 1810*, 2nd ed. (1811), 62–63.

[2] Best, *Temporal Pillars*, 213–14.

[3] D. Gray, *Spencer Perceval, the Evangelical Prime Minister 1762–1812* (Manchester, 1963), 25.

[4] J. H. Overton, *The English Church in the Nineteenth Century* (1894), 151.

country, both in Church and State, is exposed from want of places of worship, particularly for persons of the middle and lower classes'.[1] They were bolstered in their arguments by the appearance of the Reverend Richard Yates's imposing, if ponderous, study, *The Church in Danger*. Yates, Chaplain of Chelsea Hospital, drew upon a number of individual and official enquiries to describe an already widespread lack of church facilities in populous areas. Although concentrating heavily upon conditions in London, where statistics were readily available, his exhaustive compilations of other areas revealed that conditions in the Metropolis were not unique. The number of inhabitants in rural parishes within a hundred-mile radius of London averaged about 640. Yet within eight miles of St Paul's, exclusive of the City, with its surfeit of churches built after the Great Fire of 1666, there were 1,162,300 people with sittings for only 220,000 of them.[2] As most of the spaces were appropriated, the lower orders literally had no place to worship. In both the above and a follow-up study, *The Basis of National Welfare* (1817), Yates gave national prominence and authoritativeness to hundreds of individual complaints, such as that of T. F. Middleton, the future first Bishop of Calcutta, who, as Vicar of St Pancras in 1812, found himself the spiritual guardian of nearly 50,000 people and an ancient church capable of accommodating about two hundred.[3]

Parliamentary enquiries largely substantiated Yates's depressing conclusions.[4] Population growth and Church difficulties had clearly become an issue of national concern. One clergyman mysteriously concluded from parliamentary statistics that, proportionally, churches were no more numerous in 1818 than they were at the time of the Norman Conquest.[5] The government was more than sympathetic to the problem. In February 1818, Liverpool approved and endorsed the efforts of Joshua Watson and other High churchmen to establish a voluntary Church Building Society designed to give the Establishment some of the independence and flexibility enjoyed by Dissenters and which a revitalized High Church increasingly envied. Later that year, however, Liverpool, with strong support from Viscount Sidmouth and the Chancellor of the Exchequer, Nicholas Vansittart, succeeded in gaining passage of an Additional Churches Act which provided an initial £1,000,000 for the construction of new churches, authorized the raising

[1] *Ibid.*, 151.

[2] Yates, *Church In Danger*, 36 ff.

[3] C. W. Le Bas, *The Life of the Right Rev. Thomas F. Middleton, D.D., Late Lord Bishop of Calcutta* (1831), I, 25–26.

[4] Best, *Temporal Pillars*, 149.

[5] J. Brewster, *A Sketch of the History of Churches in England Applied to the Purposes of the Society for Promoting the Enlargement and Building of Churches and Chapels . . .* (1818), 78.

of subscriptions to supplement the grant, and appointed administrative commissioners.

Liverpool, who had worked out the Bill with Archbishop Manners-Sutton, Bishop Howley and several of the High Church laity, described it as 'the most important measure he had ever submitted to their Lordship's consideration'. Arguing that it was futile to educate children of the poor if they had no place to worship, he contrasted the difficulties faced by the Church with the unrestricted growth permitted to Dissenters. The part of his presentation cutting across all Establishment party lines, however, dwelt upon an accumulating reality of a 'vast increase of the population of the country within these twenty years . . . chiefly in great manufacturing towns . . .'. Liverpool and Vansittart, who introduced the Bill in the Commons, drew heavily upon Yates's studies and parliamentary statistics to prove:

> With all the advantages the country had derived from the extraordinary extension of its manufactures, it was impossible . . . to conceal . . . this fact—that great masses of human beings could not be brought together in the manner in which they were situated in these towns, without being exposed to vicious habits and to corrupting influences dangerous to the public security as well as to private morality.[1]

The measure passed without difficulty. Lord Holland, however, noted that hardships endured by Dissenters in maintaining their own clergy and chapels would increase now that, in addition to paying tithes, they would also have to contribute to the construction of churches in which they had no interest. He recommended the precedent of a 1797 Act requiring the sequestration of two prebends of Lichfield for the purpose of repairing the cathedral.[2] But, for another generation, no one of influence seriously proposed that the Church utilize its own disproportionate episcopal and cathedral revenues to provide for the lower orders in the towns. The repeal of the Test and Corporation Acts and Catholic emancipation were still a decade away. The repression of the post-war years only underlined the country's distance from parliamentary reform. The Anglican Church, still the Established Church of England, began to revive and demand the perquisites of its unique position in the machinery of state as fresh and invigorating oils lubricated its creaky, unused joints. Although Parliament granted an additional £500,000 in 1824, the interim preceding the passage of the Reform Bill of 1832 saw the Church alone raise at least an additional £1,500,000 of the nearly £3,000,000 expended in constructing more than three hundred new places of worship in populous areas.[3]

The bishops had approached the project with their usual caution,

---

[1] *Hansard*, XXXVIII (1818), 709–21.   [2] *Ibid.*, 714–17.
[3] *Census*, 1851, *Religious Worship*, 12–14.

realizing that excessive episcopal enthusiasm would not only agitate Dissenters, but might also alarm many other Englishmen, especially Evangelicals and Broad Churchmen suspicious and distrustful of High Church ambition. Since few members of the bench were sufficiently independent to exert much pressure upon the government, the initiative fell to influential laymen. Once the government recognized the problem and gave its approval for the construction of new churches, the bishops became much more active and critical in discussing urban problems and their impact upon the Established Church. Bishop Howley, for example, had been very circumspect before the passage of the Additional Churches Act, quietly participating in working out its provisions with the government. Once passed, however, he quickly criticized the measure as inadequate; especially 'when we consider that our population is doubled, and that our number of churches, after every allowance for new erections, is probably diminished, in the course of the three last centuries...'. He traced the difficulties back to 'the dawn of our commercial prosperity . . .' which not only encouraged population, but 'by the fluctuations in manufactures and commerce . . . have had the effect of transferring large masses of the people from districts well-planted with churches to places altogether unprovided with the means of religious worship'. As a result, 'the multitudes in London and other commercial towns are foregoing public prayer and instruction, or turning to Dissenters'.[1]

Walker King, the old Bishop of Rochester (1809–27) and a close friend of Edmund Burke, never discussed the inadequacies of church facilities for ten years of his incumbency.[2] Suddenly, in 1819, he issued a *Pastoral Letter* criticizing the limitations of the Church Building Act as unlikely to alleviate the great shortage of churches. As with most of his episcopal brethren, King was jolted by the Church-population statistics published over the preceding four years and the mounting unrest in many parts of the country. It was difficult not to see the obvious correlation with a 'neglected population', which might create a crisis 'dangerous to the very existence of our Established Church'.[3] But neither King, Howley nor any other complaining prelate suggested that the government provide a greater proportion of its revenue for churches. Ultimately the problem could be relieved only if the wealthy voluntarily contributed the means to minister to their Godless inferiors. With the example of

[1] Howley, *Charge* (1818), 17–19.

[2] W. King (1752–1827), son of a Lancashire clergyman, educated at Oxford. Portland elevated him to the bench in 1809 after a career in cathedral positions.

[3] W. King, *A Pastoral Letter to the Clergy and Other Inhabitants of His Diocese, In Behalf of the Society Instituted for Promoting the Enlargement and Building of Churches and Chapels* (1819), 9–15.

Peterloo still fresh in everyone's mind, Bishop King solemnly warned the rich to beware, 'lest, whilst the balm of religion is pouring over their leprous ulcers, and they intercept its healing effusion upon the sores of others, their ingratitude be not more offensive than that of the lepers, who were cleansed, and returned not to give glory to God'. More succinctly stated: 'those who are excluded from our churches, we cannot reasonably expect to be zealous supporters of it. In any case of disturbance, their weight would probably rather be thrown into some opposite scale . . .'.[1]

One bishop after another rapidly sought assurance that the balance would fall in their favor. From his diocese of Chester, George Henry Law quickly urged the building of two new churches in Manchester where he could 'with truth affirm that in no place in the Kingdom is Church room more wanted . . .'. He soon after requested funds to alleviate conditions in Preston and surrounding hamlets where the rapid increase in the manufacturing population completely overwhelmed the Established Church. New places of worship were needed in central locations throughout the diocese.[2] Henry Ryder wrote from Gloucester of the 'wild and once neglected population' who, if provided with two churches, might now be attached to a minister and made 'useful members of the community'.[3] Several of the older prelates, however, like the aristocratic James Cornwallis of Lichfield and Coventry, were cautious to the point of obstruction, and their distrust of 'parliamentary interference' repeatedly delayed the construction of new churches.[4] Others were won over.

William Van Mildert, the most influential reactionary High Church bishop on the bench, was at first frightened that the Additional Churches Act would only encourage Evangelicals to promote more churches in populous areas. Ever wary of conspiracies against the Church, he protested to Peel a section in the Act which allowed to a person building a chapel by private subscription the nomination of life trustees who would administer the patronage for the first three turns. Anyone donating fifty pounds would have a vote for the trustees. Van Mildert, aware of Evangelical appointments to many privately subscribed proprietary chapels during the preceding twenty years, knew they had a considerable fund appropriated for that project and would readily divert it to

[1] *Ibid.*, 16, 20–21.

[2] Law to Church Blg. Comm., 18 June 1820, *Minute Book*, III, 334–5, and 11 July, 405–9. Also 6 Dec. 1821, *Minute Book*, V, 376.

[3] Ryder to Liverpool, 10 April 1820, *Liverpool Ps.*, Add. MS. 38284, f. 85.

[4] Cornwallis to Liverpool, 9 and 15 June 1818, *ibid.*, Add. MS. 38272, ff. 111, 155. Cornwallis repeatedly delayed and even blocked local attempts by clergy and laity to promote funds for new churches. See Ch. Blg. Comm., *Minute Book*, III, 255, 257, 284.

buying up votes with fifty-pound donations. This would be a 'great hazard to our Ecclesiastical Establishment'; moreover, to permit the principle of popular election in the cure of souls 'is too great an *anomaly* in our Ecclesiastical System to be consistently admitted'.[1] Nevertheless, Van Mildert realized that the bishops could hardly oppose a measure so clearly devised for the benefit of their Church; especially when it seemed likely that the total of churches and chapels of Dissenters 'will probably soon equal, if not outnumber' those of the Establishment. Consequently, during his first visit to his Welsh clergy he urged them to seek funds from the Commissioners and the Church Building Society's voluntary sources. Since only nine hundred of the eighteen thousand inhabitants in the mining town of Merthyr Tydfil could enter the old church, it was not surprising that 'many of our own flocks are almost driven from Communion with the Established Church by this lamentable deficiency'.[2]

Church building rapidly became the principal panacea of Church leaders, especially the bishops, in the 1820's. Although enthusiastic Evangelicals, Broad Church liberals, and secular critics of the Establishment argued that since many existing churches were only partially filled, the success of the Church depended not upon more buildings, but upon a reformed and reinvigorated parochial ministry relevant to the needs of a new age, most prelates preferred to ignore the harsh realities of such an analysis. This, despite their awareness of the scandalous and debilitating effects of pluralism, non-residence, and ineffectual clergy available to their parishioners but one day a week. The same bishops who worked energetically to obtain grants for new churches in their dioceses knew that of the 10,583 clergymen examined in 1827, 4,530 did not reside in their cures, nor did duty; nor were they allowed to forget that ten years later the figure still exceeded 3,100.[3] During this period it is difficult to find an episcopal charge or sermon that does not lament these severe deficiencies and that does not plead, persuade, cajole and threaten the clergy into a sense of their parochial responsibilities.

The clergyman who told the Bishop of London in 1818 that the construction of new churches would be insufficient and ineffective so long as there was no rational division of large parishes into manageable sizes was not telling Howley anything new.[4] He could only nod in agreement with the Reverend John Brewster's similar complaint and conclu-

[1] Van Mildert to Peel, 30 April 1818, *Peel Ps.*, Add. MS. 40276, ff. 251–4.

[2] W. Van Mildert, *A Charge Delivered to the Clergy of the Diocese of Llandaff... in MDCCCXXI* (Oxford, 1821), 8–9.

[3] Mathieson, *Church Reform*, 127.

[4] *A Letter to the Right Reverend The Lord Bishop of London, Upon the Society For Promoting the Enlargement and Building of Churches and Chapels* (1818), 23.

sion that, 'when we live beyond the hearing of the parish bell, we forget that there is a parish Church'.[1] Such complaints had become common-place since the turn of the century. Even before the very popular High Church moralist, Sarah Trimmer, grieved:

> No circumstance in the annals of the present times is more to be lamented as detrimental to the cause of religion, than the great estrangement which has taken place between the lower orders of people and their parochial ministers, who are frequently totally unknown to each other.

But Mrs Trimmer recognized what every churchman understood: the division of parishes raised a delicate question of property rights involv-ing the question of church rates, tithes, and fees as well as the local influence of the patron and the incumbent. She sighed at the prospect of 'how easy would the task of the parochial minister become, by having his flock divided . . . into *separate congregations*, under assistants, acting in strict conformity to the doctrines of the Church, and subject to his immediate inspection . . .'.[2]

Until the Additional Churches Act of 1818, an Act of Parliament was required to alter parochial law and geography. Due to the complications involved, as well as the problems of compensating existing and future interests, such alterations were quite rare. The legislation of 1818 was but the first of a series of Acts culminating in Peel's District Churches Act of 1843, which greatly facilitated the division of parishes into manageable districts no longer financially and legally subordinate to the old parish church.[3] Nevertheless, throughout most of the first half of the century, urban parishes were grossly over-extended, the number of clergy and the administrative structure so inadequate as to preclude an effectual parochial relationship with the lower orders. An examination of thirty-four London parishes in 1836 revealed how little headway had been made against the population flood which reached its peak in the preceding decade. Four of the parishes contained 166,000 people served by eleven clergymen. In twenty-one other parishes, forty-five clergymen supposedly ministered to the needs of 739,000 souls. For the 1,137,000 in all thirty-four parishes, 139 ministered in churches accommodating a maximum of less than one-tenth the population.[4]

Although the number of subscribed proprietary chapels had grown considerably since the beginning of the century, they contributed nothing to parochial administration, and, because of their fee system, little to the alleviation of lower-class urban population problems. In London they comprised about one-fourth of the available sittings,[5]

[1] Brewster, *Sketch* (1818), 114.

[2] S. Trimmer, *The Oeconomy of Charity* (1787), II, 220 ff.

[3] Best, *Temporal Pillars*, 195–6, 408.

[4] Eccles. Duties and Rev. Comm., *Report* (1836), 59–60.   [5] *Ibid.*

reserved mainly for comfortable middle-class Evangelicals and others whose financial success permitted them to move into newer or expanding areas. Richard Yates warned that such chapels harmed the Church both indirectly, by giving the appearance of 'supplying in some measure the defect which would otherwise impress itself more strongly upon public notice, and directly, by withdrawing from ecclesiastical uses into private and secular channels those resources which might be used for supplying proper ministers. The chapels are built and conducted wholly as pecuniary and commercial speculations. The first object of the proprietor is to get the highest rent for pews; and the poor are excluded.'[1]

Such complaints, heard increasingly since the opening years of the century, were often made by High Churchmen deeply distrustful of the extra-parochial innovations of popular, soul-stirring, and fashionable preachers. As people became aware of the staggering deficiencies of parochial establishments in the populous towns, the contrast with flourishing chapels became a greater concern. At the same time, Church leaders could not ignore that the deep-rooted proprietary inroads into most parochial churches over the years more often than not excluded many of the poor from their local church. Church building seemed a marvellous compromise; while it did not modernize the archaic parochial structure of a community, it at least offered some relief to overwhelmed churches without endangering the incumbents' and their patrons' property rights and control. By proposing a large proportion of free seats for the poor, the new churches minimized the necessity for badgering wealthy churchgoers into opening their pews, thus providing a rationale for many clergymen who had no desire or intention of altering the existing arrangements with their congregations. Ultimately only about one-third of the sittings erected out of parliamentary grants were free, but the proportion was often higher in the more crowded districts. Above all, the rapid construction of new places of worship directly complemented simultaneous reform efforts to improve clerical residency, raise standards, and provide regular and more frequent services, as part of a revived sense of utility and purpose. Worried by defections and alarmed by the growth of Dissent and widespread hostility, the Church demanded, as the Established Church of England, the right to fulfil its responsibilities. Having already embarked upon education in the hopes of recapturing the rising generations of the poor, the Church realized that, once recaptured, means of holding them were needed.

3. CHURCH BUILDING, 1832–51

The bishops who warmly endorsed the construction of new churches after 1818 envisioned a new era of Church–State co-operation. It seemed

[1] Overton, *English Church*, 147.

to them that a Tory legislature, grateful for unwavering clerical support during the prolonged crisis of the preceding three decades, felt a renewed awareness and appreciation of the great advantages of its alliance with the Established Church. As a result, the legislature now intended to provide the Church with the means of fulfilling its role even more effectively. The episcopal leaders of the Establishment welcomed the support of parliamentary measures to improve clerical residence, increase clerical stipends, and erect new places of worship in populous and neglected areas. Although the passage of each measure was preceded by the expression of long-held fears of the dangers of excessive episcopal authority, the legislation unquestionably increased that authority at a time when a newer generation of prelates was willing to assume it. More and more bishops were also willing to acknowledge and cautiously rectify the deficiencies of the Georgian Church, proving at the same time that the Establishment could meet the requirements, utilitarian as well as spiritual, of the new age.

The building of new churches seemed, at first, one of the most direct and vigorous ways of demonstrating this awareness. The enforcement of clerical residency and the re-establishment of effective parochial religion was a slow, long-term development dependent upon gradual recruitment of serious parochial clergymen, improvement in their economic condition, and reform of existing ecclesiastical laws that greatly restricted the bench's disciplinary powers. But the appearance of a new church in the midst of a crowded and neglected populace was immediate evidence of an improved and vigorous Church. Bishop Blomfield, the most active and aggressive proponent of church extension in the nineteenth century, long maintained that the church building must be located at the center of any district, from which services, both spiritual and social, would radiate.[1] As the activating symbol of the Church's presence, a new edifice, he was confident, would in time draw both laity and new clergy into its orbit. This overly simplistic view, which even Blomfield eventually questioned, was eagerly accepted by the bishops. It provided a solution that obscured much more important problems deriving from the impact of economic and social change upon a Church so enmeshed in its country's political, administrative and social structure. It glossed over, for example, the uneasy awareness of lower-class alienation which, though hesitatingly acknowledged earlier, became painfully apparent to the generation of bishops who came to power in the 1830's and 1840's.

The disillusionment following the repeal of the Test and Corporation Acts in 1828, and the more controversial granting of civil rights to Catholics in 1829, only reinforced the Church's determination to press ahead with new churches as rapidly as possible. With the legislature now open to Englishmen decidedly opposed to the favored position of

---

[1] Blomfield, *Memoir*, I, 251.

U   297

the Established Church, the optimistic visions of governmental co-operation suddenly clouded. The Whig victory of 1830, together with the successful passage of the Reform Bill two years later, confirmed High Church fears that any illusions Anglicans might have had about a reinvigoration of Establishment privileges had been destroyed. The new Parliament, still the real ruler of the Church, was not only unwilling to continue granting large sums for the extension of the Establishment, but was also determined, one way or another, to reform the Church. With Dissenters and Radicals demanding disestablishment as a beginning, many bishops realized that the Church's continued expansion into populous areas would depend primarily upon its own resources and those still supporting it. This awareness, which marked the entire course of Church reform for the next decade, gave a new urgency and intensity to the whole question of extension.

At the time of The Reform Bill, the Treasury had expended £1,440,000 on 188 new churches and chapels accommodating nearly 260,000 worshippers, half of whom paid no fees.[1] The Church had voluntarily raised approximately the same amount. During the next twenty years 2,029 churches were added at an approximate cost of £6,087,000, of which only £511,385—to aid private benefactors of 386 of the new buildings—was contributed by the State.[2] Church building, like charity in the eighteenth century, became the fashion; the awareness of masses of disaffected laboring poor in the towns provided sufficient motivation. During the 1840's, when 1,409 of the new churches were erected and the building rate reached its peak, the increase in the rate of new sittings (11·3 per cent) nearly equalled, for the first time, the rate of population growth (12·6 per cent). In the larger towns sittings actually increased by more than 24 per cent, exceeding the overall rate of urban population growth by some 5 per cent. By mid-century an additional 836,000 sittings had been added to the 260,000 places provided between 1818 and 1832.[3] Nearly three-quarters of them were in the larger towns of the country.

In spite of the massive efforts of the Church to provide places for all Englishmen wishing to attend Anglican services, its efforts were steadily diluted by the much more rapid growth of the population. At the opening of the century, it was estimated that the Establishment could accommodate very nearly half (48·2) the people in England and Wales; fifty years later, it could accommodate less than a third (29·6). Although the Church increased its total provision by 24 per cent, the population grew four times as fast (101·6 per cent), and, with the exception of the 1840's, church extension never came close to the pace set by striking decennial rates of growth. The situation was, of course, considerably worse in the larger towns, where the rates of increase of population and

[1] *Parl. Ps.* (1831–2), XXIII, 309.
[2] *Census*, 1851, *Religious Worship*, 13.   [3] *Ibid.*, 75–76.

church facilities were the greatest; by 1851 only about one-fifth (21·6 per cent) of urban inhabitants were provided a place in an Anglican establishment. Although approximately half the population by that time lived in towns, the number of town churches and sittings was still considerably less than that in rural areas. Of 14,077 churches and chapels in 1851, only 3,457 of them were in large town districts. They provided sittings for nearly two million people as compared to the approximately 3,300,000 sittings available in country districts.[1]

The enormity of the problem weighed heavily upon the bench. Statistical returns, depressing enough by themselves, were exaggerated by a lack of sophisticated treatment. All too often, churchmen and their critics simply counted the number of churches and sittings and compared them with the number of people in a given district. In contrast to the religious census of 1851, they failed to take into account the age-level of the population and the number of people incapacitated by illness or old age, and lacked any real notion of how many people were worshipping in Dissenter chapels. Although Horace Mann and his statisticians concluded that approximately 58 per cent of the population could have attended religious worship on census Sunday, most worried bishops had a limited understanding of a realistic ratio of population to sittings.[2] While they might have understood that ideally there should be one church for every one or two thousand people with sittings for 50 or 60 per cent of the population, they often spoke as if there should be provision on a *per capita* basis for the entire population.

Their despair was none the less real; especially in the 1830's when the air was filled with threats of disestablishment, criticisms of glaring Church inadequacies, and schemes for basic reform. Henry Ryder, surveying his diocese of Lichfield-Coventry, in 1832, recognized that, in spite of liberal grants of money to provide new sittings in Birmingham, Derby, Coventry and Wolverhampton, no more than one-fifth of the populace could be accommodated. Of the 320,000 places available for a population of over one and a half million, most of them poor laborers, less than one-fourth were free. 'What numerous families, what densely-peopled alleys, what extensive quarters must too probably remain ignorant of their appointed minister, unconscious of his desires, and inaccessible to his efforts, for their salvation, and even almost unacquainted with his name!'[3] What primarily troubled the Evangelical Ryder was that those people would likely go to hell.

With the pressures upon them greater than ever, the bishops were often overwhelmed by the realities of the urban ministry. Whatever optimism they might have felt in the previous decade was fast disappearing. As C. R. Sumner studied the evidence of 'the dense mass of

[1] *Ibid.*　　　　　　　　　　　　　[2] *Ibid.*, 57–60.
[3] Ryder, *Charge* (1832), 30–31.

population' which had so suddenly arisen, he noted only nine ministers for the 91,500 people in the Southwark parish of his diocese of Winchester, and a similar ratio in Lambeth and Portsea. In one Surrey parish not one in forty could be seated; in another there were only 150 free sittings for fourteen thousand. Parochial religion was rapidly being destroyed. 'The shepherd, in too many instances, is so far from being able to know his own sheep, that he can scarcely count them. . . . He is disabled by the magnitude of his charge. . . .' The result is a 'neglected population, and an uneducated community . . . without check or religious restraint . . .'. A traditional and fundamental bond of social cohesion was being stretched to the breaking-point, for, as Sumner recognized, 'there is no sympathy or bond of holy union between pastor and people; [it is] despised and disowned, motives are suspect, confidence is withdrawn, respect is violated,' and the classes of society are full of enmity.[1]

Sumner reflected the episcopacy's growing awareness that the impact of urbanization upon their church was but a part of a social change they were only beginning to understand. Although Church leaders had recognized the extent of urban growth during the preceding quarter-century, few really understood its possible impact upon the traditional structure of the Church in society. They were little preoccupied with problems peculiar to the urban ministry, believing that increased population simply required increased numbers of clergy and churches. As early as 1819, however, Henry Phillpotts, troubled by disturbances in the manufacturing towns, particularly the 'uprising' on St Peter's Field, Manchester, implied that since the Church's structure and orientation was essentially rural and agricultural it could not conceivably function with the same effectiveness among the masses of industrial towns. His lifelong campaign against Poor Law reform was motivated in part by his belief that the end of outdoor relief would encourage the poor to emigrate to the towns, thereby removing 'the most numerous and the most ignorant part of the people still further . . . from the reach of religious instruction, and communication with their spiritual guides'.[2] The cities, he felt, were antithetical to the Establishment's close working alliance of gentry and clergy, for purposes of social restraint and order. As an old-school, Eldonite Tory, Phillpotts was never able to forgive the social and economic developments that created urban England and drew the lower orders from the Church. Twenty-five years later, still worried about the imminence of revolution and class warfare, he decried that materialistic motives, rather than 'Christian love and foresight', had animated 'the founders of our manufacturing greatness . . .'. He cursed

[1] C. R. Sumner, *A Charge Delivered to the Clergy of the Diocese of Winchester in October, 1833* (1834), 16–18.

[2] Phillpotts, *Letter to Bourne* (1819), 26.

the State's niggardly refusal of means to restrain spiritually 'the millions whom it has called into being for its own money-seeking purposes . . .'.[1] In 1845, as in 1819, Phillpotts was unable to see that the social implications of economic change might require the Church to establish a more meaningful relationship with the laboring poor than one based primarily upon control and regulation.

Without sharing the Bishop of Exeter's anger and inflexibility, the worried Archbishop Howley nevertheless shared the frustration, fear, and even despair of many older prelates concerning the towns. An early supporter of Church extension, Howley had long been involved with the Church Building Society's Commissioners, such as Joshua Watson, who administered the legislature's grants. Conscious, however, that relatively little progress had been made in the towns 'from the prevalence of Dissent, to the want of due provision for the spiritual care of populous places', Howley sadly confessed in a letter to Peel in 1835, that 'the greatest misfortune to the Church [was] . . . the accumulated population of large towns, which from its denseness and the peculiarity of its character can never enjoy the full benefits of religious instruction . . .'.[2] Even after the passage of numerous Church reform measures during the next five years, Howley still felt that the Church could never cope with a social structure so radically altered as to cause 'an evil of [such] formidable magnitude, destructive, as far as it extends, of the efficiency of our Church—the inadequacy of her means for the entire accomplishment of the purposes implied in a National Establishment'. It worried him that so many churchmen in the less populous counties were still unaware that 'the spiritual destitution existing in parts of the kingdom is truly appalling'. After more than two decades of expansion into urban areas the Church was still unable to cope with the changes in society. 'We can hardly conceive the want of religious ministrations which is felt in the districts where hundreds of thousands of poor and ignorant workmen, collected from all parts of the country, are employed in mines or manufactories, without places of worship for public devotion, and beyond the reach of pastoral care. . . .' Sadly, he resigned himself to the realization that irrespective of the Church's best intentions and efforts, 'multitudes must necessarily be left in a state of heathen darkness'.[3]

Well might the archbishop despair when the bishop of the largest (in area) diocese in the country (Lincoln) did not recognize until 1838 the seriousness of urban difficulties. Kaye, a devoted, hard-working prelate, confessed in an open letter to Howley that it was only as a member of the newly established Ecclesiastical Commission that he formed an

[1] Phillpotts, *Charge* (1845), 52–53.

[2] 21 Jan. 1835, *Peel Ps.*, Add. MS. 40411, f. 15, and 30 Jan., Add. MS. 40412, ff. 207–8.

[3] Howley, *Charge* (1840), 19–20.

'adequate conception of the destitution of the manufacturing districts and of the large towns . . .'.[1] Such ignorance seems all the more amazing when, since 1815, the problems had been openly discussed and referred to in episcopal charges and sermons as well as in respected reform proposals filled with jarring statistics about the lack of Church facilities in the towns. In 1834 Blomfield, who recommended Kaye as an Ecclesiastical Commissioner, had described the north-east districts of London where the ratio of churches to population was one to nineteen thousand, and of clergy one to fourteen thousand. He gave similar examples for parts of Yorkshire, Staffordshire and Lancashire.[2] While compiling the second *Report* with the Ecclesiastical Commission, Kaye learned that in 1836 the diocese of Lichfield and Coventry, with a total of 235,000 people in sixteen parishes or districts of ten thousand and over, had facilities for a maximum of about 29,000. In some of these areas the ratio of seats to population was one to fourteen, with many closed to the poor.[3] Although shocked, the Bishop of Lincoln could have prepared himself four years earlier by reading Bishop Ryder's *Charge* describing similar conditions in the diocese.[4] The jolt was sufficient to make Kaye a Church reformer who accepted the harsh reality that the Establishment might have to act alone and draw upon its own resources. After twenty years on the bench, paralleling the greatest period of industrial, social and demographic change in the nation's history, Bishop Kaye sadly conceded that much political power had shifted to the towns.[5] Thus, 'of the present generation many have been estranged from us; some it is to be feared by our own remissions; more by our inability to supply the spiritual wants of the rapidly increasing population'.[6]

If such a realization was painful to a moderate Tory High Churchman like John Kaye, it was sheer agony for a more conservative prelate like James Monk of Gloucester. Only the efforts of an old Cambridge classmate and fellow classicist like Blomfield could persuade Monk to consider the evidence and implications of the position of the Church in urban districts. When, as another of the Bishop of London's recommended appointees to the Ecclesiastical Commission, he was confronted with the formidable realities of religious life in the towns, he wavered,

[1] J. Kaye, *A Letter to His Grace the Archbishop of Canterbury, On the Recommendations of the Ecclesiastical Commission* (1838), in *Nine Charges* (1854), 171.

[2] C. J. Blomfield, *A Charge Delivered to the Clergy of the Diocese of London . . . in MDCCCXXXIV* (1834), 13–14.

[3] Eccles. Duties and Rev. Comm., *Report* (1836), 60.

[4] Ryder, *Charge* (1832), 28–29.

[5] Kaye, *Letter to Archbishop* (1838), 171–3.

[6] Kaye, *Charge* (1840), 32.

broke and fled disconsolate into the camp of the reformers. He even joined Kaye in 1840 in endorsing the unpalatable proposal to reduce the number of cathedral stalls and divert the released resources for use in urban districts.[1] Such endorsements were especially irritating to High Churchmen who were constitutionally unable to swallow the repeated charges by Evangelicals, Dissenters and secular opponents that the Church, through some inner flaw, had somehow failed to exercise its ministry. Monk, as most Tory churchmen of like mind, believed that the State was the villain: first, by allowing and participating in the looting and confiscation of Church property during the Reformation, and then by not providing the Establishment with the necessary means to over-come such severe losses. In 1835 he typically opposed the redistribution of Church wealth and was furious at the common assertion that ministers could be divided into 'working clergy' and the rest.[2] He was not unaware of difficulties caused by urban population increases and the insufficiency of parochial facilities, nor did he deny the inability of the Church to cope with the problem; but it was another five years before he and many of his episcopal brethren were willing to agree that no matter how much they might decry the rapaciousness and betrayal of the State (especially a Whig State), the Church had to turn inward if it was to expand its ministry into the blighted, heathen towns that were altering the face of the Christian England they had always known.

Even in defeat, however, Monk refused to acknowledge that the Church was perhaps responsible for its failures in the towns. The causes, as he saw them by 1841, were social and economic, as well as political, and beyond the control of a Church dependent upon legislative support. He was still unable to concede to the numerous accusations that the problems of the day largely resulted from 'a cold, lukewarm, and heart-less performance of clerical duties [that began] during the eighteenth century'. In spite of the mountains of evidence compiled by parlia-mentary committees, the Privy Council, diocesan queries and endless articles and essays all describing the evils and extent of non-residence, pluralism, single services, and the paucity of communicants, Monk still felt the evidence was insufficient to show that ministers had ever been 'negligent in their duties, or deficient in zeal and piety'. The Church was but another victim of expanding commercial and manufacturing interests that rapidly assembled masses of population in towns and districts where spiritual facilities were completely inadequate. Secular proprietary interests, the bishop added, compounded the difficulties by renting pews and sittings for the exclusive use of opulent families and

[1] *Hansard*, LV (1840), 1016–17, 1021.

[2] J. Monk, *A Charge Delivered to the Clergy of the Diocese of Gloucester ... in MDCCCXXXV* (1835), 6–8.

their servants. He admitted that it was strange that the extent and implications of the problem were not really recognized 'until somewhat more than twenty years ago; when churchmen seemed suddenly to awake, as from a long trance, and to recognize the duty of providing the means of worship for the multiplied inhabitants of the land'. 'Even then', he added, 'the actual enormity of the evil was but imperfectly understood.'[1]

More recalcitrant bishops, like Phillpotts, saw nothing strange or sudden in the awareness of the problem. The government's approach to the laboring poor had foolishly neglected the role of the Church when it implemented policies based on principles of political economy—a 'Godless, heartless and empty alternative' to spiritual understanding, providing neither comfort, security, nor social tranquillity. As a result, a vast working population had been allowed to grow up, of which, according to the Church Commissioners in 1836, over 1,330,000 were utterly deprived of a place to worship. Phillpotts angrily lashed out at a House of Commons decision to grant £150,000 *per annum* to provide five thousand more soldiers to control the poor. The bishop did not deny the danger that prompted such a measure, but took the opportunity to point out that the sum involved was 'enough to maintain 500 or 600 ministers of God's Word—Heralds of the Gospel of Peace!' As a former clerical magistrate, Phillpotts thought he knew the complementary virtues of both approaches. How have we come to such 'a wretched situation?' he asked. How have we failed 'to do our duty to God, and to our poor countrymen?' Who is to blame for 'the enormous wrongs which our national avarice—called by politicians "our social system",—has inflicted upon the bodies, and alas! upon the souls, of hundreds of thousands of our fellow-countrymen?' It is, he solemnly intoned, 'the fault of almost all the Governments, and of all the people of this land during the last half-century'.[2]

The crusty Bishop of Exeter's concern for the laboring poor was largely motivated by his fierce hatred of political economy and the Whig politicians, whom he constantly accused of trying to establish it as a new faith. Both, as far as he was concerned, were manifestations of the commercial and industrial corruption of a stable, Tory, landed society in which both Church and State were aware of their obligations to feed 'the lambs of Christ'. But the liberal offerings of the new age were a cruel, comfortless gruel to an already grossly neglected population. Phillpotts keenly felt that the 'great question of the day is, *who* shall feed these lambs?, but in it is involved an incalculably greater, *what food* shall

[1] J. Monk, *A Charge Delivered to the Clergy of the Diocese of Gloucester and Bristol . . . in August and September MDCCCXLI* (1841), 18–19.

[2] H. Phillpotts, *Charge Delivered to the Clergy of the Diocese of Exeter . . . 1839* (1839), 44–45.

they be fed?'[1] As one of the bitterest and most enduring opponents of the Church reform measures enacted by the Ecclesiastical Commissioners, there was no question in the Bishop of Exeter's mind as to the diet that would best be religiously and socially digestible.

Critical Tractarians and uncritical, unmalleable defenders of the ecclesiastical *status quo* could take comfort in the slashing, impassioned arguments raised by Phillpotts. But by the end of the 1830's most of his episcopal brethren had ceased cursing the whirlwind and were genuinely trying to understand the changes in their society and work out some safe and reasonable way for the Church to adjust with a minimum of discomfort for its settled members. Older High Church Tory bishops like Blomfield recognized in 1834 that 'we are . . . attempting to do the work of evangelists, for a population of more than 14 millions, with a machinery originally constructed for a very small portion of that number . . .' and distributed according to a bygone age. But even if 'the population and the clergy were equally distributed over the whole superficial territory of the Church, that machinery would not be sufficient for more than 11 millions, allowing each clergyman to have the care of 1,000 souls'.[2] Blomfield's mechanistic allusions to Church organization indicate his determination to bring the Establishment into line with a very different England than the one for which it was constructed. Newer Broad Church Whig bishops such as Edward Maltby were also analyzing more carefully than ever before the social problems of their dioceses. During his primary visit in 1837 to Durham he recognized how far the enlarged but scattered population had spread from the existing churches. In contrast to his unyielding predecessor, Van Mildert, Maltby understood that he administered a see in which 'rapid social movement' was a way of life for large numbers of people who flocked to new coal-mines on 'once barren moors'. He realized, as did more and more of his contemporaries, that the railroads would encourage even greater migration. It meant that 'cottages are quickly built, people flock in, but as they diligently seek their daily bread, they seek in vain for that bread, which sustains the vital principle even to everlasting ages'.[3]

Future bishops, such as Thomas Vowler Short, also understood that the urban ministry presented very different problems for the Church. It had to cope not only with larger numbers, but without that 'personal connexion, which in most country parishes forms a bond of union between all classes of society, which is a pleasure to the rich and a comfort to the poor, and which contributes to the spiritual advantages of both'.[4] He saw, in other words, what Phillpotts perceived a decade

---

[1] *Ibid.*, 48.   [2] Blomfield, *Charge* (1834), 14.

[3] E. Maltby, *A Charge to the Clergy of the Diocese of Durham, at the Primary Visitation . . . 1837* (1837), 7.

[4] Short, *Parochialia*, 20.

and a half earlier: the traditional alliance of gentry and clergy was not applicable to the towns. Also, the parochial church was no longer a center of social interchange where the inferior orders met their betters in a spirit of gratitude and benevolence. Unlike the Bishop of Exeter, however, Short was unwilling to satisfy himself with lamentations, railings and self-righteous accusations of conspiracy and betrayal. He was more typical in his belief that, like it or not, change and progress were an inevitable condition confronting the Church leaders of his generation. Either they attempted to cope with it in its new urban setting, or they would be destroyed.

4. CHURCH ATTENDANCE

As bishops became more aware of the fluidity and changing characteristics of English society, several also became less satisfied with the analyses and approaches adopted by the Church. Initially most had supported the conclusion that the basic problem was a lack of churches in overpopulated areas and warmly endorsed the Additional Churches Act and the efforts of the Church Building Society. In one diocese after another, building societies were established to accelerate the program. But it was clear to some Church leaders that the problem was more complex. The spread of either revivalism or religious indifference had been facilitated in large measure by the gross neglect of the parochial clergy, not the absence of church facilities. By the last decade of the eighteenth century even bishops complained about the large numbers of people who were outside the Church and attributed the cause not to a lack of facilities, but to a want of spiritual effort in the face of revivalistic seductions or religious apathy.

In 1790, Bishop Porteus recognized 'that some exertions rather more than common are necessary to awaken in the general mass of the people that sense of duty, and ardour of devotion, which seem almost extinguished in their breasts . . .'. He knew that the spiritual life of the 'lower classes of the community' had grievously deteriorated in many urban parishes, and urged that reinvigoration start at once before the poor were entirely beyond redemption.[1] Nine years later Bishop Cleaver of Chester more specifically complained that in one parish in his diocese 'above 40,000 persons . . . pass the Lord's day without attention to public worship under any mode whatever'. It was not a question of these people being lured away by Dissenters, nor was there any blame attributed to a lack of sittings. There was, as Cleaver saw it, simply a general decline of religious influence in the lives of a great number of people.[2] The report made by the Lincolnshire clergy the same year on their more rural diocese made the same general complaint, and

[1] Porteus, *Charge* (1790), 11, 14.   [2] Cleaver, *Charge* (1799), 10–11.

did not suggest that inadequate physical facilities were in any way responsible.

The debates, reports and legislative enactments in the early nineteenth century to improve clerical residence and increase the number and availability of religious services indicate an awareness that the fundamental problem of the Church was indeed at the parochial level, where a great many clergymen over the preceding century had lost effective contact with their parishioners. While a slowly reviving Church sought to rectify that problem, it was confronted with the realities of even more sensational deficiencies in rapidly expanding populous areas. The ensuing statistical flood of evidence, together with the simplified solution of providing more churches and sittings as quickly as possible, tended at first to submerge the realities of existing parochial deficiencies, and the hard fact that a great many Englishmen were not attending the churches already provided. Evangelical and secular critics did not hesitate to point this out. But the bishops, High Church enough to overvalue the importance of the visible church, were caught up in the drive for extension and paid little attention. From their vantage-point, the parochial ministry and its services were being improved as quickly as prudence allowed, and without the introduction of dangerous enthusiastic innovations. In the meantime, they argued, the construction of new churches and the provision for new sittings was a direct, safe way to bring the teachings of the Church into the heart of populous areas. Such an argument was predicated upon the vague assumption that if properly located, and open to the poor, the churches would somehow draw the spiritually starved to their holy tables, where a feast of eternal nourishment awaited them. After the distress, unrest and violence of the post-war years, few Church leaders were unaware that the laboring multitudes were also hungry for less exalted fare. Most prelates, however, were confident, while some merely hoped, that ravenous appetites would be appeased once they had tasted the soul-filling fruits of religious understanding and contentment.

Painfully some bishops began to realize that the laboring poor were not rushing to gorge themselves on the fare offered in the new and enlarged places of worship. The new Bishop of Gloucester (1824–30), Christopher Bethell, was the first prelate to acknowledge the fact.[1] While reviewing his primary visitation returns in 1825 he made the usual references to the need for more church building in enlarged parishes, but then recognized that even where accommodation already sufficed, there

---

[1] C. Bethell (1773–1859), son of a Surrey clergyman, educated at Cambridge, Dean of Chichester (1814–30). An able, active High Churchman, he was elevated to Gloucester by Liverpool in 1824 and briefly, by Wellington, to Exeter in 1830. When Bangor suddenly opened he was quickly translated to that more lucrative see (1830–59).

were a great many empty seats. As a High Churchman succeeding the first Evangelical bishop, Henry Ryder, in a diocese long associated with Methodist and Evangelical revivalism, Bethell's emphasis on unity of doctrine, form and discipline was greeted with little approval. Underlying his determination to enforce residence, promote additional services, establish national schools, and systematically catechize the young, however, was his awareness of the partially-filled churches throughout his new see. Even Evangelicals could agree with his conclusion that empty sittings would remain until a revived ministry could show the way to them.[1]

Another of the new generation, C. R. Sumner, was similarly troubled when he assumed his very brief tenure at Llandaff in 1827. Sumner, perhaps the most statistically-minded member of the bench, quickly sent out circular queries to his clergy and compiled the returns. Llandaff, he realized, was a much-neglected diocese with a long history of non-residence, but he was jolted upon discovering how bad things actually were. Although criticizing the lack of churches in populous mining areas, he quickly admitted that accommodation had little to do with attendance. Citing the example of three districts with more than enough sittings for their 936 inhabitants, the Bishop reported that only fifty attended, less than half of whom were communicants. In two other larger parishes of 1,646, no more than sixty attended church, while in five other parishes containing over 10,000 people, 'the deficiency is more deplorable' since only 260 appear at services and less than a third as communicants. The pattern was repeated throughout the entire diocese where, of 150,000 people (1821 Census), less than 20,000 worshipped in their parochial church, of whom only 4,134 were communicants.[2]

While preaching the general episcopal line that church extension was needed, Sumner knew that the causes for such conditions lay elsewhere: years of non-residence, negligent clergymen, the growth of a mining population away from existing facilities, and the vigorous proselytizing by Methodists and Dissenters had all contributed to the dreadful situation. But the young bishop realized that most of those absent from the Established churches were not worshipping elsewhere. They were not worshipping at all.[3] Sumner probably understood this more clearly than any of his episcopal brethren in the first half of the century, for, in spite of massive Church efforts, his private statistical enquiries repeatedly showed what the general religious census of 1851 was finally to prove:

[1] C. Bethell, *A Charge Delivered At the Primary Visitation of the Diocese of Gloucester . . . 1825* (Gloucester, 1825), 15–16.

[2] C. R. Sumner, *A Charge Delivered to the Clergy of the Diocese of Llandaff, in September, 1827 . . .* (1827), 14.

[3] *Ibid.,* 15.

the laboring poor were essentially indifferent to religion.[1] But Sumner was always somewhat of a pessimist, brooding about the statistical probabilities of his dying before his next visitation and calculating the percentage of clergy who had expired since his last one. With some surprise he announced in 1850 that he had already exceeded by four years the average term (17 years) of Winchester bishops since the Reformation, and lamented, county by county, all those of his clergy who had been less successful in overcoming the fatal odds.[2]

His elder brother at Chester, however, rarely indulged in such gloomy ruminations, though he was not much more optimistic about the state of the Church. The tumult and violence surrounding the passage of the Reform Bill caused him to pause and evaluate the degree of the Establishment's success during the preceding decade. He found that his brother's distressing calculations and conclusions about conditions in Llandaff and Winchester were even more applicable to his huge manufacturing diocese. His earlier confident assumptions that rapid population growth was part of a divine scheme of things, ultimately beneficial, were at least temporarily shaken. In spite of all the resources expended by voluntary and governmental sources, for the previous fifteen years church extension had been unable to approach the rate of population growth. Although forty-one new churches had been built in Lancashire alone, less than one-fifth of the population could be seated. The situation was far worse in the cities. Sumner, for the first time, began to argue that the problem was far too serious and complex to be solved by merely building new churches. It was no longer possible to take some negative comfort in the likelihood 'that if the people are not in the established churches, they are in the dissenting chapels, and are therefore not destitute of religious instruction. The truth is not so', the bishop warned his clergy. 'The mass of the ADULT manufacturing population is . . . without religious instruction of any kind. . . .'[3]

A grave change in English society had occurred almost imperceptibly during his lifetime. Apathy and unbelief had become a lower-class, uneducated way of life, in contrast to the eighteenth century, where it had flourished among the wealthy, the fashionable and the educated.

The unbelief of the present day has a very peculiar character. It is commonly disowned by the man of education and reflection: he may live irreligiously, but he is seldom irreligious upon principle, or through conviction. But infidelity is openly avowed by those who have no

[1] See Sumner's *Charge* (1833), 23–24; *A Charge Delivered to the Clergy of the Diocese of Winchester . . . 1837* (1837), 21–22; *A Charge Delivered . . . 1850* (1850), 32–33, 42.

[2] Sumner, *Charge* (1850), 21, 23–24.

[3] J. B. Sumner, *A Charge Delivered to the Clergy of the Diocese of Chester . . . MDCCCXXXII* (1832), xii.

knowledge, or only a smattering of knowledge. . . . To this we owe the grievous consequence, that the unbelief of the lower classes in the present day, is not merely the unbelief of vicious practice. Their principles are undermined: which renders the evil more serious, and the remedy more difficult.[1]

Sumner did not doubt that this descent of indifference and irreligion was a far greater social evil than it had been when practised by people with everything to lose by the disruption of society.

The careless apathy, or the dissolute sensuality of former times, though it had as much ungodliness in it as may be found now, was far less dangerous. Our lot has been cast upon a period, when there is nothing neutral. Every man who is not the friend, is the enemy of religion.

Like some of his episcopal contemporaries, Sumner believed that he and his generation were fated to reap the harvest of neglect, sown by earlier generations of people 'occupied with other things . . .'. Consequently, still another generation had grown up and multiplied on every side. 'That generation is now the population of our towns and cities: and the present age is lamenting, when too late, and vainly endeavouring to repair, the culpable indifference of those who lived before them.' Confronted with the masses of workers, artisans and shopkeepers who peopled Lancashire and the North and West Riding portions of Yorkshire, Sumner felt overwhelmed. He, too, realized that the construction of new churches had made little impact on 'those crowded districts where multitudes keep one another in countenance'.[2] and frankly doubted that a vast expenditure on more places of worship during the present generation 'would . . . add five hundred persons to the church'.[3]

High Churchmen, who had placed much confidence in extension, and who dominated the Church Building Society, were deeply troubled by such accounts. They agreed to the extent of exonerating their own generation, and acknowledging, as did Bishop Monk of Gloucester, that 'it was only a few years ago that . . . the nation appeared to wake as from a trance, and discovered, that for an hundred years very little addition had been made to our churches, while the population had everywhere increased . . .'. But he refused to concede to Evangelical claims of massive apathy and irreligion among the lower orders, and was sure that new churches were being filled as rapidly as they were completed. This surety convinced him that the success of Dissent in previous years was not in any way an indication of aversion to 'our religion', but rather a result of exclusion.[4]

Monk presented no evidence. His predecessors at Gloucester,

[1] *Ibid.*, 9–10.   [2] *Ibid.*, 11–13.   [3] *Ibid.*, xiii.
[4] J. Monk, *A Sermon Preached . . . June III, MDCCCXXX, At the Yearly Meeting of the Children of the Charity Schools . . .* (1830), 13.

Christopher Bethell and Henry Ryder, had found nothing to support their successor's optimistic analysis. Ryder, in his larger and more industrialized diocese of Lichfield-Coventry, found even less reason for such confidence. Since his translation from Gloucester eight years before, in 1824, he had cut non-residency by one-ninth, added forty new clergymen, and increased the number of churches and chapels providing double services on Sunday from 263 to 354. In the same period he had also consecrated twenty new churches and two that were completely rebuilt, while ten more were under construction. This meant some 45,000 new sittings. Yet Ryder knew that many of these, as well as the older places, would be only partially filled. Existing churches were filled to no more than one-third their capacity. Less than one-quarter of those attending received communion, while no more than one-twelfth of the adult population who might have been expected to come did so. The bishop, who himself often preached and even taught Sunday school in Lichfield, was saddened by this 'grievous disproportion' and saw it as 'an unfavourable sign, demanding on our part a searching examination into the cause . . .'.[1]

Many of the lesser clergy, usually High Church and in rural parishes, continued to refute such assertions. The Reverend Thomas Thorp, Senior Dean of Trinity College, Cambridge, endorsed their views when he bluntly asserted in 1834 that all the churches, new as well as old, were crowded, and encouraged even greater support for the Church Building Society.[2] With the exception of Monk, no bishop, not even Thorp's hopelessly complacent diocesan, Bowyer Edward Sparke, made such confident pronouncements on the state of the Church. Monk, moreover, by strongly defending the new churches, somehow hoped he could will their success, for he clearly lacked the accumulated evidence being presented in other dioceses. In fact, only after his experience as one of the Ecclesiastical Commissioners did he relent and finally, in 1841, call for a systematic statistical analysis of his newly combined See of Gloucester and Bristol.[3] By then he had almost come to realize that the availability of free seats was not the inducement to lower-class worship that he had long assumed it to be.[4]

Even in the face of their own statistical compilations, however, some prelates missed the point. For example, Richard Bagot, the High Church Bishop of Oxford and early friend of the Tractarians, noted in 1834 that there were over twenty thousand empty seats in 177 of 243 churches he surveyed; yet he complained that the diocese had not kept

[1] Ryder, *Charge* (1832), 32, 35–36.
[2] T. Thorp, *On Religious Education. A Sermon Preached . . . April 27, 1834 In Aid of the King's Letter for the Incorporated Society for the Enlarging, Building and Repairing of Churches and Chapels* (Cambridge, 1834), 20.
[3] Monk, *Charge* (1841), 25.   [4] *Ibid.*, 8.

up with the population increase since the beginning of the century.[1] Later, correlating the rise of Dissent in the diocese with a lack of church building, he proceeded to prove that the church was doing very well and that there had been no proportional increase in the number of Dissenters.[2] Although over one-third of the existing facilities were not being utilized, Bagot still rejoiced at the work of the Church Building Society and urged it be given greater support than ever. Considering that, of the 115,000 people in the parishes studied, less than 7,000 were communicants,[3] it is not surprising that the Bishop's sanguine conclusions were not very convincing to worried, and perhaps more realistic, defenders of the Establishment.

The uneasiness and doubts about the efficacy of concentrating on church extension as the principal way of coping with the enlarged population did not diminish the efforts of its advocates. If anything, they were intensified. When it became clear that the reformed House of Commons was unwilling to vote more church building funds, voluntary efforts more than compensated for the diminished support. Over £3,000,000 in voluntary donations were expended in the 1830's and 1840's.[4] The latter decade was the greatest period of church building in the nation's history. In too many instances the churches were built with inadequate endowments, forcing the minister to resort to a self-defeating exclusionary system of pew rents. Other new churches lacked ministers for months on end.[5] But still the buildings went up.

Some of the earlier pessimism began to abate. John Bird Sumner, who in 1832 despaired of the Church in his industrial diocese, a decade later began to see some hope. In spite of his Evangelical doubts, the Bishop of Chester had been a tireless promoter of church extension in the diocese. By 1841, 170 new churches had been built and clergy provided, especially in Liverpool and Manchester.[6] Three years later another twenty-six buildings had been consecrated and, through the efforts of various societies, more than one hundred new curates joined the growing number of lay and clerical district visitors seeking to revive parochial life.[7] Sumner was more hopeful than ever 'that instead of being overwhelmed by the swelling tide of population, we might be prepared to receive it as our own'. He felt that there were even some gratifying indications 'that we are thus recovering our population to the church'.[8] Sumner's vigorous efforts on behalf of church extension were always tempered by his deep-seated conviction that the visible presence of the church must be preceded by its spiritual presence in the hearts of

---

[1] Bagot, *Charge* (1834), 14–15. [2] *Ibid.,* 20. [3] *Ibid.,* 14.
[4] *Census*, 1851, *Religious Worship*, 75. [5] Best, *Temporal Pillars*, 354–5.
[6] Sumner, *A Charge Delivered to the Clergy of the Diocese of Chester . . . MDCCCXLI* (1841), 11–12.
[7] Sumner, *Charge* (1844), 11–12. [8] Sumner, *Charge* (1838), 21–22.

men. He shared the Evangelical emphasis on the true Church as revealed in Scripture, and it was through an activist preaching ministry assisted by the laity teaching the Gospel at home and throughout the parish at every opportunity that the laboring masses would be redeemed from apathy and unbelief. The physical church, with its ritual, form and organization, while the House of God, was by no means His only dwelling-place, and until Christ entered the hearts of men, it was unlikely that they would enter the newly consecrated edifices in their midst. Nevertheless, Sumner and other Evangelicals worked as hard as High Churchmen like Bishop Blomfield to provide places for the long-neglected flocks of poor lost sheep when, and if, they were ready to return to the fold.[1]

Blomfield, as the main episcopal advocate of Church reform, was painfully aware of the gross parochial deficiencies that had long undermined the effectiveness of old churches and continued to dilute the impact of the new. But his High Church concepts of the Establishment, and his strong belief in the necessity of episcopal and hierarchical organizational authority, caused him to place much greater emphasis on the visible physical manifestations of religion. The Church, with its history, liturgy, and life-giving authority, must stand, fully in evidence, in the midst of all communities so that it could both impress and humble all men. Moreover, to Blomfield, the physical church represented some hope of unity among a clergy and laity whose outlook, inclinations and theology were so fragmented that a meaningful dialogue between them was virtually impossible; and whose multifarious divisions seriously undermined the Establishment's effectiveness and authority. If the bishop found little practical comfort in the exclusiveness of early Tractarian writings, he certainly welcomed their enhancement of the physical church and hierarchical authority.

In the course of his long tenure at London, Blomfield consecrated nearly two hundred new churches.[2] When, in 1836, it became clear that the Church could no longer expect any repetition of 'the wise but short-lived munificence of the legislature', he copied the example of Manchester and established a voluntary Metropolis Churches Fund to solicit contributions for additional construction. He had originally hoped that it would be supported by a municipal levy of twopence a ton on coal, but soon discovered that the municipal corporations were no more co-operative than the national government.[3] Undaunted Blomfield

[1] J. B. Sumner, 'A Sermon Preached . . . May 7, 1838', in Church Pastoral Aid Society, *Report of the Committee . . . 8 May 1838* (1838), 12.

[2] Blomfield, *Memoir*, I, 250.

[3] C. J. Blomfield, *Proposals For the Creation of a Fund to be Applied to the Building and Endowment of Additional Churches in the Metropolis* (1836), 9, 14–15.

within ten years had collected £179,855. In addition he raised another £60,000 to build ten churches in Bethnal Green, where 70,000 people were served by three ministers in two churches. In those first ten years Blomfield's efforts enlarged the seating capacity in the churches and chapels of the Metropolis by 65,000. In the same period, he frustratingly announced, the population had grown by 300,000, and doubted if one-quarter of the 2,000,000 people in the area could be accommodated. Again he appealed for governmental aid, if not for religious, at least for economical reasons, pointing to the money that would be saved on prisons and convict emigration if the poor were in church.[1]

If Peel had been unwilling to approach Parliament on the matter, it could hardly be expected that Lord John Russell would come to the Establishment's aid. Blomfield, of course, knew this, but his rhetoric, reinforced by repeated disturbances in the manufacturing districts and the fear of revolution, aided the cause. In spite of suffering a stroke in 1847, Blomfield continued to drum up another £100,000 and 35,000 more sittings before his retirement and death in 1856.[2] At one point he was consecrating so many churches that some hostile papers suggested that he was receiving payment. Indignantly he assured a worried contributor to the Metropolis Churches Fund that not only was the charge untrue, but every new church actually cost him fifty to one hundred pounds in contributions.[3]

Blomfield was the dean of church-building bishops, but it was a policy that was pursued enthusiastically by most of his colleagues, irrespective of party persuasion, and handsomely supported by the laity. Since the opening of the century, the Establishment had built 2,529 churches and chapels at a cost of £9,087,000, of which more than £7,423,000 came from voluntary donations.[4] In addition, many thousands of seats were added to existing buildings to provide for the increasing population of the district. Yet on the basis of the continuing growth and shift of population distribution, there was still a deficiency of at least 1,644,734 sittings.[5] Considering the extent of torpor and neglect that plagued the

[1] C. J. Blomfield, *A Charge Delivered to the Clergy of the Diocese of London . . . in October MDCCCXLVI* (1846).

[2] C. J. Blomfield, *A Charge Delivered to the Clergy of the Diocese of London . . . in November MDCCCLIV*, 2nd ed. (1854), 25.

[3] 9 Aug. 1849, Letter Copy Book 382, f. 321, *Fulham Ps.* At one point Blomfield was acquiring funds much faster than he could provide building sites and appealed to Peel to urge the Crown to sell some of its property in the populous parts of London. The existence of a church would only enhance the value of the property, he promised. 8 May 1843, *Peel Ps.* Add. MS. 40528, ff. 151–2.

[4] *Census*, 1851, *Religious Worship*, 14.

[5] *Ibid.*, 61. Also, Blomfield, *Charge* (1854), 29.

Church well into the century, and the factionalism and party strife that at times nearly paralyzed it, the amount of voluntary support it received, especially after 1832, was extraordinary. It is clear that a great number of wealthy Englishmen, whether they found it spiritually satisfying or socially and politically necessary, believed in the preservation and extension of the Establishment. High Churchmen, Low Churchmen, Broad Churchmen rallied to its support by the mid-1830's. After 1836, as the bishops thrashed out with the government the means by which the Church would in the future draw upon its own resources to cope with the enormous problems that brought it close to disestablishment and disarray, another £5,500,000 from private sources poured in to help erect still more churches among the vast urban multitudes who had grown up beyond the hearing of ministers' pleas for patience and contentment while enduring this brief passage to a better life.[1] That those multitudes might no longer be interested in the message was a possibility that Church leaders considered, but nevertheless still did not find incompatible with their zeal for the proliferation of half-empty churches.

[1] *Census*, 1851, *Religious Worship*, 14.

IX

Parochial Innovation and Reform

1. LAY VISITORS AND ADDITIONAL CURATES

Reluctantly bishops faced the accumulating evidence that many new churches in town districts were poorly attended. When, as Dr Kay (later Kay-Shuttleworth) reported from Manchester in 1832, only 'a very small number frequent the places of worship',[1] it was difficult to avoid the conclusion that additional, perhaps less formal, institutional measures would have to be adopted in order to attract the indifferent multitudes to the empty pews awaiting them. The episcopal appointments made in the post-Reform Bill era, as well as the three Evangelical prelates already on the bench, were in general more amenable to the prospect. Usually liberal in their ecclesiastical outlook, their flexibility was often a consideration in their elevation after 1832. Although in practice their support and degree of commitment to change was far from uniform, especially with regard to education, most of the newer prelates realized that the internal reforms proposed by the Ecclesiastical Commission, while necessary, were still inadequate to cope with the multifarious problems of the urban parish. The absorption of this reality by older High Church bishops was slower and proportionate to their recognition that new churches, even when served by dedicated, resident clergy, were not attracting the poor.

A realistic adaptation to the truths of parochial life in districts overwhelmed by thousands upon thousands of immigrant and native-born workers necessitated a basic rethinking of traditional parochial relation-

[1] James P. Kay, *The Moral and Physical Condition of the Working Classes Employed in the Cotton Manufacture in Manchester* (1832), 40.

316

ships. The very concept and language of parson, parish and flock were permeated with pastoral premises of a simple, rural society that had no connection whatsoever with the sprawling, teeming manufacturing districts that had spread out around the small parochial boundaries of a different age. New concepts and a new language were needed: lay reader, district visitor, city mission, outdoor evangelist, parochial redistricting—these were the terms and innovations of a modern, industrial church no longer bound by the precedent of a squirearchical society obscured by the thick and acrid smoke of thousands of smokestacks, and the dreary rows of tenements enclosing the fetid alleys of mining and manufacturing towns throughout the country. These were the terms and innovations with which the bench had to come to grips, their eighteenth-century pastoral-social values rubbed raw by the difficult realization of their irrelevancy to millions of restless and alienated Englishmen working out their own values in an environment utterly beyond the comprehension of the majority of the clergy.

Samuel Wilberforce partially understood this as he wrestled with the psychology of urban isolation—an isolation that left the rural or small-town immigrant 'absolutely lost in this peopled wilderness . . . most entirely alone . . .'. It was a world of squalor and misery in which the evils of poverty and wealth were aggravated a thousand-fold, and in which the poor man is completely and continually degraded. He sees only others like himself, and as he cannot respect them he cannot respect himself and slips into an inner isolation. Yet, 'few and highly disciplined are those who are so entirely a law unto themselves that they are not in some measure conscious of the evil effect of feeling themselves entirely unknown'. Wilberforce, of course, believed that if the poor could but see those above them (like the squire) whom they could respect, they would be less contemptuous of themselves and more exemplary in their behavior. In the populous manufacturing society of the industrial age, however, uplifting social relationships had largely disappeared, replaced by individual competition, and 'superseded by a fierce independence on the one side, and a general abandonment of care on the other'.[1] Parochial life, in the broad social as well as religious sense, had been destroyed. The laboring man, surrounded by multitudes of others like himself, no longer had a home. He was alone, without a family. This, Wilberforce believed, was the reality of urban society. The Church, he insisted, must become that family.

Wilberforce, preaching in 1844, on the eve of his elevation to Oxford, showed remarkable sensitivity and awareness of some of the implications of that vast new urban sub-culture that the Church sought to encompass without really understanding. Although offering no concrete proposals or solutions other than the restoration of some form of

[1] Wilberforce, *Charge* (1844), 12–14.

hierarchical, paternalistic social relationship centered around the Church, he, like many of his less articulate brethren, knew that such a restoration was dependent as never before upon clerical flexibility, innovation, and social involvement. Arriving at that realization had been a slow and tortuous process for the bench. Three decades earlier, when post-war prelates first became aware of the Church's serious deficiencies in populous areas, there was little inclination to encourage innovative adjustments. George Henry Law, contrasting Liverpool and Manchester in his diocese with the towns and villages of Carlisle where he had ministered and his father, Edmund, had been bishop from 1769 to 1787, was confused and worried. In 1820 he asked his clergy to consider re-arranging their churches to make more room for the poor. Perhaps, he added, some of the wealthier parishioners could be persuaded to open their locked pews to accommodate more of the lower orders. Prospects for such co-operation were not good, and Law knew it. Consequently, with great reluctance, the prelate suggested yet another plan: the intro-duction of an additional service or lecture on Sunday evening.[1]

Evangelicals had been providing double services in some parishes for several years and the utility of such efforts was slowly being recognized by the more concerned bishops of populous dioceses with inadequate church facilities. Law was one of them; like so many of his associates, however, he still distrusted measures associated with religious enthusi-asm. While post-war disturbances drove some Church leaders further from reality, others were inched closer to it; society was changing, and the Church must also change, preferably as little as possible. In recom-mending evening services, Law assured his clergy that 'no one can view with juster abhorrence than myself the rash and uplifted hand of innovation; and it was only after the most mature and anxious investi-gation, that I could bring myself to consent to . . . the smallest altera-tion, in the ancient uses of our established church'. The bishop frankly preferred that the middle and lower orders attend church together and then spend the Sabbath eve in family prayer and domestic improvement. But, he sadly acknowledged, such days were gone, especially for the inferior orders; people 'have to be occupied' or they wander away. Consequently, with 'reluctance and fear', he approved Sunday evening lectures in Chester and the large manufacturing towns of the diocese. Casting a nostalgic glance backwards, however, Law was relieved that since country areas did not need such innovation, it was not yet neces-sary that the sexes be brought out together and at a distance from their homes.[2]

Five years later, after Liverpool had honored Law's request for trans-

[1] G. H. Law, *A Charge Delivered to the Clergy of the Diocese of Chester . . . in July and August, 1820* (1820), 8.
[2] *Ibid.*, 8–9.

lation to a more lucrative see (Bath and Wells), thereby justifying the bishop's confidence that the Prime Minister would 'wish to fill up the Preferment in that manner which will best promote the credit and the interest of the Church', Law was less reluctant to extend his innovations to his new diocese.[1] Still convinced, however, like most of his colleagues, that the lower orders would flock to church if facilities were adequate, he now unhesitatingly called upon his clergy to provide two services. His experience at Chester had taught him that 'the engagements and the habits of the working classes in society, prevent the attendance at church of every part of the family at the same time: two services, [aimed] at the the one or the other of them, might admit all'. Recognizing the realities of clerical life, however, the cautious prelate, while recommending two, insisted on at least one Sunday service.[2]

By contemporary standards, Law was a hard-working, improving diocesan administrator who visited parishes, augmented livings, built churches and parsonages, and restored the Cathedral. In 1817 he established and endowed the College of St Bees for clerical candidates unable to afford university training, but who were needed in some of the more remote and disagreeable northern and Midland parishes. Like most bishops of his generation, born shortly before or early in the reign of George III, Law's concept of Church improvement (rather than reform) was largely confined to ameliorating the most glaring deficiencies of the eighteenth-century Establishment without significantly altering it. Society was changing more rapidly than standards. Although it was still possible in the 1820's to talk about adjustments, Liverpool's younger appointments and those following began to see it as more a question of innovation and reform.

When, in 1824, the ambitious Blomfield succeeded Law at Chester, it was at once clear to him that while his kindly predecessor had increased services, his excessive caution resulted in little real improvement of clerical standards or the Church's influence in populous districts of the diocese. He inherited a clergy that were, by his more stringent standards, poor, lazy, non-resident, and engaged in a variety of secular pursuits ranging from fox-hunting to running for Mayor of Macclesfield. Several parsons were notorious drunkards—one of whom, shortly after Blomfield's arrival, fell intoxicated into an open grave while attempting to perform a funeral service! The bishop, hardly amused, wrote to Joshua

---

[1] Law to Liverpool, 27 July 1820, *Liverpool Ps.,* Add. MS. 38286, ff. 284–5.

[2] G. H. Law, *A Charge Delivered to the Clergy of the Diocese of Bath and Wells . . . 1825,* 2nd ed. (1825), 12. By the time he was translated in 1824 Law had succeeded in encouraging double services in all but sixty of the 620 churches of the diocese. See C. J. Blomfield, *A Charge Delivered to the Clergy of the Diocese of Chester . . . 1825* (1825), 7.

Watson of the 'sad want of spirit . . . in matters connected with religion . . .'.[1] Despite his pessimism, Blomfield realized that unless the Church 'imposed' itself in the minds of the working poor very quickly, places like Manchester would be lost forever. Not only did he expect double services as a matter of course in these areas, he insisted that the clergy be properly dressed and recognizable by their parishioners at all times. In 1824, Sydney Smith, like many readers of the *Edinburgh Review* who believed Blomfield had abandoned for Tory favor his earlier Whig sentiments favoring Catholic relief, parodied the bishop's stern primary Charge:

> Hunt not, fish not, shoot not;
> Dance not, fiddle not, flute not;
> But before all things, it's my particular desire;
> That once at least in every week, you take
> Your dinner with the Squire.[2]

There was much truth in the jibe, since, like most prelates, Blomfield believed an alliance of serious clergy and local gentry provided the most stable social and religious structure. Manchester, Salford and Macclesfield, however, possessed few squires and few serious clergymen. Aware of this alarming truth, the bishop replied to a protesting minister that 'the question whether such a place as Manchester shall continue to be a stronghold of the Church, or shall be converted into a vast treasure-house of Dissent, is so fearful . . .' that the clergy have no choice but to comply with his demands.[3]

Blomfield, though a vigorous diocesan administrator and a strict disciplinarian, was hardly a great innovator at Chester. His main contributions were church extension and clerical improvement. In both cases he was primarily concerned with strengthening the Establishment's image among the disaffected populace. At first stressing uniformity in dress, residence and external behavior, years later, in London, under the influence of the Oxford Movement, he engaged in a futile and stormy attempt to include uniformity of service and ritual as well. When J. B. Sumner came to Chester after Blomfield's translation to London in 1828, his impressions were very different from those of his predecessor. He was delighted to find, for the most part, a disciplined clergy performing its functions seriously and regularly.[4] During Sumner's twenty years in the diocese, standards were continually improved and implemented in the more than two hundred new churches and thousands of schools established under his direction.

From the beginning of his administration, however, Sumner realized that more churches and devoted ministers could not, in themselves, ful-

---

[1] Blomfield, *Memoir*, I, 102–7. [2] Best, *Temporal Pillars*, 171.
[3] Blomfield, *Memoir*, I, 113–14. [4] Sumner, *Life*, 159.

fil the task of reaching the great numbers of people who would continue to multiply in urban manufacturing districts; the Establishment's basically inflexible and rurally oriented parochial structure was simply inappropriate. Like his Evangelical contemporaries who were less attached to rigid parochial forms, Sumner sought expedient and effective supplements, finding some of them in the organizational work of Dr Thomas Chalmers in Glasgow. To cope with the huge population of his ancient parish, Chalmers had established District Visiting Societies employing pious laymen to visit and instruct the poor in the fundamentals of Scriptural morality. Sumner's Evangelical predilection for greater lay participation in the work of the Church was further encouraged by the possibility of extending parochial organization and influence without threatening lay and clerical proprietary interests. By the time of his initial visitation of the diocese in 1829, the new bishop had investigated his brother Charles's claim that the urban masses were not flocking to the new churches as expected and remained beyond the exhortations and teaching of the parochial ministry. He discovered that the charge was true, finding in one populous district whose church space had been recently enlarged, that only forty-three of 1,104 persons interviewed knew their clergyman or the basic principles of religion. Since half of those questioned were over twenty years of age, it appeared to the prelate that the national Church touched neither the younger nor the older generation.[1] All the Establishment's resources were required for such a task. As a start, Sumner recommended the establishment of a District Visiting Society, and the use of lay parochial visitors to seek out the poor in their homes.[2]

Sumner quickly learned how opposed the clergy were to any innovations impinging upon the parochial *status quo*. Fears for sacerdotal functions and prerogatives merged with a stubborn protection of proprietary rights. Long plagued by unregulated incursions into their parishes by Methodist and Dissenter 'fanatics', the clergy were sensitive to what appeared to be an enthusiastic scheme for introducing an organized band of lay preachers. Moreover, with the extent of non-residence still considerable in an age of conscious clerical improvement, many negligent incumbents were sensitive to the critical implications of employing a pious laity in their parishes. This clerical resistance, along with his expanded awareness of diocesan conditions, only further spurred the bishop. Essentially moderate and conciliatory, Sumner was nevertheless driven to blunt language. During his next visitation in 1832, he was appalled by the extent of lower-class apathy and irreligion; the laboring poor would be unquestionably and irretrievably lost unless maximum effort was applied immediately. No more comfort could be derived from merely providing a church and preaching a

[1] Sumner, *Charge* (1829), 37–38.   [2] *Ibid.*, 24, 33–34.

321

sermon; 'one thing is evident: the ordinary means of grace are unavailable. The church is open, but neglected: the voice of truth is raised, but never heard.' The usually mild, even diffident, prelate frankly questioned the whole trend of Church improvement when he cried out that it was a fatal error to expect those who have no faith to follow the *normal* path to the church door.

> If the minister waits . . . for times of penitence or messages of invitation, he will wait for ever. We might as justly expect that a Lazarus should rise unsummoned from the tomb, as that the man who lies in the darkness of spiritual death, should by any natural process begin to feel his ignorance, and his sin, and shake off his grave clothes, and come forth to seek religious knowledge. . . . What he needs is, not precepts, but motives: not merely a condemnation of present habits, but an effective reason why they should be changed.[1]

Sumner was not simply making the usual Evangelical appeal for soul-searing sermons to arouse a somnolent and sinful populace. On the contrary, he was appealing to his clergy to recognize that they lived in a new age where the 'normal paths of worship' were cluttered with roaring and smoking machines and huge multitudes, crowded into towns, to run them. It was urgent that the body of the faithful, clergy and laity alike, go into the streets and alleys of those blighted, heathen districts to show lost souls a different route to the empty churches waiting to receive them.[2] In the new age, statistics and spirituality composed the message. In Lancaster, one of the few places to adopt his recommendation to utilize lay visitors, the bishop noted that within two years 160 persons had been added to the church rolls, and 218 more children were enrolled in the Church's school. While hardly a spectacular achievement, there was no doubt, Sumner was sure, that the Lord had many more people ready to help His cause when the Church was ready to call them.[3]

Most of Sumner's episcopal brethren were as yet unwilling to join him in sounding the trumpet. They were certainly familiar with the scheme; not only from reading Chalmers, but from reading Lord Henley's endorsement of the plan in his very influential proposal, *A Plan of Church Reform* (1832). Henley was convinced that the conditions prompting Chalmers to institute lay visiting in Glasgow were also present in 'the recesses of St Giles, Bethnal Green, Stepney, Spitalfields, or . . . Manchester, Leeds, Birmingham, Wakefield, Halifax, Huddersfield, Wolverhampton, and our other immense and overgrown masses of population . . .'.[4] The pragmatic Blomfield, who supervised many of these parishes, knew as well as Sumner and Henley that new methods had to be employed. As was so often the case during the next two decades, Blomfield's sense of reality overcame his ecclesiastical rigidity and,

[1] Sumner, *Charge* (1832), 17–18.　　[2] *Ibid.*, 20.
[3] *Ibid.*, 8–9.　　[4] Henley, *Church Reform*, 13–15.

in 1830, he cautiously recommended to his clergy the use of lay visitors. At the same time, however, he pointedly warned that by choosing the plan, they were responsible for seeing that visitors never assumed the ministerial role of interpreting Scripture. Laymen were confined to visiting and encouraging the poor to attend church—whereupon the spiritual message of the faith could be delivered reliably by an ordained clergyman.[1] The possibility of schismatic enthusiasts confusing the lower orders under the guise of Anglican representatives was a serious worry to leaders of a Church already plagued by bitter conflict and factionalism. The Evangelical challenge had largely been absorbed by the improving Establishment; that of the Tractarians was just beginning to be felt in the 1830's. Consequently, Blomfield, like many of his associates, remained equivocal and allowed individual clergymen to associate with District Visiting Societies as they saw fit. Although not hesitating to recommend visiting to laymen interested in assisting the Church, it was not until 1843 that Blomfield finally consented to accept the presidency of the London Association for District Visiting.[2]

By then, District Visitors were fast becoming an accepted feature of overcrowded urban parishes. Seriously dedicated to the salvation of lower-class souls and upper-class property, they offered much-needed assistance to the insufficient clergy. New tasks were proposed for them in their dual quest. Bishop Short, while still Rector of Bloomsbury in 1841, recommended that visitors be utilized as gatherers of accurate information on the parochial poor in order to avoid the distribution of unmerited relief. Such an intelligence service would not only guarantee that improvident persons were denied the opportunity to take advantage of charity, but it would force them 'to exert themselves . . . , to look to their own resources'.[3] The advantages to ratepayers were obvious. Short, of course, was only confirming what many working-class people believed: the pious visitors were really additional agents of the State Church, visiting their wretched homes only to spy on them. In actuality, however, the reports of lay visitors emphasized the misery and ignorance of the urban poor much more than instances of deliberate deception. As a result, the Church gained a clearer idea of the problems confronting it. The reality only further encouraged expediency and flexibility, neither of which came easily to the leaders of the Establishment.

There was little question in the minds of some that it would be many years, if ever, before the Church would be able to provide sufficient ministers in expanding populous areas. Blomfield and C. R. Sumner

[1] C. J. Blomfield, *A Charge Delivered to the Clergy of His Diocese . . . In July, 1830* (1830), 22.

[2] 18 March 1835, Letter Copy Book 343, *Fulham Ps.*; also *Peel Ps.*, Add. MS. 40537, ff. 178–9.

[3] Short, *Parochialia*, 52, 55.

understood this by the mid-1840's and were prepared to actually license lay visitors and Scripture readers to assist the harried clergy. Blomfield had considered it ten years before, in 1835, but nothing had been done. Now, in 1845, he not only supported the idea, but believed that there might be some advantage in recruiting some of the lay assistants from among the lower orders, the very class they were trying to impress. Given the stratified nature of Anglican social thought, and the almost sacramental belief in the efficacy of exemplary upper-class association, this was an important concession. It was in part motivated not only by the recognition that the Methodists had utilized the working-class laity with great success for years, but also by the realization that many Evangelical clergy were prepared to use laymen with or without episcopal sanction. The Evangelical Sumner was not opposed, and the reluctant Blomfield saw that it was best to keep some episcopal control while it was still possible. Admittedly, there were all sorts of dangers, but, as the latter reflected, 'in these times it is not easy to devise any new plan for the public good entirely free from it'.[1]

Both prelates worked diligently to convince their brethren of the advantages. Sumner had a relatively easy time with the enlarged number of Broad Church liberals who had been elevated to the bench since the passage of the Reform Bill. Blomfield found it rougher going with High Churchmen who were cool or opposed to the idea of establishing what was, in effect, a new lay church officer—an idea tainted with schismatic implications of Dissent and Methodism and dangerous latitudinarian tendencies promoted by universalist dreamers like Thomas Arnold. The idea of formally involving the laity in traditional clerical roles, especially when, as Blomfield conceded, many of them would not be far removed 'in respect of worldly condition and manners' from those whom they instructed,[2] did not set well with bishops whose notions of ecclesiastical authority and sacerdotalism were once more stimulated, even exalted, by Tractarian descriptions of the apostolic Church. Nevertheless, by repeatedly pointing to the rise of Chartism and socialism as well as the socially disintegrating antagonisms surrounding the repeal of the Corn Laws and the agitation for the Ten Hours Act, Blomfield was able to convince influential Churchmen that desperate times required desperate measures. Bishops Denison and Wilberforce added their support, as did such diverse laymen as Gladstone, Lord Ashley, Lord Sandon, and Sir Robert Inglis. In 1847 Blomfield approached old Archbishop Howley to endorse the licensing of Scripture readers and an expanded diaconate devoted to catechizing the poor. There was no longer any question, Blomfield told the worried archbishop, that 'earnest laymen' were of

[1] Blomfield to Bishop of Nova Scotia, 19 April 1845, Letter Copy Book 376, ff. 218–20, *Fulham Ps.*
[2] *Ibid.*

great assistance in church extension; he, for one, was prepared to employ them on a wider scale than ever before.[1] Poor Howley needed time to absorb the shock of yet another new scheme to alter his beloved Establishment, and begged off by obliquely wondering about funds.[2] Within a few months Blomfield had worn him down again, and the archbishop, along with all but two of his brethren, accepted the plan.

Only Henry Phillpotts openly attacked the innovation. Driven by a deep sense of impending doom, and profoundly influenced by Tractarian glorifications of priestly functions, he believed that formal episcopal licensing of laymen was not a 'mere experiment', but one 'of a very fearful kind'.[3] By licensing readers, his associates were illegally establishing a new order of ministers without training and ordination—a scheme fraught with 'mischief and peril'. These men would not only read to the ignorant poor; they would comment as well. Who knew what schism would follow when ignorant zealots were not only permitted, but encouraged, to teach an equally ignorant populace? The prospect was especially alarming in times of grave crisis when the very survival of Church and State were in doubt. Only after Parliament had restored order and provided all the churches and clergy needed to minister to 'our heathen population', would it be possible perhaps to consider the role of lay assistants.[4]

Several of Phillpotts's High Church colleagues certainly shared his concern, even if they could no longer share his unrealistic solutions of retrenchment. The licensing of the laity, as Blomfield argued, at least gave the bishops some control over the expanding number of non-clerical assistants at work in urban parishes, and, whatever their personal feelings, most were realistic enough by the 1840's to realize they had nothing to lose as far as the poor were concerned. Bishop Longley spelled it out in 1847. After ten years of determined efforts to cope with the huge laboring population in the new diocese of Ripon, he and his clergy were as overwhelmed as ever. By summoning spiritual laymen, 'who want to do the work of an evangelist', there was at least some hope of ameliorating the crisis. Longley was desperate enough to promise that he would even admit to deacon's orders any layman, irrespective of education, who spent two years as a visitor and Scripture reader to the poor.[5]

[1] Blomfield to Howley, 11 Jan. 1847, *ibid.*, 395, ff. 326–9; also Blomfield to Ld Ashley, 17 March, ff. 362–3.

[2] Howley to Blomfield, 17 Feb. 1847, *ibid.*, f. 343.

[3] H. Phillpotts, *Scripture Readers. Letter to the Venerable the Archdeacons of the Diocese of Exeter On the Proposed Office of Scripture-Readers* (1847), 5.

[4] *Ibid.,* 10–13, 19.

[5] C. Longley, *A Charge Addressed to the Clergy of the Diocese of Ripon . . . September, 1847* (1847), 11–12.

In turning to the laity as a means of enhancing the Church's effectiveness among the laboring poor, the bishops were hopeful that it would also go a long way towards restoring some semblance of class harmony and mutual understanding in the towns. The problem of lower-class alienation and upper-class indifference or hostility to the poor portended revolution and civil war. Blomfield, in the wake of the Chartist disturbances of 1842, wrote to Peel that there was no longer any doubt that the town laborers had separated from the rest of society. Attributing that dangerous situation to the parochial system's inability to remain intact as towns grossly enlarged, he had come to accept the expediency of lay assistants. Not only could they spread Scriptural truths in beleaguered centers of heathenism, but they could also bring the middle classes once more into direct contact with their inferiors.[1] The advantages, in terms of restoring class harmony, were repeated continually in the bishop's endeavor to win episcopal support.

His efforts were considerably strengthened by Wilberforce's elevation to the bench in 1845. Although the new prelate had found one excuse after another for refusing lucrative preferments in Liverpool, London and Leeds, he was keenly aware of intense class conflicts existing in many urban parishes. True, like many well-connected clergy, he preferred contemplating them from afar, but this in no way blinded him to the fact that the Establishment had to become an urban church if it was not to become an anachronistic, rural fossil. As Archdeacon of Surrey, Wilberforce studied conditions in the urban sprawl south of the Thames and urged that the Church forge its own 'proper instruments' to deal with the great problems there and elsewhere. Though a High Churchman, he had been raised in an Evangelical environment in which the efforts of pious laymen inspired the greatest confidence; moreover, his bishop, friend and cousin, C. R. Sumner, had been one of the earliest supporters of lay visitors, and Wilberforce had been impressed with their zeal and effectiveness. If their earnest numbers could be swelled by those from 'other ranks of society', perhaps lacking much education, was it not possible that greater class co-operation might be achieved? Wilberforce conceded to critics that the Establishment had become too exclusive. Since the most populous part of the nation, the lower orders, had been gradually forced out, it was a class, rather than a national, Church. If the laity, representing all classes, were involved still further in the momentous task of renationalizing the Church, possibilities were most promising for a great spiritual uplift of towns in particular and social stability in general.[2]

The utilization of lay assistants was an expedient measure, adopted reluctantly, in many cases, by worried clergymen and bishops seeing no

[1] *Peel Ps.,* Add. MS. 40537, ff. 178–9.
[2] Wilberforce, *Charge* (1844), 28–29.

viable alternative. Church leaders would have much preferred a massive infusion of additional clergy reliably educated and ordained, to the prospect of enthusiastic laymen discussing Scripture with the impressionable poor. As in the case of church extension and parochial reorganization, however, the question of additional clergy touched the sensitive nerve of proprietary right. Incumbents and patrons shrieked in pain as they protested attempts to tamper with their livings. Although various Acts in addition to the Queen Anne's Bounty had been passed to supplement curates' stipends, they were inadequate, while many urban clergymen were still too poor or unwilling to share any part of their income with a clerical helper. The Church Building Commissioners had to be very careful not to infringe too heavily upon the rights of incumbents in whose parishes they erected new churches, since the problem of endowing the livings connected with these edifices was a constant one. The legislature attempted to encourage private endowment of churches and clergy by perpetuating the rights of lay patronage, but invariably many sittings had to be rented to support the minister and maintain the structure. After the passage of one such measure in 1831 (1 & 2 Wm. IV, c. 38), J. B. Sumner complained 'it will not raise a church in the midst of ten thousand manufacturers, where pew rents cannot be collected to the amount of one hundred pounds per annum, and where the sense of religion must be first excited, which can induce the people even to occupy the free seats'. Sumner believed that where a parish of 200,000 existed, and others had swelled to similar outlandish proportions, the only hope was the employment of 'city missionaries' on a wide and flexible scale.[1] The more acceptable term, 'additional curates', seemed hopelessly inadequate.

To bishops fearful of an Evangelical conspiracy designed to capture control of new churches in crowded areas, Sumner's terminology was most disturbing. At the time of the Additional Churches Act, Van Mildert had warned of such a plot. The establishment of a trust in 1817 by the Evangelical Charles Simeon to buy up advowsons and appoint Evangelicals to the livings continually bothered some prelates and confirmed their fears that church extension would be a means of greater Evangelical infiltration. Walter F. Hook, the future Vicar of Leeds, and the first incumbent to subdivide voluntarily and relinquish control of a large urban parish, complained to Samuel Butler in 1835 that Bishop Ryder was co-operating with 'fanatical ministers' and laymen in creating new chapels in crowded districts. Hook believed incumbents should

---

[1] Sumner, *Charge* (1832), xiv-xix. Sumner and Ryder nevertheless had already adopted the principle of rewarding munificence with patronage through their diocesan church building societies. Blomfield followed their lead in his Metropolitan Churches Fund, and it became a part of later church-building Acts. See Best, *Temporal Pillars*, 401.

vigorously resist such encroachments.[1] Butler, succeeding Ryder the following year, confessed that he had had 'too much experience of the Jesuitical proceedings to which some of the so-called Evangelical party will have recourse in order to carry a favourite point', and frankly thought that little could be done. Attributing the decline of initial support for church extension to Evangelicalism's rising influence not only in more populous areas, but within the Establishment itself, Butler favored the enlargement of existing facilities as an alternative whereby less enthusiastic incumbents could maintain control. Butler believed it time 'to open the eyes of some *old* Church of England men to the game that is going on. . . . The Evangelicals . . . have brought up, by what I think an unconstitutional, if not illegal confederacy, all the advowsons they can lay hold of in populous places. . . .'[2] Evangelicals were similarly to accuse Puseyites, under the guise of the Additional Curates Society, a decade later.

In spite of the constant bickering and recrimination that characterized the Anglican Establishment, influential spokesmen for all parties recognized the desperate need for more clerical personnel in the towns. Evangelicals were first in systematically attempting to provide them, establishing the Pastoral Aid Society in Islington in 1836. With Lord Ashley as its first President, the organization sought to increase the number of working clergy and encourage the appointment of pious laymen to assist them in populous districts. During the first year fifty new curates and thirteen lay assistants were provided in the West Riding of Yorkshire, the figures doubling in 1837.[3] Episcopal support was offered by the Sumner brothers and Ryder, as well as by the nearly extinct Bathurst and the newly elevated Stanley. When it became clear, however, that the Society intended not only to limit their support to Evangelical curates, but to pay the lay assistants, many early liberal supporters were quickly alienated.

Blomfield rejected the Society's offer to provide support in his diocese, instead initiating his own endowment fund to provide additional clergy for the new churches going up at a prodigious rate. Like most of his colleagues, the bishop deplored the confusion of lay and clerical functions, fearing that endowed lay assistants threatened the clergy's sacred position. Bishop Butler quickly repudiated the encouragement given the Society by his predecessor, Ryder, and criticized the 'ill-timed interference of the Bishop of Chester . . .' Sumner, it seemed to him, was supporting 'the principle, that a Layman is equally qualified as a Clergyman for the offices of Religion, and therefore it will in time

[1] 17 Feb. 1835, *Butler Ps.*, Add. MS. 34589, ff. 208–9.
[2] Butler to Hook, 19 Feb. 1835, *ibid.*, ff. 210–11. Also Butler to Blomfield 28 March, 1828, Add. MS. 34587, ff. 14–15, 20, 48, and *Sermon* (1830).
[3] Cornish, *The English Church*, I, 84.

be contended, that Ordination is unnecessary'.[1] When pressed by clergy for permission to apply to the Pastoral Aid Society for additional curates in their bloated parishes, Butler grudgingly acquiesced with the explicit understanding that his approval did not extend to the sanctioning of lay teachers, since it violated his 'notion of Ecclesiastical Polity'.[2]

Whatever Church leaders thought of the Pastoral Aid Society, they could not ignore the conditions leading to its establishment. Consequently, in 1837 the Society for Promoting the Employment of Additional Curates began dispensing funds within the confines of its more sacerdotal view of the Church. Broad and High Church bishops quickly lined up behind the more orthodox organization until the Tractarian controversy and accusations, that it was a principal means for the establishment of Puseyite priests throughout the Church, made them more cautious. Always somewhat suspect in the atmosphere of the 1840's, the Additional Curates Society never came close to raising the £46,000 expended by the Pastoral Aid Society during its first twenty years.[3] Party conflicts notwithstanding, the establishment of the two organizations along with an expanded use of the laity indicated the Church's growing flexibility within the institutional and political limitations upon its activities. Although the Anglican clergy were probably their own worst enemies, they were also, without doubt, aware and determined, as J. B. Sumner said, to recover 'our population to the Church'.[4]

2. A NEW 'TOUGH–MINDEDNESS'

By the 1830's Church leaders were experimenting with expedient innovations which, a decade earlier, would have been roundly rejected as alien, enthusiastic, or even fanatical. Questions of purpose and recovery were no longer conventionally answerable in eighteenth-century terms. Catholic emancipation, the overhaul of the Irish Church, the commutation of tithes, the redistribution of episcopal and cathedral revenue, and the establishment of an administrative Ecclesiastical Commission offered striking proof that standards of seriousness, efficiency and rational utility had finally penetrated the walls of unreality surrounding the old Establishment. In spite of an instinctive reluctance to tamper with established institutions, several older prelates recognized that, like it or not, tampering was a fact of life and perhaps the means of their survival in industrial England. They were soon joined by a new generation of men like Thirlwall, Denison, Short, Longley and Wilberforce, who accepted from the outset that their primary task as the first bishops

[1] *Butler Ps.*, Add. MS. 34590, f. 450.   [2] *Ibid.*, 459.
[3] Chadwick, *Victorian Church*, 449–50.
[4] Sumner, *Charge* (1838), 22, 25: also *Sermon* (1838), 15.

appointed to the reformed Church was to secure the Establishment in the hearts and minds of all classes as well as in the laws of the realm.

The new prelates, whether High like Denison and Wilberforce, or Broad like Longley and Stanley, were less attached to the eighteenth-century Church and could take a more detached view of both contemporary realities and causation. Bishop Short, for example, repeatedly claimed that the people are 'estranged from the Church', and if not hostile, they have simply 'wandered from us'. The origins of disaffection could be traced to a breakdown of clerical effectiveness in the preceding century, a collapse continuing long enough into the new age to alienate several generations.[1] It was time, said Connop Thirlwall in 1842 during his primary visitation to St David's, that we look at 'a few notorious facts', the foremost of which is 'that, within a century past, a large part of the population of this Diocese has been alienated from our communion, and is still in a state of separation from it'. The Church had looked elsewhere for explanations and blamed others—the State, Dissenters, Methodists—for the sad situation. The quest for answers had finally come full circle: 'Let us not shrink from acknowledging, that the state of things which we deplore has arisen in great measure out of neglect and abuses which we must not attempt to disguise or palliate, and may be properly regarded as a penalty which the Church has to pay for the selfishness, the supineness, and worldly spirit . . .' of her clergy.[2] Blame whom you may, the bishop argued in a sermon two years later, the truth was that the Church had allowed an entire generation to grow up without the first elements of Christian knowledge; consequently, multitudes had assembled in the great seats of manufacturing and commerce without religious provisions.[3] Thirlwall, never very popular with his clergy, did little to ingratiate himself by the blunt exposition of such pungent truths.

This type of direct confrontation reflected a tough-mindedness emerging from those on the bench who eschewed the self-righteous lamentations of clergymen who comforted themselves by attributing all their troubles to High Churchmen, Evangelicals, Dissenters, Methodists, sixteenth-century expropriators of Church property, or betrayal by the State in more recent times. Continually diverting blame, warned J. B. Sumner in 1838, was self-defeating and dangerous, for it did little to

[1] Short, *Parochialia*, 59; *Charge Delivered to the Convocation Held At Bishop's Court . . . May 19th, 1842* (Douglas, Isle of Man, 1842), 3–5; *A Charge Delivered to the Clergy of the Diocese of St. Asaph . . . July, 1850* (1850), 4.

[2] C. Thirlwall, *A Charge to the Clergy of the Diocese of St David's . . . October, 1842* (1842), 3–5.

[3] C. Thirlwall, *Anniversary Sermon Preached . . . May 30, 1844. At the Meeting of the Children of the Charity Schools . . .* (1844), 8.

correct the evils deplored by all.[1] The evidence was available for all who cared to look; myriads of lost and alienated souls swelling the great towns of the realm offered staggering testimony to realities that only the most irresponsible and obdurate minds could deny. What frustrated and angered Bishop Blomfield was the very persistence of such minds on the bench and in the Church in general. After a decade of trying to guide the Establishment to an appreciation of nineteenth-century realities, he knew as well as anyone how deeply the roots of reaction still burrowed into the eighteenth century. In 1840, after four years as a much-condemned Ecclesiastical Commissioner accused of betraying his episcopal responsibilities, he lost patience with his brethren and eloquently and bitterly pointed up some harsh truths in his defense of the Commissioners' decision to sequester revenue from cathedral stalls for use in neglected, populous districts. It was Blomfield's greatest speech and, in many ways, his finest sermon.

To defenders of the unreformed Church who contended that urban problems were exaggerated by dangerous demagogues seeking to frighten the Establishment into making destructive innovations, Blomfield suggested they 'look at the examples of Newport, Birmingham, Sheffield . . .', and dozens of other overcrowded towns. 'Inquire at the Gaol, the Hulk, the Penitentiary. . . . Hear the charges . . . and then determine whether, when we have the means of remedying these evils, in part at least, we shall suffer thousands and thousands of our fellow creatures to live in ignorance and sin, debarred from those privileges which are their birthright as members of Christ's holy Catholic Church.' It was not a fear of demagogues seeking the destruction of the Establishment that worried the bishop. The Church was again too active and faithful to its duties and obligations to be panicked by such a threat. 'The fear [is] of being found unfaithful to our trust, in leaving so many of our fellow-Christians under the pressure of evils which it was in our power to alleviate. . . . A fear, lest those classes of society which ought to be the basis and strength of the commonwealth, should become . . . its bane, and the instruments of its desolation.' No, demagogues were not the problem when Churchmen themselves firmly resisted institutional changes in the Church in spite of 'an appalling amount of spiritual destitution . . .' that left 'vast masses of . . [their] fellow creatures, living without God in the world'.[2]

During recent years, while passing by St Paul's, 'the magnificent church which crowns the metropolis, and is consecrated to the noblest of objects, the glory of God', Blomfield had found himself wondering

[1] Sumner, *Sermon* (1838), 12.

[2] C. J. Blomfield, *Speech of the Lord Bishop of London in the House of Lords . . . July 30, 1840; On the Ecclesiastical Duties and Revenues Bill* (1840), 14–15.

just how well it was succeeding. He thought of the dean and three residentiaries within, whose income totalled nearly £12,000; and the twenty-nine sinecure clergymen with an income approximately the same and growing. Weighing these facts against the avowed purpose of the Church, Blomfield continued:

> I proceed a mile or two to the E. and NE. and find myself in the midst of an immense population in the most wretched state of destitution and neglect, artizans, mechanics, labourers, beggars, thieves, to the number of at least 300,000. I find there, upon an average, about one church, and one clergyman for every 8,000, or 10,000 souls: in some districts a much smaller amount of spiritual provision; in one parish . . . only one church, and one clergyman for 40,000 people. I naturally look back to the vast endowments of St Paul's a part of them drawn from these very districts, and consider whether some portion of them may not be applied to remedy, or alleviate these enormous evils. No, I am told, you may not touch St Paul's. It is an ancient corporation . . . too valuable to be altered.

The Bishop caustically evaluated the invaluable services provided by that center of London's spiritual life: one sermon preached every Sunday by a residentiary, and another by a clergyman appointed by the bishop and paid by the corporation of London; while the non-residentiaries either preach an occasional sermon on saint's days, or pay a minor canon to do it. None of this, Blomfield sarcastically concluded, is to be disturbed in order 'to furnish spiritual food to some of the thousands of miserable, destitute souls that are perishing of famine in the neighbourhood of this abundance'.[1]

Blomfield's exasperated attack on the old guard within the Church was motivated not only by their resistance to social and economic realities, but also by their refusal to recognize political realities. Talk about the preservation of the ancient Church, while perhaps salutary, ignored the refusal by both government and legislature to continue their guarantee of the means for that preservation. The old Church-State alliance, like everything else in their dynamic age, was profoundly altered and, Blomfield asserted, unless the Establishment was prepared to draw fully upon its own spiritual and material resources, 'the Church, as an endowed Church, will cease to exist'.[2] This had almost happened, he thought, in the terrible months following the passage of the Reform Bill when a combined Radical-Dissenter challenge to the Establishment's privileged position was thwarted only by the introduction of a more effective system of centralized administration which, by offering evidence of a willingness to reform, rallied the Church's many friends to its cause. The need for further innovation and reform had not diminished, as Blomfield would have preferred; the continuing transformation of industrial England, particularly in the 1840's, clearly indicated that, like

[1] *Ibid.*, 7–9.   [2] *Ibid.*, 9.

society as a whole, the Church faced continued dangers neither 'remote nor contingent'. On the contrary, a 'present and urgent [peril] . . . has already existed too long unregarded; it is approaching, if it has not attained its height; and not a year, not a month is to be lost, in commending a remedial process'.[1]

Blomfield was trying to convince his deeply conservative associates of the necessity for the Church to recognize its altered position as an established institution and to act independently, if necessary, in fulfilling its sacred and social functions. Although legislative and judicial authority over the Church still remained in the hands of Parliament, an assertive and aggressive episcopate, willing to use its own resources, was in a better position than at any time in the preceding hundred or more years to direct the Anglican Establishment towards greater independence and flexibility. Pressures for reviving Convocation, which had not functioned since 1717, were mounting as part of a general distrust of Erastian limitations on an energetic, reforming Church. The Tractarians were, in many ways, a more sensational manifestation of the same development. Several of them, like Newman, had first become aware of the problem not from High Church divines, but under the guidance of the liberal, Broad Churchman, Richard Whately. While the frustration of coping with a transforming industrial society, especially after 1832, was deeply discouraging, it evoked from the Church a greater sense of mission and utility. Many of its leaders, in complaining of a lack of legislative support and fearing the imposition of dangerous measures by a hostile Parliament, were induced to rally all active and potential, lay or clerical, defenders of the national Church. The more perceptive prelates understood, however, that defense, rather than retrenchment, meant movement, expansion, innovation and change.

The growing aggressiveness and independence of the bench, connected in part as it was to the desperate question of Church extension, can be seen in a gradual willingness to attack directly the wealthy industrialists and mining interests transforming the face of the country. Some of this criticism was undoubtedly rooted in squirearchical prejudice and an unhappiness at the passing of a more rural, parochial England. Few prelates, however, had been prepared to criticize openly the rich manufacturers and colliery operators, for the bench was little inclined towards biting the bountiful hands, whether on estates or in towns, of the ruling classes. When it came to wealth and power, bishops were adaptable men, many of them easily accepting the natural economic arguments of middle-class progress, especially when explained so cogently by a J. B. Sumner or an Edward Copleston. Whatever their reservations about economic and social developments in the towns, they usually accommodated them to an ultimate, fatalistic confidence in the

[1] *Ibid.,* 15.

improving qualities of natural law, along with a strong clerical tendency towards acquiescence to the *status quo*. Only when conditions seemed to threaten the Church itself did its leaders begin to express second thoughts. Significantly, the first episcopal criticism came from those newer prelates elevated to the bench in the late 1820's and early 1830's— a time when the whole question of establishment was in dangerous flux.

Charles Richard Sumner, in 1827, was the first bishop of the post-war period to accuse those who profited from the accumulated energies of the laboring poor of neglecting their welfare; not their physical welfare, of course, as the new Bishop of Llandaff was too much a product of his generation to suggest interfering with the natural laws of political economy. His elder brother, after all, had explained better than anyone the divine purpose and necessity of the poverty and misery that all too often filled the abbreviated lives of those 'sheep having no shepherd', who were preyed upon by the wolves of indifference and Dissent. Sumner wanted mine- and factory-owners to provide religious facilities 'for the better instruction of those numerous families who have been brought together by their means . . .'. That it was incumbent upon them to provide these facilities 'is as certain as that parents are required to attend to the religious belief of their children, or masters of their servants'.[1] Sumner—who had sufficiently managed to accommodate his moderate Evangelical beliefs to win the favor of the dissipated George IV, and consequently, over Liverpool's reluctance, a bishopric—had no inclination to annoy the rich employers of his diocese. Gently prodding them to provide support for temporary clergy and chapels in the expanding neglected areas around their mines and factories, he then assured them that they were not solely responsible for what was a new and expanding problem.

Although a few firms responded, most owners, many of them Dissenters, were no more prepared to provide ministers and chapels than, if asked, doctors and minimal housing. No bishop yet asked. Moreover, many of the older prelates were deeply suspicious of any schemes altering established parochial arrangements. In 1831 some colliery-owners presented Bishop Van Mildert with a proposal offering land and endowments for erecting and maintaining auxiliary chapels in Durham's new mining areas. To the rigid bishop, however, such a proposal was too reminiscent of Methodist sectarianism to permit his consent. Promising to give the matter more thought, he dropped it.[2] Sumner, who had succeeded Van Mildert at Llandaff in 1826, would have jumped at the chance. Unlike his predecessor, it seemed to him that the abnormal situation in newly developed areas, which 'the Church of England has

[1] Sumner, *Charge* (1827), 8–10.

[2] W. Van Mildert, *A Charge Delivered to the Clergy of the Diocese of Durham, MDCCCXXXI* (Oxford, 1831), 10–11.

apparently never contemplated . . .', had to be recognized. Provisions were needed for instructing 'a population which ebbs and flows, collected suddenly in a given spot, to be dispersed as suddenly, after a lapse of a few years, or a few centuries, when the hidden riches which first caused the influx shall have been exhausted'. Less than a year in his new diocese before being maneuvered by the King to Winchester, a much more lucrative plum, Sumner asked, before leaving, if the poor were to be cast out, and left adrift because perpetual endowments do not exist? Are they to 'be as sheep having no shepherd, or abandoned to every blast of vain doctrine to which . . . they may chance to be exposed'? Would the wealthy employers but endow temporary clergy, he promised to license any suitable building for temporary services.[1]

Copleston, elevated to Llandaff upon Sumner's translation, rapidly surveyed the neglected diocese and concluded that it was indeed only a matter of time before the laboring poor would be completely excluded from the Established Church. What other conclusion could be drawn 'if, while the rich and middling classes have been well accommodated, our poorer brethren have been little regarded; can we wonder at them, can we blame them, for resorting to other places of worship, and to preachers from whom they certainly hear much of the word of God, although mixed with error and enthusiasm . . .'? Was it not ironic that the wealthy employers provided for their own spiritual needs, while ignoring the very classes whose labor created the riches they were able to expend on proprietary chapels and rented pews? All the new bishop could offer at that time was the hope that 'a spirit of attention' was growing among the mining rich, and which would eventually recognize 'the peculiar claims which a poor and recently collected population have upon those whose profits are created by their labour, and whose landed property is prodigiously increased in value by the same means'.[2]

Similar combinations of mild criticism and gentle persuasion began appearing more frequently in episcopal sermons, charges and pastoral letters. Henry Phillpotts, one of the few important outspoken clerical enemies of the urban middle class in post-war years, had moderated his attacks in the 1820's when it seemed less likely that newly expanded districts were ripe for social revolution. In the next decade, however, after his elevation to Exeter in 1831, he again warmed to the conflict. Talk about possible redistribution of ecclesiatical revenue to provide for the mining and manufacturing populace stung him and others into taking a more direct position. In 1833, knowing that the Church could expect little help from a reformed legislature packed with Whigs, Radicals,

[1] Sumner, *Charge* (1827), 9–10.
[2] E. Copleston, *A Sermon Preached At the Reopening of Abergavenny Church . . . September XX, MDCCCXXIX* (1830), 5–6.

Dissenters and even Catholics, Phillpotts bluntly called upon those who profited from the labor of the poor to provide for their spiritual welfare before it was too late.[1] This was mild language for the bellicose Bishop of Exeter. As he became more settled and familiar with conditions in the Church, his tongue grew sharper, honed by his hatred of industrial England and its new classes. For the time being at least, he bowed to Blomfield's more diplomatic approach in reminding the urban rich 'whose exertions in their several trades and callings have been crowned by a bountiful Providence with success, [to] remember that the very same circumstances which have swelled the amount of our population, and created the evil we desire to remedy, have caused in part the increase of their worldly substance . . .'.[2] Seeking funds for constructing more churches in the Metropolis, Blomfield believed it only just that the rich return some of their wealth to the spiritual work of God who had blessed their material endeavors.

The response was often handsome, as wealthy Englishmen contributed large amounts to a national Church obviously attempting improvements in areas that could only benefit society as a whole. Still, the clergy found themselves unable to keep pace with the growth of towns; the harder they worked, it seemed, the farther they fell behind. Confidence among many Church leaders that benefits could be derived from an expanding, unrestrained economy began to wane when it became clear that not only was the State unwilling to continue providing the means for the Establishment's adjustment, but that voluntary support in towns, where Anglicans might well be a minority, was not sufficient. Often angry, even bitter, about those conditions that apparently forced unwanted reforms upon them, several prelates were less obsequious in their discussions of the new moneyed classes. Older churchmen, loathe to accept some inner flaw within the Establishment itself, heaped recriminations upon the faithless State for abandoning its spiritual bride with millions of ill-nourished offspring. Some of them like Copleston began to wonder if they had not been cuckolded by industrialists and mine-owners whose siren calls of progress and utility had lulled them into a false sense of eventual security.

Copleston no longer felt that security when he spoke of areas which were, 'within living memory, either thinly-peopled rural parishes or uninhabitable wastes, but are now swarming with population'. Had the increase been gradual, 'through a succession of ages . . .', the needs, though the same, would not have been so striking or apparent. 'But the fact is that myriads are collected and settled on these spots within the compass of a few years, for the benefit of individuals who derive enor-

---

[1] H. Phillpotts, *A Charge Delivered to the Clergy of the Diocese of Exeter . . . 1833*, 2nd ed. (1833), 36.

[2] Blomfield, *Twenty Four Sermons*, 443.

mous wealth annually from their labours.'[1] Copleston, in charging those
individuals with abrogating their fundamental responsibilities, warned
that 'unless the capitalists who congregate this population for their own
enormous profit recognize the duty of providing for the religious instruction of the poor, there must be, and . . . there often actually is a lamentable destitution . . .'. That destitution, 'a concentration . . . of poverty
and misery of every kind . . .', was, the bishop knew, both physical and
spiritual, but he was only really troubled by the latter. The laws of
political economy explained the physical deprivation endured by fertile
laboring poor; a repudiation of Christian stewardship and common
sense explained the extent of spiritual deprivation. It was the result of a
new society in which rich and poor were separated as never before.
Still, those who create 'congregations of people' by their mercantile
efforts, 'ought surely to contribute, not only to their own immediate
neighbourhood, but still more in remote parishes which have not their
due proportion of wealthy inhabitants, and of whose swarming population the conflux of rich families to the metropolis is the cause'. By
removing themselves from the poor who congregate at their bidding, the
rich 'see them not, and therefore think they are not specially connected
with them . . .'. This, Copleston insisted, makes it especially necessary
'that the truth should be plainly told, and their own duty forcibly
pressed upon their attention'.[2]

The bishop now told it plainly and forcibly. In 1840 he confessed that
years of gentle persuasion had been 'painfully frustrated . . . either by the
apathy of the rich, or by the perverse spirit of heresy and schism . . .'.
The time for persuasion was running out; it was now imperative to
denounce 'this neglect of sacred duty'. It was time to name names.
Concentrating on the collieries in his own diocese of Llandaff, Copleston
could only cite one firm, the Rhymney Iron Company, which, after
years of pleading, finally agreed in 1838 to provide one church and a
school for the eight thousand souls it had brought together in the
desolate mountains. Although two small churches had been provided
at Danlais and Bedwelty the previous decade, people had since been
allowed to accumulate without more provision. Still worse, seventy
thousand persons connected with the iron works and collieries in
Merthyr Tydfil, Bedwelty, Mynyddysloin, Aberstruth and Trevethin

[1] E. Copleston, *Who Are the Persons Authorized to Preach the Gospel?
A Sermon Preached . . . October XXIII, MDCCCXXXVIII, at the Anniversary of the Monmouthshire District Committees of the Society for Promoting
Christian Knowledge, and the Society for the Propagation of the Gospel . . .*
(1839), 33.
[2] E. Copleston, *Church Discipline and National Education. A Charge
Delivered to the Clergy of the Diocese of Llandaff . . . MDCCCXXXIX*
(1839), 28.

were served by one church. It was no surprise that they assumed 'every form of sectarian dissent and schism, mixed with heathenism and avowed infidelity'.[1] In spite of these truths that the prelate had tried imposing upon the rich of the diocese, he looked in vain for assistance from those districts, 'reared by the skill and power of man'. and continually creating more wealth; in vain as well 'for buildings destined to the production of true riches . . .'.[2] When it was pointed out that existing churches, inadequate as they might appear, were in fact only partly filled, Copleston curtly dismissed the evidence, confidently asserting that more churches meant more congregations.[3] As a long-time supporter of church building as the principal means of Anglican revival, the prelate was not yet prepared to be disabused of his necessary illusions. Instead, he indignantly and rhetorically asked, 'whose are all those lines of houses, those arsenals of wealth . . .' inside which dwell men who have forgotten God and their responsibilities to Him? 'For whose benefit are these myriads collected, to spend their lives on this heretofore solitary ground? Can they year after year, draw additional crowds to the spot, and yet make no provision for their spiritual instruction, for the due administration of the Sacraments, and for the preaching of God's word?'[4]

Copleston's old friend and episcopal associate at Exeter, Phillpotts, knew the answers all too well as he looked out on the 'thousands and hundreds of thousands of . . . workmen of our manufactories, those miserable serfs of Mammon who now form so large a portion of the British people'. Their destitution could be attributed to 'the selfish avarice of a few . . . but which the no less selfish indolence and indifference of the many have suffered to grow to its present appalling magnitude'.[5] These were harsh words. Things must have seemed very desperate for nineteenth-century bishops to feel compelled to decry the wealthy classes, something not done since the terror of the French Revolution had brought forth some worried commentaries on the evils of luxury and the responsibilities of wealth. Copleston, conscious of the rarity of such episcopal denunciations, angrily charged rich employers to do some genuine good for a change, and reap a profit greater than that with which they were familiar. Although he expected his words might incur 'the expense of some displeasure' against him, they could no longer be

[1] E. Copleston, *Separation Either a Duty or a Sin. A Sermon Preached . . . November 6, 1840* (1840), i-iii.
[2] *Ibid.*, 23.
[3] *Ibid.*, v. Even Blomfield doubted that this could be the case in Wales. See his letter to Gladstone, 9 Sept. 1844, *Gladstone Ps.*, British Museum, Add. MS. 44361, f. 222.
[4] Copleston, *Sermon* (1840), 23.
[5] Phillpotts, *Letter* (1843), 12.

avoided.[1] Though continuing his sniping during the remainder of his life, there is little evidence that the bishop penetrated very deeply the 'arsenals of wealth' he periodically assaulted.[2]

During his repeated sallies against mine- and foundry-owners, Copleston carefully dissociated himself from criticisms of working-class social and economic conditions. The root of the problem, as he saw it, was churches, not wages. He had no intention of giving credence to the exaggerated charges of Chartists, socialists, and other socially disruptive enemies of an orderly Christian civilization. From everything he could learn, the laborers were neither economically destitute nor illiterate; in fact, 'they are plentifully supplied with materials from the Press for encouraging all their errors and all their evil passions'.[3] Copleston, then, could not understand why their employers would not co-operate with the Church in spiritually reinforcing a social and economic structure clearly beneficial to all parties concerned. Phillpotts believed he understood the reason: the new industrial classes lacked an appreciation and understanding of the harmonious qualities of a socially interdependent, hierarchical society. Blinded by the materialistic glow of a utilitarian political economy, they had lost all connection with the spiritual and social values of a pre-industrial, landed civilization. Inspired by Tractarian glorifications of the Church of that lost age, Phillpotts now sought to cope with the poor by reviving the Offertory in the service and the direct giving of alms to the needy—'whose bodily strength is wasted in labouring to acquire this affluence for us', while we suffer millions of them 'to live, and alas! to die, without God . . .'.[4] Without for a moment bowing to the need for controversial ritualistic revivals in the Church, even an old Whig, Maltby of Durham, conceded in 1845 that the greatest happiness for the greatest number had, in practice, resulted in great misery for the greatest number, and great prosperity for the few. And, if not sufficiently disillusioning, those benefiting endanger us all by not providing their workers 'with mental and spiritual food, as well as that which the labour of their own hands could procure'.[5]

Although episcopal criticism of the urban industrial classes was largely restricted to questions of religious accommodation, most prelates by the 1840's were well aware of the living and working conditions endured by the laboring poor. The great parliamentary enquiries and reports were regularly substantiated by city missionaries, district visitors and lay Scripture readers. Moreover, the bishops were increasingly concerned

[1] Copleston, *Sermon* (1840), v–vii.

[2] Copleston, *Memoir*, 200; *A Charge Delivered to the Clergy of the Diocese of Llandaff . . . August, 1848* (1848), 24.

[3] Copleston, *Sermon* (1840), iii.   [4] Phillpotts, *Letter* (1843), 10.

[5] E. Maltby, *A Charge Delivered to the Clergy of the Diocese of Durham . . . MDCCCLXLV* (1845), 15.

with the social legislation of the era. Their support of Corn Law repeal, the Ten Hours Act, and various measures to improve health in the towns, reflected an understanding that the poor's physical welfare and the success of the Church's expansive efforts could no longer be separated. Perceptive members of the hierarchy knew that maintaining this separation would, in the eyes of the poor, continue the Establishment's identification as an institution and agency of the upper classes. Chartists would continue to find 'amens' to their prayer:

> Hear us, O Lord, on behalf of a wicked and persecuting church, which exists by violence and plundering of goods, instead of the free will offerings of the heart; convert our bishops and clergy to Christianity . . .[1]

No matter how angrily a bishop might castigate the rich for denying their workers the means for spiritual sustenance, he rarely decried their social and economic attitudes and policies, even while supporting legislation and private efforts directed toward moderation and regulation. In the final analysis, the bishops themselves were still too much a part of a hierarchical social and economic system which, in spite of periodic abuses, they believed was natural and inevitable. As pillars of the Establishment, irrespective of reform, they saw their function and responsibility in maintaining that system and reconciling it with divine truth. Only when their natural lay allies in that reconciliation balked at fulfilling their responsibilities did Church leaders feel compelled to call them to task.

3. NEW MISSIONS, NEW PARISHES

Episcopal complaints about middle-class abrogations of Christian stewardship were accompanied by further innovations, including, finally, the reform of parochial boundaries. In the early 1830's, although he had his reservations, Blomfield began allowing services in unconsecrated rented rooms and buildings. Although the expediency of such measures seemed an absolute necessity, he always softened his High Church resentments with the knowledge that more permanent consecrated facilities would eventually be provided for a lower-class congregation which might not otherwise exist.[2] Most prelates coming to the bench in the 1830's and 1840's accepted such flexibility as a matter of course. While most of them were liberal churchmen whose notions of consecration

---

[1] The Chartist Circular, Sept. 19 1840, 211, in Faulkener, *Chartism*, 130.
[2] 12 Feb. 1832, Letter Copy Book 335; 16 Feb. 1833 LCB 338; 17 Nov. 1834 LCB 342, *Fulham Ps*. During his last visitation in 1854 Blomfield recalled that he had never hesitated to sanction religious services in a school or other convenient building when it was expedient to do so. *Charge* (1854), 31.

were less exalted than those of Blomfield, some of them, like Denison and Wilberforce, were no less attached than the Bishop of London to the vital importance of regular, sanctified structures. Like most of their generation, however, they simply had a much clearer appreciation of the gap existing between the ideal and the possible.

Even old High Church prelates like George Henry Law had come to understand the greatness of that gap in industrial England. Trembling in the 1820's at the prospect of establishing evening services for the laboring populace in the manufacturing towns of Lancashire, by 1838 he readily acceded to the disbursement of itinerant missionaries to minister to rough railroad navvies building the Great Western Line through his diocese.[1] This was still too much for some of his associates, however. A similar plan was presented to Bishop Butler, who not only refused permission to establish 'an institution not recognized in any way by the Church of England', but who also questioned Law's presumption and right to license railroad missions. So responsible a representative of Church order, he thought, would have opposed a scheme so 'directly adverse to the spirit of the Constitution of our Church, and [that] would soon . . . introduce the itinerant conventicle system', for which there was no canonical authority. The argument that times had changed since the last revision of the canons in 1604, and that the railway age required adjustments not foreseen in convocations of the seventeenth century, meant little to Butler. He was too worried about possible conflicts between missionaries and local parochial incumbents, not to mention the brawling and rioting that would undoubtedly result between Irish Catholic and Protestant railroad workers. Although the bishop would permit, at best, additional lectures for navvies who attended the church nearest their line-laying, he cautioned, 'for things to be done well, they must be done according to order'.[2]

Butler was determined to protect his diocese from the aggressive ministry of young enthusiasts appointed by his Evangelical predecessor, Henry Ryder. In 1837, one of these, a Staffordshire curate whose small church was inadequate for his enlarged parish, requested permission to accept the invitation of friendly Dissenters to use their facilities to deliver a series of expository lectures; Butler sharply refused. The curate could deliver them in another parish: 'if the inhabitants will not take the trouble to come . . . far to hear your sermons, and much more to hear the beautiful prayers of our Liturgy, which are superior to any sermons that were ever written, I am sure they do not deserve to have them brought to their doors'. As far as the bishop was concerned, 'they are like men who would offer sacrifice to the Lord their God of that

[1] Rev. W. H. Wayne to Butler, 29 Dec. 1838, *Butler Ps.*, Add. MS. 34592, ff. 205–6.
[2] Butler to Wayne, Jan. ?, 1839 *ibid.*, ff. 215–16.

which doth cost them nothing'.[1] By then, however, many of his episcopal brethren, without necessarily approving of co-operation with Dissenters, doubted that the troubled Establishment could afford excessive inflexibility. Consequently, with all their distrust of irregularity and innovation, prelates like Law and Blomfield were willing to change, the latter, along with several other bishops, joining Law in licensing railroad missionaries and resigning themselves to the proliferation of temporary worship places.[2]

What else could be done when even Blomfield, one of the principal proponents and most vigorous defenders of the primary necessity of church-building, conceded that many new as well as old edifices remained unfilled, sitting half-empty in the midst of an enormous, uninterested populace? To an Evangelical layman complaining in 1843 that the new churches in Bethnal Green were poorly attended, the bishop sadly replied, 'it was not to be expected that the Churches would be numerously attended for a long time to come. People nurtured in cynicism and long accustomed to darkness, will not all at once come to the light'.[3] As much as it disturbed him, Blomfield was compelled to comply with requests and even demands from his more zealous Evangelical clergy for more latitude in establishing evangelistic missions to the heathen multitudes. Although Blomfield had long distrusted the London City Mission established in 1835 by Dissenters and Evangelicals, he knew that many Anglican laymen and clergy supported its visitations, distribution of tracts, Scripture readings and even services in unlicensed rooms. Some of his brethren, like the Sumner brothers and Stanley, were openly receptive to these co-operative ventures in their dioceses. High Churchmen, however, were much less accommodating, many of whom refused any association with such ventures in the hope that the expansion of Church education, the Additional Curates Society, and the employment of lay visitors and readers would sufficiently satisfy the Establishment's evangelizing needs.[4] Blomfield was accused of bigotry, exclusiveness, and a lack of interest in the souls of the poor because he remained hostile to co-operative, interdenominational missions, but he never forbade his clergy's participation.[5] While trying to dissuade them and urging a more orthodox course of action, he also recognized that so great was the problem of communicating with the working poor that as many avenues as possible had to be kept open.

The appointments to the bench in the fourth and fifth decades of the

[1] Butler to F. E. Arden, 23 Oct. 1837, *ibid.*, 34594, ff. 152 ff.
[2] 27 March 1847, Letter Copy Book 379, ff. 177–8; 20 Nov. 1849, LCB 383, f. 44, *Fulham Ps.*
[3] 5 Sept. 1843, LCB 371, ff. 72–75; 29 Oct. 1844, LCB 375, ff. 261–2, *ibid.*
[4] 1 Dec. 1843, LCB 373, ff. 87–88, *ibid.*
[5] 14 Aug. 1847, LCB 379, f. 375; 1 Aug. 1848, LCB 381, ff. 232–6, *ibid.*

century did not have to resolve such conflicts. Men like Wilberforce, Lonsdale and Longley, as well as the powerful Archibald Campbell Tait, who joined them in the 1850's, had never experienced the sedentary beauties of the eighteenth-century Establishment. Those palmy days represented to them a romantic nostalgia, not an unforgettable reality. Their formative years and clerical careers were spent in a period of severe Church criticism, self-examination, threats of disestablishment and unprecedented reform. Social and economic transformation, especially in the towns, was an integral part of their environment, not a new and baffling experience to be grafted upon deeply ingrained assumptions learned in a different world. Consequently, while the old, pragmatic Bishop of London required years to thrash out a cautious and reluctant acceptance of lay readers, district visitors, and extraordinary evangelizing missionaries, the new Bishop of Oxford launched his career in 1845 by praising the zealous efforts of these innovations and urging the Church towards still greater changes in attempting to recreate a truly national Establishment capable of attracting and uniting all classes of Englishmen.[1] In the next decade, Blomfield's successor at London, Tait, would be out on the streets himself, preaching the working poor back to church.

All the innovations undertaken were basically designed to strengthen an overwhelmed parochial structure, too inflexible to cope adequately with the size and quality of an industrial and mercantile population. Church reform measures undertaken since the opening of the century had been oriented towards improving parochial religion. Attacks on non-residency and pluralism, the raising of curates' salaries, the construction of churches, parsonages, and schools, the redistribution of ecclesiastical revenue—all sought to improve the parochial system and extend it into the new society. These measures, as well as the jumble of local and voluntary efforts over the years, were given a legislative boost in 1843 when Peel and Sir James Graham, eager to prevent a recurrence of Chartist agitation in manufacturing towns, carried through An Act to Make Better Provision for the Spiritual Care of Populous Parishes.[2] This measure permitted the subdivision of existing parishes into new parishes upon the erection of additional churches. Moreover, in the growing evangelizing tradition, clergymen were allowed, even encouraged, to minister in new districts before the church was built in order to start the formation of congregations. By 1843 it was clear to Peel, as it was to his episcopal ally, Blomfield, that many new churches would remain empty until the town masses were once more familiarized with

---

[1] Wilberforce, *A Charge Delivered at the Ordinary Visitation of the Archdeaconry of Surrey, April 1845* (1845), 15; also *Charge* (1844), 28–29; T. V. Short, *Charge* (1850), 23–24.

[2] 6 and 7 Vic. c. 37.

the teachings of the Gospel. Incumbents and patrons, many of them well aware of the serious situation, were generally amenable to the compensation provided by the new law for loss endured through subdivision of their extended parishes.[1]

Few of them were as co-operative, however, as the dynamic Vicar of Leeds, W. F. Hook, who, in 1844, voluntarily subdivided his huge parish of 152,000 people into fourteen entirely independent new parishes.[2] Though it cost him over four hundred pounds in annual income, Hook believed the alienation of the laboring poor was so extensive as to require the most drastic action. Only the upper and middle classes, he explained, supported the Church any longer; people in the agricultural districts 'are generally indifferent . . . but in the manufacturing districts she is the object of detestation to the working classes . . . '. Hook's experience in industrial cures convinced him that the workers 'place Party in the stead of the Church; and they consider the Church to belong to the Party of their oppressors; hence they hate it . . .'. Years in Leeds lent authority to his plea that 'the Church must try for God's sake to win the people by making a great sacrifice'.[3] Hook's desire to sacrifice the wealth of the bishoprics, cathedrals and richer livings, along with his own, did not exactly endear him to the hierarchy of the Establishment, some of whom distrusted his personal decision in Leeds. Archbishop Howley, fearing that times were too dangerous to raise such issues, wrote privately to Peel that Hook's policies would stir up all sorts of controversies.[4]

No Church leader dared to question publicly such uncommon Christian behavior on the part of a clergyman, no matter how suspicious or anxious they were about the material or spiritual implications of Hook's sacrifice. The need for a systematic reorganization of a parochial structure established essentially in the sixteenth century was so obvious for so long that any serious step in that direction was welcomed with renewed hope by many prelates. As early as 1834 Blomfield had tried to persuade his old foe, the Reverend Sydney Smith, to divide the Vicarage of Edmonton for better service to the parish. Smith caustically replied that it would also help to divide the See of London. The bishop thought that a very good idea indeed, and gave Smith his 'full and free permission to urge the expediency of dividing the larger Bishoprics, and of abolishing Cathedral sinecures, as earnestly, and as sincerely, as I have urged, and shall continue to urge the propriety of dividing the Vicarage of Edmonton . . .'.[5]

[1] Best, *Temporal Pillars*, 357. [2] *Peel Ps.*, Add. MS. 40539, ff. 154–8.
[3] Hook to Wilberforce, 5 July 1843, in C. J. Stranks, *Dean Hook* (1954), 75–76.
[4] 30 Jan. 1844, *Peel Ps.*, Add. MS. 40539, ff. 152–3.
[5] 3 May 1834, Letter Copy Book 341, *Fulham Ps.*

The reorganization of dioceses and the curtailment of episcopal translation by equalizing episcopal incomes in most dioceses, enacted in 1836, were conceived as a means whereby the bishops might keep a closer eye on their parochial clergy. The attempt to rationalize and re-organize the administrative and religious functions of the parish as well as the diocese paralleled, in the broader context of Benthamite improve-ments, continual efforts to enhance the administration of the Poor Laws in parishes or united groups of parishes, and, in the select vestry move-ment, to streamline parochial government.[1] In the course of the century parochial church functions in many districts had greatly expanded from the distribution of Bibles, *Cheap Repository Tracts*, prayer-books, and from weekly Sunday schools to the introduction of regular day-school education, savings banks, benefit clubs, coal and clothing clubs, allot-ments and District Visiting Societies, often under the control and direc-tion of the local parson.[2] This congenial blending of Christian and utili-tarian values was warmly welcomed by Church reformers eager to prove by the changing standards of the age that the Establishment was not only spiritually meaningful, but useful as well.

The establishment of 'Peel districts' as a result of the legislation passed in 1843 was viewed as another important step in that direction. More-over, it heartened older churchmen who hoped that the measure indi-cated that a Tory government, after a decade of Whig regression, was prepared once more to rally parliamentary support behind the Estab-lishment. Bishop Longley thought this unrealistic and cautioned his clergy in 1844 about reviving romantic notions of a Young England, or toying with the Romish illusions of ultra-churchmen. It seemed to him that the composition of Parliament, in reflecting that of the country, largely precluded much support for Church extension. Consequently, the bishop urged the Church to be satisfied with the tangible oppor-tunity provided by the legislature to endow missionaries in populous areas where no church existed, and to welcome opportunities to build new parochial congregations. If the Establishment could 'but find zealous and devoted servants . . . who will be content to live and labour among their flock in a missionary spirit, we may humbly hope that a generation will not pass away without living proof that the Lord has of a truth raised up His power and come among them'.[3] The government had provided the legal framework for expansion, but the Church was still essentially dependent upon itself for implementation and support. Many selfless acts, like that of Hook's in Leeds, were required to reinvigorate parochial religious life.

[1] Best, *Temporal Pillars*, 145–7.

[2] *Ibid.*, 155. Also S. Best, *A Manual of Parochial Institutions*, 2nd ed. (1849).

[3] Longley, *Charge* (1844), 17–18.

z

Longley's analysis of the political situation was basically correct. Peel felt his position too weak to take a more determined stand on behalf of Church extension. The initial financing of the new districts came not from public loans, but from £600,000 of Exchequer bills borrowed by the Ecclesiastical Commissioners from Queen Anne's Bounty. When that amount was quickly exhausted with no more official support available, the Commissioners were forced to wait until 1856, when their income gave them a sufficient surplus to renew grants for new parishes.[1] In the meantime, however, many missions and hopes were raised. In 1844, J. B. Sumner, so pessimistic the previous decade, saw a new day dawning for the Church of England, one in which it would once more be effective in its national ministrations. Fifty new parishes were rapidly created in his manufacturing diocese and he predicted that in time a church and clergyman would be available for every two to three thousand persons.[2]

Wilberforce, who had refused the Vicarage of Leeds before it was offered to Hook, was also enthusiastic about what appeared to be a major step in the recapturing of the lost masses. Along with many of the new generation of prelates who would lead the Church after the middle of the century, Wilberforce realized that church-building had all too often been a case of putting the cart before the horse. What was needed were zealous clergymen working in crowded, neglected areas to form congregations before new churches were constructed.[3] Though repeatedly declining that mission for himself, he was well aware that the Church had little hold on 'the vast body of the poor and destitute in the towns'. In fact, he knew, as Hook had warned, that with the exception of the wealthy, the Church had less than keen support in the rural districts as well. Wilberforce, in spite of High Church sentiments, could not agree with Thomas Arnold's conclusion that the crowded Catholic churches, in contrast to the empty Anglican cathedrals, indicated the need for 'an external apparatus of religious services'. Also, it was not just a question of clerical discipline or more churches; rather, 'true preachers of the Gospel' were needed to go forth into the world.[4]

By the middle of the century, there was no lack of churches in England, while an appropriate division of parishes was well advanced. The population explosion of the Industrial Age had made a profound impact upon the Established Church. It had forced an essentially rurally-oriented, passive State institution to reconstruct itself in order to cope with an urban society it only partially understood, and for which it rarely felt compassion. Time after time, adjustments and reforms were grudgingly conceded as necessary to justify the maintenance of an Established Church, rather than joyously advanced as further means for serving

[1] Best, *Temporal Pillars*, 357–9.   [2] Sumner, *Charge* (1844), 13.
[3] Wilberforce, *Charge* (1844), 6–7.   [4] *Ibid.*, 24–27.

God, and providing spiritual comfort to starving multitudes. The problem was compounded by the fact that the same economic and social changes creating problems for the Church were also altering the power structure of the country, bringing into positions of authority people who had little sympathy with the privileged position of a corrupt and grossly inefficient adjunct to the State. In practical terms, it meant that after 1832 the Establishment was, to an unprecedented extent, on its own.

Considering the divisions within that encrusted institution, its response was at times remarkable. On the one hand, it was ruled by a hierarchy of men born and schooled in the eighteenth century, whose values were essentially those of the landed ruling classes rather than of the industrialists, merchants, and mine-owners whose sprawling towns they had to administer ecclesiastically. Gradually, as some of the old and many of the newer generation of Church leaders began to adopt the latter's values as well, the tensions on the bench were often no less explosive than those within the Church as a whole. In addition, the conflicting theological, sacerdotal, and ecclesiastical positions that contributed so much to the Establishment's ineffectiveness were exacerbated and heightened by its changing relationship with the State and the relentless pressures for reform. Nevertheless, thousands of new churches and chapels were built, providing more than a million new sittings. When public funds were no longer available, huge sums were raised from voluntary sources. Additional clergymen were sent into districts where the incumbent was floundering in a sea of dying souls. Bishops allowed services in schools, rented rooms, or any other viable place where a congregation could be brought together. Still other arrows, drawn from the quiver of expediency, were fired by worried episcopal archers into the dense, hostile multitudes they saw massing against divine forces of peace, order and harmony. Missions to railroad workers, an expanded diaconate, and even the organized employment of lay visitors, preceded legislative approval for subdividing swollen parishes.

By then, some of the old and most of the new generation of episcopal leaders understood and had reacted to what Walter Savage Landor had meant when he wrote in 1836:

> There is no Church, and never was there one in which the Ministers of religion have so little intercourse with the people as the English. Sunday is the only day that brings them together and not in contact. No feelings are interchanged, or sorrows or joys or hopes communicated, Unpreceded by inquiry or advice, command and denunciation follow the roll call of the day.[1]

[1] W. S. Landor, *The Letters of a Conservative: In Which Are Shown the Only Means of Saving What is Left of the English Church. Addrest to Lord Melbourne* (1836), 6.

Others, however, knew that vast numbers of working-class Englishmen were not even getting the limited benefits of denunciation on Sunday, for they were always beyond the hearing of their sometime spiritual shepherds. No one knew this better than Hook, who was completely 'convinced . . . that unless the Church of England can be made in the manufacturing districts the church of the poor, which she certainly is not now, her days are numbered, and . . . her very existence would be scarcely desirable . . .'.[1] Self-criticism and breast-beating over the alienation of the urban poor and its attendant dangers for the Church and society had become a regular tattoo by the 1840's, leading the Archdeacon of Chichester, John Garbett, to tell Oxford graduates 'there is one vocation of the Church of England: the evangelization of the manufacturing districts'. Poor old Bishop Bagot, harried by the Oxford Movement into a state of near collapse, was still around to hear Garbett add that it remained to be seen whether the Church was strong enough to make its way in the new world among the urban masses, 'unsustained by the pomp of cathedrals . . . or whether it be only fit, in its decrepitude, for the rich and for the refined, the repose of villages, and the quiet dignity of arts and letters'.[2] There were churchmen still very much alive who found that a very attractive alternative. But their influence had been eclipsed by the Blomfields and the Sumners who knew both worlds, and after, the Wilberforces and the Taits who knew mainly one. That was the one, for better or for worse, in which the Church would have to minister.

[1] Stephens, *Life of Hook*, II, 172, 175.

[2] Quoted in Brose, *Church and Parliament*, 198. Bagot was eased out of Oxford by Peel and Blomfield in 1845 in order to get a stronger, resident bishop in that diocese to deal with the Tractarians, and to break up Bagot's pluralities. Bagot was offered Lichfield in 1843, though Blomfield was not sure that he was strong enough for an industrial see, but declined. He settled for the more serene diocese of Bath and Wells in 1845. See correspondence in *Peel Ps.*, Add. MS. 40533, ff. 403–4; Add. MS. 40534, ff. 168–70, 176–8.

X

Education and Social Order, 1783–1830

1. CHARITY AND SUNDAY SCHOOLS

Church extension in the nineteenth century was largely predicated upon the assumption that the lower orders would be educated to worship in the new and expanded structures. As Church leaders became aware of the Establishment's deficiencies and recognized that a long-term process of reconstruction was necessary, they also understood that it was essential to capture and hold the younger generations. The dawning realization that the older generations were probably lost forever only intensified the Church's determination to base its recovery upon the newly catechized recruited from the swelling multitudes unaffected by the national faith. Anglican interest in the education of the laboring poor initially focused upon the relationship between social order and the Establishment's role as a guardian of the natural laws of social inequality. Gradually, however, in the decades after Waterloo, the instruction of lower-class children took on an added dimension in the minds of the Church hierarchy—the preservation of the Establishment itself.

To a Church that justified its privileges primarily in terms of eighteenth-century Warburtonian utility, and, later, Benthamite concepts of rational effectiveness, the possibility that it might no longer be the Church of the majority was most alarming. Not even Tractarian assertions of the spiritual superiority of the Anglican faith adequately convinced worried prelates that their Church's doctrines sufficiently justified its favored position with the State. They knew better. They knew that what really counted in their transformed age was the ability of the Establishment to reconcile the greatest possible number of people to a religious explanation of existing social realities. The validity of spiritual truths, in

349

other words, was manifested in the established structure of English society. The preservation of that society and its religious arm was at stake. Education seemed the most effective way to perpetuate both.

Initially, the Church was more a passive recipient than an active initiator of lower-class education. Although the episcopate, as part of its function throughout the eighteenth century, had lent its name to the voluntary charity schools in the various dioceses and paid annual homage to the efforts of the S.P.C.K., it did little else. There were exceptions, especially earlier in the century, such as bishops William Wake, Edmund Gibson, Symon Patrick and Gilbert Burnet who actively promoted schools in their sees.[1] Most prelates, however, were content to make an annual contribution to the S.P.C.K. and deliver an occasional charity school sermon. Parochial education ranked very low on the list of episcopal priorities, and eighteenth-century bishops were willing to leave it entirely in the hands of local lay subscribers, and, if he was resident or interested, the parish parson. Often he was neither.

The inadequacy of the charity schools and other independent variations like 'dames' schools' where, for a trifling sum, children were taught rudimentary reading and writing skills, weighed upon the conscience of Evangelical laymen and enlightened philanthropists before it made any indentation upon the thick hide of ecclesiastical indifference. Suspicious of innovation, and wary of Methodistical enthusiasts, Church leaders cautiously watched the emergence of the Sunday school movement in the 1780's under the guidance of the Evangelical Gloucester journalist, Robert Raikes. Troubled by swarms of idle, sinful children wandering the streets of Gloucester on the Sabbath, Raikes, in 1780, organized Sunday classes to acquaint them with the significance of that day and the blessings of salvation.[2] Although other individuals, like the Unitarian vicar, Theophilus Lindsay, and the Methodist, Hannah Ball, had started similar schools some years before, it was not until Raikes began publicizing his work in the *Gloucester Journal*, and, more importantly, the *Gentleman's Magazine*, that the idea became popular. Religious revivalism and the practical arguments of rational humanitarians gave special meaning to warnings that hundreds of thousands of children were growing up in utter ignorance, a danger to themselves and to society. For a minimal outlay of voluntary expense it was possible to provide enough instruction to these children to make them aware of the dangers of eternal damnation, and to teach them contentment with their natural station. All of this was possible without interfering in any way with their daily laboring pattern.

[1] M. G. Jones, *The Charity School Movement. A Study of Eighteenth Century Puritanism in Action* (Cambridge, 1964), 64–65.

[2] A. Gregory, *Robert Raikes, Journalist and Philanthropist. A History of the Origins of the Sunday Schools* (1877).

With such obvious benefits before them, supporters of Sunday-school education for the poor multiplied, as did the number of schools. The founding of the London Sunday School Society in 1785 by the philanthropist, Jonas Hanway, and the Dissenter, William Fox, was only the first of numerous organizations. Within twelve years it promoted nearly 1,100 schools educating 69,000 children.[1] As early as 1787, Raikes enthusiastically claimed that a quarter-million children were attending Sunday schools throughout the country, and, though his calculations were probably inflated, there is little doubt that the education of the poor was well on the way to becoming synonymous with Sunday instruction.[2] The establishment in 1803 of a Sunday School Union to coordinate the diverse societies springing up everywhere is another indication of nationwide appeal. By the end of the Napoleonic Wars, Sunday-school education had greatly eclipsed the old charity and dames' schools as the principal means of educating the lower orders. Henry Brougham's enquiries in 1818 revealed that some 452,000 children were attending 5,100 Sunday schools in England and Wales, as compared to 168,000 in charity schools and another 53,000 in local dames' schools.[3]

This rapid development of Sunday schools has been interpreted as an important aspect of a broad and growing interest in education rooted in Enlightenment concepts of rational improvement. Lockeian psychology and Rousseau's educational ideas in *Emile* have been described as paving the way for a fundamental re-evaluation of child development and the importance of formative education.[4] The child-oriented writings of Thomas Day, Richard Lowell Edgeworth and his daughter Maria, Sarah Trimmer, and even the rigidly pious Mrs Sherwood are seen emerging from this tradition. While such generalized arguments may be partially applicable to educational developments affecting the middle and higher ranks, it is questionable whether they are relevant to the expansion of lower-class education. The Sunday school movement emerged not so much from a sentimental, humanitarian, Rousseau-like tradition, as from that of puritanically-motivated charity schools founded in the seventeenth and early eighteenth century by pious and philanthropic laymen. Like the Sunday schools, the charity schools were initially open to Dissenters as well as Anglicans (until High Church vituperation drove out Dissenters), and provided a basic Scriptural and catechetical education. Both institutions were financed by voluntary subscriptions and endowments made primarily by the middle classes, but also by aristocratic patrons.

---

[1] Jones, *Charity School Movement*, 153; also *Report of the London Sunday School Society* (1797).

[2] Gregory, *Raikes*, 92.　　　　　　　　[3] *Hansard*, II (1818), 49 ff.

[4] Jacques Pons, *L'Éducation en Angleterre entre 1750 et 1800* (Paris, 1919), 20, 217. Also, Halévy, *England in 1815*, 528.

Although the stated primary motivation in establishing both the charity and the Sunday schools was religious instruction, supporters openly calculated the social benefits to be derived from the inculcation of moral principles of labor, thrift, contentment and obedience. Moreover, it was hoped that it would be possible to see those benefits reflected in declining poor rates.[1] Proponents of the charity schools earlier in the century believed their goals could be best accomplished by teaching the poor reading, writing, and basic arithmetic. Yet, in spite of the vigorous discussions about educational reform and values in the second half of the century, the conclusions were certainly not applied to lower-class instruction. Sunday-school education was actually regressive in limiting the curriculum to reading; a restriction also becoming prevalent in the charity schools. Rumblings of social discontent merged with economic fears that education would restrict the availability of cheap surplus labor, and make the working poor dissatisfied with their station in life. Hannah More, whose troubles with the local Somerset farmers opposing her charity schools are well known, indignantly assured the Bishop of Bath and Wells that she allowed no writing for the poor: 'my object is not to make fanatics, but to train up the lower classes in habits of industry and piety . . .'.[2] Whatever new educational ideas were being formulated in the Enlightenment, English educators of the poor found all the guidance they needed in Solomon's wisdom: 'Train up a child in the way he should go; and when he is old he will not depart from it.'

Given the deeply conservative emphasis of such educational thinking, few bishops were inclined to view the Sunday schools as dangerous innovations. The Church, after all, was entrusted by canon law and tradition with the education of the poor, even if many clergy did neglect that function. The religious revival of a more aggressive Protestantism was gradually encouraging the reinstitution of such responsibilities, but the clerical response was not overwhelming. Local parsons were as likely to oppose educational innovations as not, especially if they associated them with Methodists and Evangelicals. Often the incumbent or his curate simply reflected the prejudices of local farmers and dominant laymen. As eighteenth-century clergy were usually content to follow the laity's leadership and initiative, their promotion and support of schools were largely dependent upon the attitude of local patrons. Hannah More discovered the closeness of this alliance in Blagdon, where she confronted the combined hostility of angry landowners and their clerical spokesman, who accused her of being everything from a Methodist to a Jacobin revolutionary.[3]

[1] Jones, *Charity School Movement*, 28–29.
[2] Brimley Johnson, ed., *The Letters of Hannah More* (1925), 183.
[3] See M. Jones, *Hannah More* (Cambridge, 1952), and F. K. Brown, *Fathers of the Victorians*, for a full discussion of the Blagdon controversy.

Mrs More's friend, Bishop Porteus, sympathized with her complaints. As one of the earliest and most consistent episcopal advocates of Sunday-school education in particular, and lower-class instruction in general, he was well aware of the reluctance, and even antipathy, of many of his clergy to support schools in their parishes. In a diocesan letter of 1786 he tried to assuage their suspicions by describing the Sunday-school movement as an extension of the long-established charity school movement. Since the charity schools had been endowed largely in rural areas, no provision for the instruction of the poor existed in the more populous districts of the realm. This was especially evident in the manufacturing towns of Lancashire, Yorkshire and Cheshire, where 'there is the greatest number of children that want education, and who being in constant employment during the rest of the week, have scarce any leisure allowed them for instruction but on the Lord's Day'.[1]

Porteus reassured his clergy that the various attacks leveled against the Sunday schools were ill-founded, since the children were 'neither instructed in writing nor arithmetic'. Moreover, their learning to read from Scripture 'does not either indispose or disqualify them for undertaking with their *hands* the most laborious employments in town or country'. Conscious of the fears of farmers and manufacturers, he depicted the Sunday schools as complementing the use of child labor by training children, 'from their childhood, in habits of industry' which would immediately and continually be implemented during the other six days of weekly labor. 'By this wise expedient, that most desirable *union*, which has been so often wished for in Charity Schools, but which it has been generally found so difficult to introduce, is at length accomplished, the union of *manual labour* with *spiritual instruction*.' As long as 'the interests both of this life and the next . . .' could be so conveniently and co-operatively managed, the bishop could see no reason for fearing the simple education of the poor.[2] Porteus was formulating an argument that would be repeated often in the next century as both the demands for labor and education became more insistent and complex.

Similarly, the bishop raised another telling point when he suggested that the real concern should not be over what would happen if the poor were provided a rudimentary education, but what the result would be if they were left in total ignorance. Already aware of the increased population in the manufacturing towns of his diocese, Porteus had some idea of the miserable conditions in which the enlarged laboring classes lived and worked. His confidence, however, that Christian factory proprietors would 'on every principle of charity, compassion and sound policy' seek to protect their poor workers, allowed him to accept their fate with equanimity.[3] He could not, however, be so sanguine about the spiritual destitution faced by generations of poor children growing up in the

[1] Porteus, *Letter* (1786), 7–9.   [2] *Ibid.*, 10–11.   [3] *Ibid.*, 21–22.

midst of an affluent and expanding society. Methodist and Evangelical criticism only pointed out realities that Porteus and a few of his associates were gradually beginning to recognize—religion was losing its influence among the poor. This alarming development, they saw, was likely to continue and become more widespread as populous areas, based upon an economy that permitted little leisure for the laborers and their children to apply the balm of spiritual contentment, multiplied without instructional facilities. There was as yet no suggestion that anything was wrong with that economy; the problem was one of introducing principles of Scriptural morality into it.

Porteus knew that manufacturers, at least, already possessed these principles. Irrespective of the truths of natural religion and morality, most Englishmen still believed that social behavior and social harmony were rooted in basic precepts of Biblical instruction. The more learned might be able to reconcile these precepts with rational morality, but the laboring poor were too ignorant and too busy to make such cerebral connections. Furthermore, though the upper classes were increasingly assailed for their luxurious, dissipated, and often irreligious behavior, few of their critics failed to recognize that the material means to live such thoughtless and dissolute lives also firmly wedded the rich to the established social, political and economic institutions of the realm. The laboring poor, however, had no such binding interests. Only the fear of God and the Scriptural promise of eternal life kept them passive in their station. Dean Horne of Canterbury thought it time to remind the governing classes of that simple fact and urged their support of the Sunday-school movement by warning that only so long as the religious principle is present will the poor obey human laws.[1] Porteus suggested that the bonds of spiritual restraint were loose. The 'extreme depravity and licentiousness which prevails . . . among the lowest orders of the people . . .' could no longer be denied. Their manners and morals had to be reformed else 'our houses cannot secure us from outrage, nor can we rest with safety in our beds'.[2] Though he, along with the rest of the bench, supported Wilberforce's Society for the Reformation of Manners when it was established in 1787 to encourage virtuous behavior and suppress 'blasphemous and indecent publications', Porteus saw that royal proclamations against vice and the occasional prosecution of publishers and purveyors of wicked literature were more an indication of concern than an effective weapon against widespread moral corruption.

[1] G. Horne, *Sunday Schools Recommended In A Sermon Preached At the Parish Church of St Alphage, Canterbury . . . MDCCLXXV . . . With An Appendix Concerning the Method of Forming and Conducting An Establishment of this Kind* (Oxford, 1786), 6.

[2] Porteus, *Works*, VI, 235.

The bishop was aware that the attachment of the poor to the national Church was at best tenuous. Though more spiritually aroused than most of his colleagues, Porteus carefully avoided suggesting that a lack of religious ardor existed amongst the clergy. The problem was to transmit whatever did exist to the ignorant poor and to offer them a rudimentary, catechetical education which seemed the most promising means of effecting 'a great and astonishing change in the manners of the common people' in the next century, if not at once.[1] Porteus implied that the hearts and minds of the lower orders were at present closed to the Church. In 1790 he stated it directly, admitting that he had all but abandoned hope for the current generation and emphasizing the critical importance of concentrating upon the children of the poor 'to restore and invigorate the spirit of religion among the lower orders of the community'.[2] This was a strong admission by a leading prelate of the Church that something was very wrong with the Establishment. Some could be content with the knowledge that nearly 300,000 children were already attending Sunday schools, but Porteus was discouraged by the indifference, and even open resistance, he encountered in a great many parishes. In almost every district in the country, but particularly in the more populous areas, he saw 'many hundreds of ignorant, wretched young creatures . . . totally destitute of all education, totally unacquainted with the very first elements of religion, and who perhaps never once entered within the walls of a Church'.[3]

No Church leader would disagree with Porteus's argument about the social importance of religious restraints upon the inferior classes, but few of his generation were ready to acknowledge the validity of charges that the Anglican Establishment somehow failed to reach the poor. Most prelates were more restrained in the 1780's in their interpretation and endorsement of lower-class education. There was, however, no direct episcopal opposition; the bench's response ranged from neutral indifference to cautious support. The Evangelical, revivalist impetus behind the Sunday school movement was difficult for rationalistic, conservative churchmen to swallow; especially when the new enthusiasm challenged the spiritual effectiveness of the Establishment directly and its leadership indirectly. Furthermore, the fact that Evangelicalism was repeatedly confused with Methodism and the horror of schism did not enhance in cautious prelatical minds the reliability of educational innovations.

Gradually, however, a few of the more spiritually active bishops, those not unwilling to associate with Hannah More, William Wilberforce or Henry Thornton, extended their support of Sunday schools

[1] Porteus, *Letter* (1786), 25. Also *Letter* (1789), 21.
[2] Porteus, *Charge* (1790), 18.
[3] *Ibid.*, 14.

from generalized endorsements to direct encouragement. In 1788, the pious Bishop of Norwich, Lewis Bagot, looked for and found Scriptural authority in Christ's query: 'Yea, have ye never read, Out of the mouths of babes and sucklings thou hast perfected praise?' Bagot, in the face of such a divine endorsement of religious education for the poor, could not understand how clergymen could oppose its call for an immediate establishment of schools.[1] Shute Barrington, then at Salisbury, had initially favored Sunday schools in 1787 to complement the moral reform efforts of Wilberforce's Proclamation Society. Any doubts that Barrington might have felt were cleared up by the end of the decade when he saw that, in addition to their enhancement of the goals of the moral improvement societies, the schools were viable agencies of social stability. How could any clergyman withhold his support? As the proponents of the schools had promised, the limited curriculum in no way discouraged manual labor and an acceptance by the poor of their laborious station in life. On the contrary, the schools had only induced 'order, regularity and contentment'.[2] Barrington, like Porteus and Bagot, was among the earliest episcopal critics of slack parochial standards and frankly hoped that catechetical education would go a long way towards ameliorating the deleterious effects of non-residency and spiritual apathy. Optimistically, he envisioned the Sunday schools as permanent institutions, connected to the charity schools, and perhaps even supported by the counties as a 'system' of education for the poor.[3]

Barrington's casual reference to a system of public education was prompted by Morton Pitt's proposals for the creation of a county-wide educational plan.[4] Joined by the venerable John Douglas (1721-1807) of Carlisle, he saw some of the limitations of an entirely voluntary system of schooling. As Douglas explained in 1790, the schools 'are too intimately connected with the public welfare, to be left to the casual contributions of private benevolence; and highly worthy of the most effectual interference of the legislature to give them a permanent establishment, and due extent'. Unlike Barrington, old Douglas, a 'High and Dry' Tory prelate who had been a chaplain at the Battle of Fontenoy, was not much interested in the spiritual advantages to be gained from educating the poor. He simply saw a permanent school system as a rational means 'to strike at the root of that ignorant and brutal ferocity, which daily prompts so many unhappy wretches, the

---

[1] Bagot, *Sermon* (1788), 2.

[2] S. Barrington, *A Letter to the Clergy of the Diocese of Sarum . . .* (Salisbury, 1789), 9-10.

[3] *Ibid.,* 12-13.

[4] W. M. Pitt, *Plan for the Extension and Regulation of Sunday Schools* (1785).

pests of society, to acts of horrid outrage, reproachful to good government, and disgraceful to humanity itself'.[1] Most bishops, however, were still trying to digest voluntary Sunday schools, and were not in the least interested in chewing over another mouthful of innovation. Considering that the State had last supported lower-class education during the Cromwellian Protectorate of the preceding century, the precedent was not likely to enhance its palatability.

With the exception of the reform-minded Richard Watson, the bench ignored what was to become one of the most controversial questions between Church and State in the next century. Barrington, translated to Durham in 1791, henceforth concentrated on voluntary education, while Douglas, who succeeded him at Salisbury, never mentioned the subject again. Watson, however, in 1788, on one of his rare visits to his archdeaconry of Ely, informed the clergy that their poor agricultural laborers are 'remarkably perverse, stupid, and illiterate'; while the mechanics in the towns are 'debauched, and ill-mannered, and the children of both are brought up in rudeness, ignorance and irreligion'. Contemplating these realities in Ely and in his diocese of Llandaff from his permanent residence in Westmorland, the bishop concluded that the current generation was beyond social or religious redemption. The problem, he believed, was so great that only a system of free schools could effect serious improvement among the younger generation. Sunday schools, however, would be insufficient. What was needed, Watson thought, was a system of parochial weekly institutions educating children for three years.[2] He recalled that he had had some success with such a program at Cambridge and called upon the clergy to establish a fund and solicit contributions to implement a similar scheme. Unlike his episcopal associates, however, Watson frankly thought that one of the principal functions of education should be to help the children of the poor 'emerge from the gulf of poverty in which they are born'.[3] While most clerical promoters of lower-class education were trying to assure wary critics that lower-class schooling would have no impact on the economic and social position of the poor, the maverick Watson believed that such an impact would be necessary, if a generation of orderly, content and honest poor were again to be seen in England.

Not surprisingly, the clergy were insufficiently moved by the bishop's promise of 'everlasting honour' if they implemented his plan. Three years later Watson went a step further and called for the establishment of a system of publicly-financed instruction. Presenting what was to

[1] J. Douglas, *A Sermon Preached Before the Lords Spiritual and Temporal . . . January 30, 1790, Being the Anniversary of King Charles's Martyrdom* (1790), 17.

[2] Watson, *Charge* (1788), 10–11.

[3] *Ibid.*, 13–14.

become a major argument of the next generation of Church leaders, Watson, in 1791, insisted that if civil magistrates readily expended funds to punish criminals, they should also be prepared to finance the prevention of crime through education. Since the inculcation of proper social and religious values was an issue directly affecting all of society, it seemed logical to the prelate that society should be prepared to undertake the task properly. Watson recognized that the question of public education raised the thorny issue of Dissenters' participation and the State's provision of funds for other than the Established Church. Although he was the strongest episcopal advocate of complete civil equality, the bishop felt it expedient 'to assume as a principle to be admitted, that the morals of the Community will be better secured by an exclusive establishment at the public expense of the Teachers of one Sect...'.[1]

Later, under the pressure of war and a fear of revolution, Watson abandoned his limited endorsement of public education. Still, he was one of the first leaders of the Establishment to recognize that the voluntary system of financing education for the lower orders would be inadequate to provide for an expanding laboring population growing up outside of the national Church. Along with a few of his episcopal contemporaries, he saw the need for some form of public involvement. As an old Whig, Watson was much too suspicious of the State's power to envision a national system of popular education. His early imprecise suggestions conceived of some type of local public support adequate for individual parish or county needs. As usual, Watson was remote from the mainstream of clerical thought and in advance of his episcopal age. Yet, within the lifetime of some of his associates on the bench, if not his own, the issue Watson raised was to become one of the most pressing and vexatious problems for the reviving Church trying to fulfil its national role and survive as an Establishment in an age of astonishing change.

2. REVOLUTION AND EDUCATION

The French Revolution suddenly placed the question of education in a startlingly new perspective. If the propertied classes were still hesitant to extend rudimentary instruction to the laboring poor, it appeared to Church leaders that Tom Paine was not. His *Rights of Man* sold 200,000 copies in 1792, the first year of its appearance, and each copy was considered a blow against the pillars of a sane society.[2] Monarchy and aristocracy were roundly thumped, and the Church, Paine asserted, like 'all national institutions of churches . . . appear to me no other than

[1] Watson, *Charge* (1791), 11.
[2] M. D. Conway, *The Life of Thomas Paine* (1892), I, 346–7.

human inventions, set up to terrify and enslave mankind and monopolize power and profit'.[1] Established churches in particular were materially-oriented, conspiritorial institutions designed 'to hold man in ignorance of the Creator . . .' while government holds him in ignorance of his rights.[2] As the legitimate, traditional educator of the people, the Establishment was jolted by the fear that continued neglect and abrogation of its task would see it fulfilled by Paineite radicals and revolutionaries modeling themselves after the lunatic French. Moreover, as 'the Church by law established', its leaders were forcibly reminded that their positions, emoluments, and representation in the House of Lords required the fulfilment of socially stabilizing obligations, irrespective of any spiritual truths they might have to offer.

Attacks upon the structure of society in general, and upon ecclesiastical foundations in particular, rallied the bench into seizing whatever defensive weapons it could muster for the great assault that would surely come. The growing network of parochial schools suddenly assumed a new importance, with one prelate after another turning to them with hope and enthusiasm. At the same time, however, Church dignitaries became both more protective of their exclusive position and more distrustful of the co-operation with Dissenters that had prevailed in the Sunday school movement. With 'Church and King' in danger, and many Dissenters standing to benefit by the destruction of ecclesiastical privilege, latitudinarian flexibility gave way to exclusiveness and rigidity. Bishop Horne of Norwich who, as Dean of Canterbury, warmly encouraged Sunday schools as early as 1785, had never questioned the common education that was provided for Anglican and Dissenter children alike. By 1791 he was worried about contamination. The mixing of Dissenter children with those from Anglican families would 'jumble together the errors, inconsistencies, and heresies of all. This must end in indifference. . . .' Horne, like many of his colleagues, doubted that the Church could afford the risk in such perilous times. Alarmed by the progress of events, the bishop saw only one possible outcome from continued co-operation: 'it may bring the people of the Church nearer to the sects; but the present times do not give us any hope that it will bring the sects nearer to the Church'.[3] If anything, there was reason to believe that, under the leadership of men like Joseph Priestley and Richard Price, the Revolution would be viewed as an opportunity for Dissenters to lower the Establishment to their generalized level. Some High Church prelates probably had such fears earlier, which, in part, accounted for their pre-revolutionary reluctance to endorse warmly the Sunday school movement. Even the Broad Church Watson, a long-time friend of

[1] Paine, *Age of Reason*, Pt. I, in *Theological Works*, 12.
[2] *Ibid.*, Pt. II, 156.
[3] Overton, *The English Church in the Nineteenth Century*, 246-7.

toleration and co-operation, concluded in 1791 that if public funds were given to education, all teachers must be Anglican.

The pressures of the 1790's were simply too strong to permit the continuance of the uneasy co-operation between Church and Dissent that marked the early years of the Sunday school movement. As in the case of the charity schools early in the century, Church divines were unable to sustain an amicable relationship with sectarians whom they suspected were hostile to the Establishment's teachings and privileges.[1] In the 1790's Dissenters and Methodists were continually described as sectaries whose disaffection from the Establishment stood in sharp relief to the desperate need for a common, united effort against the atheistical onslaught of French republicanism. The decline of co-operation saw a vigorous rise in episcopal involvement in educational matters. Even the obscure Bishop of Bangor, John Warren (1730–1800) spoke out in 1792, describing education as the most effective way to inculcate obedience and reverence for authority among the poor. He explained to his Welsh clergy that it was good policy, 'not only for Conscience-sake, but for the sake of Interest too, as we have no other security under God, for our Religion and Liberties'.[2] A far more important voice was that of Samuel Horsley. He had said little about education during the previous decade, warily observing the influence of religious enthusiasts in the movement. In 1793, however, he was thoroughly alarmed by 'the capricious domination of an unprincipled rabble' in France and warned of the dangers if 'barbarism and irreligion are suffered to overrun the lower orders' in England. Individual liberty and civil freedom were at stake and only a basic Christian education could avert the danger: 'the Christian religion fosters and protects . . . liberty . . .', and rejects 'the absurd and pernicious doctrine of the natural equality of men'.[3]

Like Bishop Barrington, Horsley tried to calm the social and economic fears of those who believed that education would heighten the expectations of the lower classes and might, in fact, make them even more dangerous than they already were. This had not occurred, he pointed out; if anything, it was far more dangerous to exclude the poor from an elementary religious instruction providing the rudiments of Christian independence. Such independence was not a danger to a free society governed rightly by the natural laws of economic and social relationships. Those laws provided, as Locke and Adam Smith had

[1] Jones, *Charity School Movement,* 110–14, 153.

[2] J. Warren, *A Sermon Preached . . . June 14, 1792, Being the Time of the Yearly Meeting of the Children Educated in the Charity Schools . . .* (1792), 18.

[3] S. Horsley, *A Sermon Preached . . . June 6, 1793, Being the Time of the Yearly Meeting of the Children Educated in the Charity Schools . . .* (1793), 24–25.

shown, that the wealthy do not own the labor of the poor, other than by agreement. Likewise, the poor man cannot claim support from his superior, unless he is an apprentice, journeyman, menial servant or hired laborer. As a free laborer, then, he is entitled 'to the recompense of his stipulated service, and to nothing else'. Horsley believed that in such a free society the poor should be provided with sufficient education to enable them to support themselves and their families, acknowledging at the same time the inevitable natural inequality of man and the absurdity of popular sovereignty.[1] The bishop was confident that the educational programs he was endorsing would effectively contribute to that end.

No bishop reacted more hysterically to the French Revolution than did Horsley, but in the 1790's education, guided by the clergy, appeared the most potent antidote to the spread of revolutionary propaganda. Others, however, were less confident and even alarmed as they imagined thousands upon thousands of laborers reading Paine's *Rights of Man,* or the agrarian socialist offerings of Thomas Spence's *Pigs Meat or Lessons for the Swinish Multitude*; while revelations of Republican conspiracies and the success of revolutionary writings only reinforced among farmers and manufacturers eager to protect their supply of cheap, plentiful, pliable labor, stronger opposition to the whole idea of lower-class instruction. A great many more people were simply frightened and confused, and thought it best to leave things alone for the time being. Bishop Hurd of Worcester certainly felt that way.[2] Pointedly cool to the whole prospect of a literate poor, he provided little encouragement for the scheme in his diocese. He was much too busy with his literary endeavors and with editing the works of his beloved patron, Bishop Warburton, to become either Archbishop of Canterbury or a diocesan educator. Horace Walpole described him as 'a gentle plausible man, affecting a singular decorum that endeared him highly to devout old ladies'.[3] Yet, when one of those ladies, Hannah More, sought episcopal subscriptions in 1795 for her *Cheap Repository Tracts,* Hurd hesitated. Though her pious tales were specifically designed to offset the pernicious influence of Paine's writings, Hurd was not convinced that

[1] *Ibid.,* 21–23, 25–26.

[2] R. Hurd (1720–1808), son of a wealthy Staffordshire farmer, educated at Cambridge, gained Warburton's attention by dedicating his criticism of Horace to him. Owed his pluralities and advancement to Warburton and Lord Mansfield. Elevated to Lichfield-Coventry in 1775. Became preceptor to Prince of Wales and Duke of York in 1776, and became a court favorite. Translated to Worcester in 1781, and rejected Canterbury in 1783 as he considered himself unsuitable.

[3] H. Walpole, *The Last Journals . . . During the Reign of George III, From 1771–1783* (1910), I, 555.

they would have such an effect. Reluctantly he subscribed, but warned that 'these good ladies and good Bishops would needs have the poor people be taught to read: with good design no doubt: but who shall hinder them from reading bad books, as well as good; nay from giving a preference to the former?' Like his idol, Warburton, he feared that if you teach the poor to read, 'they will chuse for themselves, or suffer bad people to chuse for them . . .'.[1]

It is significant that Hurd's criticism was made in a private letter, rather than as a public statement. During the 1790's, lower-class instruction was fast becoming an orthodoxy in theory if not always in practice. No prelate spoke against it, while increasing numbers of them warmly endorsed charity and Sunday schools for every parish in their dioceses. Often they had to prod their reluctant clergy, who were not as sure as their bishops of the schools' 'tried advantages . . . too striking to need recommendation'.[2] Fears of revolution merged with eighteenth-century rationalism as one ecclesiastic after another defended education as not only necessary but natural. Bishop Courtenay, like most enlightened men, knew that everyone possessed the capacity to learn; they were born with it, and it would be as unnatural to stifle the growth of the mind as it would be deliberately to stunt the body. The mind develops from experience, Courtenay recalled; consequently, it was important that the experience of the poor be attuned to physical, social and economic realities.[3] Arguing along the same lines, other Church leaders, like George Huntingford, explained that since experience was inevitable in character, formation, its control and positive channeling was essential. He thought it a truism that uncontrolled development tends to the negative extreme; children of menial parents, for example, will not develop a 'cheerful disposition and ready obedience' necessary to their station 'unless properly guided'.[4] Recent experience had clearly shown how the human mind is 'formed for action' and there could be no question that it will function in 'a nugatory or even vicious way' if not trained properly.[5]

Reasonable advocates admitted that the poor might abuse their rudimentary knowledge; there was certainly evidence of that fact. Still,

[1] Hurd to Rev. S. Smith, 9 Feb. 1795, *Egerton MS.* 1958, f. 140, British Museum.

[2] Barrington, *Charge* (1797), 23.

[3] H. Courtenay, *A Sermon Preached . . . May 28, 1795, Being the Time of the Yearly Meeting of the Children Educated in the Charity Schools . . .* (1795), 2–5.

[4] G. Huntingford, *A Sermon Preached . . . June 2, 1796. Being the time of the Yearly Meeting of the Children Educated in the Charity Schools . . .* (1796), 6–7.

[5] *Ibid.,* 12–13.

Courtenay insisted, we must not be frightened into a defense of ignorance. 'Ignorance is [not] the best security for obedience', nor is a life of toil and labor incompatible with 'a reasonable degree of information'. If this information is erroneously or poorly taught so that industry and duty are relaxed, the remedy does not lie in 'brutish ignorance, but in more correct instruction'. Courtenay was still optimistic that progress and civilization would overcome injustice and ignorance once a reasonable renewal of confidence in natural law was transmitted throughout all levels of society.[1] Most prelates shared Courtenay's and Huntingford's Lockeian notions of learning. They were products of the same enlightenment education and had absorbed sensational psychology and environmentalism as evident truths fully compatible with natural law and Scripture. If it did not make them vigorous proponents of lower-class education before the Revolution, it certainly made the adjustment easier during that crisis and at least prevented even the most cautious prelates from opposing the educational initiatives of others.

The only significant defection came in 1800. Samuel Horsley, haunted by dark revelations of atheistical conspiracies, and fearful of the appearance of Antichrist, turned on the schools. Both in Parliament and during his diocesan visitation, he described them as possible 'nurseries of Jacobinism'. Horsley knew it to be a fact that 'schools of Jacobinical Religion, and Jacobinical Politics . . . abounded in this country; schools in the shape and disguise of Charity-Schools and Sunday Schools'. Everywhere he saw the growth of new conventicles and congregations 'of one knows not what denomination', led by 'illiterate peasants and mechanics'. He wondered where they were instructed. 'It is very remarkable that these new congregations of nondescripts have been mostly formed since the Jacobins have been laid under restraint of two most salutary statutes known by the names of the Sedition and Treason Bill; a circumstance which gives much ground for suspicion that sedition and atheism are the real objects of these institutions. . . .'[2] Horsley wanted a purging of the schools to root out any dangerous educational allies. This included all suspicious persons and Dissenters.

High Churchmen, whose principles tended to soar with the heat of the times, were disturbed that many clergymen, especially Evangelicals, had, in spite of episcopal reservations, continued to co-operate with Dissenters in the establishment and administration of schools. John Bowles, one of the High Church party's leading lay spokesmen, and an ardent government propagandist, charged, in 1800, that Dissenters 'have, with few exceptions, admired, extolled, nay even encouraged and promoted, to the utmost of their power the French Revolution, because it was founded upon their own principles'.[3] Bowles, like Horsley, was

---

[1] Courtenay, *Sermon* (1795), 9–11.   [2] Horsley, *Charge* (1800), 25.
[3] *The Anti-Jacobin*, II (Oct. 1800), 87.

also attacking by association those Evangelicals who ran the Sunday school societies, and maintained a working relationship with Dissenting sects. In the future, the bishop urged, the parochial clergy should carefully regulate all aspects of the schools in their districts and restrict them to 'children of the same class'.[1] He was not opposed to Sunday schools provided they were well regulated by proper authorities, which he feared had not been the case in very many parishes.

These and other High Church attacks severely strained whatever remnants of co-operation between Dissenters and churchmen still remained after nearly a decade of war and periodic panic. They did little, however, to alter the Church leadership's growing confidence in lower-class education as the principal means of preserving order and redirecting the poor to the Church. The depressing *Report* of the clergy of Lincoln on the state of religion in their diocese in 1799 went so far as to urge the legislature to establish a system of education for the poor in which religious instruction would be taught along with the virtues of 'industry and subordination . . .'. It appeared to those unhappy clerics that the survival of Church and State was at stake.[2] Charles Moss (1763–1811), son of the Bishop of Bath and Wells and future Bishop of Oxford (1807–11), anonymously came to the defense of the schools in 1801. Though a High Churchman himself, he was particularly disturbed by accusations leveled at Hannah More and her schools in his father's diocese. As Chancellor of the see, Moss knew that the More sisters were utterly safe and, in *A Statement of Facts*, attacked the vicious charges that their schools were dens of Methodistical and insurrectionary activity. Since the younger Moss's connection with the diocese went back to 1774 when, at age eleven, he was made sub-dean of the Cathedral, he thought he knew the clergy well enough to accept their testimonies to the effectiveness and orthodoxy of the schools. True to the clerical thinking of the times, however, Moss suggested that the enemies of lower-class education were themselves agents of that great conspiracy to destroy human restraint and the Constitution by deprecating all that effectively upholds it.[3]

By the opening of the new century the principle of lower-class instruction was firmly established. If deeply conservative bishops felt moved to defend the extension of Sunday and charity schools, opposition from the propertied classes could not have been very formidable. Moss's predecessor at Oxford, John Randolph, was only one of the numerous prelates who, in the early years of the nineteenth century, openly encouraged the schools and refuted their critics. Aside from the obvious rationalistic arguments, Randolph suggested that Christ's love of children

[1] Horsley, *Charge* (1800), 25–26.   [2] *Report*, 20–22.

[3] C. Moss, *A Statement of Facts Relative to Mrs H. More's Schools, Occasioned by some Late Misrepresentations* (Bath, 1801), 21.

compelled saving the poor from ignorance and giving them minimal instruction to enter into 'a life of daily labour, well fortified, with the principles of duty'. Like most proponents of a rudimentary reading curriculum, the bishop knew that 'all beyond that may puff up their tender minds, or entice them into a way of life of no benefit to the publick . . .'. Frankly, however he could not see how catechism, piety, industry and church attendance, the only likely results from education, could be distrusted, and agreed that anything more 'may tend to make them despise, and consequently to neglect the duties of their proper station'.[1]

The recognition by churchmen like Randolph and Bishop Pretyman that the poor were growing indifferent not only to society, but to their own fate, had caused them to re-evaluate the relationship of the lower orders to general society. In the context of the French Revolution, Pretyman's warning that the poor are essential to 'our comfort, safety and prosperity, for without their numbers there can be no society as we know it . . .' was particularly meaningful.[2] For Randolph and most of his clerical contemporaries, the implementation of a carefully controlled reading program would suffice to correct the dangerous trend towards indifference among the children of the present generation. Pretyman, however, wondered in 1804 if the curriculum could or should remain so static in an age of change. Given the expansive, commercial nature of English society, and the functional importance of the laboring classes, the Bishop of Lincoln raised the possibility that in a country in which 'the manufacturers and commerce . . . are among the brightest ornaments of its glory, and the firmest bulwarks of its strength [it] cannot even exist without the assistance of honest, industrious, and . . . intelligent persons in the inferior classes of life'. Cautiously, he suggested that some consideration might be given to extend the curriculum to include at least an introduction to science and the various branches of trade.[3]

Pretyman was not only refuting the critics of education for the poor, but was also trying to indicate that the industrial and commercial growth of the nation was altering the forms, if not the function, of lower-class labor. Adjustments, it seemed to him, had to be made if the expanding instructional program was to be utilized effectively. Most of Pretyman's episcopal contemporaries were too closely wedded to the values and outlook of the landed squirearchy to appreciate the implications of a

---

[1] J. Randolph, *A Sermon Preached in the Parish Church of St Mary le Bow . . . May 20, 1802, Before the Society for Promoting Christian Knowledge* (1802), 19.

[2] *Pretyman Family Archives*, T 108/24.

[3] G. Pretyman, *A Sermon Preached . . . May 31, 1804, Being the Time of the Yearly Meeting of the Children Educated in the Charity Schools . . .* (1804), 9–13.

changing economy. In spite of the expanding body of literature in the second half of the eighteenth century calling for a more extensive program of basic vocational instruction for the poor, there is no evidence that it made much impression on the bench. Since modern, practical education was associated with Dissenter schools and academies, it raised little enthusiasm even in the higher levels of Anglican instruction. Given churchmen's vigorous defense of a fossilized, classical system of education in the universities and the grammar schools, it was unlikely that eighteenth-century parsons would be much interested in an advanced curriculum for the poor, if, in fact, they showed any interest whatsoever in educating them. Earlier in the century, schools of industry had been established in some areas in conjunction with charity schools, but the hostility of local tradesmen and the indifference of most parishes soon saw them fall by the wayside.[1] Various attempts to revive them in the second half of the century generally proved abortive, as did Pitt's effort to include vocational instruction in his Poor Law reform proposals of 1795. That was an unpropitious year for reform of any kind, as employers worried about the loss of their cheap, surplus labor market, and ratepayers were determined to resist any scheme likely to increase their taxes.

If the opening of the new century saw little inclination on the part of clerical educators to expand curriculum in the charity and Sunday schools to include writing and perhaps a little arithmetic, most Church leaders were convinced that the schools had already proven to be a great boon. Bishop Porteus, an energetic supporter from the start, during the peace of 1803 credited the charity and Sunday schools with saving the nation. He interpreted their rise and progress in the final decades of the century as providential. With revolution and anarchy lurking unforeseen, Englishmen, for some reason, had begun to construct an important means of defense and had already educated more than 300,000 children before the storm struck. Divine guidance was undoubtedly behind that fortuitous development, and, rather than being 'nurseries of disaffection and enthusiasm', as some charged, the schools were bulwarks of the Constitution. They not only taught the laboring poor to read and comprehend Scripture, but prepared them to read 'those admirable discourses, sermons, and tracts . . .' composed for the lowest classes as antidotes to revolutionary propaganda.[2] Porteus was so relieved and enthusiastic that he was convinced that there could no longer be any question that 'in *some way or other*, in Sunday schools, in charity schools, in day schools, in schools of industry, or whatever species of school, the poor *ought to be educated*'.[3] So critical was the 'public concern' in the matter, the bishop felt, that he proposed that if voluntary support was

[1] Jones, *Charity School Movement*, 83.
[2] Porteus, *Charge* (1803), 27–28.   [3] *Ibid.*, 23.

inadequate, the 'government itself (as many ancient governments have done) ought to take it into their own hands'. Raising what was to become a stock argument for opponents of voluntary education in the post-war years, Porteus briefly alluded to the very low crime rate in Scotland, where national educational establishments had long been in existence.[1] Before the Revolution *foreign* systems of national education were viewed by Church leaders as exactly that: they were unsuited to the English Constitution with its long tradition of decentralization, localization, and voluntary endowment.

Porteus's flirtation with foreign innovation was brief, and was not revived by episcopal spokesmen until Liberals like Edward Stanley began to appear on the bench in the 1830's and 1840's. When, in 1807, the government attempted to pass legislation establishing a national system of education for the lower orders, Porteus joined his brethren in defeating the measure in the House of Lords. The philanthropic brewer, Samuel Whitbread, had proposed in his Bill the establishment of parish schools financed by local rates under the direction of the local magistrates to supplement the voluntary schools already established. As in the case of Pitt's abortive measure a decade before, the new Bill was conceived as part of a larger scheme to reform the Poor Laws by educating a more responsible, self-reliant, industrious poor who would be less likely to follow their parents to the parish relief tables. In spite of opponents' hoary predictions that education would only teach the poor 'to despise their lot in life . . .', and would 'render them factious and refractory', susceptible to 'seditious pamphlets and vicious books', the Bill passed the Commons on August 6th.[2] The members were more convinced by evidence showing that in contrast to the rebellious behavior of the ignorant French and Irish poor, English laborers had remained loyal as their educational facilities increased. Reading had not enticed them from their necessary station in life; in fact additional instruction might permit more of the poor living off the rates to function without assistance from the burdened parish.

The Church had no quarrel with these aims. Its successful resistance to the Bill was motivated by a slowly emerging sense of social and religious responsibility. Nearly three decades of educational discussion and expansion, much of it under the threat of revolution and invasion, had made many clergymen aware of their canonical responsibilities and rights. Praised on all sides for having kept the lower orders content during the tumultuous events of the revolutionary years, churchmen took pride in the belief that their efforts had saved the nation. As Porteus explained, the schools were certainly a major weapon in the arsenal of social stability, which, under the guidance of the local clergy, had proven most effective. Moreover, the establishment of 'Church and King

[1] *Ibid.*, 30.   [2] *Hansard*, IX (1807), 798.

Societies' to counteract the reformist activities of the Corresponding Societies and the more moderate 'Friends of the People', did much to reassert the intimate relationship between the Establishment and the State. The Church had both fulfilled its social and political responsibilities and justified its emoluments and privileges.

Also of considerable importance was the growing recognition that lower-class education might well prove critical in re-establishing an Anglican influence among *all* classes of society. The Evangelical Revival breathed a new energy and sense of religiosity into clergy and laity alike, and gradually affected every party in the Church. In time High churchmen like Joshua Watson, Henry Handley Norris and William Stevens were as active on behalf of the faith as were William Wilberforce, Henry Thornton and Zachary Macaulay. The Hackney Phalanx was as devoted to improvement as was the Clapham Sect, and had the added advantage of close relations with the most important prelates on the bench.[1] Whatever High Churchmen or Broad Churchmen thought of the Evangelical enthusiasts who upset the spiritual equanimity of the Georgian Establishment, they were profoundly affected, if only negatively, by the religious revival. Not only did it make them conscious of many of the defects earnest revivalists sought to correct, but it forced them to encourage their clergy to counteract Evangelical and Methodist successes by an even more diligent devotion to parochial duty.

Whitbread's Bill, by placing control of parochial education in the hands of local magistrates, ran headlong into this improving sense of clerical function and responsibility. The bishops, including Porteus, interpreted the measure as an assault on Establishment prerogatives and responsibilities at a time when many clergymen were again ready to assume both. Archbishop Manners-Sutton spoke for the bench when he condemned the Bill passed by the Commons for subverting the first principle of education in the country—control by the parochial clergy. The archbishop emphasized that neither he nor the Church 'should . . . be considered hostile to the principle of diffusing instruction among the poor', and pointed to educational projects flourishing in every diocese, including his own. But the measure before the House of Lords was something else: it was a dangerous innovation threatening the very foundations of religion in the country.[2] Whitbread, by placing control of the schools, like the poor rates, in the hands of the magistrates, was trying to gain broad support from all religious denominations. Churchmen, more sensitive to the position of the Establishment than at any time in the preceding half-century, and relieved that it had survived so

[1] A. B. Webster, *Joshua Watson, the Story of a Layman 1771–1855* (1954), 26.

[2] *Hansard*, IX (1807), 1177–8.

many assaults by political and religious enthusiasts, were in no mood to compromise the privileges they so recently feared might be lost.

Although the bishops' old foe, Lord Stanhope, angrily denounced the 'abominable principle that no part of the population in this country ought to receive education unless in the tenets of the Established Church', he missed the point.[1] The prelates were not denying Dissenters the right to provide for the education of those children whose parents chose to send them to Nonconformist schools. They were merely asserting their conviction that as an Established Church, with canonical and legal rights and responsibilities to educate the people, any system of public education must be under the control and guidance of the Anglican clergy. The fact that generations of that clergy had chosen not to fulfil those responsibilities in no way altered their legality. In any event, new generations of churchmen were once more prepared to assume that traditional role, and it would be another sixty-three years before the passage of the Forster Education Bill in 1870 would force them to relinquish part of it to complete public control.

The implications of Whitbread's proposals even frightened old, broadminded bishops like Watson, if not the new episcopal defender of toleration and reform, Henry Bathurst. Watson, who years before had advocated a national system of public education, had, by 1807, lost his enthusiasm for the idea. In contrast to his brethren, however, Watson argued exclusively in economic and social, rather than ecclesiastical, terms. He wrote to the archbishop that he did not believe that the instances of educational neglect were sufficient to warrant legislative interference: this in spite of the fact that of 208 parishes queried in his diocese, only eighty-five reported a school. Furthermore, as a great landowner, he was opposed to any further increase in the rates. Citing census statistics, Watson concluded that as there was an average of nine births for every two marriages, there were very few peasants or manufacturers who could not spare threepence a week for each of their four or five children to be educated for two or three years. If any family was too impoverished to afford even that pittance, the bishop was sure 'it would readily be supplied to them by their richer neighbours, if from their sobriety and industry they appeared to be deserving objects of such benevolence and munificence'.[2] Underlying Watson's change of mind was fear of class disharmony, and suspicion of the extent of the poor's attachment to the English social structure. Years of revolutionary fervor and war, the success of Tom Paine and others who sought to incite the poor against their betters, and the vituperation and contempt heaped on the 'factious rabble' in return, indicated to Watson deep social rifts that would not soon be healed. Education was too important a means for

[1] *Ibid.* [2] Watson, *Anecdotes*, II, 318–20.

ameliorating these social tensions to be ignored. Voluntary support for the improvement and elevation of the inferior classes would go a long way to re-establish social trust and harmony, as it 'tends to unite the rich and poor together in bonds of benevolence and subordination, of good will and gratitude; and it tends also to generate in them both, that Christian disposition of mutual laws, and of respect for religion as a rule of life'.[1]

Watson's arguments for a change fell on sympathetic episcopal ears. Social cohesiveness and the protection of the Establishment were advantages of voluntary education that few churchmen were inclined to surrender to a religiously diverse political system. Only Bishop Bathurst, after learning that 'nearly two-thirds of the children of the laboring poor in this kingdom . . . have little or no education . . .', was willing to push on with legislative plans for making education a part of poor relief. There was no denying that vast numbers of people were idle and deplorably ignorant. It seemed to him that since these miserable folk are so important to 'our welfare and domestic comforts', they ought to have 'an unanswerable claim upon us, not only for necessary food and clothing, but also for education'.[2] Church leaders disagreed with the method, not the sentiment. That being so, it was clear to many of them that, having resisted a public solution, they had best come up with one of their own.

3. THE NATIONAL SOCIETY

Whitbread's scheme for parochial education was only one of several proposed in the opening decade of the new century. Wilberforce and some of his Evangelical friends spent two years on a plan for an Anglican school program before they bowed to the hostility or indifference of Rationalists, Dissenters and High Churchmen.[3] As early as 1798 the Quaker, Joseph Lancaster, had established for the poor in London a small non-denominational school utilizing the monitorial system of instruction developed by the Anglican clergyman, Andrew Bell, while teaching in Madras. By employing the older pupils to teach the younger students, Lancaster was able to provide an inexpensive, rudimentary introduction to reading, writing and arithmetic. The 'Madras system', as Bell and Lancaster both recognized, promised an economical way to educate great numbers of children at a minimal expenditure for staff and facilities. In their more euphoric moments, proponents of the monitorial

[1] Watson, *Charge* (1809), 20–22.
[2] H. Bathurst, *A Sermon Preached . . . June 7, 1810, Being the Time of the Yearly Meeting of the Children Educated in the Charity Schools . . .* (1810), 16–18.
[3] Wilberforce, *Life,* III, 72.

method estimated that one master, through proper supervision of his student monitors, could teach a thousand pupils.[1]

Lancaster's school and reputation steadily expanded, and in 1810 his friends and supporters, with the endorsement of the royal family, established the Royal Lancastrian Institution as a more effective way to promote the stability and expansion of lower-class education. Although it drew most of its support from wealthy Dissenters, the new society also attracted secular utilitarians like Jeremy Bentham, James Mill, and the leading parliamentary proponent of educational reform, Henry Brougham.[2] As Lancaster's schools eschewed religious controversy by limiting spiritual instruction to Bible reading, they also attracted many Evangelical and Broad Church supporters who had no quarrel with so wise and prudent a policy. The Church hierarchy, however, watched the development with mounting concern. Pious Sarah Trimmer had early denounced the schools for destroying the fear of man and God, while training an army for the approaching revolution, but her immediate conclusions received no endorsement from the bench.[3] On the contrary, Bishop Bathurst, in his primary *Charge* at Norwich in 1806, went out of his way to praise Lancaster's 'humane and benevolent intentions', as well as the 'ingenuity of his system'. He regretted the absence of the catechism, Creed and the Lord's Prayer in the schools, but felt the advantages overcame these concerns.[4] Bathurst's liberalism was fast becoming an anachronism on the bench and would remain so until the last years of his long life, when a few Evangelicals and more Broad Churchmen began to occupy episcopal thrones. Charles Daubeny, the High Church Archdeacon of Sarum, spoke more accurately for the hierarchy when, in 1809, he described the Lancastrian system as a conspiracy calculated to achieve the amalgamation of 'the great body of the people into one great deistical compound'.[5] When the Institution was established the following year, Daubeny added that Lancaster was himself a new Julian the Apostate and an emissary of Satan.[6]

These portentous descriptions of the Lancastrian movement were substantiated by the Lady Margaret Professor of Divinity, Herbert Marsh, when, in 1811, he not only condemned the new Institution, but

[1] Halévy, *England in 1815,* 529–30.

[2] E. Halévy, *The Growth of Philosophic Radicalism,* M. Morris, trans. (Boston, 1955), 285–6.

[3] Halévy, *England in 1815,* 531.

[4] H. Bathurst, *A Charge Delivered to the Clergy of the Diocese of Norwich . . . in 1806* (Norwich, 1806), 18–19.

[5] C. Daubeny, *A Sermon Preached . . . June 1, 1809, Being the Time of the Yearly Meeting of the Children Educated in the Charity Schools . . .* (1809), 17.

[6] Halévy, *England in 1815,* 531.

vigorously insisted that the Established religion must be the basis of any system of national education.[1] Citing the 77th and 79th canons of the Church requiring episcopal licences for schoolmasters, the teaching of the catechism, and the deliverance of the children to church, Marsh insisted that they still applied to parochial education. The reformers of the sixteenth and seventeenth centuries, he asserted, saw the importance of parish schools when they drafted the canons and, had their plans been carried out, the defections long experienced and still continuing would never have occurred. With the possibility of rational education at last becoming a reality, it would be madness, a betrayal of the Reformation, if it was not under the direction of the national Church. It 'would involve, not only an absurdity, but a principle of self-destruction; it would *counteract* by authority what it *enjoins* by authority'.[2]

Marsh charged that churchmen who lent their support to the Lancastrian schools were contributing to the destruction of the Establishment. What they described as religious neutrality was, in fact, religious indifference; the very idea of neutrality was, in Marsh's mind, a rejection of a canonically directed education in the principles of the Church. It was as illusory to suppose that children of the poor would receive religious instructions from their parents as it was to believe that a weekly Sunday lesson sufficiently overcame the 'generalized Christianity [taught] during six days in the week'. Marsh had no criticism of the monitorial method of instruction; on the contrary, he believed that the very effectiveness of the system accentuated the danger. It could reach so many children so rapidly that it would multiply indifference and even dislike of the Church at a frightful pace. Consequently, he warned, unless the Church utilizes it on its own behalf, the Bell system will prove 'the most powerful engine, that ever was devised against . . . [the Establishment], and is now at work for its destruction'.[3] Certain that the enemies of the Church appreciated the power of their new weapon, Marsh saw them launching a subtle offensive under the guise of religious neutrality. Now that they were exposed, he urged that the Church should

[1] H. Marsh (1757–1839), son of a Kent vicar, educated at Cambridge and at Leipzig. While in Leipzig wrote a history of English and French relations, pub. in 1798. Had to hide from Napoleonic agents in 1799. Pitt was pleased by the book and gave him a pension. Was Lady Margaret Professor in 1807, elevated to Llandaff in 1816 and Peterborough in 1819. Was a rabid anti-Calvinist, continually in conflict with Evangelicals like Simeon and Milner, and embroiled in controversy over his attempts to weed out Calvinist clergy from his diocese. Though a vigorous, improving bishop, he was not free from nepotism or pluralism.

[2] H. Marsh, *The National Religion, the Foundation of National Education. A Sermon Preached . . . June 13, 1811, Being the Time of the Yearly Meeting of the Children Educated in the Charity Schools . . .* (1811), 3–6.

[3] *Ibid.,* 10–13.

also adopt the Bell method and create a national system of Establishment day schools in which the children of the poor for a nominal fee would be expeditiously and inexpensively taught reading, writing, and numbers, but in a religious atmosphere that would adhere them to the Church while providing them 'ample leisure for *manual labour*'.[1] By the class standards of the day, it was a system that had everything.

Marsh was not simply belaboring the old High Church war-cry that it was once more in danger. Eighteenth-century hyperbole was giving way to nineteenth-century realities, which for the Church meant that thousands upon thousands of laboring families had deserted the national faith and were utterly beyond recall. Marsh's contempt for Methodists and Evangelicals did not blind him to the evidence for their criticism, nor the reasons for their success. They were, in his opinion, filling a vacuum created by the unwillingness of the State to provide adequately for the religious supervision of its subjects. But things were going too far when churchmen—lay and clerical alike—could support a non-Anglican system of instruction for the most populous class in society. They were rejecting the alliance of Church and State, with all its mutual advantages, and playing into the hands of those who wished to destroy it. Marsh pleaded that 'whether men consider Religion as *merely* an engine of the State, or regard it also, as they ought, for its own excellence and truth . . . they must in either case admit that its alliance with the *State* implies *utility* to the State'. The very principle of establishment required that both the secular and religious interests of the participants had to be upheld, else the entire structure would crumble. If the continued defection of people from the Church was encouraged much longer, it would 'create divisions in the *State* which may end with the dissolution of both'. Marsh recalled that they fell together under Charles I, and rose together under Charles II, supporting each other ever since. Which direction was preferable was obvious, but it was time to remind even statesmen that they were imagining things if they believed 'that the Church may fail without danger to themselves'.[2]

When he spoke of Establishment education, Marsh was not advocating legislative action to create a national system of schools under the direction of the Anglican clergy. Instead, he was calling upon the propertied classes of English society, most of whom he assumed were attached to the Church, to avoid strengthening the forces of religious indifference by financing non-denominational instruction for the poor. The lower orders already had 'less than ever a predilection for the Established Church'.[3] This was one of what Archdeacon Daubeny called the 'two striking circumstances of the times: namely, that increasing

[1] *Ibid.*, 18. [2] *Ibid.*, 39.

[3] H. Marsh, *A Vindication of Dr Bell's System of Tuition, in a Series of Letters* (1811), 9.

indifference to our excellent Establishment, together with that unprecedented zeal for the general propagation of Christianity'. The Church had to resolve this contradiction before still another generation was able to grow up outside of its influence, not only in traditional parishes, but in the manufacturing towns and in the Metropolis itself. What Marsh emphasized, however, was that the Church would not only be denied an opportunity to bring the saving truths of the Anglican faith to the poor, but that it would also lose its utility to the State, and imperil its privileged status. 'Our *utility* will cease', he warned. 'We shall lose the *power* of doing good. No residence, no preaching, no catechizing will further avail. Our flocks will have deserted us; they will have grown wiser than their guides; and the *national* Creed will have become too narrow for minds accustomed to the liberal basis.'[1] Unless the Church was prepared to assert its rights and show itself more useful to society than any of its enemies, then Dissenters, radicals and other enthusiasts of all types would assume the task.

Marsh's warning still rang in the ears of Joshua Watson, Henry Norris, John Bowles, Archbishop Manners-Sutton, and several other prelates when they met on 16 October 1811 to work out plans for a National Society for the Education of the Poor in the Principles of the Established Church. This was clear in the private memorandum that Bishop Randolph of London attached to an account of that organizational meeting. He and all the participants were motivated by the certainty that if the 'great body of the Nation be educated in other principles than those of the established Church, the natural consequences must be to [disassociate] . . . the minds of the people from it or render them indifferent to it'. In succeeding generations this would very likely 'prove fatal to the Church and the State itself'.[2]

Although the National Society was the conception of the High Church party, it quickly received the support of churchmen of all persuasions. Henry Ryder, then Dean of Wells, established two schools at once, and by 1813 was working on a third.[3] Elevated to Gloucester the following year, the first Evangelical to reach the bench, Ryder continued his enthusiastic efforts on behalf of the new society. Henry Bathurst, who never pretended to possess the energy and dedication of his new colleague, nevertheless warmly endorsed the new schools while resisting the vain attempts of his more narrow brethren to limit them to Anglican children. As he and others realized, a restrictive policy would merely drive the multitudes who floated between Methodism and the Church into Lancastrian schools, and irrevocably into Dissent.[4] The tolerant Bath-

[1] Marsh, *Sermon* (1811), 39–40.
[2] *Randolph Ps.,* Bodleian Library MSS. Top. Oxon. b. 170, f. 50.
[3] Ryder to Dudley Ryder, 12 Sept. 1813, *Harrowby MS.,* V, f. 122.
[4] Halévy, *England in 1815,* 532.

urst could see no possible advantage in exclusion, but several of his High Church associates, after too many years of revolutionary and religious enthusiasm, were unable to view Dissenters with anything but suspicion and hostility. With eminent churchmen like Marsh claiming that the Lancastrian Institution and the non-denominational British and Foreign Bible Society (established in 1804) were simply part of a leveling conspiracy to destroy the Established religion, Evangelicals and more moderate clerics like Bathurst had their work cut out for them.[1] In the charged atmosphere of the age, the Lady Margaret Professor's prediction, that in another generation the majority of the kingdom would no longer reside in the Establishment, strengthened the resolve of many Church defenders to prevent any further dilution of ecclesiastical and religious principles.[2]

Although the founding of the National Society was initially defensive, it rapidly became, along with church-building, the major offensive weapon of the reviving Church. Like it or not, the Establishment was challenged by the standards of its competitors, whether Evangelicals within the Church or religious and philanthropic enthusiasts without. Before the National Society was established, Lancaster charged that Bell in particular, and the Church in general, favored the ignorance of the poor by restricting the curriculum in existing schools to basic reading. Marsh sharply refuted the Quaker educator's claim by proving that Bell, in describing his monitorial system, favored 'the useful arts of writing and arithmetic' as well, and insisted that they should be taught in all Church schools. Sensitive, however, to contemporary prejudice on the subject, Marsh assured critics that the natural laws of hierarchical relativity would prevent any alteration of necessary social relationships. The expansion of the curriculum to include writing and numbers might elevate the poor within their stations, but relative class proportions would remain unaffected. 'The *higher* orders of society by a still superior education, will always remain at a sufficient distance from their poorer brethren'; consequently it would be cruel and unjust to deprive the lower orders of what minimal advancement they might attain. Furthermore, the growing complexity of daily life meant that if our domestics cannot write, 'we are perpetually inconvenienced'.[3]

The transformation in 1814 of the Royal Lancastrian Institution into the more powerful and effective British and Foreign School Society caused much less concern among Church leaders than did its reorganization four years earlier. The National Society had already attracted

[1] H. Marsh, *A Reply to the Strictures of the Rev. Isaac Milner, D.D., Dean of Carlisle* (Cambridge, 1813), 121.

[2] Marsh, *A Vindication*, 8.

[3] *Ibid.*, 14–15. See also A. Bell, *A Sketch of a National Institution for Training up the Children of the Poor* (1808).

sufficient contributions to provide for 360 new schools, educating 60,000 pupils. By 1818 the figures were tripled, and by 1824 400,000 children were being instructed in 3,054 schools united directly with the National Society.[1] In addition, thousands more were receiving rudimentary lessons in Sunday schools and charity schools which, though not formally united with the organization, nevertheless followed its principles and, in most schools, its mechanical practices. Well might the seventy-eight-year-old Bishop of Chichester, John Buckner, be amazed by the 'spirit of zeal for the education of the Poor [that] has sprung up, which watered by a widely-diffused beneficence, and flowing through different channels must tend to produce a fruitful harvest of soul-saving knowledge to future generations'.[2]

When bishops spoke of 'soul-saving', they also meant society-saving, and most of Buckner's colleagues, including the new Bishop of London, Howley, could not help but wonder what else the harvest would bring. Elevated to the bench in the midst of Luddite disturbances, and conscious of the poor's declining attachment to the Church, the nervous Howley was particularly conscious of dangers to the Establishment. By endorsing the National Society he believed he was placing a powerful weapon in the hands of the national Church. At the same time, however, Howley made it clear that he could see no way to improve upon the Bell system as currently employed, trusting that no more educational innovations would be necessary. Things had gone far enough; he had no interest in extending the schools or their curriculum beyond existing social and pedagogical levels. He simply hoped that they would continue to avoid Dissenter influences endangering the purity of Church instruction so recently achieved.[3] Howley's deeply conservative attitude was typical of the episcopal bench: having finally acted to preserve what it still possessed, it was best if the Church held the line at that point. The dynamics of the age were not very kind to line-holding. Men were continually re-examining and altering their views about social institutions, and education was no exception. By the end of the war, the *Rights of Man* had little novelty; they were assumed by large numbers of

---

[1] Walmsley, *Sermon* (1817), 12; Howley, *Charge* (1818), 24 ff.; Overton, *The English Church*, 241.

[2] John Buckner, *A Sermon Preached Before the Lords Spiritual and Temporal . . . February 5, 1812, Being the Day Appointed For A General Fast* (1812), 15.

Buckner (1734–1824) was an extraordinarily long-lived pluralist who was chaplain to the Duke of Richmond at the taking of Havana in 1762. He collected Church livings at a prodigious pace, culminating his preferments with Chichester in 1798.

[3] Howley's Letter Book 1, 10 Jan. 1815; HLB 31, 12 Sept. 1815; HLB 65, 21 July 1816; also *Charge* (1818), 25.

workers, even if they as yet had little opportunity to implement them.[1] In addition, many of Paine's old readers and a great many new literate laborers were extending their education under the tutelage of William Cobbett and the far more dangerous T. J. Wooler and Richard Carlile. Cobbett bluntly explained to Bishop Van Mildert in 1820 that his Lordship 'is very much deceived in supposing the People, or the vulgar, as you were pleased to call them, to be *incapable of comprehending argument*'. As if it was necessary to remind worried prelates, Cobbett pointed out that the minds of the poor 'have, within the last ten years, undergone a very great revolution . . .'.[2] The patronizing of the poor as if they were stunted children was a grave error.

Middle-class utilitarians, also suspecting that it was a great waste of improving energy, increasingly denounced a clerically dominated, haphazard system of education that was so inadequate in preparing the lower orders for the realities of life. Confident that individual understanding of economic and social realities would enhance the implementation of individual practices of enlightened self-interest, people like Bentham, James Mill, Dr Kay, Malthus and their parliamentary ally, Brougham, saw in popular education a necessary concomitant of an expanding industrial society. Adam Smith had understood this earlier when, on the basis of his experience in Scotland, he recommended the establishment of parish schools in which the laboring classes could be taught to understand their role in the social economy, as well as provided with some practical instruction. In Smith's time a little geometry and mechanics would suffice to embellish the three R's.[3] This would not interfere with the necessary mechanistic drudgery of repetitive industrial labor, but would in fact make it more acceptable if workers were convinced that their true interests were bound up with the accumulation of capital in an expanding society. The idea that an understanding of the natural laws of society and economics would reconcile the lower orders to these laws was fundamental to the educational schemes of radical utilitarians and political economists. Malthus repeated Smith's proposals, including them in his discussion of population restraints, and, in contrast to most of the clergy, supported Whitbread's Bill.[4]

Bentham and Mill, even before their first meeting in 1808, had concluded that a system of instruction was needed to enlighten the poor about their own interests, and consequently, those of the national welfare. Mill, as the principal utilitarian spokesman on education, believed that the laboring poor could be educated to see that their interests

[1] Thompson, *English Working Class*, 603.   [2] *Ibid.*, 745-6.

[3] *Wealth of Nations*, Bk. V, Chap. 1, art. ii.

[4] *Essay On Population*, Bk IV, chap. 9: also *A Letter to Samuel Whitbread, Esq., M.P., On His Proposed Bill for Amendment of the Poor Laws* (1807).

lay with middle-class leadership and the economic system it encouraged.[1] This meant that the curriculum should be rational, scientific and secular, stressing those subjects that would best prepare the children of the laboring classes for a practical role in society. Initially, Mill, along with Brougham, Joseph Hume and Francis Place, supported the Lancastrian schools as the best hope, and attacked the National Society as narrow and exclusive, seeking to reconcile the poor to the domination of clerical and Tory landowning interests.[2] The most abusive and persuasive attacks on the National Society's exclusiveness came from Bentham himself in his provocative *Church of Englandism and Its Catechism Examined* (1818). Whigs readily co-operated with the Radical critics, seeing in their educational proposals a means for encouraging contentment among the poor while weakening the Tory-clerical alliance so many of them abhorred. Not yet appreciating the implications of Ricardian rent economics, many Whigs believed that utilitarian self-interest would reconcile the laboring classes to an understanding and continued acceptance of hereditary, aristocratic domination, of Whig rather than Tory persuasion. While the Radicals dreamed of integrating the workers into a new society led by industrialists, bankers, merchants and professional people, Whig aristocrats dreamed of acquiescence.[3] Both, however, spelled trouble for the Church's newly discovered role as educator of the people.

The early utilitarian hope placed in the Lancastrian schools gradually gave way to disillusionment as spiritually revived Dissenters began to dominate the British and Foreign School Society. It became clear to Mill and Bentham that the foundations of a useful system of universal secular education had not been established. Through the efforts of Brougham, the Whig-Radical educational alliance turned to Parliament, where, in 1816, the Commons agreed to establish a Select Committee on the Education of the Lower Orders in the Metropolis. Its controversial report in 1818 was followed two years later by an attempt to legislate a parochial system of compulsory education permitting the erection of school houses and the payment of schoolmasters from local rates as well as from already established voluntary sources. Although Brougham's proposals drew heavily upon Mill's educational ideas, an attempt was made to win Anglican support by accepting the incumbent's right to

[1] 'Education', *Encyclopaedia Britannica*, 5th ed. (1818), Supplement. Also, Brian Simon, *Studies in the History of Education 1780–1870* (1960), 143–4.

[2] James Mill, *Schools for All not Schools for Churchmen Only* (1812).

[3] Simon, *Studies*, 134–5. Whigs were especially fascinated by the educational schemes of the Swiss pedagogue, von Fellenberg, whose model schools carefully delineated between aristocratic and lower-class subjects. Brougham, who visited the schools, wrote a series of articles for the *Edinburgh Review*, XXXI, No. 61 (Dec. 1818), XXXII, No. 64 (Oct. 1819).

veto any schoolmaster in the parish selected by local householders. Moreover, the minister was granted the right of superintendence over the schools under the visitation of his bishop. This sufficed to alienate Dissenters and the more ardent Radicals, who saw in the measure nothing more than the establishment of Church schools. The requirement that the Bible alone be read, with all distinctive catechisms excluded from the class-room, also ended all hope of Church support. That was exactly the kind of leveling indifference Marsh, now Bishop of Peterborough, and others had been condemning throughout the preceding decade. At Lord Castlereagh's request, the Bill was dropped after the first reading. Unlike Whitbread's Bill, which passed the Commons thirteen years earlier, this second attempt at public education never came to a vote. Denominational lines were being more sharply drawn as political and economic lines were becoming blurred. To the Church, the underlining of the former would somehow clarify and preserve the latter, with society and the Establishment its benefactors.

4. UTILITARIAN ADVANTAGES AND SECOND THOUGHTS

If in 1820 the bishops were hostile to Brougham's Education Bill, some of their successors were at least strongly sympathetic to the utilitarian motives behind the measure. As early as 1803, Robert Gray, later Bishop of Bristol, had been convinced by Adam Smith's arguments in favor of a national system of parochial schools to insure that the minds of laboring poor would be allowed some expansion.[1] Gray was particularly struck by the Scottish economist's contention that

> where dexterity in particular trades is acquired at the expense of intellectual and social virtues . . . [the result *is*] that stupid torpor, incapable of generous sentiments and just judgement concerning the ordinary duties of private life, and much more of the extensive interests of the country, and that debasement of the national courage and activity. . . .

Ignorance, Gray argued, was a far greater cause of social unrest than learning, and, like Smith, he believed the poor would be more content and productive if they understood the natural laws creating their laborious station.[2]

Other early propoponents of political economy, like J. B. Sumner, Edward Copleston and William Otter, shared similar views, but were inspired more directly by Malthus than by Smith. In his important analysis of Malthusian law in the *Records of Creation*, Sumner

[1] R. Gray, *A Sermon Preached . . . May 26, 1803, Being the Time of the Yearly Meeting of the Children Educated in the Charity Schools . . .* (1803), 16.

[2] *Ibid.*, 13. *Wealth of Nations*, Bk. V, Chap. I.

envisioned education as an important adjunct of poor relief and population control. The principles of political economy, when presented in a simple religious framework, would suffice to convince the poor that it was in their own self-interest to co-operate with the truths of natural law that had been established for a comprehensible divine purpose. 'If labour is heavy, or distress severe, how greatly is the load lightened by the conviction that man is not the sport of chance, or accidental circumstances, or human enactments, but the work of a wise and benevolent Creator, and the object of his paternal care!'[1] The inculcation of that conviction through a regularized program of education would make the poor agents of their own self-improvement. Education was, in effect, a 'preventive check' providing the lower orders an opportunity to evaluate their own condition realistically and, in accordance with natural laws of enlightened self-interest, to determine the most beneficial course of personal betterment for themselves and their families. Copleston described the check as 'moral alleviation—a spirit of industry, of self-respect, of moral decency . . .' that would provide the discipline for 'that preventive check upon marriage which, whether deliberately imposed or adopted only through habit and custom, is absolutely essential to the well-being of society'.[2] So long as that check was under religious control, Sumner was confident that the poor's conclusion would provide a natural blending of self-interest and social harmony. Consequently, it seemed obvious to clerical economists that the upper classes must recognize that ignorance is the enemy of industry, as stupidity is the foe of subordination.[3]

The National Society promised to fight these opponents and, in addition, strengthen the position of the Establishment. This was made clear in 1817 when T. T. Walmsley, Secretary to the Society, cited as a principal goal of the organization the eventual elimination of the poor rates. As the children of the poor were taught prudence and responsibility, they would develop a self-discipline and restraint that would lead to their general economic as well as social improvement.[4] The expansion of statistical enquiries facilitated the evaluation of such a plan, For example, churchmen seeking meaningful and measurable proof of their educational successes attended to the worrisome problem of increased urban crime. If a significant correlation between rising educational opportunities and a declining crime-rate could be established, was it not likely that the poor were being improved by the expansion of their intellect? Many supporters of the National Society certainly thought so. Bishop Ryder, in 1819, quoted Society statistics showing that of 497 juveniles committed to Newgate Prison between 1814 and 1818, only 14

---

[1] Sumner, *Treatise*, II, 294, 297.
[2] Copleston, *Second Letter*, 102–3.
[3] Sumner, *Treatise*, II, 295. [4] Walmsley, *Sermon* (1817), 8–9.

had ever attended a National School, and 6 of them had left after only one week.[1] Bishop Jenkinson of St David's, Liverpool's cousin, offered similar figures for Millbank Penitentiary, where he was delighted to learn that, of some 400 inmates examined, only one had been educated in a National or Sunday school.[2]

The quoting of such favorable statistics became a standard item of episcopal exhortation and justification in the 1820's. Shortly before his translation to London in 1828, Bishop Blomfield suggested that the National Society's schools had been so successful in reducing juvenile crime among their students that the government should consider supporting them as a less expensive and more effective method of crime-prevention. As an old admirer of Jeremy Bentham's prison reform schemes, the bishop had long been interested in questions of penal improvement. He endorsed the utilitarian emphasis upon preventive law enforcement and prisoner rehabilitation, and saw the Church's schools playing an important correlative role in that area. Appealing to the frugal sentiments of complaining ratepayers, Blomfield indicated that 'a moderate expenditure, bestowed upon the education of poor children, might be the means of curtailing, and rendering unnecessary, the cumbrous and costly machinery of punishment, which is now employed to constrain, or to crush, as useless or noxious members of society, those who have become so for want of early instruction and discipline'.[3] Radical reformers had been saying the same thing for several years, but without conceding the Church's essential point that the most important ingredient of success was catechetical instruction rather than an expanded practical curriculum.

In spite of clerical utilitarian promises, the disturbances and riots of the post-war years, as well as the Radical challenge to religious education, certainly caused second thoughts, among some churchmen, about the value of an educated poor. Most recognized, however, that there was no turning back; the alternatives were even less appealing. William Otter in 1820 ridiculed waverers who blamed recent disturbances, like that at Manchester the preceding year, on people deluded by 'an excess of information'. He was concerned that many supporters of the schools had suddenly withheld contributions while they 'anxiously and doubtfully' re-examined the wisdom of their beneficent act. Otter found it

[1] H. Ryder, *A Charge Delivered to the Clergy of the Diocese of Gloucester ... 1819* (Gloucester, 1819), 18–19.

[2] J. B. Jenkinson, *A Sermon Preached . . . June V, MDCCCXXVIII, At the Yearly Meeting of the Children of the Charity Schools . . .* (1828), 7.

[3] C. J. Blomfield, *The Christian Duty Towards Criminals. A Sermon Preached . . . For the Benefit of the Society for the Improvement of Prison Discipline, and for the Reformation of Juvenile Offenders, On Sunday June 22, 1828* (1828), 16–17.

incredible that such great work, so recently begun, might perish 'under the influence of dark surmises, and of insidious unfounded fears'.[1] As all men are endowed with natural privileges and capacities, mental cultivation being among them, only despotic societies dare contradict nature and providence by neglecting the education of the inferior orders. Ignorance and immorality will sweep us all away in time, he warned, but even sooner in a country where the press is free, communication is rapid and sedition can spread freely.[2] Otter asserted that it was no longer possible to ignore the truth: if we abandon the effort, others will readily assume it. Radical schools are already planting seeds of infidelity and disloyalty in the populous cities of the north.[3] Otter, as a Whig and an early convert to Malthusianism, felt more strongly than many about the importance of lower-class instruction. But even that old nepotistic Tory, Majendie, agreed that there were, in the new age, two essential needs for the preservation of the Constitution: 'each Parish should have its appropriate resident Minister, and every town, at least, its Established school'.[4] Both seemed distant.

Most prelates by the end of the second decade of the nineteenth century knew that it was 'a superfluous task' to preach the early instruction of the poor. The Church was already doing it, and only prayed it could proceed more quickly than its various enemies. The new Bishop of Llandaff, and later Durham, Van Mildert, wished it were otherwise; he recoiled at the 'leveling tendencies' of modern education. The advocates of Brougham's proposals were 'levellers of rank and property [who] . . . aim at accomplishing their purpose by lowering others as well as raising themselves, and learning in the one case, as wealth in the other, is made a subject of opprobrium and contempt'. Proponents of popular education, in the frightened prelate's mind, were seeking to diminish the poor's respect for superior attainments and the benefits they had so long derived 'from deference to the judgement of those who are best qualified to direct them'. Van Mildert shuddered as he envisioned the new application of 'intellectual machinery' that could produce instruction 'with a rapidity, and with a precision also, of which our forefathers had no conception'. The mechanistic implications of the Bell monitorial system deeply frightened conservative Tory churchmen like Van Mildert, who saw in it the same dire threats to old England that others saw in the mechanized industrialization of the Midlands and the north. Reluctantly, the bishop acknowledged there was no turning back; it was 'neither safe nor practicable . . .', since both were now the standards by which measurements were made. 'Perseverance is become necessary for self-

---

[1] Otter, *Sermon* (1820), 3–4. [2] *Ibid.,* 7–8.
[3] *Ibid.,* 26, 29.
[4] H. Majendie, *A Charge Delivered to the Clergy of the Diocese of Bangor . . . 1817* (Bangor, 1817), 29.

defense. The machine is even now in motion, and upon prudence and discretion of the hand that guides it must the result depend.'[1]

Van Mildert, as one of the prelates least able to come to grips with post-war England, in contrast to most Church leaders of the 1820's and 1830's rarely mentioned the question of lower-class education. As far as he was concerned, it had proceeded far enough, and he could not abide the receptivity of his colleagues to plans for still greater expansion. In 1834, two years before his death, and after what seemed to him a life-time of evil innovations, he was sure that his distrust had been vindi-cated. The education of the poor had indeed proven to be dangerous and mischievous.[2] This was as close as any bishop came to open opposi-tion. Not even the security of the National Society and its dedication to Church principles reconciled Van Mildert, and his coolness towards the schools was only exceeded by his bitter hostility to reform of any kind.

Ambivalence, however, rather than opposition characterized the feelings of those strong conservatives of Van Mildert's generation respon-sible for encouraging the expansion of lower-class instruction. George Henry Law, for example, found his enthusiasm rising and falling in direct proportion to the intensity of popular disturbances. In 1813 he wholeheartedly supported 'framing the heart and stamping the charac-ter of the future man', by educating children as early as possible.[3] By 1820, however, he felt frightened and overwhelmed by the magnitude of problems in his manufacturing diocese, and the realization that laborers were reading Paine, Volney, Voltaire, and even Thomas Spence. The latter's visions of land redistribution were especially upsetting, for 'the poor . . . will always lend a ready ear to arguments, the intention of which is to prove, that they are justly entitled to the superfluities of the rich'. Perhaps education had gone too far when 'the universality of reading, combined with the licentiousness of the press . . .' endangered society.[4] Van Mildert would have been content to say 'I told you so'; Law, however, like most of his colleagues, especially those who had risen to power since the war, concluded that the only antidote to 'the deadly poison' was a more vigorous application of religious and moral instruction in the schools.[5] Three years later Law was again very optimis-tic about that 'most important experiment', and boasted that 'ere long

[1] W. Van Mildert, *True and False Knowledge Compared. A Sermon Preached . . . June 8, 1820, Being the Time of the Yearly Meeting of the Children Educated in the Charity Schools . . .* (1820), 12–13.

[2] W. Van Mildert, *A Sermon Preached . . . at the Assizes, July 27, 1834* (Durham, 1834), 16–17.

[3] Law, *Sermon* (June 1813), 9. Also *A Charge Delivered to the Clergy of the Diocese of Chester . . . 1817*, 2nd ed. (Chester, 1817), 6–7.

[4] Law, *Charge* (1820), 24–25.   [5] *Ibid.*, 29–30.

the British Isles may exhibit an instance never before known, of a whole nation educated, and able to read and write'.[1] When, however, in 1828, the orientation of the teaching of arithmetic in particular, and the curriculum in general, towards slightly 'higher scholastic attainments' was suggested, the prelate feared it would cause the poor to 'puffeth up' suddenly and seek employment for which they were unqualified. The result would be a 'dangerous and pitiable frustration' among educated youths.[2] It was best to leave things alone. Law had gone as far as he dared.

Like so many churchmen of his generation, Law had been raised with an eighteenth-century confidence in the efficacy of rational improvement within the context of an established hierarchical social structure governed by unvarying natural laws. He never feared that the betterment of the human condition would in any way invalidate inequitable social realities necessary for the benefit of all. If the French Revolution had shaken his optimism, it did not radically alter his faith. The establishment of Church-directed schools was seen as a reaffirmation of the belief that the human mind, no matter how lowly, was receptive to truths, especially those in accord with evident natural laws of society. As in the hierarchy of life, all things were relative, and so long as the instruction of the poor was predicated upon that relativity, without in any way violating it, the necessary harmony of a progressive society could be maintained. This was a static eighteenth-century faith in an era of nineteenth-century motion. The previous generation of bishops, Porteus, Barrington, Watson and Horsley, were never really confronted with the social implications of industrial change. The disruption of an agrarian society, the development of a working-class consciousness, the emergence of a more aggressive, intellectually powerful middle-class radicalism no longer content with the traditional landed patterns of political, social and economic leadership, were not yet realities to those Church leaders who dominated the revolutionary years. In a way the French Revolution had protected them from seriously confronting the changes occurring in a nation supposedly held together by their ameliorative skills.

The post-war generation, lacking such protection, saw unprecedented changes; though they were still men of the eighteenth century, differing little in terms of education and outlook from their predecessors. Attempting to interpret and adjust to the nineteenth century in the usual

---

[1] G. H. Law, *On Education. A Sermon Preached . . . At the Anniversary Meeting of the Bath and Wells Diocesan School, On Tuesday, October 9, 1827* (1827), 18–19.

[2] G. H. Law, *The Spiritual Duties of a Christian Minister. A Charge Delivered to the Clergy of the Diocese of Bath and Wells . . . July, 1828* (Wells, 1828), 24.

eighteenth-century way they reaffirmed the necessitous truths of natural law and the relativistic nature of the social structure. For some, political economy was the logical outcome—a political economy reconciled to the natural laws of Scriptural revelation. Education was cast in the same light and, so long as it could be reconciled to the natural laws of hierarchical stratification, there was no problem. When, however, it appeared that an advancement of knowledge incompatible with the existing natural relationship between classes endangered the relative relationship between the various levels of society, there was very great concern indeed. This is what led Bishop Law into a retreat from his earlier educational optimism. Sounding very much like a High Church prelate of the 1780's warning his clergy about Rousseauist visionaries, Law recalled in 1831 that:

> the Almighty has given to his creatures different faculties and endowments, both of mind and body. There must be the Philosopher, the Statesman; the Artizan; and . . . at the same time, the hewers of wood and the drawers of water. On the combined operation of all, grounded in the conviction of mutual interest and utility, depends the proper working, and the harmony, of the great machine of the world.

Law saw that education gave power to all who received it, even the poor. But by going beyond the dictates of natural law and social harmony, 'we render them dissatisfied with their station, we lay the foundation of civil insubordination, and discord'. Consequently, we dare proceed no further; a basic religious education is enough for them 'to discharge the duties of that station of life, in which it hath pleased Almighty God to place [them]'.[1]

What Law and other opponents of curricular extension failed to see was that the relative societal scale upon which they weighed their arguments and reactions was loaded against them. It had been balanced in a different age and in a different world in which the calculations, though reassuring, were hopelessly irrelevant. The National Society had been established in 1811 on eighteenth-century standards, which modern critics stridently pointed out by the 1820's. Utilitarians and other rational reformers argued that the narrowness and inadequacy of the Church schools were as anachronistic as the classical-clerical obscurantism and pedantry of the grammar schools. Many of the Lancastrian and Dissenter schools were providing basic instruction in science and mechanics as well as other trades, while the appearance of Mechanics Institutes and other programs for adult education further pointed up deficiencies of Anglican schools. Moreover, within the National Society itself there were a few reform voices concerned about curricular rigidity and the wretched quality of instruction provided by the monitorial method. As

[1] Law, *Charge* (1831), 16–17.

Bishop Jenkinson concluded in 1828, the education of the poor was no longer an issue as such; of what it should consist, and how it should go, were the meaningful questions.[1]

Samuel Butler, Archdeacon of Derby and Headmaster of Shrewsbury School since 1798, lent considerable weight to the argument that it had gone far enough. Butler, the most famous schoolmaster of the early nineteenth century, was not simply an educational reactionary. On the contrary, before leaving Shrewsbury to become Bishop of Lichfield in 1836, Butler had anticipated many of the curricular reforms Thomas Arnold later applied at Rugby. Through a judicious introduction of modern languages, geography and history to its basically classical curriculum, Butler transformed the school from a declining, debt-ridden, poorly endowed institution into one of the most flourishing and respected grammar schools of the day. Even Brougham, who had raised Butler's ire in 1820 by his scheme for national education, considered the headmaster among the most enlightened of educators and was his principal supporter for a bishopric.[2] Nevertheless, they were far apart on the question of lower-class education, with Butler, better than anyone else, representing conservative ecclesiastical thinking on the subject in the 1820's.

Like most churchmen, Butler, while believing great progress had been made in creating a literate laboring class during the preceding forty years, recognized that a critical point had been reached. It is, he told his clergy in 1826, as rare to find an adult who cannot read and write today as it was to find one who could forty years earlier, but 'I am not afraid to confess that I think there is something too vague and indefinite in the benevolence of those who would wish to go much farther'. He was deeply alarmed by the beneficial and exaggerated schemes for the improvement of mankind, as well as the increase in chimerical attempts to spread wisdom to all classes through shorter roads to learning, by 'almost instantaneous technical illuminations'. The wisdom and experience of ages have revealed that real learning is a slow and gradual process, so what useful purpose can really come from educating the poor beyond reading, writing and religion?[3]

Butler recognized what many advanced educational reformers of the period failed to consider. The social structure and its economic requirements could not afford the luxury, nor risk the disruptive dangers, of an

[1] Jenkinson, *Sermon* (1828), 2.

[2] Brougham to Butler, 3 April 1831, *Butler Ps.,* Add. MS. 34588, f. 28; Butler to Maltby, 9 Oct. 1834, Add. MS. 34589, ff. 127-8. Also S. Butler, *A Letter to Henry Brougham, Esq., M.P., On Certain Clauses in the Education Bills Now Before Parliament* (Shrewsbury, 1820).

[3] S. Butler, *A Charge to the Clergy of the Archdeaconry of Derby . . . 1826* (1826), 6-8.

educated laboring class. The lower orders must, by necessity, be excluded from the required leisure and opportunity for proper education. 'Time, patience, talent and opportunity' are the prerequisites of meaningful instruction. 'How much of these can be commanded by the lower orders, who must always be under the necessity of working for their daily bread, and whose intervals of labour must generally be spent in that rest, which is necessary to qualify them for its resumption?' It would be both cruel and dangerous to introduce to the poor what can be only superficial educational attainments whose further pursuit social and economic requirements forbid. At the same time they would not be prevented from exaggerating their little learning, from feeling competent to speculate and propose on the most difficult and profound questions answerable only by years of slow, accumulated study.[1]

Butler, typically viewing society as hierarchical and relative, did not believe that social change could affect one part of the hierarchy without relatively affecting the other segments. Applied to education, this meant that expanded opportunities for the lower orders would not in reality alter their 'relative degree of ignorance', and things would remain much as they were. 'For beyond [a] . . . point those who knew nothing, would still be held as ignorant; and those who knew more, and those who knew most, as most informed. So that the equalization of learning is as great, and considering the various degrees of talent and capacity which God has given to mankind, a greater chimera, than that of property.'[2] Consequently, without really altering the realities of the existing social structure, educational expansion would seriously threaten it; 'for the possession of knowledge without the power of exercising it, must not only be unprofitable, but a source of restlessness and uneasiness to its possessor. It must tend to make him dissatisfied with his condition. . . .'[3]

To those who argued that a more expanded, practical education would create more skilled and efficient laborers, beneficial to themselves and society, Butler appealed in 1829 to Scripture and political economy, both of whose validity he felt assured was beyond question. After reminding his clergy, as if they required it, of what followed from eating fruit from the tree of knowledge, he indicated his hostility to the 'sentimentality' that encouraged further education for the poor along with 'other acts of charity and benevolence'. Was it not possible that more education would, in fact, so alienate the poor from their established role that they would

withdraw . . . from useful and honest industry, to idle and unprofitable speculation; from cheerful and active employment in the duties of their

[1] *Ibid.*, 9–10.   [2] *Ibid.*, 11.
[3] Butler, *Charge* (1829), 10.

calling, to a reluctant and dissatisfied discharge of so much labour as the wants of nature required, or to lazy and degrading dependence on the bounty and services of others?[1]

In a way, Butler never recovered from the fright of Brougham's attempt in 1820 not only to establish public education, but to revise the grammar school statutes by requiring the modernization of their curriculum and the admission of more of the local poor as their founders and endowers had often stipulated.[2] It seemed to the headmaster part of a wicked plot to equalize education; although he was not opposed to introducing some modern subjects, he believed that classical studies were not only the pillars of a sound education, but a principal means of excluding the lower orders from sharing in benefits above their station. His deep contempt for the poor, so evident among many of the clergy of the time, came through in his angry complaint that 'the parents of all boys above the lowest class who wish to avail themselves of the benefactions of their ancestors must do it at the price of having their children's manners contaminated by association with the very dregs of society'.[3] Butler never modified his hostility in spite of the many changes in English society before his death in 1839. As far as he was concerned, education for the lower classes had been settled in 1811 with the establishment of the National Society. When, in 1836 as Bishop of Lichfield, he was asked to support a society for the promotion of normal schools to train teachers to educate the poor, he condemned the plan as a European innovation which would lead to a compulsory, leveling system of education. This not only violated traditional English concepts of freedom, but the mixing of classes would inevitably lead to 'that detestable mediocrity which is the *summum bonum* of dullness . . .'.[4]

Butler's influential ideas were shared by many Church leaders in the decade before the Reform Bill, although the realities of the 1830's and 1840's forced many to re-evaluate their earlier policies. Bishop Howley who as early as 1822 was very uneasy about increasingly introducing the mass of people to the 'systematic culture of intellect', warmly thanked Butler in 1826 for his 'very judicious, and masterly remarks on the

[1] *Ibid.*

[2] See Butler's *Letter to Henry Brougham* (1820). Butler argued that rather than open the grammar schools to the poor on a wider basis the government should provide a system of lower-class instruction. See also Butler to Master of St John's, 19 Sept. 1820, *Butler Ps.,* Add. MS. 34585, ff. 33–35.

[3] Butler to H. G. Bennett, 20 Sept. 1820, *Butler Ps.,* Add. MS. 34585, f. 36. Butler had second thoughts about this intemperate description of the poor and crossed it out.

[4] Butler to E. Strutt, M.P., 29 Nov. 1836, *ibid.,* Add. MS. 34590, ff. 439–42, and Strutt to Butler, 5 Dec. 1836, ff. 451–3.

education of the lower orders'.[1] As Archbishop of Canterbury throughout the second quarter of the century, however, Howley and most of his contemporaries on the bench came to recognize that the poor would be exposed to wider education with or without the co-operation of the Church. Again, the triple motivations of social utility, Church revival, and the preservation of the Establishment began to affect the settled complacency and self-satisfaction of the bench. Stimulated by the mounting hostility towards an institution that seemed utterly indifferent to the real needs of a large segment of society, charges of callousness, neglect, materialism and uselessness both confused and angered churchmen who felt the Establishment was making remarkable progress in eliminating such abuses. As pressure for more dramatic reforms mounted, the Church was able to find protection in its alliance with the State; the repeal of the Test and Corporation Acts, however, followed by the shock of a Tory government emancipating Catholics in 1829, made even the dullest churchmen aware that they could no longer count on old arrangements. The worst was yet to come. The electoral setback suffered by the Tories the following year threatened to unleash those archdemons of the well-ordered society—enthusiasm, innovation and reform. It appeared to some panicked churchmen that their enemies were on the verge of their greatest triumph since the French Revolution. One of their foes' first tasks, it was assumed, would be to deprive the Church of its educational role; the next, in all probability, would be to complete the job of disestablishment. The success of the first would unquestionably assure the success of the second.

---

[1] Howley to Butler, 2 Oct. 1826, *ibid.,* Add. MS. 34586, f. 232. Also Howley, *A Charge Delivered to the Clergy of the Diocese of London . . . July, 1822* (1822), 10–12.

XI

<<<<<<<<<<<<<<<<<<<<<<<<<<<<<<<<<<<<<<<<<<<<<<<

Education and Establishment, 1830–51

<<<<<<<<<<<<<<<<<<<<<<<<<<<<<<<<<<<<<<<<<<<<<<<

1. CHURCH SCHOOLS CRITICIZED

The inauguration of Whig government in 1830 meant neither the end of Anglican education nor the destruction of the Establishment, though for some churchmen it certainly portended both. Earl Grey was no more committed to that policy than the Duke of Wellington. Both, however, did believe that reform of the Establishment was necessary and inevitable. Wellington, before his departure, and Grey shortly after his arrival, tried to impress upon Church leaders the need to 'put their own house in order'. Some of the newer, more perceptive prelates understood the implications of this even earlier and frightened their less resilient colleagues. Bishop Lloyd warned Peel in 1828 that the Bishop of London, Blomfield, was considering rash reform measures. 'No Act must pass through Blomfield's hands *alone*. . . . He . . . does not sufficiently take the advice of his brethren.'[1] Blomfield, during the months before Wellington's government fell, tried to convince prelates like Kaye and Monk that the Church must be prepared to reform itself. Soon after the election of 1830 he warned Kaye that unless the leaders of the Establishment began to act on its behalf, others would do it for them.[2]

Blomfield, concerned with internally reorganizing Church resources to enhance its efforts in the populous towns of the country, was able to convince the archbishop as well as Kaye, Monk, J. B. Sumner and a few others that it would be prudent for the bench to welcome a parlia-

[1] 26 Feb. 1828, *Peel Ps.*, Add. MS. 40343, ff. 178–9; also ff. 319–20.

[2] Blomfield to Kaye, 29 Sept. 1830, *Kaye Dep.*, I, 5/1; also Blomfield, *Memoir*, I, 162–3.

mentary enquiry into the amount and use of Church property. Several prelates believed the same kind of flexibility should be shown in the area of education as well, for the same changes in society that required a critical appraisal of Church utility in general also necessitated an examination of vital parts in particular. By the end of the 1820's very few churchmen would deny that education for the laboring multitudes was vital to the Establishment, though many agreed with Samuel Butler that in matters of content it had gone far enough.

Charles Richard Sumner, the new Bishop of Winchester, realized how closely this restrictive mentality was connected to the numerous charges of clerical indifference and contempt for the poor that were levied against churchmen in the post-war years. During his first visitation to his new diocese in 1829, Sumner urged that the Church accept the realities of the new age and be ready 'to condescend to men of low estate, whether of mind or fortune'. In matters of instruction it was necessary the clergy recognize that a period of unprecedented intellectual expansion, in which rigid formulas were no longer meaningful, was upon them. 'I know not why we should be backward in opening our eyes to it, that the fountains of human knowledge have been broken up, and the full tide is poured forth with such irresistible rapidity, that it may well be questioned whether there is an earthly power which can stay the torrent within its legitimate boundaries. . . .' To clergy still shaken by the bitter struggle over Catholic emancipation these were difficult words. They were too well aware of the instability of the age when their new diocesan warned them to 'mark the signs of the times, and to guide the current, which it was hopeless for them, if desirable, to attempt to stem'. Whether we think it a blessing or a curse, the 'rising curiosity of man' will continue.[1] It was absolutely essential that its progress be guided and regularized by the national Church.

Although Tory clerics doubted that Whig reformers would continue to welcome their voluntary educational efforts, it soon became clear that there was little sentiment in the country for a national system of compulsory public education. Churchmen were surprised and greatly relieved in 1833 when Roebuck's proposal to establish a rate-financed system of parochial instruction found little support even in the feared reformed House of Commons. The old alliance between Radicals and Whigs had gone as far as it could and quickly disintegrated after the passage of the Reform Bill. Most Whigs were satisfied with the voluntary system of education and distrusted the foreign models of national instruction some dissatisfied Radicals urged them to adopt. Even Henry Brougham had lost his enthusiasm for public education, no longer able to see any reason for supplementing, and eventually replacing, the expanding voluntary societies. On the contrary, he sought to strengthen

[1] Sumner, *Charge* (1829), 31-32.

391

their efforts when, in place of Roebuck's Bill, he proposed and carried a measure granting the societies £20,000 a year to assist in the construction of new schools in populous areas. Although in retrospect the annual grant marked the beginning of direct government involvement in the education of its people in England and Wales, it established no new principle at the time. Similar grants had regularly been distributed to Irish societies before 1830, and few people in the reformed Parliament could see anything wrong with extending the same type of assistance to the National and the British and Foreign School Societies.[1]

Whatever relief churchmen felt at the passage of Brougham's modest Act was short-lived. Parliament's endorsement of voluntary, denominational education—in effect the *status quo*—was but a brief prelude to years of bitter wrangling between Church and State. The growing complexity of English society magnified the diversity of interests in the advantages to be gained by popular education. Liberal reformers thought these advantages too important to be dominated by an Established Church unwilling to train the labouring poor for the age in which they lived and worked. Consequently, agitation increased, often supported by Dissenters who quickly perceived that since the amount of the grant received was proportionate to the amount of money raised by each society voluntarily, the apparently neutral distribution of public funds actually favored the Establishment. The Church consequently received 70 per cent of the first £100,000 distributed by the government.[2] Supported more strongly each year by numerous attacks on the inadequacy and incompetency of the National Society schools, Roebuck continued to propose plans for a system of public instruction. These attacks were not the work of Radicals and Dissenters only—the latter's schools were themselves often criticized—but appeared more frequently in the columns of *The Poor Man's Guardian*, in the workers' co-operatives, in the Owenite Halls of Science, and finally in the Chartist literature and rhetoric of the 1840's. When the working classes—the supposed beneficiaries of Church education—began disparaging the Establishment's efforts on their behalf, Anglican educators sensed that their troubles were just beginning.

The accumulation of crime-rate statistics, so impressive in the previous decade, were less encouraging to the bench in the 1830's. The agricultural riots of 1830–1 and the anti-clerical disturbances accompanying episcopal resistance to the Reform Bill caused prelates to take another look at the figures. C. R. Sumner was the first to admit that the Church had perhaps exaggerated the influence of education in preventing crime and violence. Drawing upon statistics compiled by the Poor Law Com-

[1] G. F. A. Best, 'The Religious Difficulties of National Education in England, 1800–70'. *Cambridge Historical Journal*, XII, No. 2 (1956), 164.
[2] Chadwick, *Victorian Church*, 338.

missioners in 1831, rather than those of the National Society, Sumner noted that of 332 persons jailed in his cathedral city, Winchester, 131 could both read and write; another 96 could read, while 105 could do neither. Even more distressing, of the 85 Hampshire parishes in which they lived, 81 had Anglican schools.[1] Sumner was a hard-working prelate who knew his diocese well. He was sophisticated enough to recognize that severe agricultural distress had driven laborers to riot and pillage, but, like most of his contemporaries, he could not understand how economic conditions could really overcome right attitudes. It was clear to him now, as he had suspected a few years before, that the schools were not imparting those attitudes in a way meaningful to the poor.

Episcopal defenders of Anglican education faced a continual dilemma over this problem. Having made crime-prevention an important utilitarian justification for the extension of denominational education, they were repeatedly embarrassed by the agitation, disturbances and periodic riots that were often led by literate laborers who had been educated in Sunday or day schools. Advocates of a national system of public education agreed with churchmen that education could be a major antidote to worker unrest and crime, but only if pupils were provided with a practical, useful curriculum that would both prepare them for their task in life, and help them understand the reasons for it. The formation of the secular Central Society of Education in 1836 to pursue this goal caused considerable consternation to worried episcopal leaders. C. R. Sumner, the following year, noted the danger from such an organization and warned that there was mounting pressure for the establishment of a general system of education under a central board. As it was no longer possible for the clergy to deny the considerable dissatisfaction with the quality of instruction provided in Church schools, Sumner feared that unless there was rapid improvement, their task of educating the people would be usurped. The solution did not lie in simply building new schools, especially since in some areas those already in existence were only partially filled, and in others there was actually a decline in attendance. During the previous four years, Sumner revealed, the number of pupils attending National Society schools in the diocese had actually fallen, despite the construction of thirty-two new class-rooms.[2] He was discovering what advocates of church-building were soon to learn: the existence of physical facilities were a secondary problem for the Church where the poor were concerned. The quality and character of their relationship were more important, and it was in this area that the Establishment continued to have its greatest difficulties. Such diverse prelates as Sumner, Maltby, Blomfield, Bathurst, Otter and Stanley

[1] Sumner, *Charge* (1833), 57.

[2] Sumner, *Charge* (1837), 25.

appreciated this in varying ways, and urged a reorganization of Church education to make the curriculum more relevant to the poor.

Maltby, for example, in 1834 explained that it was perfectly natural for the poor to be led from one subject to another once they were introduced to new information. Instead of fearing their curiosity, the Church should encourage and control it.[1] The alternative, as C. R. Sumner saw it, was to continue 'to live in the center of an ignorant and reckless population—reckless because ignorant'.[2] Without denying the truth of these words, or the failures of the schools, it was still distressing for Church leaders to contemplate continuing with more experiments. The extension of learning, as another prelate complained, had not ended the poor's 'thrill of excitement which is shaking our institutions to their base'; was there any prospect that more learning would satisfy their aroused appetites? Was it true, as educational innovators in the Church warned, that unless the Establishment continued with their plans, the laboring classes would pull free of religious roots entirely and bring disaster upon themselves and the rest of society?[3] The powerful Blomfield thought so; there was little time to be lost if the Church was to continue to have any voice in the matter. He concluded in 1834 that 'the extension and improvement of the National system will probably decide the question, whether the education of the poorer classes shall be suffered to remain, where it ought to remain, in the hands of the parochial clergy; or whether an attempt will be made, to place it under the control and direction of the government, with a compulsory provision for its maintenance'.[4]

Specifically, the bishop felt it was now time to introduce such subjects as history, geography and elements of useful practical science. There was no longer any reason 'why the education given the poor should differ from the education of their superiors, more widely than the different circumstances and duties of their respective conditions in life render absolutely necessary'. Unless the Church acted in this age of expansive learning, there was a danger that the lower orders would conclude 'that there is . . . an opposition between the doctrines and precepts of our holy religion, and other legitimate objects of intellectual inquiry; or that it is difficult to reconcile a due regard to the supreme importance of the one, with a certain degree of laudable curiosity about the other'.[5]

Blomfield, like most churchmen, believed an adequate national system

[1] Maltby, *Charge* (1834), 10–12.

[2] Sumner, *Charge* (1837), 28.

[3] P. N. Shuttleworth, *The Carnal Mind Is Enmity Against God. A Sermon Preached in the Parish Church of Bideford, August 9, 1835, On the Occasion of the District Committees of the Society for Promoting Christian Knowledge* . . . (1835), 16–17, 22.

[4] Blomfield, *Charge* (1834), 37.   [5] *Ibid.*, 34–36.

of instruction could be built upon existing voluntary, denominational foundations. It was simply a question of tacking on a few modern subjects to a Scripturally grounded, catechetical framework. Only one bishop, the indulgent old Bathurst, questioned the role of denominational instruction if a truly national system of useful education was a desirable goal. It seemed to him that so long as diverse religious interests were involved in the instruction of the poor, a comprehensive plan for lower-class education was unlikely. He had long believed that the State had no right to inflict capital punishment on any of its subjects, unless it had previously educated them to such a level that they were aware of alternatives. This, he felt, was done in Scotland and Switzerland where true national education existed and where children were not excluded from learning because of religious opinions. Denominational beliefs could be inculcated through Sunday schools, or whatever arrangements churches cared to make; national education, however, should be the business of the nation.[1]

After Bathurst's death in 1836, his successor, Edward Stanley, kept up the unpopular fight by arguing that public instruction did not preclude catechetical instruction by individual denominations. In his installation sermon the new prelate praised the advantages of religious education, but claimed that secular instruction also had great value in raising people 'in the scale of being, by exalting them above sensual and profligate habits, and by thus preparing the soil . . . for future fruits, and by a still further renewal and regeneration of their minds, rendering them more fit recipients for those higher sentiments associated with devotion'.[2] Stanley had had too much experience with the catechetical instruction lauded by his colleagues to believe that the memorizing of doctrinal points really had much lasting effect on the poor. He readily conceded, however, that he was virtually alone on the bench in his advocacy of instruction in any shape or form, so long as it was free from party factionalism and primarily concerned with the mental improvement of the lower orders.

Stanley was asking churchmen to support education not so much for the inculcation of complacent Christian virtues, but rather as a great opportunity to improve the mental, and, correspondingly, the physical condition of the working poor. The social results the clergy so desperately expected from religious exhortation and catechism would be a byproduct of intellectual uplifting. By supporting mechanical and industrial schools as well as other vocational institutions, the parochial ministers could provide a critical connecting link between the higher and humbler classes of the community—a link many feared had already

[1] Bathurst, *Memoir*, II, 70–71.
[2] E. Stanley, *A Sermon Preached At His Installation . . . 1837*, 2nd ed. (Norwich, 1837), 16–17.

snapped. They would be the 'medium by which the influence and refinements of the former are brought home to the wants, the necessities, the domestic economy, and even the recreation of the latter. And to the omission of this valuable accessory cultivation of the mind, do I attribute that disappointment too frequently complained of by the most sanguine and zealous supporters of . . . national education.'[1] During his primary visitation the following year, 1838, Stanley continued to pound the realities of a new political and social age into the minds of those clergy still preferring to ignore them. The 'circumstances of the age' have placed the relationships of society into new forms, and whatever opinion one might have about expanded political rights, and extended knowledge, they are here to stay. If the Church continued to reject every new experiment in education for lack of complete agreement with it, others will assume control. All the signs of the times, Stanley continued, point out that in education as in so many other areas, the salvation of Church authority does not depend upon resistance to innovation, but upon advocacy and guidance of new proposals.[2]

The expansion of education among the laboring classes appeared to clash with the much-belabored promise that the instruction of the poor would never be allowed to interfere with their passive acceptance of their laborious station in life. Stanley saw the conflict and listened to the fears; they were, he believed, irrelevant to an expansive, progressive era in which alternatives for improvement were continually being offered the lower orders. The Church could no longer resist. He confessed he had long 'considered and advocated education, and those various institutions more or less calculated to raise the people of this land above low and degrading pursuits, as the great means of civilization and reformation, as a *desideratum* with which the vital interests and welfare of the British empire were closely interwoven and identified'.[3] Clerics and laymen of all denominations, he pleaded, should unite in this common purpose. Stanley received some support from a future prelate, T. V. Short, who, as Rector of St George's, Bloomsbury, in 1835 had insisted that it was time for the Church to ask some hard questions about its position on the instruction of the poor. If it was afraid to teach the children of the laboring classes as much as time permitted, the Church would not long endure as the instructor of the working people. Like Blomfield, he could see no reason why the Establishment should be unwilling to provide the poor with as sound an education as the upper classes provided their children. But he went further than his bishop when he bluntly stated the reason he knew was most convincing

[1] *Ibid.*, 16.

[2] E. Stanley, *Charge Delivered to the Clergy of the Diocese of Norwich . . . July, 1838* (Norwich, 1838), 18–21.

[3] Stanley, *Sermon* (1837), 20–21.

to many of his brethren: 'it will be beneficial to society to prevent the mechanic from rising above that rank of life in which he was born, and that ignorance is likely to promote religion and good order in the state.'[1]

Short and Stanley, along with some others of their episcopal generation, believed that just the opposite would occur: the only hope of retaining meaningful class distinctions and religious authority lay in a recognition of 'the degree of power which has, of late years, been distributed to the people . . .'. It could then be made more 'coherent' by an educational system appreciative of economic and political change; one in which the rich man would appreciate the benefits derived from an improved condition of the poor, and the poor man would be convinced 'that his own interests are best consulted when the well-being of the rich is advanced'. Unlike Bathurst or Stanley, however, Short was still firmly convinced that this could best be accomplished within the structure of voluntary Church schools, for only Christianity could ameliorate 'the jarring interests of mankind . . . without that clash of selfishness which must terminate in anarchy and despotism'.[2]

Liberal bishops of the 1830's and 1840's were much more conscious of the utilitarian precepts of enlightened self-interest than were their old Tory predecessors. When they preached about social balance and class harmony, they were also concerned with a balance of interests—interests that economic changes and opportunities were altering, thus confusing both traditional relationships and traditional interests of individuals and classes. Church educators could not afford either to ignore the lessons or to fail to modernize their schools by more closely conforming them to the necessary interests of society. In 1838, shortly after his elevation to Chichester, Otter urged the National Society to revise its limited curriculum to conform to the new Poor Law by providing an education that would permit the poor to live on their own mental and physical resources: 'as the children in the workhouses, formerly the most destitute and hopeless of their race, are now so carefully instructed and educated, as to bid fair to become a credit and a comfort to the society . . . instead of a disgrace and an injury . . .'. The paternalism and over-protectionism of a bygone era was anachronistic in an age of political economy and unprecedented intellectual and material expansion. This, Otter said, had to be recognized in planning lower-class instruction. 'Hitherto the poor have been treated as children—they must now be considered as men'; but, if they are to become independent and mature, they must be properly trained and educated—not only for religious and economic security, but because, as the Reform Bill suggested, most of the poor in the National Schools would

[1] Short, *National Education*, 19.
[2] *Ibid.*, 4–5.

eventually be called upon to exercise the vote.[1] It is questionable how much Otter spoke for the Church when he thought such a prospect gave cause for rejoicing, but there is little doubt that few of his brethren would deny his claim that grounds for fearing that eventuality also existed. The real danger, however, was not that the laboring children, who would comprise the next generation of workers, would learn history, geography, philosophy and political economy, but that they would learn them under non-clerical tutelage.[2]

Otter's endorsement of an expanded curriculum had become standard episcopal fare by the later 1830's. As usual, the bench was trying to adjust realistically, but as little as possible, to the pressures of the age. The bishops were more astute in analyzing and posing problems than formulating and implementing meaningful solutions. There was little sympathy for Stanley's comprehensive schemes of national secular education, nor did many prelates relish the prospect of the laboring classes being educated out of their determined station in life. In spite of his support of a modernized curriculum, Short, for example, opposed public education as harmful to the 'strong bond of union between rich and poor' created by the charitable relationships of a voluntary system.[3] Still, pressures were mounting and criticism was becoming more severe. Bishop Maltby acknowledged this in 1838 when he agreed to present and support a petition from Manchester containing 24,000 names which urged the establishment of a national system of education to help alleviate the misery of the poor. Not only did the bishop concede that the monitorial system of instruction was superficial and ineffective, but he expressed sympathy for the principle of compulsory education. If English schools were ever to improve and approach the higher standards of Continental education, the government must take a much more active role in their improvement, beginning with the funding and establishment of normal schools to train competent teachers. Furthermore, Maltby argued, with a shortage already of fifteen thousand instructors for existing schools, only a large expenditure could alleviate the problem. Ever optimistic about the utility of education, the bishop was certain that the savings from reduced crime and prison maintenance would compensate for the cost.[4]

Maltby and the petitioners knew that the crux of the problem in any educational proposal was the question of religious instruction. They favored Bible readings without commentary, while reserving catechetical instruction for the denominational Sunday schools. The bishop

---

[1] W. Otter, *A Charge Delivered to the Clergy of the Diocese of Chichester in June 1838* . . . (1838), 50–51. Also, *A Sermon Preached . . . June 1, 1837 At the Yearly Meeting of the Children of the Charity Schools* . . . (1837), 14–15.

[2] Otter, *Sermon* (1837), 18–19.   [3] Short, *National Education*, 8.

[4] *Hansard*, XLII (1838), 937–42.

was not in the least optimistic, however, that the times were conducive to co-operation between Dissenters and churchmen. Stanley, alone, believed that some agreement might be reached on the essentials of Christianity which could be presented to the lower classes without denominational confusion. If Arminians and Calvinists can exist within the Establishment, he argued, was it not possible to find a common meeting ground with all Christians that would permit educational co-operation! Quoting reports on education in Holland and Belgium indicating that a co-operative approach was possible, Stanley urged its attempt in England.[1] As Maltby suspected, it was a futile cause.

The real strength of Stanley and Maltby's argument did not lie in the religious proposals they vainly advocated, but in the social conservatism they represented. Compulsory education seemed the best means of avoiding a serious alteration of the country's relative social composition. What bothered Maltby was that some laborers were receiving an education while many more were not. If, as some people charged, this made the educated laborers feel superior and therefore discontented with their station, the only answer was to educate all laborers so as to reduce relative comparisons. There was no evidence to prove that the ability to read the Bible and write a little, as well as understand something of figures, was incompatible with handling a plow or doing manual or mechanical work. Was it not unreasonable and unnatural to believe that because a man better understands his duty, he will be less inclined to practise it? Maltby thought so; moreover as his was an age when all classes were more learned and educated, there was a great danger that the relative social scale would be more seriously disrupted if the poor were excluded from a relative share. The entire intellectual level of society was rising, Maltby believed, so 'by advancing the lower in the scale of intellect, we shall not be in danger of breaking in upon the distance, by which different ranks were separated some years ago. The same gradation will continue; the same superiority in mental acquirements will still distinguish those of a higher rank. . . .'[2] National compulsory education, then, was not only in tune with economic and political changes in English society, but was also in harmony with the balanced laws of social relativity so important to nineteenth-century churchmen. In the post-Reform Bill years, however, Church leaders were not just concerned with social harmony; they were also concerned with the reform and preservation of their Church. Bishop Marsh's formulation of the argument early in the new century, to most Church leaders had greater meaning than ever.

[1] Stanley, *Charge* (1838), 23.

[2] E. Maltby, *The Early Training and Education of the Poor, Truly Christian Objects. A Sermon Preached . . . August 26, Being the Sunday Following the Meeting of the British Association . . .* (Newcastle, 1838), 13–14.

2. GOVERNMENT INTERFERENCE

Churchmen feared it was only a matter of time before agitation for public education would result in legislative action. Bishop Bagot, in 1838, believed his clergy should start organizing a major protest campaign.[1] In the same year Wilberforce privately noted that the government was planning to remove education from Church control, and predicted 'it must be the ruin of our land'.[2] The bishops, however, had not remained passive in the face of mounting criticism. In accordance with new principles of rational organization, they created twenty-four diocesan and sub-diocesan boards of education to co-ordinate and encourage the development of improved voluntary schools. The needs of the population, however, far exceeded the quantitative and qualitative capacities of existing voluntary societies. In 1839 Lord John Russell proposed increasing the annual education grant from £20,000 to £30,000, and extending it to all reputable schools, even those outside the two principal societies. To guarantee that the money would be well spent, the government now insisted on the right of school inspection under the direction of a special Educational Committee of the Privy Council. Religious affiliation did not enter into the composition of the Committee, nor was the bench represented. Russell, at the urging of Dr Kay, also proposed the establishment of a normal or model school to train competent teachers. As in all previous interdenominational schemes, religious instruction was to be limited to Biblical generalities rather than catechetical indoctrination. The bishops steeled themselves for a bitter battle, only to discover that they were outmanœuvered from the outset. By law the government only needed the consent of the Commons to spend less than a million pounds. Three thousand petitions, many of them clerical in origin, were submitted against the measure which, only after the normal school provisions were deleted, passed by two votes.[3] There was no chance that the Act would have survived the episcopal wrath in the Lords.

The usually benign Archbishop Howley was stung into action, bluntly accusing the government of trying to by-pass Parliament to establish an unpopular system of national education excluding Church influence. He felt reasonably safe as long as the grants were made directly to the two great educational societies, but the establishment of a secular committee, appointed by government ministers (especially Whig ministers)

[1] R. Bagot, *A Charge Delivered to the Clergy of the Diocese of Oxford . . . 1838* (Oxford, 1838), 16.

[2] Wilberforce to C. Anderson, 7 Dec. 1838, *Wilberforce Ps.,* Dep. C. 191, I.

[3] G. Monk, *A Charge Delivered to the Clergy of the Diocese of Gloucester and Bristol . . . MDCCCXLVII* (1847), 15.

was an innovation designed to threaten the Church. Frustrated that the Bill did not come to the Lords for consideration, Howley successfully carried a motion for an address to the Queen asking that a discussion be permitted in both houses on so momentous a national issue.[1] Only three Whig prelates, Otter, Maltby and Stanley, voted against the gesture. Arguing that the Committee of Council was merely a more efficient way to administer public funds, they refused to concede that it was a step towards the destruction of Church education.[2]

Maltby claimed that the English lower classes were far more ignorant than those in Continental countries, where the government took an active role in providing adequate facilities.[3] The revolutionary disposition of the Continental poor was not convincing testimony of the advantages of foreign methods. Recalling how the Church had so often resisted change and improvement in education, Stanley took a different tack. He still remembered when it took real moral courage to advocate any instruction for the lower orders, when even infant schools for the poorest children were decried by Churchmen as 'engines to undermine the Church . . ., a danger to the Church from puerile delinquents and from delinquents in the nursery!' Great changes had occurred since then, and Stanley looked forward to the day when his brethren would welcome them as benefiting all men and would practise as well as profess toleration. Until that happy day, the Establishment should at least acknowledge the hard fact that it was in no position to implement its grandiose assertion that it was the educator of the poor. How was this even remotely possible when there were parishes in which one clergyman served 15,000 people? For the genuine good of those people, Stanley thought that the Church should join in a national effort to educate all poor children irrespective of their religious persuasion. Optimistically, he prayed for the day when all passion and bitterness would cease, when, rather than fight one another, all would unite to fight the common and more powerful enemies—ignorance, vice and profligacy.[4]

Bishop Blomfield had no such visions, nor admitted to such prayers. He saw wicked conspiracies and prayed for their failure. Speaking more accurately for the Church hierarchy, he rejected co-operation with Dissenters who had so recently urged disestablishment, and suggested that Russell's schemes were part of a broader plot aimed at the subversion and eventual overthrow of the national faith. The government was under the influence of parties and persons dedicated to the destruction of the Church without realizing that the destruction of the monarchy was also involved.[5] Diluting religious instruction was another step on the fatal path of secularism, and, though he claimed to feel no hostility

[1] *Hansard*, XLVIII (1839), 1234–55.   [2] *Ibid.*, XLIX, 321–5.
[3] *Ibid.*, XLVIII, 1282–3.   [4] *Ibid.*, 1287–92.
[5] *Ibid.*, 1292–1313.

towards Dissenters, modifying the instruction of the poor to satisfy their demands was out of the question.

After years of citing crime statistics at home and abroad to support his pleas for expanded lower-class education, Blomfield now rejected similar evidence presented by supporters of the government. He specifically referred to Guerry's *Statistique Morale de la France*, in which the crime rate was shown to be much higher in areas of widespread education.[1] The reason given for the high incidence of crime in the south-east and Alsace, compared to the ignorant areas of Berri, Limousin and Brittany, was the absence of a sound religious basis of instruction.[2] Blomfield, though not prepared to assert that more education meant more crime, did insist that instruction, without religion, certainly did not diminish it. Actually non-religious instruction merely altered the character and complexion of crime, reducing violence and increasing duplicity and fraud. Guerry had shown that of 5,800 crimes studied in backward Russia during a certain period, 3,500 of them were violent. Yet in Pennsylvania, where education was general, there were only 640 acts of violence out of 7,400 crimes recorded.[3] For those suspicious of a Frenchman's figures, Blomfield also had a report from the chaplain at the new prison at Clerkenwell confirming the opinion that educated criminals were indeed the most wily and depraved.[4]

Blomfield was terribly agitated throughout the debate, his notions of conspiracy often bordering on hysteria. Yet the old, shrill cry of 'Church in danger' was not his style, and in contrast to that other power on the bench, Phillpotts, he rarely lost control and lashed out at vague plots. An ability for dispassionate and realistic evaluation, as well as a willingness to compromise, were the ingredients of his success. After nearly a decade of reform battles, fighting threats of disestablishment by co-operating with Whig ministers he never trusted, Blomfield was frightened and angered at the prospect that his efforts might be undermined by the loss of control over one of the Church's principal means for rejuvenation—the education of the poor. If he and his colleagues understood how critical the catechizing of the coming generation was for strengthening the Establishment, was it not also evident to the enemies of the Church? Blomfield and most of the bench thought so. He had not lost his confidence in the social utility of educating the poor and, when calmer, he clarified his belief that proper instruction was still a major

[1] A. M. Guerry, *Essai sur la statistique morale de la France* (Paris, 1833).

[2] C. J. Blomfield, *Speech of the Lord Bishop of London in the House of Lords, July 5, 1839, On the Government Plan For promoting National Education* (1839), 4–6.

[3] *Ibid.*, 11. See also Phillpotts, *Charge* (1839), 21–22, 25–27, in which he used Blomfield's statistics to prove that education is not a crime-deterrent.

[4] Blomfield, *Speech* (1839), 14.

weapon against crime and social disorder—'by far the cheapest, as well as the most effective measure of police which any Government can adopt'.[1] But it must not be separated from clerical supervision. Although Blomfield agreed that the National Society had failed to improve and modernize its limited curriculum and low teaching standards, he could not accept reform at the expense of religious instruction.

In contrast to Archbishop Howley, who preferred the *status quo*, Blomfield admitted the need for greater governmental expenditure in education, adding that its initiation fifty years earlier would have cost one-tenth the amount since spent on prisons, asylums and houses of correction. Consequently, he welcomed an enlarged grant of public funds, provided it was absolutely clear that it was not tied to provisions oriented towards eventual compulsory national education. The bishop recoiled at the thought of a Whig administration becoming a 'universal pedagogue'. At the same time, however, merely giving an enlarged contribution to the national Church as the 'great instrument of education' in the country would not only improve the condition of the schools, but would strengthen the weakened notion of establishment. Moreover, Blomfield had no objection to Dissenters and others receiving grants as long as it was absolutely clear that such public funds were charitable contributions, not concessions to legal rights.[2] The Established Church alone had the right to expect government funds. As usual, Blomfield was trying to arrange a compromise through this type of sophistic rationalization which promised to improve the Church's financial position and, at the same time, to reassert its privileges. It did not, however, compromise on the more important issue: the right of government inspection.

Brougham acidly deplored the exaggerated panic, obstructionism, intolerance and class prejudices of the bishops. He hoped that a system of interdenominational schools would follow and could not comprehend how churchmen could seriously object to Anglican and Dissenter children being educated together so long as separate hours were provided for religious instruction. Nor could he see how regularized inspection could be other than a benefit to the children of all persuasions.[3] The reason Brougham and others like him could not understand the Church's position, according to Phillpotts, was their involvement in the grand secular conspiracy that moved inexorably towards the destruction of the Establishment. Like Blomfield, Phillpotts argued that the State was obligated to provide the Church with adequate means to educate the people, including Dissenters if they chose to accept the opportunity. But he gave it a bitter twist when he insisted that had the State returned the wealth confiscated from the Church during the Reformation all the

[1] *Ibid.*, 15.   [2] *Ibid.*, 16–19.
[3] *Hansard*, XLVIII (1839), 1313 ff.

people would have been educated long ago. A plundered clergy had done all they could on their limited resources; the abject ignorance that now existed in so many manufacturing towns was stark testimony to the refusal of the State to provide its spiritual arm with the means to catechize the blighted heathen hordes, who now threatened them all with a just retribution.[1]

Phillpotts' ultra-High Church indignation acquiesced in the distribution of funds to Dissenters in 1833, but not in 1839. After nine years of Whig experiments, it was time to draw the line while time still remained. In contrast to most of his brethren, who were more realistic about the position of the Establishment, Phillpotts challenged the legality of the government's distribution of public funds to any religious group not belonging to the Established Church. The broader question of Establishment lay at the root of the argument. Catholic emancipation, the repeal of Dissenter liabilities, the reform of the Irish Church, and the establishment of Ecclesiastical Commissioners weighed heavily upon High Church consciences stimulated by Tractarian explanations and descriptions of the true Church. In this context, the Education Bill appeared as another humiliating diminution of ecclesiastical responsibility and authority. Could any scheme of national instruction be founded on any other than the national religion without acknowledging that the Established Church was merely another English denomination? Phillpotts, quoting from a pamphlet, *Recent Measures for Promotion of Education in England*, endorsed by the Privy Council, focused on the promise that 'the *established Church shall suffer no detriment* . . . but should *hold its position among the religious denominations of the Country*, as the Church whose head is the Sovereign, and whose institutions are interwoven with those of the temporal power'. This interpretation, the prelate solemnly explained, diminished the Anglican Establishment even further, and gave Dissenters 'A LEGAL RIGHT TO EQUAL DISTRIBUTION of all the secular advantages derivable from a Government supported by the public funds'. In endorsing this leveling notion, the Education Committee of the Privy Council had acted on behalf of a sovereign whose coronation oath bound her to the protection and maintenance of the national faith. How could the Council, in all good conscience, ask the queen to endorse a system of national education that would, in effect, force her to violate her solemn promise?[2]

Ever hungry for another of the legal battles his belligerent constitution fed upon, Phillpotts demanded a judicial decision on the legality of the Committee of Council's activities. The prelate did not wish to compel Dissenter children to attend Anglican services, learn the catechism, or anything else to which their parents objected; nor did he wish to keep them out of the schools. He only wanted to avoid the legal recognition

[1] *Ibid.*, 1277–82.   [2] Phillpotts, *Charge* (1839), 33, 35–36.

of their doctrines that public support of Dissenter schools implied. 'The contest', Phillpotts told his clergy, 'is not whether the children of the poor shall be taught, and well taught, but whether Papists, Unitarians, Jumpers, Ranters, Irvingites, Socialists, shall be henceforth recognized, as having a legal right—be it a legal right or not—to an equal distribution of the privilege of educating and being paid by the State for educating, the rising generation of Englishmen.'[1] If the Established Church was to lose this contest, it had best understand its full implications.

Actually the government had gone as far as it could in 1839. When Brougham, undeterred by fierce episcopal opposition, tried on July 15th to obtain approval to increase the regulatory and supervisory functions of the Committee of Council and to establish parochial school committees with rate-levying powers, he found little support. Even the usually sympathetic Bishop Otter condemned the moves as a direct threat to clerical control of the schools.[2] Charles Longley, the new Bishop of Ripon, was right in concluding a year earlier that a public school system on an interdenominational basis was simply against the wishes and interests of a very large proportion of the population.[3] England was still wedded to the voluntary mass-production of elementary literacy that had characterized popular education since the eighteenth century and, though the curriculum was slowly expanding, the voluntary principle seemed as entrenched as ever. Government inspection was viewed as a more effective way of obtaining some minimal standards within the voluntary framework.

Nevertheless, the education battle of 1839 was far more important than the decision of 1833 to provide £20,000 annually to the two great educational societies. Although Dr Kay's plan for a model normal school, and Brougham's proposal for rate-supported parochial schools, were victims of Church opposition and legislative indifference, the principle of State inspection, already applied to factory legislation, was established now in education. Furthermore, the increased government grant of £30,000 was made available to all schools conforming to established standards, irrespective of societal or religious affiliation. Also the involvement of the Privy Council, by asserting the right of the government to establish national standards, provided a nucleus for national public education, dealing at the same time another critical blow to Church notions of independence and privilege. As many bishops feared, the government successes of 1839 were seen by Whigs as important steps 'to prevent the growth of inordinate ecclesiastical pretensions . . . to vindicate the rights of conscience, and to lay the foundation of a

[1] *Ibid.,* 37–38.
[2] *Hansard,* XLIX (1839), 321–5.
[3] C. Longley, *A Charge Delivered to the Clergy of the Diocese of Ripon . . . 1838* (1838), 23.

system of combined education in which the young might be brought up in charity with each other, rather than in hostile camps'.[1]

Led by an aroused Archbishop Howley, many of the clergy adopted tactics of passive resistance, refusing to apply for government grants. Several prelates sympathetic to the Whig administration tried by reasoning with their clergy to convince them that the inspectors were empowered to judge only the teaching of secular subjects, not religious instruction. The new Bishop of Hereford and future Archbishop of York, Thomas Musgrave, endeavored during his primary visitation in 1839 to explain that some compromise would have to be reached if an effective system of national education based upon religion and morality was ever to be achieved. No person must be abandoned to 'hopeless and dangerous ignorance', even if the State working with all denominations separately or together must provide the means.[2] Old Samuel Butler, ill and dying, could not understand the resistance, provided government inspectors were excluded from religious questions. They were a threat to the inadequate, not the well-run school. Frankly, possessing little sympathy with the exaggerated claims of High Churchmen, he did not know why 'it is unreasonable that while one half of the sum voted for educational purposes is appropriated to the Established Church the remaining half should be divided among all the various classes of Dissenters, who are equally British subjects with ourselves, and who it must be a benefit to ourselves to see brought up as moral and intelligent beings'.[3]

Butler, never much of a friend of lower-class instruction, did not feel that the education of the laboring poor was as critical for the Church as some of his brethren claimed. Actually, he always thought it prudent and economical to let the Dissenters carry much of the educational load to permit the Church to concentrate its limited resources in more important areas. For most of the bench, however, there were few areas as important as education. Whatever their individual feelings, the bishops generally permitted each minister to make his own decision about requesting funds, even though the intensity or indifference of diocesans could not help but influence that decision.[4] A few of the more moderate prelates like Blomfield, Kaye and Denison, realizing that the confusion and confrontation of Church and State only benefited the Dissenters and other enemies of the Establishment, convinced the archbishop of

[1] Chadwick, *Victorian Church*, 340.

[2] T. Musgrave, *A Charge Delivered to the Clergy of the Diocese of Hereford . . . 1839* (Hereford, 1839), 20.

[3] Butler to Archdeacon Hodgson, Oct. 1839, *Butler Ps.*, Add. MS. 34592, f. 397. Butler was replying to a query of Hodgson (ff. 395–6) asking if the clergy should apply for funds from the governmental grant.

[4] See, for example, Blomfield, Letter Copy Book 356, f. 39. *Fulham Ps.*

the importance of a compromise. Although, in a brief moment of magnanimous condescension, Bishop Phillpotts had offered to call a conference to work out difficulties, Lord John Russell would have nothing to do with a prelate he utterly detested.[1] Russell did, however, welcome the initiative taken by Blomfield in 1840, agreeing that if Church and government continued to squabble, both would be injured without promoting educational advance. A meeting was arranged at the home of Lord Lansdowne, chairman of the Education Committee, between the Prime Minister, Howley, Blomfield and Denison, who finally decided that the archbishop of the province would have a veto over the appointment and continuance of inspectors connected with National Society schools.[2] Although the Church thereby maintained control over the inspectors, it conceded the right of inspection.

Churchmen saw the implications of the compromise. C. R. Sumner wrote to Wilberforce, 'I do not yet see my way in this. It seems to me to recognize what practically is the most objectionable part of the Government plan—the interference of Government, as a Government, in the management of education.'[3] Bishop Murray, a Tory aristocrat, and Bishop Allen (1770–1845), a Whig Banker's son, both saw conspiracy afoot, and felt it might be best thwarted if the archbishops appointed the inspectors directly and permitted the Privy Council the right of veto.[4] Tractarians pointed to yet another pathetic example of the Church's unhappy subservience to the State, and Joshua Watson, a principal founder of the National Society, resigned as treasurer. Most Church leaders, however, agreed that compromise was inevitable and acquiesced in the decision of the National Society to renew its application for government funds. In the end there was nothing else to do. Bishops might praise the splendid work being done by Anglican schoolmasters, given the limited resources provided and the magnitude of the problem, but they also knew that much more had to be done. Critics were already complaining about quality, while Church leaders were still desperately trying to provide quantity.

Although Blomfield, bowing to changing standards, urged a more extensive curriculum in National Society schools, many parishes in his

[1] Phillpotts to Russell, 16 Oct. 1839, and Russell to Phillpotts, 18 Oct., quoted in Phillpotts, *Charge* (1839), 94–95.

[2] Lord John Russell, *Recollections and Suggestions, 1813–73* (1875), 375–6.

[3] 10 June 1840, *Wilberforce Ps., Dep. C. 195.*

[4] G. Murrary, *A Charge . . . to the Clergy of his Diocese . . .July, MDCCCXL* (1840), 35–7: J. Allen, *A Sermon Preached . . . June III, MDCCCXLI at the Yearly Meeting of the Children of the Charity Schools . . .* (1841), 4–5. Blomfield had favoured a similar plan earlier, but recognized that it would not be acceptable. See 2 Dec. 1839, Letter Copy Book 356, ff. 84–85, *Fulham Ps.*

huge diocese still had no school at all.[1] Henry Ryder, reluctant though he was to antagonize a clergy already cool to his Evangelical leanings, nevertheless bluntly accused them of a serious 'ministerial defect' apparent in his visitation queries in 1832, which revealed fifty parishes without schools.[2] J. B. Sumner, surveying his huge industrial diocese in 1838, offered what he thought to be an optimistic estimate of 112,000 children who had never seen the inside of a class-room.[3] As evidence mounted, it became clear to some prelates that government assistance would have to be extended if the Church was ever to keep pace with the educational needs of the age.

They had to overcome the reluctance of their brethren to concede the failure of the Church's voluntary efforts and its attendant risk of secular interference. Copleston, for example, was worried not only about the violation of religious instruction, but the violation of the natural laws of political economy as well. Although there were admittedly an inadequate number of schools in some populous districts, he believed that generally the National Society had kept up with the demand. If anything, Copleston argued, the poor were not taking advantage of existing facilities and, as some prelates complained, the number attending was less than in previous years. The 'novelty is passed away', and the interest has languished as parents have discovered that no other benefit than that of instruction is obtained from sending their children to school. The poor, being as they are, always expect some 'secular advantage', some favor or reward, as if they were conferring a favor in sending their children to school. Other motivations influenced the behavior of the lower orders, of course, but 'a sense of secular advantage . . . like the great law of gravitation in the system of the universe, is the only one that can be reckoned upon as a constant self-acting power. There must be an external impulse from individuals, renewed from time to time, like that of muscular action in the animal body, or the motion once given soon dies away, and torpor gradually succeeds to a state of activity and energy.'[4] Consequently, it was perfectly natural that the ignorant poor, weighing the schools in the balance of self-interest, would conclude that there was no further advantage in sending their children to be educated; it was more profitable to send them to work.

Copleston did not suggest any new 'external impulse'. He did, however, think that government interference, the introduction of centralizing regulation, and the extension of aid to all denominations would only exacerbate the situation. It smacked of compulsory education, that 'offspring of despotic governments', and he was certain that local needs and free educational competition would eventually lead to solutions more in accordance with natural law and compatible with local problems. Unlike

[1] Blomfield *Charge* (1834), 33–4.   [2] Ryder, *Charge* (1832), 33.
[3] Sumner, *Charge* (1838), 38.   [4] Copleston, *Charge* (1839), 26, 29.

Benthamite economists, with whom he agreed on many things, Cople-ston believed that centralization and administrative regulation would interfere with, rather than facilitate, the beneficial functioning of the laws of political economy. Describing the clergy's fight against govern-mental regulation of the schools as analogous to merchants' resistance to Colbert's mercantilist controls, Copleston cried, 'Laissez nous faire!' Failing the fulfilment of this laudable policy, the prelate reluctantly accepted government funds for Church schools, but only so long as it was clearly recognized that 'we are the almoners of the State for religious purposes'.[1] He resisted the extension of grants to other schools as a step towards centralized, compulsory instruction.

The attempt to turn the question of education into a discussion of utilitarian, lower-class psychology did not find much support. To bishops like Phillpotts, who also deplored the extension of govern-mental interference, political economy was a cause of that interference, not a reason for avoiding it. It was utilitarian confidence in the power of practical, secular instruction that was causing the country's abandon-ment of the stabilizing and saving virtues of religious education. Phill-potts thought it complete lunacy that 'the *sole* means' of correcting the moral evils of the nation would be the instruction of 'the working people in the true causes' of the way matters are. 'In plain English, Political Economy is henceforth to be the Poor Man's Gospel; and the true way of making him contented under all his privations in this life, is to open to him no prospect of an inheritance of happiness and glory beyond the grave!'[2]

Copleston, of course, had no intention of suggesting that political economy should become the basis of the lower-class's educational curriculum, and his selective reading of those iron laws permitted him to exclude the possibility. But his brethren listened to the proposals of utilitarian reformers and feared that men in government were acting upon them. Wilberforce, in an open letter to Brougham in 1840, asked:

> Can any reasonable man believe that the subtleties of political economy can be a fetter enough to bind down successfully the heaving masses of society? Can the maxims of the economist stand between hunger and property? Will a man see his children want, and hear patiently the racking of their cries, because he believes that he should disturb the natural and easy flow of capital by helping himself?[3]

Believing that only religious instruction could provide that kind of acquiescence, the frightened Wilberforce pleaded with Brougham not to pursue educational policies that endangered the catechetical inculcation of spiritual restraints.

It was no longer possible for bishops, in making smug pronouncements

[1] *Ibid.*, 30–32. [2] Phillpotts, *Charge* (1839), 28–29.
[3] Wilberforce, *Letter to Brougham*, 39–40.

on the ingratitude and selfishness of the poor, to feel that they had explained the problems of Church education. In 1821, early in his career and when the National Society was only ten years old, Bishop Kaye could, like Copleston and others, resent the poor for not really appreciating the wonderful schools the rich provided for them. Instead, the ungrateful people merely saw themselves complying with the latest wishes of their betters and assumed they 'are conferring rather than receiving a favour'. When the blessings of charity were no longer appreciated, but grudgingly accepted, it was time for beneficent people to examine their policies. Kaye also charged that parents of the poor used the schools as a way to neglect their own responsibilities, and by continuing their own dissolute, irreligious lives, undermined the teachings of religious education. Suspicious as they are of their betters, the lower classes are merely waiting to see if they would be exploited, and will support education only so long as they see some definite advantage to themselves. Kaye had opposed the educational proposals of 1820 because the use of public funds would not only be difficult in a diverse country, but would tend to frustrate 'those great and moral purposes, which the distinction of mankind into rich and poor was intended to answer'. The rich benefit from their benevolence; the poor from their feelings of gratitude. Both are united 'in the bonds of mutual charity and affection', and only absolute necessity would ever warrant any deviation from an exclusive voluntary system.[1]

By 1840 the necessity was clear. With other influential prelates he argued that it was no longer possible to separate the spiritual and the temporal in education as much as some High churchmen preferred, any more than it was possible to separate the clergy and laity as much as some recommended. Fearful that the controversy over education would pry Church and State even further apart, Kaye joined Blomfield, Denison and others in praising the spirit of mutual compromise and friendly concession that had proven so beneficial in the past. While it was obvious that churchmen could not sanction strictly secular education, there was no reason why it could not be blended with religious instruction, with the State regulating the temporal sphere. In any event, like it or not, the Educational Committee of the Privy Council was a fact, and it controlled the funds. It was also a fact, Kaye noted, that 'of the present generation many have been estranged from us; some, it is to be feared, by our own remissness; more by our inability to supply the spiritual wants of the rapidly increasing population . . .'.[1] Exclusiveness and inflexibility would do nothing to change these facts, and most bishops had to agree.

[1] J. Kaye, *A Sermon Preached . . . June 13, 1822, At the Yearly Meeting of the Children of the Charity Schools . . .* (1823), 7–10.

[2] Kaye, *Charge* (1840), 27–29, 32.

3. CHILD LABOR AND THE FACTORY ACT OF 1843

Church educators assumed from the outset that children would be unable to remain in school more than two or three years before entering the employment they would undertake for the rest of their lives. As this was natural and inevitable, only the most sublime, freethinking, and perhaps revolutionary optimist would have challenged a truth both tested by Scripture and experience and confirmed by the natural laws of economic and social necessity. Educators repeatedly guaranteed that lower-class instruction would not interfere with this process. When, during the 1830's, clergymen like T. V. Short were urging the National Society to improve its curriculum, they still assumed that the early age at which children began to labor precluded any great extension of ordinary education to the working classes.[1] Like most churchmen, they simply accepted the inevitability of the poor becoming involved very early in what J. B. Sumner called the 'perplexing labyrinth of the business of life . . .'.[2]

Considering these realities, defenders of the National Society often complained that the Church was being unfairly criticized for not pursuing a course of instruction that would have been incompatible with social and economic reality. It was one thing to condemn the poor quality and limited scope of Anglican instruction, but it was another to offer realistic alternatives when pupils were available sporadically for no more than a few months of their lives. In making this point, Sumner reminded critics of the difficulty of getting parents to send their children to school, let alone the difficulty of keeping them long enough to be taught the rudiments of reading, writing, and arithmetic. Like many churchmen, Sumner resented the poor's attitude that they were doing the clergy a favor in sending their children to free schools; he thought they were more appreciative when a small fee was added. Blomfield had made this same point in explaining National Society policies to a Parliamentary Committee in 1834.[3] Either way, however, in too many districts the 'low and degraded state of their parents rendered them totally reckless of their children's welfare'. Sumner realized, however, that it was more than selfishness that forced parents 'to increase their means of subsistence by the premature employment of their children's labour'.[4] He had spent too many years as the active diocesan of a large manufacturing complex not to have seen that the general economic values and demands of the age were at least as responsible for the exploitation of young children as were the individual debased and material standards of their parents.

Realism is what Sumner preached to his clergy in 1838—a realism

[1] Short, *National Education*, 19.　　[2] Sumner, *Charge* (1835), 12–13.
[3] *Parl. Ps.* (1834), IX, 189.　　[4] Sumner, *Charge* (1838), 11–12.

411

that pointed to the 'community's requirement for young labourers' as the most serious impediment to extensive education. All our plans 'for educating the poor in factory towns' must take into consideration the fact 'that all the children, both male and female, can have profitable employment in the factories as soon as they are eleven years of age, and we can never expect to retain them in our day schools after that age'.[1] Obviously, a reduction in the use of child labor would be of great benefit in educating the young, but the requirements of their station in life precluded any such advantage. We must be content to provide a 'partial and imperfect education' that ill prepares the lower orders for life; still 'exposes [them] to temptation . . . [and] leaves the hours of leisure so few, that the advantages of exertion are sadly overmatched by the inclination to idleness'. Sumner's gloomy prognosis led him to conclude that 'new schemes of education would be a waste of labour, and parliamentary schools, a fruitless expenditure' so long as the demands for child labor were so great.[2] Ultimately, it all went back to 'the first transgression' and no amount of legislation would change the basic cause of man's necessity to labor in an unequal world.[3]

Church leaders readily accepted their society's priorities; if they complicated their work with the laboring classes, they tried to adapt, despite the increasing difficulty of doing so, as the century wore on. Bishop Allen, for example, recommended the wider adoption of infant schools in order to commence the education of poor children at an age earlier than seven or eight. After all, he argued, 'it is in vain, and indeed unreasonable, to expect parents with large families, to continue their children at school when they are of an age to contribute to their own support by their daily labour'.[4] There was no faulting that logic, and the willingness of many clergymen to encourage instruction for four- and five-year-old children indicated that the Church was continuing to seek ways of adapting to the laws of economic necessity. The picture was nevertheless spotty. Many existing schools were only partially attended, while in some areas like Manchester, facilities were woefully inadequate. Although some of his episcopal associates were no longer as sanguine, Sumner hoped that the laws of enlightened self-interest would show industrialists and colliery-owners the advantages of a more extensive education for their young employees. Manufacturers, in fact, might even encourage longer time in school as more of them recognized the direct

---

[1] *Ibid.*, 39.   [2] *Ibid.*, 12–13.   [3] Sumner, *Charge* (1835), 13.
[4] J. Allen, *A Charge Delivered to the Clergy of the Diocese of Ely . . . June, July and August, 1841* (1841), 15–16.
Joseph Allen (1770–1845), son of a Manchester banker, educated at Cambridge. A mediocre prelate, he was one of the few to hold an urban living before his elevation to the bench. He owed his appointment to Bristol in 1834 to his former pupil, Lord Althorpe, and was translated to Ely in 1836.

association between the regulation and discipline of the monitorial system and the factory economy. 'Beautiful and affecting is the sight which [the schools] . . . present, containing as they do, many hundreds, in some cases even thousands of children, arranged with the exactness of the factory itself, and conducted with no less regularity.'[1]

The easy transition from class-room to mill or mine obviously appealed more to Sumner than to employers who were less confident about the benefits to be derived. Furthermore, like many of his colleagues, he was staggered by the evidence of working and living conditions endured by the laboring poor revealed in parliamentary reports and underlined by the rapid spread of worker agitation in the depression, racked towns of the 1840's. The threat of Chartism and the exaggerated pronouncements of Owenite socialists added to the conviction that Church and State had best take another hard look at the extent and quality of instruction offered the poor. The inclusion of an educational plan in the Factory Act of 1843 was an immediate result. Sir James Graham proposed that children between the ages of eight and thirteen be instructed three hours a day in rate-supported schools, with the addition of a small fee to keep the demons of slothful dependency in check. Despite the compulsory clauses of the plan, the bishops were prepared to co-operate. Although enthusiasm varied, no prelate disputed Longley's conclusion that the education clauses would be a blessing for young factory workers, 'these too much neglected children . . .'.[2] If English liberties and the rights of the Establishment were endangered, the events of recent years indicated that there were even greater dangers from ill-instructed working masses. Moreover, to calm the fears of older prelates, this was a Tory measure, the nearest Peel's Cabinet came to helping the Church in an old-fashioned Tory way.[3] Not only was the schoolmaster to be an Anglican, but he was permitted to teach the catechism and prayer-book an hour a day and three hours on Sunday. Dissenter children could be exempted if their parents so stipulated, and licensed ministers would attend one day a week to instruct the children of their respective denominations. The schools were to be managed by seven trustees, including the Anglican schoolmaster and two churchwardens.

Although some High Churchmen balked at State funds being used to support any Dissenter instruction, Archbishop Howley, Blomfield, and most other influential High Church prelates had endorsed the plan. Broad Churchmen and Evangelicals saw it as a step in the right direction, encompassing utility and toleration for what had become a necessary end. Whatever qualms J. B. Sumner had about compulsory education were overcome by reports in his diocese showing that only 6 per cent of

[1] Sumner, *Charge* (1838), 43.
[2] 19 Jan. 1843, *Longley Ps.*, I, ff. 235–6, Lambeth Palace Library.
[3] Chadwick, *Victorian Church*, 340.

the children living in many rural areas and less than 3 per cent in some towns were receiving daily instruction.[1] Many more had but a brief association with a day school before disappearing into the labor market forever. The Factory Act of 1843 at least raised the possibility of improving the percentages. It provided more time in which to expose the poor to moral and religious subjects, because, as Phillpotts explained, since the children were 'consigned by Providence to the laborious occupations of life', there was no reason to waste precious time on too many secular subjects.[2] As the poor, whose 'besotted ignorance' made them almost brutally indifferent 'to everything but the objects of sense', were so fated, extensive curriculum and vague interdenominational instruction were dangerous and irrelevant. The evidence cried out for a return to teaching strong denominational religious principles to 'those great manufacturing classes . . . whom it is the nature of our social system to accumulate, but for whom, unhappily, it has not hitherto been a part of our social system to provide the means for Education'.[3] From Phillpotts's High Church vantage-point, this was another instance of the State's betrayal of the Establishment by sequestering its resources and depriving it of the means to fulfil its canonical obligations in order to take them over for secular purposes.

It seemed to churchmen of that persuasion that the State was now reaping the harvest of riot and chaos that its growing religious neutralism and secularity had sown. The reason for danger in the large towns, 'those hot-beds of population, those strongholds of liberal principles, enlarged views and new systems', is precisely because it is there that the Church is weakest. In making this analysis, young Wilberforce complained that endowments had not been increased with the population; instead 'liberality and political economy have used men as if they were machines for making or modelling wealth; have let the adults fall back into heathenism, and the young grow up on the food of cotton-looms and vice'.[4] The Whigs were responsible, periodically threatening to destroy the Church once and for all by imposing foreign despotic systems of compulsory instruction upon the liberties and birthrights of every free-born Englishman. Wilberforce shuddered and invoked the spirit of a formidable ally to shame his wicked successors:

> Shade of the mighty Burke! could such sounds as these break upon thy rest, how would the thunder of thy eloquence arouse itself, and roll in crashing peals to the utter discomfiture of thy degenerate party![5]

[1] Sumner, *Charge* (1844), 16–17.

[2] H. Phillpotts, *National Education. Speech . . . in the House of Lords, July 5, 1839*, 2nd ed. (1839), 8; also *Hansard*, XLVIII (1839), 1276.

[3] Phillpotts, *Charge* (1839), 38–39.

[4] Wilberforce, *Letter to Brougham*, 25.

[5] *Ibid.*, 7–8.

While such invocations stirred the hearts of like-minded clergy, Wilberforce's distaste for compulsory education cut across episcopal party lines. Few prelates, however, offered anything more imaginative than that a greater effort be made by the already overburdened voluntary societies. Some bishops were establishing voluntary normal schools to improve teaching, but most knew higher standards would not solve the crushing problem of overpopulation and inadequate private resources. The emphasis, however, focused as much on the inability to keep the poor long enough to make any impression, as it did upon the lack of facilities. As Thirlwall told his clergy, until the parents of poor children were willing to do without the 'petty, immediate advantages' of added income, little could be done.[1] Schoolmasters repeatedly made the same complaint. C. R. Sumner, a long-time critic of Church education, summarized many feelings when, in 1841, he reflected on the probable reactions of a Continental visitor to English schools. 'He might take them for the nurseries of our youngest population. Tell him that they are the chief seminaries of sound learning and religious education for the offspring of our peasantry, and that the infants whom he sees before him, ... will become in a few short years the industrial classes of our land ...', and the stranger will justifiably be very sceptical about the results. Yet Sumner firmly opposed the adoption of a Continental State system requiring seven or eight years of instruction for all children. Under the present system of social life in England, it was obvious to him that the parents of poor children could afford neither the financial contribution nor the wages lost to provide a similar education for their unfortunate offspring. 'I see for the evil in question', he concluded, 'no adequate remedy.'[2]

Analysis and complaint, not solution, were the episcopal way in the 1830's and 1840's. Ever more conscious and critical of the social conditions compounding the very problems seeming to overwhelm them, Church leaders were unable or unwilling to suggest that some fundamental alteration in the social order might be necessary. It was easy to blame the parents of the poor for callously surrendering their children to the factories instead of the Church, but those who complained also knew of the economic and social conditions that forced that decision. The laws of political economy explained it for some, but they were really unsatisfactory to active clergymen who, while wanting to do something about the limited appeal of their Church, were incapable of truly understanding and communicating with those who viewed them as bulwarks of a social and economic system predicated upon the inevitability of their misery. In the final analysis, the Establishment, with all its new

[1] Thirlwall, *Charge* (1842), 32.

[2] C. R. Sumner, *A Charge Delivered to the Clergy of the Diocese of Winchester ... September, 1841* (1841), 9–11.

churches, schools, visitors and missions, really had little to say to the laboring poor. The clergy were talking to and for themselves and the higher orders they served and represented.

This unconscious, and sometimes conscious, awareness in the midst of the turmoil of the early 1840's made the bench much more receptive to the educational schemes of Graham's Factory Act, in spite of the introduction of compulsory and integrated instruction. Dissenters wanted no part of a measure that appeared so decidedly in favor of the Establishment. Petitions poured in. Already angered by criticisms leveled by school inspectors at the poor quality of instruction observed in their schools, Dissenters were convinced that State aid, as recommended by Graham, was only another means for promoting the Established Church. They did not need Lord John Russell to tell them that the Tories were creating a public office, financed by public funds, but excluding many qualified schoolmasters for religious reasons. In the eyes of many Whigs and Dissenters this was a subtle attempt to revive a test Act.[1] No government, including Peel's, would have dared propose a revival of grants to build new churches in populous districts. Dissenters, more confident than ever of their strength, had no intention of allowing their rates to be used to finance an Anglican system of education as an alternative.

Peel and Graham badly miscalculated, but even Dr Kay-Shuttleworth, once a Dissenter himself, failed to appreciate the intensity of feeling over the issue. It was clear that the Factory Act could not be carried with the educational clauses included. Dissenter and churchman alike saw that public education was out of the question in their religiously fragmented country. Wilberforce, disappointed, concluded that 'the question is plainly at rest'. He thought public education might have been instituted during the Reformation under Edward VI, but, 'we are now too free and too divided to agree on any system of coercive instruction'. Since all men realize 'that education is indeed the great and awful power of training man . . .', it has become too critical an issue to permit cooperation without religious compromise. At the same time, though the burden had become enormous, the nation was too much at odds with itself to accept responsibility for educating the poor. Wilberforce, two years away from the bench, concluded that the clergy of his generation would have to do it themselves, though the burden was all the heavier because of their predecessors' failures.[2]

It was no longer possible to hope that a friendly Tory government would find some way to finance Church schools at the level required. This was particularly distressing to prelates who noted that during the riots in manufacturing towns in 1842 those districts where Anglican schools were located tended to remain comparatively peaceful, while no

[1] Chadwick, *Victorian Church*, 341.
[2] Wilberforce, *Charge* (1843), 24–26.

person educated in a National School had been arrested. Bishop Denison recognized that the situation in towns, where 'vast multitudes of our people are growing up without any instruction at all', remained explosive. Distressed by figures showing that there were areas in some towns where ninety thousand wage-earners were assembled without a single public day school for their children, Denison asked: Is it any wonder that 'a turbulent, restless, discontented spirit not only agitates the surface, but threatens to break up the very foundations of society'?[1] Longley was equally upset, especially when his visitation returns indicated that of children attending schools in the diocese of Ripon the best ratio was one in eleven, the worst one in forty. With the national average probably less than 50 per cent, he was particularly saddened by the failure of Graham's plan.[2]

Angered by the resistance of *laissez-faire* advocates, as well as Dissenters, Denison bluntly asserted that there was no comfort to be found in the self-righteous individualism of political economy. Sounding a new and critical tone to be heard increasingly after the middle of the century, he claimed that the evils and dangers of English society could no longer be blamed on the poor; the fault lay with their betters, including those in the Church. The poor 'are the victims of a state of things, for which they are not themselves responsible', and unless the upper classes really understood it, it would be impossible to bring 'the untrained multitudes' under control.[3] Like several of his colleagues, Denison felt frustrated by social and economic conditions, 'which are beyond our control, [and] the deep poverty of the labouring class . . . which incapacitates them from providing for the education of their own children'.[4] At best, he resigned himself to the painful realization that the education of the poor 'will be sadly defective. What should we say ourselves, if we were told that the education of our own children must terminate at eight, nine, or even ten years of age?' In spite of agitation all around him favoring greater restrictions on child labor and the establishment of a ten-hour work-day, the bishop never suggested anything other than passive resignation:

> It is useless to lament this, however much we may regret the pressure of that poverty which is its cause. It is useless to strive against it, or to blame parents for it, as if they were indifferent to the education of their children, because they are constrained by urgent necessity to avail themselves of whatever trifling assistance even little hands can give in providing a scanty supply for their bodily wants.[5]

[1] E. Denison, *Report of the Society For Promoting Christian Knowledge for 1843; to Which is Prefixed the Anniversary Sermon Preached . . . June 1, 1843* (1843), 7.
[2] Longley, *Charge* (1844), 11–13.   [3] Denison, *Sermon* (1843), 10–11.
[4] Denison, *Charge* (1845), 21.   [5] *Ibid.*, 33–34.

Modern episcopal heads, wigs discarded for several years now, nodded sadly at this recurring lament.[1] Though some of them still suspected the poor were more responsible for their poverty than Denison claimed, the end-result remained the same.

Within three weeks of the government's decision to drop the educational classes from the Factory Act, Archbishops Howley and Harcourt on July 5th joined with several other prelates in urging the National Society to recognize reality and make a special effort in blighted manufacturing and mining districts. It was clear that the legislature would not rally behind the Church. It was also clear that, since the problem extended far beyond the parochial level, the parochial clergy would need much greater support from the Church as a whole. The Church had to raise funds from the laity in unprecedented amounts. The problem was not merely religious; it was social and political, and the laity had best understand that churches and ministers were presently unable to guarantee the security of the laboring classes.[2] Howley even dropped his long-held objections to the mixing of denominations and, in spite of some High Church groans, accepted the right of Dissenters to send their children to Anglican schools while retaining the right to absent them from the reading of the catechism and the prayer-book.[3]

Peel, welcoming the new campaign and personally contributing £1,000, knew that any remaining illusions Howley, Kaye, Phillpotts, or any other old prelate might have had about resuscitating the Tory alliance were out of the question.[4] The bishops knew it too. The appointment of fifteen new bishops by Grey and Melbourne since 1832 had gone a long way towards reconciling Church leadership to the great social and political changes that had occurred in the nineteenth century. An unreconstructed Tory like Phillpotts might still rail at those changes, look for new allies in the Oxford Movement or in a promising cleric like Wilberforce complaining about the loss of a bygone age. But even Wilberforce belonged to the Establishment of the present and future, not the past. Dissenters were now able to force a Tory government led by Peel, the Church's best friend, to abandon objectionable legislation that might benefit the national faith. Moreover, by the end of 1843, Dissenters had even extracted from the Education Committee of the Privy Council the same right of veto over school inspectors enjoyed by the Established Church.

[1] Blomfield, who led the way in the elimination of the episcopal wig, tried in vain to get George IV to sanction his modern innovation. William IV was more accommodating and permitted prelates to discard the wearing of the wig. S. C. Carpenter, *Church and People, 1789–1889* (1933), 25.

[2] *Peel Ps.,* Add. MS. 40530, ff. 413–14.

[3] Howley to Peel, 11 July 1843, *ibid.,* Add. MS. 40531, ff. 46–47.

[4] *Ibid.,* 13 July, ff. 52–53.

4. MANAGEMENT AND COMPROMISE

The failure of 1843 only heightened episcopal determination to make the Church the educator of the people. During the remainder of the decade they campaigned as never before on behalf of the National Society. In 1844 alone, £160,000 was raised to provide schools in populous areas, and the contributions kept coming in.[1] Blomfield, the dean of episcopal fund-raisers, personally managed an appeal for the construction of fifty new schools in London.[2] In addition, he agreed to support the establishment of free infant ragged schools in the Bethnal Green slums, persuading a suspicious London Diocesan Board of Education that enrolment in the National Schools, where a small fee was charged, would actually be encouraged. Understanding the power of status in all classes, the bishop reasoned that parents who really cared for their children, and could afford it, would rather pay for instruction in a more respectable National School than have their offspring mingling with the lowest common denominator. It was hard to resist the promise that 'many little Tradesmen and Mechanics would send their children to a National School if the most destitute and ragged children went elsewhere—the respectability of the school would in their estimate be increased'.[3]

Much of the money collected was used to expand the number of diocesan normal schools providing qualified teachers for the expanding educational system. As the monitorial method was widely recognized as inadequate for quality instruction, since the late 1830's various dioceses had been training the most promising pupils for a teaching career in the Anglican schools. The attempt by Dr Kay in 1839 to establish a public, non-denominational normal school had prodded many prelates to introduce the innovation within the controllable confines of the National Society. In addition to increased voluntary contributions, the Church benefited from a steady, if inadequate, increase in the size of the government's annual grant. By 1846 the Education Committee was distributing £75,000, raising it to £100,000 the next year, and adding another £25,000 in 1848.[4] Although the government increased its contribution more than four-fold in a decade, it still represented a small proportion of the total expenditure for education and did little to meet the pressing needs of the times. With children still increasing more rapidly than schools and teachers, no one knew it better than the clergy who were trying desperately to keep the Church in evidence.

[1] Hammond, *Age of the Chartists*, 201.
[2] Blomfield, Letter Copy Book 395, f. 277, *Fulham Ps.*
[3] *Ibid.,* LCB 381, ff. 218–19.
[4] J. W. Adamson, *English Education 1789–1902* (Cambridge, 1930), 146.

Although the bulk of educational operating and expansion funds came from voluntary sources, the returning Whig government in 1846 was determined to impose still greater controls over the grants it was prepared to increase. This time, however, Lord John Russell brought the Church into the planning stage and permitted Dr Kay-Shuttleworth, Archbishop Howley and leaders of the National Society to work out a series of school management clauses. Every Anglican school was to be governed by a committee of Anglican laymen, which, in co-operation with the parish incumbent, was designed to provide continuity of management and to minimize the exclusion policies practised by some clergy against Dissenters. The growing influence of Tractarians in the National Society made the government and some bishops wary of Puseyite parsons running inadequately supervised schools. Although the incumbent retained complete authority over the moral and religious instruction presented in the schools, many clergymen, usually High Church, and some prelates charged that the management clauses were a devious means of prying the schools away from clerical control. The Oxford Movement had intensified the whole question of the Erastian position of the Church, and many clergymen were convinced that the only hope for a return to true Church principles was ecclesiastical independence and control over the Establishment's institutions, policies and theology. This lay at the root of the struggle over the management clauses, as it did the Hampden controversy and the Gorham decision.

In spite of the support given the management clauses by the respectable, super-cautious Howley, many churchmen refused to accept the conditions. The National Society was torn by internal strife. George Anthony Denison, the Puseyite Vicar of East Brent, Somerset, and brother of the Bishop of Salisbury, battled in the Society meetings of 1849 and 1850 to persuade the Church to refuse all government funds and co-operation so long as parish clergymen and their bishop were not allowed sole control of the schools. His diocesan, Richard Bagot, shaken from his experience with the Tractarians at Oxford and incapacitated most of the time now by a nervous breakdown, nevertheless roused himself to encourage Denison and to protest against the clauses as a dangerous threat to clerical authority.[1] It was a serious dilemma for the bench. Though several of its members were themselves suspicious of the government's plans, knowing that Russell was opposed to the ecclesiastical domination of national education, they also realized that the voluntary system was hopelessly inadequate. Individual clergymen might think that they were providing adequate instruction in their parishes, but their diocesans recognized that a great many more parishes were

[1] Chadwick, *Victorian Church*, 343-4.

languishing in ignorance with no hope of alleviating the situation without increased assistance. They also knew, however, that the existing school system had been greatly aided by the efforts of a tireless, invigorated clergy, many of them distrustful of the State and now alarmed that their work would be undone. Bishop Gilbert was deeply worried by the seven hundred petitions of complaint he had received in his diocese alone.[1] With the Church already battered and bitterly fragmented by the Oxford Movement and sensational defections to Rome, even the most ardent party men on the bench saw the need for caution.

Bishop Denison, High Churchman though he was, could not agree with his brother. His episcopal experience had taught him that all of the Church's voluntary efforts could not overcome the greater needs of the poor. The management clauses, challenging neither the voluntary system nor the authority of the Church, actually provided local schools with a greater prospect of support and permanency. Like many of his episcopal brethren, Denison warned the clergy against resistance and excessive jealousy over their educational prerogatives. It was a luxury the Church could no longer afford, any more than it could expect government support without conditions.[2] No bishop was prepared, however, to concede Walter Hook's sensational conclusion that the voluntary system was an utter failure. His experience as Vicar of Leeds had convinced him by 1846 that Dr Kay-Shuttleworth and others like him were right in advocating a national system of secular schools which allowed the various denominations to instruct children on Sundays and during special weekly hours. Furthermore, in his proposal, made to Bishop Thirlwall, Hook endorsed public normal schools, an apprentice system for teachers, and subsequent government licensing. The entire system would be financed by national and local funds and administered by county boards of management.[3] Hook concluded that unless there was a clear separation of Church and State in the area of education, both would be unable to fulfil their respective responsibilities to the unlettered populace.

Neither Anglicans nor Dissenters were willing to surrender their critical prerogatives in so important an evangelizing sphere. Moreover, there is little evidence that Englishmen were as yet much interested in taking on the expense of educating the laboring multitudes. Nevertheless

---

[1] *Hansard*, CIX (1850), 299-304. Ashurst T. Gilbert (1786-1870), son of a Bucks. naval officer, contemporary of Peel at Oxford, Fellow and Principal of Brasenose College (1822-42), and Vice-Chancellor of Oxford (1836-40). At Wellington's request, was elevated by Peel to Chichester in 1842, where he was a conscientious High Church diocesan.

[2] Denison, *Charge* (1848), 14-17.

[3] W. F. Hook, *On the Means of Rendering More Efficient the Education of the People. A Letter to the Lord Bishop of St David's* (1846).

Hook's willingness to trust the secular education of the poor to the State found at least one interested episcopal listener, if not an outright endorser. Bishop Thirlwall in 1848 struck out at resistance to the management clauses by insisting that it was preposterous for clergymen still to contend that the State had no right or responsibility to educate its people. He argued that the enormous rise of population in preceding decades, compared to the obvious insufficiency of denominational education, ought to provide evidence to the contrary. Thirlwall, one of the most unconventional thinkers on the bench, took a step that his fellow bishops, in spite of their often sensitive analyses, were unwilling to take by proposing that it was time for a basic rethinking of the political and economic assumptions of the age. The State, he argued, can no longer be considered 'a necessary evil' and an enemy of freedom and individual liberty. It should be appreciated as 'an eminently sacred institution' with the rights and obligations not only of protection, but of promoting progress for *all* its members.[1] In Thirlwall's opinion, a sound, economical public education was the best way of fulfilling this role for the lower classes. A proper system of national instruction would permit each child to pursue knowledge as far as his leisure and talents allowed. Not only would the entire level of civilization be raised, but quiet and contented citizens who would view the State as a source of opportunity, rather than as an instrument of repression, would be produced. The clergy, so long as they blocked this march of progress, would be associated with that repression. Public education would always include sufficient time for the various denominations to catechize the young. As a result, religion and intellectual progress could proceed hand in hand instead of in opposition, as was so often the case over the preceding years.[2]

Thirlwall, cold, aloof, never very popular with his clergy or fellow bishops, sounded more like a prelate of the 1880's than the 1840's. His defense of public education, however, was raised in the context of a general episcopal reconsideration of the problem. The preceding year Bishop Longley had conceded that the country could no more support education by voluntary contributions than it could provide adequate armies, navies and courts by such a system.[3] The analogy is revealing. Longley concluded that education had become so vital an institution that the State could no longer entrust it to the fluctuations of public beneficence. Yet less than ten years before, he had rejected similar arguments against the inadequacy of voluntary education.[4] A decade of experience and statistics now revealed his error, and he urged the government to maximize its efforts, 'if ever it hoped to see our vast population

---

[1] C. Thirlwall, *A Charge Delivered to the Clergy of the Diocese of St David's . . . 1848* (1848), 32–33.

[2] *Ibid.,* 42.   [3] Longley, *Charge* (1847), 14.   [4] Longley, *Charge* (1838), 23.

trained up in the fear of God, in the faith of Christ, and with a proper knowledge of their duties as Christian citizens'. Even Dr Chalmers, whose work in Glasgow had inspired innumerable churchmen to examine the problems of the urban cure, reportedly lamented on his deathbed the conclusive failure of the voluntary system. Longley quoted his conclusion that 'the system has been fairly on its trial for nearly half a century', and all attempts to give it the impetus needed to cope with the emergency only led to 'the inevitable conclusion that more extensive aid on the part of the government was indispensable if any effectual remedy were to be applied to the mass of moral evil which prevailed'.[1]

There was no suggestion of supplanting the existing voluntary schools —everyone appreciated the reciprocal social and religious advantages of charity—but it was necessary to support and supplement them with government funds and constructive inspection. Longley, for example, thought the management clauses were an acceptable condition and did not 'relieve the Church and Dissenters alike from all responsibility in providing for the better education of those children of the poorer classes'.[2] Public education, he was certain, would remain for the foreseeable future a co-operative institution in England, although the government would have to play a greater role in years ahead as the population and its expectations continued to grow.

In contrast to the episcopal resistance to inspection in 1839–40, the bench in 1846 was generally acquiescent, if not openly favorable. Although Howley, Blomfield, Kaye, and even Phillpotts were far from endorsing the advanced notions of a Hook or a Thirlwall, like Longley they saw the inevitability of co-operation and pledged the support of the National Society. There was grumbling: Wilberforce privately expressed his 'intense dissatisfaction with the government, and especially with Mr Kay-Shuttleworth', but publicly supported the new arrangements and urged his clergy to co-operate.[3] It was an age of reappraisal for the Church—theologically, socially and politically. The adjustments were easier for Wilberforce and younger prelates just coming to power and whose entire careers had been built in an era of reform. It was more difficult for the older prelates of Kaye's generation, for whom reform had always been an imposition and reality a disappointment. In education, as in so many other areas of Church involvement, reality had to be acknowledged once again; Kaye, who had, from the earliest days of his episcopal career, defended Anglican educational prerogatives on the basis of canonical responsibility, had to tell churchmen—especially High Churchmen—that the canons of 1603, in matters of popular instruction, were now only a legal fiction. Many people were no longer

---

[1] Longley, *Charge* (1847), 14–15.　　　　[2] *Ibid.,* 16.
[3] Wilberforce to Phillpotts, 15 June 1848, *Wilberforce Ps.,* Dep. C. 187, ff. 22–23; also *Charge* (1848), 21–23.

members of the Established Church and, whatever our pretensions, would continue to receive State grants to educate their children. Kaye still found some comfort in the continued separation of denominations, especially for religious instruction, and still hoped that Church principles could be protected within the framework of expanded public support.[1]

Episcopal pleas for co-operation and acquiescence went unheeded by many aroused High Churchmen, who continued to view the management clauses as another Erastian scheme to strip the Church of its sacred functions and privileges. The intense sacerdotalism of the Oxford Movement clashed with the expanded role given the laity in the management of parochial schools. Some clergy, tottering on the brink of defection to Rome, prayed for disestablishment and salvation; many more were simply determined not to surrender the control of schools they had labored to establish. Though some bishops certainly sympathized, they could offer little encouragement. Kaye told his angry clergy that while he too was deeply disturbed by the 'spirit of interference' implied in the clauses, he hoped that he and his brethren would be the final arbiters in *all* questions pertaining to the schools and not just those concerned with religious instruction.[2] In any event, he made it clear that even if these hopes were not fulfilled, the Church was in no position to reject State assistance.

The government made some concessions. Kaye allowed a three-man appeal board on all school matters, two of whom would have episcopal approval. In addition, the members of the management committees would have to be not only members, but communicants as well, of the Church of England. Howley's successor to Canterbury in 1848, John Bird Sumner, was satisfied, as were many leaders of the National Society. Sumner's endorsement, however, was not likely to calm the fears of High Churchmen who loathed his Evangelical theology almost as much as they did his patron, Lord John Russell. Defections to Rome after the Gorham decision in 1850 and the subsequent 'Papal Aggression' seriously weakened the demands of High Church clergymen for clerical control of anything as critical as education. Although Evangelicals and liberals were able to defeat George Denison's motion for non-co-operation at the uproarious meeting of the National Society in 1851, the bitterness remained. In 1853 many moderate churchmen felt compelled to form a separate Church Education Society based upon more general Protestant principles than were acceptable to High Churchmen within the older Society.[3]

By the middle of the century, popular education represented a com-

[1] J. Kaye, *A Letter to the Clergy of the Diocese of Lincoln On the Subject of the Recent Minutes of the Committee of Privy Council* (Lincoln, 1847), 3–5.
[2] Kaye, *Charge* (1849), 381–3.   [3] Chadwick, *Victorian Church*, 344–5.

posite of compromises resulting from the sharp, often bitter, religious divisions in the country. The voluntary system remained at the core, and, in spite of its obvious inadequacies, continued to expand. At the same time, State grants, proportionally distributed annually to the various denominational schools and societies, increased sharply, rising from £150,000 in 1851 to £663,435 in 1858. In the same period, expenditures for teachers' salaries and training instituted in 1846 rose from £93,474 to £256,739. By 1861 the government had distributed £4,400,000 for national education—approximately half the amount raised by voluntary societies.[1] Moreover, the State had clearly established the right of inspection and administrative forms, although they were compromised considerably by the veto powers retained by each denomination. As long as Englishmen insisted upon religious foundations for national education, little else could be done—a fact the government recognized and accepted after 1846; until 1870 the real problem it faced was to ensure that education reflected the nation's religious beliefs. National education, in spite of Anglican hopes, could never be based upon a national faith; there was no such thing in England. The very revival of the Establishment accentuated this truth as the Church fragmented into feuding parties whose religious beliefs and concepts of the Church often differed as much as those of the Dissenters. In spite of the hopes of a Thomas Arnold, Edward Stanley, Frederick Denison Maurice, or even Lord John Russell, Protestantism was not sufficient as a national faith, their ideas of comprehensive Christianity finding little support in the camps of warring churchmen. By 1870 the concept of a national faith had become so generalized as to be virtually meaningless.[2] Forster's Education Bill of that year, allowing local boards of education to levy rates for non-denominational elementary instruction, marked the government's abandonment of attempts to reconcile education with the varieties of national belief.

The Church had resisted such a course since 1851, when permission to levy a compulsory local rate to educate all the poor in the Manchester-Salford area was proposed. The bishops feared that such action would end voluntary support, and eventually destroy denominational schools.[3] Blomfield privately appealed to Spencer Walpole to give the National Society a chance to alleviate the great problems in Manchester-Salford, on the grounds that after forty years' service the Society deserved a hearing before passing a Bill which would result in its destruction.[4] The

---

[1] Adamson, *English Education*, 202, 205.

[2] Best, 'Religious Difficulties', *CHJ*, 170–1.

[3] See S. Wilberforce, *A Charge to the Clergy of the Diocese of Oxford . . . November, 1851* (1851), 26, and J. Kaye, *A Charge Delivered . . . in 1852*, in *Nine Charges*, 469–70.

[4] 26 March 1852, Letter Copy Book 398, ff. 255–6, *Fulham Ps.*

Church had much to lose. The census of 1851 showed that of the 10,595 schools receiving State aid, 81 per cent were Anglican and instructed 76 per cent of the 1,048,851 children in attendance.[1] Blomfield, in his final *Charge*, nevertheless confessed that 'our systems of education have not yet effectually reached that class which stands most in need of instruction—the very poorest'.[2] Even where the schools were available, prelates like Wilberforce questioned whether the education provided made much impression on either the intellectual or spiritual character of the laboring classes. It seemed to him that still greater efforts had to be made 'to get the poor to love their pastor and church'.[3]

The Newcastle Commission's report in 1861, after a three-year study of education, while long on statistics, was very short on hopeful solutions. There was much satisfaction in the knowledge that of 2,655,767 school-age children in the country, only 120,000, mostly in the newer manufacturing towns, were completely cut off from any instruction.[4] It was regrettable that another 860,000 children in poor and rural areas were confined to some 16,000 private schools of such wretched quality that they could not qualify for government support. There was, however, some consolation in knowing that many of these children also attended one of the 33,872 Sunday schools that had appeared since the 1780's and which were currently providing rudimentary reading instruction for 2,411,554 pupils.[5] The Commissioners reported with satisfaction that only Prussia, with compulsory education, had a greater proportion of its population in school. While encouraging to Church opponents of compulsory national education, it was difficult to ignore the figures showing that in all states with public instruction children remained in school three to four years longer than in England and Wales.

The Newcastle Report statistically verified what every thinking critic had known for the past twenty years—the superficiality and brevity of schooling in England was seriously undermining the effectiveness of educational efforts. With the majority of pupils leaving school before the age of eleven, and 95 per cent by the age of thirteen, attendance averaged four years and even less in factory and mining towns.[6] In spite of repeated appeals for extension, the curriculum was still largely restricted to religion and the three R's—a limitation made virtually permanent after the decision in 1862 to limit grants to those schools whose pupils demonstrated a rudimentary proficiency in those areas alone: few schools were prepared to risk disqualification by spending time on other subjects.

[1] Blomfield, *Charge* (1854), 8–9.   [2] *Ibid.*, 10.

[3] S. Wilberforce, *A Charge to the Diocese of Oxford . . . November, 1854* (1854), 45–46.

[4] *Report of the Commissioners Appointed to Inquire Into the State of Popular Education in England,* 6 vols. (1861), I, 84–86.

[5] *Ibid.*, 204 ff.   [6] *Ibid.*, 172, 187.

Bishop Thirlwall had warned that it was not possible to begin educating people and then expect to stop their development at some arbitrary age. It will not stop, he promised; it will not be confined by your pleasure and limitations. 'Intelligent curiosity' is the mark of a civilized man, and if by science, geography and history we can elevate the poor from their 'animal wants and enjoyments', we should rejoice.[1] C. R. Sumner, coming to a similar conclusion by mid-century, believed that Church schools had reached a crisis of 'quality and purpose' that would not permit relegating lower-class instruction to the rote learning of reading, writing and basic arithmetic. It was no longer feasible or desirable to restrict intellectual development to the upper classes; 'you must act on the same principle upon the mind of the child of the labourer or the mechanic'.[2] Thirlwall's treatment of the subject cut more deeply into the conservative hierarchical assumptions of the age. Was it not clear from the events of the 1840's that the Church was trying to minister old truths to a new populace 'irreconcilably hostile to all privileges of caste, and to all monopolies of things which may and should be common'? Education was perhaps the most important of those 'things', and it was no longer possible 'to appropriate the light of knowledge to one class or portion of the community'. Flying in the face of deeply entrenched attitudes about the charitable nature of lower-class instruction, Thirlwall insisted that education 'is as much their birthright as the light of day; and that it not only ought not to be kept from them, but ... it is a national duty to diffuse it as widely as possible among them'. Rudimentary instruction was sufficient for the past, but not for the future. The bishop urged that the best minds and the most arduous research be devoted to educating the laboring multitudes.[3]

Thirlwall was no leveler, but he thought the times were. Rank and fortune, he concluded, would no longer suffice to assure the preservation of relative social positions. Talent, study and labor were the determining factors of the new age and, like it or not, the Church and the society it represented had to understand that they were possessed by people in all ranks of life.[4] The exciting and provocative liberality of such rare episcopal views did not alter the fact that, to a great extent, they were irrelevant. Rank and privilege continued to dominate English society, and not always with demonstrable evidence of talent, study and labor. Education for the lower orders remained simple and grossly inadequate for many years to come; the Church was prepared no more than society as a whole to consider the instruction of the poor as anything other than a useful, but essentially charitable, obligation of rank. Moreover, idealistic

[1] Thirlwall, Lecture (1849), 15–16.   [2] Sumner, *Charge* (1850), 56–57.
[3] C. Thirlwall, *The Centre of Unity. A Sermon Preached ... December 13, 1850* (1850), 13–14.
[4] *Ibid.*, 15.

enthusiasts like Thirlwall forgot that the working classes had to work. As one of the Assistant Commissioners for the Newcastle enquiry, James Fraser, bluntly concluded: 'we must make up our minds to see the last of [the poor] . . . as far as the day school is concerned, at ten or eleven . . .'. Fraser, who was to become the second Bishop of the new diocese of Manchester in 1870, thought all educational planning must conform to that reality, confidently adding 'that it is quite possible to teach a child soundly and thoroughly . . . all that is necessary for him to possess in the shape of intellectual attainment, by the time that he is ten years old'. Intellectual attainment meant the ability to read a newspaper paragraph, write a legible and intelligible letter, make out a shop bill, have some idea where other countries are, be sufficiently acquainted with the Bible to follow 'a plain Saxon sermon', and remember enough of the catechism to know one's duty to God and man. Whatever the exaggerated visions of some churchmen, Fraser and the Commission saw 'no brighter view of the future or the possibilities of an English elementary education floating before [their] . . . eyes than this'. The 'peremptory demands of the labour market' required confining any additional education for the poor to evening schools.[1]

Henry Ryder had made the same suggestion as early as 1816 when he noted that 'manufactories and other avocations' prevented children from attending day schools.[2] The proposal was largely ignored until the 1840's, when a newer generation of Church leaders, sensitive to their inability to keep the poor in school and fearful of Chartist, Owenite, and other radical schemes for filling the gap, tried to attract former pupils to evening classes. Edward Denison saw more than one hundred evening schools established in his diocese at various times which workers would not attend.[3] The two archbishops, Sumner and Musgrave, had also endorsed similar plans in their earlier sees, but had met with the same results.[4] More often, however, there was little clerical enthusiasm for schemes usually associated with radicals, socialists and irreligious workers' co-operatives. In many of the overcrowded industrial districts, the Church was fortunate to establish and maintain a National Society school without attempting to support an additional burden.

As in the case of church extension, the Establishment marshalled enormous voluntary resources for education in order to fill these newly constructed edifices in populous areas. The more than 8,500 schools

[1] *Report,* 243.

[2] H. Ryder, *A Charge Delivered to the Clergy of the Diocese of Gloucester . . . 1816,* 3rd ed. (Gloucester, 1816), 30–31.

[3] E. Denison, *A Charge Delivered to the Clergy of the Diocese of Salisbury .. . September, 1842* (1842), 11–12; also *Charge* (1845), 42.

[4] J. B. Sumner, *The Charge to the Clergy of the Diocese . . . 1853* (1853), 9–10, and Musgrave, *Charge* (1853), 15–17.

established in the first half of the century under the auspices of the National Society provided at least a minimal elementary education for millions of children.[1] Such minimal education, however, did not stimulate its recipients to fill the empty pews awaiting them. For a great many laboring children their first and last contact with the national faith came during their brief interlude in a National Society school where they learned little that was relevant to the life into which they were soon plunged; not enough, in any event, to encourage their return to the Church for further enlightenment. Many Church leaders knew this, and by mid-century the Religious Census of 1851 confirmed it. Since the 1820's, bishops had been discussing education in terms of a new age of 'restless curiosity and searching enquiry', and many of them saw that innovation and experiment, rather than a tenacious adherence to ancient opinions and practices, would be necessary to make Church school instruction relevant to the laboring classes. Time and again, however, they rejected the implications of their own arguments. In this they reflected the general pattern of episcopal social thought in the first half of the nineteenth century. After analyzing the evidence and recognizing the implications of their analyses, prelates often drew critical and perceptive conclusions about the relationship of social and economic problems to the effectiveness of their Church. There they stopped, however, unwilling or unable to take the next logical step: the proposal of a solution or policy that might have made them appear genuinely interested in the total welfare of the laboring masses they endeavoured to reach.

Churchmen were really unable to separate themselves from that upper-class society whose attitudes, prejudices, fears and anxieties they so closely mirrored. Complain as they did about the economic requirements of society constantly undermining their educational efforts, no bishop was prepared to *demand* that instead of sending ten-year-old children to work, they should be sent to school. But then that was not the function of an Established Church dedicated to reconciling all classes to one another and, especially, to the natural order of things. For a half-century, the Church had been trying to accomplish this task from below by educating the children of the laboring poor away from both dissatisfaction with their station in life as well as from Methodism, Dissent, hostility, or indifference. Old prelates like Blomfield, the Sumner brothers, and Kaye, who had been elevated in the decade after the National Society's establishment and who had guided it through the difficult years

[1] Ollard, *Dictionary*, 198. The passage of the Education Act of 1870 stimulated the Church's quest for voluntary support so that by 1904 it was maintaining 11,874 schools. Not until 1900 did the average attendance in the rate-supported schools, established by the 1870 Act, reach the number of pupils attending Anglican schools.

of political and ecclesiastical reform, realized that their hopes had not been fulfilled. Along with the next generation of prelates, men like Wilberforce, Denison, Thirlwall and Longley, they already knew in the 1840's that their limited, voluntary system was inadequate to achieve the spiritual and social goals set by the Church early in the century. They also knew many of the reasons, and, after discussing them at great length, proceeded to plod along the same disappointing path.

XII

❖❖❖❖❖❖❖❖❖❖❖❖❖❖❖❖❖❖❖❖❖❖❖❖❖

Conclusion: Old Truths and
New Realities

❖❖❖❖❖❖❖❖❖❖❖❖❖❖❖❖❖❖❖❖❖❖❖❖❖

RELIGIOUS CENSUS: 1851

At mid-century Bishop Blomfield surveyed the impressive accomplishments of the Church he had witnessed during his long clerical career. He pointed with pride to the thousands of churches and schools, 'which are now so many centers of light and holiness in regions where the powers of darkness long held undisputed sway . . .', and declared the Establishment revived and militant. Remembering the laxity and indifference characterizing the Establishment of his youth, Blomfield noted that the Church's 'inherent energy' had not been sapped, but had been merely dormant. When the opportunities arose, the Church, 'without assistance, almost without encouragement from the State . . .', vigorously undertook to fulfil its sacred and political obligations.[1] Perhaps dazzled by the 'many trophies which the Church Militant has been permitted to erect over the enemies of man's salvation', Blomfield failed in retrospect to see how often the improvement of the Establishment had been encouraged, and even demanded, by both Tory and Whig governments. Although he would not have denied the positive contributions of the former, he would have been reluctant to give much credit to the latter party.

Half of Blomfield's colleagues in the final years of his life were in fact Whig appointments, but they seemed to take no less pride in the vigorous extension of the Church. Henry Pepys, Bishop of Worcester, and brother of the Whig peer, Lord Cottenham, believed the Establishment

[1] C. J. Blomfield, *The Charge to the Clergy of His Diocese . . . On the Occasion of His Sixth Visitation* (1850), 34.

431

healthier and more efficient than at any time since the Reformation.[1] Less exalted in his ecclesiastical notions than Blomfield, Pepys had long recognized that the revival of the Church was part of a wider religious revival affecting all segments of English society. During his ordination of new clergy in 1844, Pepys told them they were fortunate to minister in a religious age and in a religious nation. Comparing spiritual life to that of fifty years ago, the bishop welcomed the genuine religious zeal that 'pervades the minds and actuates the conduct of individuals'.[2] Ten years later he believed the evidence to be even more obvious. Not only was the physical extension of the Church testimony to the religiosity of the era, but the zealousness and energy of the clergy was without parallel in living memory. 'The sporting clergyman, so common a character in former days, is now rarely to be met with; and Fielding, were he alive now, would look in vain for the antitype to his Parson Trulliber.'[3] Whether Archdeacon Grantly or the Reverend Obadiah Slope were any improvement is doubtful.

In spite of bitter party strife exacerbated by conflicts with Tractarians and the Gorham decision, most Church leaders not only took considerable pride in the progress of the Church, but were confident that it had a future. The revolutionary upheavals on the Continent had not proven infectious, and the portentous fears of a great confrontation had largely dissipated. If all classes were not living in blessed harmony, it at least seemed possible after the 1840's that they would not tear each other apart. The different ranks of society seemed to have reached an understanding about their responsibilities and priorities. As Blomfield explained during his last visitation in 1854.

> the spirit of insubordination and tumult has nearly disappeared from amongst us. The labouring classes appear to have discovered, that in every struggle against the established laws of social order they are sure to be the chief losers. The higher classes have seen and recognized the duty and advantage of exerting themselves to promote the real interests, temporal and spiritual, of the lower.

This could be seen in the social legislation of the previous decade as well as in the great contributions made to educate the poor and provide them with churches and clergy. Blomfield thought it possible to discern on the part of the laboring classes an increased attachment to those 'who are intrusted with a larger share of worldly advantages, and who seem to use them as good stewards of the gifts of God'. If true, the clergy deserved great thanks as 'the chief instruments in bettering the condi-

[1] H. Pepys, *A Charge Delivered to the Clergy of the Diocese of Worcester . . . July, 1854* (1854), 8.

[2] H. Pepys, *A Charge Addressed to the Candidates For Priests and Deacons Orders . . . August, 1844* (1844), 9–10.

[3] Pepys, *Charge* (1854), 8.

tion of the poor . . .'. It meant that the lower orders again recognized 'in the parochial clergy their true friends and helpers; the kind and disinterested mediators between them and their worldly superiors . . .'.[1]

From an episcopal vantage-point the vigorous extension of clerical activity, coupled with the diminution of working-class agitation, certainly suggested a victory for the useful, ameliorative policies of the Church. The passage of social legislation in the 1840's and the gradual improvement of the economy during the next decade were, however, probably more important than clerical explanations of social inevitability. Yet, if bishops often confused the Church's ministrations with the effects of social and economic causation, it was because they still desperately believed that the inculcation of right attitudes was the key to social harmony. The Church seemed in a stronger position than ever to turn that key to advantage. Although, as Blomfield said, 'vast masses of human beings' were jammed into the cities and towns still beyond the reach of the clergy, even the most pessimistic churchmen were confident that the net could be cast more widely than ever.[2] The expanding network of schools promised to lead many of the untouched poor into the nearly 2,700 new churches constructed during the preceding half-century; more than 2,000 of them since 1831.[3] In addition thousands of the 11,379 churches already in existence at the opening of the century were enlarged or rebuilt. While the most important strides in parochial reorganization came in the second half of the century, the Church Building Commissioners between 1818–56 managed to assign 1,077 districts in established parishes to the new churches.[4]

Of greater importance was the marked increase in both the number and quality of the clergy. From 1831 to 1851, the period of greatest Church extension, the number of beneficed clergy rose from 10,718 to 17,621.[5] While remnants of old abuses lingered on, they were scandalous exceptions among a clergy more respectable, spiritual and obedient than at any time since the early eighteenth century. In this they reflected the values and controls of Victorian society and public opinion from without as well as the serious standards posed by Evangelicals and Tractarians from within. In an age of improving standards and professionalism, the Anglican clergy had become a respected profession earnestly dedicated to improving their Church and society as a whole.[6] Pluralism and non-residency had been cut virtually in half during the last twenty-five years, though nearly two thousand ministers were still

[1] Blomfield, *Charge* (1854), 4–5.
[2] *Ibid.*, 6.
[3] *Census*, 1851, *Religious Worship*, 75.
[4] G. Kitson Clark, *The Making of Victorian England* (1965), 169.
[5] *Census*, 1851, *Religious Worship*, 12; *Census*, 1851, 128.
[6] Best, *Temporal Pillars*, 398–400.

non-resident at mid-century.[1] Curates were mandatory in such cases, however, and instances of prolonged and total neglect had become very rare. Pluralism was closely regulated by legislation, and the strengthening of ecclesiastical discipline had gone a long way towards confining it to manageable and proximate parishes.

Although Wilberforce might complain of the inferior quality of individual bishops appointed to the bench in recent years, in defense, he could be stung to defend the high level of episcopal performance in general.[2] Whether or not he liked his colleagues personally, the critical prelate knew that they were much better disciplinarians than their predecessors, and usually devoted primarily to the administration and improvement of their dioceses. Though still subservient to Parliament, the episcopate was becoming less political in its interests, and concentrated more upon ecclesiastical matters. In spite of the intense party factionalism inflamed by Tractarians and Evangelicals, most bishops by the middle of the century had a strong appreciation of the importance of Church unity and ecclesiastical decision-making. They realized that the traditional alliance of Church and State, though preserved in form, was greatly weakened in substance. The ability of the Establishment to accept some reform and to rally voluntary support to its cause had greatly eased its adjustment to that reality. The hesitant revival of Convocation in 1852, in spite of considerable episcopal trepidation that it would only exacerbate party factionalism, was a further indication that the leadership of the Church was determined, with parliamentary approval, to bring greater cohesiveness and directed purpose to the heterogeneous national Establishment.

The publication in 1854 of Horace Mann's report of the results of the religious census taken in 1851 provided a unique opportunity for the Church to evaluate more precisely how effective its extensive efforts had been. Moreover, an examination of attendance at religious worship conducted by all denominations placed the question of establishment on a different level—that of quantitative utility. That is what frightened churchmen who initially opposed the religious census, when it was suggested that religious affiliation be included as one of the questions on the general census of 1851. Nonconformists were equally upset by the realization that many non-churchgoers would in all probability still consider themselves as nominal members of the Church of England and would answer the questions accordingly. The decision to organize instead a great voluntary count of attendance to be taken on Sunday, 30 March 1851, was more welcome to the sects who had nothing to lose. Wilberforce, however, spoke for many churchmen when he warned that

[1] Kitson Clark, *Victorian England,* 152.

[2] Wilberforce to Gladstone, 26 Dec. 1851, *Wilberforce Ps.,* Dep. D. 204, ff. 281–6; also, *Gladstone Ps.,* Add MS. 44343, ff. 137–40.

the returns would be unreliable and incomplete, and suggested that in some vague way they would be used to the disadvantage of the Establishment. Bishop Denison agreed, but rejected charges that the Church was trying to hide from reality. Since the returns were to be made voluntarily by clergymen or their appointees, there was no way to guarantee reliability, and Denison predicted that 'unjust, mischievous and dangerous' inferences would be drawn.[1]

Wilberforce and Denison were familiar enough with the remaining weaknesses of the Church to realize that a national survey would reveal the many deficiencies continually described in diocesan enquiries. By making excuses in advance they were preparing for the worst. Yet, when the remarkable *Report* appeared in 1854, it was still a shock to ecclesiastical sensibilities. Particularly upsetting were the figures on non-attendance, and the size of Nonconformist congregations. Out of a total population of 17,927,609 in England and Wales, Mann calculated that approximately 12,549,326 persons, those not too young, too ill or otherwise legitimately occupied, could have attended one of the three services provided by the various denominations on census Sunday. The returns indicated that only 7,261,032 Englishmen availed themselves of the opportunity and many of them attended more than one service.[2] While it does not appear to the modern reader of these figures that the country was consumed by heathenism, contemporaries believed themselves a churchgoing people and were appalled to learn that some 5,288,294 persons among them did not share their religious inclinations. Churchmen were particularly distressed by the figures showing that of those who chose to worship, 3,773,474 attended an Anglican service, while 3,487,558 were in Dissenter chapels.[3] Whatever justifications defenders of the Establishment might make in the future for the privileges enjoyed by the Church, the assertion that it was first in the hearts of most Englishmen was no longer supportable. Nonconformists were delighted.

Adding insult to injury, the *Census* also showed that the availability of facilities was not an important factor. Despite the continual proliferation of sittings for nearly half the century, the Church, at its best-attended service (morning), utilized no more than 47·8 per cent of its total accommodation. An analysis of attendance at afternoon and evening services, as well, indicated that overall, 66 per cent of the seats in Anglican churches were not filled. The Nonconformists fared about as well, with the Wesleyan Methodists having the highest utilization (45 per cent).[4] These statistics proved that during the past half-century of Church extension the Dissenters had worked at least as hard, not simply to hold their relative position in English religious life, but to improve it considerably. They had been most successful in the expanding

[1] *Hansard*, CXV (1851), 630–2.
[2] *Census*, 1851, *Religious Worship*, 87–88.   [3] *Ibid.*, 91.   [4] *Ibid.*, 92.

manufacturing towns. Since the opening of the century Dissenting congregations had constructed 16,689 new places of worship with 4,013,408 sittings.[1] Of the nearly 30,000 ministers in the country in 1851, more than 12,000 were Nonconformists, and their ranks were supplemented by innumerable lay preachers.[2]

Church leaders, stung by charges that the Establishment could no longer claim to be the national Church, nor the guardian of national belief, struck back by questioning the honesty of Dissenter returns, and impugning the accuracy and fairness of their figures. Wilberforce had warned of these dangers in 1851;[3] three years later he claimed that Anglican returns were understated, since many vicars and curates who opposed the census had refused to co-operate at all. He had in fact urged them not to. The Nonconformists, he charged, exaggerated their attendance; but the bishop was not surprised, since 'many of their ministers were not often in the same rank of life as the clergy of the Established Church'.[4] Actually Mann had gone to considerable lengths to encourage accurate returns, and where clergy balked at replying he sent additional queries. He recognized that his figures could not be precise, and in some instances reflected approximate estimates rather than exact returns. Nevertheless they were based upon a surprisingly high number of replies. Out of 14,077 places of Anglican worship only 989 continued to refuse any co-operation.[5] Whatever criticism could be made about the exactitude of Mann's compilations, the general picture they revealed seems fairly reliable.[6] Even Wilberforce reluctantly conceded this to be true. During his visitation in 1854 he pointed to the religious census as proof that the majority of people were not in church —any church. Of those claiming to be members of the Church of England, only one-quarter actually attend services—a proportion far below that enjoyed by Dissenter congregations. The bishop also pointed to the more ominous revelations of the Mann *Report* that even he never questioned: the working classes generally did not go to church or chapel. In spite of the massive campaign of the past half-century, the Establishment had not yet removed 'the many hindrances to the worship of the poor which the selfishness of wealth, or the decays of age, have brought into our churches . . .'.[7]

---

[1] E. Halévy, *Victorian Years 1841–1895*, E. I. Watkin, trans. (1961), 392.
[2] *Census*, 1851, 122, 137.   [3] *Hansard*, CXV (1851), 629–31.
[4] *Ibid.*, CXXXV (1854), 25.   [5] *Census*, 1851, *Religious Worship*, 110.
[6] K. S. Inglis, 'Patterns of Religious Worship in 1851', *The Journal of Ecclesiastical History*, XI, April (1960), 76–77. For a brief discussion of some problems in using the census returns see D. M. Thompson, 'The 1851 Religious Census: Problems and Possibilities', *Victorian Studies*, XI, No. 1, Sept. 1967, 87–97.
[7] Wilberforce, *Charge* (1854), 39–41.

Mann not only compiled figures, he analyzed their significance. It was clear to him from his study of attendance in urban working-class districts that the more than five million Englishmen absent from religious worship were mainly from the lower orders. They formed an 'absolutely insignificant . . . portion of the congregations . . .'. Though they filled the day and Sunday schools, the laboring classes 'soon become as utter strangers to religious ordinances as the people of a heathen country . . .' so that this 'vast, intelligent, and growingly important section of our countrymen is thoroughly estranged from our religious institutions . . .'.[1] Mann had conservatively estimated that if all persons capable of attending a service had in fact done so, some 58 per cent of the populace would have worshipped on census Sunday. In theory many of them could not have been accommodated, especially in the towns where seating facilities were still far from adequate.[2] In practice it had not been a problem.

In some of the large manufacturing towns, like Birmingham and Manchester, only around a third of the population attended any service. Of the 83,985 persons who worshipped in Birmingham, less than 40,000 were in Anglican churches. In Manchester the Establishment accounted for only 36,244 of the 105,383 worshippers reported. The same proportions held for nearby Salford, where Dissenters reported two and a half times as many worshippers. Yet only 23,000 of nearly 64,000 people bothered to attend at all. In Leeds, where Hook had labored so diligently, nearly half the population of 172,000 was present, but not in Establishment facilities. Anglican services managed to attract only around 28,000 of the more than 53,000 who attended that day. The returns from the industrial areas of the north-west were no more comforting to the urban ministry. In Liverpool, where the extension of religious facilities had already been undertaken on a municipal level in the eighteenth century, only 45 per cent of the nearly 376,000 people in the city attended a service. Anglican congregations accounted for slightly more than 69,000 of them. Far more depressing was the situation in Preston, where only one-quarter of the population of 69,542 were accounted for, and of these only 3,610 attended an Anglican service.[3]

The Church was much more successful in the small towns and rural areas, largely in the south, and largely unaffected by industrial expansion. There it has been estimated that on the basis of adding all attendances and expressing them as a percentage index of the total population, better than 71 per cent attended services as compared to an average index of just under 50 per cent in towns of more than 10,000 people. The average index for the entire nation was 61 per cent. A few larger towns in the south exceeded even the rural average, and several others the national average. In addition another twenty-one towns exceeded 50 per cent.[4]

[1] *Census.,* 1851, *Religious Worship,* 93.   [2] *Ibid.,* 60–61.
[3] *Ibid.,* Table F, 113 ff.   [4] Inglis, 'Patterns', *JEH,* 80.

Most of the large manufacturing districts, however, as well as the parliamentary boroughs of London, were populated with a majority of people who displayed no religious preference on census Sunday. The archiepiscopal palace at Lambeth sat at the edge of a borough in which only 31 per cent of the 251,345 inhabitants attended services. There was perhaps some consolation in the knowledge that the majority of them were Anglican. This was not the case in Southwark, however, where of the 37 per cent who attended less than half were in Establishment churches; or in Tower Hamlets, where the same was true and where out of a total population of over 539,000 less than 69,000 were counted in Anglican churches.[1]

If most people in the large towns were not enticed to worship with any congregation, of those who did most preferred Nonconformity, usually Methodist. A tentative survey of the twenty-nine largest manufacturing towns indicates that in all but three (Halifax, Kidderminster and Warrington) Anglican worshippers were in the minority. In twenty of these towns Nonconformists alone comprised the church-going majority, and in six others Roman Catholic attendances, combined with those of the Dissenters, sufficed to keep the national Church in the minority.[2] The picture in Wales was even more disheartening for churchmen. There the statistics added up to a monument to Establishment indifference. Not only did less than half the populace attend any service, but of those who did, no more than one-fifth were in Anglican churches.[3] With the exception of Tower Hamlets, Southwark, and perhaps Finsbury, the Establishment could at least claim to be the church of the majority of those attending services in the parliamentary boroughs of the Metropolis.[4] It could not, however, claim to be the church of the people, and it was this reality that old and new bishops alike had to confront.

C. R. Sumner weighed the charges of error and miscalculation leveled against the *Report* and decided that it was 'undeniable, as Mr Horace Mann concludes, that a sadly formidable portion of the English people are habitual neglectors of the public ordinances of religion'. Diocesan investigations substantiated the broad conclusions of the *Report*. On one street of 200 families, only 10 adults were in church; on another 7 of 312 adults were in attendance. Scripture readers' reports were equally depressing. In 1849 they had shown that of nearly 500,000 people studied in the Metropolis, less than a third of them had any religious affiliation. The census two years later confirmed such reports, and, Sumner told his clergy, if you examine your own parishes carefully, you will see these 'fearful facts' corroborated. Heathenism was literally infecting all parts of the country. Like Mann, he believed it was largely the result of a

[1] *Census*, 1851, *Religious Worship*, Table F.
[2] Inglis, 'Patterns', *JEH*, 82–83.
[3] *Census*, 1851, *Religious Worship*, Table N, 142.   [4] *Ibid.*, Table F.

'negative, inert indifference' on the part of the laboring masses. 'They are *unconscious Secularists*—engrossed by the demands, the trials, or the pleasures of the passing hour, and ignorant or careless of a future.' Contrary to what many churchmen believed and feared, the weaknesses of the Establishment had not really been remedied by evangelizing Dissenters; most of the wretched poor still knew nothing of that 'future life as a time when the rich will find the tables turned, and the poor [will] be exalted . . .'.[1]

Church leaders were not only confronted with statistical confirmation of their worst fears, they were provided with explanations that must have sounded depressingly familiar to some of them. Mann noted that social distinctions had become so sharp that class lines were too great to be effaced even on Sundays. The working classes live in a world apart, and feel it is 'wholly uncongenial' to that of their betters. As the rich were equally uncomfortable if the poor were in church with them, or not in church at all, the best solution seemed to be the spread of worker churches—'Ragged Churches', as they were called. Mann found this term perhaps objectionable, but could think of none better. There was evidence, nevertheless, 'that the multitudes will readily frequent such places, where of course there is a total absence of all class distinctions . . .'.[2]

Another major impediment to lower-class religiosity cited was the widespread belief among the poor that professed Christians were not really interested in alleviating the oppressive burdens of poverty, disease and ignorance. Years of preaching social resignation could not be overcome by still more promises of charity. Mann recognized, as did several prelates, that ministers were increasingly at the forefront of efforts to improve the living and working conditions of the lower orders, but the general impression of the clergy among the poor was still one of selfish secularity. Clerical failings were especially exaggerated in an atmosphere of grinding poverty that dulled the mind and senses to Christian principles. Mann pointed to improved housing as one way to provide some privacy for solitude and reflection.[3] Some Church leaders had been pushing their clergy in that direction throughout the previous decade, and the census *Report* reinforced the changing conviction that it was no longer meaningful to preach a religion of social statics. As C. R. Sumner reflected on Mann's words, he saw that the Church of the future had to concern itself with improving the quality of life on this earth if men were to place any value on the one that followed. An examination of the census certainly indicated that those who found material and intellectual satisfaction during this transitory passage were much more amenable to

---

[1] Sumner, *Charge* (1854), 6–10. Also, *Census*, 1851, *Religious Worship*, 93.

[2] *Ibid.*, 94. [3] *Ibid.*, 95–96.

contemplating, at least on Sundays, the possibilities of a more permanent environment. Sumner argued that the parochial clergy must, as never before, involve themselves in sanitation, housing, adult education, and the further reduction of working hours. Moreover they must provide reading-rooms, libraries, lectures, displays of nature and art, all in an effort to show the poor man that he is appreciated.[1]

The main thrust of Mann's analysis of lower-class religious alienation was towards maximum flexibility on the part of the Church to evangelize those whom Sumner called 'the godless multitude ... without the gates of the city'.[2] An aggressive missionary offensive had to be launched, utilizing the lay as well as clerical resources of the Church. Mann suggested that it was time the Establishment learned not only from past mistakes, but from the successes of Dissenters like the Methodists, who marshalled all their resources to assist their overburdened clergy. The Scripture Readers Association and the Pastoral Aid Society were not yet utilized extensively by the Church. The Methodists, however, the most successful denomination among the poor, utilized 20,000 lay preachers. Even the excesses of the Primitive Methodists 'will most likely be forgiven when it is remembered that perhaps their rough, unformal energy is best adapted to the class to which it is addressed, and that, at all events, for every convert added to their ranks, society retains one criminal, one drunkard, one improvident the less'. Was it not possible that the rougher Dissenters actually civilized the lower classes to the extent that they might be more susceptible to the less exciting, but more refined worship of other churches? If the Anglican clergy adopted greater flexibility they might discover that the Dissenters are providing 'a sort of preliminary education' for eventual worship in the Established Church.[3]

This theme of missionary flexibility pervaded the episcopal thinking of the early 1850's as it did the remainder of the century. Wilberforce, for example, lamented the past rigidity of Anglican preconceptions about the Church's sphere of influence. The clergy had never really overcome its rural, pastoral orientation and accepted the cities as places worthy of a vigorous moral and religious life. For too long the ministry had resigned itself to the belief that the towns were beyond redemption; that it was really futile to try and impress 'these vast hives of life, and industry, and production, and intellectual activity'. England, at mid-century, however, was an urban country, and it was in the cities that Christianity must flourish. Wilberforce saw that it would require unprecedented pliability to escape from 'a certain unbending rigidity of external form' that interferes with the Church's true needs. Although he

---

[1] Sumner, *Charge* (1854), 32–33.   [2] *Ibid.,* 20.

[3] *Census*, 1851, *Religious Worship*, 97–100; also Sumner, *Charge* (1854), 22–23.

had the Tractarians in mind, the bishop was speaking generally when he called for the setting aside of rigid formularies when they interfered with the primary goal of the spiritual revival of 'our lost multitudes'.[1] Inflexibility had driven the Wesleyans from the Establishment in the preceding century; it threatened a much greater loss in the present age.

The emphasis upon flexible, evangelizing missions was in effect a recognition that church-building, the main instrument of the Church's revival for the past thirty-five years, had proven largely futile. Evangelicals and some Broad Churchmen had been criticizing that emphasis since the 1820's even as they themselves were caught up in the momentum of building churches in populous districts. The census of 1851 showed that if there was one thing the Establishment did not need in the towns, it was more churches. Many of them were already virtually empty, and formed what Mann described as 'too conspicuous a difference between accommodation and attendants . . .'.[2] Criticism of appropriated sittings seemed irrelevant when the evidence showed that the existing open accommodations were hardly utilized. Bishops were already aware of the situation to some extent before the *Report* illustrated it so clearly. Both Blomfield, the principal proponent of church-building, and Wilberforce admitted in 1851 that the free seats in new churches were rarely occupied to any great extent; consequently in spite of their earlier attacks on appropriated pews, they reluctantly allowed many of them to be rented in order to increase operating revenue.[3] Not only had church extension made little impact upon the urban masses, but the large size of many of the new edifices compounded their emptiness. Mann thought it far more sensible to use licensed rooms and then build smaller churches in subdivided parishes when it was clear that a congregation actually existed to fill them.[4] Peel's Act of 1843 provided the legal mechanism; it was up to the Church to provide the congregations.

This meant not only the use of lay visitors and readers working with aggressive parochial clergymen; it also meant in 'the terrible emergency' the possible introduction of outdoor preaching missionaries.[5] In contrast to the minister who tends to deal with his parishioners as if they were in a safe state of grace, the missionary, C. R. Sumner explained, knows his charges are not. As a result he must use different weapons in the assault.[6] Sumner saw that before a congregation could even be

---

[1] S. Wilberforce, *I Have Much People In this City. A Sermon Preached . . . October 13, 1853* (1853), 11, 17. Also A. Ollivant, *A Charge Delivered to the Clergy of the Diocese of Llandaff . . . August, 1854* (1854), 43.

[2] *Census*, 1851, *Religious Worship*, 96–97.

[3] *Hansard*, CXVI (1851), 859–60.

[4] *Census*, 1851, *Religious Worship*, 97–98.

[5] *Ibid.*, 97.   [6] Sumner, *Charge* (1854), 13.

formed its members in the towns 'must be sought as the wounded and the dying upon the battlefield . . .', and be brought to safety. The language of militancy reflected the emphasis upon the Church militant that gradually appeared in the ecclesiastical thought of mid-century England. It meant that an Evangelical prelate like Sumner could join with an institutionally-minded High Churchman like Blomfield to endorse that most extravagant of enthusiastic innovations—open-air preaching. It also meant that they were to some extent faced with a *fait accompli*, since some zealous missionaries were already in the streets and alleys of the populous slums exhorting the heathen poor wherever they could find them. Sumner cautiously predicted that public opinion approved of outdoor evangelizing, 'though long associated in men's minds only with fanaticism and extravagance'. Although there was still 'little modern example in connexion with our own Church', it was now being attempted, and 'must be looked upon as a remarkable testimony to the exigencies of the case'. Undoubtedly there would be resistance to this innovation, but it 'indicates the general feeling that the time has come when something must be ventured beyond the ordinary routine of ministerial work, and sinners followed, as Archbishop Leighton said, to their homes, and even to their alehouses'.[1]

To walk the streets in search of congregations would mean, Sumner conceded,

> to walk in the wake, if not to share the obloquy, of the Wesleys and Whitefields, who, as one of them said, thought they saw 'abundant reason to adore the wise providence of God in thus making a way for myriads of people, who never troubled any church or were likely to do so, to hear that Word which they soon found the power of God unto salvation'.

The nature of the episcopal bench and ecclesiastical thought had changed greatly when bishops could invoke Wesley and Whitefield as allies in the Church's cause. Sumner, of course, cautioned that those early Methodist divines were itinerants whose example was not suitable to the parochial system. Even the Wesleyans themselves had abandoned much of their earlier irregularity. Still, there was much room for zealous activity within the parish. Conscious of the Tractarian challenge to such a Low Church view, Sumner recalled the many cases of outdoor preaching and services during the Reformation. Though Puseyite churchmen might prefer to forget that era, Sumner described Latimer preaching his seven sermons before Edward VI in the Privy Garden when the Chapel Royal proved too small.[2] Furthermore outdoor preaching was canonical so long as it was licensed by the bishop, and did not employ the whole use of the liturgy. Obviously it should be an occasional rather than a continuous innovation, and employed only by trusted and gifted

[1] *Ibid.*, 19–21. [2] *Ibid.*, 22–24.

ministers who were seeking to bring people into the parochial churches, not attract them to listen without.[1]

Sumner had long believed that church-building should be a secondary rather than a primary stage in parochial reconstruction. Blomfield, throughout his career, believed that the physical presence of a church was essential to attract congregations. Both men recognized the importance of education, and with varying degrees of enthusiasm supported the various parochial innovations introduced in the 1830's and 1840's to attract the urban poor. For Blomfield, however, the emphasis was always on providing a church first, and when critics complained that ecclesiastical resources could be better utilized evangelizing in less institutional ways, he insisted that it was only a matter of time before a new generation of Church-educated people would fill the new edifices. When, in the 1840's, his prophecy remained unfulfilled, he complained that appropriated sittings were responsible for the absence of the lower classes. Sometimes he insisted that the descriptions of half-empty churches were exaggerated, and that the new buildings were 'extremely well attended'. He might then turn around and complain that, given the accumulated neglect in so many parishes, it was impossible to fill the new churches in so few years.[2]

Blomfield became increasingly uncertain of his position as he suggested that the motivations for religious worship were perhaps more complex than he had realized. Class antagonisms and feelings of social inferiority made the unwashed and ill-clad poor 'ashamed of appearing amongst their richer neighbours'; their ignorance left them incapable of understanding the service. One of the things that frightened him about Tractarian-inspired ritualism was the confusion that the more ornate services would cause in the minds of the poorer worshippers. Blomfield appealed to Puseyite incumbents to keep their services for the lower orders 'solemn, earnest, reverential, [and] not needlessly at variance with established usage'.[3] The same year, 1851, that he confessed that the free sittings in many churches were empty week after week, he complained that the poor were not in church because of an absence of open pews. Blomfield's inconsistency reflected his troubled awareness of the Church's parlous condition in London and most of the large towns of the realm. Yet he was still unable to accept the evidence that the vast church-building program to which he devoted so much of his life, fortune and prestige was in fact a monument to the Establishment's failure among the greater populace. Certainly the administrative and financial reforms he promoted with such effectiveness went a long way towards restoring middle- and upper-class confidence in the Church, and the enormous

[1] *Ibid.*, 29–31.
[2] Blomfield, *Memoir*, I, 246–7.
[3] 2 Jan. 1851, Letter Copy Book 384, ff. 285–8, *Fulham Ps.*

contributions made to support its extension programs indicated the extent of that confidence and attachment.

It meant little to the poor, however, as the religious census revealed. In the aftermath of the *Report* Lord Shaftesbury, one of Blomfield's old philanthropic allies, in 1855 seriously questioned the wisdom of the bishop's enthusiasm for church-building.[1] Blomfield, in his *Charge* of the previous year, not only questioned Mann's statistics, but continued to complain about the lack of 'proper accommodation' and the importance of more free sittings in good locations as if the *Report* had never appeared.[2] His response after so many years was like a knee-jerk reaction. Yet the old bishop, weakened by stroke and shaken by the *Report*, was still realistic enough to concede Mann's assertion that 'the myriads of our labouring population [are] really as ignorant of Christianity as were the heathen Saxons at Augustine's landing . . .'.[3] Perhaps now as then an extraordinary missionary effort was necessary to evangelize the non-believers. So many different innovations had been introduced in recent years that it did not seem illogical to try still another, even if it was something as irregular as outdoor preaching. Blomfield doubted that it would be very effective, and questioned its durability when compared with catechizing in schools or lectures in licensed buildings. He clearly was not enthusiastic, but agreed not to prohibit open-air preaching so long as it was restricted to parochial boundaries and had the incumbent's consent. His successor, Tait, not only approved, but did some of the preaching himself.

To a prelate like Blomfield, however, for whom a sermon was a finely tuned explication rarely, if ever, delivered extemporaneously, this was a major concession. It was as much an acknowledgment of the impact of the religious census as was C. R. Sumner's direct endorsement of Mann's conclusion. Blomfield had been saddened to discover that in Bethnal Green, where he raised funds for ten churches in as many years, only 6,024 persons out of a population of 90,193 attended any service.[4] Several proposals had been made to establish churches comprised entirely of the poor, but it appeared that the poor would worship neither with the rich nor with each other. Disappointed and puzzled, Blomfield now expressed 'some doubts as to churches to be used exclusively by the poor; a provision which seems to mark more strongly the already too wide distinction between them and the upper classes'. His expectations were hardly answered in Bethnal Green, 'where there are no pew rents nor appropriated sittings in the new churches'.[5] Yet he could think of nothing else, and, in spite of his experience, thought that churches exclusively for the poor were still worth trying. Blomfield,

[1] *Hansard*, CXXXIX (1855), 490 ff.   [2] Blomfield, *Charge* (1854), 22.
[3] *Ibid.*, 38.   [4] Kitson Clark, *Victorian England*, 163.
[5] Blomfield, *Memoir*, II, 169.

after thirty years of attempting to revitalize the Establishment as the church of all classes, was prepared at the end of his life to donate another £5,000 and launch still another campaign to construct more churches to reflect the class divisions that he and many churchmen like him thought so inimical to their efforts to minister to all the people. It was an upper-class solution. Blomfield and his generation, in spite of their occasionally remarkable insight into the nature of their problem, knew no other.

Between 1860 and 1885 the Church expended another £35,000,000 of voluntary funds on the building, restoring and endowing of more churches. An additional £21,000,000 went into elementary schools and training colleges, while £7,000,000 were utilized in the establishment of home missions.[1] There is little question that the Church's influence among the wealthier classes was greater than ever. There is little evidence, however, to suggest that its relationship with the working classes was much more improved than indicated in the religious census of 1851. The Church was unwilling to co-operate in the taking of another religious census based on attendance although it was recommended every ten years from 1860 to 1910.[2] As Professor Inglis has shown, it would only have revealed the continued futility of the Establishment's efforts to capture the working masses.[3] Churchmen could perhaps find some solace in the knowledge that their Dissenting opponents were not much more successful, but the consolation was bitter when it meant that millions of laboring Englishmen were uninterested in the saving truths preached by any Christian denomination.

The revived Church in the nineteenth century had not lost the working classes; it never had them. Consequently it was faced with the enormous problem not of holding their allegiance, but of winning them to the faith in the first place. The laxity of eighteenth-century parochial religion had permitted generations of English laborers to grow up with only the most superficial association with the national Church. By the latter years of the century that association had often been broken completely, as worried churchmen noted. When thousands upon thousands of laborers migrated to the growing manufacturing towns they easily shook off what remnants of the Anglican faith might still have remained. They found nothing in the towns to encourage their already tenuous association with the national Church. They quickly became part of a new, secular culture with interests and values more closely associated with their immediate earthly needs and concerns. More often than not there was neither clergyman nor church close enough to provide complementary spiritual encouragement. In many parts of indus-

[1] Kitson Clark, *Victorian England*, 170.　　[2] Inglis, 'Patterns', *JEH*, 74.
[3] K. S. Inglis, *Churches and the Working Classes in Victorian England* (1963).

trial England, and in some rural areas as well, generations grew up in an environment virtually cut off from any meaningful association with a religious body. Religious worship, in other words, was in no way an integral part of their experience; they grew to maturity in a non-church-going culture. This meant that the Church's task was especially difficult, since it was not primarily one of recapturing for the faith those who had merely wandered away, but of evangelizing and proselytizing millions who had never been in the fold.

The Establishment and its leadership in the first half of the nineteenth century were ill-prepared to undertake so difficult a missionizing role. Knowing virtually nothing of the working-class culture they sought to influence, earnest clergymen set about restoring and building thousands of churches and schools, reorganizing dioceses and parishes, redistributing ecclesiastical revenue, all in the hope of re-establishing the spiritual and utilitarian validity of the national Establishment. To supplement its efforts, the Church gradually sanctioned lay visitors and Scripture readers, the use of unconsecrated rooms and buildings, the employment of detached missionaries. Decade after decade, millions of pounds poured in to support these and other innovations. Guided by bishops who had grown to maturity and began their careers in what often seemed to them to have been a different world, the Church was dragged into an era of unprecedented change. Fundamentally a rural institution closely attached to the values, principles and administration of a landed society, the Establishment, in less than a few decades, was compelled to become an urban institution and minister in an environment it found hostile and bewildering. The religious census of 1851 indicated the extent of its success as well as its failure. Though many bishops were distressed by the size of Dissenter congregations, and their near parity with the extent of Anglican attendance, they were most appalled by the millions of working-class folk in the towns who did not worship at all. Whatever the Church had to say, it is reasonably clear that it was saying it to middle- and upper-class Englishmen, not to the laboring sort.

Although the evidence collected at mid-century spurred the reinvigorated Church to still greater efforts in the years ahead, they were often only more extensive variations on themes already developed and instituted. Few Church leaders were yet able to consider that the Establishment's inability to arouse the working masses might be less a question of its methods and more the irrelevancy and purpose of its message. The inculcation of principles of spiritual equality in an ecclesiastical atmosphere of pervasive class distinctions was perhaps further compromised by an often greater emphasis upon social rather than religious values. It is difficult to avoid the conclusion that from the later eighteenth to the middle of the nineteenth century the bishops and their clergy were more interested in social security than in the salvation of equal souls. To the

446

more engaged working-class activists, the Anglican clergy appeared as the ordained, paid representatives of the propertied classes, who, in spite of bitter doctrinal differences, at least agreed on their role as social pacifiers charged with the responsibility of reconciling the lower orders to the inevitable inequities of a hierarchical social structure. Most clerics, while rejecting the pejorative implications, would have acknowledged the importance of that function.

Promises of an ultimate reward for passive resignation in this life seemed to be no more inspiring to the workers than rationalistic appeals to understand the natural laws of political economy. From the workers' standpoint it added up to the same thing, and did little to turn them away from the secular alternatives of agitation, organization, riot and strike. The propertied classes who flocked to the revived Church and to Dissenter chapels in such great numbers found little difficulty in reconciling spiritual truths with material prosperity, and generously supported the efforts of the clergy to bring those truths to the unconvinced. The fact that cathedral as well as parochial pulpits increasingly rang with criticisms of the use of wealth did not seem to discourage or anger the rich. Ashamed, penitent, they gave even more to the Church, certain that it was a sound investment that would reap rewards not only in the improved security of this life, but in the one hereafter. Though Church spokesmen professed to speak to all classes, and certainly made a great effort to do so, they were often only carrying on a dialogue with each other and with the laity who shared their particular social and religious explanations of the human condition. Millions of other Englishmen, however, mainly working-class, remained what they had been at least since the latter years of the eighteenth century—indifferent. They raised their children the same way, and neither charity nor Sunday schools seemed to make a great difference. The practice of religious belief in Victorian England had become, as so many other facets of that society, a characteristic and function of class. Few ecclesiastics failed to understand this by the middle of the century, and in their usual perspicacious way analyzed its significance for a national Establishment. Perhaps a little less condescending and sincerely troubled by the disaffection of the laboring classes, a new generation of bishops earnestly and enthusiastically set about trying to create a national Church more representative of all the people. Given the nature of their Church, and the structure of their society, as the census of 1851 suggested, the prognosis was not encouraging.

Bibliographical Note

This bibliographical note refers only to the principal manuscript collections and printed primary sources utilized in this book. Many of the important secondary works pertinent to the subject have been cited in the footnotes, but they constitute only a portion of the large body of literature relevant to a study of Church and society in the nineteenth century.

The major sources for an examination of ecclesiastical thought are the published works of churchmen. The revival of the Church and its growing interest in social as well as ecclesiastical problems was accompanied by a striking revival of clerical publications covering an ever-widening variety of subjects. Bishops were no exception. Leaving aside several scholarly works, usually on classical subjects, the charges, sermons, pastoral letters, books, essays, pamphlets and articles published by prelates before and after their elevation to the bench between 1783–1852 total well over nine hundred separate items. More than three-quarters of them appeared after 1815. None of the prelates of this period have had their works published in comprehensive collected editions, although a few limited collections of sermons and charges are available. Most of the bishops' publications as well as the relatively small number of biographies and memoirs about them are available in the British Museum. While the general catalogue is quite complete, several items listed were in fact destroyed during World War II. These gaps can usually be filled at the Bodleian or Lambeth Palace Libraries.

Manuscript materials are less abundant and less conveniently centralized. In contrast to the second half of the nineteenth century, the papers of relatively few bishops of the later eighteenth and first half of the nineteenth century have survived intact. Prelates of this earlier period apparently destroyed many of their papers themselves, or requested that they be destroyed after their deaths. There is also some evidence that their more earnest Victorian descendents, embarrassed by the politics, place-seeking and bitter recriminations that abounded in the clerical correspondence of the preceding generations, saw fit to consign much of it to the fire. Consequently, although the papers of Samuel Butler, John Kaye, and the earlier correspondence of Samuel Wilberforce, along with the Letter Copy Books of C. J. Blomfield, provide rich and sizeable manuscript collections for students of the period, the surviving papers of most prelates are limited in extent or exist as correspondence appearing in other collections of manuscripts. Moreover, with the exception of Lambeth Palace Library, where Mr E. G. W. Bill and his staff have done much valuable work in collecting and cataloguing sources for the study of the Church of England, most ecclesiastical repositories do not contain episcopal papers. Diocesan registries and Cathedral libraries, though often rich in source material for the history of dioceses, were not utilized by bishops who preferred to keep their official and private correspondence in their private residences.

As a result the quest for manuscript material must lead to a wide variety of locations and collections, as the following list indicates. The bishops were, like many important people of their age, inveterate correspondents; their letters therefore crop up in the papers of many leading contemporaries. I have only cited those collections found to be of some use in developing the attitudes and policies of the bench towards the problems of Church and society in the later eighteenth and the first half of the nineteenth century.

Principal MS. Sources

Lambeth Palace Library
Fulham Papers: Blomfield's Letter Copy Books, 1830–54
Howley's Letter Book, 1815–24
Royal Letters to Archbishop Howley, 1815–48
Longley Papers
Manners-Sutton Letters (film)
Moore Papers

British Museum

Aberdeen Papers	Chichester Papers
Auckland Papers	Douglas Papers
Babbage Correspondence	Egerton MS.
Bentham Papers	Ellis Papers
Berkeley Papers	Gladstone Papers
Bliss Correspondence	Grenville Papers
Butler Papers	Hardwicke Papers

BIBLIOGRAPHICAL NOTE

British Museum

Huskisson Papers
Liverpool Papers
Maskell Papers
Napier Papers
Nelson Papers
Newcastle Papers
Peel Papers

Perceval Papers
Phelps Letters
Ripon Papers
Windham Papers
Wellesley Papers
Young Papers

Bodleian Library

Bagot Papers
Burgess Letters
J. Butler Correspondence
Jackson Correspondence
Legge Correspondence
Lloyd Correspondence
Moss Papers
Parsons Papers

Randolph Papers
Smallwell Papers
Wilberforce Papers
C. Wordsworth Papers
MS. Top. Oxon. contains several
miscellaneous letters

Cambridge University Library
Several letters of Bishops Barrington, Cornwallis, Mansel, Pelham,
Porteus, Stanley and Watson

Trinity College Library, Cambridge
Several letters of Bishops Allen, Bathurst, Blomfield, Burgess, Good-
enough, Huntingford, Kaye, Maltby, Mansel, Marsh, Musgrave,
Otter, Stanley, and C. R. Sumner

Durham University Library
Barrington Papers
Van Mildert Papers

University of London Library
Fisher Letters

Office of the Church Commissioners
Minute Books of the Church Building Commissioners

Exeter Cathedral Library
Phillpotts Papers

Priors Kitchen, Durham Cathedral
Grey of Howick MS.

Salisbury Diocesan Record Office
Douglas Papers

BIBLIOGRAPHICAL NOTE

Public Record Office
Chatham Papers
Ellenborough Papers
Home Office Papers, Series 40, 42–44

Bedfordshire Record Office
Williamson Papers (correspondence of Bishop Gray)

Devon Record Office
Copleston Correspondence
Phillpotts Letters

Ipswich and East Suffolk Record Office
Pretyman Family Archives

Lincolnshire Archives Office
Kaye Deposit

Worcestershire Record Office
Hurd Papers

Sandon Hall, Stafford
Harrowby Papers (correspondence of Bishop Ryder)

Index

INDEX